# THE DICTIONARY OF MODERN PROVERBS

THE DICTIONARY OF MODERN

# Proverbs

Compiled by Charles Clay Doyle,
Wolfgang Mieder, and Fred R. Shapiro

## Yale

UNIVERSITY PRESS
New Haven and London

Yale University Press books may be purchased in quantity for educational, business, or promotional use. For information, please e-mail sales.press@yale.edu (U.S. office) or sales@yaleup.co.uk (U.K. office).

Set in type by Scribe Inc.

Printed in the United States of America.

*Library of Congress Cataloging-in-Publication Data*

Doyle, Charles Clay, 1943–
The dictionary of modern proverbs / compiled by Charles Clay Doyle, Wolfgang Mieder, and Fred R. Shapiro.
    p. cm.
  Includes bibliographical references.
  ISBN 978-0-300-13602-9 (alk. paper)
    1. Proverbs, English. 2. Proverbs, American. I. Mieder, Wolfgang. II. Shapiro, Fred R. III. Title.
  PN6421.D69 2012
  398.9'2103—dc23                          2011051982

A catalogue record for this book is available from the British Library.

This paper meets the requirements of ANSI/NISO Z39.48-1992 (Permanence of Paper).

10 9 8 7 6 5 4 3 2 1

# CONTENTS

# ACKNOWLEDGMENTS

The compilers thank the following individuals for their contributions to the project: Shirley L. Arora, Simon J. Bronner, Robin DuBlanc, Jane Garry, Elissa R. Henken, Susan Laity, Jonathan Lighter, Jay Mechling, Bill Mullins, Elliott Oring, Garson O'Toole, Barry Popik, Kelly Revak, Thomas Skinner, Victor Steinbok, Patricia Turner, and Benjamin Zimmer.

# INTRODUCTION

*The Dictionary of Modern Proverbs* is the culmination of a unique project: an extensive, focused effort to collect proverbs that, as far as the compilers have been able to ascertain, originated in English no earlier than 1900 and to present them in a systematic fashion with illustrative quotations.

A frequently used synonym for the word *proverb* in sixteenth-century England was "old said saw." While rightly acknowledging the fundamentally *oral* character of proverbs (in fact, *said* and *saw* are cognate "saying" words), the phrase "old said saw" also voices the common impression that proverbs, by their nature, must be *old* expressions, somehow encapsulating the venerable wisdom of long-ago times. The very concept of a *modern proverb,* then, would seem anomalous or paradoxical.

However, there must have existed a time when even an "old said saw" was a *new* said saw! Like other kinds of folklore, and like words themselves, new proverbs are continually being fashioned or "coined" (while others lapse into obsolescence). Such is the nature of human creativity as expressed in oral tradition, where proverbs exist before someone thinks to write them down.

While folklorists know that new proverbs continually arise, published compilations of proverbs have not kept up with the expanding repertory. In contrast, lexicographers compiling dictionaries of words search relentlessly for new coinages and new uses of words, taking as their database the whole panoply of current language acts: newspapers, magazines, books, technical journals, television, radio, popular music, motion pictures, e-mail, snail mail, junk mail, and oral discourse. The makers of major English dictionaries maintain their own computerized databases, which are constantly being updated and expanded.

"Dictionaries" of proverbs, on the other hand, have mostly been compiled from fixed—and often rather old—collections of data, and even in their implicit policies governing what expressions to regard as proverbs, they have tended to rely on what earlier proverb dictionaries included. The process becomes circular, then: a *proverb,* almost by definition, is an expression certified as such by its inclusion in proverb dictionaries!

B. J. Whiting's magisterial compilation *Modern Proverbs and Proverbial Sayings* (1989) was based on notes Whiting took as he detected proverbs in the course of his career-long "recreational" reading, especially mystery novels; most of his citations come from works published in the first two-thirds of the twentieth century (with some from the 1970s and early 1980s). The vast *Dictionary of American Proverbs* (1992), edited by Wolfgang Mieder, Stewart A. Kingsbury, and Kelsie B. Harder, derived its entries from an extensive collecting project sponsored by the American Dialect Society, in which academicians and laypeople were encouraged to mail in expressions they had heard that sounded proverbial to them; mostly the items were submitted between the mid-1940s and the mid-1970s. Even for expert paremiologists, and even more for the largely untrained contributors to the American Dialect Society's project, it can take time for the consciousness to register a new expression as proverbial and thus for it to be "collectable" from oral or written sources. Proverbs of recent coinage have inevitably been slighted.

The term "modern proverbs" in Whiting's title is ambiguous, but it is intended to mean "proverbs (of whatever age) current in modern times," though the dictionary does include some that appear to have originated in the twentieth century. Likewise with the *Dictionary of American Proverbs*: among its fifteen thousand (or so) entries, several dozen "modern" coinages are found, but the bulk of the entries testify to the twentieth-century currency of older sayings.

Most other recent proverb dictionaries have relied heavily on the *Dictionary of American Proverbs* for their entries. An important exception is the *Random House Dictionary of America's Popular Proverbs and Sayings,* compiled by Gregory Titelman (1996, 2000). Another exception is the *Oxford Dictionary of Proverbs,* currently in what is called the fifth edition (2008),

the first three editions (1982, 1992, and 1998) having borne the title *Concise Oxford Dictionary of Proverbs*. The editor, Jennifer Speake, notes, "It is a reflection of the proverb's vitality that new ones are continually being created as older ones fall into disuse" (x). The Oxford University Press's online catalog in 1999 rashly claimed that the third edition (a "concise" one) had been "updated to include every major proverb in use in the twentieth century." The advertisements emphasized the inclusion of recently coined proverbs. However, as regards proverbs originating in "modern" times, the *Oxford Dictionary of Proverbs* falls short in two respects. First, it includes comparatively few proverbs that the dictionary's own entries trace back no further than 1900. Second, many of those "new" proverbs, upon further scrutiny, turn out to be older than 1900.

Even for the 2008 edition, the compilers of the *Oxford Dictionary of Proverbs* seem to have made hardly any use of the indispensible new technology for language study: computer searches of the numerous electronic full-text databases that are available—the size, number, and scope of which will continue to burgeon.

The present compilers have taken advantage of those resources. *The Dictionary of Modern Proverbs* is the first proverb dictionary ever to be based on such research. For the proverbs entered here (as well as the great many others that were considered but rejected on account of their age or lack of frequency), we have searched ProQuest Historical Newspapers, Newspaperarchive, America's Historical

Newspapers, 19th Century U.S. Newspapers, LexisNexis Academic, Google News, Google Books, JSTOR, and other databases—seeking the earliest available instance of the proverb in print (or in other media), hoping to get as close as possible to the time when the proverb existed only in oral tradition, or, in some cases, when the expression passed from print (or film, or popular song, or the reported words of a famous person) into oral tradition as a proverb.

Of course, we have also employed more traditional methods of research, such as combing through published and archival collections of proverbs and heightening our own vigilance for "new said saws" in the discourse and popular culture surrounding us.

Our compilation is limited to proverbs in English, including ones from North America; Great Britain and Ireland; Australia and New Zealand; and Anglophone parts of Asia, Africa, South America, Central America, and the Caribbean—though resources for identifying proverbs from some of those locations are unfortunately limited. We have included only what folklorists call "true proverbs": full sentences (or, in a few cases, elliptical sentences), formulaic though variable in their wording, that express general observations, assertions, or propositions, usually (but not always) with the presence of some figurative aspect or application.

We have excluded not only proverbial phrases ("push the envelope"; "Monday-morning quarterbacking") but also wellerisms ("'I see,' said the blind man"; "It won't be long now, as the monkey said when it backed into the fan") and sarcastic interrogatives ("Is the pope Catholic?" "Does

a chicken have lips?"). At the last minute, we excised a number of expressions that seemed just barely (or not quite) proverbial, some that are not (yet) abundantly attested in print, and a few that are more like statements of superstitions or folk practices than actual proverbs (though the distinction can blur).

Two special types of new proverbs should be mentioned, both of which, originally, would have depended on the audience's or readers' familiarity with older sayings. In 1982 Wolfgang Mieder coined the term *anti-proverb*. An anti-proverb is an allusive distortion, parody, misapplication, or unexpected contextualization of a recognized proverb, usually for comic or satiric effect. Anti-proverbs occur frequently in commercial advertising, on greeting cards, in the captions of cartoons, and as the punch lines of "shaggy dog" jokes. Sometimes they pass into oral tradition as proverbs in their own right: for example, "Absence makes the heart go wander"; "Beauty is only skin"; "No body is perfect"; "Do unto others before they do unto you"; "Dynamite comes in small packages."

In 1972 Charles Clay Doyle coined the term *counter-proverb*. A counter-proverb is simply an overt negation or sententious-sounding rebuttal of a proverb, an explicit denial of the proverb's asserted truth. A counter-proverb does not typically aim for any ironic effect, other than calling into doubt whatever wisdom it is that proverbs are supposed to encapsulate. For example, in the twentieth century we find, with some frequency, "One rotten apple does not spoil the whole barrel," rebutting the very old proverb "One rotten apple spoils the whole barrel." Sometimes it is impossible to determine which is the original proverb and which the counter-proverb: "Good enough is not good enough" seems to be about the same age as "Good enough is good enough"; the sayings "Life is (just) a bowl of cherries" and "Life is not a bowl of cherries" are contemporaneous.

The earliest instance discovered of "Life is just a bowl of cherries" occurs in a popular song of circa 1931 (the same year as the earliest for "Life is not a bowl of cherries"). A number of other proverbs also appear to have entered oral tradition from lines in popular songs, motion pictures, literary works, commercial advertising, or celebrity remarks. Most often, however, we cannot be certain whether the song, movie, play, novel, slogan, or quotation originated the proverb—or just famously adopted (or adapted) a proverb *from* oral tradition.

Of course, by its very nature a project like this is open-ended. New proverbs will continue to be coined as the twenty-first century progresses. There certainly exist other modern proverbs that the present compilers have failed to identify as such or to locate. Further research and newer means of searching will no doubt show that some of the proverbs included here are actually older than 1900—sayings that must in later editions be consigned to our appendix, which lists proverbs previously thought (by the present compilers or other collectors) to be newer than 1900 but now are known not to be. And for some of the genuinely "modern" proverbs in this volume, earlier twentieth-century instances will be discovered.

To assist in the ongoing project, we have created a Web site: www.yalebooks.com/ modernproverbs. Readers are invited to contribute potential new entries there, as well as earlier examples of proverbs appearing in *The Dictionary of Modern Proverbs*. We suggest that contributors emulate the format of our entries, which we have found to optimize the necessary combination of clarity, specificity, and compactness.

# HOW TO READ THE ENTRIES

The entries are alphabetized according to the *first noun* in each proverb. (For this purpose, although grammarians and lexicographers lack consensus on the point, the word *nothing* is regarded as a noun.) If no noun occurs, then the *first finite verb* is taken as the key word. If the proverb contains neither a noun nor a finite verb, then its key word is the first significant word of another kind. That arrangement follows the prevailing practice of scholarly compilers of proverbs, and it best facilitates a reader's locating a given expression.

Regarding key words, a plural or a possessive noun is alphabetized as if it were the singular "nominative" form (for example, *men* or *man's* as *man*), an inflected verb as if it were the base form (*gets* or *got* as *get,* for example, though the gerund *getting* should be considered a noun). For key words, when a noun is homophonous (and homographic) with a corresponding verb (for example, *fish* n. and *fish* v.), they are treated, for purposes of alphabetizing, as the same word. For multiple proverbs having the same key word, the alphabetical sequencing depends on the first word of the proverb as entered but ignores initial articles (*A, An, The*). For cases in which variants of a proverb may have differing key words, entries appear at the alphabetical positions of the alternative key words, cross-referencing the main entries.

Each main entry begins with the proverb itself (with some principal variants shown in parentheses). Next, introduced by its date, appears an early attestation of the proverb (in most cases, the earliest that the compilers have been able to authenticate). In most of the entries, further dated examples follow. Multiple examples are included (1) if the "proverbiality" of the expression as illustrated in the earliest given instance is questionable (in fact, in some cases the earliest citation will reveal what might best be called a precursor to the actual proverb); (2) if the given saying is not well known as a proverb or is not recorded as such in any of the standard published compilations of proverbs; (3) if important variants can be efficiently illustrated; or (4) if instances besides the earliest reveal significant information about the origin, meanings, common attributions, or evolution of the proverb.

Next, the entry cites major compilations or dictionaries of proverbs that register the item, followed by other collections or studies that give dated quotations from printed sources or other information. The "major" cited works have the following abbreviations:

*DAAP*   Bryan, George B., and Wolfgang Mieder. 2005. *A Dictionary of Anglo-American Proverbs & Proverbial Phrases Found in Literary Sources of the Nineteenth and Twentieth Centuries.* New York: Peter Lang.

*DAP*   Mieder, Wolfgang, Stewart A. Kingsbury, and Kelsie B. Harder. 1992. *A Dictionary of American Proverbs.* New York: Oxford UP.

*MP*   Whiting, Bartlett Jere. 1989. *Modern Proverbs and Proverbial Sayings.* Cambridge MA: Harvard UP.

*ODP*   Speake, Jennifer. 2008. *The Oxford Dictionary of Proverbs.* Fifth edition. Oxford: Oxford UP. (The first three editions—1982, 1992, and 1998—were titled *The Concise Oxford Dictionary of Proverbs.*)

*RHDP*   Titelman, Gregory. 2000. *Random House Dictionary of America's Popular Proverbs and Sayings.* Second edition. New York: Random House.

*YBQ*   Shapiro, Fred. 2006. *Yale Book of Quotations.* New Haven CT: Yale UP.

The other secondary citations refer to the "Works Cited" list at the back of the volume.

Finally, where deemed advisable, the compilers' brief comments are added. Some of those comments include references to analogous or related proverbs, given roughly in the order of their perceived degree of affinity.

## You can get straight (all) **A's** and still flunk life.

1980 Walker Percy, *The Second Coming* (New York: Farrar, Straus & Giroux) 93: "I didn't get a job. I didn't get married. . . . I didn't move on like I was supposed to. I made straight A's and flunked ordinary living." 1983 Robert Coles, "Alienated Youth and Humility for the Professions," in *Preventing Adolescent Alienation*, edited by L. Eugene Arnold (Lexington MA: D. C. Heath) 6: "The qualities of compassion, of self-respect, of disciplined behavior in a moral purpose— . . . these capacities we must conclude do not necessarily come with education. As Walker Percy the American novelist put it, 'one can get all A's and flunk life.'" 1994 Peter Kreeft, *Handbook of Christian Apologetics* (Downers Grove IL: InterVarsity) 316: "Jesus said, 'What does it profit a man if he gains the whole world but loses his soul?' No one in history ever asked a more practical question. In other words, don't get all A's but flunk life." 1998 W. Jay Wood, *Epistemology* (Downers Grove IL: InterVarsity) 67: "As Walker Percy writes, 'one can get straight A's in school and still flunk life.'" The attribution to Percy has been persistent.

## **Ability** (Talent) can take you to the top, but character is what will keep you there.

1980 George W. Knight, *Church Bulletin Bits*, vol. 2 (Grand Rapids MI: Baker Book House) 44 (in a collection of sayings): "Ability may get you to the top, but only character will keep you there" (the proverb is ambiguously titled "Character's Holding Power"). *DAP* 3(4): "Ability will enable a man to get to the top, but character will keep him from falling." In recent times, the expression is often attributed to the basketball coach John Wooden. Wooden eventually did use the proverb in print: "I believe ability can get you . . . to the top, but it takes character to keep you there. A big part of character is self-discipline. . . ."; 1997, *Wooden: A Lifetime of Observations* (Lincolnwood IL: Contemporary) 99. Cf. "PUSH can get you there, but it takes character to stay there."

## **About** is not close enough.

See "ALMOST is not good enough."

## **Absence** is the mother of disillusion.

Champion (1938) 296 lists the saying as a Spanish proverb; it has been borrowed into English (and other languages). An interesting variant (perhaps arising from the nominal occurrence of *disillusion* as an uncommon substitute for *disillusionment*): 2007 Rodney Dale, *Sayings Usual and Unusual* (Ware UK: Wordsworth) 1 (in a list of sayings): "Absence is the mother of delusion." In light of the substitution of that psychological term *delusion*, we might compare this: 1913 Havelock Ellis, "Sexual Problems and Their Nervous and Mental Relations," in *Modern Treatment of Nervous and Mental Diseases*, edited by William Alanson White and Smith Ely Jelliffe (Philadelphia: Lea & Febiger) 1: 115: ". . . [I]t is true that absence is 'the mother of ideal beauty,' and that many a lover thus frustrated cherishes the belief that he or she thus missed happiness in life." *DAP* 3(4).

## **Absence** makes the heart go wander.

1908 *Washington Post* 18 Oct.: "It is the separations that make the trouble. Absence makes the heart go wander. Sometimes the necessity of an engagement takes the wife away." The proverb originated as an anti-proverb based on "Absence makes the heart grow fonder." *DAP* 3(6); Litovkina and Mieder (2006) 82.

## Abuse it and lose it.

1985 *Los Angeles Times* 10 May: "Factwino was born in 1981 as a waitress who had the human frustration of not being able to respond to arguments she knew were wrong. . . . The motto then was, 'If you abuse it, you lose it.'" 1986 *Philadelphia Inquirer* 2 Mar. (quoting from the Pennsylvania Department of Corrections *Inmate Handbook*): "This [telephone use] is a privilege for your use and benefit. Use it wisely and enjoy it or abuse it and lose it." The proverb originated as an anti-proverb based on "Use it or lose it." Doyle (2009).

## Accomplishment is a journey, not a destination.

See "SUCCESS is a journey, not a destination."

## Act first, think later (afterward).

1965 Dorothy Westby-Gibson, *Social Perspectives on Education* (New York: Wiley) 76: "Most Americans, on the other hand, tend to value 'getting things done' or 'doing something' about a problem. Indeed, sometimes 'act first, think later' has appeared to be our cultural adage." Baldwin (1965) 131 lists the saying as a Pennsylvania proverb. *DAP* 6(2). Perhaps it originated as a rebuttal of the old proverb "Think, then act" or "Act first, think afterward, repent forever"—sayings that advise *against* hasty, ill-considered action. Cf. the older "Shoot first and ask questions later."

## Act like you've been there before.

1984 *Spokesman-Review [Spokane WA]* 2 Feb.: "On a player who spikes the ball after a touchdown [football referee Jim Tunney says]: 'I don't like them either. I always tell the player, act like you've been there before.'" 1986 *New York Times* 7 Dec.: "'But I never spiked the ball in college,' he [football player Stacy Robinson] said, because my coach, Dan Morton, used to tell us, 'Act like you've been there before.'" 1990 Ed Rushlow, *Get a Better Job* (Princeton

NJ: Peterson's Guides) 103: "A National Football League coach was quoted as saying to his team, 'I really don't care what kind of dance you guys do in the end zone. Just be sure you act like you've been there before.' The same is true when you're on the telephone [seeking to obtain an interview with a prospective employer]: you have to act like you've been there before."

## Get your act together.

1972 *New York Times* 12 Apr. (ad for women's clothing): "Get your act together at Plaza 2." 1974 *Los Angeles Times* 1 Jan. (ad): "We know how you want to dress. So get your act together with these famous gotogethers." *RHDP* 108; Lighter (1994– ) 1: 7–8.

## There are no second acts.

1941 The saying probably entered oral tradition as a proverb from F. Scott Fitzgerald's posthumously published *The Last Tycoon* (the author died in 1940): "There are no second acts in American lives." *YBQ* F. Scott Fitzgerald (46).

## Action (Activity, Work) is worry's worst enemy (is the best antidote for worry).

1930 *Washington Post* 20 Oct.: "Hard work is the best antidote to worry, and like most busy people, you are not a worrier" (in a prognostication for persons born on 20 Oct.). 1942 W. M. E., review of *The Retarded Child at Home* by Katharine Ecob (n.d.), *American Journal of Mental Deficiency* 46: 280: "Outline as many possible definite things the parents can do to help the child from day to day. Constructive action is a good antidote to worry." *DAP* 6(7).

## Activity is worry's worst enemy.

See "ACTION is worry's worst enemy."

## Don't advertise what (if) you cannot fulfill (deliver).

1919 Frederick Houk Law, *Mastery of Speech*

(New York: Independent Corporation) 8: 12 (in a list of "business maxims"): "Don't advertise what you can't fulfil." 1929 E. V. Shepard, *Correct Contract Bridge* (Garden City NY: Doubleday, Doran) 52: "*Never advertise what you cannot deliver. A pass denotes weakness; a bid indicates ability to fulfill contract, willingness to be assisted, and either one sure trick held or holdings justifying further contracting . . .*" (italics—and wording—as shown). *DAP* 9(1).

## Free **advice** is worth (exactly) what you pay for it (Free advice is worth the price).

1913 Nathaniel C. Fowler, *Handbook of Journalism* (New York: Sully & Kleinteich) 194: "While much of free advice is worth just what is paid for it,—nothing,—the advice of competent persons should not be despised." *DAP* 10(16). The variant, "Free advice is worth the price" occasionally means something like the *opposite*: since there is no "cost" to receiving free advice, one might as well give consideration to such advice. 2004 Mark Everson, commissioner of Internal Revenue, addressing the Securities and Exchange Commission, *States News Service* 8 Nov.: ". . . [T]he non-profit sector does not need one-size-fits-all regulations imposed on it, so what to do? If I can offer some unsolicited advice—'free advice is worth the price'—I think you should take a measured and wise approach. . . ."

## Act (Be) your **age**.

1925 *New Yorker* 25, no. 32 (26 Sep.) 18: An illustration of a "suggested bookplate"—"Ex Libris Scott Fitzgerald" (just turned forty-six years old)—shows a tuxedoed man with a skull for a head, dancing spryly amid confetti and streamers, playing a saxophone; the motto at the top of the bookplate reads, "Be your age." 1928 Lida Larimore, *Tarpaper Palace* (New York: Grosset & Dunlap) 166: "Bantering remarks, fragments of conversation, the senseless patter of the 'crowd' struck her ears: 'Gentlemen prefer blondes' . . . 'Who do you think I am, a big butter-and-egg man?' 'Knows her onions!

You bet.' 'Did you ever hear that one about the old maid and—' 'Go on now. Act your age.'" 1932 J. Louis Kuethe, "Johns Hopkins Jargon," *American Speech* 7: 328 (in a glossary): "act your age—'don't be childish'; 'stop the foolishness.'" *MP* A44.

## Act your **age**, not your IQ.

1995 Lisa Vice, *Reckless Driver* (New York: Dutton) 221: "'Oh, grow up why don't you?' That's all she ever says. That or 'act your age not your IQ.'" The proverb originated as an anti-proverb based on "Act your AGE."

## Act your **age**, not your shoe size.

1967 Barbara Schoen, *A Place and a Time* (New York: Thomas Y. Crowell) 57: "'Why don't you act your age, not your shoe size?' said Paul. He made a disgusting face and ran out and slammed the door." 1981 *Pittsburgh Post-Gazette* 5 Feb.: "The high school students put their feelings succinctly, when they made signs which urged the negotiators to 'act your age, not your shoe size.'" The proverb originated as an anti-proverb based on "Act your AGE."

## **Age** (Old age) is a high price (too high a price) to pay for maturity (Maturity is a high price to pay for growing up).

1969 Tom Stoppard, interviewed in David Bailey and Peter Evans, *Goodbye Baby & Amen* (New York: Coward-McGann) 205: ". . . [I]t is a very immature thing to worry about one's sinking youth, but I don't care: I think age is a very high price to pay for maturity." 1970 Tom Stoppard, *Where Are They Now* (radio play), in *Artist Descending a Staircase and Where Are They Now* (London: Faber & Faber, 1973) 77: ". . . [E]verywhere I looked, in my mind, *nothing was wrong*. You never get that back when you grow up; it's a condition of maturity that *everything* is wrong *all the time*. . . . Maturity is a high price to pay for growing up" (italics as shown).

## Age is just a number.

1957 James Beasley Simpson, ed., *Best Quotes of '54, '55, '56* (New York: Thomas Y. Crowell) 194 (attributing the saying to Bernard Baruch on his eighty-fifth birthday in 1955): "Age is only a number, a cipher for the records. A man can't retire his experience. He must use it." 1959 *Sunday Herald [Bridgeport CT]* 24 May: "I don't feel that age should be a deciding factor in anything. Age is just a number. What counts is how compatible you are."

## Old age (Getting old) is better than the alternative (Old age sucks, but it's better than the alternative).

1960 *Los Angeles Times* 15 May (quoting Maurice Chevalier): "Old age isn't so bad when you consider the alternative." Cf. "LIFE sucks, but it's better than the alternative."

## Old age is hell.

1952 Virginia Moore, *The Unicorn: William Butler Yeats' Search for Reality* (New York: Macmillan, 1954) 424; Maud Gonne is being interviewed: "For ten years heart trouble had kept her immobile, she said. 'Old age is hell. So boring.'" Dundes and Pagter (1987) 194.

## Old age is not for sissies.

1969 Eugene P. Bertin, "Ravelin's: Threads Detached from Texture," *Pennsylvania School Journal* 17: 546 (in a series of witty sayings commemorating Senior Citizen Month, May): "Old age is not for sissies." 1974 Mark H. Ingraham, *My Purpose Holds* (New York: Teachers Insurance and Annuity Association) 62 (in a series of remarks from interviews about retirement): "I like least the process of aging, living with 'ailing and aging flesh.' As some one has said, 'Old age is not for sissies.'" The proverb's origin is often attributed to the actress Bette Davis.

## If you aim for it, you will miss it (you will lose it, you are turning away from it).

1998 Maxwell Craig, *For God's Sake—Unity* (Glasgow: Wild Goose) 163: "The philosopher Aristotle teaches that happiness is a byproduct. If you aim for it, you will miss it." The saying often occurs with an identification of it as an Asian proverb (rather than a précis of Aristotle's philosophy); a version appeared in an 1808 Chinese Taoist commentary by I-ming (Yiming) Liu, translated (by Thomas Cleary) as *The Inner Teachings of Taoism* (Boston: Shambhala, 1986) 13: "Because this opening is most abstruse and subtle, in ecstasy and deep abstraction, if you aim for it, you lose it; if you conceptualize it, that is not it."

## Alcohol and gasoline (driving) do not mix.

See "GASOLINE and whiskey do not mix."

## Alcohol will preserve anything but a secret.

1904 Charles Wayland Towne (pseudonym "Gideon Wurdz"), *A Foolish Dictionary* (Boston: John W. Luce) [fol. 6v] (unpaginated; in an alphabetical list of words followed by jocular definitions): "ALCOHOL[:] A liquid good for preserving almost everything except secrets." *DAP* 14(2).

## Be all (the best) that you can be.

1956 Pauli Murray, *Proud Shoes* (New York: Harper & Row) 117: "The Fitzgerald boys considered this course, but it would have been an act of disloyalty to their father. . . . He'd always taught them, 'Never be ashamed of what you are. Just be the best you can be and show what colored men can do when they have the chance'"; the book is a partly conjectural memoir of an African American family in the nineteenth century, and the quotations are mostly invented—in the present case (almost certainly) uttered anachronistically. 1968 and 1969 American Library Association: "Be all you can be—read"; the slogan was adopted and promoted (on posters and other literature) for National Library Week. 1970 David W. Augsburger, *Be All You Can Be* (Carol Stream IL: Creation House). 1971 Paul F. Dietzel, *Coaching Football* (New York: Ronald) 241: "Be a champ! Be the best that you can be! Hit your own zenith." 1973 Joseph Gerard Brennan, *Ethics and Morals* (New York: Harper & Row) 157: "The young soul hears his conscience call, 'Be yourself! Be all that you can be!' But the exhortations of his parents, his teachers, his friends and peers all too easily drown out that call. . . ." Since 1980, "Be all that you can be" has ubiquitously appeared as the recruitment slogan for the U.S. Army and the Army Reserves.

## It's (They're) **all** pink on the inside.

1971 Breyten Breytenbach, "Vulture Culture," in *Apartheid: A Collection of Writings on South African Racism*, edited by Alex La Guma (New York: International) 138: "Apartheid is the White man's night. . . . What one doesn't see doesn't exist. Also, at night one doesn't balk at the skin deep peculiarities of the girl you sleep with. They are all pink on the inside." 1983 David Allen, "Now Since Fear and Goodness Are Different Things, " *Denver Quarterly* 18, no. 2 (Summer) 55–56: "She lead [*sic*] me by the hand to the bedroom, she lay down, she spread her legs. . . . I said, 'They ARE all pink on the inside.' And we laughed" (capitalization as shown). The proverb ungallantly asserts—from the male point of view—the sameness of all women for sexual purposes.

## Kill them **all**, and let God sort them out.

See "Kill them all, and let GOD sort them out."

## Let it **all** hang out.

See "LET it all hang out."

## **Almost** doesn't count.

See "CLOSE doesn't count."

## **Almost** (Close, Nearly, About) is not good (close) enough (Close doesn't cut it).

1921 *American Artisan and Hardware Record* 1 Jan.: "'Nearly' is not good enough." 1926 Frank H. Gardner, "Teddy Lands a Big Job," *Herald of Gospel Liberty* 118, no. 32 (12 Aug.) 759: "It was an awful bitter lesson, but I've learned that *almost* is not good enough when *perfectness* can be obtained at the same price or nearly so" (italics as shown). 1935 *Independent [St. Petersburg FL]* 26 Aug.: "Close isn't close enough, and the boys want undisputed possession of the trophy. . . ." 1985 *Los Angeles Times* (San Diego County edition) 15 Dec.: "Some recent headlines in Philly newspapers: . . . 'Close Doesn't Cut It.'" *DAP* 15(1): "Almost made it never made the grade." Cf. "CLOSE doesn't count," "BETTER is not good enough," "CLOSE enough is close enough," "GOOD enough is good enough," and "JUST is good enough."

## We are not **alone**.

The locution, prevalent in the discourse of UFO enthusiasts and science fiction fans since the late 1950s, acquired popularity among the general public from the television series *The X-Files* (1993–2002). The proverb means "Some kinds of creepy occurrences, otherwise inexplicable, must be attributable to the presence of extraterrestrial or supernatural creatures."

## Getting old is better than the **alternative**.

See "Old AGE is better than the alternative."

## Never (Don't) sell **America** short.

1922 *Atlanta Constitution* 8 Jan.: "Don't sell America short! is the advice Mr. [J. H.] Tregoe gives his audiences." Stevenson (1948) 60(4) attributes the saying "Never sell a bear on the United States" to Junius Spencer Morgan, though no actual record exists; the famous industrialist J. P. Morgan used a version of his father's purported remark (including its jargon from stock trading) in 1908: "Never sell a bear on the United States." *RHDP* 242; *YBQ* J. P. Morgan (2).

## All **animals** are (created) equal, but some are more equal than others.

1945 The saying entered oral tradition as a proverb from George Orwell's *Animal Farm*. *RHDP* 4; *YBQ* Orwell (25); Pickering et al. (1992) 179; Rees (1995) 7; Rees (2006) 17.

## There are no final **answers** (solutions).

1916 Carl Kelsey, *The Physical Basis of Society* (New York: D. Appleton) 395: "Adopt democracy and there are still plenty of political problems. . . . Adopt anarchy, socialism, single-tax or any other of the compounds advocated today and the result will only be a new set of problems for the future to solve. . . . This merely means that there are no final solutions for social ills." 1929 Frankwood E. Williams, *Mental Hygiene* (Chicago: American Library Association) 30: "There are no such books [that give 'final answers' regarding mental health], for the simple reason that there are no final answers, nor will there be for a long time, if ever." Of course, by the 1940s the term "final solution" had acquired a specialized meaning in reference to Nazi atrocities.

## To get the right **answer**, ask the right question (Finding the right answer starts with asking the right question).

See "You have to ask the right QUESTIONS to get the right answers."

## An **apology** is a sign of weakness.

See "Don't apologize; it's a SIGN of weakness."

## **Applause** is the beginning of abuse.

1936 Carl Sandburg, *The People, Yes* (New York: Harcourt, Brace) 246 (in a poetic montage of sayings, many of them proverbs). 1991 Diane Wood Middlebrook, *Anne Sexton* (Boston: Houghton Mifflin) 283: "He [Ted Hughes] went on to compile a catalogue of the harms produced by favorable reviews: 'They tend to confirm one in one's own conceit. . . . Also they create an underground opposition: applause is the beginning of abuse.'" Champion and Mavrogordato (1922) 38 give the saying as a Japanese proverb; Sandburg could have found it there (it reappears in Champion [1938] 438). *DAAP* 23.

## Big **apples** come to the top of the barrel.

See "Little APPLES go to the bottom of the barrel."

## Do not (You cannot) compare **apples** and oranges.

1949 *Housing Amendments of 1949: Hearing before the Committee on Banking and Currency, House of Representatives* (Washington DC: Government Printing Office) 236; Congressman Clinton McKinnon speaks: "I do not think much can be gained by trying to compare oranges and apples and trying to find out which is best[,] because they are different. . . . Now, if we compare apples and apples and oranges and oranges and go over your cost sheet, I do not see where you are going to make a lot of savings." *RHDP* 42–43. By the last decades of the twentieth century, the sequence "apples and oranges" had become standard.

## Little **apples** (always) go to the bottom of the barrel (Big apples come to the top).

1912 Charles A Siringo, *A Cowboy Detective: A True Story* (Chicago: W. B. Conkey) 468: "With outstretched arms ready for action, the President [Theodore Roosevelt] sprang forward and grabbed some of the urchins . . . , and with a smile he said, 'Look out boys, little apples always go to the bottom of the barrel!' Of course, he put himself in the big apple class. . . ." 1931 Virginia Woolf, letter to Ethel Smith (27 Jun.): ". . . [W]hy is this so, even in the case of Wagner, so often during their life time? Somehow the big apples come to the top of the basket . . ."; in *The Letters of Virginia Woolf*, edited by Nigel Nicolson, 6 vols. (London: Hogarth, 1975–80) 4: 348. 1948 E. Wright Bakke, "The Goals of Management," in *Unions, Management, and the Public*, edited by Bakke and Clark Kerr (New York: Harcourt, Brace) 250: ". . . [In] this competition, the fittest will survive. Given competition, 'the big apples will come to the top and the little apples will go to the bottom.'" *DAP* 24(15): "Shake the barrel and the big apples will come to the top."

### One rotten (bad) **apple** does not spoil the whole barrel (crate, basket).

1955 Kathleen Moore Knight, *The Robineau Look* (Garden City NY: Doubleday) 186: "She went on, her voice shaking. 'One rotten apple does not spoil the barrel, but it must not happen again.'" 1959 Lawrence Levine, *The Great Alphonse* (New York: W. W. Norton) 342: "Oh, well, a single bad apple. Won't spoil the barrel." 1973 *Wall Street Journal* 6 Apr. [Quoting a person on the street in Ohio, explaining that the Republican Party shouldn't be held accountable for the actions of a few individuals]: "One rotten apple doesn't spoil the whole barrel. . . . You can't attack an entire system because of one incident [the Watergate scandal]." Baldwin (1965) 132 lists the saying as a Pennsylvania proverb. It probably originated as a (figurative) counter-proverb rebutting the old (figurative) proverb "One rotten apple spoils the whole barrel."

### There is (at least) one rotten (bad) **apple** in every barrel (box).

1943 *Los Angeles Times* 7 Oct.: "The proverbial one rotten apple in every barrel has already done its rotten work and corrupted most of its fellow apples" (combining the proverb with an older one, "One rotten apple spoils the whole barrel"). 1945 "Editorial by a Soldier," *News from Belgium and the Belgian Congo* 5: 115: "There's a rotten

apple in every barrel, and the Belgian barrel is no exception." *MP* A112; *DAP* 24.

### What one is least up on, he is **apt** to be most down on.

See "The MAN most down on a thing is he who is least up on it."

### Every **argument** has three sides.

See "There are three SIDES to every question: my side, your side, and the right side."

### The more **arguments** you win, the fewer friends you will have (own).

1945 *Public Relations Journal* 1, no. 1 (Oct.) 24 (filler item): "The more arguments you win, the fewer friends you have." 1968 Jacob M. Braude, *Braude's Source Book for Speakers and Writers* (Englewood Cliffs NJ: Prentice-Hall) 18 (in a collection of categorized pithy utterances): The sentence is attributed to one Ruth Smeltzer, a figure to whom numerous "sayings" have been credited but about whom no information can be ascertained. *DAP* 26(12).

### You can't win an **argument** with a man (someone) who buys ink by the barrel (gallon).

See "Never argue with a MAN who buys ink by the barrel."

### Your **arms** are too short (not long enough) to box (fight, spar) with God.

1912 James Weldon Johnson, *Autobiography of an Ex-Coloured Man* (Boston: French) 174: "He [an African American preacher] struck the attitude of a pugilist and thundered out: 'Young man, your arm's too short to box with God!'" Johnson repeated the proverb in a 1927 poem, "The Prodigal Son." *YBQ* James Weldon Johnson (4).

A singing **army** is invincible (is a fighting army).

1918 Edward Frank Allen, *Keeping Our Fighters Fit for War and After* (New York: Century) 83: ". . . [A]ll stand at rigid attention as the band plays 'The Star Spangled Banner.' Our boys are singing. A singing army is invincible." 1920 William J. Robinson, *Forging the Sword: The Story of Camp Devens* (Concord NH: Rumsford) 60: "It has been an army adage that 'A singing army is a fighting army.' That is true. If you don't believe it, ask the Germans." *DAP* 27(2): "A singing army and a singing people cannot be defeated."

The unaimed **arrow** never misses.

2001 Kinky Friedman, *Steppin' in a Rainbow* (New York: Simon & Schuster) 140: "'What the old kahunas say is something I've taken somewhat to heart as regards this case. "The unaimed arrow never misses."' 'That's the stupidest thing I've ever heard in my life.'" 2002 *Hartford Courant* 28 Jul.: "'Only an unaimed arrow always hits its target.' . . . An unaimed arrow is also an apt metaphor for Frank Ruddle's own education." 2003 Jack E. Edwards et al., *Human Resources Program-Evaluation Handbook* (Thousand Oaks CA: Sage) 266: "It is said that the unaimed arrow never misses its mark, but in modern organizations, that archer will not get a second chance to shoot."

Don't **ask**, don't tell.

1993 *Chicago Tribune* 31 Jan.: "Sociologist [Charles] Moskos suggested this formula as a compromise for both sides to help them deal with the question of homosexuality in the military: 'Don't ask, don't tell, don't seek, don't flaunt.'" *YBQ* Moskos. (When the editor of *YBQ* queried Moskos, the latter replied that he coined this phrase in a letter to Senator Sam Nunn, about Jan. 1993.) As a proverb, the expression has come to be used (sometimes in a jocularly allusive way) for situations other than homosexuality in the armed forces.

If you have to **ask** how much it costs, you can't afford it.

See "If you have to ask the PRICE, you can't afford it."

If you have to **ask**, you'll never know (you can't understand, I can't tell you).

1947 *Washington Post* 17 Jul.: "[Eddie] Condon tells of the time a lady approached [Thomas] Fats Waller and asked him to explain jazz. Waller replied, 'Lady, if you got to ask, you ain't got it.'" *YBQ* Thomas Waller (2).

**Ass**, gas, or grass: Nobody rides for free.

See "GAS, grass, or ass: Nobody rides for free."

There's an **ass** for every seat.

1979 Robert G. Kaiser and Jon Lowell, *Great American Dreams* (New York: Harper & Row) 80: "We have a term here [at a car dealership], 'There's an ass for every seat.' Once in a while you get a car that's ugly. . . . It's a car that you think, Oh my gosh, nobody's ever going to buy *that* one. And sure enough, somebody'll come in and say, 'Just what I've always wanted'" (italics as shown). 1982 Remar Sutton, *Don't Get Taken Every Time* (New York: Viking) 111: "Car people say it a little more succinctly: 'There's an ass for every seat.'" 2002 *Entertainment Weekly* 27 Sep.: "'I can't even get a ticket for my girlfriend,' [Dennis] Quaid lamented the day before its gala screening [of *Far from Heaven*]. 'There's an ass for every seat.' (Fortunately, a last-minute chair was found for her rump.)"; there the proverb is comically recontextualized in the manner of an anti-proverb.

When you're up to your **ass** in alligators, it's hard to remember you're there to drain the swamp (it's too late to start figuring out how to drain the swamp).

1971 William Moore Jr., *Blind Man on a Freeway* (San Francisco: Jossey-Bass) 32: The community college administrator "must keep uppermost in his mind that the improvement of the quality of education is his main objective. This is difficult. When one is up to his ass in alligators, it is easy to forget that his original objective was to drain the swamp." Dundes and Pagter (1987) 91 show a version of "this extremely popular folk notice" that was found in an office at the University of California (Berkeley), also in 1971: "The objective of all dedicated company employees should be to thoroughly analyze all situations, anticipate all problems prior to their occurrence, have answers for these problems, and move swiftly to solve these problems when called upon— However—when you are up to your ass in alligators, it is difficult to remind yourself that your initial objective was to drain the swamp." The proverbial phrase "up to one's ass (neck) in alligators"—meaning "extremely busy, hassled, or confused"—is the basis of this proverb; Lighter (1994– ) I: 19.

## You have to bring **ass** to whip (get) ass.

1959 Frank London Brown, *Trumball Park* (Chicago: Regnery) 352: "'The thing to do,' Kevin said, 'would be for us to get ourselves a bunch of forty-fives, get out of those squad cars, and start walking in. That way we'd show these people that if they want to whip ass they'll have to bring ass. . . .'" Lighter (1994– ) I: 39, defining the phrase *bring ass to get ass* as "to risk one's well-being in order to defeat someone else," suggests an origin in boxing. 1974 Rubin "Hurricane" Carter, *The Sixteenth Round* (New York: Viking) 129: ". . . [H]e wasn't going to just whup on me without getting whupped on himself. I was going to let him know that he would have to bring ass to get ass; that he couldn't leave his in the corner when he came out to get mine." Lighter (1994– ) I: 39.

## *Assume* makes an ass of you and me (u and me).

1975 *Fairbanks [AK] Daily News-Miner* 11 Feb.: "If you read this commissioner, I say to you

what a good man here in Fairbanks said to me when I assumed something: 'If you break down the word assume it makes an "ass" out of "u" and "me." How true it was then and now.'" Occasionally the playful "folk etymology" implied in the proverb seems actually to be *believed*: "'You can't assume anything,' she [an Atlanta social worker] says. 'Assume makes an ass out of you and me. That's where that verb comes from'"; quoted by Linda Bird Francke, *The Ambivalence of Abortion* (New York: Random House, 1980) 28.

## There are no **atheists** in foxholes.

1942 *Los Angeles Times* 13 Apr., an "eye-witness" article by Col. Warren J. Clear: "When the attack was over, I turned to him and said, 'Sergeant, I noticed you were praying.' 'Yes, sir, I was.' There are no atheists in fox holes." There, the punctuation indicates that Col. Clear himself claims credit for the expression. However, an article of the same date in the *New York Times* attributes it, instead, to the sergeant: "They said he [Clear] and a sergeant, who shared the same fox-hole, prayed. . . . The sergeant, Lieut. Col. Clear related, observed afterward that 'There are no atheists in fox-holes.'" An account by Clear published in the *Reader's Digest* (Jul. 1942) 2 likewise assigns the words to the sergeant: "When the attack was over I said: 'Sergeant, I noticed you were praying.' 'Yes, sir,' he answered, without batting an eye, 'there are no atheists in foxholes.'" During 1942, 1943, and 1944, the saying was frequently quoted with a specific reference to Col. Clear or his sergeant. Subsequently, however, it has been more commonly attributed to a military chaplain; according to Carlos Romulo, *I Saw the Fall of the Philippines* (Garden City NY: Doubleday, Doran, 1943) 263: "Then I saw Father William Thomas Cummings standing on a chair over this scene of bedlam and death. . . . It was he who had said in one of his field sermons on Bataan: 'There are no atheists in the fox holes.'" Perhaps Father Cummings garnered the saying from one of the aforementioned articles or from Col. Clear himself. Already in 1943 it was being referred to as an "adage"—for instance, in Ernie Pyle's *Here's Your War* (New York: H. Holt) 287, where no specific attribution appears. With variant wording, the germ of the proverb is older than World War II. 1917 *Olean [NY] Evening Herald* 22 Dec.: "There are no atheists over there when those big shells come over their heads." 1918 *Oakland Tribune* 6 May: "There are no atheists in trenches." The proverb may even owe something to the very old Christian commonplace (which has different implications) that there are no atheists in hell. *DAP* 31; *YBQ* William Cummings; Stevenson (1948) 107; Pickering et al. (1992) 26; Pickering (2001) 30.

## It pays to pay **attention**.

1902 William H. Hills, editorial column, *The Writer* 14: 184: "It pays to pay attention to details in any business." 1929 *Port Arthur [TX] News* 21 Jul. (real estate advertisement): "IT PAYS TO PAY ATTENTION! And if you want to get located near DeQueen school before the fall term opens, you will do well to look over 2235 9th Street" (capitalization as shown).

## You can't bluff someone who is not paying **attention**.

1977 Dale Armstrong, *Win at Gin and Poker* (New York: Winchester) 94 (in a list of principles entitled "When and How to Bluff"): "You can't bluff them if they're not paying attention." 1987 David Mamet, *House of Games: A Screenplay* (New York: Grove) 69: "You can't bluff someone who's not paying attention" (the person to whom the character Mike addresses the line immediately shoots him).

## Question (Always question) **authority**.

1958 William Eastlake, *The Bronc People* (New York: Harcourt, Brace) 158: "Now the old man said, 'Never shoot a man in the back—his brother may be walking behind you.' The old man . . . looked at the ceiling and smiled. 'Always question authority. It's the way the ignorant have of covering up.'" 1979 *New York Times* 8 Apr.: "It was like a replay of a Vietnam War protest: a crowd of earnest young people in blue jeans, carrying signs and signing folk songs, wearing buttons that read 'Question Authority,' all in front of the television cameras."

face nature had given her at birth. . . ." 1935 Harry Middleton Hyatt, *Folk-Lore from Adams County[,] Illinois* (New York: Alma Egan Hyatt Foundation) 126 (in a section listing folk beliefs about the "physical characteristics of babies"; given as a pair of verses): "Ugly babies make pretty ladies, / Pretty babies make ugly ladies." The paired beliefs— though not expressed in proverbial form—are cited by Margaret Cannell, "Signs, Omens, and Portents in Nebraska Folklore," *University of Nebraska Studies in Language, Literature, and Criticism* 13 (1933) 34. Whiting (1952) 363. Each proverb comments figuratively on the relationship between beginnings and outcomes.

## A **baby's** smile (A smile, One smile) pays the bill.

1936  Carl Sandburg, *The People, Yes* (New York: Harcourt, Brace) 106 (in a poetic montage of sayings, many of them proverbs): "The baby's smile pays the bill." A reported reminiscence from c. 1916: One afternoon, visiting in Columbia, South Carolina, Woodrow Wilson "became thirsty and stopped at a drugstore. When the party had been served and the President prepared to pay the bill, the clerk serving him said, 'One smile pays the bill.' The smile was forthcoming"; 1958 Woodrow Wilson Centennial Commission, *Woodrow Wilson Centennial* (Washington DC: for the Commission) 78. *DAAP* 33.

## **Baby** steps first.

See "Baby STEPS first."

## To a **baby** with a hammer, everything is a nail (everything needs pounding).

See "When all you have is a HAMMER, everything looks like a nail."

## An ugly **baby** makes a pretty girl (A pretty baby makes an ugly girl).

1903 C. F. Marsh, "Broken Glass," *Longman's Magazine* 42: 162: "She had given the lie to the popular notion that an ugly baby makes a good-looking woman, for she had grown up with the

## Always polish the **backs** of your shoes (because that's what people will see when you walk away).

1917 William Edgar Geil, *Adventures in the African Jungle Hunting Pigmies* (Garden City NY: Doubleday, Page) 55: "The man who does not polish the heels of his shoes is as foolish as the ostrich that hides its head in the sand when an enemy approaches. It is well to keep your back yard as clean and tidy as your front yard." 1994 Jeanne Swanner Robertson, *Mayberry Humor* (Houston: Rich) 217 (quoting from episode 118 of *The Andy Griffith Show*, which aired 9 Mar. 1964; Barney Fife addresses Gomer Pyle): "Now an old German soldier once told me, always polish the backs of your shoes 'cause that's the last people see of you and remember." 2004 William Bridges, *Under the Heaven Tree* (College Station TX: Virtualbookworm.com) 34: "And he gave me a piece of advice from his banking days: 'Always polish the backs of your shoes. That's what people see as you walk away.'" 2008 *Moscow [ID]–Pullman [WA] News* 31 Mar. (quoting the basketball coach Bob McKillop): "My father was a New York City cop. He used to always tell me to polish the backs of your shoes 'because that's the last thing people see of you.'" Cf. the older "You can judge a man by his shoes."

## Strong **back**, weak mind.

1929 *Jefferson City [MO] Post-Tribune* 16 Nov.: "It appears that the professor has sent a-skittering that 'strong back, weak mind' contention in regard to modern college athletics." *DAP* 34(6) and 583(6): "Some tasks require a strong back and a weak mind."

## Clean up your own **backyard** (first).

1943 "4–H Clubs Find War Work to Do," *Extension Service Review* 14: 133: ". . . Larimer County, Colo., 4–H Clubs have been doing a 'bang-up' job of collecting and delivering scrap. Members are following a plan of 'Clean up your own back yard first, and then your neighbor's,' with the neighbor's permission, of course." That use of the proverb seems like a playful literalizing of its traditional figurative sense. 1946 Fred T. Wilhelms, "Advertising: Help or Hindrance to Smart Consuming?" *NEA Journal* 35: 89: "Incidentally, there's a good point of leverage for consumers who want to promote reforms. Why not work in your own backyard first?" *DAP* 35.

## Your **backyard** should look as pretty as your front yard.

1917 William Edgar Geil, *Adventures in the African Jungle Hunting Pigmies* (Garden City NY: Doubleday, Page) 55: "The man who does not polish the heels of his shoes is as foolish as the ostrich that hides its head in the sand when an enemy approaches. It is well to keep your back yard as clean and tidy as your front yard." Daniel et al. (1987) 502; Mieder (2004) 112.

## Grab them (If you've got them) by the **balls**, their hearts and minds will follow.

1967 *Sheboygan [WI] Press* 24 May: "After the Presidential visit, related one of the fliers, Navy crews had painted this slogan on some fighter-bombers: 'Grab 'em by the throat[,] the hearts and minds will follow." 1969 *Pacific Stars and Stripes* 15 Mar.: "Samuel Ichiye Hayakawa interrupted the interview to send an aide to fetch a cigarette lighter he had received from admiring members of a tank battalion in Vietnam. The lighter bore an inscription to the effect that when you have men by a vulnerable part of the anatomy, 'their hearts and minds will follow.'" 1974 *Los Angeles Times* 4 Jun.: "In the den of his Tudor-style home on two wooded acres in McLean, Va., he [Chuck Colson] tacked up a plaque with a Green Beret slogan: 'When you've got 'em by the balls, their hearts and minds will follow.'" The proverb, widely attributed to President Lyndon Johnson, satirizes the Kennedy administration's hope of winning "the hearts and minds" of the Vietnamese people. *YBQ* Modern Proverbs (38); Keyes (1992) 85–86.

## It is not how hard you hit the **ball** but where you hit it (where you put it, where it goes) that counts.

1964 Maryhelen Vannier, *Physical Activities for College Women* (Philadelphia: W. B. Saunders) 242: "Make all [tennis] strokes smooth and rhythmical rather than trying to 'kill' the ball, for it is not how hard you hit the ball that counts but rather *where* you place it on the court" (italics as shown). The saying, in a literal sense, could have originated in tennis, baseball, golf, volleyball, or another sport. As a proverb, it often applies to nonathletic endeavors.

## That's how the **ball** bounces.

See "That's the WAY the ball bounces."

## You can't hit the **ball** (get a hit) if you don't swing (the bat).

1943 John R. Tunis, *Keystone Kids* (New York: Harcourt, Brace) 141: "'Get your bat offa your shoulders, Jocko. You can't expect to hit if you don't swing at 'em.'" 1949 Frank Bettger, *How I Raised Myself from Failure to Success in Selling* (Englewood Cliffs NJ: Prentice-Hall) 16: "'You can't hit 'em if you don't swing at 'em,' I found was just as true in selling as in baseball." Cf. "You can't SCORE if you don't shoot."

You can't score unless you have the **ball**.

1907 Albert Bushnell Hart, "Saving the Cities," *Proceedings of the Providence Conference for Good City Government and the Thirteenth Annual Meeting of the National Municipal League*, edited by Clinton R. Woodruff ([Providence?]: National Municipal League) 70: ". . . [I]f a private citizen, he is confronted with the great principle, as true in civic affairs as on the gridiron, that you can't score unless you have the ball; you cannot reform a city government unless you can get control of it." 1939 Forrest C. Allen, "Winning Success in Basketball," in *Boy Scouts Book of Indoor Hobby Trails*, edited by Franklin K. Mathiews (New York: D. Appleton-Century) 113: "You can't score unless you have possession of the ball, and only a team whose players know their fundamentals is able to get possession of the ball and keep possession of it."

No matter how (thin) you slice (cut) it, it's still **baloney**.

1924 Edward Verrall Lucas, *A Wanderer in Holland*, "18th edition" [the 2nd, actually] (New York: Macmillan) 18: "All Dutch cheese is good, but the cheese of Gouda I prefer to all others. But I have not yet learned to care for slices of it for breakfast, however thin it is cut." 1926 *Sun [Baltimore]* 9 May: "'No matter how thin you slice it.' Which, as every flapper knows, is merely bologna (pronounced 'bolognie') served in the grand manner." 1927 Billy Rose (song), "No Matter How You Slice It It's Still Bologney." 1927 *New York Times* 7 Sep.: "Well, as Bobby Randall [a character in the 1927 stage musical *Good News*, by Laurence Schwab and B. G. DeSylva] says on a less exciting occasion, 'No matter how you slice it, it's still bologna.'" 1928 *Washington Post* 1 May: "If the elation expressed in his note was real and not just so much of that which is still what it is no matter how thin it is sliced, I have no doubt that Saturday's achievement was at least in part the result of walking on air." 1928 *Delmarvia Star [Wilmington DE]* 22 Jul.: "Al Smith says he will pose for no boloney pictures. He believes

boloney is boloney no matter how thin you slice it." *MP* B56; *DAP* 36; *DAAP* 39; Lighter (1994– ) 1: 82. The attribution to the politician Alfred E. Smith is now common.

Don't ask a **barber** if you need a haircut.

1972 Daniel S. Greenberg, "Don't Ask the Barber Whether You Need a Haircut," *Saturday Review: Science* 55, no. 48 (Dec.) 58 (the article is subtitled "Greenberg's First Law of Expertise"). 1973 Arnold H. Vollmer, "The Numbers Game," in *Environmental Impact: Proceedings of the ASCE Urban Transportation Division, Specialty Conference . . . 1973* (New York: American Society of Civil Engineers) 85: "One of the basic laws of reasoning, discourse or argument can be summarized as 'Don't ask the barber whether you need a haircut.' Try though we may to be completely objective, there is no denying that an engineer has an inherent bias toward and a vested interest in engineering." 1975 Selwyn Enzer, "Policy Analysis," in *Perspectives on Technology*, edited by Sherry R. Arnstein and Alexander Christakin (Jerusalem: Science and Technology) 108: "Dan Greenberg's first law is 'never ask a barber if you need a haircut.'"

**Barely** is good enough.

See "JUST is good enough."

A **bargain** is something you don't need at a price you can't resist.

1964 *Christian Science Monitor* 10 Feb.: "Do you know the cynic's definition of a bargain? 'Something you can't use—at a price you can't resist.'" There exist other proverbial warnings about "bargains," some of them older than the twentieth century: "A bargain is usually worth no more than you pay for it"; "A bargain usually costs more in the end"; "On a good bargain think twice." *DAP* 37–38.

**Barking** saves biting.

Beckwith (1925) 17 gives the saying as a Jamaican proverb, as do Anderson and Cundall (1927) 15: "Barkin' save a bitin'." Whiting (1952) 365 lists it as a North Carolina proverb. Cf. the older "Barking dogs don't bite."

Even an old **barn** looks better with fresh (a new coat of) paint.

1972 *Newark [OH] Advocate* 25 Sep.: "This liberal cynic in a country church tried to trap the old parson by asking him if it were O.K. for her to wear face make-up. Since she was the largest contributor in the church, he wanted to be tactful, yet hold his ground. He thoughtfully replied, 'Even an old barn looks better with a little paint.'" 1996 Lynn F. Price, *Bless Mom in Whatever She Does* (Bountiful UT: Horizon) 29: ". . . [T]his is not to suggest that mothers should not exemplify good grooming habits. As someone once said, 'Even a barn looks better painted.'" 1998 Kate Welsh, *For the Sake of Her Child* (New York: Steeple Hill): "What was it her grandmother used to say about women and makeup? 'Even an old barn looks better with a fresh coat of paint.'"

You can't argue (It's hard to argue, Don't argue) with the **barrel** of a gun (with a gun, with a forty-five).

1937 Milward W. Martin, *Flood Control*, in *Twenty Short Plays on a Royalty Holiday*, edited by Margaret Mayorga (New York: Samuel French) 430: "SLIM. Get back there. Get back there, or I'll kill you! / KELLY (stopping short). I can't argue with a 45, can I?" 1943 Cleve F. Adams, "Up Jumped the Devil," *Cosmopolitan* 114: 165: "'All right,' he said timidly, 'I can't argue with a gun.'" 1986 Charlotte Hinger, *Come Spring* (New York: Simon & Schuster) 196: "There was a man waiting for me when I got to my claim. Said the land was his. . . . Knew he was lying, but it's hard to argue with the barrel of a gun."

You can't steal first **base**.

See "You can't steal FIRST BASE."

You can't steal second **base** while your foot is on first base.

See "You can't steal SECOND BASE while your foot is on first base."

Don't hang your **basket** higher than you can reach.

Anderson and Cundall (1910) 2 give the saying as a Jamaican proverb: "Ebery man hang him bonkra wha' him han' can ketch" (gloss: "Every man hangs his basket where his hand can reach it"). 1919 Elsie Clews Parsons, "Proverbs [from Eleuthera, Bahamas]," *Journal of American Folklore* 32: 441: "Don't hang yer basket higher than you can reach 'em." Whiting (1952) 366 lists the saying as a North Carolina proverb.

Don't let the **bastards** wear (grind) you down. (The saying also occurs frequently in a pseudo-Latin version.)

1952 Louis Adamic, *The Eagle and the Roots* (Garden City NY: Doubleday) 351, recounting a 1949 conversation with the Yugoslav leader Tito and one of his aides, who had asked about Gen. Joseph Stilwell: "In an aside, I mentioned that during World War II he [Stilwell] had adopted as his motto a labor union slogan: '*Illegitimati non carborundum*—Don't let the bastards grind you down.'" *YBQ* Sayings (42). Partridge (1977) 114 asserts that the proverb originated in the British army's intelligence corps during the early years of World War II, but he gives no documentation.

Nobody **bats** a thousand.

1930 *Los Angeles Times* 15 Jul.: "Nobody bats a thousand in everything." 1938 *Washington Post* 18 Apr.: "One wonders what was the matter with Mr. Atwell that he never mentioned it. But even at that, nobody bats a thousand." 1940 Clarence

Budington Kelland, "Golden Lady [part 5],"
*American Magazine* 129, no. 1 (Jan.) 88:
"' . . . [H]ow many times have I been wrong?'
'Nobody bats a thousand per cent [*sic*]'" (in
baseball parlance, "batting 1000" refers to
hitting 100 percent—not 1000 percent!—of the
times at bat). Nussbaum (2005) 33. Cf. "You can't
hit a HOME RUN every time."

## It isn't over till the last **batter** is out.

See "The GAME is not over until the last man is
out."

## Choose (Pick) your **battles** (wisely, carefully).

1972 Richard A. Lacey, *Seeing with Feeling: Film
in the Classroom* (Philadelphia: W. B. Saunders)
96: ". . . [Y]ou must nurture your innovation
separately and systematically, or you may
jeopardize the larger program you have worked
so hard to create. Choose your battles wisely."
1974 Paul W. Engstrom, "Conflicts of Law:
For the Defendant," in *Small Aircraft Accident
Litigation*, edited by Richard S. Maurer (Chicago:
American Bar Association) 150: "The only caveat
is to pick your battles carefully, because it is the
controversies over cases in which little chance of
success exists that creates [*sic*] the law which in
turn catapults down the mountain like a snowball
to bury the defense Bar in an avalanche."

## The harder the **battle**, the sweeter the victory.

1906 John Wilbur Chapman, *S. H. Hadley of
Water Street* (New York: Fleming H. Revell) 244:
"I find the Christian life is a fight from start to
finish, but thank God, the harder the battle,
the sweeter the victory." *DAP* 39(3); Prahlad
(2001) 238.

## In **battle** there is no second place.

See "There is no second PLACE."

## You can lose a **battle** and (still) win the war (It is better to lose the battle and win the war).

The proverb also occurs in the reverse: "You can
win the battle and still lose the war." 1918 George
Bernard Shaw, "Irish Conscription," *Living
Age* 10 (8 Jun.) 617: "Conscription is always an
extremely delicate operation because nothing is
easier, as an eminent German authority has just
reminded us, than to win the battle and lose the
war." *RHDP* 167.

## You must fight one **battle** at a time (Wars are fought one battle at a time).

1903 California Construction League, "Defeat of
the Water Speculators," *Out West* 18: 120: "One
battle at a time! The battle now is to prevent a
long and dangerous step in the wrong direction."
1917 Eden Phillpotts, *Green Alleys* (New York:
Macmillan) 223: "She could only fight one battle
at a time, and, much to Nathan's surprise, his
confession did not overwhelm her."

## A **bayonet** is a weapon (tool) with a worker on each end.

1942 Max Burns, "Detroit (Mich.) Mailers, No.
40," *Typographical Journal* 100, no. 5 (May) 889:
"This, like every war, is the worker's onus. It
has been said 'that there is a worker on each
end of the bayonet and a worker makes the
bayonet. He fights the wars, he dies in them
and he pays for them. Rarely does he start the
war.'" 1987 *Guardian [UK]* 21 Aug.: "The 1914–
18 pacifist slogan that a bayonet was a weapon
with a worker at each end could be applied with
even more precision to the postwar German
phenomenon of the Freikorps." Manser (2002)
14: The proverb "originated in 1940 as a British
pacifist slogan" (no documentation offered).

## **Be** all (the best) that you can be.

See "Be ALL that you can be."

Don't put **beans** (peas) in the baby's ears (up the baby's nose).

1905 Martin G. Brumbaugh, *The Making of a Teacher* (Philadelphia: Sunday School Times) 295–96: "A very well-disposed mother, but not wise, on leaving her home one day, said to the older children, 'Now be sure to put no beans in the baby's ears.' The children had never thought of such a thing, but when she returned the baby's ears were well filled with beans!" Doyle (1983) 28; Cassidy and Hall (1985–) 1: 184. The proverb warns about the power of suggestion.

Sometimes (Some days) you get the **bear**, sometimes the bear gets you.

1970 *Florence [AL] Times–Tri Cities Daily* 8 Jul.: "'Like they say in South Carolina, where I'm from,' [Dick] Dietz, a native of Greenville, said in summation, 'some days the bear gets you and some days you get the bear.'" 1975 *Pittsburgh Post-Gazette* 4 Jun.: "And Larry Liprando . . . shot a booming 79-73-152. 'Sometimes you get the bear,' he sighed, 'and sometimes the bear gets you.'" In a literal (though perhaps intentionally comical) way, the wording had been anticipated in an elementary geography textbook of 1939 Carl Sauer, *Man in Nature* (New York: Charles Scribner's Sons) 80: "The Eskimo like the warm fur and the meat and fat of the bear, and so usually, the man gets the bear. But sometimes the bear gets the man."

We killed a (the) **bear**.

1939 Paul G. Brewster, "Folk 'Sayings' from Indiana," *American Speech* 14: 262: "A braggart, boasting of his feats, is silenced (at least temporarily) by a sarcastic '*We* killed a bear. . . .'" The fuller form of the proverb is "We killed a bear, but Papa (Brother, etc.) shot it." 1941 V. E. Gibbens, "Notes on Indiana Speech," *American Speech* 19: 206: "We killed the bear—but Johnny shot it." *MP* B124.

The **beat** goes on.

1967 The saying probably entered oral tradition as a proverb from the title and refrain of a song by Sonny Bono. It means either that time and events move forward ineluctably or that someone is being annoyingly repetitive.

To be the best, you have to **beat** the best.

1971 *Windsor [Ontario] Star* 5 Jul.: "To be the best, you have to beat the best and the top [tennis] players all come to Wimbledon to prove it." 1981 *Spokane [WA] Daily Chronicle* 14 Nov.: "If you're going to be the best, you have to beat the best, is how the adage goes."

You can't **beat** somebody with nobody.

See "You can't beat something with NOTHING."

You can't **beat** something with nothing.

See "You can't beat something with NOTHING."

You don't get **beaten** unless you quit.

See "You never LOSE unless you quit."

**Beauty** does not buy happiness.

1989 Rebecca Manley Pippert, *Hope Has Its Reasons* (New York: Harper & Row) 52: "But can beauty buy happiness? What happens if she gets what she wants and still is not content?" 1994 *Kingsport [TN] Daily News* 24–26 Jun.: "People Magazine senior editor Charles Leerhsen agrees and says that public interest in the [O. J. Simpson] story is so great because 'it's a story with a moral—money and beauty can't buy happiness.'" 2000 Sally Dalton-Brown, *Voices from the Void: The Genres of Liudmila Petrushevskaia* (New York: Berghaha) 118: ". . . [I]n 'Devushka-Nos' ('The Girl with the Big Nose'), the moral is that beauty cannot buy happiness or true love." The proverb is probably modeled on the older "Money can't buy happiness."

**Beauty** is only skin.

1963 Sidney M. Jourard, *Personal Adjustment*, 2nd ed. (New York: Macmillan) 129: ". . . [I]n the words of a homely twelve-year-old girl at a summer camp, 'After all, beauty is only skin. Be a beautiful *person*, and don't worry so much about how you look!'" Litovkina and Mieder (2006) 101. The proverb originated as an anti-proverb, a clipping of "Beauty is only skin deep."

**Beauty** is pain.

1978 Ron DeChristoforo, *Grease*, a "novelization" of the screenplay (New York: Simon & Schuster) 82: "We heard Frenchy telling her, 'Sandy, Sandy, come on now. Beauty is pain!' Frenchy stuck her head out of the bathroom and said, 'Hey, Jan, get me some ice cubes to numb Sandy's earlobes.'" The current sense of the proverb is that the acquisition and maintenance of physical (especially feminine) beauty requires the endurance of (or obliviousness to) pain. In other occurrences of the locution, a person's beauty—or beauty of a more general "aesthetic" kind—*imparts* pain to someone else: 1932 Terrence Armstrong (pseudonym "John Gawsworth"), *Kingcup: Suite Sentimentale* (London: Twyn Barlwm) 7: "You are too lovely to remember. / Beauty is pain and I, I would forget; / But your eyes gaze upon me for ever, / And your kisses linger yet." Cf. "No BEAUTY without pain," "BEAUTY knows no pain," "If it HURTS, it's good for you," "PAIN is beauty," and the older "No pain, no gain."

**Beauty** knows (feels) no pain.

1920 *Syracuse Herald* 4 Dec.: "Morning in the beauty parlor. . . . It was a nerve-wracking job, but beauty knows no pain. Her hair was pretty with her long curls." Baldwin (1965) 133 gives the saying as a Pennsylvania proverb. 1971 *Beauty Knows No Pain*, title of a documentary film about the training of college majorettes. This proverb seems like the opposite of "BEAUTY is pain," but it actually makes the same point: A woman is expected to suffer silently the discomfort of making herself beautiful; she must either be oblivious to the required pain or acknowledge it as necessary and endure it stoically. Cf. "No BEAUTY without pain."

**Beauty** may open doors but only virtue (strength, etc.) enters.

2000 *Daily Mail [London]* 24 Mar.: "Beauty can open doors—but it takes a strong personality to actually be able to walk through them." Perhaps the proverb originated as an anti-proverb enlarging on the old "Beauty opens locked doors."

Every **beauty** needs her [a] beast.

1973 Jeff Jacks, *Find the Don's Daughter* (Greenwich CT: Fawcett) 56: "'Tell me how you and Melody got together.' 'Every beauty needs her beast.'" 1976 Dorothy Jongeward and Dru Scott, *Women as Winners* (Reading MA: Addison-Wesley) 58: "Every Beauty needs a Beast. . . . The woman who plays a Victim role will be attracted to the man who plays Rescuer or Persecutor." The proverb alludes to a common title or plot of the international folktale cycle "Beauty and the Beast."

No **beauty** (There is no beauty) without pain.

1987 *New York Times* 12 Sep.: "Miss Way retains the individual expression that originally impelled modern dance as an art form. . . . Her opening concert . . . demonstrated her favorite theme—there is no beauty without pain." 1991 Doris Rochlin, *In the Spanish Ballroom* (New York: Doubleday) 5–6: "Sometimes the ladies [clients at an electrolysis parlor] cried aloud or whimpered. . . . 'Courage,' Juanita used to tell them. 'There's no beauty without pain.'" Cf. "BEAUTY is pain."

Never get caught in **bed** with a dead girl or a live boy.

1966 Larry L. King, "Joe Pool of HUAC," *Harper's* 233, no. 1398 (Nov.) 64: "'Hell,' I said, 'the only way you can lose this election, Joe, is to get caught in bed with a live man or a dead woman.' Pool boomed with laughter." 1984 *Pacific Stars and Stripes* 20 Dec.: "Throughout his 1983 campaign, [Edwin] Edwards entertained voters with such boasts as: 'The only way I can lose is if I'm found in bed with a dead girl or a live boy.'" 2000 Laura Lippman, *Sugar House* (New York: HarperCollins) 298: "Never get caught with a dead girl or a live boy. You left Dahlgren with a dead boy. . . ."

The **bee** that gets (makes) the honey doesn't hang (loaf, stand, stay) around the hive (The roving bee gathers the honey).

1906 Ed Rose (song title), "The Bee That Gets the Honey Doesn't Hang around the Hive." 1906 Anonymous verses (parodying Longfellow's "Psalm of Life"), *Gleanings in Bee Culture* 34: 722: "Let us, then, be up and doing; / Thrift comes to those who strive; / The bee that gets the honey / Doesn't loaf around the hive." 1912 *Manitoba Morning Free Press [Winnipeg]* 10 Dec.: "A roving bee gathers honey." *DAP* 42–43(11); *DAAP* 50.

Don't let the same **bee** sting you twice.

1911 The saying occurred as the title of a song in the musical comedy *In the Jungle,* lyrics by Will Marion Cook and Alex Rogers. *DAP* 42(5): "If a bee stings you once, it's the bee's fault; if a bee stings you twice, it's your own damn fault"; Prahlad (1996) 209. Cf. "Don't let the DOG bite you twice."

Where's the **beef**?

1984 The saying entered oral tradition as a proverb from an advertising slogan for Wendy's hamburgers. *RHDP* 368; *YBQ* Advertising

Slogans (132); Barrick (1986) 43–46; Lighter (1994– ) 1: 125; Rees (1995) 504; Room (2000) 745; Winick (2003) 571–601; Rees (2006) 728. In the proverb, the word *beef* is understood to mean "substance" in various senses.

Being born is only (just) the **beginning**.

1919 J. Ritchie Smith, *The Wall and the Gates, and Other Sermons* (Philadelphia: Westminster) 251: "To be born is only the beginning of living. The cradle is neither the dwelling place nor the goal, but the starting point of life. God gives life, we must live it." 1936 Carl Sandburg, *The People, Yes* (New York: Harcourt, Brace) 4 (in a poetic montage of proverbs and other sayings): "Five hundred ways to say, 'Who are you?' / Changed ways of asking, 'Where do we go from here?' / or of saying, 'Being born is only the beginning.' . . ." *DAAP* 53.

Good **behavior** is the last refuge of mediocrity.

1940 Albert Jay Nock, *Mediations on Wall Street* (New York: W. Morrow) 135 (in a list of sayings). 1995 *New Straits Times [Malaysia]* 7 Aug.: "It was a kind of kaizan (the Japanese word for continuous improvement or evolution or organic growth) that could-not-be-entirely-eliminated, even by the claustrophobic manners of the colonial, bureaucratic hierarchy. Good behaviour, someone once said, being the last refuge of mediocrity." *DAP* 46(3). The expression may derive from nineteenth-century locutions like "Consistency is the last refuge of mediocrity" and "Dignity is the last refuge of mediocrity." It is sometimes attributed to Henry S. Haskins.

It's better to belch the **belch** and bear the shame than squelch the belch and bear the pain.

See "Better to burp and bear the SHAME than swallow the burp and bear the pain."

## Don't **believe** everything you think.

1948 Clayton Rawson, "From Another World," *Ellery Queen's Mystery Magazine*, no. 55 (Jun.): 24: "*Don't believe everything you see* is excellent advice; but there's a better rule: Don't believe everything you *think*" (italics as shown). 1984 *Mother Jones* 9, no. 2 (Feb.–Mar.) 61 (slogan in an advertisement for printed T-shirts): "Don't believe everything you think." The proverb originated as an anti-proverb based on "Don't believe everything you hear (read, see)."

## If you don't **believe**, you won't (don't) receive.

1990 *Portland Oregonian* 6 Feb.: "Dear Mr. J.: If you don't believe, you don't receive. I only help those who are willing to help themselves." 1995 David Comfort, *Just Say Noel: A History of Christmas* (New York: Simon & Schuster) 178: "'We have a motto at our house,' Mrs. Jones [of Kansas City] told a reporter. 'If you don't believe, you don't receive. And so my children, who are now in their thirties, have never admitted there's no Santa Claus.'"

## Whether you **believe** you can or not, you are probably right.

See "Whether you THINK you can or not, you are probably right."

## The dinner **bell** is always in tune.

See "The DINNER BELL is always in tune."

## You can't unring a **bell**.

1912 *Oregon [Law] Reports* 62: 40: "It is not an easy task to unring a bell, nor to remove from the mind an impression once firmly imprinted there, and the withdrawal of the testimony should be so emphatic as to leave no doubt in the mind of the juror as to the unequivocal repudiation by the court of the erroneously admitted matter." DAP 47.

## The blacker the **berry** (meat), the sweeter the juice.

1929 *Chicago Defender* 2 Mar.: "They tell me that 'The blacker the berry, the sweeter the Juice:' is that so?" 1929 Wallace Thurman, *The Blacker the Berry* (New York: Macaulay) [3]; an epigraph to the novel gives the full form, presented as verse: "The blacker the berry / The sweeter the juice"—identifying it as a "Negro folk saying." 1934 Zora Neale Hurston, *Jonah's Gourd Vine* (Philadelphia: J. B. Lippincott) 234: "Ah could uh married one uh dem French women but shucks, gimme uh brown skin eve'y time. Blacker de berry sweeter de juice." DAP 48; RHDP 29; Daniel et al. (1987) 503, 505; Page and Washington (1987); Taft (1994); Prahlad (1996) 209–10; Williams (1997) 216–18; Prahlad (2001) 239–40; Prahlad (2006) 1022–27. The proverb praises blackness, usually in regard to sexual desirability. Cf. "The blacker the MEAT, the sweeter the bone."

## Be the **best** that you can be.

See "Be ALL that you can be."

## Buy the **best** and you only cry once (If you buy quality, you only cry once).

1959 *Abilene [TX] Reporter-News* 13 Sep.: Advertisement for A-1 Building Supply company—"Where you buy the best and cry but once." 1979 Blaine M. Yorgason and Brenton Yorgason, *The Bishop's Horse Race* (Salt Lake City UT: Bookcraft) 106: "'And I like a man who cares about his livestock, who cares enough to buy the very best. . . .' 'Well,' Soderberg replied, somewhat embarrassed. 'I've always said that a man ought to buy the best and cry once.'"

## To be the **best**, you have to beat the best.

See "To be the best, you have to BEAT the best."

## **Better** (Being better) is not good enough.

1925 *New York Times* 26 Nov. (title of article): "Better Is Not Good Enough"—about "the fact that the state courts make better use of fingerprints than do the federal courts." Cf. "ALMOST is not good enough."

## When you fall off a **bicycle**, you must get right back on.

See "When you fall off a HORSE, you have to get back on."

## You never forget how to ride a **bicycle**.

1933 *Spokane [WA] Daily Chronicle* 8 Aug.: "But once you had learned to balance yourself it seemed easy and you will never in the future forget how to ride a bicycle. The same is true of swimming." 1950 *Los Angeles Times* 3 Nov.: "I had thought that the wearing of long underwear, once learned, was never forgotten, just as a man never forgets how to ride a bicycle. . . ." The proverb is often figuratively applied to an activity, such as performing sexually.

## **Big** is beautiful.

1927 Willard H. Wright (pseudonym "S. S. Van Dine"), *The Benson Murder Case* (New York: Charles Scribner) 277: "The American aesthetic credo is: Whatever's big is beautiful. These depressin' gargantuan boxes with rectangular holes in 'em, which are called skyscrapers, are worshipped by Americans simply because they're huge." 1968 Peter F. Drucker, review of *The Myth of the Machine* by Lewis Mumford (1967), *Technology and Culture* 9: 94: "He [Mumford] has fought valiantly against the common tendency to believe that what is big is beautiful." Flavell and Flavell (1993) 16; Pickering (2001) 47. Cf. "SMALL is beautiful."

## When (If) they are **big** enough, they are old enough.

1932 Tiffany Thayer, *Three-Sheet* (New York: Liveright) 185: "'These two aren't much to look at,' Wade warned the boy as they hurried downstairs, 'but they are sure fire . . . The short one is mine. The other one wants you.' 'Yeah? Gee! How old are they?' Hek foresaw that his own youth might prove embarrassing in this adventure which he had always regarded as strictly for adults. 'Old enough . . . When they're big enough, they're old enough; and when they're old enough, they're big enough'" (ellipsis dots as shown). *MP* B205; *DAP* 50. Cf. "Old enough to BLEED, old enough to breed" and "If there's GRASS on the field, play ball."

## **Big Brother** is watching you.

1949: The saying entered oral tradition as a proverb from George Orwell's *1984*. *RHDP* 27; *YBQ* Orwell (34); Rees (1984) 89; Pickering et al. (1992) 48; Rees (1995) 54; Rees (2006) 82.

## **Bigger** is not always (necessarily) better.

1928 *Chicago Daily Tribune* 20 Mar. (the article is titled "Power Industry Finds That Bigger May Not Be Better"): "Publicists of the electric power industry have, naturally enough, chanted the praises of 'bigger and better.' . . . [B]ut we are being reminded every day that bigger is not always better. . . ." The proverb perhaps originated as counter-proverb responding to "The bigger the better." Cf. "SIZE doesn't matter" and "SIZE does matter."

## No one (No child) is born a **bigot** (racist).

1945 "San Francisco Conference Neglects Important Step," *Science News-Letter* 47: 338: "Race prejudice is not instinctive. No child is born a bigot." 1974 Herbert Aptheker, "Response," in *From Hope to Liberation*, edited by Nicholas Piediscalzi and Robert G. Thobaben (Philadelphia: Fortress) 52–53: "Racism . . . is a system of ideas. It is not self-made; no child is born a racist."

A **billion** (million) here and a billion (million) there—pretty soon it adds up (begins to add up) to real money.

1938 *New York Times* 10 Jan. (filler item): "Well, now, about this new budget. It's a billion here and a billion there, and by and by it begins to mount up into money." An earlier analog, from 1917, in the *Iowa Daily Statesman [Des Moines]* 23 Jun.: "Congress never appropriates less than a thousand of them [millions] for any military activity, a billion here, a billion there until billions are getting common." The saying is commonly attributed to Senator Everett Dirksen; however, his use of it would almost certainly have occurred later than 1938. *YBQ* Dirksen.

A **bird** may love a fish, but where would they live (build a home, build a nest)?

1964 Joseph Stein, *Fiddler on the Roof* (New York: Crown) 100: "As the good book says, 'Each shall seek his own kind.' Which, translated, means, 'A bird may love a fish, but where would they build a home together?'" 2009 Dennis F. Mahoney, "'The Bird and the Fish Can Fall in Love . . . ': Proverbs and Anti-proverbs as Variations on the Theme of Racial and Cultural Intermingling," in *The Proverbial "Pied Piper,"* edited by Kevin J. McKenna (New York: Peter Lang) 245–56 ("The bird and the fish could fall in love. Building the nest would go on forever").

A **bird** never flies so far that his tail doesn't follow.

Wilson (1969) 13 lists the saying as a Kentucky proverb. *DAP* 51(5). The proverb may be related to a Norwegian saying: "A cow never goes so far that her tail does not follow" (Speight [1911] 215).

**Birds** sing after a storm (so why shouldn't we?).

1974 Rose Fitzgerald Kennedy, *Times to Remember* (Garden City NY: Doubleday) 496:

"Birds sing after a storm; why shouldn't people feel as free to delight in whatever sunlight remains to them?" 1983 *Pittsburgh Post-Gazette* 30 Jun. (quoting Rose Kennedy): "No matter what, God wants us to be happy. He doesn't want us to be sad. Birds sing after a storm. Why shouldn't we?" 1996 Carmen Renee Berry, *Coming Home to Your Body* (Berkeley CA: Circulus) 40: "Reflect on the fact that day always follows night, gravity always keeps you connected to the earth, and birds always sing after a storm." 2005 *Calhoun [GA] Times* 7 Dec. (a published e-mail to the newspaper from a local teenager): "Birds sing after a storm. Why can't we?" The attribution to Rose Kennedy frequently adheres to the proverb.

Dead **birds** don't fall out of nests.

1952 Hugh Dalton, diary entry (19 May): "A. J. Irvine tells a good story of Winston [Churchill] at some function with his fly-buttons undone. When his attention was tactfully drawn to this, he said, 'A dead bird won't fall out of the nest'"; in *Political Diary*, edited by Ben Pimlott (London: Jonathan Cape, 1986) 587. Rees (1984) 108.

Sometimes you're the **bird**, and sometimes you're the windshield.

See "Sometimes you're the WINDSHIELD, and sometimes you're the bug."

You can't keep **birds** (crows) from flying over your head, but you can keep them from building a nest in your hair (on your head).

Anderson and Cundall (1910) 28 give the saying as a Jamaican proverb: "You can't keep crow from flyin', but you can keep him from pitchin' 'pon you head." *DAP* 5; Beckwith (1925) 124; Prahlad (2001) 239.

A little **bit** of powder and a little bit of paint makes a woman look like what she ain't.

See "A little POWDER and a little paint makes a woman look like what she ain't."

## **Black** is beautiful.

1927 *New York Amsterdam News* 20 Nov.: "Marcus Garvey made black people proud of their race. In a world where black is despised he taught them that black is beautiful." *DAAP* 70; *YBQ* Political Slogans (8); Parker (1975); Rees (1984) 215; Pickering et al. (1992) 54; Rees (1995) 59; Room (2000) 71. In 1926 Langston Hughes had declared it the "duty of the younger Negro artist . . . to change . . . that old whispering 'I want to be White,' hidden in the aspirations of his people, to 'Why should I want to be white? I am a Negro—and beautiful!'"; "The Negro Artist and the Racial Mountain," *The Nation* 122: 694.

## Once you go **black**, you'll never go back (Once black, never back).

1978 William P. Nye, "The Emergent Idea of Race," *Theory and Society* 5: 350: "One need not look very far or very hard to discover everyday examples of how Americans view social color. For example: 'If you're white, you're right; if you're brown, stick around; if you're black, stay back.' 'Once you go black you'll never go back.'" 1981 John Sacret Young, *The Weather Tomorrow* (New York: Random House) 75: "Murphy said, 'You know he's part black.' He wanted to surprise her. 'M-mm. Well, why not. Once you go black you never go back. So I'm told.'" Initially, the reference was to the supposed superiority of black persons (male and female) in sexual performance. Now the proverb can have wider applications.

## You can't think (talk) **black** and sleep white.

See "You can't THINK black and sleep white."

## You can't **blame** someone for trying.

See "You can't blame a FELLOW for trying."

## If it **bleeds**, it leads (What bleeds leads).

1983 Herbert Benson, "The Unity of Body, Mind, and Soul," in *Marriage and the Family*, edited by John T. Chirban (Brookline MA: Holy Cross Orthodox Press) 75: "The near assassination of a president, the near assassination of a Pope, rampant violence, the gruesome material in our nightly local news, where the credo of some of the local stations is, 'If it bleeds, it leads,' where uncertainties come repeatedly . . . take, for example, this Tylenol business. How do you respond to it?" (ellipsis dots as shown). 1996 Daniel Cotton, *Ravishing Tradition* (Ithaca NY: Cornell UP) 67: "'What bleeds leads' is a joking catch-phrase among journalists at the moment I write this." The proverb is often uttered as a critique of journalism and a comment on gossip and sensationalism in general.

## Old enough to **bleed**, old enough to breed (butcher, stick, etc.).

1971 David Selbourne, *The Damned* (London: Methuen) 86 (a girl speaks): "I'm not a kid. / Old enough to bleed, old enough to butcher." 1972 Bruce Rodgers, *The Queen's Vernacular: A Gay Lexicon* (San Francisco: Straight Arrow) 39 (at the entry for *butcher* in the sense of "penetrate sexually"—"especially to deflower a young man"—illustrating the usage, unaccountably, with the proverb): "If they're old enough to bleed, they're old enough to butcher." 1976 Thomas York, *Snowman* (Toronto: Doubleday) 15–16: "She couldn't have been more than fifteen though she claimed to be twenty. . . . The girl had just smiled and nodded, so Bard said, 'Old enough to bleed, old enough to stick,' and turned her over to them." 1980 Jon Sharpe, *Seven Wagons West* (New York: Signet) 25: "'Isn't she a little young for you?' the woman prodded. 'Old enough to bleed, old enough to breed,' he answered laconically." 1983 Ellen Bass, *I Never Told Anyone*

(New York: Harper & Row) 41: "One man who had molested his stepdaughter . . . told us he'd heard many times growing up, old enough to bleed, old enough to slaughter." The verb *bleed* refers to menstruation. All the variant forms of the proverb seem to allude to different aspects of livestock raising. Currently, the *breed* form appears to be the most common. Cf. "When they are BIG enough, they are old enough" and "If there's GRASS on the field, play ball."

## Follow your (own) **bliss**.

1971 Joseph Campbell, interview in *Psychology Today* (Jul.) 91: "To find your own way is to follow your own bliss. This involves analysis, watching yourself and seeing where the real deep bliss is—not the quick little excitement." 1988 Bernie S. Siegel, *Love, Medicine & Miracles*, 2nd ed. (New York: Harper & Row) xii: "Allow the development to occur to its fullest; grow and bloom. Follow your bliss and be what you want to be." *YBQ* Joseph Campbell.

## **Blondes** have more fun.

1939 *Lowell [MA] Sun* 25 Aug.: "'Blondes have more fun.' That's why Jane Wyman is a brown-eyed blonde." *YBQ* Advertising Slogans (29, for Clairol hair coloring: "Is it true blondes have more fun?").

## Buy when (the) **blood** is running in the streets.

1964 Harry D. Schultz, *Bear Markets* (Englewood Cliffs NJ: Prentice-Hall) 164: "Rothschild once advised, '*Buy* when the blood is running in the streets.' He said it all. I can only expand on this theme" (italics as shown). 1988 *Los Angeles Times* 29 Aug. (quoting Kathleen Odean): "There's an old stock market proverb, 'Buy when the blood is running in the Street.'"

## No **blood**, no foul.

See "No HARM, no foul."

## **Bloom** (Grow, Grow and bloom) where you are planted.

1971 *Appleton [WI] Post Crescent* 4 Apr.: "There's a lot of truth in the statement: 'Bloom where you are planted.'" 1974 James Lawrence Nicholson, *Views from the Mountain* (Tracy City TN: Herald) 23 (section title): "Grow Where You Are Planted." 1976 *Washington Post* 27 May: "One of them [churches in Damascus MD] has a sign outside the door below an electric cross perched high on the steeple. 'Grow and bloom where you are planted,' says the sign."

## Don't (Never) dance in a small **boat**.

See "GOD is good, but don't dance in a small boat."

## Whatever floats your **boat**.

1981 *Sunday Herald [Chicago]* 16 Aug.: "Fly, drive, row, or read. Whatever floats your boat." 1984 *Times Daily [Florence AL]* 18 Nov.: "[Scott] Waterhouse explained the principles of Satanism as doing whatever feels good: 'Whatever floats your boat, turns your crank.'" This is perhaps the prototype of such formulaic expressions, which assert, "You should (or may) do whatever you wish, whatever interests you." It has spawned a number of analogous expressions, such as "Whatever tickles your pickle," "Whatever butters your biscuit," "Whatever blows your skirt up."

## No **body** is perfect.

1958 *Los Angeles Times* 1 Jun. (advertisement): "No body is perfect . . . every body needs Peter Pan [brassieres]." Litovkina and Mieder (2006) 239. The proverb originated as an anti-proverb playing on "Nobody is perfect"; it has come to be widely used in connection with anxieties about "body image," especially those affecting young women.

## No **body** (corpse), no crime.

1947 L. Ron Hubbard, "The End Is Not Yet," *Astounding Science Fiction* 40, no. 1 (Sep.)

125: "'And there was no body at all,' cried the sergeant . . . 'No body, no crime!'" 1950 Edmund Bergler, "Myth, Merit, and Mirage of Literary Style," *American Imago* 7: 281: ". . . [T]he artist performs his 'magic gesture' according to the established judicial principle, 'no corpse, no crime.'"

## No matter how you slice it, it's still **bologna**.

See "No matter how you slice it, it's still BALONEY."

## **Boots** (Shoes) are made for walking.

1966 The saying probably entered oral tradition as a proverb—or at least gained popularity from—the title and refrain of a song by Lee Hazelwood, sung most prominently by Nancy Sinatra: "Well, these boots are made for walking / And that's just what they'll do / One of these days these boots / Are gonna walk all over you." 1980 Shirley O. Steele, "Shoes Are Made for Walking": title of a short story, rpt. in *Home Girls: A Black Feminist Anthology*, edited by Barbara Smith (New York: Kitchen Table, 1983) 260. 1983 *Washington Post* 13 Feb.: "'As shoes are made for walking, we're made for counterinsurgency,' explained a captain in the Ramon Bellose Battalion, trained last year at Ft. Bragg, N.C." 2000 "These Boots Are Made for Walking: Why Most Divorce Filers Are Women," *American Law & Economic Review* 2: 126–69. 2002 Sue Blundell, "Clutching at Clothes," in *Women's Dress in the Ancient Greek World*, edited by Lloyd Llewellyn-Jones (London: Duckworth) 148: "If shoes are made for walking—and some of the literature already quoted certainly indicates that putting your shoes on was associated with leaving the home for the wider world—then the difference that is being highlighted in both scenes may be one of status." 2006 Linda Rogers, *Joe Rosenblatt: Essays on His Works* (Toronto: Guernica) 59: "Like the prisoners of war who walked across Europe when his relatives were burning in the ovens of Auschwitz, his boots were made for walking."

The proverb means "One can leave anytime one resolves to" or "One must prepare to be mobile."

## You **booze**, you lose.

1986 *Los Angeles Times* 14 Dec.: "Choose booze . . . you lose." 1989 *Portland Oregonian* 5 Jan.: "The slogans 'If You Booze, You Lose' and 'Don't Pop 'Em, Drop 'Em' decorated the halls at Sam Barlow High School." 1990 *San Diego Union-Tribune* 30 Aug.: "You booze, you lose, under Surf City's municipal code." 1991 *Boston Globe* 27 Oct.: "Keliher eschewed alcohol, saying 'you booze, you lose.'" The rhyming proverb may have originated as an anti-proverb based on "You SNOOZE, you lose."

## **Bosses** are (will be) bosses.

1907 Albert Payson Terhune, *Caleb Conover, Railroader* (New York: for the Author and Newspaper Association) 183: "Because they'd rather be led than lead themselves. Can you find a flaw in that? Facts is facts, and history is history. Bosses is bosses, and the people are sheep." c. 1929 Desmond Morse-Boycott, *Ten Years in a London Slum* (London: Skeffington & Son, n.d.): "There is an absence of kindliness in the Temple of the God of Mammon. 'Business is business,' employers say. . . . 'Bosses are bosses,' the foremen say." *DAAP* 96.

## The **boss** is always right.

1918 Daniel J. Hauer, *Modern Management Applied to Construction* (New York: McGraw-Hill) 173: "Contractors, like other employers, go too much on the principle that the boss is always right. He can be at fault just as much as the man." Dundes and Pagter (1987) 106. The proverb is often uttered sarcastically.

## If you are at the **bottom**, the only way is up.

See "When you're down, the only WAY is up."

When you **bow** (If you must bow), bow low.

1980 Edgar Ray, *The Grand Huckster: Houston's Judge Roy Hofheinz* (Memphis: Memphis State UP) [564] (in a collection of "Sayings by the Judge"): "Regarding entertainment of prospective sponsors: 'When you bow bow low.'" Often referred to as a Chinese (or "Eastern") saying, it is probably a loan proverb in English (Champion [1938] 351). Sometimes it refers not to manipulative obsequiousness but to a Christian's humble abasement before God.

## Think outside the **box**.

1971 Michael R. Notaro Jr., "Management of Personnel: Organization Patterns and Techniques," *Data Management* 9, no. 9 (Sep.) 77 (section subtitle): "THINK OUTSIDE THE BOX / If you have kept your thinking process operating inside the lines and boxes [of organization charts], then you are normal and average, for that is the way your thinking has been programmed" (capitalization as shown).

## Anything **boys** can do girls can do better.

The proverb may have originated as a generalization of the title line of the song "Anything You Can Do I Can Do Better," in the 1946 stage musical *Annie, Get Your Gun* by Irving Berlin, in which the famous sharpshooting proto-feminist Annie Oakley aggressively serenades her marksman rival/boyfriend. 1971 Clem Philbrook, *Ollies's Team and the Alley Cats* (New York: Hastings House) 87: "'We're having a girls' liberation movement here at Willowdale.' 'We believe anything boys can do, girls can do better,' Deedee contributed." 1981 Charles Le Baron, *Gentle Vengeance: An Account of the First Year at Harvard Medical School* (New York: Richard Marek) 126: "Grace [Vanda, a lecturer] . . . proceeded to peel it off in one sinuous wiggle, revealing another T-shirt underneath that said, 'Anything boys can do, girls can do better!'"

Occasionally the proverb takes the undactylic form "Anything a boy can do a girl can do better."

## **Boys** and school do not mix.

1930 *Hamilton [OH] Evening Journal* 6 Sep.: "We are two girls in our teens. We have both boy and girl chums, but are not too chummy with the boys, but think boys and school do not mix very well, when you are really interested in getting an education." 2006 Carol Gilligan, "Mommy, I Know You," *Newsweek* 147, no. 5 (30 Jan.) 53: "Having read 'Tom Sawyer' and 'Catcher in the Rye,' I know that boys and school don't mix."

## A **boy** cannot do a man's work.

1904 Charles Richmond Henderson, *Introduction to the Study of the Dependent, Defective, and Delinquent Classes*, 2nd ed. (Boston: D. C. Heath) 180: "Mr. A. Johnson makes a distinction, however, which should be noted. A boy cannot do a man's work; if he could he would be more than self-supporting, for a man must support several persons by his labor." DAP 64. In contrast to the (slightly) older "Don't send a boy to do a man's job," the proverb "A boy cannot do a man's work"—in one of its applications, at least—has more to do with economics than with competence.

## **Boys** just want to have fun.

See "GIRLS just want to have fun."

## **Boys** (Men) seldom (don't) make passes at girls who wear glasses.

1926: The saying entered oral tradition as a proverb from Dorothy Parker's poem "News Item": "Men seldom make passes / At girls who wear glasses." DAP 65(12), 251(13), 253(3), 402(172); YBQ Dorothy Parker (7).

## Never get caught with a live **boy** or a dead girl.

See "Never get caught in BED with a dead girl or a live boy."

You can take a **boy** (man, girl, etc.) out of the country, but you can't take the country out of a boy (man, girl).

1916 Burr S. Stottle, *Hunting the Tango* (Kansas City MO: Burton) 10: "You know the old saying, Hazel, that you can take a man out of the country but you can't take the country out of a man, and I guess that is true of your old uncle." 1917 R. A. Underwood, "Country Banking," *Texas Bankers Record* (Mar.) 22: "I am reminded of the old saying, 'you can take a man out of the country, but you cannot take the country out of a man,' and equally true might we say that we can take banks out of the country, but we cannot take the country out of banking" (i.e., "the broad and high minded underlying principals [*sic*] of banking"). 1921 Nate Cordova and Cleofas Calleros, "El Paso," *Santa Fe Magazine* 15, no. 5 (Apr.) 73: "You can take the boy out of the country but you can't take the country out of the boy: Leche left his 'Jew Packard' motor hitting on all four cylinders in front of the court house the other morning." 1924 Ruth Cross, *The Golden Cocoon* (New York: Harper & Brothers) 69: "She learned among other things that she was still a very crude and ignorant little country girl. 'You can take the girl out of the country, but you can't take the country out of the girl,' Stephen reminded her teasingly. . . ." 1934 John O'Hara, *Appointment in Samarra* (New York: Harcourt, Brace) 12: "He . . . had been born in a tiny coal-mining village, or 'patch,' as these villages are called; and Reilly himself was the first to say, 'You can take the boy out of the patch but you can't take the patch out of the boy.'" 1963 John O'Hara, *The Hat on the Bed* (New York: Random House) 100: "I'm the same, you're the same, and Dale's the same. You know the old saying, you can take the boy out of Ohio but you can't take Ohio out of the boy." 1965 Langston Hughes, "Roots and Trees," *Simple's Uncle Sam* (New York: Hill & Wang) 46: "Joyce was setting up in the library all last Saturday reading up on that old problem of how to solve the question 'you can take a Negro out of the country but you can't take the country out

of the Negro.' . . ." *DAP* 66(36), 119(13), 251(22); *RHDP* 379–80; *YBQ* Baer; *ODP* 33. Cf. "You can take the MAN out of Texas, but you can't take Texas out of the man."

## The **brain** is the most important erogenous zone.

See "The most important erogenous ZONE is the brain."

## Engage (Turn on, Use) your **brain**, (then) open your mouth (before opening your mouth, before putting your mouth in gear).

1960 *Milwaukee Sentinel* 18 Aug.: "A modern touch was a wall sign over the rolltop desk: 'Be sure your brain is engaged before putting mouth in gear.'" 1991 *Los Angeles Times* 18 Aug.: "One must remember to engage brain before putting mouth in gear or risk gagging on one's foot." 1994 Leo Reilly, *How to Outnegotiate Anyone: Even a Car Dealer!* (Holbrook MA: B. Adams) 46 (paragraph heading): "Use your brain before you open your mouth."

## If you're too open-minded, your **brains** will fall out.

1960 William Henry Burton et al., *Education for Effective Thinking* (New York: Appleton-Century-Crofts) 226: "No one wants to be so open-minded that his brains fall out, but in far worse state is he who cannot open his mind at all." 1968 *Los Angeles Times* 4 Aug.: "There is nothing wrong with being 'open minded'—as long as you aren't so open minded that your brains fall out."

## No **brain**, no pain.

1917 Anonymous review of *The Problem of Pain in Nature* by Charles F. Newell (1917), *Nature* 99: 103: "For the humblest animals, 'no brain, no pain' seems good sense; and the animals of the little-brain type, such as insects, the behavior of which is predominantly reflex and instinctive, often go on as if they were callous to serious injury." 1976 *European Stars and Stripes* 23 Feb.: "Like they say, no brain, no pain." Usually the proverb refers insultingly to a person's insensitivity.

## If it ain't **broke**, don't fix it.

See "If it ain't broke, don't FIX it."

## You **break** it, you buy (bought, own) it (If you break it, it's yours).

1952 *Long Beach [CA] Press-Telegram* (*Parade Magazine* insert) 16 Mar.: "In Miami Beach, the Marcia Kaye Gift Shop . . . displays rows of fragile gifts with this warning: 'If you break it, you've bought it.'" 1957 *Los Angeles Times* 8 Feb.: "A nice little inconspicuous sign in his place that seems to be all-encompassing reads: 'If you break it—You bought it.'" Sometimes the proverb is called "the Pottery Barn rule." Cf. the older proverb (and legal maxim) "He who breaks pays."

## Don't burn your **bridges** in front of you (before you get to them).

1917 *McClure's Magazine* 49, no. 2 (Jun.) 39 (advertisement for Miller Tires): "You wouldn't burn your bridges before you—and yet it would be as logical as buying tires without making sure that the mileage, the strength, and the vitality are really there. . . ." 1966 Robert Heinlein, "Free Men," in *The Worlds of Robert A. Heinlein* (New York: Ace) 31: "Dad grinned, wryly. 'Sounds like the United Nations before the Blow Off. Cheer up, Ed. Don't burn your bridges before you cross them.'" *MP* B428; *DAP* 71(1); *RHDP* 60; Daniel et al. (1987) 503. This proverb has a fundamentally different meaning from the earlier "Don't burn your bridges behind you"— even though both *MP* and *DAP* collapse the two proverbs into a single entry. The proverb may have originated as an anti-proverb, a blending of "Don't burn your bridges behind you" with "Don't

cross your bridges before you get to them" or "Never cross the stream before you come to it."

## If you can't dazzle them with **brilliance**, baffle (blind) them with bullshit (B.S.).

1972 James H. Boren, *When in Doubt, Mumble: A Bureaucrat's Handbook* (New York: Van Nostrand Reinhold) 127: "At every opportunity the probu [professional bureaucrat] should use the years of experience, the knowledge of the specialty language, and other devices to reflect indispensible expertise. . . . A distinguished leader of an operating foundation once stated, 'If you cannot dazzle them with your brilliance, baffle them with something else.'" 1973 Edwin E. "Buzz" Aldren Jr. and Wayne Warga, *Return to Earth* (New York: Random House) 259: "There is a sign he [astronaut Mike Collins] recently made and hung in his bathroom that contains, I think, Mike's wry comment on life. It says IF YOU CAN'T DAZZLE THEM WITH BRILLIANCE, BAFFLE THEM WITH BULLSHIT" (capitalization as shown). 1974 David Batterson, "So You Wanna Be a Star," *Take One* 4, no. 11 (May–Jun.) 18 (epigraph): "If you can't dazzle them with brilliance, baffle them with bullshit."

## The wider the **brim**, the smaller the property.

See "The bigger the HAT, the smaller the property."

## Don't get caught with your **britches** down.

See "Don't get caught with your PANTS down."

## **Bros** before hos.

1993 *Anchorage [AK] Daily News* 29 Jul.: "Put 'bro's before ho's.'" 1998 Sharon Bohn Gmelch, *Gender on Campus* (New Brunswick NJ: Rutgers UP) 56: "When someone makes sexist comments (e.g., 'Bros before hos') . . . , speak up." *Bro* and *ho* are lexified slang pronunciations (originally or putatively African American) of *brother* "male friend" and *whore* "woman," respectively. Cf. "CHICKS before dicks" and "SISTERS before misters."

## B.S. can get you to the top, but it can't keep you there.

See "BULLSHIT can get you to the top, but it won't keep you there."

## The **buck** stops here.

1942 *Wisconsin State Journal [Madison]* 26 Apr. "The buck stops here" (quoting a sign above the desk of Army captain Spencer Z. Hillyard). *RHDP* 31–32; *YBQ* Truman (11); Rees (1984) 70; Allinson and Minkes (1990) 179–87; Pickering et al. (1992) 7; Rees (1995) 73–74; Mieder and Bryan (1997) 62–65; Room (2000) 109; Rees (2006) 107. The proverb is popularly associated with President Harry S. Truman; beginning about 1945 he kept a sign inscribed with the proverb on his desk. It is based on the idiom "pass the buck."

## It's not a **bug**; it's a feature.

1980 David Howarth, reply to a letter to the editor, *Computer Music Journal* 4, no. 2 (Summer) 4: "Entries do not correspond to global entry points and are not similar to subprograms except in external appearance (a feature, not a bug)." 1981 *CoEvolution Quarterly* (Spring) 30 (in glossary of "Computer Slang"): "FEATURE *n.* 1. A surprising property of a program. . . . 'That's not a bug, that's a feature!' A bug can be changed to a feature by documenting it." 1983 Jerry Pournelle, "A BASIC and Pascal Benchmark, Elegance, Apologies, and FORTH," *Byte* 7, no. 10 (Oct.) 277: "Pascal dumps your program. And believe it or not, the language's designers seem to think that's not a bug but a feature." *YBQ* Sayings (50).

## Sometimes you're the **bug**, and sometimes you're the windshield.

See "Sometimes you're the WINDSHIELD, and sometimes you're the bug."

## If you **build** it, they will come (Build it and they will come).

1979 The saying probably entered oral tradition as a proverb—or at least gained popularity—from W. P. Kinsella's story "Shoeless Joe Jackson Comes to Iowa" and the motion picture based on it, *Field of Dreams* (1989). *YBQ* Kinsella (1); Rees (1995) 238; Rees (2006) 330.

## A little **bull** goes a long way.

See "A little BULLSHIT goes a long way."

## Play (Mess, Fuck) with a **bull** and you will get the horns.

1967 George W. Boswell, "Folk Wisdom in Northeastern Kentucky," *Tennessee Folklore Society Bulletin* 33: 14 (in a list of proverbs): "Play with the bull and you will get the horns." 1976 Pete Rose and Bob Hertzel, *Pete Rose's Winning Baseball* (Chicago: Henry Regnery) 68: ". . . I try to bowl him over. I don't like to do that, but if the catcher is going to mess with the bull, he's going to get the horns." 1976 Jack Kramer, *Travels with the Celestial Dog: A Documentary* (London: Wildwood House) 156: ". . . [I]t was a Corpsman, a big quiet Guamanian, who had the answer on Easter Day . . . , 1967. A trooper wondered out loud why Indian country had to be Indian country. What made the natives so deadly. 'Fuck with the bull,' said the Corpsman, 'and you get the horns.'" *DAP* 73(4): "If you play with the bull, you will get a horn in the arse."

## Take (Grab) the **bull** (life, the world) by the balls.

1954 Robert Lowry, "The Day He Got Fired," in *Happy New Year, Kamerades! 11 Stories* (Garden

City NY: Doubleday) 212: "I guess it included seeing everything around that people said you ought to see . . . and feeling I had life by the balls after all those years the army had *me* by them." 1994 Marisa De Franceschi, *Surface Tension* (Toronto: Guernica) 313: "'*Carpe diem*,' she would quote from the ancient Romans. 'Grab the bull by the balls while he still has them,' she would say." T-shirts advertised c. 2000 were inscribed with the proverb as parodically paraphrased in Latin: "Carpe scrotum." The proverb may have originated as an anti-proverb based on the older "Take the bull by the horns" (and, by one variant or interpretation of that expression, "Take life by the horns"). In a literal sense, grasping a bull by the horns will allow a certain measure of control that would be absent in the grabbing of a bull by the balls!

## The **bullet** (shot) you don't hear is the one that gets (kills) you.

1905 William Brooke Rawle et al., *History of the Third Pennsylvania Cavalry* (Philadelphia: Franklin) 50 (an imagined first-person account of Civil War campaigns): "As some of the men dodged their heads, he said, 'Tut, tut; you never hear the one that hits you.'" 1916 A. John Gallishaw, "Gallipoli: The Adventures of a Survivor," *Century* 92: 376: "When you hear the zing of a spent bullet or the sharp crack of an explosive, you know it has passed you. The one that hits you you never hear." In later instances, the proverb is often figurative: 1994 Bert O. States, "Notes on the Poststructural Code," *American Scholar* 63: 11: "As an even older proverb goes, 'You don't hear the shot that kills you.' We have all had the experience of one day noticing that a heretofore inconspicuous, if not forgotten, word—*reify, valorize, discourse*—is unaccountably appearing with unusual regularity" (italics as shown).

## **Bullshit** can get you to the top, but it won't keep you there.

1999 *Herald [Glasgow UK]* 19 Aug. (in the "shaggy dog" sort of joke, a turkey has fortified itself by eating bull dung until it is strong enough to fly to the top of a tree): "Soon, though, the turkey was spotted by the farmer, who shot it out of the tree. Moral: Bullshit might get you to the top, but it won't keep you there." Cf. "PUSH can get you there, but it takes character to stay there" and "ABILITY can take you to the top, but character is what will keep you there." Whether the proverb alludes to the joke or the joke is built upon the proverb cannot be determined.

## A little **bullshit** (bull, exaggeration) goes a long way.

1943 *Lethbridge [Alberta] Herald* 31 Jul.: "A little bull goes a long way." 1946 L. Ó B., book review, *Irish Monthly* 74: 179: "It [the depiction of impossibilities] can be excused when the subject or the manner of treatment is obviously playful or fantastic, but even then a little exaggeration goes a long way." 1959 *Washington Post* 14 Mar.: "Mrs. Robert Levering (D-Ohio) . . . declared 'a little bull goes a long way,' after relating how she and her husband trucked their cattle along on campaign tours in his fifth try for Congress" (there the speaker playfully literalizes the proverb). 1960 Manohar Malgonkar, *Distant Drum* (Bombay: Asia) 48: "'A little bullshit goes a long way;' that was what Colonel Jones used to tell his officers." *DAP* 73(1). The proverb has two meanings: insincere compliments or feigned interest can be advantageous; if you choose to employ exaggeration (or "bullshit")—for instance, inflating a résumé for a job application or telling a tall tale (or an Irish "bull"!)—you will be most credible or effective if you exercise some measure of restraint.

## Don't (You can't, Don't try to) bullshit a **bullshitter**.

1973 Michael E. Abramowitz, "Bureaucrats and Lawyers," *The Bureaucrat* 2: 266: "[A] bureaucrat with a lawyer on his staff may also benefit from the legal profession's equivalent of the venerable maxim, 'Don't bullshit a bullshitter.'" 1975 Robin Moore, *The Set Up* (New York: Pyramid) 64: "'Don't bullshit a bullshitter, son,' the man in front of him said." Cf. "You can't con a CON" and "You can't kid a KIDDER."

## If you stand up to a **bully**, he will back down (stand down, give way, etc.).

1947 *Washington Post* 29 Sep.: "Tito is a bully, and when you stand up to a bully, he comes off his high horse." 1960 Ian Stevenson and Joseph Wolpe, "Recovery from Sexual Deviations through Overcoming Non-sexual Neurotic Responses," *American Journal of Psychiatry* 116: 740: "Most people discover for themselves that if you stand up to a bully he becomes a pigmy, whereas if you run from him he becomes a giant. The principle deserves better understanding and acceptance in psychopathology." *DAAP* 114. Cf. the older "A bully is always a coward."

## It's better to burp the **burp** and bear the shame than swallow the burp and bear the pain.

See "Better to burp and bear the SHAME than swallow the burp and bear the pain."

## There will always be another **bus** (streetcar).

1925 Laurence W. Meynell, *Mockbeggar* (New York: D. Appleton) 11: "'It is . . . comparable to that old question of whether one should run to the corner of the road in order to catch the next bus. . . .' 'But after all,' he said, 'there is always another bus just coming'" (there the proverb is employed more or less literally). 1936 John Milton Caldwell, "The Fraternal Bond," in *Forty-Minute Prize Plays*, edited by Albert McCleery (New York: Dodd, Mead) 83: "Well, when you're young and frisky like I am, there's always another street car along in a few minutes." 1958 Betty Smith, *Maggie-Now* (published with

*A Tree Grows in Brooklyn* in a single volume, continuously paginated; New York: Harper & Row) 531: ". . . I don't want you to throw yourself away on the first man what says, 'Ah there,' to you. Remember, he's not the only pebble on the beach. . . . There's always another streetcar coming along." Cf. "Never run after a WOMAN or a streetcar; if you miss one, another will come along soon."

## **Business** goes where it is invited and stays where it is well treated.

1910 *Newport [RI] News* 1 Dec.: "The retail business is sensitive—it goes only where it is invited and stays where it is well treated." *DAP* 75(4).

## The **business** of America is business.

1928 *New York Times* 28 Aug.: "As President Coolidge declared in his first notable utterance after his inauguration, 'The business of America is business.'" *RHDP* 34; *YBQ* Coolidge (3). In a 1925 speech, Coolidge had uttered a different form of the saying: "After all, the chief business of the American people is business" (*New York Times* 18 Jan.).

## There's no **business** like show business.

1946 The saying entered oral tradition as a proverb from the title and first line of a song by Irving Berlin. *RHDP* 325; *DAAP* 117; *YBQ* Irving Berlin (14); Rees (2006) 662.

## Get **busy** living or get busy dying.

1973 John Thomasson, *White Hope, White Saddhu, White Trash* (Santa Barbara CA: Christopher's) 50 (in a poem): "May I ever remain in suspense / to opt one way / or the other / . . . / 'Who is not busy living's busy dying' / says Dylan." The lines in Bob Dylan's 1965 song "It's Alright, Ma (I'm Only Bleeding)" actually say ". . . he not busy being born / is busy dying," but they are widely misquoted (often with attribution) to match the proverb. 1980 Karl Albrecht, *Brain Power* (Englewood Cliffs NJ: Prentice-Hall) 117: "A person who isn't busy living is busy dying. Each of us *chooses* to be happy or unhappy" (italics as shown). 1982 Stephen King, *Different Seasons* (New York: Viking) 100: "It always comes down to just two choices. Get busy living or get busy dying." *YBQ* Stephen King (1).

## What **butter** and whiskey won't cure, there's no cure for.

1939 Christopher Morley, *Kitty Foyle* (Philadelphia: J. B. Lippincott) 303: "I caught myself the grippe that was prevalent then, and remembered Pop's remedy, hot whiskey and water with sugar and a lump of butter. He always said, 'What butter and whisky won't cure, there's no cure for.'" The saying has been referred to both as an Irish proverb and as a Scottish one (also as a toast). It is unclear whether it has had (or can have) any extended or figurative application.

## Float like a **butterfly**, sting like a bee.

1964 *New York Times* 19 Feb.: "'Put the poison on him,' yelled Drew (Budini) Brown, Clay's spiritual adviser and assistant trainer. 'Float like a butterfly, sting like a bee. Oh, beautiful, Cassius, you should see yourself.'" *YBQ* Ali (3); Rees (1984) 222. The saying has generally been attributed to Muhammed Ali (né Cassius Clay) himself.

## C's get degrees.

1990 Douglas S. Looney, "The Minefield," *Sports Illustrated* 73, no. 10 (3 Sep.) 56: "Says [football player Todd] Marinovich, 'One of the first things the older guys laid on me when I got here [to college] was that C's get degrees, and sometimes D's.'" 2005 Tom Kealey, *Creative Writing MFA Handbook* (New York: Continuum) 124: "I'd been a lame student in high school, one whose motto was 'Cs get degrees.'"

## As **California** goes, so goes the nation.

1940 Eugene McAuliffe, *Railway Fuel* (New York: Simmons-Boardman) 197–99: "With California producing 30 per cent of the nation's output in 1925, the bulk of the fuel oil now consumed for steam-making purposes coming from that state, . . . it is safe to paraphrase the old political expression by saying, 'as California goes, so goes the nation.'" Cf. the older "As Maine goes, so goes the nation." The "California" proverb often refers not just to electoral politics but to fashions and fads of various kinds.

## **Call** (You've got to call) them like you see them.

1941 *Los Angeles Times* 29 Oct. (advice to a neophyte baseball umpire from a senior colleague): "Nothing to worry about, kid. You've been doing fine. Just loosen up and call 'em like you see 'em." 1949 *Pittsburgh Press* 27 Mar.: "Sort of sounds like the old umpire's code that

[Bill] Klem made the by-word of the business. He used to say, 'Call 'em like you see 'em and walk away tough.'" 1951 *Hartford Courant* 12 Apr.: "A man of more than passing wisdom has a word of advice for young baseball umpires. 'Call them as you see them and never tell why,' is the sound advice." 1967 *Herald-Tribune [Sarasota FL]* 27 Aug.: "[President Lyndon B.] Johnson takes comfort in the advice of an Austin, Tex., federal judge who recently wrote him: 'Call them like you see them boy—even if the stars fall.'"

## He who **can** does; he who can't teaches (Those who can do; those who can't teach).

1903 The saying entered oral tradition as a proverb from George Bernard Shaw's *Man and Superman* (the appended "Maxims for Revolutionists"). *MP* C24; *DAP* 81; *RHDP* 331–32; *DAAP* 127; *YBQ* Shaw (17); *ODP* 42. The proverb has acquired various codas: ". . . he who can't teach teaches others to teach"; ". . . he who can't teach, administrates"; etc.

## A **candle** loses nothing by lighting another candle.

1918 Orison Swett Marden, *Love's Way* (New York: Thomas Y. Crowell) 146–47: "A candle loses nothing by giving its light to light another's candle which has gone out. We never lose anything by a kindly deed. . . ." *DAP* 82(9): "To light your candle from mine won't take any off my brilliance."

## A **candle** that burns (shines) twice as bright burns (shines) half as long.

See "A LIGHT that burns twice as bright burns half as long."

## Better to light a (one, the) **candle** than to curse the darkness (dark).

1907 W. L. Watkinson, *The Supreme Conquest and Other Sermons* (New York: Fleming H. Revell) 218: "But denunciatory rhetoric is so much easier and cheaper than good works, and proves a popular temptation. Yet it is far better to light the candle than to curse the darkness." *DAP* 82(5); *RHDP* 167; *YBQ* James Keller; *ODP* 23. The saying is sometimes referred to as a Chinese or a Hindu proverb.

## Candy is dandy but liquor is quicker.

1931 The saying passed into oral tradition as a proverb from Ogden Nash's poem "Reflection on Ice-Breaking." *DAP* 82; *YBQ* Nash (4).

## *Can't* never could.

1952 Leon Wilson, *This Boy Cody and His Friends* (New York: Franklin Watts) 50: "'I know a saying that will match yours,' he told Uncle Jeff. 'My mother taught it to me: "Can't never could do anything."'" 1959 Thomas William Duncan, *Big River, Big Man* (Philadelphia: Lippincott) 496: "'That's impossible,' he used to say, about projects that were not impossible at all. 'It can't be done.' 'Can't never could,' Myrtle told him." *DAP* 81(6). Cf. the older "*Can't* never did anything."

## If you **can't** be good, be careful.

See "If you can't be GOOD, be careful."

## If you **can't** be good, be good at it.

See "If you can't be GOOD, be good at it."

## If you **can't** be good, be lucky.

See "If you can't be GOOD, be lucky."

## Big **car**, small dick (prick).

1991 Bruce Jones, *In Deep* (New York: Crown) 52: "What happened, Hartley—her husband leave too big a path to follow? You get frustrated, was that it? Big car, little dick?" 1992 Noel Virtue, *Eye of the Everlasting Angel* (London: Peter Owen) 79: "Well, you know what they say, George, don't you? Big car, small prick." Cf. "Big MOUTH, small pecker."

## Nobody washes (We don't wash) a rental (rented) **car**.

1985 Tom [Thomas] Peters, "A Necessary Revolution in American Management: People, People, People" (a printed version of a speech given in June 1984), *Selections from the Second National Labor-Management Conference*, edited by Peter L. Regner (Washington DC: US Department of Labor) 18: "The General [William Creech] . . . said, 'You used to be a specialist expert practicing your trade. Now you're just responsible for a couple of planes: why does it make so much difference?' And the NCO's response, which ought to go down in history: 'General, when's the last time you washed a rental car?' That is what ownership is all about or not about." 1985 Thomas Peters and Nancy Austin, *A Passion for Excellence* (New York: Random House) 239: "The NCO's to-the-point reply: 'General, when's the last time you washed a rental car?' We think that may say it all. None of us washes our rental cars." 1986 *Chicago Sun-Times* 7 Oct.: "He favors applying to public policy the axiom that 'no one washes a rental car.' Which means: Ownership encourages rational maintenance of resources." Less specifically, the proverb usually advises against spending time, effort, resources, or worry on anything temporary or transitory.

## You can't judge a **car** by its paint (job).

1908 "Buying an Old Car," *Gas Engine* 10: 338: "Finally, do not judge a car by its outside appearance. Paint and varnish are cheap, and often cover up a multitude of sins" (credited to *The Motor Car*). 1955 "What Makes a Good Slide Projector Good?" (advertisement by Kodak), *Popular Science* 166, no. 5 (May) 236: "You can't judge a car by its coat of paint. Likewise, there's more to making a good color slide projector than meets the eye." Barbour (1965) gives the saying as an Illinois proverb. 1988 *Washington Post* 15 Jan.: "The car had an engaging personality. I liked it. . . . I guess it all comes down to a reworked cliche: You can't judge a car by its paint." *DAP* 83(6). Cf. the older proverb "You can't judge a book by its cover."

## Cards have no memory.

1962 Edward O. Thorp, *Beat the Dealer* (New York: Random House) 41: "If we draw one card again, the chance that it will be the Four of Spades is no greater than, and no less than, the chance of it being any one of the other 51 cards. This fact has made popular the phrase 'the cards have no memory.'" 1963 Ian Fleming, *On Her Majesty's Secret Service* (New York: New American Library) 31: "And it was time for the man's run of luck to end. After all, cards have no memory." 1965 Billy E. Goetz, *Quantitative Methods: A Survey and Guide for Managers* (New York: McGraw-Hill) 102: "What happened on the first draw has no effect on the second. Or as statisticians say, 'The cards have no memory.'" Besides its use specifically in card playing and figuratively as a principle of statistics, the proverb can express a generalized skepticism about luck.

## A card laid is a card played.

1975 Frank Snare, "Consent and Conventional Acts in John Locke," *Journal of the History of Philosophy* 12: 34: "*Perhaps* it is the case that consent acts must be voluntary to be consent. *Perhaps* the consenter must know what he is doing or it will not count as consent. (N.B. that in cards, on the other hand, 'a card laid is a card played')" (italics as shown). As translated into English in 1978, a journal entry by Kierkegaard from 1847 used the expression: "People are busily engaged in insulting me and ridiculing me, but they are not aware at all that a card laid is a card played, that in the end I will still have made an impression on them"; *Søren Kierkegaard's Journals and Papers*, edited and translated by Howard V. Hong and Edna H. Hong (Bloomington: Indiana UP) 1: 382.

## Trust everyone (all men), but cut the cards.

1900 The saying passed into oral tradition as a proverb from Finley Peter Dunne's *Mr. Dooley's Philosophy* (in a list of "casual observations"): "Trust ivrybody—but cut th' ca-ards"—unless Mr. Dooley's dialect aphorism was itself an adaptation of an existing proverb. *RHDP* 342. Cf. "TRUST but verify" and "Trust GOD, but lock your door."

## You play the cards you are dealt.

See "You play the HAND you are dealt."

## *Don't care* was made to care.

See "*DON'T CARE* was made to care."

## The caribou and the wolf are one; for the caribou feeds the wolf, but it is the wolf who keeps the caribou strong.

1963 Farley Mowat, *Never Cry Wolf* (Boston: Little, Brown) 124–25: "The wolf and the caribou are so closely linked, he [an Eskimo friend] told me, that they were almost a single entity. . . . Here, paraphrased, is Ootek's tale. '. . . And this is what happened, and this is why the caribou and the wolf are one; for the caribou feeds the wolf, but it is the wolf who keeps the caribou strong.'" 1972 John Hillaby, "Don't Cry Wolf," *New Scientist* 54: 31: "By killing the weakest and slowest of their prey, nowadays largely deer, they [wolves] help to maintain the survival of the fittest. As the Chipewyans used to say: 'The wolf and the caribou are one for the caribou feeds the wolf, but it is the wolf who keeps the caribou strong.'" 1978 Merle Shain, *When Lovers Are Friends* (Philadelphia: J. B. Lippincott) 15: "The Eskimos have a legend about the caribou and the wolf. The caribou feeds the wolf but the wolf keeps the caribou strong. And so it is with people too" (the analogy with "people too" is not clear!) *ODP* 45.

## Every case has a winner.

See "Every GAME has a winner."

The first **casualty** of war is truth.

See "TRUTH is the first casualty of war."

**Cats** look down on you, dogs look up at you, pigs look at you as equals.

1937 William Ralph Inge, *The Rustic Moralist* (London: Putnam) 319: "A North Country farmer summed up the characteristics of his animals as follows: 'You see, cats look down upon you, dogs look up to you, but pigs is equals.'" *ODP* 84. The saying has sometimes been attributed to Sir Winston Churchill.

Even a dead **cat** will bounce.

1987 "Shrinking Profit Margins Increase Risk of Aerospace Investments," *Aviation Week & Space Technology* 127, no. 9 (31 Aug.) 64: "'If dropped far enough, even a dead cat will bounce,' one aerospace analyst said about the recent firmness in aerospace stock prices." 1990 *The Advertiser* [Adelaide, Australia] 8 Apr.: "One analyst said the short-lived recovery was nothing more than a technical recovery or 'dead cat bounce.' 'Even a falling dead cat will bounce, but not far and not for long,' he said." Possibly the proverb was the basis of the financial term "dead cat bounce," even though the noun phrase appeared earlier in a column by Chris Sherwell and Wong Sulong, "Singapore Stock Market Stages a Modest Recovery," in the *Financial Times* [London] 7 Dec. 1985: "Despite the evidence of buying interest yesterday, they said the rise was partly technical and cautioned against concluding that the recent falls in the market were at an end. 'This is what we call a "dead cat bounce,"' one broker said flatly."

Sleeping **cats** catch no mice.

1903 Andrew Lang, *Crimson Fairy Book* (London: Longman's, Green) 108: "The old man laughed. . . . I do not exactly see where your riches are to come from if you do not work for them. Sleeping cats catch no mice." Based on a German translation of an Estonian folktale,

"Tiidu the Piper," Lang's English version either paraphrases the German "Läuft doch die Maus einer schlafenden Katze nicht in den Rachen" or substitutes for the German expression what was already recognized as an English proverb. *DAP* 87.

Who cares if a **cat** is black or white as long as it catches mice?

1968 "When Workers and Peasants Study Together," *China Reconstructs* 17, no. 8 (Aug.) 18: "But a handful of class enemies in the vegetable company . . . ran it in a capitalist way. . . . This handful openly declared, 'So long as a cat catches mice it is a good cat, whether it is black or white. Never mind how the money is made so long as the profit target is met.'" 1977 "Cat and Mouse," *New Society* 39: 267: "Teng [Hsiao-p'ing] was accused of being a pragmatist. His famous remark, 'It doesn't matter whether a cat is black or white as long as it catches mice,' was quoted against him *ad nauseam*" (italics as shown). 1978 Rita Mae Brown, *Six of One* (New York: Harper & Row) 248: "'For all you know, the father could be black as spades.' Cora quietly replied, 'Don't matter if a cat is black or white as long as it catches mice.'" *ODP* 46. The proverb was probably Chinese in its origin, and it is often so designated in English. In its Maoist uses, it derogated the "pragmatic" tolerance of cats of various kinds. More recently, the proverb has lost any awareness of the Chinese use; it now endorses tolerance in general, especially racial tolerance.

You cannot herd **cats**.

1992 *Globe and Mail* [Toronto] 29 Aug.: "You can't herd cats, and Canadians are cats on constitutional matters. Political strategies that work well with Americans (a people of more canine proclivities) are counterproductive in Canada (especially among anglophones)." 1997 Spider Robinson, *The Callahan Chronicles* (New York: Tom Doherty) 393 (in a fictional song): "Water ain't dry, the sky goes up high, / And a booger makes a pretty good glue / You can't herd cats, bacteria don't wear hats / —and I love you." As a simile betokening difficulty or impossibility ("like trying to herd cats," "as easy as herding cats"), the image or conceit of herding cats is probably older; certainly the motif of herding hares (rabbits, grasshoppers, etc.) is.

## You **catch** (caught, killed) it, you clean it.

1962 *Hartford [CT] Courant* 1 Aug.: "Excavations in Mexico indicate that primitive man hunted the mastodon. And primitive woman said, 'you killed it; you clean it.'" 1981 John T. Thurmond, *Fossil Vertebrates of Alabama* (University: U of Alabama P) 16 (heading of a section on the field cleaning of paleontological specimens): "Preparation: or, You Caught It, You Clean It" (in its unconventional and jocular application, that instance is an anti-proverb). Casselman (2002) 91.

## The **cemetery** is full of indispensable people.

See "The GRAVEYARD is full of indispensable people."

## Don't rearrange the deck **chairs** on the *Titanic*.

1991 Jonathon Kozol, *Savage Inequalities* (New York: Crown) 80: "'You don't dump a lot of money into guys who haven't done well with the money they've got in the past,' says the chief executive officer of Citicorps Savings of Illinois. 'You don't rearrange deck chairs on the *Titanic*.'" As a simile and a verb phrase suggesting futility, the conceit is older.

## Never miss a **chance** to relieve yourself.

See "Never miss an OPPORTUNITY to relieve yourself."

## Never miss a **chance** to sit down and rest your feet.

1951 Edward Windsor, *A King's Story* (New York: G. P. Putnam's Sons) 134: "Perhaps one of the only positive pieces of advice that I was ever given was that supplied by an old courtier who observed: 'Only two rules really count. Never miss an opportunity to relieve yourself; never miss a chance to sit down and rest your feet.'" Rees (1984) 4. Cf. "Never miss an OPPORTUNITY to relieve yourself."

## You never get a second **chance** to make a first impression.

1952 Harry Simmons, *Successful Sales Management* (New York: Prentice-Hall) 127: "Naturally, in calling on prospects, a good first impression is important—you don't always get a second chance to correct a bad first impression." 1966 *Winona [MN] Daily News* 3 Jun.: "A fellow seldom gets a second chance to make a good first impression." Cf. the older proverb "First impressions are lasting."

## The **chase** (hunt) is better than the kill.

1904 Henry F. Cope, "In the Home of the Elk," *The World To-day* 7: 1291: "But the true sportsman loves the chase, the patience, the skill, the endurance more than the kill." 1910 Stafford Harry Northcote (Viscount St. Cyres), *Pascal* (New York: E. P. Dutton) 876: "We do not care for things once they are ours; what we enjoy is running after them. The excitement of the chase is worth far more to us than the kill." *MP* C146; *DAP* 93(1).

## Better to **cheat** than repeat.

1966 *Salt Lake Tribune* 25 Sep.: "Frances M. Briggs, Associate Professor of English Education at Richmond Professional Institute, is convinced that over-emphasis on grades encourages widespread cheating. She cites a motto found one morning on a high-school blackboard: 'It's better to cheat than repeat.'" Cf. "When in DOUBT, look about."

## If you are not **cheating**, you are not trying.

1982 Alastair Fowler, *Kinds of Literature* (Cambridge MA: Harvard UP) 99: "Even our sayings are prefaced by opening formulas ('*Like they say*, if you're not cheating you're not trying'; '*As the saying goes* . . .')" (italics and ellipsis dots as shown). 1992 *Boston Globe* 27 Dec.: "First of all, rules are made to be broken, I don't care what you're getting involved with. If you're breaking it [*sic*], you're trying to win. If you're not cheating, you're not trying to win." The proverb is most often used in reference to athletic competition. Cf. "If you are not LYING, you are not trying."

## Don't write a **check** that your ass can't cash.

See "Don't let your MOUTH write a check that your ass can't cash."

## There's always free **cheese** in a mousetrap.

1962 *Dispatch [Lexington NC]* 2 Jun.: "Mousetraps furnish free cheese. But the mouse's happiness there is short-lived. For mice and men there is no such thing as a free lunch." 1962 *Nevada [MO] Daily Mail* 1 Oct.: "Looking for a government handout? There's always free cheese in a mousetrap, but you never saw a happy mouse there." 1971 Jacques Leslie, "H. R. Gross: The Conscience of Uncle Sucker," *Washington Monthly* 3, no. 6 (Aug.) 38: "One sign on the wall [of Republican congressman Gross's office] says 'Nothing is easier than the expenditure of public money.' . . . Another says, 'There's always free cheese in a mousetrap.'"

## Never trust a skinny **chef** (cook).

1976 *Augusta [GA] Chronicle* 4 Mar.: "The French use lots of whipping cream, pure butter, cheese,

wines and liqueurs in their cooking. But as Chef [Marcel] Carles pointed out, 'You wouldn't trust a skinny chef, would you?'" 1977 *Washington Post* 8 Dec. (filler item): "Sound advice[:] Paul Sweeny counsels, 'Never trust a skinny cook.'"

## Good at **chess**, bad at life.

2002 The saying may have entered oral tradition as a proverb from a line in the motion picture *Dirty Pretty Things*, written by Steven Knight—or the character in the movie may have been uttering a proverb. In the proverb chess represents a cerebral expertise unrelated (or detrimental) to "life." Perhaps it originated as a variant of "Lucky at cards, unlucky in love."

## **Chicks** before dicks.

2002 *Daily Vanguard [Pennsylvania State University]* 9 Apr.: "Tomorrow Art Explores CBD—Chicks before Dicks, HMB—High Maintenance Boys and More in Further Survey of College Slang." The slang term *chicks* refers to "young women"; *dicks* is a slang anatomical reference, a synecdoche for "men." The proverb (usually uttered from a woman's point of view) asserts the preferability of female companionship. It is the counterpart of "BROS before hos."

## **Chicken** today, feathers tomorrow.

1958 *New York Times* 8 Aug.: "There's an old [horse] racing expression: 'Chicken today, feathers tomorrow.' This was a feather day for Sunny Jim Fitzsimmons, the 80-year-old dean of the trainers." 1980 Barry Fell, *Saga America* (New York: Times) 314: "The English proverb answering to this Greek and Pima fable . . . is 'Chicken today, feathers tomorrow,' and the sentiment is basically 'Live for today, let tomorrow take care of itself.'" Cf. "A ROOSTER one day, a feather duster the next."

When the **chicken** is merry (happy), a hawk is near.

Anderson and Cundall (1910) 20 give the saying as a Jamaican proverb: "When fowl merry, hawk ketch him chicken" (gloss: "Said also of pigeons. When one is prosperous one should guard against trouble"). Beckwith (1925) 118; Prahlad (2001) 243.

**Chicken Little** (Licken, Lickin') was right.

1950 Max Steele, *Debby* (New York: Harper, 1950) 270 (the protagonist looking up at the dark sky, which seems to have "split wide open"): "Smack-dab across the center of darkness was a band of sunlight. 'Chicken Little!' Debby whispered aghast. She had always known that Chicken Little was right; that the world would come to an end; that the sky would someday fall in on their heads." 1956 *Victoria [TX] Advocate* 6 Feb.: "The poultry flock decides that Chicken Little was right about the sky falling, and takes off for the tall timbers." 1965 *Los Angeles Times* 16 Dec.: "A bumper sticker with the odd message, 'Chicken Little Was Right,' given him by a friend, has been drawing curious reactions since Jack T. Pickett of the California Farmer put it on his car." 1971 *Chicago Tribune* 11 Apr.: "And when a Disney film takes up revolutionary causes . . . , maybe Chicken Licken was right." *YBQ* Sayings (5).

**Children** (Our children, The children) are our future.

1920 W. E. B. Du Bois, *Dark Water* (New York: Harcourt, Brace and Howe) 212: "If we realized that children are the future, that immortality is the present child, that no education which educates can possibly be too costly, then we know the menace of Kaiserism. . . ." 1921 Marguerite E. Harrison, *Marooned in Moscow* (New York: George H. Doran) 78: "Like many other thoughtful Communists, she [Alexandra Kolontai] believes the present generation is hopeless . . . and that, as the Communists express it, 'the children are our future.'"

**Children** should be seen and not had.

1928 *Life Magazine* 91 (16 Feb.) 30 (filler item): "Modern Version: Children should be seen and not had" (credited to *College Humor* [magazine?]). Litovkina and Mieder (2006) 115. The proverb originated as an anti-proverb based on "Children should be seen and not heard."

Never work with **children** or animals.

1964 *Humboldt Standard [Eureka CA]* 30 Oct.: "'Young man,' Ray Milland once told Brian Kelly, 'let me give you a piece of advice. If you want to get anywhere as an actor, never work with children or animals. They'll kill you.'" Rees (1995) 340–41; Pickering (2001) 255.

No **child** is born a bigot (racist).

See "No one is born a BIGOT."

Teach your (Parents must teach their) **children** to walk then to walk away.

1964 C. W. Brister, *Pastoral Care in the Church* (New York: Harper & Row) 223: "While parents have taught their children to walk, then to 'walk away' in marriage, the minister can point the young couple to God. . . ." 1971 C. W. Brister, *It's Tough Growing Up* (Nashville TN: Broadman) 31: "Your parents teach you to walk, then to walk away from them as you mature."

There are no bad **children**, only bad parents.

1910 "Personalities," *Hampton's Magazine* 24: 573: "Now, working along the same theory as Father [Peter J.] Dunne's, comes Mrs. Frederick Schoff, of Philadelphia. 'There are no bad children, only bad parents, bad guardians, and evil surroundings.'" Cf. "There are no bad DOGS, only bad owners" and "There are no bad STUDENTS, just bad teachers."

To a **child** with a hammer, everything looks like a nail.

See "When all you have is a HAMMER, everything looks like a nail."

Don't lead with your **chin**.

1931 *Washington Post* 26 May: "I believe in the silver lining, the rainbow after the storm, . . . the infallibility of the slogan 'Never lead with your chin.' . . . I believe the worst is over and that it never was as bad as it was advertised." *DAP* 98; *RHDP* 63–64. The proverb makes figurative and general a sentence of conventional advice from boxing.

The **chip** doesn't (Chips don't) fall far from the block.

Anderson and Cundall (1910) 7 give the saying as a Jamaican proverb: "De chip never fall too furr from de block." Champion (1938) 289 gives it as a Slovakian proverb. Prahlad (2001) 237. Cf. the older "An apple doesn't fall far from the tree" and the proverbial phrase "a chip off the old block."

A **chip** on the shoulder is a good indication of wood higher up.

1926 *Christian Science Monitor* 10 Nov. (in a collection of "random ramblings"): "A chip on the shoulder often advertises the existence of more wood higher up." *DAP* 98.

When the **chips** are down, the buffalo (cow) is empty.

1997 *Copley News Service* 3 Dec.: "Everything seemed to be going wrong, management was in a funk and stock prices lost wattage from $34 to $18 a share this year. The chips were down and the buffalo was empty." Casselman (2002) 91. The proverb plays punningly on the idiom (from poker) "the chips are down" (in other contexts, *chips* is a slang euphemism for "feces").

Our **choices** define us.

c. 1985 Edmund D. Pellegrino, "Philosophical Groundings for Treating the Patient as a Person," in *Changing Values in Medicine* (papers from a 1979 conference), edited by Eric J. Cassell and Mark Siegler (Frederick MD: University Publications of America) 100: "No two persons make precisely the same choices and so our choices define us as unique beings, as *this person*, not the universal person" (italics as shown). 1990 Jess Feist, *Theories of Personality*, 2nd ed. (Fort Worth TX: Holt, Rinehart & Winston) 672: "Ultimately, each of us is responsible for the choices we make and those choices define us as unique human beings." 1992 Barry Baldwin, "Classicism, Content, and Contemporaneity in Michael Italicus," *Byzantion* 62: 110: "But anyone who indites a monody on a dead pet is saying something about himself—our choices define us."

**Choose** it or lose it (Choose or lose).

1979 *H. R. 5424. National Publications Act of 1979 . . . Committee on House Administration* (Washington DC: Government Printing Office) 11: "The present system of 'choose it or lose it' causes many libraries to choose marginally useful documents at great expense. . . ." 1985 *New York Times* 7 Dec.: "Early this year some telephone users were asked to choose a long-distance company. . . . The new campaign marks an important change in the telephone company's approach, one that it sums up in its new catch phrase—'Choose or lose.'" The proverb probably originated as an anti-proverb based on "Use it or lose it"; Doyle (2009).

**Church** is not out till the fat lady sings.

1976 Fabie Rue Smith and Charles Rayford Smith, *Southern Words and Sayings* (Austin: for the authors) [fol. 10r] (unpaginated): "*Church ain't out 'till* [sic] *the fat lady sings*—It ain't over yet" (italics as shown). *YBQ* Ralph Carpenter. Keyes (1992) 40–42 reports oral recollections of similar sayings from the American South in the 1950s and 1960s. The proverb "Church is not out till the fat lady sings" may represent a variant of "CHURCH is not out till they sing"—or a conflation (based on faulty memory or deliberate wit) of that proverb with "The OPERA isn't over till the fat lady sings" or "The GAME is not over till the fat lady sings."

## **Church** is not out till they sing.

1966 Larry L. King, *The One-Eyed Man* (New York: New American Library) 198: "The governor wallowed coffee in his mouth and swallowed, nodding. 'All that might be true,' he said. 'But church ain't over till they sing.'" *DAP* 99(4).

## Sometimes a **cigar** is just a cigar.

1950 Allen Wheelis, "The Place of Action in Personality Change," *Psychiatry* 13: 139: "One errs, however, in inferring on every occasion, under whatever circumstances, that such a state of affairs obtains. This is still an occupational hazard of psychoanalysis—thirty years after Freud's famous remark that 'a cigar is sometimes just a cigar.'" 1954 Robert V. Faragher and Fritz F. Heiman, "Price Controls, Antitrust Laws, and Minimum Price Laws," *Law and Contemporary Problems* 19: 656: "This search for significant meanings where none are to be found recalls the reply made by Sigmund Freud to overzealous disciples who felt that there must be a significant meaning behind his cigar smoking. 'Sometimes a cigar is just a cigar,' the Father of Psychoanalysis reminded them." *YBQ* Freud (24); Keyes (1992) 173. The proverb discourages overanalyzing. The factuality of its attribution to Freud is questionable.

## Every **circus** needs a ringmaster.

1993 *St. Petersburg [FL] Times* 2 Nov.: "Any circus needs a ringmaster. Tradition assigns that role to the governor. So does the Constitution." 1996 Sandra P. Aldrich, *Men Read Newspapers, Not Minds* (Wheaton IL: Tyndale House) 151 (quoting a young married man): "Equal partnership sounds good in theory, but in practice somebody has to run the show. Every circus needs a ringmaster."

## You can't fight **city hall**.

1933 A. H. Shoenfeld, *The Joy Peddler* (New York: for the author) 23: "'How can you fight the church? . . . You know what they say goes,' added Mrs. Beeman. 'Try and fight City Hall.'" 1939 *Administration and Operation of the Civil Service Laws: Hearings before a Special Committee . . . Senate* (Washington DC: Government Printing Office, 1941) 306; Lee K. Frankel testifies: "I was advised by friends in the Bureau that you could not fight city hall, and that it was best to preserve my job by keeping quiet. . . ." *MP* C220; *RHDP* 381–82; *YBQ* Modern Proverbs (30).

## We may achieve **climate**, but weather is thrust upon us.

1912 The saying entered oral tradition as a proverb from the posthumously published story "A Fog in Santone" by O. Henry (William Sydney Porter, who died in 1910). *DAP* 101.

## **Close** (Almost, Nearly) doesn't count (won't cut it).

1916 *Forest and Stream* Aug.: "Trapshooting is the one sport where luck doesn't figure. You have got to deliver the goods in shooting at the targets. Close doesn't count." 1932 *Rhinelander [WI] Daily News* 11 Jun.: "Local fans who have watched the home-made Rhino team play some excellent games this season, believe the local club should cop tomorrow afternoon. Almost doesn't count in the season's standings, but the Rhinos almost defeated Medford." Cf. "ALMOST is not good enough."

## Close doesn't count except in horseshoes (and hand grenades) (and nuclear bombs).

1914 *Lincoln [NE] Daily News* 15 Aug.: "Close does not [*sic*] count only in horseshoes." 1921 *Decatur [IL] Daily Review* 3 Oct.: "Close counts in horseshoes only." 1932 *Washington Post* 8 Jul.: "Close doesn't count except in horseshoe pitching." 1970 *Guthrian [Guthrie County IA]* 26 Jan.: "Close only counts in horse shoes and grenades." *DAP* 102; *YBQ* Frank Robinson. The proverb, with its various accretions, probably originated as an anti-proverb based on "CLOSE doesn't count."

## Close enough is close (good) enough.

1978 J. W. LaPatra, *Analyzing the Criminal Justice System* (Lexington MA: D. C. Heath) 23: "As a body of knowledge, mathematics tries to be clear, elegant, and rigorous, but as a tool it is sometimes sloppy, and 'close enough' is good enough." 1981 I. Gormezano and E. James Kehoe, "Classical Conditioning and the Law of Contiguity," in *Predictability, Correlation, and Contiguity*, edited by Peter Harzen and M. D. Zeiler (Chichester UK: John Wiley & Sons) 14: ". . . [S]uch a vague specification of CS-US contiguity was able to evade the problems of trace conditioning and stimulus asynchrony with an implicit close-enough-is-good-enough principle. . . ." 1998 Robin Dellabough, *Beardstown Ladies' Pocketbook Guide to Picking Stocks* (New York: Hyperion) 126–27: "Again, people's numbers will vary here, because their estimated high earnings per share will vary. This is a case where close enough is close enough." Cf. "GOOD enough is good enough."

## Close is not close enough.

See "ALMOST is not good enough."

## Always be closing.

1971 Frederick E. Webster, *Marketing Communication* (New York: Ronald) 308:

"A salesman may learn a 'rule' of spelling (for example, 'ABC,' 'Always Be Closing') long before he learns how to apply that rule." 1977 Richard Smith, "Birth of a Salesman," *New Society* 42: 609: "Salesmen have a penchant for mnemonics. . . . There is ABC: Always Be Closing. The close is the goal of all salesmen, the point when the customer agrees to part with the money."

## Everybody loves a clown.

See "All the WORLD loves a clown."

## The cock's mouth kills the cock.

Anderson and Cundall (1910) 22 give the saying as a Jamaican proverb: "Cock mout' kill cock" (gloss: "Applied to the evil effects of jealousy and gossip"). Beckwith (1925) 25; Prahlad (2001) 243–44. Glossing the proverb, Beckwith cites a Swahili proverb in an 1891 collection, translated "A man is betrayed by his own tongue."

## Wake up and smell the coffee.

1943 *Chicago Daily Tribune* 18 Jan.: "A few years ago, when a wife told her husband to 'wake up and smell the coffee,' it usually was said in utter derision." 1960 *Evening Courier [Prescott AZ]* 1 Feb. ("Ann Landers" advice column): "Wake up and smell the coffee. Irving loves you—like a sister."

## The bigger they come, the harder they fall.

See "The bigger they are, the harder they FALL."

## *Come see me* is one thing; *come live with me* is a different thing.

See "*SEE me* is one thing; *come live with me* is a different thing."

### You have to **come** from somewhere before you can go back.

1966 Louise Bennett, "Back to Africa," in *Jamaica Labrish*, edited by Rex Nettleford (Kingston, Jamaica: Sangster's Book Stores) 214 (the poem satirizes the "Back to Africa" movement popular among Rastafarians and others): "Back to Africa Miss Matty? / Yuh noh know wha yuh dah-sey? / Yuh haffe come from some weh fus, / Before yuh go back deh?"; the editor says, "This poem was written in 1947," but evidently it was not published then. Prahlad (2001) 244.

### Everybody loves a **comeback** (a comeback story).

1941 *Christian Science Monitor* 4 Apr.: "Sentimentally he [hockey player Mel Hill] was the people's choice—a crowd always loves a comeback." 1943 "The Gaudy Touch," *Time* 41, no. 15 (12 Apr.) 74: "Everybody loves a comeback. Last week flat-faced, chocolate-colored little Henry Armstrong . . . endeared himself to the ring fans. . . ." 1987 *New York Times* 17 Apr.: "Everyone loves a comeback story, and the old fans [of a reopened restaurant] can be expected to come back in droves."

### Never **complain**, never explain (Never explain, never complain).

1903 Benjamin Disraeli, as quoted in John Morley's *Life of William Ewart Gladstone* (London: Macmillan) 1: 222–23: "What Mr. Gladstone carried away in his memory was a sage lesson of Lyndenhurst's . . . —'Never defend yourself before a popular assemblage . . . ; the hearers, in the pleasure which the assault gives them, will forget the previous charge.' As Disraeli himself put it afterwards, *Never complain and never explain*" (italics as shown). 1915 Robert T. Morris, *Doctors versus Folks* (Garden City NY: Doubleday Page) 6: "It is well to follow the rule to never explain and never complain. A man is judged by his character as a whole—not by individual acts." *MP* C314; *DAAP* 174; *YBQ* Disraeli (32).

### You can't (Don't try to) con a **con** (con man).

1942 *Oakland Tribune* 30 Jun.: "Don't try to con a con'man, sucker." 1970 Howard James, *Children in Trouble* (New York: David McKay) 150: "'We decide when it's time for a guy to go home,' said one 15-year-old, who has been in institutions for a third of his life. 'You can't con a con.'" The noun *con* or *con man* usually means "confidence man," though occasionally, either punningly (in an anti-proverb) or by a misunderstanding, it might mean "convict": 1976 *Daytona Beach [FL] Morning Journal* 27 Nov.: "Steve Smith, a university professor who taught some of the courses the three convicts attended, said: '. . . you have to know what you are talking about. You can't con a con.'" Cf. "Don't bullshit a BULLSHITTER" and "You can't kid a KIDDER."

### A clear **conscience** is (usually) a sign of (usually comes from) a bad memory.

1953 Joseph Nuttin, *Psychoanalysis and Personality*, translated from the German (of 1949) by George Lamb (New York: Sheed & Ward) 69: "Perhaps the saying 'All too often a clear conscience is merely the result of a bad memory' is applicable to the father of the [Freudian] theory that absent-mindedness comes from repression?" 1961 *Chicago Daily Tribune* 8 Nov.: "What might pass as a clear conscience might be just a case of bad memory."

### **Conscience** gets a lot of credit that belongs to cold feet.

1911 *Fort Worth [TX] Star Telegram* 9 Aug. (filler item): "Conscience gets a good deal of credit that belongs to cold feet." *DAP* 113(12). Cf. Shakespeare's Hamlet's "Conscience doth make cowards of us all."

A **conservative** is a liberal who has been mugged (A liberal is a conservative who has not been mugged).

1973 *Oakland Tribune* 30 Apr.: "I sort of like Curtis Stewart's definition of a conservative. 'It's a liberal who got mugged last night.'" 1979 Frederick J. Hamilton, letter to the editor, *Black Belt Magazine* 14, no. 12 (Dec.) 10: "We have a saying in Harlem that a Liberal is a Conservative who has not been mugged." Ratcliffe (2006) 104. Cf. "A LIBERAL is a conservative who has been arrested."

The most important **considerations** for buying (selling) a home are location, location, and location.

1926 *Chicago Daily Tribune* 27 Sep. (classified ad): ATTENTION, SALESMEN, SALES MGRS. LOCATION LOCATION LOCATION[.] Close in to Rogers Park" (capitalization as shown). 1952 *Washington Post* 20 Mar. (advertisement): "The 3 Most important Considerations of the Wise Home Investor[:] 1. location: Walking distance of shopping center. . . . 2. location: Rapid transportation to city. . . . 3. location: Convenient to schools, churches and hospitals." 1953 *Los Angeles Times* 6 Dec.: "There's an old saying in the home-buying field. It goes: 'The ten most important things to look for in a house are location, location, location, location, location, location, location, location, location and location.'" *YBQ* Sayings (37). The maxim (sometimes designated "the first three laws of real estate"), especially in the elliptical form "Location, location, location," can be applied more broadly to baseball (both hitting and fielding) and football (punting), as well as to the advantageous selection of a region or country in which to locate a factory or other business.

Every **contest** has a winner.

See "Every GAME has a winner."

The (latest) **convert** is the greatest zealot.

See "There is no ZEALOT like a convert."

Never trust a skinny **cook**.

See "Never trust a skinny CHEF."

That's how the **cookie** crumbles.

See "That's the WAY the cookie crumbles."

The winner gets the **cookie** and the loser gets the crumbs.

1986 *News-Journal [Daytona Beach FL]* 29 Aug.: "'They [racing pigs] know there's an Oreo cookie at the finish line[;] that's why they race,' said [fair] Manager Dave Williams. 'The loser gets the crumbs, just as in real life.'" 1987 *Chicago Tribune* 23 Jul.: "'The winner gets the cookie,' [Al] Pringle added. 'The loser gets the crumbs. That's the way it is in life.'"

You can't get all your **coons** up one tree.

Bradley (1937) 67 lists the saying as a South Carolina proverb, with the gloss "You can't gain all the advantages thru one act, stroke or operation." 1938 Marjorie Kinnan Rawlings, *The Yearling* (New York: Charles Scribner's Sons) 10: "'A buck, Jody. I near about run him down.' Again he was furious. 'Why'n't it wait 'til I got home?' 'Didn't you pleasure yourself at the Forresters? You cain't git all your 'coons up one tree.'" *MP* C328; *DAP* 116.

If you don't believe in **cooperation**, watch what happens to a wagon (car) when one wheel comes off.

1921 *Locomotive Engineers Journal* 55: 754 (filler item): "If you don't think co-operation is necessary, watch what happens to a wagon when a wheel comes off." *DAP* 116(3,4).

## Even the **corn** has ears.

1905 Lilian M. Heath, *The Red Telephone* ([Chicago]: W. R. Vansant) 64: "He will never need a scarecrow if he will only stay in his cornfield himself. But, as even the corn has ears, we should hate to think of what it must endure when the Northeast Man gets to talking." *DAP* 117(6). The quoted example is an anti-proverb, ironically misinterpreting (or reinterpreting) the proverb, which ordinarily cautions against uttering secrets. Cf. the older "Walls have ears."

## I throw out **corn**, but I don't call the fowl.

Franck (1921) 103 lists the saying as a Jamaican proverb: "Me trow me corn a door me no call neighbour fowl fe pick it up." Beckwith (1925) 84 paraphrases: "'I throw my corn, I don't call my neighbor's fowl to pick it up'; employed as a retort to one who, although no names have been used, thinks himself the one abused." Anderson and Cundall (1927) 32; Prahlad (2001) 244. The meaning resembles "If the shoe fits, wear it."

## You have to throw (put, plant) the **corn** where the hogs can get it.

1990 *Technology Transfer and Challenges Facing Small Business: Hearing before the Committee on Small Business . . . Senate* (Washington DC: Government Printing Office) 207; Senator Dale Bumpers speaks: "He [Senator Herman Talmadge] said, Dale, it has been my experience that if you want people to understand, you have got to throw the corn where the hogs can get to it." 1993 *New York Times* 27 Mar.: "Besides policy advice, Mr. [Bill] Clinton has also gleaned some of his best down-home Arkansasisms from his two friends, including . . . 'You gotta throw the corn where the hogs can get to it,' a [Dale] Bumpers saying often used in reference to making aid more easily available to the Russians." 1993 President Bill Clinton, "Remarks at the Congressional Black Caucus Dinner" (18 Sep.), *Weekly Compilation of Presidential Documents* 29: 1814: "And he

[Dale Bumpers] said, 'Well, you know, every now and then Joycelyn [Elders] may be a little too outspoken, but you can say one thing for her: She plants the corn where the hogs can get at it.'"

## Live fast (hard), die young, leave (have) a good-looking **corpse**.

1930 Courtenay Terrett, *Only Saps Work: A Ballyhoo for Racketeering* (New York: Vanguard) 29: "There was an old cowboy proverb . . . that it was glorious to 'live hard, die young, and make a hell of a good-looking corpse.'" 1947 Willard Motley, *Knock on Any Door* (New York: D. Appleton-Century) 157: "When the beer came Nick lifted and tilted the brown liquid in past the yellow foam. 'Live fast, die young, and have a good-looking corpse!' he said with a toss of the head. That was something he had picked up somewhere and he'd say it all the time now." 1954 Clyde B. Vedder, *The Juvenile Offender* (Garden City NY: Doubleday) 156: "A large part of this code [of 'gang morality'], as publicized by such motion pictures as 'Knock on Any Door,' is supposed to be expressed by the slogan: 'Live fast, die young, love all the girls, hate all the cops, and have a good-looking corpse.'" The shorter locution "Live fast and die young" is older.

## No **corpse**, no crime.

See "No BODY, no crime."

## If you have to ask the **cost**, you can't afford it.

See "If you have to ask the PRICE, you can't afford it."

## It **costs** nothing to dream (Dreaming doesn't cost anything).

1920 W. C., "Make Known the Facts and Silence the Propagandist," *Santa Fe Magazine* 14, no. 7 (Jun.) 33: "Such dazzling ambitions are not to be easily quenched, and it costs nothing to dream, and talk." 1932 Beulah Marie Dix, *Pity of God*

(New York: Viking) 36: "Dreams cost nothing. She dwelt fondly on the roadster she would like to give Jonny on her graduation." 1945 Dorothy Fields (lyricist), "It Doesn't Cost You Anything to Dream"—song in the stage musical *Up in Central Park* (music by Sigmund Romberg). Cf. the older "It costs nothing to look."

## Coughs and sneezes spread diseases.

1918 *Daily Leader [Grand Rapids WI]* 9 Oct.: "UNCLE SAM'S ADVICE ON FLU . . . Coughs and Sneezes Spread Diseases" (capitalization as shown). Pickering et al. (1992) 122.

## It's what's up front that counts.

c. 1957 The saying entered oral tradition as a proverb from an advertising slogan for Winston cigarettes—playing on the older proverb "It's what inside that counts." 1960 *Washington Post* 23 May: "'Tis said 'It's what's up front that counts' and to check the fractional clocking [for timing race horses] is to wonder if father time wasn't on a treadmill."

## Not everything that can be counted counts (Not all things that can be counted count, Not everything that counts can be counted, Some things that count cannot be counted).

1955 Robert Gordis, *Judaism for the Modern Age* (New York: Farrar, Straus, & Cudahy) 74–75: "Many aspects of life and the world are forever beyond the power of the scientific method. There are more things in heaven and earth than can be weighed or measured. The things which count cannot be counted." 1957 William Bruce Cameron, "The Elements of Statistical Confusion," *AAUP Bulletin* 43, no. 1 (Spring) 34: "Equally obvious, 100 evening college students taking one two[-]hour course each are in no meaningful way equivalent to 100 day students, each with a sixteen[-]hour load. The moral is: Not everything that can be counted counts." 1963 William Bruce Cameron, *Informal Sociology*

(New York: Random House) 13: "It would be nice if all of the data which sociologists require could be enumerated because then we could run them through IBM machines and draw charts as the economists do. However, not everything that can be counted counts, and not everything that counts can be counted." 1968 Richard Harvey Wood, *U. S. Universities: Their Role in AID-Financed Technical Assistance* (New York: Education and World Affairs) 48: "One of the major difficulties encountered in attempting to evaluate the results of any institution building project is that often the things that really count can't be counted." Versions of the saying have been attributed to Sir George Pickering and Albert Einstein.

## Ask not what your country can do for you—ask what you can do for your country.

The saying (often slightly misquoted) entered oral tradition as a proverb from President John F. Kennedy's inaugural address, 20 Jan. 1960. An 1884 speech by Oliver Wendell Holmes Jr. is sometimes cited as a prototype of Kennedy's wording, since it anticipates the (commonplace) idea and the parallel phrasing, the chiasmus: ". . . [W]e pause . . . to recall what our country has done for each of us, and to ask ourselves what we can do for our country in return." A closer prior analog: 1922 Isaac Doughton, *Preparing for the World's Work* (New York: Charles Scribner's Sons) 4: "But as good citizens you are not so anxious to know what your country does for you as you are to know what you can do for your country." The eeriest anticipator of both Holmes's and Kennedy's wording occurred in 1858, except that the writer, one Rev. M. Thomson, was engaging in satire, proffering ironic advice—and thus inverting the clauses—in "Our Youth: Their Principles and Prospects," *Ladies' Repository* 18: 285: "Fetter the noblest powers and impulses of the soul; turn all your genius into cunning; prefer your wages to your work; study not what you can do for your country, but what your country can do for you." *YBQ* John Kennedy (16); Rees (1984) 76–77; Hoffman and Honeck (1987); Mieder (2005b) 172–73.

**Courage** is fear that has said its prayers.

1922 The saying probably passed into oral tradition as a proverb from an epigram titled "Courage" by Karle Wilson Baker, *Burning Bush* (New Haven CT: Yale UP) 69: "Courage is armor / A blind man wears; / The calloused scar / Of outlived despairs: / Courage is Fear / That has said its prayers." *DAP* 120(8).

**Courtesy** pays dividends (compound interest).

1922 Edward Hungerford, *Our Railroads Tomorrow* (New York: Century) 132: "Yet he too has found long since that courtesy pays dividends, plain dollars-and-cents dividends." Barbour (1965) 40 gives the saying as an Illinois proverb: "Courtesy pays compound interest." *DAP* 121(15). The proverb originated as an anti-proverb elaborating on the proverb "Courtesy pays."

Better a good **cow** than a cow of a good kind.

1922 John Buchan, *Huntingtower* (London: Hodder & Stoughton) 203 (a fictional Scotsman is speaking): "I'm no weel acquaint wi' his forbears, but I'm weel eneuch acquaint wi' Sir Erchie, and 'better a guid coo than a coo o' a guid kind,' as my mither used to say." *ODP* 20.

Sacred **cows** make great (good, the best, gourmet) hamburgers (burgers).

1965 *Daily Collegian [Pennsylvania State University]* 19 Oct. (regarding a feature titled "Bottom of the Birdcage"): "Birdcage's newly-adopted theme, borrowed from Aardvark magazine, is 'Sacred cows make the best hamburger.' Each issue will have something to offend each member of the family." 1968 *Lowell [MA] Sun* 25 Jan.: "An old newspaper adage says 'Sacred cows make the best hamburger.'" The conceit of butchering a "sacred cow"—but not the proverb—can be found in the first half of the twentieth century.

Salt (Feed, Pet, Court, Woo, Buy) the **cow** to get the calf.

1949 T. M. Cranfill, "Barnaby Rich and King James," *ELH* 16: 74: "Reversing the strategy recommended in the old proverb 'Salt the cow to get the calf,' Rich dedicated yet another work . . . to Prince Henry in 1612." *DAP* 123(19).

**Crab** say him no trust no shadow after dark.

See "You cannot trust SHADOWS."

If you sift through enough **crap**, you may find gold.

See "If you sift through enough DIRT, you may find gold."

Ninety percent of everything is **crap**.

See "Ninety percent of everything is CRUD."

**Crime** doesn't pay and neither does farming.

1975 *Bemidji [MN] Pioneer* 7 Mar.: "A newspaper clipping received recently showed a time and temperature sign from a Wisconsin bank. Printed on the sign was the message: Crime Doesn't Pay—Neither Does Farming." 1977 *Lawrence [KS] Journal-World* 12 Dec.: "The signs also told of the plight of farmers, who are demanding parity prices for their products. . . . 'Crime doesn't pay and neither does farming.'" Casselman (1999) 74. The proverb originated as an anti-proverb based on "Crime doesn't pay."

**Don't do the crime if you can't do the time (If you can't do the time, don't do the crime).**

1957 *Lowell [MA] Sun* 23 May: "Don't do the crime if you can't do the time." 1973 *Fort Scott [KS] Tribune* 24 Aug. (in a letter to the "Dear Abby" advice column): "There is an old saying: 'If you can't do the time, don't do the crime!'" *YBQ Modern Proverbs* (17).

**It's not the crime but the cover-up.**

1973 *Bulletin [Bend OR]* 17 May: "The [Watergate] scandal now involved not only the crime but the coverup." 1994 *New York Times* 23 Jan.: "'It isn't the crime it's the cover-up,' goes the truism that has routinely been applied to political scandals since the Watergate cover-up forced President Richard M. Nixon from office two decades ago." 1994 Ward S. Just, *Ambition & Love* (Boston: Houghton Mifflin) 11: "'I haven't had a show in a while.' 'But I saw a review——.' 'Yes, there were plenty of those. I never lacked attention. As they say, it's not the crime but the cover-up.'"

**The only crime is getting caught (It isn't a crime unless you get caught, It isn't against the law if they don't catch you).**

1940 George H. Bender, *The Challenge of 1940* (New York: G. P. Putnam's Sons) 69: "Youthful Americans are growing into manhood and womanhood with the vicious theory that violation of the law is not a crime; that crime is 'getting caught.'" 1948 *Washington Post* 26 Apr.: "They're still throwing spitballs [in baseball] despite the fact that the spitter was outlawed nearly 30 years ago. The only crime is getting caught."

**A criminal (murderer) (always) returns to the scene of the crime.**

1905 *Washington Post* 24 Apr. (a joke beneath a drawing that illustrates the joke): "Poet—They say a criminal always returns to the scene of

the crime. Wife—I wonder if that's why your poems come back?" *MP* C406; *YBQ* Modern Proverbs (18).

**A crisis is an opportunity (With crisis comes opportunity).**

1900 S. B. Rossiter, "A Message to the Auxiliaries of the McAll Association of America," *American McAll Record* 18, no. 1 (Feb.) 7 (in a quoted letter that the author says he wrote the previous Dec.): "What is crisis? One of two things. Opportunity or defeat. Can God suffer defeat? No. Then crisis is opportunity." 1904 C. P. Middleton, "The Present Crisis," *Women's Missionary Magazine* (of the United Free Church of Scotland) 37: 286: "A crisis is an opportunity; and our chief concern should be lest we should fail to use this opportunity aright." 1943 [Carl E. Purinton?], "Dostoevsky, Novelist of Crisis" (editorial), *Journal of Bible and Religion* 11: 248: "In conclusion, it is helpful to recall the Chinese proverb: 'Crisis is opportunity.' This is a thought that is basic to Dostoevsky and, we might add, to the New Testament." 1950 Geoffrey Parrish, "Revolution and Reformation," *Contemporary Review* 177, pg. 118: "With every crisis comes opportunity, and the natural accompaniment of social revolution in the secular sphere should be a renewal of vigour by every Christian body of people. . . ." Cf. "TRAGEDY is an opportunity," "There are no PROBLEMS, only opportunities," and "Don't waste a CRISIS."

**Don't waste a crisis (Never let a crisis go to waste).**

1976 Myron F. Weiner, "Don't Waste a Crisis— Your Patient's or Your Own," *Medical Economics* 53, no. 5 (8 Mar.) 227: "If you have a myocardial infarction, or any other overwhelming crisis in your own life, whatever you do, don't waste it" (that is, use the medical "crisis" to improve aspects of personality, mental health, and lifestyle). 1993 Luther P. Gerlach, "Crises Are for Using: The 1988 Drought in Minnesota,"

*The Environmental Professional* 15: 279: "He [an unnamed official of the Minnesota Department of Natural Resources] agrees with the posted motto of a DNR colleague, 'Don't waste a crisis.'" The proverb has commonly been applied to ecological, economic, or diplomatic crises that can be exploited. Cf. "A CRISIS is an opportunity."

## There is never a **cross** you can't bear.

See "GOD sends no cross that you cannot bear."

## You can't keep a **crow** from flying, but you can keep it from building a nest on your head.

See "You can't keep BIRDS from flying over your head, but you can keep them from building a nest in your hair."

## Ninety percent of everything is **crud** (crap, shit).

1958 Theodore Sturgeon, "On Hand: A Book," *Venture Science Fiction* 1, no. 5 (Sep.) 78: "Sturgeon had a revelation. . . . It came to him that s f [science fiction] is indeed ninety-percent crud, but that also—Eureka!—*ninety-percent of* everything *is crud*. All things—cars, books, cheeses, hairstyles, people and pins . . . " (italics as shown). 1960 *Chicago Tribune* 3 Apr.: "We are all too aware of the validity of Sturgeon's law: 'Ninety per cent of science fiction is crud. In fact ninety per cent of *everything* is crud'" (italics as shown). 1969 Harlan Ellison, "The Glass Teat," *Los Angeles Free Press* 16 May: "Sturgeon's Law holds true, especially for writers. The Law says: 90% of EVERYthing is shit. . . . That is, ninety per cent of everything is merely average. Merely sufficient" (capitalization as shown). When Ellison revised the column for a collection of his essays, the percentage increased: 1975 *The Glass Teat* (New York: Pyramid) 178: "The Law says: 94% of *every*thing is shit" (italics as shown). 1975 Ellison, *The Other Glass Teat* (New York: Pyramid) 8: "I like to think of Theodore Sturgeon's Law when I hear the snobs

badrapping tv: '90% of everything is crap.' That means 90% of everything is mediocre, as I read the Law. And that goes for books, plays, cars, puddings, people and movies. The percentage is probably higher for politicians."

## There's no **crying** in baseball.

1992 The saying probably entered oral tradition as a proverb from the motion picture *A League of Their Own*, screenplay by Lowell Ganz and Babaloo Mandel. *YBQ* Film Lines (109). The proverb can apply to the resisting of tearfulness in situations other than baseball.

## There is no **cure** for a fool.

1909 Chase S. Osborn, *The Andean Land* (Chicago: A. C. McClurg) 2: 262 (in a list of "Andean" proverbs, with English translations): "There is no cure for a fool" (translating "El mal que no se cura es la locura"—or, perhaps, offering an equivalent English proverb). 1910 Louis Joseph Vance, *The Fortune Hunter* (New York: Dodd, Mead) 309: "He reviewed the encounter and laughed quietly. 'There's no cure for a fool,' he mused." *MP* C447. Cf. "STUPID is forever" and "You can't fix STUPID."

## The **customer** gets what the customer wants.

2001 *Irish Times [Dublin]* 2 Oct.: "I do not care if we're selling beef or chicken or vegetarian, the customer gets what the customer wants." 2004 *The Age [Melbourne, Australia]* 28 Aug.: "The customer gets what the customer wants, rescue calls and cover-ups included. Just call it a full-service package."

## The **customer** is always right.

1905 *Boston Daily Globe* 24 Sep.: "Broadly speaking, Mr [Marshall] Field adheres to the theory that 'the customer is always right.'" 1905 *Corbett's Herald* 11 Nov.: "One of our most successful merchants . . . recently summed up his business policy in the phrase, 'The customer is always right.'" *MP* C456; *DAP* 132(3); *RHDP* 45; *DAAP* 188; *YBQ* Modern Proverbs (212); *ODP* 68; Taylor (1958); Pickering et al. (1992) 130; Flavell and Flavell (1993) 62; Chlosta and Grzybek (1995); Rees (1995) 106; Room (2000) 168; Pickering (2001) 88.

## A clean **cut** heals soonest.

1913 Eden Phillpotts, *The Shadow: A Play in Three Acts* (London: Duckworth) 70: "A clean cut is soonest healed. We'll part clean, not ragged." 1952 John Steinbeck, *East of Eden* (New York: Viking) 417: "'You'll let us hear from you?' 'I don't know. I'll have to think about it. They say a clean cut heals soonest.'" The figurative proverb evolved from a literal aphorism in medicine and horticulture; as a proverb, it counsels that an abrupt departure or a complete severing of a human relationship can be advisable.

## Dance as if no one is watching.

1989 The saying probably entered oral tradition as a proverb from a line in the song "Come from the Heart," by Susanna Clarke and Richard Leigh (popularly recorded by Kathy Matea, Don Williams, Guy Clark, and others): "You've got to sing like you don't need the money / Love like you'll never get hurt / You've got to dance like nobody's watchin' / It's gotta come from the heart if you want it to work." The saying has been referred to as an Irish proverb and, even more improbably, a quotation from Mark Twain.

## Dance with whoever brought you.

See "Dance with the ONE who brought you."

## You need more than **dancing shoes** to be a dancer.

Kin (1955) 63 lists the saying as an American proverb. 1981 *Uniontown [PA] Morning Herald* 24 Aug.: "Wisdom in fortune cookies at Pearls restaurant: . . . 'Remember you need more than dancing shoes to be a dancer.'" *DAP* 133.

## Murder your **darlings**.

1916 The saying entered oral tradition as a proverb from an aphorism by Arthur Quiller-Couch, *On the Art of Writing* (New York: G. P. Putnam's Sons) 281: ". . . [I]f you here require a practical rule of me, I will present you with this:

'Whenever you feel an impulse to perpetuate a piece of exceptionally fine writing, obey it—whole-heartedly—and delete it before sending your manuscript to press. *Murder your darlings*'" (printed from a 1914 lecture; italics as shown). *YBQ* Quiller-Couch; Collins (1959) 34. Cf. "When in DOUBT, throw it out" and the older proverb, specifically about writing, "When in doubt, leave it out."

## Another **day**, another dollar.

1907 *Logansport [IN] Reporter* 11 Mar.: " I sat up and stretched and yawned. 'Oh, hum! The same old grind. Another day, another dollar. If I could only sleep two more hours.'" *MP* D30; *DAP* 135(6); *RHDP* 11; *YBQ* Modern Proverbs (22); Rees (1995) 20.

## Any **day** above ground is a good day.

1973 *The Transcript [North Adams MA]* 29 Sep. (quoting Tom Snyder): "I guess I can attribute my ability to enjoy life to the philosophy of my grandmother: 'Each day above ground is a good day.'" 1977 Don Rhodes, "Weekend at Walnut Valley," *Bluegrass Unlimited* 12, no. 6 (Dec.) 31: "'And today started out to be such a good day.' [Dan] Crary said[;] at that, the other good guy turned to the person who had arranged the ill-fated ambush and said, 'Son, any day above ground is a good day!'" 1991 *Buffalo [NY] News* 7 Feb.: "Keep writing and keep in mind the old GI saying, 'Any day above ground is a good day.'"

## Different (New) **day**, same shit.

See "Same SHIT, different day."

## Don't burn the **day** away.

1998 The saying perhaps entered oral tradition as a proverb from a line in the song "Pig" by the Dave Matthews band ("Don't burn the day away" represents the group's 1998 revision of a line in an earlier version of the song: "Don't burn the pig.")

On any given **day**, any team can beat any other team.

See "On any given SUNDAY, any team can beat any other team."

Some **days** you get the bear, other days the bear gets you.

See "Sometimes you get the BEAR, sometimes the bear gets you."

Some **days** you're the dog, and some days you're the fireplug.

See "Sometimes you're the DOG, and sometimes you're the fireplug."

Some **days** you're the windshield, and some days you're the bug.

See "Sometimes you're the WINDSHIELD, and sometimes you're the bug."

There is no **day** but today.

1979 Georgia Elizabeth Taylor, *The Infidel* (New York: St. Martin's) 449; "Today I love you, no one but you. There is no day but today, no past, no future—just this moment." 1991 Kofi Natambu, *The Melody Never Stops* (Detroit: Past Tents) 61 (beginning of a poem titled "Men Women Money Promises & Death: NYC, 1989"): "Welcome to the city / called no text but subtext / no way but subway / no say but hearsay / no lay but waylay / no day but today." The saying was further popularized in a song featured in the 1996 stage musical *Rent*, by Jonathan Larson.

Whatever gets you through the **day**.

See "Whatever gets you through the NIGHT."

You can buy anything except **day** and night.

1900 Hugh Percy Jones, *New Dictionary of Foreign Phrases and Classical Quotations*

(Philadelphia: J. B. Lippincott) 304 (in a list of French aphorisms): "(Money can buy everything but night and day.) Life cannot be bought." 1936 Carl Sandburg, *The People, Yes* (New York: Harcourt, Brace) 167 (in a poetic montage of proverbs and other sayings): "You can buy anything except day and night." *DAP* 77(8); *DAAP* 197.

Better **dead** than Red.

1961 *Oakland Tribune* 27 Apr.: "About 1,000 spectators gathered in San Francisco's Union Square to hear Robert Du Rord, a University of San Francisco senior, lash out against students who conducted pro-Castro demonstrations in the same place last week. . . . The platform yesterday was covered with signs stating 'Better Dead than Red' and allied sentiments." Barrick (1979); Rees (1984) 214; Rees (1995) 52. The proverb perhaps derives from (at least it was anticipated by) a parallel German expression, "Lieber tot als rot"—a propaganda slogan during World War II. In 1938 a similar German slogan was given in English as "Better dead than red-white-red"; Eugene Lennhoff, *Last Five Hours of Austria* (New York: Frederick A Stokes) 155. In the early history of the saying, *Red* (like German *rot*) means "Communist" (or "leftist"). Since the demise of the Cold War, the English proverb has been used as a playground taunt directed at red-haired children, sometimes in the form "Better dead than red on the head." Cf. "Better RED than dead."

A **deadline** is a deadline.

1933 *Chicago Daily Tribune* 29 Sep.: "Now go on with the story and let us have no more interruptions. A deadline is a deadline." 1940 Ely Culbertson, *The Strange Lives of One Man: An Autobiography* (Chicago: John C. Winston) 609: "'You know, Jo,' I finally said, 'an earthquake is an earthquake, but a deadline is a deadline. Why not go back and finish our job?'" *DAAP* 201.

**Death** is nature's way of telling you to slow down.

1960 "Brainstorms: Sicker, Sicker, Sicker," *Newsweek* 55, no. 17 (25 Apr.) 70: "Madison Avenue's latest definition of death, bouncing around New York last week, will hardly tempt the conservative editors of Stedman's [Medical] Dictionary: 'It's nature's way of telling you to slow down.'" *YBQ* Sayings (29); Rees (1995) 336. The proverb perhaps originated as a jocular anti-proverb based on "PAIN is nature's way of telling you to slow down."

A single **death** is a tragedy (misfortune); a million deaths is a statistic.

1947 *Washington Post* 20 Jan. "One official arose and made a speech about this tragedy— the tragedy of having millions of people dying of hunger. He began to enumerate death figures. . . . Stalin interrupted him to say: 'If only one man dies of hunger, that is a tragedy. If millions die, that's only statistics'" (ellipsis dots as shown). 1948 Charles J. Rolo, "Reader's Choice," *Atlantic* 182, no. 4 (Oct.) 106: "A Frenchman has aptly remarked that 'a single man killed is a misfortune, a million is a statistic.' How to encompass [in fiction] the emotional reality of that aggregate of horrors which so easily becomes 'a statistic' . . . ?" 1958 *New York Times* 28 Sep.: "'A single death is a tragedy, a million deaths is a statistic.' Stalin's epigram is admirably illustrated by Ernest Schnabel's pointilliste portrait of Anne Frank. . . ."

No one on his **deathbed** has ever said, "I wish I'd spent more time at the office (at work, on business)."

1984 Paul Tsongas, *Heading Home* (New York: Random House) 159–60: ". . . [T]he family was where I fulfilled my human aspirations. . . . Or, as an old friend, Arnold Zack, wrote to me in a letter, 'No one on his deathbed ever said, "I wish I spent more time on my business."'" 1986 *Adweek* 7 Apr.: "If you're not having as much fun out of life as you ought to, you should do something about it. Nobody on their deathbed ever said, 'I wish I had spent more time at the office.'"

Don't rearrange the **deck chairs** on the *Titanic*.

See "Don't rearrange the deck CHAIRS on the *Titanic*."

No good **deed** goes unpunished.

1938 James Agate, *Ego 2* (London: George G Harrap) 275 (diary entry): "[Isidore Leo] Pavia was in great form today: 'Every good deed brings its own punishment.'" 1942 *Tucson [AZ] Daily Citizen* 5 Oct.: "Reminds me of the line diplomats use: 'No good deed goes unpunished in Washington.'" *RHDP* 244; *YBQ* Claire Boothe Luce (7); *ODP* 136; Rees (1995) 348. The proverb may have originated as an anti-proverb based on the moralistic "No bad deed goes (remains) unpunished"; or it might be regarded as an updating of an old anti-proverb "Virtue is its own punishment" (which, in turn, parodied the Augustinian maxim "Sin is its own punishment"). It has often been attributed to Oscar Wilde or to Walter Winchell.

**Defeat** is not bitter if you don't swallow it.

1935 "From North, East, West and South," *Gleanings in Bee Culture* 63: 348: "Someone has wisely said, 'Defeat isn't bitter if you don't swallow it.' If beekeepers in northern California have never heard this saying, they will be thankful to see it now. . . ." *DAP* 142.

You don't get **defeated** unless you quit.

See "You never LOSE unless you quit."

Take what the **defense** gives you.

1960 *Christian Science Monitor* 29 Sep. (quoting the football coach Chuck Studley): "'We'll throw short,' Studley volunteered. 'You know, take what the defense will give us.'" 1979 *Washington Post* 26 Nov. (on rush-hour driving): "Don't try to beat the competition. Let the other guy have his rights, and all of yours too. Take what the defense gives you, as they say. You'll learn to feel smug, not beaten." The proverb originated as a football or basketball maxim.

## Delay is the deadliest form of denial.

1966 *Times [London]* 15 Sep.: "PARKINSON'S LAW OF DELAY BY C. NORTHCOTE PARKINSON . . . Delays are thus deliberately designed as a form of denial and are extended to cover the life expectation of the person whose proposal is being pigeon-holed. DELAY IS THE DEADLIEST FORM OF DENIAL" (capitalization as shown). 1969 Neil V. Sullivan, *Now Is the Time: Integration in the Berkeley Schools* (Bloomington: Indiana UP) 164: "But how well I know, as former board member Judge Avakian quoted later, that 'Delay is the deadliest form of denial.'" *YBQ* Parkinson (13).

## Don't tell me about the delivery; just show me the baby.

See "Don't tell me about the PAIN; just show me the baby."

## You cannot tell the depth of the well by the length of the handle on the pump.

1915 *Electric Railway Service* 17 Dec.: "You can never judge the depth of a well by the length of the pump handle. Inaugurate the system. Try it out." *DAP* 144.

## A messy (cluttered) desk is a sign of a messy mind (person).

1974 *Register-Guard [Eugene OR]* 3 May: "'They say a cluttered desk bespeaks a cluttered mind,' observed Paul Freund. 'But I much prefer to think a clean desk bespeaks an empty mind—that is my solace.'" 1995 *Worcester [MA] Telegram & Gazette* 26 Sep.: "Some people with clean

desks say, A messy desk is the sign of a messy person." 1999 *Boston Globe* 23 Sep.: "If a messy desk is a sign of a messy mind, then what is an empty desk a sign of?"

## A messy (cluttered) desk is a sign of intelligence (brilliance, genius, creativity, productivity, a busy person, etc.).

1973 "Dental Dean," *Ebony* 28, no. 5 (Mar.) 84: "There is little wonder, then, that on the desk in her [Juliann Bluitt's] Chicago office there is a sign reading, 'A cluttered desk is a sign of genius.'" 1979 John Peers, *1,000 Logical Laws* (Garden City NY: Doubleday) 114: "Bill's Note: A cluttered desk = a man of genius." 1987 *Chicago Tribune* 15 Mar.: "Pohl's office, . . . in a converted bedroom of his home, makes an argument for the theory that a messy desk is the sign of a creative mind." 1992 *Boston Herald* 27 Sep.: "The idea that a messy desk is the mark of intelligence finally has a defender." The proverb possibly originated as an anti-proverb based on "A messy desk is a sign of a messy mind"—or vice versa. Another anti-proverbial version appeared in 1988: Dru Scott, *The Telephone and Time Management* (Los Altos CA: Crisp) 52 (as a section heading): "A Messy Desk Is a Sign of a Messy Desk."

## A neat desk is a sign of a sick mind.

1973 *El Paso Herald-Post* 9 Nov. ("Dear Abby" advice column): "There's a sign on my friend Sidney Ascher's office bulletin board that reads: 'A neat desk is the sign of a sick mind.'" 1980 *Post and Evening Times [Palm Beach FL]* 1 Feb.: "If a neat desk is a sign of a sick mind, then I'm outrageously healthy." Dundes and Pagter (1987) 110.

## The devil is in the details.

1963 Richard Mayne, *The Community of Europe* (New York: W. W. Norton) 92: ". . . [O]n the principle that 'the devil is in the details', what should have been a merely formal occasion developed into a debate about the Community's official languages and the site of its headquarters." 1966 Peter Batty, *The House of Krupp* (London: Secker & Warburg) 271: ". . . [N]othing had been definitely signed or agreed on in detail—as [Berthold] Beitz [general manager of the German company] has said, 'The devil is in the details. . . .'" *YBQ* Modern Proverbs (24); *ODP* 74. Cf. "GOD is in the details." (One of the two proverbs probably originated as an anti-proverb based on the other.)

### Do not greet the **devil** till (before) you meet him.

1905 *Detroit Free Press* 4 Aug.: "Still, a man told me a long while ago that there's no use worrying about shaking hands with the devil until he meet [sic] his satanic majesty." 1956 J. Frank Dobie, "His Looks and My Ways Would Hang Any Man," *Southwest Review* 41: 213: ". . . Grandpa would cheer up the world around him by saying, 'Now, Mattie, don't greet the devil until you meet him.'" *MP* D141.

### Go to the **devil** for truth and to a lawyer for a lie.

1930 J. S. Fletcher, *The Investigators* (New York: Edward J. Clode) 136: "'Go to the devil for truth and to a lawyer for a lie,' said Mr. Hopps. 'Give me this chap's address, Jeffcott. He seems likely to suit me.'" *MP* D143.

### If you dance with the **devil**, you will get burned.

1996 *Philadelphia Inquirer* 22 Apr.: "'When you dance with the devil, you're going to get burned,' [the basketball coach John] Lucas said. 'And I've sure danced with the devil.'" 1997 *Contra Costa [CA] Times* 12 Oct.: "When you dance with the devil, prepare to get burned. That's the lesson Oakland and Alameda County are learning as their deal with the Raiders takes another painful romp through the coals." 1999 *Star-Times [Auckland, New Zealand]* 16 May: "If you dance with the devil enough, eventually you're going to

get burned. And yesterday . . . the Highlanders [rugby team] were well and truly scorched." 2003 John Price and Joe Nicholas, *AS Media Studies* (Cheltenham UK: Nelson Thomes) 164 (quoting "the head of a celebrity agency"): "Sure you can ask for privacy and decency. Will you get it? No. If you dance with the devil, you get pricked by the horns." Cf. the older "If you dance with the devil, you will have to pay (the piper, the fiddler)."

### If you keep knocking on the **devil's** door, (sooner or later) somebody's going to answer."

1999 *Washington Times* 5 Jul. (quoting the competitive cyclist Miguel Indurain): "It takes too much hard work to build up a reputation in sport to risk ruining it in 15 seconds. . . . It is much better not to knock on the devil's door" (ellipsis dots as shown). 2005 *Four Brothers* (motion picture): The character Lt. Green says, "You keep knocking at the devil's door long enough, somebody's going to answer you." 2006 Sherrilyn Kenyon, *Dark Side of the Moon* (New York: St. Martin's) 48: "'You don't knock on the devil's door, boys, unless you want him to answer,' he said, his voice deep and evil. He wiped the blood from his chin."

### If you lie down with the **devil**, you will wake up in hell (you will get burned, you'd better be ready to fuck, etc.).

1972 Andrew Sinclair, *Magog: A Novel* (London: Hodder & Stoughton) 269: "I do know one thing. Lie down with the Devil and you get fucked by the Devil too. And something else. I also know you've lost." 2002 *Herald Sun [Melbourne, Australia]* 9 Jan. (summary of a soap opera episode): "Meanwhile, Thorne is busy telling Sally his marriage to Brooke has been annulled. Sally's response is simply this: If you lie down with the devil, you deserve to get burned." 2005 *Daily Telegraph [Sydney, Australia]* 22 Jun.: "You know what they say: 'You lie down with the devil, you wake up in hell.'"

**Diamonds** are (A diamond is) a girl's best friend.

1949 The saying entered oral tradition as a proverb from the title and refrain of a song by Leo Robin. *DAAP* 209; *YBQ* Robin (2).

A **diamond** is (Diamonds are) forever.

1948 The saying entered oral tradition as a proverb from an advertising slogan of the DeBeers company. *YBQ* Advertising Slogans (39); Rees (1984); Rees (1995) 117; Room (2000) 182.

The **dictionary** is the only place where success comes before work.

See "The only PLACE where success comes before work is in a dictionary."

Never say **die**—say damn.

1922 *Duluth [MN] News Tribune* 15 Aug. (verses): "Never say 'die,' say 'damn.' / It isn't classic, it may be profane. / But we mortals have need of it time and again; / And you'll find you'll recover from fate's hardest slam. / If you never say 'die,' say 'damn.'" The proverb originated as an anti-proverb based on "Never say die."

Just because you're on a **diet** (Just because you've ordered; Just because you've already eaten) doesn't mean you can't look at the menu.

1959 "Words of the Week," *Jet* 16, no. 15 (6 Aug.) 30: "Lionel Hampton, remarking that it is good for husbands to look at pretty girls: 'Even when you're on a diet you can still look at the menu.'" 1980 James Applewhite, "The Mary Tapes" (a poem), in *Following Gravity* (Charlottesville: UP of Virginia) 61: "I remember him standing on a pier at White Lake, / A beer in his fist, looking at the girls / In tight shorts. 'Just because you've ordered, don't mean / You can't look at the menu,' was what he said." Cf. "Just because you're MARRIED doesn't mean you're blind."

The (only) **difference** between men and boys is the price of their toys.

1963 Millard Dale Baughman, *Educator's Handbook of Stories, Quotes and Humor* (Englewood Cliffs, NJ: Prentice-Hall) 335 (in a list of witty sayings): "The biggest difference between men and boys is just the cost of their toys." 1964 *Professional Boxing: Hearings before the Subcommittee on Antitrust and Monopoly . . . Senate* (Washington DC: Government Printing Office) 1618; boxing promoter Garland D. Cherry testifies: ". . . [H]e [boxing promoter William B. McDonald] is the kind of individual who strikes me as not being afraid to lose a couple of hundred thousand as he puts it. He once said that the difference between men and boys is the price of their toys, and this apparently was the price of his toy."

A **difference** that makes no difference is no difference.

1907 William James, "What Pragmatism Means," in *Pragmatism: A New Name for Some Old Ways of Thinking* (London: Longmans, Green) 49–50: "It is astonishing to see how many philosophical disputes collapse into insignificance the moment you subject them to this simple test of tracing a concrete consequence. There can *be* no difference anywhere that does not *make* a difference elsewhere" (italics as shown). 1940 J. F. Brown, *The Psychodynamics of Abnormal Behavior* (New York: McGraw-Hill) 51: "Modern research in philosophy, however, has shown that differences of opinion which may not be decided by some experimental criterion are meaningless. To put this viewpoint in a slogan: 'A difference which makes no difference is no difference'" (the author adds a footnote, "For this slogan I am indebted to Prof. H. Feigl"). 1949 Carrol C. Pratt, review of *Der Toncharakter* by Jacques Handschin (1948), *Musical Quarterly* 35: 487: "Yet Handschin insists that *d* is more fundamental in any system of tonal relations than is *c*. But a difference that makes no difference cannot be a difference."

The only **difference** between a rut and a grave is that a grave is a little longer.

1905 *New York Times* 15 Apr.: "Nothing new attempted to increase the business, the same old rut; and there's but precious little difference between the rut and the grave, except for its length and breadth." *DAP* 520.

What a **difference** a day makes (can make)!

1914 L. A. Talbot, *Jehane of the Forest* (Philadelphia: J. B. Lippincott) 116: "Ah, if our mothers would only think what a difference a day makes to a man!" 1917 Homer Alvan Rodeheaver, *Song Stories of the Sawdust Trail* (New York: Moffat, Yard) 37: "There was a trial— and I was sent up for five years for murderous assault. Funny, isn't it, what a difference a day can make in a man's life?" 1934 The proverb occurs as a line in a song (translated from Spanish) by Stanley Adams. Rees (1995) 496.

The **dinner bell** is always in tune (to the hungry man).

Champion (1938) 624 lists the saying as a "Negro" proverb: "The dinner-bell's always in tune." Whiting (1952) 395 lists it as a North Carolina proverb: "The dinner bell's always in tune to a hungry man." Paul Green, *Paul Green's Wordbook* (Boone NC: Appalachian Consortium, 1990) 1: 314 includes a version in a list of Appalachian sayings: "There never was a fieldhand that found the dinner bell out of tune."

When all else fails, read the **directions** (instructions).

1954 *The Aeroplane* 86 (9 Apr.) 453 (filler item): "Pencilled advice seen alongside a fire extinguisher on a hangar wall at H.M.S. 'Peregrine,' Royal Naval Air Station, Ford: 'When all else fails, try reading the instructions.'" 1957 *Ironwood [MI] Daily Globe* 22 Mar.: "When all else fails, read the directions." 1959

*Approach* (Naval Safety Center) 5, no. 6 (Dec.) 14 (filler item): "Thought for the Month: Before everything else fails read the instructions." *YBQ* Sayings (61). Cf. "If at first you don't succeed, try reading the INSTRUCTIONS."

He who slings **dirt** loses ground (When you throw dirt you lose ground).

See "MUD thrown is lost ground."

If you sift through enough **dirt** (mud, crap), you may find gold (a diamond, etc.).

1997 Eric Land and Nina Shengold, *Take Ten: New 10–Minute Plays* (New York: Vintage) 216: "If you sift through enough crap, you may find a few genuine spiritualists here" (perhaps a parody of the proverb). 2008 *Ottawa Citizen* 12 Apr. (headline): "Sift through Enough Dirt and You Find Gold." Cf. "There is a PONY there somewhere" and the older "Where there's muck there's money."

A little **dirt** never hurt (you, anyone).

1904 *Outing* 43: 408: "'Sure,' said the landlady, smiling, 'a little clane Irish dirt never hurt anny one.'" 1914 Jean Dawson, *The Boys and Girls of Garden City* (Boston: Ginn) 237: "You are getting altogether too particular, Mabel. Why, a little dirt won't hurt a fellow." Cf. "GOD made dirt; dirt don't hurt."

You can **disagree** without being disagreeable.

1927 *Youngstown [OH] Vindicator* 8 Feb. (in a small collection titled "Remarkable Remarks"; this one is unattributed): "The final test of gentility is the ability to disagree without being disagreeable." 1944 *Atlanta Constitution* 29 Apr. (caption of a cartoon by Ed Reed; a juror emerges from the jury room and addresses the judge): "I want to go home, your honor—One of the jurors can't disagree without being disagreeable." 1958

*Washington Post* 2 Sep.: "The four [panelists on a television show] demonstrated that persons can disagree without being disagreeable."

## You are not your (the) **disease**.

1984 *Los Angeles Times* 26 Aug. (ad for Adventist Health Systems): "If you are bulimarexic, you are not your disease. You are an important person." 1988 Anne Wilson Shaef and Diane Fassel, *The Addictive Organization* (San Francisco: Harper & Row) 155: "In the AA program, there is a saying, 'You have a disease; you are not your disease.'" The proverb commonly applies to addictions and various intractable physical afflictions like cancer and muscular dystrophy; it encourages sufferers not to define themselves and their lives solely by their disorders.

## Don't **dish** it out if you can't take it (If one dishes it out, he should also take it).

1930 Fred D. Pasley, *Al Capone* ([New York]: Ives Washburn) 77 (regarding the gangland "enforcer" John Torrio): "'Johnny's the same as a lot of fighters in the ring,' said a straight-talking Chicagoan who knows him. 'He can dish it out but he can't take it.'" *MP* D179; *DAP* 153; Stevenson (1948) 957.

## **Do** it (first), then talk about it.

Whiting (1952) 396 lists the saying as a North Carolina proverb. 1978 *Washington Post* 12 Jan. (quoting the football coach Red Miller): "Our motto was, 'Hey, do it, then talk about it.' We're happy to be in the Super Bowl."

## **Do** unto others before they (can) do unto you (before they do you).

1915 *Indianapolis Star* 29 Oct.: "The Golden Rule in war seems to be, Do unto others before they can do it unto you." *DAP* 154–55(9); *RHDP* 52; Litovkina and Mieder (2006) 124. The proverb originated as an anti-proverb responding to the biblical "Golden Rule" (Matthew 7:12).

## If you always **do** what you've always done, you'll always get what you've always gotten (If you keep on doing what you've always done, you will keep getting what you've always gotten).

1985 Robert J. Kursar, "Transportation Professionals Delve into Challenges of the Next Decade," *Traffic World* 204, no. 2 (6 Oct.) 133: "Awareness that the 'person closest to the work knows it best can have excellent results,' Mr. [Frank] Pfeifenroth said, declaring that 'if you always do what you've always done, you'll always get what you've always gotten.'" 1990 *Dallas Morning News* 24 Jun.: "We must realize that if we keep on doing the things we've always done we're going to keep on getting what we've always gotten." Cf. "INSANITY is doing the same thing and expecting a different result."

## Just **do** it.

1988 The saying entered oral tradition as a proverb from an advertising slogan of the Nike shoe company. *YBQ* Advertising Slogans (93); Nussbaum (2005) 69.

## They'll **do** it every time.

1919 Corinne Lowe, *Saul* (New York: James A McCann) 183: "'Got to keep your eye on these *ganuffs* every minute or they'll carry off everything in your place. . . .' 'Sure, they'll do it every time,' responded Gersten sympathetically." The proverb acquired special popularity starting in 1929 from Jimmy Hatlo's comic strip with the title (and theme). Doyle (1996) 74.

## You can **do** anything you want to if you want to (badly) enough.

1961 Wallace Stegner, *A Shooting Star* (New York: Viking) 255: "Whenever I get feeling sorry for myself I'll take a midnight swim or walk a few miles. You can do anything you want to, if you want to bad enough." *DAP* 156(39).

**Dogs** don't bark at parked cars.

1993 *USA Today* 23 Aug.: "'Dogs don't bark at parked cars,' he [Congressman Don Johnson of Georgia] says, 'and this car's moving. If they want a parked car, they need to elect somebody else. What we're doing is making changes, and there are going to be some unsettling complaints about it.'" 1993 Jim Dator, title of the keynote address at the Nov. conference of the World Futures Studies Federation: "Dogs Don't Bark at Parked Cars."

A **dog** is for life, not just for Christmas.

1978 The saying entered oral tradition as a proverb from a slogan introduced by the UK's National Canine Defence League to discourage the giving of puppies as Christmas presents. *ODP* 82–83. It (and its allusive adaptations) can refer metaphorically to concerns other than the disposition of puppies.

A **dog** knows better than to chew a razor.

Anderson and Cundall (1910) 13 give the saying as a Jamaican proverb: "You never see darg chaw razor" (gloss: "Don't play with edged tools"). Whiting (1952) 396 lists it as a North Carolina proverb. Beckwith (1925) 126.

**Dogs** look up to you, cats look down on you, pigs look at you as equals.

See "CATS look down on you, dogs look up at you, pigs look at you as equals."

Don't let the (same) **dog** bite you twice.

1932 *Coshocton [OH] Tribune* 2 Jul.: "Never allow the same dog to bite you twice." 1948 "Never Let the Same Dog Bite You Twice" was the title of a song, lyrics by Jack Yellen (popularized by Sophie Tucker). *DAP* 160(82); Prahlad (1996) 223. Cf. "Don't let the same BEE sting you twice."

If the **dog** hadn't stopped to shit (rest, etc.), he would have caught the rabbit.

1919 Francis J. Reynolds and Allen L. Churchill, eds., *World's War Events*, vol. 3 (New York: P. F. Collier & Son) 20: "I nearly bagged a submarine for you. . . . If she had only—but, as the saying goes, if the dog hadn't stopped to scratch himself, he would have got the rabbit. . . ." *DAP* 160(70); Prahlad (1996) 185. The proverb usually means that excuses or explanations do not avail. It may have originated as a translation of the German "Wenn der Hund nicht geschissen hätte, hätte er den Hasen gefangen."

If you aren't the lead **dog**, the scenery (view) never changes.

1980 Paul Dickson, *The Official Explanations* (New York: Delacorte) 202: "Sgt. Preston's Law of the Wild: The scenery only changes for the lead dog." 1985 *Washington Post* 13 Jan. (quoting the Georgia humorist Lewis Grizzard): "Just remember this one thing: Life is like a dog-sled team. If you ain't the lead dog, the scenery never changes." Ratcliffe (2006) 256 (where the expression is identified as a "Canadian saying"); Dundes and Pagter (1996) 149 give a rare variant: "If you ain't the lead reindeer, the view never changes."

If you can't run with the big **dogs**, stay on (under) the porch.

1985 *Globe and Mail [Canada]* 29 Aug.: "The Jays, who have proved they can come off the porch and run with the big dogs this season, were fifth . . . in the American League East when they departed on the trip." 1987 *Washington Post* 20 Sep.: "As they say, 'Run with the big dogs or stay on the porch.' The folks in places like Knoxville understand things like that." *RHDP* 156.

It's a **dog**-eat-dog world.

See "It is a dog-eat-dog WORLD."

## It's a foolish **dog** that barks at a flying bird.

1975 The proverb occurs in a song by Bob Marley and Lee Perry, "Jah Live," occasioned by the death of the deific (to Rastafarians) Haile Selassie; the song comprises a pastiche of proverbs and other sayings: "The truth is an offence / And not a sin, / And he who laughs last / Is he who wins, / It's a foolish dog / Barks at a flying bird." There the imagery satirizes the folly of those who scoff at spiritual realities. More commonly, the proverb refers to futility or pointless hostility of more secular kinds. 1989 *The Guardian [UK]* 8 Dec.: "'I would like to beat him [boxer Derek Williams] because of what he's been saying about me,' [Gary] Mason said. 'All I'll say is that only a foolish dog barks at a flying bird.'" Prahlad (2001) 247.

## It's a poor **dog** that won't wag its own tail.

1922 Emily Grant Hutchings, *Indian Summer* (New York: Knopf) 123: "'You might have waited for some one else to say that,' Larimore rebuked. 'Huh! it's a poor dog that can't wag its own tail.'" *DAP* 160(77); Whiting (1952) 398. Cf. the older "It's an ill (tired) horse that cannot whinny or wag its tail."

## Someone who kicks his **dog** will beat his wife.

See "A MAN who kicks his dog will beat his wife."

## Sometimes (Some days) you're the **dog**, and sometimes (some days) you're the fireplug (Sometimes you're the fireplug, and sometimes you're the dog).

1989 Paul Dickson, *New Official Rules: Maxims for Muddling through the Twenty-first Century* (Reading MA: Addison-Wesley) 135: "McCabe's Observation. Sometimes you're the dog, sometimes the hydrant" (attributed to Joseph M. McCabe). 1999 Timothy V. Rasinski, "Outside of a Dog, a Book Is Man's Best Friend," in *Advancing the World of Literacy: Moving into the 21st Century*, edited by JoAnn R. Dugan et al. (Carrolton GA: College Reading Association) 3: "And then there is the way that literary quotes always seem more vivid and memorable when they involve dogs. Take for example: Some days you're the dog, some days you're the hydrant. (Unknown)."

## There are no bad **dogs**, only bad owners.

1949 *Los Angeles Times* 4 Aug.: "There are no bad dogs; there are only bad owners. So says a man who is best described as a dog psychologist." Cf. "There are no bad CHILDREN, only bad parents" and "There are no bad STUDENTS, just bad teachers."

## You can't run with the (big) **dogs** if you pee like a pup.

1986 *Washington Post* 15 Mar.: "'If you want to run with the big dogs, you've got to go potty in the tall grass,' said [Glenn] Brenner by way of explaining [Bernie] Smilovitz's need to go elsewhere." *RHDP* 159. Not infrequently the proverb is amalgamated with "If you can't run with the big DOGS, stay on the porch"—to yield something like "If you want to pee like the big dogs, you've got to get off the porch."

## Anything worth **doing** is worth overdoing.

See "Anything WORTH doing is worth overdoing."

## A **dollar** in the bank is worth two in the hand.

1904 *Indiana County [PA] Gazette* 17 Feb. (a bank advertisement): "One Dollar in the Bank Is Worth Two in the Hand." *DAP* 163. The proverb originated as an anti-proverb based on "A bird in the hand is worth two in the bush."

You can only spend a **dollar** (spend money, spend earnings) once.

1913 Herbert Joseph Davenport, *The Economics of Enterprise* (New York: Macmillan) 52: "It is a peculiar and exasperating fact about a dollar that you can spend it only once." 228: "There is no need for a greater rationality in the case than that he realize the quality proper to the dollar everywhere—that it can be spent only once. . . ." 1921 *Wall Street Journal* 24 Dec.: "'However,' he [chairman of Royal Dutch-Shell] continued, 'the unpleasant quality of the guilder being that it can only be spent once, we shall not be able to pay a dividend in cash'" (because of Dutch East Indian taxes). 1932 Louis Bader, "Economics of Marketing," in *Economic Principles and Problems*, edited by Walter E. Spahr (New York: Ray Long & Richard R. Smith) 1: 293: "Earnings can be spent only once, and when spent in advance they are likely to give an artificial stimulus to demand. . . ." 1936 Dora S. Lewis, "What Is Required of Efficient Homemakers?" in *Our Homes*, edited by Ada H. Arlitt (Washington DC: National Congress of Parents and Teachers) 40: "Families must . . . face squarely the fact that money can be spent only once."

### *Don't care* was made to care.

1927 The proverb is detached from a children's rhyme: "Don't Care was made to care, / Don't Care was wild: / Don't Care stole plum and pear / Like any beggar's child. // Don't Care was made to care, / Don't Care was hung: / Don't Care was put in a pot / And boiled till he was done"; Robert Graves, ed., *Less Familiar Nursery Rhymes* (London: Ernest Benn) 18. The proverb usually comments on (or retorts to) the assertion "I don't care." *ODP* 44–45; Ratcliffe (2006) 138.

### Don't miss the **donut** by looking (shooting) through the hole.

1999 Roger Clark et al., "The Liberal Bias in Feminist Social Science Research on Children's Books," in *Girls, Boys, Books, Toys*, edited by

Beverly Lyon Clark and Margaret Higonnet (Baltimore: Johns Hopkins UP) 79: ". . . [H]aving shown that in 1989 women characters were much more likely to be depicted in a broad range of occupations than their 1972 counterparts, Powell and Stewart seem to miss the donut for the hole. . . ." 2007 John Bradley Jackson, *First, Best, or Different: What Every Entrepreneur Needs to Know about Niche Marketing* (Indianapolis IN: Dog Ear) 191 (epigraph at the head of a chapter): "'Don't miss the donut by looking through the hole.' Author Unknown." Cf. "Keep your EYE on the donut and not on the hole."

### Don't shit on your own **doorstep**.

1967 Eric Partridge, *Dictionary of Slang and Unconventional English*, 6th ed. (New York: Macmillan) 1356: The proverb is glossed with an allusion to an older proverb: "You don't 'foul your own nest.'" 1975 John Becker, *After Geneva* (London: London Magazine Editions) 14: "He said there was a tall woman across the hall, red haired, a good-looker. She would come out with her negligee half open and it wasn't hard to see what she was after. But Schultz never went in. 'Why?' 'Never shit on your own doorstep, Jaimie.'" 1976 Colin Dexter, *Last Seen Wearing* (New York: St. Martin's) 124: "There's an old saying, isn't there—if you'll excuse the language—about not shitting on your own doorstep. Surely it would be far too risky?" *MP* D282. Cf. "Don't SHIT where you eat" and the older "A bird does not foul its own nest."

### **Dot-com**, dot-bomb.

2000 Neil Cavuto, "Your World with Neil Cavuto," Fox News Network 21 Aug. (LexisNexis transcript of the television program): ". . . [D]o not tell Kay Koplovits that dot.coms are dot. bombs." 2000 Christopher Palmery, "Stock Info for the Masses," *Business Week*, no. 3708 (20 Nov.) "e.biz" supplement, 104: "Clearly, not all dot-coms are dot-bombs." 2001 James Battey, "Infoworld e-Business 100 Update," *Infoworld* 23, no. 12 (19 Mar.) 37: "'First, dot-coms turned into dot-bombs, and second, regulators didn't make it easy,' [John] Egan says." The term *dot-com* (or sometimes, iconically emulating a Web address, *dot.com*) refers to a company involved in Internet commerce—a volatile sector of the economy that especially suffered financially in the 1990s. *Dot-bomb* is an echoic construction based on the verb *bomb* in the sense of "crash, collapse financially."

## When in **doubt**, look about.

1902 *The S.W.P.* [trade magazine of the Sherwin Williams Paint company] 4, no. 1 (Jan.) 183 (in an anonymous poem about Sherwin Williams paint): "It's a paint that won't fade / In the sun's bright rays— / It is known in each zone / Where it's used always. / When in doubt, look about— / Ask for S. W. P." 1996 Laurie Powers et al., *On the Road to Autonomy* (Baltimore: Paul H. Brookes) 165: "Even adults watch their dinner partners to determine which fork to use with which course. The old sayings 'when in doubt, look about' or 'when in Rome, do as the Romans do' apply as much to children and teenagers as they do to adults." *DAP* 165(8b). Besides the awareness of one's physical and social surroundings, the proverb now commonly refers to students' cheating on a test.

## When in **doubt**, punt.

1924 Robert C. Zuppke, *Football Techniques and Tactics*, 2nd ed. (Champaign IL: Bailey & Himes) 137: "Crangle, drawn in slightly by the feint, met the jump with a reverse turn. The result is depicted above. '*When in doubt, punt*'" (italics as shown). 1940 *Atlanta Constitution* 1 Oct.: The proverb appears as the title of an episode of the comic strip *Terry and the Pirates*; the strip has nothing to do with football. *DAP* 166(11). In the 1940s and after, the proverb refers to a wide range of nonathletic activities, such as legal pleadings and medical diagnoses. It is sometimes attributed to John Heisman, Bobby Dodd, or other figures prominent in the history of football.

## When in **doubt**, throw (toss) it out.

1919 Fred E. Tracy, "Some Reflections of a War-time Inspector of Army Gunstocks," *The Wood-Worker* 38, no. 6 (Aug.) 50: ". . . [O]ur motto was, 'If in doubt, throw it out.' The idea in inspecting is to see that the blanks have the proper dimensions, that dry-rot, knots, . . . etc. don't run too deep. . . ." 1930 *Los Angeles Times* 22 Jun.: "Never taste canned food to see if it is spoiled. . . . When in doubt, throw it out." Cf. the older advice for writers, "When in doubt, leave it out."

## No **dough**, no go.

1952 Maxwell Griffith, *Port of Call* (Philadelphia: J. B. Lippincott) 198–99: "They've all got the same price. Just like a union. No dough, no go." 1962 Iris Murdock, *An Unofficial Rose* (New York: Viking) 146: "Don't forget your practical thinking. No dough, no go."

## Don't miss the **doughnut** by looking through the hole.

See "Don't miss the DONUT by looking through the hole."

## **Down** is not (always) out (A man may be down but not out).

1910 *Chicago Daily Tribune* 9 Oct. (caption to a drawing of a shabbily dressed man, which accompanies an "inspirational" essay): "A man may be down but not out." 1917 Albert W. Atwood, *How to Get Ahead* (Indianapolis IN: Bobbs-Merrill) 76: "A man may be down but he is not out until every method of self-improvement has been exhausted." 1919 H. W. Kellog, "Our Reformatory—An Introduction and an Interpretation," *Ohio State Institution Journal* 2, no. 4 (Jul.) 77: "The bitter heart of men had to be changed to accept the truth that a 'man may be down but is never out.'" 1964 Carl A. Lefevre, *Linguistics and the Teaching of Reading* (New York: McGraw Hill)

107: "Adverbs [*sic*] also occur in both N functions in the same pattern, as in *Down is not out . . .* " (italics as shown). *DAP* 166(1), 397(34); Whiting (1952) 400. The proverb is probably related to the idiomatic phrase from boxing "down but not out."

## What one is most **down** on, he is apt to be least up on.

See "The MAN most down on a thing is he who is least up on it."

## When you're **down**, the only way is up.

See "When you're down, the only WAY is up."

## Sometimes the **dragon** wins.

1981 *Chicago Tribune* 14 Oct.: "A needlepoint pillow in Steve Pistner's former office at Dayton Hudson Corp. reportedly showed a battlefield with an obviously well-fed dragon facing an empty suit of armor. The legend: 'Things my mother never told me. . . . Sometimes the dragon wins.'" 1994 John M. Capozzi, *Why Climb the Corporate Ladder When You Can Take the Elevator: 500 Secrets for Success in Business* (New York: Villard); the unpaginated book consists of numbered business "maxims": "310 'Some days the dragon wins.'—Peter Rogers, former chairman, Nabisco Brands." Dundes and Pagter (1996) 58–61.

## Don't get your **drawers** in a twist.

See "Don't get your PANTIES in a twist."

## **Dreams** can't (won't) come true unless you wake up (and go to work).

1928 *Evening Independent [St. Petersburg FL]* 2 Jul. (in a collection of notable sayings): "Your dreams of honors, success and happiness will never come true unless you wake up." 1966 Herbert V. Prochnow, *The Successful Toastmaster* (New York: Harper & Row) 223 (in a collection of "Epigrams and Quips"): "No dream comes true until you wake up and go to work." *DAP* 167(10).

## If you can **dream** it, you can do it (be it, have it).

1970 Sam L. Sebesta, "The Library, Nongrading, and Individualized Reading," *School Libraries* 19, no. 3 (Spring) 29: "In technology the rule is fast becoming this: 'If you can dream it, you can have it!'" Starting in the early 1980s the General Electric corporation waged a campaign of inspirational ads (directed at young people) that featured the slogan; an early example: 1983 *Senior Scholastic* 115, no. 14 (18 Mar.), inside front cover: ". . . Now take your imagination a step further. Give your robot muscles, a skeleton and a nervous system. . . . If you can dream it, you can do it." Sometimes the proverb is attributed to Walt Disney. Cf. "If you can SEE it, you can be it."

## **Dreaming** doesn't cost anything.

See "It COSTS nothing to dream."

## First up, best **dressed**.

See "FIRST up, best dressed."

## If you keep a **dress** long enough, it will come back in style.

See "If you keep anything long enough, it will come back in STYLE."

## Keep your **dress** down and your panties (drawers) up.

1975 James P. Comer and Alvin F. Poussaint, *Black Child Care* (New York: Simon & Schuster) 315: "In the past, before dates girls were told 'keep your dress down and your pants up.' . . . Not only was the advice often ignored, it created much discomfort and contributed to unhealthy attitudes about sex." 1976 Alice Walker, *Meridian* (New York: Harcourt Brace Jovanovich) 53: "When Meridian left the house in the evening with her 'boyfriend' . . . her mother only cautioned her to 'be sweet.' She did not realize this was a euphemism for 'Keep your panties up and your dress down,' an expression she *had* heard and been puzzled by" (italics as shown). 1980 Dindga McCannon, *Wilhelmina Jones, Future Star* (New York: Delecorte) 111: "'I'll get her back on time,' said Joe politely. 'Well, you better! And you, miss, keep your dress down! And your drawers up!'" Currently, the proverb is often used to epitomize and ridicule the kind of instruction about sexuality that previous generations of parents and teachers offered.

## Finish (You have to finish) the **drill**.

2002 *St. Petersburg [FL] Times* 25 Aug. (quoting the football player Kendyll Pope): "That's the thing here at Florida State. You play four quarters and finish the drill." 2002 *Atlanta Journal-Constitution* 3 Nov.: "In all kinds of situations, [the University of] Georgia [football team] had lived up to its team motto: 'Finish the Drill.'" The proverb means "Don't quit."

## If you **drink**, don't drive; if you drive, don't drink.

See "If you DRIVE, don't drink; if you drink, don't drive."

## **Drinking** and driving do not mix.

1928 Dixon Merritt, "Control on Canada's Countryside," *Outlook and Independent* 150, no. 12 (21 Nov.) 1191: "All people but fools know that drinking and driving don't mix. But how can you drive anywhere and get back home now without drinking?" 1934 *Charleston [WV] Gazette* 44 May: "The drunken driver should be deprived of the privilege of driving until he learns that drinking and driving do not mix." Cf. "GASOLINE and whiskey do not mix."

## **Drinking** and thinking do not mix.

1992 *DAP* 168 gives the saying as a proverb from Indiana. 1998 Edward O. Phillips, *Sunday's Child* (Toronto: Riverbank) 53: "Good judgement dictated I give him [a robber] the watch and the

money. But drinking and thinking don't mix." The proverb probably originated as an anti-proverb based on "DRINKING and driving do not mix."

## If you **drive**, don't drink; if you drink, don't drive (If you drink, don't drive; if you drive, don't drink).

1935 *New York Times* 3 Feb.: "It would help to enforce the entirely sensible dictum, 'If you drive, don't drink; it you drink, don't drive,' upon which both repealists and prohibitionists can stand as on common ground." *DAP* 168(2).

## For every **drop** of rain that falls a flower grows.

1953 The saying may have entered oral tradition as a proverb from the song "I Believe," by Ervin Drake and Jimmy Shirl, who reported having written it to console a woman whose son was killed in the Korean War. Among others, Frankie Laine recorded it in 1953. 1971 Stanley Reynolds, "End of the World Sale—What Offers?" *Punch* 260: 60: "For a number of years, I firmly believed, among other things, that a stitch in time saved nine, that for every drop of rain that fell a flower grew . . . , so who am I to laugh at another's faith?" 1975 Sam Koperwas, "Ball," *Esquire* 83, no. 2 (Feb.) 100: "A flower grows for every drop of rain that falls. Don't tell me no." 1982 George V. Higgins, *The Patriot Game* (New York: Alfred A. Knopf) 81–82: "'How do you know that?' 'Well, . . . I just know it.' 'Right, . . . and I know that for every drop of rain that falls, a flower grows.'" The proverb is often uttered ironically, in a way that calls attention to either its saccharine sentimentality or its "scientific" inaccuracy.

## Get your **ducks** in row.

1956 *The Al Sarena Case: Joint Hearings before a Special Committee on the Legislative Oversight Function* (Washington DC: Government Printing Office) 222; Senator Kerr Scott is questioning J. A. McDaniel: "In fact, you mentioned some time ago that somebody . . . came to you and said that you had better be ready for a hearing. They did not say, 'Get your ducks in a row,' but you have it that way." As an idiom, the verb phrase "get (one's) ducks in a row" may antedate the proverb (that is, the imperative sentence). 1911 Kate Langley Bosher, *Miss Gibbie Gault* (New York: A. L. Burt) 63: "You had your ducks in a row, all right."

## Go hunting where the **ducks** are.

1930 Robert W. Jones, *The Editorial Page* (New York: Thomas Y. Crowell) 58: "To hunt ducks one must go where the ducks are. To clip good 'reprint copy' for use on the editorial page . . . , one must turn to some worth-while exchanges." 1962 "Mr. Nixon and the Negro Voters," *U. S. News & World Report* 52, no. 15 (9 Apr.) 20: "Last year Senator [Barry] Goldwater told a Republican meeting in Atlanta, Ga., that the party 'is not going to get the Negro vote as a bloc in 1964 or 1968, so we ought to go hunting where the ducks are.'" *RHDP* 113. The saying is often attributed to Goldwater. Cf. "Fish where the FISH are" and "If you are looking for ELEPHANTS, go to elephant country."

## If it looks like a **duck**, walks like a duck, and quacks like a duck, it's a duck.

1948 *New York Times* 3 Sep. (quoting the labor union leader James B. Carey): "A door-opener for the Communist party is worse than a member of the Communist party. When someone walks like a duck, swims like a duck, and quacks like a duck, he's a duck." *RHDP* 152; Pickering (2001) 219.

## It is better to be a big **duck** in a little puddle (pond) than a little duck in a big puddle (pond).

1934 George Ade, "This Thing of Living in the Country," *Atlanta Constitution* 18 Mar. (an anti-proverbial version of the proverb): ". . . I'll explain why I am still guessing as to whether it is better to be a big duck in a little puddle or a sardine in the Atlantic ocean. I was born on the outskirts of a very small town in Indiana. . . ." *DAP* 170. Cf. "Better a big FISH in a little pond than a little fish in a big pond."

## A wise **duck** takes care of its bill.

See "NOTHING ruins a duck but its bill."

## **Dynamite** comes in small packages.

1937 *Tyrone [PA] Daily Herald* 15 Feb.: "Tagged with the nickname 'Little Corporal,' because of his minuteness, Dominic Dallesandro of Reading, Pa. will try to prove the old saw, 'Dynamite comes in small packages,' when he battles for a berth with the Boston Red Sox." 1938 *Washington Post* 15 Sep. (regarding actress Florence Enright): "She proves that dynamite comes in small wrappers—she's but 4 feet 10." *DAP* 172. The proverb probably originated as an anti-proverb based on "Good things come in small packages."

## It is hard to soar with the **eagles** when you are surrounded by (scratching with, running with, etc.) turkeys.

1980 *Washington Post* 27 Mar.: "The hostility between the two sides was so great that some of the committee liberals prepared and mailed a 'hate letter' to each of their conservative opponents late last week. The message[,] spelled out in letters clipped from newspapers, read, 'You can't soar with eagles when you have to work with turkeys  signed, the Crazies.'" 1980 *Milwaukee Sentinel* 25 Apr.: "Ralph Szablewski said he was compiling a book of some of [James] Keeley's more memorable remarks about the chorus, including his observation that 'It's hard to soar with the eagles when you have to work with such turkeys.'" Dundes and Pagter (1991) 72–75. Cf. "In any GROUP of eagles, there will be at least one turkey."

## You can only spend **earnings** once.

See "You can only spend a DOLLAR once."

## It's not **easy** being easy.

1982 Mark Gray and Les Taylor (song, popularized by Janie Fricke), "It Ain't Easy Being Easy." 1990 Andrea Rothman, "The 'Prince of Play' Gives Up His Title," *Business Week*, no. 3178 (17 Sep.) 78: "[Martin F. C.] Emmett has earned a 'master's degree from the Don Meredith School of Leisure,' boasts his friend. The Meredith credo: 'It ain't easy being easy.'" 1993 Timothy Philipps, "It's Not Easy Being Easy: Advising Tax Return Positions," *Washington and Lee Law Review* 50: 589. The proverb (often associated with the football player turned sportscaster Don Meredith) commonly refers to the difficulty of making a performance (such as an athletic feat) look easy. However, in the 1982 song, *easy* means (from the perspective of an amorous woman) "disinclined to resist a man." The proverb may be regarded as an anti-proverb based on "It's not EASY being hard."

## It's not **easy** being green.

1970 The saying entered oral tradition as a proverb from a song by Joe Raposo, sung by the character Kermit the Frog of the Muppets. The proverb laments the pain of being "different"— perhaps including differences in color or race. Eventually it came to apply to the difficulty of efforts to save the environment and perhaps to other kinds of figurative "greenness."

## It's not **easy** being hard.

1913 "Be Hard, My Friends" (the title is attributed to Nietzsche), *English Review* 14: 309 (an editorial, probably by Austin Harrison): "Everywhere, every day it is the hard and prompt decision that carries the business of mankind. . . . It is not easy to be hard by any means, or there would be little mediocrity and no subjection." 1990 June Francis, *Friends & Lovers* (Littley Green UK: Riverside) 263: "'You've got to be the strong one if he ever comes trying it on. I know you won't find it easy being hard but—' 'My mother's caused a hell of a lot of trouble, hasn't she?' interrupted Viv." 2005 Danny Ticali, "It Ain't Easy Being Hard" (section title), in *The Courage to Be Yourself*, edited by Al Desetta (Minneapolis: Free Spirit) 101. The word *hard* in the proverb can have several different senses. The 1967 stage musical *Hair* (lyrics by James Rado) featured the song "Easy to Be Hard," sung by a rejected lover, imputing cruelty; perhaps the line is a counter-proverb responding to "It is not easy being hard." Cf. "It's not EASY being easy."

**Eat** it up (Use it up), wear it out, make it do, or do (go) without.

1933 Irving Bacheller, *Uncle Peel* (New York: Frederick A. Stokes) 5: "He had taught me this ancient maxim in which were the four dark threads that went into the weaving of New England life: / Eat it up. / Wear it out. / Make it do. / Do without." 1933 Edwin Brant Frost, *An Astronomer's Life* (Boston: Houghton, Mifflin) 26: "The spirit of New England has been summarized in the words, 'Eat it up. Wear it out. Make it do.' All of this is in strong contrast to the modern tendency to extravagant buying. . . ." 1937 Malcolm M. Willey, *Depression, Recovery and Higher Education* (Boston: McGraw-Hill) 129: "Emerson's wife is said to have given this advice concerning the way to meet economic adversity: 'Eat it up, wear it out, make it do.'" 1938 Odell Shepard, *Connecticut Past and Present* (New York: Alfred A. Knopf) 225: "Under the conditions of Colonial life frugality became a major virtue because a necessary one. 'Wear it out! Use it up! Make it do!' was deeply characteristic in those remote and segregated towns. . . ." *DAP* 626(2).

**Eat** right, stay fit (don't smoke, etc.), die anyway.

1990 *Environmental Nutrition* 1 Feb.: "A popular T-shirt message proclaims: 'Don't smoke, exercise, eat right, and die anyway.' No truer words have been spoken." 1991 *Los Angeles Times* 11 Aug. (reporting a bumper sticker in San Diego): "Eat Right, Stay Fit and Die Anyway."

Just because you've **eaten** doesn't mean you can't look at the menu.

See "Just because you're on a DIET doesn't mean you can't look at the menu."

You've got to **eat**.

1907 Clara E. Laughlin, *Felicity* (New York: Charles Scribner's Sons) 181–82: "Felicity demurred at first. 'I can't go anywhere,' she said fretfully, 'everywhere I go people stare at me.' . . . 'I'll take you to some little old place where nobody'll know you from a hole in the wall. . . . You've got to eat, you know.'" 1938 Allis McKay, *Woman about Town* (New York: Macmillan) 269: "'Well!' Don said. 'Darling, you've got to eat, you know. Twenty-Six first, for just a minute, and then dinner.'" The proverb has a different meaning from the older expression "A man has to eat (to live)." The modern "You've got to eat" means something like "If we dine together, it won't be an imposition on your time or sensibilities—since you have to eat anyhow," typically spoken by a person who has extended an invitation to a meal and been tentatively or implicitly rebuffed.

**Education** is a journey, not a destination.

1936 Mary B. Harris, *I Knew Them in Prison* (New York: Viking) 383: "Reformation, like education, is a journey, not a destination." 1946 Bess Goodykoontz, "The Elementary School of Tomorrow," *Childhood Education* 22: 220: "Then education will be not a destination, but a journey, with teachers and learners always enroute." Cf. "SUCCESS is a journey, not a destination" and "LIFE is a journey, not a destination."

Never let (your) **education** interfere with your intelligence (with learning, with college) (Never let school interfere with education).

1900 Edward Clodd, *Grant Allen: A Memoir* (London: Grant Richards) 53: "One of his original axioms . . . was, 'You must never let schooling interfere with education'" (the conceit appears in various works by Allen, but not as a general proposition). 1911 Charles Franklin Thwing, *Universities of the World* (New York: Macmillan) 2: "Oxford is the best illustration of the value of the remark not uncommon in American colleges, 'Don't let your education interfere with your college life.'" 1922 Gordon Laing,

"The Humanities and the Trend of Education," *University [of Chicago] Record* n.s. 8, no. 1 (Jan.) 10: "The college boy who inscribed on a placard fastened on the wall of his room 'Don't let your education interfere with your development' is typical of thousands of university alumni. . . ." *DAP* 177(8); *YBQ* Twain (151).

## A boiled (fried, cooked) **egg** won't hatch.

1901 Josiah Keep, *Shells and Sea-Life* (San Francisco: Whitaker & Ray) 160: "But hard boiled eggs never hatch, and when it was found that the number of birds was decreasing, the gathering of eggs [for human consumption] was stopped by government officers." 1954 Lawrence L. Bethel et al., *Essentials of Industrial Management* (New York: McGraw-Hill) 294: "If you speed up the process (apply more heat), you can get a hard-boiled egg but no chicken! New ideas incubate in much the same way." 1967 George W. Boswell, "Folk Wisdom in Northeastern Kentucky," *Tennessee Folklore Society Bulletin* 33: 15 (in a list of proverbs): "A boiled egg never hatches." *DAP* 177(11): "From fried eggs come no chickens."

## An **egg** today (yesterday), a feather duster tomorrow.

See "A ROOSTER one day, a feather duster the next."

## You can't unscramble **eggs**.

1911 *Chicago Tribune* 12 Oct. (headline "Morgan Makes an Epigram"): "When the conferees were talking over the proposed 'voluntary dissolution' of the steel trust, Mr. [J. P.] Morgan asked: 'How can you unscramble eggs?'" 1911 *Waterloo [IA] Times-Tribune* 15 Oct. "You can't unscramble eggs." *MP* E48; *DAP* 178(26); *RHDP* 386; *DAAP* 242; Pasamanick (1985).

## Your **ego** is not your amigo.

1979 The saying perhaps entered oral tradition as a proverb from a song written and performed by Terry Allen, "My Amigo" (on the album *Lubbock*); it contains the line "My ego ain't my amigo anymore." In the form "Your ego is not your amigo," the proverb has become common in addiction "recovery" circles. 2005 *Las Vegas Weekly* 21 Apr. (quoting George Carlin, regarding his "rehab" experiences): "You don't control the universe—period—and your ego is not your amigo."

## Every **election** has a winner.

See "Every GAME has a winner."

## If you are looking for (hunting) **elephants,** go to elephant country (go where the elephants are).

1954 Paul Dean Proctor, Edmond P. Hyatt, and Kenneth C. Bullock, *Uranium: Where It Is and How to Find It* (Salt Lake City UT: Eagle Rock) 20: "However, the trite saying that if you must hunt for elephants go to elephant country seems appropriately applied to one's chances for greatest success in the search for deposits of uranium." 1954 H. E. Hawkes, *Geochemical Prospecting: Investigations in the Nyeba Lead-Zinc District[,] Nigeria* (Washington DC: U.S.G.P.O.) 239: "It has long been a maxim in the exploration business that 'if you are looking for elephants, go to elephant country.'" 1997 Guy Alvarez, *What the Small Office Practitioner Must Know about Legal Resources and Client Development on the Internet* (New York: Practising Law Institute) 130: "The famous adage, 'if you want to shoot elephants, you have to go where the elephants are' applies precisely to the new age of lawyering." Cf. "Fish where the FISH are" and "Go hunting where the DUCKS are."

## It is possible to swallow (You can eat) an **elephant**—one bite at a time (Don't try to swallow an elephant whole).

1921 Frank Cody, "What One Representative American City Is Doing in Teaching Americanism," *Journal of the New York State*

Teachers' Association 8: 56: ". . . [N]othing has been more clearly demonstrated than that there is a limit to our national powers of assimilation during any given period. It is entirely possible for a man to swallow an elephant one bite at a time and it will make him a bigger, stronger man, too. But he cannot swallow it all at once. . . ." 1947 Paul Peach, *Introduction to Industrial Statistics*, 2nd ed. (Raleigh NC: Edwards & Broughton) 158: "The job may be lengthy, but, in the words of the great Kung Fu Tze, a man can eat an elephant if need be, one bite at a time." 2005 Larry Bond, *Dangerous Ground* (New York: Tom Doherty) 78: "Don't try to swallow an elephant whole. Take this one bite at a time." The proverb often takes the form of a question + answer, a pseudo-riddle: "'How do you swallow an elephant?' / 'One bite at a time.'"

## When all **else** fails, pray.

See "When all else FAILS, pray."

## Every **employee** tends to rise to his level of incompetence.

1967 One article of the so-called Peter principle, articulated by Laurence J. Peter—quoted in the *Wall Street Journal* 8 Jun. *RHDP* 83; *YBQ* Peter (1).

## Well **endured** is half cured.

1926 "Lord" George Sanger, *Seventy Years as Showman* (New York: E. P. Dutton) 73: ". . . [T]he poorest trick may come in useful some day, if it is only that of knowing how to tumble down without hurting yourself. If you do hurt yourself, remember, 'well endured is half cured.'" 1946 David Liebovitz, *The Canvas Sky* (New York: Harcourt, Brace) 23: "An' there was Hackeliah Bailey. He used to say, 'Well endured is half cured.' So it was with me, sinner, only it's all cured!" *DAAP* 247.

## Forgive (Love) your **enemies**, but remember (never forget) their names.

1981 Nancy McPhee, *Second Book of Insults* (New York: St. Martin's) 13: "Always forgive your enemies—but never forget their names"; attributed to Robert F. Kennedy. 1982 "Playboy Interview: Edward Koch," *Playboy* 29, no. 4 (Apr.) 76: "PLAYBOY: No, no, what we're getting at is what we've heard as your motto: 'Forgive your enemies but never forget their names.' KOCH: That's not my quote. Mine is, 'I'll never forget and I rarely forgive.'" 1984 Edward I. Koch, *Mayor* (New York: Simon & Schuster) [second page of photographs, following page 97; caption]: ". . . [Robert] Kennedy thought I had opposed him in his campaign for the Senate. This photo proved I had supported him. . . . I remembered what his brother Jack had said: 'Forgive your enemies, but never forget their names.'" *YBQ* Robert Kennedy. Perhaps both Kennedy brothers used the same proverb, which plays on the expression "forgive and forget."

## We have met the **enemy**, and it is us.

1953 Walt Kelly, "Foreword," *The Pogo Papers* (New York: Simon & Schuster) [ii]: "Resolve, then, that on the very ground, with small flags waving and tinny blasts on tiny trumpets, we shall meet the enemy, and not only may he be ours, he may be us." 1960 Russell I. Thackrey, "Some Responsibilities of the State University," *Educational Record* 41: 202: "We are in the position immortalized by Pogo in this phrase: 'We have met the enemy—and he is us!'" 1965 *Conditions and Problems in the Nation's Nursing Homes: Hearings before the Subcommittee on Long-Term Care . . . Senate* (Washington DC: Government Printing Office) 607; reprinting a letter from John H. Knowles to the *Boston Herald*, 3 Aug. 1965: "It dismays me that anyone in the medical profession will attempt to speak for the public. . . . Perhaps, as Pogo said, 'We have met the enemy, and they are us.'" 1966 *New York Times* 1 May: "The noted author and teacher Saunders Redding concluded a speech on assimilation by quoting from Pogo on the oneness of man: 'We have met the enemy,' Pogo related to his friends, 'and they is US'" (capitalization as shown). 1968 Interdepartmental Committee on the Status of Women and Citizens' Advisory Council on the Status of Women, *1968: Time for Action* (Washington DC: Government Printing Office) 4 (quoting Secretary of Labor Willard Wirtz): "What I have to say could perhaps be suggested more aptly, more directly, and more lightly in the terms of Pogo, that philosopher of the southern swamplands, who one day proudly announced, 'We have met the enemy, and it is us.'" 1968 Harold W. Sobel, "The New Wave of Educational Literature," *Phi Delta Kappan* 50: 110: "Pogo's famous epigram, 'We has met the enemy and he is *us*,' applies to many teachers" (italics as shown). *RHDP* 253; *YBQ* Walt Kelly (3). The proverb is based on Adm. Oliver Hazard Perry's famous dispatch to President William Henry Harrison at the end of the battle of Lake Erie in 1813: "We have met the enemy, and he is ours." The best dictionaries of quotations, as well as studies of the cartoonist Walt Kelly, seem to concur that Kelly's use of the popular form of the proverb first appeared in an Earth Day poster in 1970. Obviously, though, by the 1960s the saying already belonged to popular tradition (usually attributed, specifically, to Kelly's comic-strip character Pogo the 'Possum). Was Kelly in 1970 quoting a popular misquotation (and misattribution) of his own saying? It seems more likely that he was alluding to an existing Pogoism of his own creation—though it has not been found in the published collections of the *Pogo the 'Possum* strip. Despite the variability in the pronoun and the auxiliary verb, the attribution of the proverb to Pogo is highly stable.

## Your worst **enemy** could be your best friend (Your best friend may be your worst enemy).

1970 Richard Gardner, *Grito! Reies Tijerina and the New Mexico Land Grant War of 1967*

(New York: Bobbs-Merrill) 244: "Asked how the villagers [in Rio Arriba NM] were reacting to the murder [of Reies Tijerina], a man replied, 'Something like this is not taken lightly,' and walked away. 'Your best friend might be your worst enemy,' explained one young woman. 'You never know who is listening, who is on which side, who might be next.'" 1976 Bob Marley, "Who the Cap Fit" (song), on the album *Rastaman Vibration*: "Children, y'all don't know who to trust / Your worst enemy could be your best friend / And your best friend your worst enemy." Beckwith (1925) 126 gives a variant as a Jamaican proverb: "You wus enemy lib in a you house wid you." Anderson and Cundall (1927) 49; Prahlad (2001) 248.

## The most important **erogenous zone** is the brain (mind).

See "The most important erogenous ZONE is the brain."

## Don't make **excuses**; make good.

1909 *Wilson's Photographic Magazine* 46: 144 (a notice of "decorative mottoes, maxims, and wise sayings of prominent photographers" for sale as wall hangings): "What would be better to keep before the eyes of your receptionist . . . than H. H. Pierce's brief but crisp *Don't make excuses; make good*" (italics as shown). *DAP* 188(3). Stevenson (1948) 720(5) attributes the saying to Elbert Hubbard, citing that author's "*Epigrams* (1905)," but the date seems to be erroneous; the only edition of Hubbard's *Thousand and One Epigrams* was published in 1911.

## **Excuses** are like assholes (armpits); everybody has them (and most of them stink).

1974 Robert Reisner and Lorraine Wechsler, *Encyclopedia of Graffiti* (New York: Macmillan) 290: "Excuses are like assholes—everybody's got one!" (said to have been recorded in Detroit in 1971). 1982 Greg Barron, *Groundrush* (New York:

Random House) 17: "Pap hadn't blamed the refs. 'Excuses are like assholes,' he told Jason. 'Ever'body's got one, and they all stink.' But the adage was wasted on Jason, who didn't blame the refs either." Cf. "OPINIONS are like assholes—everybody's got one."

## Expedience is the best teacher.

1966 *Corpus Christi [TX] Times* 8 Oct. "Some of the bumper stickers say things like . . . 'Expedience is the Best Teacher.'" Litovkina and Mieder (2006) 144. The proverb originated as an anti-proverb based on "Experience is the best teacher."

## One ought to try every experience once except incest and folk dancing.

See "One ought to try everything once except INCEST and folk dancing."

## An expert is only a fool a long way from home.

1926 "Unit Costs for Measuring the Efficiency of City Administration: Round Table Session," *City Manager Magazine* 8: 155: "A young chap whom I [C. E. Douglas] had met in the army introduced me as an 'expert.' He also gave the definition for 'expert.' He said an expert was a darn fool a long ways from home." 1931 *Congressional Record* 74: 7097; Senator Ellison D. Smith speaks: "I do not propose to define, as some one has done in modern times, what an ordinary expert is. He said he was a 'blamed fool away from home.'" *DAAP* 251.

## Never explain, never complain.

See "Never COMPLAIN, never explain."

## Close (Shut) your eyes and think of England (the Empire, the queen, Old Glory, etc.).

1943 *Washington Post* 18 May: "Stanley Baldwin's son tells this story of the day his sister went out

with a young man who wanted to marry her. She asked her mother for advice, in case the young man should want to kiss her . . . 'Do what I did,' said her mother, reminiscing of the beginning of her romance with the man who was to become Prime Minister. 'Just close your eyes and think of England'" (ellipsis dots as shown). 1972 Jonathan Gathorne-Hardy, *The Rise and Fall of the British Nanny* (London: Hodder & Stoughton) 71 (epigraph at the head of a chapter): "I am happy now that Charles calls on my bedchamber less frequently than of old. As it is, I now endure but two calls a week and when I hear his steps outside my door I lie down on my bed, close my eyes, open my legs and think of England." (Gathorne-Hardy attributes the quoted matter to Lady Alice Hillingdon's "journal," but no such journal appears to exist, and the quotation is probably apocryphal.) The common male counterpart of the proverb, regarding sexual intercourse with a homely partner: 1969 Myles Ludwig, *Golem, a Hero for Our Time* (New York: Weybright & Talley) 166: "Ah, what's the big deal anyway? They all look alike in the dark. One hole's as good as another. Put a flag over her head and fuck for old glory." Doyle (2007a) 199.

## Every shut eye is not asleep.

1900 *Nebraska State Journal [Lincoln]* 19 Nov.: "He keep still, but we say, 'Every shut eye no asleep.'" *DAP* 190(11); Whiting (1952) 404; Prahlad (1996) 227. Bohn (1857) gives an analogous Italian proverb (115) and an analogous German proverb (147).

## An eye for an eye leaves the whole world blind.

1948 Louis Fischer, *Gandhi and Stalin* (New York: Harper & Brothers) 61: "The shreds of individuality cannot be sewed together with a bayonet; nor can democracy be restored according to the Biblical injunction of an 'eye for an eye' which, in the end, would make everybody blind." 1950 Louis Fischer, *Life of Mahatma Gandhi* (New York: Harper & Brothers) 77:

"'Satyagraha' means truth-force or love-force. Truth and love are attributes of the soul. . . . Satyagraha is the exact opposite of the policy of an-eye-for-an-eye-for-an-eye-for-an-eye which ends in making everybody blind." *YBQ* Fischer. The saying is commonly credited to Mohandas Gandhi, though neither of Fischer's books on Gandhi specifically makes the attribution, and no instance in Gandhi's own writings has been found.

## Keep your **eye** on the donut and not on the hole.

1908 "Splinters from Speeches" [this "splinter" is attributed to one "Dr. Richards"], *The Home Missionary* 82: 472: "A prosperity association is touring the country. . . . Their emblem is that most toothsome of New England products, the doughnut, and under the picture is the motto, 'Keep your eye on the doughnut, and not on the hole.'" The proverb grew into (or was extracted from) four lines of verse (though not printed as verse): 1939 *Food Industries* 2: 540 (in a miscellaneous collection of tidbits): "The doughnut industry has a good slogan for young hopefuls: 'As you go through life, no matter what your goal, keep your eye on the doughnut and not on the hole.'"

## When six **eyes** meet, the story is over.

Anderson and Cundall (1910) 17 give the saying as a Jamaican proverb: "When six yeye meet 'tory done" (gloss: "The intervention of a third person stops many a story"). Whiting (1952) 404 lists it as a North Carolina proverb. Beckwith (1925) 121.

## The **eyebrow** is older than the beard.

1925 H. H. Finlay, "Folklore from Eleuthera," *Journal of American Folklore* 38: 294 gives a version of the saying as a Bahaman proverb: "Eye winkers older than beard, but when beard come, beard grow the longest." Anderson and Cundall (1927) 49 list it as a Jamaican proverb: "Yeyebrow older dan beard." Whiting (1952) 405 lists it as a North Carolina proverb (and cites Haitian French analogs). 1961 John Jacob Niles, *The Ballad Book* (New York: Houghton Mifflin) 319–20: "She [a singer in North Carolina] wanted to make sure I got the moral: 'He thought he was shed of her, but she learned 'im! Women like that are powerful old and powerful smart, and as folks do say, the eyebrow is older than the beard, and a heap smarter.'" The proverb may have evolved from an older expression, "The hair (head) is older than the beard."

### Beware (of) a smiling **face**.

1955 *Chicago Tribune* 23 May (in a small collection of wise or witty sayings): "Beware of a smiling face: A frown could easily take its place" (attributed to "Leo the Lion"; perhaps intended as a rhymed couplet). 1975 Song by the Jamaicans Horace Andy and JoJo Hookim: "Beware of a Smiling Face." 1998 Juan Delgado, *El Campo* (Santa Barbara CA: Capra) 31 (in a poem titled "Raul"): "Our camp is full of thieves. / You can start with our boss. / . . . / Raul, beware of a smiling face / and what's hiding behind it." Cf. "Beware a smiling MAN."

### You don't fuck the **face**.

1984 Julian Wood, "Groping toward Sexism: Boys' Sex Talk," in *Gender and Generation*, edited by Angela McRobbie and Mica Nava (Houndmills UK: Macmillan) 60: "Don't worry, you don't fuck the face! She's got a nice body." 1985 Andrew H. Vachss, *Flood* (New York: Donald I. Fine) 29: "'She's got some beautiful body, you know, but her face's ugly as shit.' 'Man, you don't fuck her *face*'" (italics as shown).

### Never let **facts** (the truth) get in the way of (interfere with) opinions.

1998 *St. Louis Post-Dispatch* 24 Aug.: "When Littell continued complaining that the city should not be giving a break to a new business by giving them taxpayer money, O'Keefe finally said: 'Never let facts get in the way of a good opinion, sir.'" 1999 *Macon [GA] Telegraph* 16 Jan.: "Fact is—and Skippy doesn't know this, for why should facts interfere with opinions?—Atlanta played a schedule hardly different from most other playoff teams." 2002 *Virginia Pilot [Hampton Roads]* 1 May: "Let us not let facts stand in the way of opinion." This cynical or satiric proverb may be related to "Never let the FACTS stand in the way of a good story."

### Never let the **facts** stand in the way of (spoil, ruin) a good story (the truth) (Don't spoil a good story with facts).

1924 Louis Ludlow, *From Cornfield to Press Gallery* (Washington DC: W. F. Roberts) 360: "Persons whose opportunity gave them a close-up of the real President Harding in action marvel that even partisan spellbinders could be so reckless with the truth, and their conduct is only to be explained on the theory, to which many politicians are devoted, that it is best not to let the facts stand in the way of a good story on the opposition." 1965 Winston Bode, *Portrait of Pancho* (Austin TX: Pemberton) 104 (photograph caption): "'The Lord loveth a cheerful liar,' [J. Frank] Dobie would say, with such an emphatic gesture as this. 'Never let facts stand in [the] way of the truth!'" Rees (1995) 339. Cf. the older "Truth is more important than facts."

### There are no **facts**—just interpretations (of facts).

1915 William Mackintire Salter, "Nietzsche and the Problem of Reality," *Mind* 24: 415 (summarizing points from Nietzsche's *Will to Power*): "We can conceive only a world that we ourselves have made. . . . There are no facts, only interpretations; we cannot fix any fact in itself—perhaps it is absurd to wish to." The standard translation of Nietzsche by Anthony Ludovici (1910) lacked the epigrammatic phrasing that would become proverbial in English: "In opposition to Positivism, which halts at phenomena and says, 'Those are only *facts* and nothing more,' I would say: No, facts are precisely what is lacking; all that exists consists of *interpretations*" (§481; italics as shown).

## If you **fail** to prepare, you prepare to fail (If you fail to plan, you plan to fail).

1919 "The Church and the World," *Biblical World* n.s. 53: 81 (quoting Rev. H. K. Williams): "There is positively no excuse for wasting another's time by going to the meeting unprepared and rambling helplessly in your talk. Remember, if you fail to prepare, you are preparing to fail." 1940 *Newsweek* 16, no. 17 (21 Oct.) 41: Ad for Babson's Reports, ". . . [A] service designed to help you plan more soundly and to make your plans effective with increasing success. *Those who fail to plan are planning to fail*" (italics as shown). 1942 Maurice M. Smith et al., *Junior High School Education* (New York: McGraw-Hill) 244: "The successful teacher knows that to fail to plan is to plan to fail."

## When all else **fails**, pray (try prayer).

1957 Henry Miller, *Big Sur and the Oranges of Hieronymus Bosch* (New York: New Directions) 397: "If you have the vision and the urge to undertake great tasks, then you will discover in yourself the virtues and capabilities required for their accomplishment. When everything fails, pray!" 1962 *Lakeland [FL] Ledger* 26 Apr.: "I finally walked into a church . . . got down on my knees and prayed to God to deliver me of the habit [smoking]. . . . When everything else fails, try prayer."

## You can't **fail** unless you quit.

See "You never LOSE unless you quit."

## **Failure** is not falling down but staying down.

1936 *St. Petersburg [FL] Times* 25 Jan. (a column by the actress Mary Pickford): "However, if you have made mistakes, . . . there is always another chance for you. . . . [F]or this thing we call 'failure' is not the falling down but the staying down." *DAP* 195(6). Cf. "It's not how many TIMES you get knocked down that matters but

how many times you get back up" and "To win, you only have to get up one more TIME than you fall down."

## Respect **faith** (knowledge), but doubt is what gives you an education.

1935 The proverb is recorded in a list of "Miznerisms" by Edward Dean Sullivan, *The Fabulous Wilson Mizner* (New York: Henkle) 266: "I respect faith, but doubt is what gets you an education." *DAP* 354(31); *YBQ* Mizner (2).

## **Fake** it till you make it.

1972 *Anniston [AL] Star* 8 Jun.: "One slogan repeated at many of the meetings, the attorney general's office said, was 'Fake it until you make it.'" 1973 *Federal [Law] Reporter*, 2nd ser., 474: 480: "He [a 'purchaser-salesman'] is told to 'fake it 'til you make it,' or to give the impression of wealth even if it has not been attained."

## The bigger they are, the harder they **fall**.

1905 H. R. Dur[ant], "A Quitter," *Everybody's Magazine* 12 (Jan.–Jun.) 230: "When the manager returned to the champion's dressing room he said: 'Looks as if he could step some, eh? A big gazabo, ain't he?' 'The bigger they are the harder they fall.'" *MP* B206; *DAP* 51; *YBQ* Fitzsimmons; *ODP* 26; Albig (1931); Jente (1932); Mieder (1992); Mieder (1993b) 41–57; Mieder (1994) 297–316; Taft (1994); Prahlad (1996) 218–19; Prahlad (2001) 244. In more literal phrasing, the concept may be a little older: 1900 *Brooklyn Daily Eagle* 11 Aug. (quoting the English-born New Zealand boxer Robert Fitzsimmons): "He is a monstrous big fellow, but you know the old saying, 'The bigger they are, the further they have to fall.'" 1902 *National Police Gazette* 27 Sep.: "'If I can get close enough,' he [Robert Fitzsimmons] once said, 'I'll guarantee to stop almost anybody. The bigger the man, the heavier the fall.'" Cf. the much older "A great tree has a great fall."

Don't **fall** before you're pushed.

1922 John Symonds Udal, *Dorstshire Folk-lore* (Hertford UK: Stephen Austin) 296, gives the proverb with the gloss "A piece of advice not to anticipate troubles." Champion (1938) 27 lists it as a Wiltshire proverb.

**Fame** has a price.

1932 *Atlanta Constitution* 17 Apr. (picture caption): "FAME HAS A PRICE / Beautiful Ann Harding, Film Star. She Was One of Many in the Movie Colony Who Received Anonymous Threats . . ." (capitalization as shown). 1937 Elmer Rice, *Imperial City* (New York: Coward-McCann) 159: "He knew that fame has its price and that the acceptance of tribute is one of the inescapable responsibilities of greatness." Cf. "GLORY has a price" and "POWER has its price."

**Fame** is a bitch.

1961 Louis Zara, *Dark Rider: A Novel Based on the Life of Stephen Crane* (Cleveland: World) 290: "Any woman who makes up her mind to catch Stevie Crane will land him like a prize fish! . . . Watch out. Fame is a bitch." 1986 *Los Angeles Times* 12 Jan. (in an ad for the "Ninth International Imitation Hemingway Competition"): "Winter is coming. Fame is a bitch. Writing is Playing Hurt."

**Fame** is a powerful aphrodisiac.

1961 Graham Greene, *A Burnt-Out Case* (New York: Viking) 138: "You are famous among your readers and fame is a potent aphrodisiac. Married women are the easiest, Parkinson." *YBQ* Graham Greene (6). If Greene originated the saying (rather than himself adapting a proverb), then it is popularly misquoted, though often still attributed to Greene. Cf. the older (in French, at least) "Power is an aphrodisiac."

**Fame** is better than fortune (Better fame than fortune).

1932 Jean Marsh, *Murder Next Door* (London: John Long) 277–78: "'You've done pretty well, I consider,' Rodney said. . . . 'It will make your name. . . .' 'Well, they say fame's better than fortune any day,' Tony exulted." 1981 *Philadelphia Inquirer* 2 Jul.: "World Boxing Association heavyweight champion Mike Weaver has decided that fame is better than fortune. Weaver will give in to the WBA orders, fight second-ranked James 'Quick' Tillis. . . ." 1990 Jacques Ellul, *The Reason for Being: A Meditation on Ecclesiastes* (Grand Rapids MI: W. B. Eerdmans) 78: "'Fame is better than perfumed oil.' Many consider this [biblical] proverb trite and empty (some have compared it to 'better fame than fortune'). . . ." *MP* F23; *DAP* 198(5). Cf. the old proverb "A good name is better than gold."

The **family** that prays together stays together.

1947 The proverb possibly originated as a slogan on *Family Theater of the Air* (radio program), 6 Mar. It is said to have been invented by a professional ad writer, Al Scalpone, for Rev. Patrick Peyton's Roman Catholic Family Rosary Crusade, initiated in 1942, but no evidence of the use of the slogan occurs from that early. 1947 Marie Appleton, in one of ten prize-winning essays on the topic "How Can We Strengthen the American Family," *Town Meeting* 13, no. 5 (29 May) 33 (in an enumerated list of instructions for parents, on the basis of which "their home will be the better"): "14. Pray with your family. A family that prays together, stays together." *DAP* 198; *RHDP* 92; *DAAP* 262; *YBQ* Scalpone; *ODP* 109; Rees (1984) 50; Pickering (2001) 129.

Every **family tree** has a nut on it.

See "There's a NUT on every family tree."

Everyone thinks his own **farts** smell sweet.

See "Nobody minds the SMELL of his own farts."

Why go out for **fast food** when you can get steak at home?

See "Why go out for HAMBURGER when you can get steak at home?"

**Fatigue** is nature's way of telling you to slow down.

See "PAIN is nature's way of telling you to slow down."

**Feast** today (makes) fast tomorrow.

1908 *Bar Association of the State of Kansas: Proceedings[,] Twenty-fifth Annual Meeting* (Jan.) 38 (the proverb appears as an epigraph on a banquet program—presumably intended ironically): "Feast today makes fast tomorrow." *DAP* 204. The proverb has been applied metaphorically to economic matters; currently, it sometimes refers to calorie intake. Cf. the older proverb "After the feast comes the reckoning."

**Feed** them or amuse them.

1908 George Middleton, "The Librettist and His Profits," *The Bookman* 28: 116: "'Sonny,' the fat man said, 'if you ain't in politics, and you want to make money, feed them or amuse them.' The comic opera has no aim but sheer amusement." *MP* F67. Cf. the ancient phrase "bread and circuses."

If it **feels** good, do it.

1968 *Rowan and Martin's Laugh-In* (New York: Samuel French) 62 (in a list of "graffiti and sign material"): "If it feels good, do it." 1969 *Los Angeles Times* 27 Mar.: "In contemporary society, the word 'love' has taken on new dimensions. One of these seems to be an attitude of 'If it feels good, do it.'" Nussbaum (2005) 43.

You can't blame a **fellow** (a guy, a man, someone) for trying.

1906 Gamaliel Bradford Jr., *Between Two Masters* (Boston: Houghton, Mifflin) 198: "But it [the world] needs making over, does n't it? If that is so, you can't blame even the little, weak, pitiful ones for trying—with God to help them." 1918 Charles Bernard Nordhoff, "More Letters from France," *Atlantic Monthly* 121: 125: "They can never shoot quickly enough to hurt any one at this point, Jean thought, but after all, 'You can't blame a fellow for trying.'"

The **female** of the species is deadlier than the male.

1911 The saying probably passed into oral tradition as a proverb from Rudyard Kipling's poem "The Female of the Species" (unless Kipling in his poem was elaborating on a proverb). *DAP* 206; *DAAP* 270; *YBQ* Kipling (34); *ODP* 112.

Don't take (tear) down a **fence** (wall) unless you are sure why it was put up.

1964 J. M. Juran, *Managerial Breakthrough* (New York: McGraw-Hill) 35: "The Inhibitor will not tear down an old fence: to him old fences are sacred. The Conservative may tear it down, but only after he knows why it was put up." 1964 Walter Dean Burnham, "Democracy and the Court," *Commonweal* 80: 503: "It seems more than likely that the development of such a party system would be accompanied step by step by a decline in the Supreme Court's policy making function. But until that day arrives, it would be well to remember that a wise man does not tear down a fence until he learns why it is up." 1965 Arthur M. Schlesinger Jr., *A Thousand Days* (Boston: Houghton Mifflin) 105–6 (said to be quoted from "a looseleaf notebook that John F. Kennedy kept in 1945–46"): "Don't ever take a fence down until you know the reason it was put up." *RHDP* 69. Kennedy's reported attribution of the saying to G. K. Chesterton cannot be verified.

One **fence** at a time (Take your fences one at a time).

1928 Archibald E. Fielding, *The Net Around Joan Ingilby* (New York: A. L. Burt) 283: "'You don't think he also impersonated Waddy at the theatre? . . .' Blair asked eagerly. . . . 'One fence at a time, Blair, or we'll never get home!'" *MP* F71; Stevenson (1948) 794(14). Cf. the older "One step at a time."

Show me a fifty-foot **fence**, and I'll show you a fifty-one-foot ladder.

1986 *Issues Relating to Drug Trafficking in the New Jersey Area: Hearing before the Select Committee on Narcotics Abuse and Control . . . House of Representatives* (Washington DC: Government Printing Office, 1987) 85; David Kerr testifies (11 Apr.): "My feeling as far as supply and demand is that I like to try to stop the supply—someone said a law enforcement officer says, if you build a 30-foot wall around the United Sates, it will take a drug pusher 30 seconds to build a 31-foot ladder. . . ." 1987 *Narcotics Trafficking through John F. Kennedy Airport: Hearing before the Select Committee on Narcotics Abuse and Control . . . House of Representatives* (Washington DC: Government Printing Office) 37; Robert M. Stutman testifies (10 Jul.): "I have used the analogy many times: If you build a 13 foot wall around the United States the dope peddlers would realize all you need is a 14 foot ladder to get over a 13 foot wall." The height of the fence and of the ladder, obviously, can vary. Currently, the proverb is applied not only to drug trafficking but also (more literally) to illegal immigration from Mexico, which abounds despite the construction of fences and walls along the southern border of the United States.

You win a **few**, you lose a few (You win some, you lose some; Sometimes you win, sometimes you lose).

1912 *Oakland Tribune* 21 Jul. (heading over a list of professional baseball standings): "Sometimes You Win, Sometimes You Lose." 1945 Kenneth Davis, *Soldier of Democracy: A Biography of Dwight Eisenhower* (Garden City NY: Doubleday, Doran) 91 (referring to Six MacDonell, Eisenhower's childhood and college friend, after a bad play by Ike had cost his Kansas University team a victory): "Six tried to soothe him. It was just a game, Six said. You win some. You lose some." 1958 *New York Times* 11 Mar.: "Basketball and politics are somewhat similar in that you win a few, you lose a few. In the former it's a game. In the latter it's votes." *MP* A70 (intermingled with "You can't win them all"); *DAP* 656(5); *DAAP* 844; *YBQ* Modern Proverbs (99); *ODP* 346–47; Pickering (2001) 374. Cf. "You can't WIN them all."

The **fewer** the sooner.

1906 Stephen Moore, "Morituri Te Salutamus" (a verse meditation on Psalms 90:10), *The Watchman* 88, no. 16 (19 Apr.) 17: "If the years shall be few and fleeting, / What matter and why despond? / The fewer, the sooner the meeting / With Christ and the loved ones beyond." 1928 Carl Sandburg, *Good Morning, America* (New York: Harcourt, Brace) 15 (in a poetic montage of proverbs and other sayings): "The higher they go the farther they drop. / The fewer the sooner. Tell 'em. Tell 'em." *DAAP* 272. In its syntax, the proverb parallels the old proverb "The more the merrier."

The older the **fiddle** (violin), the sweeter (finer) the tune (melody, sound).

1909 William J. Luby, *The Vandal* (Chicago: J. S. Hyland) 328–29: "We are all getting old, but we must console ourselves with the beautiful thought that the older the violin the better the melody." 1934 *Parliamentary Debates: Commons* 295: 12; Noel Lindsay speaks (20 Nov.): "If he [Winston Churchill] may properly be described as an old man, I am sure that the House will have appreciated and understood the old country proverb which says, 'The older the fiddle, the sweeter the tune.'" *DAP* 206(2). Cf. the older proverb "There's many a good tune played on an old fiddle."

## Don't start a **fight** you can't finish (unless you finish it).

1921 E. S. Chamberlayne, *The Little Back Room* (New York: Frederick A. Stokes) 227: "I think he has it in for me; and if he has, that means a fight. And I don't want to start a fight unless I can finish it." 1941 *Pittsburgh Press* 19 Oct.: "So the old common sense of the people is very much in order now. It says: . . . Don't start a fight you can't finish. . . . We offer these homely adages to the President and Congress. . . ." 1947 Marie Small, *Four Fares to Juneau* (New York: McGraw-Hill) 70: "He arranged a somewhat swollen mouth into a grin. '. . . Never start a fight but always finish it.'"

## Anything worth **fighting** for is worth fighting dirty for.

1979 John Peers, *1,001 Logical Laws* (Garden City NY: Doubleday) 138: "Bert's Bulwark: If it is worth fighting for, it is worth fighting dirty for." 1996 *San Jose [CA] Mercury News* 1 Jun.: "The following words of wisdom came to us under the title 'Everything I Need to Know . . . I Learned in Corporate America': . . . Anything worth fighting for is worth fighting dirty for" (the first set of ellipsis dots as shown). The proverb originated as an anti-proverb based on "Anything worth fighting for is worth dying for."

## Everyone **finds** someone.

1943 Cornell Woolrich, *The Black Angel* (Garden City NY: Doubleday, Doran) 265: "Well, it's like this. Everyone finds someone. But most men, they just find women. . . . I've found an angel." 1945 Tom Hanlin, *Once in Every Lifetime* (New York: Viking) 5: "Jibbing at going through life alone, nearly everybody finds somebody. But it's seldom the somebody. It's usually just somebody they could get."

## **Find** them (etc.), fuck them, and forget them.

See "FUCK them and forget them."

## The hottest **fire** makes the hardest steel (The hardest steel comes from the hottest fire).

1980 *The Sun [Baltimore]* 1 Sep. (quoting Bill Thomas, on the difficulty of performing at a comedy club): "Still, if you love it you keep coming back for more. It's like they say—the hardest steel is tempered in the hottest fire." 1995 *Austin [TX] American-Statesman* 24 Aug. (quoting the football coach Gary Darnell): "But everybody has heard that the hottest fire creates the hardest steel."

## Keep the home **fires** burning.

1914 The saying may have entered oral tradition as a proverb from a line in the song "Till the Boys Come Home!" by Lena Guilbert Ford— or the song may have been quoting a proverb. *DAP* 210.

## You cannot fight **fire** with fire.

1917 Achmed Abdullah, *The Blue-Eyed Manchu* (New York: Robert J. Shores) 140: "You cannot fight fire with fire, nor water with water. Listen master!" (the character speaking is a "Goanese half-cast"). 1919 John Cournos, *The Mask* (New York: George H. Doran) 222: "But other fires came, fires of pity, which overwhelmed this other fire [of shame, frustration, anger] but did not put it out. For you cannot fight fire with fire." The proverb perhaps originated as a counter-proverb rebutting the very old "Fight fire with fire" or "You've got to fight fire with fire." The modern proverb has a Turkish counterpart, quoted by President Barack Obama (Mieder [2010a] 31–32).

Sometimes you're the **fireplug**, and sometimes you're the dog.

See "Sometimes you're the DOG, and sometimes you're the fireplug."

Everyone can't be **first**.

1955 Oliver St. John Gogarty, *Start from Somewhere Else* (Garden City NY: Doubleday) 28: "In Cuba he [Jimmy Walker, mayor of New York City] had to speak at a lunch, but . . . he lay asleep until nearly one o'clock. . . . [He] apologized for being late. 'After all,' he said, 'everyone can't be first: George Washington married a widow'" (Mayor Walker died in 1946; the anecdote may be apocryphal). *DAP* 211(1).

**First** up, best dressed.

1919 E[rnest] Classen, *Outlines of the History of the English Language* (London: Macmillan) 263: "The same dislike of assertiveness is responsible for much of the characteristic brevity of expressions in English, and for the frequency of such short pregnant phrases as, 'first come, first served,' 'first up, best dressed,' 'better late than never,' and many more." 1930 Samuel Hopkins Adams, *The Godlike Daniel* (New York: Sears) 18: ". . . [T]he group [of Dartmouth students] . . . shared indiscriminately their food, bedding, firewood, textbooks, and apparel. First up, best dressed was their accepted principle." *ODP* 117.

If you are not **first**, you are (you might as well be) last.

1987 *Telegraph [Sydney, Australia]* (21 Jan.): "In this game [yacht racing] you're first or last. There's no in-between." 1999 *Detroit Free Press* (13 Jan.): "According to [motion picture] industry insiders, early interest in the stories in the works often translates into acquisition. The adage 'if you're not first, you're last' applies here." Cf. "There is no second PLACE" and "Second PLACE is first loser."

You can't steal **first base**.

1915 *Ogden [UT] Standard* 7 Aug.: "'A wonderful fielder and a great base runner,' a scout will say to his manager. 'How does he hit?' asks the manager. 'Only about .200,' says the scout dolefully, 'but he stole 57 bases in the Michigan State league last year.' 'Well, you can't steal first base,' replies the manager." 1925 *St. Petersburg [FL] Independent* 20 Oct.: "You must get on the bases to take advantage of speed. . . . It's an old and true saying that you can't steal first base." 1959 Joseph P. Lyford, *Candidate* (New York: Henry Holt) 8: "I told him [Democratic Party leader John Morgan Bailey] that if I were nominated and elected that I could be much more useful to the party in Washington than someone who was nominated solely because he met the accepted nationality and religious tests. . . . 'I know what you mean,' he said. 'You have a feeling that you're the greatest base runner in the world but you can't steal first. What you need to do is get on first base.'"

Better a big **fish** in a little pond (puddle, pool) than a little fish in a big pond (mighty ocean).

1903 *New York Times* 20 Apr.: "Is it better to be a big fish in a little pond or a little fish in a big pond? Of course, there have been instances where the big fish from a little pond has been able to remain a big fish when transferred to a big pond, but there is always a risk." *DAP* 212(6); *RHDP* 23; *YBQ* Modern Proverbs (7). Cf. "It is better to be a big DUCK in a little puddle than a little duck in a big puddle."

A **fish** in the net (creel) is worth two in the water (sea, river).

1902 W. Payne Collier, "A Devon Stream," *Badminton Magazine of Sports and Pastimes* 15: 527–28: "However . . . you may rest assured I will never again play with 'fire,' or, rather, fish, and ever since this mishap have always considered that a fish in the 'net' is worth two in the water." 1937 Henry Randolph Latimer, *The Conquest of Blindness: An Autobiographical Review* (New York: American Foundation for the Blind) 47 (recounting a school exercise of "capping" proverbs—one student's quoted proverb being answered by another student with an equivalent proverb): "One evening, I responded with the proverb 'A bird in the hand is worth two in the bush.' The next boy gave a groan as he rose to deliver his selection. After a moment's hesitation, he said in a matter of fact tone, 'A fish in the net is worth two in the sea.'"

## Fish where the **fish** are.

1901 Sir Edward Grey, *Fly Fishing* (London: J. M. Dent) 159: ". . . [W]henever sea trout do show themselves in this way, it is an invaluable help to the angler, whose first object is to fish where the fish are. . . ." 1912 Nathaniel C. Fowler Jr., *The Boy: How to Help Him Succeed* (New York: Moffat, Yard); a panel of "successful" men responds to a series of questions, one of which is "Would you advise a country boy to go to a great city, if his home is in a sparsely settled district where there is little or no opportunity for business?" (135); Joseph C. Hendrix answers, "Yes; fish where the fish are" (200). Cf. "Go hunting where the DUCKS are," "If you are looking for ELEPHANTS, go to elephant country," and "You've got to FISH while they are biting."

## A **fish** wouldn't get caught if it kept its mouth shut.

1921 T. J. R[uddy], "Gossip Is a Form of Insanity," *Western Osteopath* 16, no. 5 (Oct.) 41: "This man in turn was threatening a slander suit. Perhaps he was justified, but we all can agree with the editor of Whiz Bang [Wilford H. Fawcett?] that 'Even a fish won't get caught if it keeps its mouth shut.'" *DAP* 211(30); Prahlad (2001) 249. Cf. "Smart FISH don't bite."

## Half a **fish** is better than none (at all).

See "HALF a fish is better than none."

## Only dead **fish** go with the flow.

1989 Bobbie Louise Hawkins, *My Own Alphabet* (Minneapolis: Coffee House Press) 135 (in a list of sayings by unknown authors): "Only dead fish go with the flow." 2000 Michaelann Martin, *Women of Grace* (Steubenville OH: Emmaus Road) 81: "I like to remember that in the river of life, only dead fish 'go with the flow.'" Cf. the older proverb "A dead fish can float downstream, but it takes a live one to swim upstream." The modern variant (among other implications) satirizes—and sometimes retorts to—the proverbial advice "Go with the FLOW."

## Smart **fish** don't bite (don't get caught, keep their mouth shut).

1935 *Chicago Tribune* 2 May: "Most fishermen never saw a highfin or a carp, either, or yet a buffalo fish, for those smart fish bandits won't bite at a hook." 1938 *Hartford Courant* 25 Dec.: "Dr. [Charles M.] Breder would like to say, 'the smart fish doesn't get caught.'" 1995 Ronald T. Potter-Efron and Pat Potter-Efron, *Letting Go of Anger* (Oakland CA: New Harbinger) 115: "If you are a rageaholic, remember these four words: Smart fish don't bite." 1998 *Chicago Sun-Times* 20 Feb.: "I am sure you will agree that the line, as I perceive it, does make sense: a smart fish tends to keep its mouth closed." Cf. "A FISH wouldn't get caught if it kept its mouth shut."

## You can't catch a **fish** without baiting a hook (putting the line in the water, etc.).

1921 Joseph C. Lincoln, *Galusha the Magnificent* (New York: A. L. Burt) 75: "No harm in tryin', was there? Never catch a fish without heavin' over a hook, as the feller said." *DAAP* 281. The proverb refers to taking necessary steps toward achieving a desired end; it is different from the older "You can't catch a fish without bait." Dora Sakayan, *Armenian Proverbs* (Delmar NY: Caravan, 1994) 218 translates an Armenian proverb, "You can't catch a fish without getting wet."

## You've got to **fish** while they are biting.

1921 W. Livingston Larned, "Going to It after Gar," *American Angler* 6: 420: "I observed, 'anybody can catch fish when they're biting.'" 1941 *St. Petersburg [FL] Times* 21 Dec.: "Dazzy [Vance] has only one theory about fish: 'The surest way to catch fish is when they are biting, and I never found anything that made any difference if they weren't.'" Person (1958) 177 lists the saying as a Washington State proverb: "You've got to fish while they are biting." Beyond its application to angling, the proverb can advise the seizing of opportunities in general. Cf. "Fish where the FISH are."

## If it (If the glove) doesn't **fit**, you must acquit.

1995 The saying entered oral tradition as a proverb from its use as a mantra by the defense lawyer Johnnie Cochran Jr. in his closing argument at the murder trial of O. J. Simpson (27 Sep.). 2002 Jonathan Franzen, *How to Be Alone* (New York: Farrar, Straus & Giroux) 253–54: "Good sex writing, it turns out, is a lot like good fiction writing in general. . . . Avoid clichés, she advises—or at least 'give them a unique twist.' Try to 'make the writing interesting.' Don't forget: 'You need not be explicit but you must be specific.' And if it doesn't fit, you must acquit." 2007 Bruce Jackson, *The Story Is True: The Art and Meaning of Telling Stories* (Philadelphia: Temple UP) 135: "In real life, if everything fits but one thing, then that one thing is what is aberrant and what is tossed out; in court, if everything fits but one thing (and if you've got a good lawyer), then it is the other side's story that is tossed out. 'If it doesn't fit, you must acquit.' The court, like the world of drama, requires perfection in narrative." 2008 Peter Charles Hoffer, *The Historians' Paradox* (New York: New York UP) 188: "Verification test: the philosophical version of the infamous slogan, 'If it doesn't fit, you must acquit.' For a word to have meaning, its sense must be testable in the real world." Winick (2003); Prahlad (2006) 1022–27.

The proverb means "You must reject, abandon, or discard a belief or plan that does not 'fit' with realities, goals, or purposes." The proverb is less commonly applied in specifically jurisprudential discourse.

## It is always **five o'clock** somewhere.

See "It is five O'CLOCK somewhere."

## If it ain't broke (isn't broken), don't (why) **fix** it (If it works, don't fix it).

1960 L. C. Sheetz, "Is Communications Reliability Possible?" *Signal* (Armed Forces Communications Association) 14 (May) 33 (in a facetious footnote glossing a reference to Murphy's Law, said to have been propounded by one "M/Sgt Murphy, a crew chief of many years experience"): "Although originally advanced in connection with aircraft maintenance, subsequent investigations by M/Sgts Shultz, Cohen and Dabnovich have proven its applicability to C-E ['communications electronics']. The latter, by the way, is the author of the Dabnovich axiom, 'If it works, don't fix it'" (presumably, M/Sgt Dabnovich is fictional). 1964 "Notes and Comments on Maintenance," *Approach: The Naval Aviation Safety Review* 9, no. 10 (Apr.) 42: "But be sure it's real leakage that you're measuring. As someone recently said, 'if it ain't broke don't fix it.'" 1968 James K. Van Fleet, *Guide to Managing People* (West Nyack NY: Parker) 159: "If It Ain't Broke—Why Fix It?" (section heading); the section ends, "If you had an alarm clock that was still running well and had gotten you up every morning on time for the last twenty years, would you suddenly decide to take it apart and check just to see if it would ring for sure tomorrow morning? I wouldn't either. *So if it ain't broke—don't fix it!*" (italics as shown). 1973 *Implementation of Transportation Controls: Hearing before the Subcommittee on Air and Water Pollution . . . Senate* (Washington DC: Government Printing Office, 1974) 259; Senator Jack L. Gockel speaks: "I might add that the average cost for the tuneups performed on 300 cars was only $27, and the reason why the cost was so low was that the criteria of, if it isn't broke, don't fix it, was the main criteria that we taught." 1979 *New York Times* 26 Sep.: "Governor [Lee S.] Dreyfus and others argue that no one has made a serious case against the Wisconsin primary. 'If it works don't fix it,' said the Governor." In the form "If it ain't broke, don't fix it," the saying has often been attributed to Bert Lance; however, the earliest record of his use of the expression appeared in the *Washington Post* on 23 Dec. 1976. *RHDP* 152; *DAAP* 109; *YBQ* Lance; *ODP* 38; Flavell and Flavell (1993) 30–31; Rees (1995) 238; Pickering (2001) 58; Rees (2006) 329.

## You can't **fix** everything.

1933 John P. Marquand, *Haven's End* (Boston: Little, Brown) 284: "'I've looked into that.' 'Look here,' said Tom, . . .'You can't fix everything.'" 1967 Frank G. Slaughter, *Doctors' Wives* (Garden City NY: Doubleday) 219: "'You may be right at that,' he admitted . . .' 'So you admit you can't fix everything?'" 1969 Martha Gellhorn, *The Lowest Trees Have Tops* (New York: Dodd, Mead) 196–97: "They have the right to live their own lives or ruin them in their own way. You cannot fix everything for everybody." Cf. the older "You can't save the world."

## Put a **flag** over her head (face) and fuck for Old Glory (our country).

See "Close your EYES and think of England."

## Run it up the **flagpole** and see who (if anybody) salutes.

1957 J. Harvey Howells, *Good-bye, Gray Flannel* (a television play that premiered 22 Oct. 1956), in Writers Guild of America, *Prize Plays of Television and Radio 1956* (New York: Random House) 60: "I've written a little something here. I'd like to run it up the flagpole and see if you salute it." 1957 J. P. Shanley, "Television," *America* 96, no. 17 (Jan.) 491: "The second

program in the series [Bergen Evans's *The Last Word*] was devoted to examples of contemporary English usage, including what has come to be known as 'Madison Avenue talk.' Specimens of this jargon, said to be in widespread use among advertising men in New York and elsewhere, include . . . 'Let's run this up the flagpole and see who salutes.' . . ." 1957 Reginald Rose, *Twelve Angry Men* (screenplay), in *Film Scripts Two*, compiled by George P. Garret et al. (New York: Appleton-Century-Crofts, 1971) 221: "I mean it's the weirdest thing in the whole world sometimes the way they [ad agency personnel] precede the idea with some kind of phrase. Like . . . Oh, some account exec'll say, 'Here's an idea. Let's run it up the flagpole and see if anyone salutes it'" (ellipsis dots as shown); the saying does not occur in Rose's television play of 1955 or in Sherman Sergel's 1956 adaptation of it for the stage. 1957 James Kelly, response to Geoffrey Wagner's article "The Decline of Book Reviewing," *American Scholar* 26: 214: "As that mass communicator on the Boston train would probably say if anybody asked *him*: Lets run this one up the flagpole and see who salutes, Mr. Wagner" (italics as shown). *YBQ* Sayings (35); Lighter (1994– ) 1: 762.

## **Flattery** will get you everywhere (anywhere).

1926 Henry T. Finck, *My Adventures in the Golden Age of Music* (New York: Funk & Wagnalls) 50: "Flattery will get you most anywhere, but it should be *honest*; mine always was. I have made a specialty of discovering people's best points and focusing their attention on those" (italics as shown). 1955 *Los Angeles Times* 28 Oct. (advertisement for men's clothing store): "*Flattery will get you* everywhere! The flattery of GGG's new, imported fabrics, that is" (italics as shown). 1956 John Keats, "This Smoke Gets in My Eyes," *Coronet* 40, no. 2 (Jun.) 133: "'That's he-man food, and we little girls know nothing about it.' Since flattery will get you anywhere, I arranged the logs, lit the fire, and threw a split chicken on the grill.'" *MP* F169; *DAP* 215(17). The proverb probably originated as a counter-proverb rebutting "FLATTERY will get you nowhere"—or the reverse.

## Flattery will get you nowhere (nothing).

1938 Charles Yale Harrison, *Meet Me on the Barricades* (New York: Charles Scribner's Sons) 5: "Unappeased by appreciation of his wit, he continued: 'You are not compelled to laugh, gentlemen. Flattery will get you nowhere.'" *MP* F169; *DAP* 215(17); *YBQ* Modern Proverbs (33). Cf. "FLATTERY will get you everywhere."

## If you've got it, **flaunt** it.

See "If you've GOT it, flaunt it."

## In any **flock** of eagles, there will be at least one turkey.

See "In any GROUP of eagles, there will be at least one turkey."

## Go with the **flow**.

1962 *Military Cold War Education and Speech Review Policies: Hearings before the Special Preparedness Subcommittee of the Committee on Armed Services . . . Senate* (Washington DC: Government Printing Office) 2533; Col. Benjamin Wylie Tarwater testifies: "One thing about them [Communists], however, is that they do not have any particular master plan nor time schedule. They try to go by what they call going with the flow; don't go against the tide, but rather go with the flow." 1968 Tom Wolfe, *Electric Kool-Aid Acid Test* (New York: Farrar Straus & Giroux) 176–77: "Go with the flow—and what a flow—these cats, these Pranksters—at big routs like this the [Hell's] Angels often had a second feature going entitled *Who Gets Fucked?* . . . [T]hen he lurches and mounts her and slides it in, and the Angels cheer Haw Haw—but that is her movie, it truly is, and we have gone with the flow." 1969 Edmund Schiddel, *Good Time*

*Coming* (New York: Simon & Schuster) 422: "All right, Baby, let's get with it. Don't fight it, let it come. . . . That's it, Baby. Heist it. There. A little. Go with the flow." *RHDP* 114; *YBQ* Modern Proverbs (36); Room (2000) 296.

## Flowers leave fragrance in the hand that bestows them.

1944 *Los Angeles Times* 23 Jul.: "As a Chinese friend once replied when I paid him a compliment, 'Flowers leave part of their fragrance in the hand that bestows them.'" *DAP* 216, 99–100.

## Say it with **flowers**.

1917 The saying entered oral tradition as a proverb from an advertising slogan of the Society of American Florists. *DAP* 217(14); *DAAP* 289; *YBQ* Advertising Slogans (112); Rees (1984) 202.

## Stop and smell the **flowers** (roses).

1951 Alfred E. Hoffmann, "Try This on Your Young Musicians!" *Educational Music Magazine* 30 (Jan.–Feb.) 40: "He must go slowly enough to give him a chance to enjoy the skills he already has, to quote the famous and beloved Dr. F. Melius Christiansen, 'We mustn't always rush on! We must sometimes stop to smell the flowers along the wayside' (a rehearsal 1942)." 1954 Grantland Rice, *The Tumult and the Shouting* (New York: A. S. Barnes) 73: "'Freddie,' he [Walter Hagen] said [to Freddie Corcoran], 'relax. Don't worry—don't hurry. You're here on a short visit. Be sure to smell the flowers.'" 1956 Walter Hagen (as told to Margaret Seaton Heck), *The Walter Hagen Story* (New York: Simon & Schuster) 319 (epigraph to the final chapter): "You're only here for a short visit. Don't hurry. Don't worry. And be sure to smell the flowers along the way" (attributed to Hagen himself). 1974 Mac Davis, "Stop and Smell the Roses" (title of a song). *DAAP* 647; *YBQ* Hagen.

White **folks** got the money and black folks got the signs.

1934 Zora Neale Hurston, *Jonah's Gourd Vine* (Philadelphia: J. B. Lippincott) 289: "Don't set on de do' step Elder, heah's uh chear. . . . If you set on de steps you'll git all de pains in de house. Ha, ha! Ah reckon you say niggers got all de signs and white folks got all de money." 1966 Marshall Stearnes and Jean Stearnes, "Frontiers of Humor: American Vernacular Dance," *Southern Folklore Quarterly* 30: 229 (from the ballad "The Sinking of the *Titanic*" as performed by Budd "Stringbeans" LeMay, c. 1915, stanza 3): "White folks got all the money / Colored folks got all the signs / Signs won't buy you nothin' / Folks, you better change your mind." Prahlad (1996) 259–60. The *signs* are superstitious beliefs that falsely promise prosperity or success.

Why go out for fast **food** when you can get steak at home?

See "Why go out for HAMBURGER when you can get steak at home?"

Everybody is somebody's **fool**.

1947 In the motion picture *The Lady from Shanghai*, the character Michael (played by Orson Welles) says near the end, "Well, everybody is somebody's fool. The only way to stay out of trouble is to grow old. . . ." 1950 William B. Richter, "Everybody's Somebody's Fool" (rhythm and blues song, recorded by Jimmy Scott and later by the Heartbeats). 1951 Alistair Cooke, *Letters from America* (London: Rupert Hart-Davis) 84: "Now, everybody is somebody's fool, if only his wife's." c. 1960 Howard Greenfield, "Everybody's Somebody's Fool" (song, recorded most famously by Connie Francis). Bryan (2001) 25.

**Fools** seldom differ.

1945 Arthur Thrush, *Representative Majority: Twenty-one Years of the B.P.R.A.* (London: Book Publishers' Representative Association) 69: "He did not know who coined the expression 'Great minds think alike'—neither did he know who said 'Fools seldom differ.' . . ." *DAP* 223(83).

It is better to be thought a **fool** than to open your mouth and let the world know it.

1907 Maurice Switzer, *Mrs. Goose, Her Book* (New York: Moffat, Yard) 29 (printed as an uncontextualized aphorism): "It is better to remain silent at the risk of being thought a fool, than to talk and remove all doubt of it." 1921 James A. Davis, response to the welcoming address at the annual meeting of the Kentucky State Medical Association (20 Sep.), *Kentucky Medical Journal* 19 (1921) 690: "While listening to the beautiful words of welcome of Dr. Meyers we were wondering whether or not to sit still and look like fools, or endeavor to speak and remove all doubt." 1922 H. C. Perry, discussion of "The Maine Medical Association's Plan for Coordinating Health Activities with State Associations" at the annual convention of the American Medical Association (12 Nov. 1921), *American Medical Association Bulletin* 16, no. 1 (Jan.) 81: "The only thing that has kept me from speaking has been the recollection of two aphorisms I have heard, one of which is that silence is the wise man's strength and the fool's refuge, and the other is that it is better to remain silent at the risk of being thought a fool than to speak and remove all doubt of it." *DAP* 224(120); *YBQ* Lincoln (67). The saying is often credited to Abraham Lincoln and even to Samuel Johnson, but no corroborative evidence exists, and the attributions themselves are no more recent than the 1930s.

It takes a **fool** to know a fool.

1901 *Laredo [TX] Times* 9 Nov.: "It takes a fool to know a fool and a crank to know a crank." *DAP* 224; Doyle (2001a) 464–65.

Never argue with a **fool**; people might not know the difference.

1975 Conrad Schneiker, "An Abridged Collection of Interdisciplinary Laws," *CoEvolution Quarterly*, no. 8: 138: "The First Law of Debate[:] Never argue with a fool. People might not know the difference." Sometimes the proverb is identified as one of "Murphy's Laws."

## No **fool**, no fun.

1918 Fergus Stikeleather Jr., "North Carolina," *Postal Record* (National Association of Letter Carriers) 31: 162: "We replied that we had quite a little practice in swatting the fly, and that we would take a shot at the mosquito for a night or two. No fool, no fun." 1942 Marjorie Kinnan Rawlings, *Cross Creek* (New York: Charles Scribner's Sons) 148: "I said, a little irritated, '. . . This was foolish.' 'Well,' he said, and chuckled, 'no fool, no fun.'" *DAP* 244(122).

## Walk with a **fool**, you'll be a fool yourself.

Anderson and Cundall (1927) 54 list the saying as a Jamaican proverb: "Walk with a fool, you shall be fooler." Prahlad (2001) 250. Cf. the Old Testament *Proverbs* 26:4: "Answer not a fool according to his folly, lest thou also be like unto him."

## Don't shoot yourself in the **foot**.

1980 *St. Petersburg [FL] Times* 21 Jan.: "The former ambassador joined other campaigners in this farm state saying that canceling grain shipments to the Soviet Union was hurting American farmers more than it was the Russians. 'What I'm saying is, don't shoot yourself in the foot,' [George H. W.] Bush said." 1984 *Sacramento Bee* 19 Jul.: "But just remember that some [Gary] Hart people wore these stickers saying 'Don't shoot yourself in the foot.'" The figurative idiom "shoot [oneself] in the foot" may be older than the proverb.

It is better to die on your **feet** than to live on your knees.

1924 Roberto Habermann, "Bandit Colonies," *The Survey* 52, no. 3 (1 May) 148: "The day he [Emiliano Zapata] was murdered, and the news of it reached Cuernavaca, a barefooted peon scratched with his penknife in crude letters on one of the posts of the Boarda Garden, the old Maximilian palace, the following: 'Rebels of the South, it is more honorable to die on your feet than to live on your knees.'" The saying is commonly credited to Zapata himself (assassinated in 1919), but the narrative of the penknife-wielding peon does not make that attribution. *DAP* 227(30); *YBQ* Ibarruri (1); Whiting (1952) 411; Rees (1984) 227–28.

## Move your **feet** (meat), lose your seat.

1987 *Philadelphia Inquirer* (6 Dec.): "In the world of the homeless, there is a universal law: Move your feet, lose your seat. Thomas Davis lost his life." 1999 *Washington Post* (13 May): "When I came back, my cousin was sitting in my chair. I asked for my place back, and his response was 'Move your meat, lose your seat.'" The phrase "move your meat (feet)" means "get up" or "move from a space that you had occupied and claimed." Cf. "You MOVE, you lose."

## When you pray, move your **feet**.

1936 John Erskine, *The Influence of Women and Its Cure* (Indianapolis IN: Bobbs-Merrill) 88: "'I'd like to tell you what my philosophy has done for me!' How often have you heard the testimony! Do they ever tell you what they've done for their philosophy? Personally, I prefer the advice of the Quakers, 'When you pray, move your feet.'" 1961 *Beaver County [PA] Times* 25 May (advice column by Helen Worden): "Have the courage to take the aggeessive [sic] and you'll be surprised at the miraculous way in which constructive forces rally to back your [sic] up. Practice the philosophy of my favorite proverb, 'When you pray, move your feet.'" In recent times, it is regularly referred to as an African or an African American proverb. It asserts the importance of virtuous action to complement prayerfulness.

## It's easier to get (ask) **forgiveness** than permission.

1966 Keith Coulbourn, "Panzer Division in the Poverty War," *Southern Education Report* 2, no. 1 (Aug.) 29: "[David] Hernandez began advertising for bids on the mobile classrooms even before the money to pay for them had been approved. 'It's easier to get forgiveness than permission,' he explained." 1977 Leslie R. Gue, *Introduction to Educational Administration in Canada* (Toronto: McGraw-Hill Ryerson) 160: "His oft-repeated stance, 'It's easier to get forgiveness than permission[,]' did not endear him to a staid central office." 1979 Keith DeGreen, *Creating a Success Environment* (Phoenix AZ: Summit Enterprises) 288: "An old Jesuit saying provides, 'It is better to ask forgiveness than permission.'" *YBQ* Hopper (2). The proverb has come to be regarded as one of "Murphy's Laws."

## It is easy to (You don't need to) hold the **fort** when it is not (being) attacked.

Kin (1955) 99 lists the saying as an American proverb. 2005 Martin R. Carbone, *Teach the Short Words First* (Carlsbad CA: for the author) 133 (in a section titled "Short Word Proverbs, Aphorisms and Quotations"): "It is easy to hold the fort when you are not at war." *DAP* 229. The proverb plays on the idiomatic phrase "hold the fort."

## You can't argue (It's hard to argue, Don't argue) with a **forty-five**.

See "You can't argue with the BARREL of a gun."

## A **fox** does not smell his own stench.

Champion (1938) 80 lists the saying as a Welsh proverb. 1990 Patricia Cornwell, *Postmortem* (New York: Charles Scribner's Sons) 240: "'Ever heard the expression, "A fox never smells its

own"?' I added. 'You mean he could stink and not know it?' she asked." *DAP* 231. Cf. "Nobody minds the SMELL of his own farts."

## **Freedom** is not for sale.

1949 George A. Fallon, review of *The Plight of Freedom* by Paul Scherer (1948), *Religion in Life* 18: 302: "It [freedom] can be saved only if men will fulfill the conditions which are set by the plans and purposes of God. . . . Freedom is not for sale on the bargain counter." 1969 H. Rap Brown (subsequently Jamil Abdullah Al-Amin), *Die, Nigger, Die!* (New York: Dial) 140: "Freedom is not for sale. Freedom can only be bought with revolution." An older wording of the idea is "Freedom cannot be bought." Cf. "FREEDOM is not free."

## **Freedom** is not free.

1943 *American Forests* 49 (May) 195 (advertisement for war bonds): "Freedom is not free—It is Priceless." 1943 *New York Times* 23 Sep. (ad for war bonds): "Freedom isn't free. We must fight for it."

## **Freedom's** just another word for nothing left to lose.

1969 The saying probably entered oral tradition as a proverb from the song "Me and Bobby McGee," written by Kris Kristofferson and Fred Foster (popularized by Janis Joplin, Willie Nelson, and others). *YBQ* Kristofferson.

## Fifty million **Frenchmen** can't be wrong.

1927 The saying passed into oral tradition as a proverb from the title of a song by Billy Rose and Willie Ruskin (popularized by Sophie Tucker). *RHDP* 93–94.

## Fast pay (payment) makes (for) fast **friends**.

1980 Norman Krasna, *Full Moon* (New York: Dramatists Play Service) 38: "Fast pay makes fast friends. I went to a bookmaker once who had that printed on his cards." 1987 John O. Whitney, *Taking Charge: Management Guide to Troubled Companies and Turnarounds* (Homewood IL: Dow Jones-Irwin) 56: "The best policy is to pay all bills when due. As the country sage said, 'Fast pay makes fast friends.'" 1989 Paul D. Zuelke, *Cash or Credit? A Nuts and Bolts Guide to Effective Credit Management* (Tulsa OK: PennWell) 161: "There is an old adage: 'Fast pay makes fast friends.' This certainly applies with staff bonuses and incentive plans."

## Friends don't let friends drive drunk (ride drunk [that is, on motorcycles], drink and drive).

1976 *Teacher* 93, no. 5 (Jan.) 138 (bold print at the bottom of a full-column ad from the U.S. Department of Transportation, National Highway Safety Administration): "FRIENDS DON'T LET FRIENDS DRIVE DRUNK." 1993 Center for Substance Abuse, *Prevention Primer* (Rockville MD: National Clearinghouse for Alcohol and Drug Information) 116: ". . . [A] familiar campaign to reduce drinking and driving problems focused its message not on the drinking driver, but on others with its 'Friends Don't Let Friends Drink and Drive' slogan."

## Friends don't need explanations (You do not need to explain to a friend).

1912 Elbert Hubbard, "William Marion Reedy," *The Fra* 9 (Mar.) 163: "He knows that explanations never explain, and that your friends do not require explanations and your enemies will not believe you anyway." 1948 Lillian Eichler Watson, *Standard Book of Letter Writing* (New York: Prentice-Hall) 112: "There is an old familiar saying: 'You never need to explain to a friend.' But that doesn't apply to dinner invitations!" Person (1958) 177.

## A friend's frown is better than a foe's smile.

Listed by Dwight Edwards Marvin, *The Antiquity of Proverbs* (New York: G. P. Putnam's Sons, 1922) 78, as an English proverb. *DAP* 234. The proverb perhaps derives from a mishearing (or misreading) of the older proverb "A friend's frown is better than a fool's smile."

## A (true, good) friend walks in when (all) others walk out.

1994 *The Advertiser* 24 Oct.: "From Skyman in cyberspace, this thought: A true friend walks in when others walk out." 2002 Greg Laurie, *The God of Second Chance* (Wheaton IL: Tyndale House) 201: "An old adage says that a true friend walks in when others walk out."

## A friend with weed is a friend indeed.

1968 *Evergreen Review* 12 (Mar.) 98 (ad for slogan-bearing buttons): "A friend with weed is a friend indeed." 1969 Tom Nolan, "Groupies: A Story of Our Times," in *The Age of Rock*, edited by Jonathan Eisen (New York: Random House) 90: "They [two young rock music fans] go into the girls' room of the Hullabaloo . . . and (along with general information like 'Bullwinkle lives on acid' and 'A friend with weed is a friend indeed') leave anonymous judgments [as graffiti]. . . ." 1970 Roger D. Abrahams, "Such Matters as Every Man Should Know, and Descant Upon," *Proverbium* o.s. 15: 425: "Witness the recent use of the proverb, 'A friend in need is a friend indeed.' The force of the proverb in this form is underlined yet particularized in the rephrasing, 'A friend with weed is a friend indeed' ('weed' is a slang term for marijuana)." The proverb originated as an anti-proverb.

## If you want a friend, get (buy) a dog.

1941 *Dunkirk [NY] Evening Observer* 22 Jan.: "And then there was Frank Fay's advice to Rene Clair, the newly arrived [in Hollywood] French director. Said Fay, 'If you're going to stay in this town and want a friend, go out and buy a dog.'" 1973 Erma Bombeck, "Coed Dorms," *Ledger [Lakeland FL]* 27 Nov.: "Women! Could you have a meaningful relationship with a boy . . . who belches before breakfast? And hangs his trousers under the mattress? A housemother once told me, 'There is nothing that attracts the opposite sex like a busy signal, a locked door, and the word "No." If you want a friend, get a dog." 1975 *Daily Collegian [Pennsylvania State University]* 26 Sep. (in a list of witticisms ascribed to President Harry S. Truman): "Truman on banks: 'They're happy to lend you money when you prove you don't need it. If you want a friend, get a dog.'" The proverb alludes to the old saying "A dog is man's best friend." It usually suggests that, in some particularly hostile or competitive setting (Hollywood, Washington DC, Wall Street), a dog will be the *only* friend that a person can hope to find—and that (human) friendship itself is a quality not only improbable but even undesirable.

## Keep your **friends** close and (but) your enemies closer.

1974 The proverb probably entered oral tradition from a speech in the motion picture *The Godfather, Part II*: "There are many things my father taught me here in this room. He taught me: Keep your friends close, but your enemies closer." Occasionally it is referred to as an ancient Chinese proverb.

## Little **friends** may prove (become) great friends.

1903 *First Book of Song and Story*, introduction by Cynthia Westover Alden (New York: P. F. Collier & Son) 455: "Little friends may prove great friends," given as the "moral" to the Aesopic fable "The Lion and the Mouse." That text found its way into the Harvard Classics volume *Folklore and Fable* (New York: P. F. Collier & Son, 1909) 14. 1903 Huber Gray Buehler and Caroline

Hotchkiss, *Modern English Lessons* (New York: Newson) 133 (the conclusion of the fable): "In a few moments the lion was free. 'I have learned,' said he, 'that little friends may become great friends.'" *DAP* 237.

## Make **friends** when you don't need them (before you need them).

Anderson and Cundall (1927) 60 give the saying as a Jamaican proverb: "Mek fren' when you no need dem." 1946 "Word to the Wise," *Business Education World* 27: 56 (filler item): "The time to make friends is before you need them." 1966 "Ed Florio's Career Brings Honors," *The Refresher* [Coca-Cola company magazine] o.s. 13, no. 1 (Jan.–Feb.) 9: "Here are a few of his [corporate vice president Florio's] philosophic axioms: 'Make friends before you need them. Dig a well before you are thirsty.'"

## Only your **friend** knows your secret.

1976 Bob Marley, "Who the Cap Fit" (song), on the album *Rastaman Vibration*: "Only your friend know your secret / So only he could reveal it." 1990 Norman B. Schwartz, *Forest Society* (Philadelphia: U of Pennsylvania P) 233–34: "Children [in rural Guatemala] can depend on their parents, but beyond this[,] relationships are faculative, not firm, and everything is equivocal. An elderly informant explains that '*el más amigo es el más traidar*' (one's best friend is the most traitorous)—your most intimate friend knows your secrets, the better to betray you" (italics as shown). Prahlad (2001) 250.

## A true **friend** is one who knows all your faults and still loves (likes) you.

1917 Francis C. Kelley, *Letters to Jack* (Chicago: Extension) 61: "The real friend is the man who knows all about you and loves you in spite of it." 1922 Lawrence Wickes Conant, *Tackling Tech* (New York: Ronald) 194–95: "True friendship is not a superficial acquaintanceship; it is something deep and firmly founded in one's character. A friend is a man who knows all your faults—and likes you just the same." *DAP* 234.

## You cannot use your **friends** and have them too.

1954 Edmund Bergler, *Revolt of the Middle-Aged Man* (New York: A. A. Wyn) 272: "Experience proves that the less one asks, the better cemented the friendship becomes. As someone said, 'You cannot use your friends and have them too.'" *DAP* 239(189). The proverb probably originated as an anti-proverb echoing "You cannot have your cake and eat it too."

## You can pick your **friends,** and you can pick your nose, but you can't pick your family.

See "You can pick your NOSE, but you can't pick your family."

## You can pick your **friends,** and you can pick your nose (You can pick your nose, and you can pick your friends), but you can't pick your friend's nose.

1975 Jane Boyar and Burt Boyar, *World Class* (New York: Random House) 46: "He resumed, 'In conclusion, let me offer this simple thought. You can pick your friends, and you can pick your nose, but you can't pick your friend's nose.'" 1978 Noel Coppage, "Is Country Going to the Dogs?" *Stereo Review* 41, no. 5 (Nov.) 102 (an anti-proverbial version that occurs with some frequency): "The guitar and bass were from the Joey Davis Band, which plays progressive country music in the persons of Joey Davis himself, a singer, songwriter, guitarist, and philosopher ('You can pick your nose and you can pick your friends, but you can't wipe your friends on the couch'). . . ." The proverb itself perhaps originated as an anti-proverb based on the older "You can choose your friends, but you cannot choose your family." Cf. "You can pick your NOSE, but you can't pick your family."

## Your best **friend** may be your worst enemy.

See "Your worst ENEMY could be your best friend."

## Don't fatten **frogs** for snakes.

1922 Thomas W. Talley, *Negro Folk Rhymes* (New York: Macmillan) 97 (anonymous verses titled "Fattening Frogs for Snakes," the second stanza of two): "W'y don't you git some common sense? / Jes git a liddle! Oh fer land sakes! / Quit yo' foolin', she hain't studyin' you! / Youse jes fattenin' frogs fer snakes!" Prahlad (1996) 227–28.

## If **frogs** had wings, they wouldn't bump their tails (butts, etc.) on rocks (logs, the ground, etc.) (If frogs had wings, they could fly).

1914 J. D. Hellums, letter to the editor, *Railway Carmen's Journal* 19: 723: "I have an idea what you will say; you will say if the European war hadn't broken out, sugar would not have gone up. Yes, and if a frog had wings, he would not be bumping his bottle end on the ground, so that is the trouble." 1935 Zora Neale Hurston, *Mules and Men* (Philadelphia: J. B. Lippincott) 158: "'If, if, if,' mocked Jim Allen. 'Office Richardson, youse always iffin'! If a frog had wings he wouldn't bump his rump so much.'" 1990 Sam Hamill, *A Poet's Work* (Seattle: Broken Moon) 46: "In blessed moments the poet . . . becomes 'inspired,' but without discipline, the Mind refuses to speak. If frogs had wings, they could fly." *DAP* 241(4); *RHDP* 151. Cf. the older proverb "If pigs had wings, they could fly."

## If you're going to swallow (have to swallow) a **frog**, don't look at it (don't think about it) too long.

1986 Martha Grimes, *I Am the Only Running Footman* (Boston: Little, Brown) 24: "Mar poured the inch and a half into a tumbler. 'I try not to look at it at all. If you're going to swallow a frog,

better not stare at it too long, as they say.'" 1987
N. S. Xavier, *Two Faces of Religion* (Tuscaloosa AL:
Portal) 37: "Our imagination can help or hinder
will power depending on whether it is working
in favor of or against our desired goal. As Mark
Twain advised, if one has to swallow a frog, one
shouldn't look at it for too long." *DAAP* 302. The
common attribution to Mark Twain appears to
be spurious.

## You have to kiss a lot of **frogs** (toads) to find a prince.

1976 *Coshocton [OH] Tribune* 10 Feb.: "Pithy
mottoes and worthy sayings are needlework
favorites: . . . 'Before you Meet your handsome
Prince, you'll probably have to Kiss lot [*sic*]
of Toads.'" 1977 James M. Smith, "Madness,
Innovation, and Social Policy," *Hastings Center
Report* 7, no. 5 (Oct.) 9: "The recognition that
there are many [diagnostic and treatment]
alternatives and that they require serious
assessment are the important outcomes. As
one participant said: 'You have to kiss a lot of
frogs to find a prince.'" 1977 (purchase date).
Hallmark greeting card: "Thought of the day:
Before you discover your handsome prince . . .
you have to kiss quite a few toads!" (ellipsis dots
as shown). 1978 *Washington Post* 28 Jul. (in a
classified ad for housing): "You would have to
kiss a lot of toads to find a 'Prince Charming' of
a home like this." 1980 *Good Housekeeping* (Jan.)
196 (cartoon: a young woman wearing a crown
speaks from a psychiatrist's couch): "I started
out looking for a prince, but now I just like to
kiss frogs." Most often the proverb refers to the
difficulty of a woman's finding suitable male
companionship, but (as some of the quotations
illustrate) it can apply to other kinds of searches
as well. The prevalence of the *toads* form of the
proverb is surprising, given the fact that the
popular tale to which it alludes is nearly always
referred to as "The *Frog* Prince"; perhaps, in the
popular mind, toads better exemplify extreme
unattractiveness.

## Turn a **frown** upside down (A smile is just a frown turned upside down).

1931 Joe Young, song (music by Sam Stept):
"Turn That Frown Upside Down, Smile at the
Cock-eyed World." 1931 *Leader-Post [Regina,
Saskatchewan]* 6 Feb.: "In the poem entitled
'Smile,' Barton Pogue defines the real meaning
and worth of a smile. He says, 'A smile is a frown
turned upside down and what's in the heart turns
it over.'" 1933 Leo Robin, song in the motion
picture *The Way to Love* (music by Ralph Rainger):
"Turn That Frown Upside Down." 1941 (copyright
date) A. F. Giebel (pseudonym "Al Gable"), song
(music also by Gable): "Turn Your Frown Upside
Down" (there can be found no evidence that the
song was ever recorded or printed).

## **Fuck** them (Find them, fuck them) and forget them.

1922 John Gunther, "The Higher Learning in
America VI / The University of Chicago," *The
Smart Set* 67, no. 4 (Apr.) 73: "A fair proportion
of the men are now what are technically known
as 'Charlie.' They make a profession of lines.
The unofficial motto of this group is something
like F. F. F. (Find 'em, Fool 'em, and Forget
'em)." 1936 Harry Graffis, "A Breast of the
Times," *Esquire* 6 (Sep.) 195: ". . . [T]here are
definite, frequent evidences of a complete
reversal of form in the employment of the
cynical slogan of seduction: 'fool 'em and forget
'em.'" 1949 August B. Holingshead, *Elmtown's
Youth* (New York: John Wiley & Sons) 422: "The
high school students refer to them as 'clippers'
and wolves. . . . They call themselves the Five
F's—'find 'em, feed 'em, feel 'em, f—— 'em,
forget 'em.'" 1953 Lester V. Berrey and Melvin
Van den Bark, *American Thesaurus of Slang*, 2nd
ed. (New York: Thomas Y. Crowell) 325: ". . .
[T]he four F's, *high-pressure romancing—find
'em, fool 'em, frig 'em, and forget 'em*" (italics as
shown). 1960 Donald Windham, *The Warm
Country* (London: Rupert Hart-Davis) 101: "'Not
me,' Dusty answered. 'I'm through with girls.'
'Sure,' Robinson agreed. 'Find them, feel them,

frig them, and forget them.'" 1967 Norman Martien, "Norman Mailer at Graduate School," *New American Review* 1: 236 (recounting Mailer's conversation with a group of students): "Finally, I didn't know quite what he meant: Posture and Action, Wharton and Dreiser, the Artist and the Man, Fuck 'em and Forget 'em?—Any number of things probably." Most often the proverb has (it is supposed) been uttered by men, but currently no such limitation obtains. It may have originated as a dysphemistic anti-proverb based on "Love them and leave them," or "Love them and leave them" may represent a polite variant of the *F*-proverb.

## Always leave (quit) while you're still having **fun**.

See "Always leave the PARTY while you're still having fun."

## It's all **fun** and games till someone loses an eye (gets hurt, etc.).

1990 Title of a musical album by the Australian band The Bedridden: *It's All Fun and Games until Someone Loses an Eye*. 1992 *Jerusalem Post* 2 Oct. (title of an article): "The Ninth Commandment: It's Always Funny until Someone Loses an Eye." 1992 Jim DeFilippi, *Blood Sugar: A Novel* (New York: HarperCollins) 118: "'So, partner mine, what d'you think? We having any fun?' 'Hey, it's all fun and games, till somebody gets their eye poked.'"

## The **future** is not (is no longer) what it used to be.

1948 Paul Valéry, "Our Destiny and Literature," in *Reflections on the World Today*, translated by Francis Scarfe (New York: Pantheon) 135: "The future, like everything else, is no longer quite what is used to be. By that I mean we can no longer think of it with any confidence in our inductions" (Valéry's "Notre destin et les lettres" was published in 1937; there the sentence reads, "L'avenir est comme le reste: il n'est plus ce qu'il était"). 1950 Mordecai M. Kaplan, "Random Thoughts," *The Reconstructionist* 16, no. 2 (Mar.) 30: "Men say the future isn't what it used to be. Neither is the past. Both are in need of reconstruction, if we are to have a livable present." *YBQ* Friedrich Hollander.

## It is dangerous (difficult) to prophesy, especially about the **future**.

See "Never make PREDICTIONS, especially about the future."

## There is no **future** like the present.

1909 *Los Angeles Times* 23 Apr. (in an advertisement for a haberdashery): "Don't wait until the assortment is all shot to pieces. Remember, there is no future like the present. Come today." *DAP* 244(17). The proverb probably originated as an anti-proverb based on "There is no time like the present."

## Being nice doesn't win **games**.

See "NICE doesn't win games."

## Every **game** (contest, etc.) has (to have) a winner (and a loser).

1943 "News Report on a Test Case," *Billboard* 55, no. 3 (16 Jan.) 55: "The [pinball] player gets exactly what he bargained for. . . . Every game has a winner and a loser. . . ." 1962 Loren P. Beth, *Politics, the Constitution, and the Supreme Court* (Evanston IL: Row, Peterson) 42: "With rare exceptions every [Supreme Court] case has a winner and a loser." 1965 Theodore Sorensen, *Kennedy* (New York: Harper & Row) 219: "Every election has a winner and a loser, he [John F. Kennedy] said in effect." 1971 *Sumpter [SC] Daily Item* 27 Oct.: "The fact that Hillcrest defeated Hartsville is not that earth shaking. Every game has a winner and a loser. . . ."

## The **game** is not over till it is over.

See "It's not OVER till it's over."

## The **game** is not over till the fat lady sings.

1984 *Sunday Times [London]* 17 Jun. (regarding golf): "He [Seve Ballesteros] played . . . well behind after a few holes. 'Never mind,' rasped [David] Graham consolingly, 'The game ain't over till the fat lady sings.'" The proverb probably originated as a conflation (deliberate or unwitting) of "The OPERA isn't over till the fat lady sings" with "The GAME is not over until the last man is out." Cf. "CHURCH is not out till the fat lady sings."

## The **game** is not over until the last man is out.

1965 "Norfolk and Western Railway Company and New York, Chicago and St. Louis Railroad Company—Merger, etc. Decided June 24, 1964," *Interstate Commerce Commission Reports* (May–Jun.) 324: "As in a baseball game, under the case-by-case approach, even in proceedings of this magnitude, you can never tell who will win the game until the last batter is out." 1982 Mary Vetterling-Braggin, *"Femininity," "Masculinity," and "Androgyny"* (Totowa NJ: Rowman & Littlefield) 108: "Alternatively, they can be praised for having the courage of their convictions or for not giving up the ball game until the last batter has been retired." 1997 William Safire, *Watching My Language* (New York: Random House) 36: "In a speech following the debate on October 15 [1992], [President George H. W.] Bush compared himself to the pennant-winning Atlanta Braves, saying that politics is like baseball: 'It ain't over till the last batter swings.'" *DAP* 246(6). Cf. "It's not OVER till it's over."

## **Game** recognizes (knows, respects) game.

1986 Carol Bruchac, Linda Hogan, and Judith McDaniel, eds., *The Stories We Hold Secret* (Greenfield Center NY: Greenfield Review) 21 (quoting a long-term penitentiary inmate as she addresses a new convict regarding a third inmate): "Personally, I liked the fat bitch. . . . I understand she was a crook and I always did understand. Game recognizes game, Baby Cakes, all over the world." 1995 "Game Recognizes Game," title of a song by the Atlanta rap duo Tag Team. 1995 *Game Recognizes Game*, title of a musical album by Daddy D. 1995 "Game Recognizes Game," title of a song by Kino Watson. 1997 *Albuquerque [NM] Journal* 12 Dec. "[The singer] Usher said he was glad to have such successful producers on board but not surprised that they were willing to work with him. 'Game recognizes game. From one professional to another.'" 1999 Jennifer Nine, *Bush: Twenty-seventh Letter* (London: Virgin) 164: "There's an old expression in pool circles: 'game knows game.' That is, if I play a certain game in a pool room, and if I'm a specialist in a certain game and I'm talking to somebody, I can tell whether or not he's versed in the game." 2004 Dave Gardetty, "The Game of Vice," *Los Angeles Magazine* (Dec.): "'Game knows game' Hollywood prostitutes will say of their vice squad. 'Game respects game.'" 2005 Sherman D. Manning, *From the Palace to the Prison* (New York: HarperCollins) 44 (quoting the millionaire swindler Kenneth Lay): "When all is said and done, most of us know they are screwing us. We take it as a given. But as the Black people say, 'game respects game' and truth be told we the CEO's are very often screwing everybody we can." In the proverb *game* has the slang sense of "skill, savvy, wile" as applied to a variety of activities—ranging from music and sports to business and criminal activity.

## Hate the **game**, not the player.

See "Don't hate the PLAYER; hate the game."

## If you can't win, don't play the **game**.

See "If you can't WIN, don't play."

## If you don't play the **game**, you can't (shouldn't) make the rules.

1963 Joan Didion, *Run River* (New York: Ivan Obolensky) 34: "I said you play the game, you make the rules. I said if a lot of people a long time back hadn't said what they wanted and struck out for it you wouldn't have been born in California." 1969 Gwendolyn Midlo Hall, "Africans in the Americas," *Negro Digest* 18, no. 4 (Feb.) 38: "The educational institutions in this country are like everything else. They make the rules and make blacks play the game." 1972 *Los Angeles Times* 6 May: "Attending a Los

Angeles civic organization luncheon last year, Bishop [Juan] Arzube listened to a comic's talk that included a reference to Pope Paul's birth control encyclical: 'Those who don't play the game shouldn't make the rules'" (the bishop's purported riposte was "I don't lay eggs, but I can cook them better than any chicken"). 1972 Joey Adams, *Joey Adams' Speaker's Bible of Humor* (Garden City NY: Doubleday) 8: "Pat Henry, at a dinner for [Terence] Cardinal Cooke, said: 'Talking about the Pill, Your Eminence, if you don't play the game—don't make the rules.'" Cf. "My GAME, my rules."

## It isn't how you play the **game** that counts; it's whether you win or lose.

1967 *Wall Street Journal* 11 Apr.: "To its more extreme critics, however, college athletics . . . has reversed the old maxim to read: It's not how you play the game that counts, but whether you win or lose." 1972 Mel Brooks, *All American: A Musical Comedy* (Woodstock IL: Dramatic) 55: "When you go out on that field, men, I want you to remember one thing. It's not how you play the game, it's winning that counts!" 1973 Walter Wells, *Tycoons and Locusts* (Carbondale: Southern Illinois UP) 17: "The same motif of corrupted values pervades *They Shoot Horses*. It's not how you play the game, but winning that counts." The proverb originated as an anti-proverb satirizing "It isn't whether you win or lose; it's how you play the GAME."

## It isn't whether you win or lose (that counts); it's how you play the **game** (It's not winning that counts, it's playing the game).

1913 Alfred E. Chirm, *Burton Dane* (New York: Alice Harriman) 249: ". . . Father used to tell me that whether you win or lose counts but little compared to the kind of fight you put up." 1925 Leigh H. Irvine, *Follies of the Court* (Los Angeles: Times-Mirror) 117: "Often one sees placards in business offices, on which the sentiment is quoted to the effect that it isn't whether you win or lose that counts, but how you play the game." The proverb may have originated as a response to the old (and cynical) "He plays well that wins."

## My **game**, my rules (Your game, your rules).

1963 Ron Levin, "By the Sea," *December* 4: 96: "You keep out of this. It's my game and my rules, and if Walter can't get them crossed, I'll understand." 1970 Donald Westlake, "The Winner," in *Nova 1: An Anthology of Original Science Fiction Stories* (New York: Delacorte) 225: "You mean I can't win. But I won't lose. It's your game, your rules, your home ground, your equipment; if I can manage a stalemate, that's pretty good." 1977 Jeanne Paslé-Green and Jim Haynes, *Hello, I Love You! Voices from within the Sexual Revolution* (New York: Times Change) 93 (Edwin Atchison is being interviewed): "I felt a requirement each time I was with a girl that it be my game, my rules, so to speak, and I had to make them up as I went along. . . ." 1984 Peter C. Gronn, "I Have a Solution," *Educational Administration Quarterly* 20, no. 2 (Spring) 84: "Until resolution 69.8 there had been a game without rules, or as Hughes [the principal of an Australian primary school] put it, it was 'my game, my rules.'" Cf. "My HOUSE, my rules."

## Nice doesn't win **games**.

See "NICE doesn't win games."

## A **gap** in the ax shows in the chip.

Champion (1938) 621 lists the saying as a "Negro" proverb: "Gap in the axe show itself in the chip." 1949 Paul Green, *Dog on the Sun* (Chapel Hill: U of North Carolina P) 119: "'Well,' my mammy said, as she looked round and about at us chillun—'mark my word that a gap in the axe allus shows in the chips.'" Whiting (1952) 413. The proverb asserts that a fault or other quality in a parent will be passed down to offspring.

## Mind the **gap**.

The proverb originated in the late 1960s as a warning (posted and vocally announced) at London train stations, for the safety of passengers who must traverse the *gap* between the train car and the edge of the platform. 1970 Elisabeth Elliot, "Mind the Gap," *Christian Herald* 93, no. 7 (Jul.) 54: "Mind the gaps— between men and women (God help us all if the idea of Unisex gets hold of us), between the stage and audience in a theater (I don't want an actor coming up *my* aisle), between those who know and those who don't know (let teachers teach, please, don't make them forever ask, What do *you* think?), and between generations. . . ." 1972 Victor Kryston and Portia Meares, *Know What I Mean?* (San Francisco: International Society for General Semantics) 35: (chapter title): "Mind the Gap" ("This chapter invites you to consider reasons why we so often don't understand one another . . ."). 1992 James E. Sabin, "'Mind the Gap': Reflections of an American Health Maintenance Organisation Doctor on the New NHS," *British Medical Journal* 305: 514 (subsections of the essay have titles like "Gap between What You Want and What You Will Pay For"). 2001 Richard Wilkinson, *Mind the Gap: Hierarchies, Health and Human Evolution* (New Haven CT: Yale UP); the first page explains, "This book is about . . . the socioeconomic factors that make some societies, and some groups within societies, healthier and longer-lived than others." 2004 Ferdinand Mount, *Mind the Gap: The New Class Divide in Britain* (London: Short). Perhaps on account of the perceived quaintness of its diction, the British locution struck the fancy of American speakers, and it became popular as a cryptic motto on wall hangings. The proverb commonly directs attention to figurative "gaps" between groups or populations (in terms of education, income, communication, etc.).

**Garbage** in, garbage out. (Often abbreviated with the acronym GIGO.)

1957 Ernest E. Blanche, "Applying New Electronic Computers to Traffic and Highway Problems," *Traffic Quarterly* 11: 411: "When the basic data to be used by a computer are of questionable accuracy or validity, our personnel have an unusual expression—GIGO—to characterize such information and the answers the computer produces. It simply means 'garbage in—garbage out.'" 1959 B. A. Wilson, "Operations Research and Management," *Business Quarterly* 24, no. 4 (Winter) 215: "The attempt to use existing records and data in O.R. studies may eventually indicate the inadequacy or inconsistency of existing data, but any results derived from using such data can be no better than the basic data. As one consultant puts it, 'Garbage in, Garbage out.'" *DAP* 246; *YBQ* Modern Proverbs (35); *ODP* 127; Wescott (1981); Kanfer (1983); Mieder (1991); Pickering et al. (1992) 221; Mieder (1993b) 3–17; Rees (1995) 176; Room (2000) 278; Pickering (2001) 149; Winick (2001); Mieder (2005a).

It's not enough for a **gardener** to love flowers; he must hate weeds.

1950 "The Editor's Page," *NEA Journal* 39: 250 (in a list of sayings): "It is not enough for a gardener to love flowers; he must also hate weeds." 1958 Joe H. Cerny, *Courtroom Know-how* (Cincinnati OH: W. H. Anderson) 255: "The persistent use of common slang is tantamount to a person's watering of weeds in a garden. Incidentally, horticulturists tell us that, in order to have a beautiful garden, it's not enough for us to love flowers; we must hate weeds." *DAP* 247(2).

**Gas**, grass, or ass: Nobody rides for free.

1978 Advertisement for bumper stickers, *Baseball Digest* 37, no. 5 (May) 91: "Gas—Grass Or Ass / Nobody Rides Free!" 1979 Edward Abbey, *Abbey's Road* (New York: E. P. Dutton) 159: "The bumper sticker in front of me read: Ass, Gas, or Grass—Nobody Rides for free.' I liked that sentiment. . . ." The nouns can occur in different sequences. Cf. "There is no such THING as a free ride."

**Gasoline** and whiskey (Alcohol and gasoline, etc.) do not mix.

1915 *Lowell [MA] Sun* 8 Jun.: "Gasoline and whiskey don't mix. The truth of this statement was vividly shown last week when a car from Lowell was smashed into bits in New Hampshire by a swiftly moving car driven by an irresponsible party who was under the influence of liquor." 1930 *Christian Science Monitor* 28 May: "Even wets generally admit that 'alcohol and gasoline do not mix.' . . ." 1944 *Soda Springs [ID] Sun* (16 Mar.): "'Alcohol and driving don't mix' may still be a worthy admonition." *DAP* 14(1), 247, 650(2). Cf. "DRINKING and driving do not mix."

**Generals** (Soldiers, etc.) always fight (prepare to fight, are condemned to fight) the last war.

1934 Edward P. Warner, "Present Conditions under the N.R.A. [National Recovery Act]," *American Marketing Journal* 1: 12: "There is a saying that is rather common among the critics of the military profession that 'soldiers are always preparing to fight the last war.' Business must not incur the rebuke that it is devoting itself to preparing to sell goods under the conditions of the last economic cycle." 1938 Valentine Williams, *World of Action* (Boston: Houghton Mifflin) 208: "If Clemenceau was right when he observed that the military always fight the last war over again, I do not anticipate that in the next war it will be found that matters in this respect have changed much. . . ." 1943 *Chicago Tribune* 7 May: "Generals have a proverbial weakness for fighting the last war." 1951 Earl Butz, *Price Fixing for Foodstuffs* (New York: American Enterprise Institute) 25: "Other consequences have followed from the disposition of economic generals to fight the last war."

## What is good for **General Motors** is good for America (the country).

1953 The proverb originated as a misquotation from U.S. Senate testimony of Charles E. Wilson (former president of General Motors): "For years I thought what was good for our country was good for General Motors, and vice versa. The difference did not exist." *RHDP* 359; *YBQ* Charles Wilson; Rees (1984) 234; Pickering et al. (1992) 239. The proverb most often satirizes the concept that the well-being of giant corporations is inextricably and benevolently connected with the welfare of the nation and its populace.

## Each **generation** is better than the last.

1954 Eleanor Roosevelt, *It Seems to Me* (New York: W. W. Norton) 63: "I have lived more than sixty years and I have heard young people condemned many times. I think nearly every generation is better than the last, and I certainly admire the present one." 1984 Frederick Samuels, *Human Needs and Behavior* (Cambridge MA: Schenkman) 149: "An eighty-two-year-old woman said her second most important need was: Not to live too long. I'm no longer useful. Each generation is better than the last."

## You can't put the **genie** back in the bottle.

1919 George Matthew Adams, cartoon, *American Review of Reviews* 49, no. 1 (Jan.–Jun.) 141 (caption, in reference to a big, dark, shaggy, possibly ursine-looking genie designated "Bolshevism"): "Can Germany put the genie back in the bottle?" (credited to the *Spokesman Review* of Spokane WA). 1945 *Parliamentary Debates [Great Britain]: Commons* 416: 638; Scholefield Allen speaks (22 Nov.): "The atomic bomb is with us, and we cannot put that genie back in the bottle, much as we should like to do so." *RHDP* 205. Cf. the somewhat older "You can't put the bullet back in the gun."

## **Gentlemen** prefer blondes.

1925 The saying passed into oral tradition as a proverb from the title of a novel by Anita Loos (the basis of the 1953 motion picture starring Marilyn Monroe). *MP* G28; *DAP* 249; *DAAP* 311; *YBQ* Loos (1); Rees (1984) 194; Rees (1995) 178; Room (2000) 274.

## Can't we all just **get** along?

See "Can't we all just GET ALONG?"

## Don't **get** mad, get ahead.

1986 *Wall Street Journal* 21 Jul. (title of column): "Don't Get Mad. Don't Get Even. Get Ahead!" 1986 Susan Littwin, *The Postponed Generation* (New York: William Morrow) 109: "When things like that happened, she would say, 'Don't get mad. Get ahead. Act in your own interest.'" The proverb originated as an anti-proverb based on "Don't GET mad, get even."

## Don't **get** mad (angry), get even.

1956 *Newport [RI] Daily News* 14 Jun. (in a list of various individuals' "Favorite Expressions"): "Cathy Janes 'Don't get mad—get even.'" 1960 Philip D. Eastman, *Are You My Mother?* (New York: Random House) 49: "He thought of all the time he had wasted in the office wallowing in depression and said, 'Don't get mad. Get even.'" *RHDP* 60–61; *YBQ* Joseph P. Kennedy; Rees (1995) 127. The proverb is often related to the Kennedy family.

## **Get** along to go along.

See "GET ALONG to go along."

## **Get** them young, treat them rough (and tell them nothing).

1920 A. H. Deute, "Should the Cub Salesman Be Treated Rough?" *Printers' Ink* 113, no. 7 (18 Nov.) 70: "One particularly 'hard boiled' sales manager sums it up with the borrowed phrase: 'Get them

young; treat them rough and tell them nothing.'"
1922 Dorothy Parker, "The Flapper" (a poem),
*Life Magazine* 79 (26 Jan.) 22: "Her golden rule
is plain enough— / Just get them young and
treat them rough."

## If it is for you, you will **get** it (What is for you, you will get).

1959 L. D. Reddick, *Crusader without Violence: A
Biography of Martin Luther King, Jr.* (New York:
Harper & Brothers) 98: "This early in her life,
Coretta [Scott] had begun to believe in a kind of
destiny. 'What is for you, you will get, providing
you strive for it as best you can.'" 1968 "Like
It Is: Pressures in a Ghetto School," *Theory
into Practice* 7: 21: "Their [minority students']
attitude is a sort of rule of nature—nature takes
its course. 'If you go, okay.' And, 'if it's for you,
you'll get it'—elusive results." 1982 Dennis
W. Folly, "Getting Butter from the Duck," in *A
Celebration of American Family Folklore*, edited
by Steven J. Zeitlin et al. (New York: Pantheon)
233 (the author discusses his African American
family): "Many times my great-grandmother
used them [proverbs]. . . . 'If it's for you, you'll get
it,' she'd sometimes say if we became obsessed
with a particular goal."

## If (When) you've **got** it, flaunt it.

1968 The saying may have entered oral tradition
as a proverb from the motion picture *The
Producers*: "That's it, baby! When you got it,
flaunt it!" (or the character in the movie may
have been uttering a proverb). 1987 Lance
Humble and Ken Cooper, *World's Greatest
Blackjack Book* (Garden City NY: Doubleday)
173: "As a Texas University bumper sticker
proclaimed during its football team's long
winning streak of the late 1960s, 'If you've got
it, flaunt it!'" *RHDP* 159–60; *YBQ* Mel Brooks
(2); Rees (1984) 202; Pickering et al. (1992)
201; Pickering (2001) 163. Most frequently the
proverb refers to the display of an individual's
sexuality.

## In order to **get** where you want to go, you have to start from (know) where you are now.

1965 John A. T. Robinson, *The New Reformation?*
(Philadelphia: Westminster) 26: "There is
no easy answer to this—and the more one is
involved in the machine, as I am, the more
one sees how impossible it is simply to put it
into reverse or to start anything from scratch.
To get where you want to go, you have got
to begin from where you are." 1977 John A.
Hutchison, *Living Options in World Philosophy*
(Honolulu: UP of Hawaii) 190: "An old adage
asserts that to get where you want to go, you
have to start from where you are. Accordingly, to
move toward global philosophy we must begin
from our present situation." What may be a
variant, but with a different meaning (printed
as an uncontextualized epigram): 2001 Gerald
G. Jampolsky and Diane V. Cirincione, *Simple
Thoughts That Can Change Your Life* (Berkeley
CA: Celestial Arts) 30: "If you want to get where
you want to go, you first have to leave where
you are." Cf. "You can't KNOW where you're going
unless you know where you've been."

## It's not what you've **got**, it's what you do with it (how you use it).

1934 *Manchester [UK] Guardian* 24 Mar.: "What
I always tell customers, It ain't what you got, it's
what you do with it." In more recent times, the
proverb often has a sexual application (cf. "SIZE
doesn't matter"): 1973 Marion Meade, *Bitching*
(Englewood Cliffs NJ: Prentice-Hall) 84: "A
scrawny penis should deserve no comment. . . .
However, sooner or later the man with an
anemic scallion forces his bed partner into
playing critic-at-large whether she wants to or
not: Anemic: I guess you've been with a lot of
guys before? Critic: Um, enough. It's not what
you've got, it's what you do with it." 1983 Cynthia
Heimel, *Sex Tips for Girls* (New York: Simon &
Schuster) 187: "Stop any girl on the street and
ask her if she cares if a man is well hung, and

she will look at you aghast. 'Of course not,' she'll say, 'it's not what you've got, it's how you use it. It's not the meat, it's the motion.'" Cf. "SIZE doesn't matter" and the older sententious expression "It's not what you've got that matters, it's what you are (what you've done)."

## When you've **got** to go, you've got to go.

See "When you've got to GO, you've got to go."

## You are not late till you **get** there.

1980 Paul Dickson, *The Official Explanations* (New York: Delacorte) 94: "Huhn's Law. You're not late until you get there." 1989 *Washington Post* 10 Apr.: "They proved, therefore, the old truism: 'You're never late until you get there.'"

## You can't **get** there from here.

1927 Louise Moore, "College Women in Business," *Annual Convention Series* (American Management Association), no. 61: 13: "When I first moved to Poughkeepsie I got lost among our narrow winding streets. A passerby answered my question about the shortest way to the factory, 'Why, you can't get there from here.'" 1955 *Washington Post* 12 Sep.: "That classic advice to the lost motorist, 'You can't get there from here.'"

## You haven't **got** it (You don't know you've got it) till you get it.

1905 J. Hickory Wood, *Dan Leno* (London: Methuen) 183: "Promotion in the army is very like a whack on the nose; you never know you've got it till you get it." 1994 *West African*, no. 4002 (13–19 Jun.) 1041 (advertisement for M-NET television): "All this makes for the very best in pay-TV in Africa. But remember, you haven't got it till you get it!"

## You have to **get** in it to win it.

See "You have to be in it to WIN it."

## You've either **got** it or you don't.

See "You either HAVE it or you don't."

## Can't we all just **get along**?

1992 The saying entered oral tradition as a proverb from an utterance (somewhat misquoted) of Rodney King, victim of brutality inflicted by Los Angeles policemen: ". . . [C]an we all get along? Can we get along?" *YBQ* Rodney King.

## **Get along** to (and) go along (If you want to go along, you have to get along).

1971 John Neary, *Julian Bond: Black Rebel* (New York: William Morrow) 245 (quoting Bond): "Put it in its most cynical light: . . . These guys would then have to say, 'Well, we need somebody who will go along with most things. Who will go along with us?' Get along and go along, yeah!" 1971 *Christian Science Monitor* 3 Jul. (quoting Senator Birch Bayh Sr.): "Yes, 'Get along and go along,' was my position." 1978 *Washington Post* 5 Feb. (quoting Leo E. Green): "I'm not part of the thing that you've got to get along to go along." 1997 Julie Leiniger Pycior, *LBJ & Mexican Americans* (Austin: U of Texas P) 43–44: "At first [John Nance] Garner had cooperated with the New Deal, following Sam Rayburn's maxim, 'You have to get along to go along.'" The proverb possibly originated as a simple misquotation (or misunderstanding) of "You've got to GO ALONG to get along."

## **Getting** there is half the fun.

1952 *Capital Times* [Madison WI] 23 Jan.: "We feel, to plagiarize the Cunard line ad, 'Getting there is half the fun.'" Pickering et al. (1992) 215. The proverb often construes the "getting there" as a figurative journey. Cf. "HAPPINESS is a journey, not a destination" and "The JOY is in the journey."

## Get while the **getting** is good.

1911 *Chicago Daily Tribune* 15 Jun.: "We seem to detect a disposition to reproach Mr. [Johnny]

Kling because he isn't catching for his health. But Mr. Kling, being on the inside, knows how much bunk there is in the g. o. g. ['Grand Old Game'—baseball]; therefore his motto is: 'Get while the getting is good.'" 1912 Rollo Walter Brown, "A Word-List from Western Indiana," *Dialect Notes* 3, pt. 8: 576: "[G]et while the gettin(g)'s good . . . To get while one has an opportunity." *DAP* 250(1). Cf. "Go while the GOING is good" and "Take while the TAKING is good."

## Girls (Guys, Boys) just want to have fun.

1979 The saying probably entered oral tradition as a proverb from the title and refrain of a song by Robert Hazard, especially after Cyndi Lauper's wildly popular recording of the paean to frivolity and hedonism in 1983. The *guys* (or *boys*) variant perhaps developed as an anti-proverb. 1985 Katharine Blood, "Boys Just Want to Have Fun," *Forbes* 135, no. 12 (3 Jun.) 92—an article about new models of sporty cars.

## Never chase **girls** or busses; another will be along shortly.

See "Never run after a WOMAN or a streetcar; if you miss one, another will come along soon."

## Never get caught with a dead **girl** or a live boy.

See "Never get caught in BED with a dead girl or a live boy."

## Never **give** anything away that you can sell (Why give something away when you can sell it?).

1953 The saying may already have belonged to oral tradition when Cole Porter adapted it in his song "Never Give Anything Away": "Never give anything away, away, away, / That you can sell." 1962 Theodore M. Bernstein, *More Language That Needs Watching* (Manhasset NY: Channel) 33: "The problem of when to use commercial names in the news columns is a ticklish one.

The adage—and if there isn't such an adage there should be one—'Why give it away if you can sell it?' is still valid."

## The **glass** is either half empty or half full.

1930 Lewis E. Lawes, "Crime and Rehabilitation," *New York State Bar Association Bulletin* 2: 27: "I told him of the lady who drove into a filling station and said the indicator pointed to one-half, but she didn't know whether that meant half-full or half-empty." 1935 *New York Times* 12 Nov.: "I came recently upon a graphic distinction drawn by Sir Josiah Stamp [economist, 1880–1941] between an optimist and a pessimist: 'A pessimist looks at his glass and says it is half empty; an optimist looks at it and says it is half full.'" *RHDP* 112–13.

## Through rose-colored **glasses** the world is always bright.

1977 Marlene Kramer and Claudia Schmalenberg, *Path to Biculturalism* (Wakefield MA: Contemporary) 5: "During the honeymooon phase, the new graduate looks at the world through rose-colored glasses: the world is all good; everything is wonderful." *DAP* 253(5). Of course, the metaphor of seeing through rose-colored (and other-colored) glasses is older than the proverb; Doyle (2001b).

## **Glory** has a price.

1917 William Harvey Allen, *Universal Training for Citizenship and Public Service* (New York: Macmillan) 262: "Today, in 1917, in the midst of time's most devastating and least justifiable war, . . . the future is glorious, but that glory has its price." 1924 Maxwell Anderson and Laurence Stallings, *What Price Glory?* (title of a play). 1960 Charles de Gaulle, *War Memoirs*, translated by Richard Howard (New York: Simon & Schuster, 1955–60) 3: 171: "'At this very moment,' he [Gen. Eisenhower] said, 'I am having a lot of trouble with Montgomery, a general of great ability, but

a bitter critic and a mistrustful subordinate.'
'Glory has its price,' I replied. 'Now you are
going to be a conqueror'" (de Gaulle's French
was "La gloire se paie"). Cf. "FAME has a price"
and "POWER has its price."

## If the **glove** doesn't fit, you must acquit.

See "If it doesn't FIT, you must acquit."

## No **glove**, no love.

1982 Steve Tesich (author of the screenplay),
*The World According to Garp* (the saying does
not appear in John Irving's novel of 1978); the
character Cushie in dialog with the sexually
naïve Garp: "'Where's your thing?' 'Where's
what?' 'Your thing.' 'My thing. Don't you have a
hold of it?' 'No, your glove.' 'My glove?' 'Look,
I don't want babies. No glove, no love.' 'You
mean rubbers.'" 1984 Laurence Paros, *The Erotic
Tongue: A Sexual Lexicon* (New York: Henry
Holt) 214: "No glove, no love" (Paros erroneously
attributes the saying to Irving's 1978 novel).
1986 "Sex and Schools," *Time* 128, no. 21 (24
Nov.) 63: "[Seventh-grade teacher Thomas]
Lundgren talks about condoms ('No glove, no
love' is a popular class mnemonic), and abortion
is presented as a fact of life." Mieder (2005a).

## Go all the way or don't go at all.

1968 Patrick Hayes, "The National Music
Council as Music Propagandist," *Bulletin*
(National Music Council) 28, no. 3 (Summer)
10: "So, I suggest that as you go about this
campaign of propaganda . . . be militant—go all
the way or don't go at all." 1972 *Montreal Gazette*
5 Feb. (horoscope): "Don't do things halfway. No
lukewarm methods. Go all the way or don't go at
all." 1975 *Bryan [OH] Times* 16 Apr.: "'If you are
going to go,' [Congressman Arthur] Wilkowski
said, 'you either go all the way or don't go at all.'"
Cf. "GO big or go home" and "GO hard or
go home."

## Go big (large) or go home.

1965 *Chronicle Telegram [Elyria OH]* 23 Mar.: "An
old pinochle saying, 'Go big or go home,' was
followed by Lauretta Moore last night. She went
big with a 590 series in the Monday Night Ladies
[bowling] League." 1986 *Chicago Sun Times* 9
Jan.: "'Go big or go home.' 'Go all the way or
don't go.' (Pick a cliche and live by it)." Cf. "GO
hard or go home."

## Go hard or go home.

1990 *Toronto Star* 11 Apr.: "It was either go hard
or go home and the Leafs [Toronto Mapleleafs
hockey team] opted for the former." 1990
*Philadelphia Inquirer* 20 Sep.: "[Roger] Clemens
slipped on a T-shirt that said, 'Go hard or go
home.'" 1990 *Washington Post* 6 Nov.: "The
Magruder field hockey team showed up at the
Maryland State Class 3A semifinals . . . wearing
shirts emblazoned with 'Go Hard or Go Home!'
across the back." Mieder (2009a) 268. Cf. "GO
big or go home."

## Go strong or don't go at all (or go home).

1995 Gregg Easterbrook, review of *Prodigal
Soldiers* by James Kitfield (1995), *Washington
Monthly* 27, no. 1 (Jan.–Feb.) 52: "Horner learned
the basic military lesson of Vietnam: Either go
strong or don't go at all." 2000 *St. Petersburg [FL]
Times* 2 Feb. (epigraph for an article): "Go strong
or go home" (credited to Brian Tomlin). Cf. "GO
big or go home" and "GO hard or go home."

## Go with what you've got (You have to go with what you've got).

1960 John Hohenberg, *The Professional Journalist*
(New York: Henry Holt) 5: "They [journalists]
must know that no edition will wait for a
perfectionist—that newspapermen often must,
as the saying is, 'Go with what you've got.'" 1963
*Ludington [MI] Daily News* 18 Nov. (quoting the
local basketball coach, regarding his team's poor

free-throw shooting): "That's going to kill us one of these nights. We have to live with it, thought [*sic*]. You have to go with what you've got."

## If anything can **go** wrong, it will.

See "If anything can GO WRONG, it will."

## If you don't know where you are **going**, you might not get there (you might end up somewhere else).

1969 Lawrence J. Peter and Raymond Hull, *The Peter Principle* (New York: William Morrow) 159: "In my lecture *Destiny Lies Ahead*, I tell my students, 'If you don't know where you are going, you will probably end up somewhere else.'" 1972 Willys H. Monroe, "Helping School Staffs Perform under an Accountability System," *Colorado Journal of Educational Research* 11, no. 3 (Spring) 9: ". . . I would like to quote from that eminent philosopher Yogi Berra . . . : 'If you don't know where you are going, you might wind up someplace else.'" 1979 Kateri Heckathorn and Sharon A. Smith, "Management," in *AACN Organization and Management of Critical-Care Facilities*, edited by Diane C. Adler and Norma Shoemaker (St. Louis: C. V. Mosby) 157: "It has been said that if you do not know where you are going, you probably will not get there. It is important to develop a philosophy and determine goals and objectives. . . ." As with most "Yogi-isms," the attribution to Berra is unreliable.

## What **goes** around comes around.

1961 *Proceedings of the Fourteenth Biennial Convention of the International Longshoremen's and Warehousemen's Union* 242: "The need has always been for the Negro to be a full part of the Labor Movement, and I don't think you can deny him this right. And if you do, you are taking away the rights belonging to you, because the old saying goes, 'What goes around comes around.'" 1962 Paul Crump, *Burn, Killer, Burn!* (Chicago: Johnson) 132: "'Yeah,' he sneered, 'I'll hang tough. Only you guys remember—What goes

around, comes around.'" *RHDP* 355–56; *DAAP* 831; *YBQ* Modern Proverbs (37); *ODP* 134–35; Bassin (1984); Daniel et al. (1987) 504; Page and Washington (1987); Prahlad (1994); Prahlad (1996) 205–6. Also occurring is a variant (or counter-proverb?—but the meaning seems to be the same): "What comes around goes around." 1974 Title of a "soul" song by Dr. John: "What Comes Around (Goes Around)." 1983 Karen Payne, *Between Ourselves: Letters between Mothers and Daughters* (Boston: Houghton Mifflin) 267 (in a letter dated 1 Dec. 1980): "It seemed significant, having lost three friends that past winter, that three new lives would enter the valley next winter. What comes around, goes around, right?"

## When you've got to **go**, you've got to go.

1937 *Atlanta Constitution* 20 Apr. [the journalist Arthur Cain refers to himself in the third person]: "No sooner did we accustom ourselves to one place than that wretched sense of duty of ours appeared like an evil genii [*sic*] and prodded Cain aggravatingly in the shapely ribs. Well, when you gotta go you gotta go, so Cain assembled the bones and prepared to get a flying start to Hamburg." 1937 Olga J. Martin, *Hollywood's Movie Commandments* (New York: W. W. Wilson) 220 (elaborating on the Motion Picture Production Code of 1930): "The following represent some of the most commonly deleted subjects, which violate both the Code and censorship rulings: . . . Toilet gags, views of toilets in washrooms; doors marked 'Ladies,' or 'Gentlemen' (even in foreign language); remarks like 'I gotta see a man about a dog'; and 'When you gotta go, you gotta go.'" 1939 *Washington Post* 21 Jul.: "Fellows, the doctors say I'll soon be wearing a lot of these [roses] on my chest. I'll be out in Flatbush Cemetery. Well, what the hell, thousands die every minute. When you gotta go, you gotta go." The verb *go* probably denoted "depart" or "proceed" in various senses before the proverb came to focus principally on urinating or defecating.

Wherever (No matter where) you **go**, you are there (there you are).

1955 "Oddities," *Hazleton Collegian* (Pennsylvania State University, Hazleton) 4 Mar. (humorous tidbits, with local allusions): "Jim Russell wants to know why it is that no matter where you go, there you are." 1962 Lyn Coffin, "Wherever You Go, There You Are" (title of poem), *Cross Currents* 6 (Michigan Slavic Materials 28): 245.

You have got to **go** along to get along.

See "You've got to GO ALONG to get along."

You only **go** around (round) once.

See "You only go around once in LIFE."

You've got to **go along** to get along (Go along and get along, Go along to get along, If you want to get along you have to go along.).

1952 *Kerrville [TX] Times* 14 Oct.: "Claude Gilmer of Rocksprings, chairman of the Democrats for Eisenhower, last night blasted at [Congressman Sam] Rayburn's claims of Democratic prosperity. 'It is sickening to see Get-Along, Go-Along Sam Rayburn and his coterie of Trumanites traveling all over Texas gloating over the blood-stained dollars that are now in circulation and calling it prosperity.'" 1953 *Chicago Tribune* 25 Nov. (quoting Willis McCarthy): "'I think they [the employers] simply said to themselves, "black is white, and we'll go along to get along,"' said McCarthy, who was an employers' spokesman at the Chicago meeting" (square brackets as shown). 1955 *New York Times* 19 Feb.: "At the meeting, according to one member who was there, the Speaker [Sam Rayburn] did not 'order' the members to support the unmodified bill. . . . [H]e simply put it this way: 'If you want to get along, go along.'" 1960 James Reichley, "1960: Failure of Social Imagination," *The Nation* 190 (6 Feb.) 121: "Those among them [progressives]

who were elected to Congress in the huge Democratic sweep of 1958 seemed willing enough to accept 'Go along to get along' for their motto. 'My first job is to get re-elected,' said a Democratic freshman. . . ." *YBQ* Rayburn. Cf. "GET ALONG to go along."

You only **go around** (round) once.

See "You only go around once in LIFE."

If anything can **go wrong**, it will (Anything that can go wrong, will go wrong; anything that can possibly go wrong usually does).

1908 Nevil Maskelyne, "The Art in Magic," *The Magic Circular* (Jun.) 25: "It is an experience common to all men to find that, on any special occasion, such as the production of a magical effect for the first time in public, everything that *can* go wrong *will* go wrong. Whether we must attribute this to the malignity of matter or to the total depravity of inanimate things, whether the exciting cause is hurry, worry, or what not, the fact remains" (italics as shown). 1951 Anne Roe, "Child Behavior, Animal Behavior, and Comparative Psychology," *Genetic Psychology Monographs* 43 (May) 204: "As for himself he realized that this was the inexorable working of the second law of the thermodynamics which stated Murphy's law 'If anything can go wrong it will.' I always liked Murphy's law." 1955 Lee Corey, "Design Flaw," *Astounding Science Fiction* 54 (Feb.) 54: "'Reilly's Law,' Guy Barclay said cryptically. 'Huh?' 'Reilly's Law,' Guy repeated. 'It states that in any scientific or engineering endeavor, anything that can go wrong *will* go wrong'" (italics as shown). *DAP* 21; *RHDP* 150–51; *YBQ* Modern Proverbs (102); *ODP* 6–7; Rees (1984) 56–57; Pickering et al. (1992) 419; Rees (1995) 236; Pickering (2001) 26. In popular legend, Murphy's Law originated in 1949 at Edwards Air Force Base in California, coined by project manager George E. Nichols after hearing Edward A. Murphy Jr. complain about a wrongly wired rocket-sled experiment. However, there is no documentation of that connection until 1955. The idea embodied in Murphy's Law (less often, "Reilly's Law" or "O'Reilly's Law") has appeared in numerous forms, in reference to a variety of activities, from antiquity forward (see the cross-references at the *YBQ* entry). For example: 1878 Alfred Holt, "Review of the Progress of Steam Shipping during the Last Quarter of a Century," *Minutes of Proceedings of the Institution of Civil Engineers* 51: 8: "It is found that anything that can go wrong at sea generally does go wrong sooner or later." 1941 George Orwell, "War-time Diaries," in *Collected Essays, Journalism and Letters*, edited by Sonia Orwell and Ian Angus (New York: Harcourt, Brace & World, 1968) 2: 400–401: "Iraq, Syria, Morocco, Spain, Darlan, Stalin, Raschid Ali, Franco—sensation of utter helplessness. If there is a wrong thing to do, it will be done, infallibly. One has come to believe in that as if it were a law of nature." The term "Murphy's Law" has come to designate a range of seemingly reasonable but often paradoxical or absurd propositions.

## Even **God** gets tired of too much hallelujah.

1936 Carl Sandburg, *The People, Yes* (New York: Harcourt, Brace) 106 (in a poetic montage of proverbs and other sayings). 1958 Glenn Coulter, "Billy Holliday," reprinted from *Jazz Review* in *Jazz Panorama*, edited by Martin T. Williams (New York: Crowell-Collier, 1962) 150: "*Fine and Mellow* is one of twelve songs done [by Billie Holiday] for Commodore now newly released on LP. Even God gets tired of too much alleluia, and it would be fruitless to invent fresh ways of commending performances which Commodore rightly calls classic" (italics as shown). 1987 Helen Papanikolas, *A Greek Odyssey in the American West* (Lincoln: U of Nebraska P) 123: "'Enough's enough, Koula,' Hrisoula said sharply. 'Even God gets tired of too much Kyrie, eleison.'" *DAAP* 318.

## **God** ain't choosy.

Whiting (1952) 415 lists the saying as a North Carolina proverb. 1998 John V. Taylor, *The Uncancelled Mandate: Four Biblical Studies* (London: Church House) 20: "God isn't choosy. And if God chooses his human agents so indiscriminately then who are we to refuse as fellow partners those who do or don't ordain women, do or don't separate the orders of bishops and presbyters. . . ."

## **God** can make a way out of no way.

1922 Coe Hayne, *Race Grit* (Philadelphia: Judson) 109: "God can make a way out of no way. Pray to him, and he will open a way." 1925 Edgar Garfield Thomas, *The First African Baptist Church of North America* (Savannah GA: for the author) 32: "But believers in a wonder-working God, hope against hope, trusting an all wise Providence to make a way out of no way." 1957 Martin Luther King Jr., "The Rewards of Worship" (sermon delivered 28 Apr.), in *Papers of Martin Luther King, Jr.*, edited by Clayborne Carson et al. (Berkeley: U of California P, 1992–2007) 6: 301: The poet William Cowper, entering a Paris cathedral, "saw a man mount the throne, and he started talking about the man who could make a way out of no way." Preponderantly, the proverb (as well as the phrase "make a way out of no way" in other uses) has occurred in African American speech; it may have originated (in the rhetoric of preachers) as a paraphrase of Isaiah 43:10, "I will even make a way in the wilderness. . . ." Mieder (2010b) 171–86.

## **God** doesn't love ugly.

Anderson and Cundall (1910) 23 list the saying as a Jamaican proverb: "Godamighty no lub ugly" (gloss: "God almighty does not love bad deeds"). 1913 Kelly Miller, "Moral Pedagogy," *Education* 34: 139: "Men of taste and refinement of feeling abhor vice because it is unseemly. The old fashioned maxim tells us that 'God does not love ugly.'" 1930 Langston Hughes, *Not without Laughter* (New York: Alfred A. Knopf) 75: "'One thing sho, de Lawd ain't prejudiced!' 'No,' said Hager; 'but He don't love ugly, neither in niggers nor in white folks.'" 1976 James Thomas Jackson, "My Africa—It Is All This and More," *Los Angeles Times* 12 Feb.: "As we blacks are fond of saying, 'God doesn't love ugly.' (To which someone will always answer, 'Naw, and he ain't too crazy about pretty, either.')." In light of the obvious African American association of the proverb, it is perhaps significant that Kelly Miller, who in 1913 referred to it as an "old fashioned maxim," was a professor at the predominantly African American Howard University.

## God doesn't make junk (trash).

1975 Joseph Breault, *Seeking Purity of Heart* (Locust Valley NY: Living Flame) 76: "This love of ourselves is . . . a deep respect, acceptance and confidence in the basic goodness the Lord has placed there. God does not make trash and he has made us." 1975 *Prescott [AZ] Courier* 14 Feb. (in a Valentine's Day "Heart-o-gram"): "M. E. COMMUNITY, We love you. God doesn't make junk. From, I'M LOVABLE" (capitalization as shown). 1976 Elizabeth M. Gough, *Who Are You? A Teen-ager's Guide to Self-Understanding* (New York: William Morrow) 52: "A priest once counseled a woman when she felt very low, 'Remember this: God made you, and God doesn't make junk.'"

## God doesn't make land anymore.

See "They don't make LAND anymore."

## God doesn't play dice.

1926 The saying probably entered oral tradition as a proverb from a remark in a letter from Albert Einstein to Max Born: "Quantum mechanics is certainly imposing. . . . The theory says a lot, but does not really bring us any closer to the secret of the 'old one.' I, at any rate, am convinced that *He* is not playing at dice" (italics as shown); *The Born-Einstein Letters*, translated by Irene Born (London: Macmillan, 1971) 91. (The German says, "Jedenfalls bin ich überzeugt, dass der [Gott] nicht würfelt.") *YBQ* Einstein (8). Christy (1888) 1: 5 gave as a proverb "Nothing with God is accidental," attributing it (spuriously) to Longfellow.

## God is good, but don't dance in a small boat.

1995 Sean Desmond, *A Touch of the Irish: Wit and Wisdom* (Stamford CT: Longmeadow) 108 (in a list headed "Proverbs"): "God is good, but never dance in a small boat." The proverb can occur without the first clause: 2002 Andrew Frothingham, *Great Toasts* (Franklin Lakes NJ: Career Press) 159 (a toast): "May you never dance in a small boat." The proverb is often identified as Irish.

## God is in the details.

The saying may have entered English-speaking oral tradition as a proverb from German or French. 1925 Aby Warburg, announcing the title or topic of a seminar at Hamburg University, 11 Nov.: "Der liebe Gott steckt im Detail," in *Schriften und Würdigungen*, edited by Dieter Wuttke (Baden-Baden: Valentin Koerner, 1992) 618, 623–25. 1955 Erwin Panofsky, *Meaning in the Visual Arts* (Garden City NY: Doubleday) v: "Neither have I tried to make them [essays in a collection] appear less pedantic by expunging scholastic argument and documentation (if anything at all can be gained from reading essays like these, it is a certain respect for Flaubert's conviction that *'le bon Dieu est dans le détail'*). . . ." 1958 Peter Blake, "The Difficult Art of Simplicity," *Architectural Forum* 108, no. 5 (May) 129: "[The architect Ludwig] Mies [van der Rohe] likes to say that 'God is in the Details.' By this he means that a building 'declares itself' through its details—features such as visible joints and trim and projection or recession—and that the details of a building are a creative force in themselves." *RHDP* 116; *YBQ* Warburg, Flaubert, Rohe; Rees (2006) 264. The attribution of the French saying to Flaubert cannot be corroborated. Cf. "The DEVIL is in the details." (One of the two proverbs probably originated as an anti-proverb based on the other.)

## God isn't choosy.

See "GOD ain't choosy."

## God made dirt; dirt don't hurt.

1994 Clarence Major, *Juba to Jive: A Dictionary of African-American Slang* (New York: Penguin) 204: "God made dirt and dirt don't hurt (1970s–1990s)[:] a children's saying used after they drop food on the ground or floor and brush it off and eat it." 1997 Brian Keith Jackson, *The View from Here* (New York: Simon & Schuster) 105: "'Goodness gracious. Look at this sheet,' said Momma, getting off the white sheet that was now covered with dirt and grass stains. . . . 'Is it ruint, Momma?' 'No, baby. It's not ruined. God made grass. God made dirt. Dirt and grass can't hurt.'" Cf. "A little DIRT never hurt."

## God protects the working girl.

See "HEAVEN protects the working girl."

## God sends no cross that you cannot bear.

1985 William Sears, *Christian Parenting and Child Care* (Nashville: Thomas Nelson) 156: "I began to imagine what God says to mothers. . . . 'Trust in Me with all your heart and lean not on your own understanding. I will not give you a cross you cannot bear.'" 1993 *Chicago Tribune* 3 Jan.: "'Sometimes it's not always for us to understand,' [basketball coach Marianna] Freeman said. 'My grandma says there is never a cross you can't bear.'" 1995 Ralph G. Martin, *Seeds of Destruction: Joe Kennedy and His Sons* (New York: G. P. Putnam's Sons) 565 (quoting Dave Powers, in reference to Rose Kennedy): "Having had two sons assassinated, and one killed in the war, and Kathleen dying in a plane crash. . . . And

going on to say that God never gives you a cross that you cannot bear. See, that's what makes her great!" (ellipsis dots as shown). 1995 Mickey Clement, *The Irish Princess* (New York: G. P. Putnam's Sons) 97: "'Clare, my dear,' he said to me as he took my hand, 'God does not give you a cross you cannot bear.' 'Well, he has!'" Cf. the old proverb "God fits the burden to the shoulders."

## God wants spiritual fruit, not religious nuts.

1978 *Abilene [TX] Reporter-News* 7 Feb. (advertisement): "Pioneer Drive Baptist Church . . . God wants spiritual fruit, not religious nuts." 1978 *Los Angeles Times* 9 Apr. (filler item): "Sign seen outside a church in North Redondo Beach reads: 'God Wants Spiritual Fruit, Not Religious Nuts.'"

## Kill them all, and let God sort them out.

1932 Emile Saillens, *French History* (Philadelphia: J. B. Lippincott) 42: "'Kill them all,' said Simon [de Montfort], 'God will sort them out!' Albi, Carcassonne and other cities fared hardly better." 1981 *Lewistown [ME] Journal* 7 Nov.: "Two former members of Delta Force, the hostage rescue team, . . . work for him [Col. Charles Beckwith]. On his desk is a plaque that reads, 'Kill 'em all. Let God sort 'em out.'" 1983 Stephen King, *Christine* (New York: Viking) 112–13: "A sleazy-looking guy in a cracked leather jacket was dorking around with an old BSA bike. . . . The back of his jacket displayed a skull wearing a Green Beret and the charming motto KILL EM ALL AND LET GOD SORT EM OUT" (capitalization as shown). The proverb is the modern version of a Latin declaration attributed to the leader of the Albigensian Crusade of the early thirteenth century, "Kill them all; God will know his own!" (Russell [1999] 287–93). Numerous individuals recall the ". . . let God sort them out" version from the battlefields of Vietnam in the 1960s, and as a tattoo and T-shirt slogan in the 1970s. However, the record in print from those decades is very scarce; there is this allusion from 1978 in Piero Gleijesus, *The Dominican Crisis: The 1965 Constitutionalist Revolt and American Intervention* (Baltimore: Johns Hopkins UP) 318: "The principle governing the [Trujillo regime's] repression was to arrest them all and let God sort them out."

## Let go; let **God**.

1923 "Sermonic Literature," *Homiletic Review* 86: 340 (section title, paraphrasing Romans 6:13): "Let go—Let God / . . . And what God did for Dwight L. Moody he will do for all of us who yield ourselves to him. There is only one condition to this divine enduement of power, and that is that we let go of self and take hold on God." 1926 George Bennard, "Let Go—Let God" (title of a hymn; words and music by Bennard). 1930 E. Stanley Jones, *The Christ of Every Road* (New York: Abingdon) 174: ". . . [T]he gospel . . . ends with a self-finding, life's supreme affirmation. Its word is, 'Let go, let God.'" In recent years, the proverb has been most prevalent among participants in "recovery" programs for addicts.

## Only **God** can make a tree.

1913 The saying entered oral tradition as a proverb from Joyce Kilmer's poem "Trees." *DAAP* 319; *YBQ* Kilmer (2).

## "Take what you want," says **God**, "and (but) pay for it."

1955 Gladys Mitchell, *Watson's Choice* (London: Michael Joseph), 13: "The Englishman had had what he wanted of Manoel's mother. Take what you want, says God, and pay for it. The Englishman had taken what he wanted. Now, thought Manoel, . . . he should pay." 1958 Sean O'Casey, letter to May Keating, in *Letters*, edited by David Krause (New York and Washington DC: Macmillan and Catholic U of America P, 1975–92) 3: 546: "Well, they [the Roman Catholic clergy] are having their own way, but they are paying heavily for it. . . . Hundreds of Parishes are perishing for want of parishioners. Take

what you want, says God; take what you want, and pay for it." *DAP* 580(3); *DAAP* 755. The saying is sometimes referred to as a Spanish proverb. Without the attribution to God, the saying is older.

## Trust (in) **God**, but lock your door (your car).

1991 *Hartford [CT] Courant* 19 May: "There's a saying: 'Trust in God, but lock your door.'" 1993 H. Jackson Brown Jr., *Life's Little Instruction Book*, vol. 2 (Nashville: Rutledge Hill), no. 757 (unpaginated): "Trust in God, but lock your car." *RHDP* 275. Cf. "TRUST but verify" and "Trust everyone, but cut the CARDS."

## Where **God** goes (is), the devil goes (is).

1926 T. F. Powys, *Innocent Birds* (New York: Alfred A. Knopf) 77: "A large bird flew out of it [a thorn bush] that wasn't a rook. Solly started. Where God was expected he knew the Devil might appear too; for where God goes the Devil goes." 1989 Lynette Dreyer, *The Modern African Elite of South Africa* (New York: St. Martin's) 131 (quoting a black African religious leader): "To many people Christianity is taken to be the White man's religion. . . . If God is for every one why can't there be justice for everyone? We must explain that where God is, the devil also is." *MP* G124.

## Go while the **going** is good.

1911 *New York Times* 17 Jul.: "And what every woman knows is that, matrimonially speaking, a girl's greatest assets are beauty and youth; therefore this wise mother wanted her daughters to 'go while the going is good!'" 1913 Witter Bynner, *Book of Plays* (New York: Alfred A. Knopf) 60: "Go while the going's good. You're wasting time." 1914 W. Cecil Price, "The Development of the Boy Scout Movement," *Living Age* 282: 520: ". . . [H]e probably knew that to carry out even a large part of his political programme he must, as the old frontiersmen used to say, 'go while the going is good.'" *Room* (2000) 296. Cf. "Get while the GETTING is good" and "Take while the TAKING is good."

## When the **going** gets tough (If you can't dodge trouble), step on the gas.

1924 Thomas Lansing Masson, *Tom Masson's Annual* (Garden City NY: Doubleday, Page) 71 (in a list of trenchant sayings): "If you see you can't dodge trouble, step on the gas and hit it head-on" (credited to the *Florence Herald*). 1994 *Ottawa Citizen* 10 Jun. (review of the motion picture *Speed*): "It's a candy bar of a film, pure sugar, whose main point seems to be that when the going gets tough, the tough step on the gas." 2005 *U.S. Competitiveness: The Innovation Challenge. Hearings before the Committee on Science, House of Representatives* (Washington DC: Government Printing Office, 2006) 39; prepared statement by William R. Brody (21 Jul.): "*We should greatly increase both government and private funding in research. . . . It's just like Dale Earnhardt Jr. would tell you—when the race gets tough, step on the gas*" (italics as shown).

## When the **going** gets tough, the tough get going.

1954 *Charleston [WV] Daily Mail* 4 May: "Frank Leahy, now an actor, is back coaching football in front of a camera and the material is as good as it used to be at Notre Dame. . . . He also inserted his own personal football motto into the dialogue: 'When the going gets tough, the tough get going.'" 1956 *Los Angeles Times* 24 Aug.: "Former Notre Dame Coach Frank Leahy in seconding Ike's nomination stirred the audience with a motto for football and politics: 'When the going gets tough, the tough get going.'" *RHDP* 364; *DAAP* 320; *YBQ* Leahy; *ODP* 135; Bassin (1984); Rees (1984) 238; Pickering et al. (1992) 235; Rees (1995) 501; Pickering (2001) 157. Beginning in the 1960s, the attribution of the saying to Joseph P. Kennedy became common.

## Go for the **gold**.

1963 Frank Rose, *West of Eden: The End of Innocence at Apple Computer* (New York: Viking) 40: "The semiconductor industry prided itself on its 'go-for-the-gold' mentality. This was the new Gold Rush." 1971 Garry Hoyt, *Go for the Gold: Somebody Has to Lose . . . But Why You?* (Chicago: Quadrangle; ellipsis dots as shown).

## He who has the **gold** makes the rules (Whoever has the gold rules).

1967 Earl H. Brill, *Sex Is Dead* (New York: Seabury) 83: "The best I ever heard it stated was in a recent comic strip, 'The Wizard of Id.' The King was finishing up a speech with the exhortation, 'And let us all remember to live by the Golden Rule.' Someone asked the Wizard what was the Golden Rule, and he answered: 'The one who has the gold makes the rule.'" 1969 M. J. Cetron and D. N. Dick, "Producing the First Navy Technological Forecast," *Technological Forecasting* 1: 194–95: "The Navy Technological Forecast is being used by people who live by the golden rule: 'He who has the gold, makes the rules.' As such, it is becoming a valuable aid to planning and funding technology." 1970 Todd Gitlin and Nanci Hollanader, *Uptown: Poor Whites in Chicago* (New York: Harper & Row) 301 (an interviewee speaking): "I've not eaten for nine days in Chicago once. You get real faint. The golden rule: whoever has the gold makes the rules." Often the proverb includes the satirical designation "The Golden Rule" (Matthew 7:12).

## All the **good** ones are (already) taken.

See "All the good ones are TAKEN."

## Anything **good** (in life) is either illegal, immoral, or fattening.

1933 *Reader's Digest* 24 (Dec.) 109 (in a list of witticisms): "All the things I really like to do are either illegal, immoral, or fattening" (attributed to Alexander Woollcott). 1934 *Six of a Kind* (motion picture, released 9 Feb.), screenplay by Walter DeLeon and Harry Ruskin; however, W. C. Fields is reported to have been ad-libbing on the set (in his character Sheriff John, conversing with the hosteler): "'Now listen to me, Honest John, why do you drink so much?' 'Because I like it!' 'Everything you like to do is wrong!' 'According to you, everything I like to do is either illegal, immoral, or fattening.'" 1934 *Evening Tribune [Albert Lea MN]* 1 Mar.: "We all have to admit that women get the worst of the deal, as one said today that most women now find that what they do is either illegal, immoral or too fattening." 1934 Mary Channing Coleman, "Our Unique Contribution: Presidential Address [American Physical Education Society]," *Journal of Health, Physical Education, and Recreation* 5, no. 6 (Jun.) 4: ". . . [F]rom prim little Jane Austen—herself surely one of our immortals—comes the flapper's lament that life was hardly worth living since everything she really liked to do was either illegal, immoral, or fattening." The attribution of "the flapper's lament" to Jane Austen is certainly erroneous, though the proverb may loosely resemble something said in an Austen novel. *YBQ* Woollcott (4).

## Do **good** (You can do good) by doing well.

1973 R. A. Labine, "Besides Being Charming, They're Ecologically Sound," *Old-House Journal* 1, no. 3 (Dec.) 2: "While few people buy an old home to make a social statement, its [*sic*] nice to know you can do good by doing well." 1974 *New York Times* 16 Mar.: "The other group comprised more secular types with overtly economic motives for migrating to the New World. Even so, these settlers . . . were also children of the Reformation, and they too hoped to do good by doing well." Perhaps originating as an anti-proverb responding to the benevolently capitalistic "Do well by doing GOOD," the proverb usually means that one who becomes wealthy stands in a better position to behave

altruistically—though it can also suggest that the general well-being of society is somehow mystically enhanced by individual wealth.

## Do well (You can do well) by doing **good**.

1963 Paul Rink, *Building the Bank of America: A. P. Giannini* (Chicago: Encyclopaedia Britannica) 107: "A. P. had never been more right. 'To do well by doing good' hits the nail on the head." 1963 *New York Times* 10 Sep. (advertisement for Alcoa): "Above all, we hope this proves that corporate good citizenship pays. That it makes good business sense to help in preserving our cities. That it is possible to do well by doing good." *RHDP* 54–55. Cf. "Do GOOD by doing well."

## **Good**, better, best: never let it (them) rest until your (the) good is better and your (the) better is best.

1904 Julia Richman, "Graded Work in Dictation for All Grades," *School Work* 3, no. 2 (Jun.) 143 (dictation exercise): "Good, better, best, / Never let it rest, / Till your good is better, / And your better, best." 1905 W. W. Wilkinson, "The Veil Lifted," *Ohio Educational Monthly* 54: 400 (imagining a happy future for education in the state): ". . . I find . . . a simple, profound faith that the best is not yet and that Ohio has adopted as her motto: 'Good, better, best; / Never let her rest / Till your *good* is better, / And your *better*, *best*'" (italics as shown). *DAP* 258.

## **Good** enough (What's good enough) is good enough (If it's good enough, it's good enough).

1910 Clayton Hamilton, "The Younger American Playwrights," *The Bookman* 32: 254: "We make no concerted and organised effort to improve the technique of our drama, because we carelessly assume that whatever is good enough is good enough." 1915 *Washington Post* 14 Feb.: "Modesty is very well in maids, but it is utterly useless in the present circumstance [a vaudeville show]. Good enough is good enough, but a whole lot is immense." The proverb may be regarded as a counter-proverb rebutting "GOOD enough is not good enough"—or vice versa. Cf. "CLOSE enough is close enough."

## Good enough (Sometimes good enough) is not good enough.

1907 Waldo Pondray Warren, *Thoughts on Business* (Chicago: Forbes) 226 (in a list of sagacious sayings): "Good enough is not good enough for the man who would make his mark." 1911 "Metal Sectional Furniture and Loose-Leaf Records," *Bankers Magazine* 83: 371: ". . . [E]very operation is influenced by the Baker-Vawter idea that 'Good Enough' is *not* good enough, but that only the best will be accepted" (italics as shown). The proverb may be regarded as a counter-proverb rebutting "GOOD enough is good enough"—or vice versa. Cf. "ALMOST is not good enough."

## If it hurts, it's doing you good.

See "If it HURTS, it's good for you."

## If you can't be good, be careful.

1902 George Ade, *Forty Modern Fables* (New York: R. H. Russell) 185: "Just one word of parting. Always count your Change, and if you can't be Good, be Careful." 1903 Arthur M. Binsted, *Pitcher in Paradise* (London: Sands) 197–98: "Never be above counting your change; and always bear in mind what the country mother said to her daughter who was coming to town to be apprenticed to the Bond Street millinery: 'For heaven's sake be good; but, if you can't be good, be careful.'" *MP* G137; *DAP* 259(10); *DAAP* 325; *ODP* 136; Pickering et al. (1992) 239; Rees (1995) 239; Pickering (2001) 161; Prahlad (2001) 251–52. The proverb may represent an updating of "If not chastely yet charily."

## If you can't be good, be good at it.

1986 *Daily Collegian [Pennsylvania State University]* 14 Feb. (among "Lovelines"—brief paid Valentine's messages): "Have a fantastic Valentine's! Be good and if you can't be good, be good at it!!" 1995 *Herald Sun [Melbourne, Australia]* 9 Feb.: "I just say to them, take it one game at a time and if you can't be good, be good at it."

## If you can't be good, be lucky.

1935 *Los Angeles Times* 3 Apr.: "The Angels should have won the game . . . , but the Cubs, weighted down by horseshoes and rabbits' feet, staved off a deserved defeat. . . . The moral, if any, seems to be: If you can't be good; be lucky." Cf. "It's better to be LUCKY than good."

## If you want good, your nose must run.

Anderson and Cundall (1910) 23 give the saying as a Jamaican proverb: "You wuk good you nose mus' run" (gloss: "Wuk good = work well. Cf. Nihil sine labore"). Beckwith (1925) 74 gives the form (as a Jamaican proverb) "If you want good, you' nose mus' run" (with the gloss "You must work hard for it."). Prahlad (2001) 251.

## Sometimes the good you do does you no good.

2003 *Law and Order* (television series on NBC) 26 Nov. (the district attorney addresses his subordinates): "Sometimes the good you do won't do you any good." 2005 *Sun-Star [Cebu, Philippines]* 25 Nov.: "There's an old proverb that says: 'Sometimes the good you do doesn't do you any good.'" 2009 *Daily Telegraph [Sydney, Australia]* 27 Jun. (quoting "Dr. Phil" McGraw): "My dad used to say 'sometimes the good you do does you no good.'"

## When you're good, you're good.

1967 *Miami News* 27 Mar.: "Stan [Stanczyk] said several other bowlers compete in both leagues. 'When you're good, you're good all the way through the night.'" 1977 "'Goldfinger' and Dove," *Ebony* 32, no. 6 (Apr.) 88: "But when you're good, you're good, and no one cares what color you are." The proverb may playfully allude to the old nursery rhyme (sometimes attributed to Longfellow) "There was a little girl / Who had a little curl / That hung in the middle of her forehead. / When she was good, / She was very, very good, / But when she was bad, she was horrid." In the proverb, however, *good* means not "well behaved" or "virtuous" but "skillful" or "accomplished." Cf. "When you're HOT, you're hot."

## Good-bye (Every good-bye, Everybody who says good-bye) is not gone.

1929 Kemp Malone, "Negro Proverbs from Maryland," *American Speech* 4: 285 (collected from a "negro washerwoman"): "Every good-bye ain't gone." Whiting (1952) 416 gives the saying as a North Carolina proverb. *DAP* 261.

## New **goods** are better than bargains.

1919 W. R. Hotchkin, *Manual of Successful Storekeeping* (Garden City NY: Doubleday, Page) 51: "Show them [customers] that you have goods that can COMMAND FULL PRICE, and which they must HURRY for before their more lucky and prompt neighbors have bought them all. Show by your own attitude of mind that you have SOMETHING FAR BETTER THAN BARGAINS to sell" (capitalization as shown). 1923 John Wanamaker, *Maxims of Life and Business* (New York: Harper & Brothers) 23 (listed as a "maxim"): "New goods are better than bargains." *DAAP* 327.

## Where does a five hundred–pound (eight hundred–pound, etc.) **gorilla** sit?

1976 *Corporate Rights and Responsibilities: Hearings before the Committee on Commerce . . . Senate* (Washington DC: Government Printing Office) 393; statement by David L. Ratner: "The

reason lies in the relationship between the giant corporations and the states. An eight billion dollar corporation is like an eight hundred pound gorilla: 'Where does an eight hundred pound gorilla sit?' We all know the answer: 'Anywhere it wants.'" *RHDP* 178. The proverb derives from the riddle-joke summarized in the quotation.

## Anyone who **gossips** to (with) you will gossip about you.

1994 Roger Haywood, *Managing Your Reputation* (London: McGraw-Hill) 197: "Keep any off-the-record comments to an absolute minimum. . . . Remember that 'who gossips with you, will gossip about you.'" Earlier occurrences (beginning in the 1960s) most often designate the proverb as Spanish or Arabic.

## **Gossip** is the lifeblood of society (the community, etc.).

1932 Nels Anderson, review of *Small Town Stuff* by Albert Blumenthall (1932), *American Journal of Sociology* 38: 294: "Gossip is the lifeblood of the town[,] which makes every person's tongue a whip to discipline his neighbor. . . ." 1941 David Kent, *Jason Burr's First Case* (New York: Random House) 68: "Gossip is the lifeblood of society—and Armitage's domestic infelicities are about as secret as Prexy Hillier's telephone number." 1945 *Hearings on Science Legislation . . . before a Subcommittee of the Committee on Military Affairs . . . Senate* (Washington DC: Government Printing Office) 298; J. R. Oppenheimer testifies: "The gossip of scientists who get together is the lifeblood of physics, and I think it must be of all other branches of science." 1957 Elsa Maxwell, *How to Do It; or, The Lively Art of Entertaining* (New York: Little, Brown) 199: "Gossip can scarcely be condemned as a party-killer; indeed good clever amusing gossip is the lifeblood of any party." *DAP* 262–63(2). The proverb may respond playfully to older expressions (none of them quite proverbial) like "Credit (Commerce) is the lifeblood of society."

**Gossip** is vice enjoyed vicariously.

1904 Elbert Hubbard, *The Philistine* 19: 104: "Gossip is vice enjoyed vicariously—the sweet, subtle, satisfaction without the risk." *DAP* 263(3).

A **government** big enough to give you everything you want is big enough to take everything you have.

1952 Paul Harvey, *Remember These Things* (Chicago: Heritage Foundation) 57: "Why shouldn't I take their offer of free medicine, money for work I don't do and crops I don't grow? Why not? Here's why not, and don't ever forget this. 'If your government is big enough to give you everything you want, it is big enough to take away from you everything you have.'"

**Grades** (Good grades) aren't everything.

1939 E. G. Williamson, *How to Counsel Students* (New York: McGraw-Hill) 177: "Indeed he [the school counselor] may be in all the more need since he, along with many teachers and administrators, may fail to realize that 'grades are not everything.'" 1945 William Maxwell, *The Folded Leaf* (New York: Harper & Brothers) 248: "So comic, the combination. One all brains and no brawn, the other all brawn and—but grades aren't everything, are they, Mr. Latham?" 1945 Edwin M. Robinson, *Business Organization and Practice* (New York: McGraw-Hill) 10: "'After all, money isn't everything.' That expression is reminiscent of the college sophomore returning home on his Christmas recess and greeting his father with these words, 'After all, Dad, grades aren't everything in college.'"

Little **grains** of powder and little dabs of paint make a girl of forty look like what she ain't.

See "A little POWDER and a little paint makes a woman look like what she ain't."

You can tame a **grapevine**, but you won't take the twist out of it.

Champion (1938) 634 gives the saying as a "Negro" proverb: "You can't take the twist out of the grape vine by cultivating it." Whiting (1952) 417 lists it as a North Carolina proverb: "You can tame a grapevine but that won't take the twist out." 1996 Clarence Major, *Dirty Bird Blues* (San Francisco: Mercury House) 237: "And he suddenly now knew . . . : I wants to live. And he knew this was at the center of the plan always in the back of his mind. May not be able to take the twist out of the grapevine, but you sho can cultivate it."

**Grass**, gas, or ass: Nobody rides for free.

See "GAS, grass, or ass: Nobody rides for free."

The **grass** is (looks) greener on the other side of the fence (road).

1913 *Janesville [WI] Daily Gazette* 25 Jan.: "The breachy cattle evidently think the grass is greener in the next pasture." 1918 Fred R. Jenkins, "Educational Work—A Means to War-time Efficiency," in *Proceedings of the Second War Convention, National Electric Light Association* 41: 347: "When an employee feels that he has been sidetracked, that he would have more opportunities elsewhere, or that the 'grass looks greener on the other side of the fence,' he needs the stimulus represented by a systematic method of training. . . ." 1919 Eleanor Mercein Kelly, *Why Joan?* (New York: Century), 68: "She was . . . [a] rolling stone by nature and profession; and to such, 'the grass is always greener down the road.' New York, Boston, swam before her dreamy vision; even London, Paris. . . ." 1924 Raymond B. Egan, song (music by Richard A Whiting) "The Grass Is Always Greener (in the Other Fellow's Yard)." *MP* G173; *DAP* 265(9); *RHDP* 121; *DAAP* 333; *YBQ* Proverbs (128); *ODP* 140; Nierenberg (1983); White (1987); Flavell and Flavell (1993) 116–17; Folsom (1993); Mieder (1993a); Mieder (1994) 515–42, 543–61; Prahlad

(1994); Chlosta and Grzybek (1995); Rees (1995) 196; Petrova (1996); Prahlad (1996) 229; Scott (1996); Hernadi and Steen (1999); Pickering (2001) 164. Cf. the older "Hills are green far off," "Distant fields are always green (greener)," "The apples on the other side of the wall are the sweetest," and (much older) "Our neighbor's ground always yields better corn than our own."

## If there's **grass** on the field, (you can) play ball.

1998 Clive Barker, *Galilee* (New York: Harper-Collins) 110: ". . . Mitchell's taste for girls ran to the barely pubescent. 'If there's grass on the field, play ball, that's what he used to say,' the 'classmate' remembered." 1998 Chris Simunek, *Paradise Burning* (New York: St. Martin's Griffin) 80: "'You see the way she looks at you? What are you, some kind of faggot?' 'She's fifteen, man.' 'If there's grass on the field you can play ball.'" 1998 Tobias Wolff, "You Can't Kill the Rooster," *Esquire* 129, no. 6 (Jun.) 94: "The work puts him in contact with . . . men who offer dating advice like 'If she's old enough to bleed, she's old enough to breed' and 'If there's grass on the field, I say it's time to play ball.'" *Grass* refers metaphorically to female pubic hair. Doyle (2007a) 199. Cf. "When they are BIG enough, they are old enough" and "Old enough to BLEED, old enough to breed."

## The **graveyard** (cemetery) is full of indispensable people.

1951 Omar N. Bradley, *A Soldier's Story* (New York: Henry Holt) 205: "In the army we often scoff at the myth of the indispensable man, for we have always maintained that Arlington Cemetery is filled with indispensable men." In 1912 Woodrow Wilson had declared, "There is no indispensable man"; *YBQ* Woodrow Wilson (5).

## If **greedy** waits, hot will cool.

1902 James Speirs, *The Proverbs of British Guiana* (Demerara Guyana: Argosy) 22: "If greedy wait,

hot sa ['shall'] cool." 1971 Austin Clarke, *When He Was Free and Young and He Used to Wear Silks* (Toronto: Anansi) 24: "I don't have time to wait. That is old slave talk. Wait, wait, wait. If the greedy wait, hot going cool! If you patient, God going bring you through in the name o' the Lord" (the character, speaking sarcastically, is—like the author—a Barbadian immigrant living in Toronto). 1982 Margot Blackman, *Bajan [i.e., "Barbadian"] Proverbs* (Montreal: Cedar) 7: "If greedy wait, hot will cool."

## **Grief** is the price we pay for love (loving).

1912 Mary Ridpath Mann, *The Unofficial Secretary* (Chicago: A. C. McClurg) 40: "Then we pass out of life, worldly and satisfied or still longing and unsatisfied. . . . Grief is the price we pay for Love." 1972 Colin Murray Parkes, *Bereavement* (New York: International Universities) 5–6: "The pain of grief is just as much a part of life as the joy of love; it is, perhaps, the price we pay for love, the cost of commitment." 1978 James Mathers, review of *The Grief Process* by Yorick Spiegel (1978), *Theology* 81: 462: "Spiegel considers that grief is a disease entity, but his reasoning is not entirely convincing. Grief is the price we pay for loving, and love would be cheapened if grief were less. So it may be thought of as normal and healthy as love itself." Ratcliffe (2006) 300–301.

## In any **group** (flock) of eagles, there will be at least one turkey.

1979 Paul Dickson, "The Official Rules: The Murphy Center Rides Again," *Washingtonian* 15, no. 2 (Nov.) 140: "Allan's Theorem: In any group of eagles, you will find some turkeys" (credited to Allan B. Guerrina). 1980 *Miami News* 25 Sep. (title of an article): "A Gathering of Eagles Is No Place for Turkeys" (the first sentence explains, "'A Gathering of Eagles' is what sponsors call the Nike-Oregon Track Club Marathon"). The word *turkey* in the proverb is (partly) to be understood in its slang sense of "foolish, inept, or socially awkward person." Cf. "It is hard to soar with the EAGLES when you are surrounded by turkeys."

### Grow where you are planted.

See "BLOOM where you are planted."

### If it **grows**, chop it down; if it moves, shoot it.

See "If it MOVES, shoot it; if it doesn't, cut it down."

### To **grow** is to change.

1908 Hugh MacDonald Scott, "The Development of the Seminary," *Chicago Theological Seminary Register* 1, no. 3 (May) 20–21: "The Seminary has from the beginning regarded itself as the servant of the churches. . . . But it has not hesitated to receive new light, adopt new methods, add new courses. . . . It agrees with Newman that 'to grow is to change. . . .'" 1912 Percy MacKaye, *Tomorrow: A Play in Three Acts* (New York: Frederick A. Stokes) 146: "MANA . . . Father Peter, only *you* are the same. All other things have changed. PETER To grow is to change. MANA And to die!" (capitalization and italics as shown). Not infrequently, early instances of the proverb attribute it to John Henry Newman. However, what Newman actually said, in *Essay on the Development of Christian Doctrine* (1845), was, "In the higher world it is otherwise, but here below to live is to change, and to be perfect is to have changed often."

### Don't draw a **gun** unless you're going to use it.

1905 *New York Times* 21 May: "That it [a proposed tariff reform] chills Wall Street is no reason why it should not be done, but is a fair reason why it should have been done without unnecessary bungling. . . . Cowboy etiquette is not to draw a gun unless it is used." Cf. the older aphorism,

common among policemen (and others), "If you (must) shoot, shoot to kill."

### **Guns** don't kill people; people kill people.

1959 *Chicago Daily Tribune* 32 May: "'Our big concern,' says Roff, son of a police chief, 'is to make sure that guns get into the hands of only those who know how to safely use them. Guns don't kill people. People kill people.'" *YBQ* Political Slogans (18).

### It's the unloaded (empty) **gun** that kills people.

1921 Warren Hilleary, "Safety Features of Steam Boiler Accessories," *Safety Engineering* 41 (1921) 152: ". . . [W]ater column stop valves will eventually be closed at a time when they should be open; at least we are led to that conclusion when we remember that it is always the unloaded gun which kills." *DAP* 271(3, 4).

### You can't argue (It's hard to argue, Don't argue) with a **gun**.

See "You can't argue with the BARREL of a gun."

### No **guts**, no glory.

1945 *New York Times* 30 Aug. (quoting Lt. Col. John R. McCray, as he cites the names of airplanes): "We came [to Shanghai] in our own B-17, The Headliner, . . . escorted by a single-engine Mustang fighter, No Guts, No Glory. . . ." 1955 John Maling, "The Stanford Alpine Club," *Appalachia* 30: 400: "The spirit of the old club was represented in the motto, 'No guts, no glory.' The consequences of this spirit had been almost disastrous [*sic*] to the club." *DAP* 271; *YBQ* Modern Proverbs (40); Prahlad (1994); Mieder (2005a). The proverb parallels a series of alliterating Christian commonplaces that were assembled in a single sentence by William Penn: "No pain, no palm; no thorns, no throne; no gall, no glory; no cross, no crown" (*No Cross, No Crown*, 1669). Cf. the older "No pain, no gain."

## Go home with the **guy** who brought you.

See "Go home with the ONE who brought you."

## **Guys** just want to have fun.

See "GIRLS just want to have fun."

## Nice **guys** (always) finish last.

1948 Leo Durocher, "Nice Guys Finish Last," *Cosmopolitan* 124, no. 4 (Apr.) 40. 1948 *Christian Science Monitor* 26 Apr. (in a cartoon, which shows a figure that represents Durocher uttering the statement; over the cartoon appears the heading "Durocher Is Back with the Dodgers"):

"NICE GUYS FINISH LAST!!" (capitalization as shown). The incident that occasioned a remark of Durocher's that would evolve (in Durocher's own phrasing and that of others) into the proverb "Nice guys finish last" occurred 5 Jul. 1946. *RHDP* 243; *YBQ* Durocher (2); Rees (1984) 220; Pickering et al. (1992) 431–32; Rees (1995) 342. The series of events and formulations is discussed (though poorly documented) by Keyes (1992) 142–44.

## Some **guys** got it, and some guys don't.

See "You either HAVE it or you don't."

## You can't blame a **guy** for trying.

See "You can't blame a FELLOW for trying."

## Half a fish is better than none (at all).

1905 Philip Geen, *What I Have Seen while Fishing and How I Have Caught My Fish* (London: T. Fisher Unwin) 172: "We got the photo I give you here after many failures, and, on the principle that half a fish is better than none, I felt as 'sadly thankful' as a friend of mine said he was when a salmon, having taken all his line down Glenlyon Pass, left him the rod and winch." 1919 Jack London, "The Bones of Kahekili," in *Complete Short Stories*, edited by Earle Labor et al., 3 vols. (Stanford CA: Stanford UP, 1993) 3: 2372: "'We cannot send Kahekili on his way with only the tops of the taro.' 'Half a fish is better than none.' Aimoku said the old [Hawai'ian?] saying." *DAAP* 279. The proverb corresponds to the older "Half a loaf is better than none."

## Talk half, leave half.

1962 Carlton Robert Ottley, *Legends: True Stories and Old Sayings from Trinidad and Tobago* (Port-of-Spain, Trinidad: College Press) 23: "*Talk half, lef half.* You should not say everything that comes into your head but leave half of what you know in your head" (italics as shown). Daniel et al. (1987) 504 ("Leave half of what you know in your head"). The proverb has been reported from several parts of the Caribbean and Anglophone Africa.

## Why go out for hamburger (for a hamburger, fast food) when you can get steak at home?

1971 Muriel Davidson, "Joanne Woodward Tells All about Paul Newman," *Good Housekeeping* 168, no. 2 (Feb.) 126: "Newman says, 'I don't like to discuss my marriage, but I will tell you something which may sound corny but which happens to be true. I have steak at home. Why should I go out for hamburger?'" 1979 Anthony Pietropinto and Jacqueline Simenauer, *Husbands and Wives* (New York: Times Books) 386 (a wife is answering a survey): "I do not believe in extramarital sexual activity in any way. If my husband decided to have an affair I would separate from him. Why go out for a hamburger when you have steak at home!" The proverb parallels the older "Why buy the cow when milk is cheap?" Often, in many variants, it is attributed to Newman, explaining his long and faithful marriage to Joanne Woodward. Cf. "Why buy MILK when a cow is so cheap?"

## When all you have is a hammer (When you are good with a hammer, When you are a hammer), everything looks like a nail (needs to be pounded) (To a baby with a hammer, everything is a nail).

1962 Milton J. Horowitz, "Trends in Education," *Journal of Medical Education* 37: 637 (in a brief report—headed "The law of the instrument"—of a banquet speech by Abraham Kaplan): "Because certain methods happen to be handy . . . is no assurance that the method is appropriate for all problems. He cited Kaplan's Law of the Instrument: 'Give a boy a hammer and everything he meets has to be pounded.'" 1963 Silvan S. Tomkins, "Simulation of Personality," in *Computer Simulation of Personality*, edited by Tomkins and Samuel Messick (New York: Wiley) 8: "If one has a hammer one tends to look for nails, and if one has a computer . . . one is more likely to concern oneself with remembering and with problem solving than with loving and hating." 1964 Abraham Kaplan, *The Conduct of Inquiry* (San Francisco: Chandler)

28: "In addition to the social pressures from the scientific community there is also at work a very human trait of individual scientists. I call it *The law of the instrument*, and it may be formulated as follows: Give a small boy a hammer, and he will find that everything he encounters needs pounding" (italics as shown). 1966 Abraham Maslow, *The Psychology of Science* (New York: Harper & Row) 15–16: "I suppose it is tempting, if the only tool you have is a hammer, to treat everything as if it were a nail." 1991 Richard A. Brealey and Stewart C. Myers, *Principles of Corporate Finance*, 4th ed. (New York: McGraw-Hill) 256: "Why is an MBA student who has learned about DCF like a baby with a hammer?" *YBQ* Maslow; *ODP* 145–46. Besides the "Law of the Instrument" or "Kaplan's Law of the Instrument," the concept embodied in the proverb is sometimes called the "Golden Hammer," the "Law of the Hammer," or the "Law of the Tool."

## Busy **hands** are happy hands.

1956 Harold W. Kennedy, "The Philosophy of Recreation," *Recreation* 49: 53: ". . . [L]et us not be stifled by the negative approach. This approach is characterized by the same sort of 'busy hands are happy hands' or 'man's idle mind is the devil's workshop' philosophy." 1962 Robert Lee, "Religion and Leisure in American Culture," *Theology Today* 19: 44: ". . . [T]here is considerable agitation for legislation which would allow young people to start work earlier, based on the supposition that idle hands lead to temptation. As the children's song goes, 'Busy hands are happy hands; hands that cannot go wrong.'" *DAP* 275(9).

## Cold **hands**, warm heart (Warm hands, cold heart); dirty feet, no sweetheart.

1927 Hilda Roberts, "Louisiana Superstitions," *Journal of American Folklore* 40: 167 (printed as verse): "Cold hands, warm heart, / Dirty feet, and no sweetheart." 1949 Henry Hornsby, *Lonesome Valley* (New York: William Sloane) 151: "'Your

hands feel cold,' he said. 'Did you even hear the saying about cold hands?' She laughed, and Johnny thought she squeezed his hand. 'Warm hand, cold heart; dirty feet, no sweetheart,' she said." *DAP* 274(3). The proverb represents a practical extension of the old superstition "Cold hands, warm heart."

## Give a **hand** up, not a handout.

1938 *Washington Post* 16 Oct.: "'Give a Hand Up—Not a Handout' is the slogan adopted for the 1938 [Washington DC] Community Chest appeal." 1962 *New York Times* 23 Mar. (title of an editorial in defense of New York City's welfare system): "A Hand Up, Not a Handout."

## The **hand** will not reach for what the heart does not long for.

Champion (1938) 81 lists the saying as a Welsh proverb (along with a probable variant, "The hand reaches not what the heart does not wish to give"). Ratcliffe (2006) 3. Perhaps the proverb originated as an anti-proverb responding to the older "What the eye does not see the heart does not long for" (or, in a rhyming variant, "What the eye does not admire the heart does not desire").

## Shit (Pee, Spit) in one **hand** and hope (wish) in the other; see which one fills up first.

1971 Helen McAvity, *Everybody Has to Be Somebody* (New York: Dramatists Play Service) 26: "Huh! Hope in one hand and pee in the other and see which one gets filled the fastest." 1973 Carol Hill, *Subsistence USA* (New York: Holt, Rinehart & Winston) 164 (the text attempts to represent the speech of a young African American man in New Jersey): "My grandmother tole me when I was a boy, like as knocked ma shoes off, she said, 'You can plan an plan an wish an wish, but shit in one hand an plan an wish in the other an see what you feel [for "fill"?] first.'" 1986 Jonathon Green, *Slang Thesaurus* (London: Elm Tree) 83 (under the subject heading "Displeasure" and the subheading "Sullenness, Depression"): "US black—'shit in one hand, wish in another, see which fills up first.'" The *shit* version of the proverb is obviously primary—in that peeing or spitting would fill a hand not much more effectively than hoping or wishing.

## Two (Both) **hands** for beginners.

1910 *Trenton [NJ] Evening Times* 12 Jul.: "Keating had one hand in a sling Saturday—at least that's the way it looked to the crowd. Always two hands for beginners." The baseball proverb—advice on catching or fielding a ball—has been widely applied to other activities as well, such as firing a gun, climbing a ladder, driving a car, or riding a horse: 1962 Stephen Longstreet, *The Flesh Peddlers* (New York: Simon & Schuster) 282: "Vanessa was ebullient, and rude about my riding. 'Two hands for beginners.'"

## You play the **hand** (the cards) you are dealt.

1953 Polly Adler, *A House Is Not a Home* (New York: Rinehart) 316: "'Seems to me,' said Vicki slowly, 'it's a waste o' breath bellyachin' about the cards being stacked. You still got to play the hand that's dealt you. And the way I look at it, *somebody's* got to be a madam'" (italics as shown). 1953 Richard C. Hertz, *Our Religion above All* (Detroit: Temple Beth El) 58: "You play the game of life with the hand you are dealt." 1975 Al Reinert, "Loser Take All," *Texas Monthly* 3, no. 12 (Dec.) 26: "'I think you have to play the cards you've been dealt,' said [Senator Lloyd] Bentsen. 'I'm just trying to be realistic.'" Cf. "LIFE deals us each a hand."

## A **handicap** is what you make it.

1946 Alanson H. Edgerton, *Readjustment or Revolution?* (New York: McGraw-Hill) 140: "A handicap is what you make it, a challenge or an insurmountable hurdle." 1959 *Beaver County [PA] Times* 27 Feb.: "In his talk, entitled 'Your Handicap Is What You Make It,' he [Harold Wilke] told of the ways in which a handicapped person wants to be responded to as an individual."

## Putting a **handle** on the gourd does not make it a dipper.

1943 Bernice Kelly Harris, *Sweet Beulah Land* (Garden City NY: Doubleday, Doran) 20: "'You ought to call him "Mister," Mammy.' . . . Miss Partheny looked at the girl sharply. 'Cush! Puttin' a handle on a gourd don't make it no dipper.'" *DAP* 277.

## Anything can **happen** and probably will (usually does).

1926 Floyd Dell, *An Old Man's Folly* (New York: George H. Doran) 217: ". . . [O]ur world isn't fixed and changeless and eternal, after all. Anything can happen—and probably will!" 1928 *Decatur [IL] Herald* 22 Aug.: "Anything can happen, and usually does, as we reflected sadly again yesterday upon observing another gravel truck driver go right past a boulevard stop sign without being either arrested or hit." Pickering et al. (1992) 20. The proverb probably originated as an anti-proverb based on the older expression "Anything can happen."

## **Happiness** is a journey, not a destination.

1937 Fay H. Arnold, *A Woman's Approach to Business* (Los Angeles: Arnold Sales Training Institute) 97: "The business woman who develops her personality . . . will find herself blessed with some measure of success—some degree of happiness. 'Happiness is a journey, not a destination.'" Cf. "SUCCESS is a journey, not a destination" and "The JOY is in the journey."

## **Happiness** is where you find it.

1937 "Twenty-five Years in Bed," *Health Bulletin* (State Board of Health, North Carolina) 52, no. 9 (Sep.) 7: "Like gold, happiness is where you find it, and you can find it in bed if you look for it industriously enough." 1941 *New York Times* 13 Apr. (in a classified ad for housing): "Happiness is where you find it but there is joy in a home of your own." 1941 *Atlanta Constitution* 15 May: "Happiness is where you find it—or where you seek it—or something to that effect. . . ." *DAP* 280(28). As the first quotation may suggest, the proverb possibly derives from "Gold is where you find it." Cf. "LOVE is where you find it."

## No **harm**, no foul.

1956 *Hartford Courant* 2 Dec.: "The conference coaches also agreed that Big Ten officials this winter should emphasize a principle of 'no harm, no foul.'" 1972 Dave Wolf, *Foul! The Connie Hawkins Story* (New York: Holt, Rinehart & Winston) 304: "The league's [National Basketball Association's] philosophy is 'No harm, no foul.' . . . The players call it 'No blood, no foul.'" The maxim from basketball refereeing is applied proverbially to other matters: 1966 *Los Angeles Times* 1 Jan.: "Strolling through the quiet Valley bargain counters [featuring after-Christmas sales], I kept thinking of Chick Hearn's famous line of 'No harm, no foul.' And there we'd be with a broken bone sticking out of one elbow and a hand ripped off at the wrist." 1975 Brown Meggs, *The Matter of Paradise* (New York: Random House) 39: "So they quietly divorced: no harm, no foul. Mainly, no children." The expression was coming to be used as a sort of legal maxim as early as 1972: "José O. Lizama v. Bank of America," *Reports [of legal opinions] of the Trust Territory of the Pacific Islands* 6: 56: "The delay in furnishing the bank with the second year policy . . . , in view of the fact that there was no loss on the policy, may be compared to the call in professional basketball—'no harm, no foul'—for a rule infraction not affecting the game." The saying (as in the 1966 quotation) is sometimes attributed to the California sportscaster Chick Hearn. The 1972 quotation from Dave Wolf implies that "No blood, no foul" represents a jocular variant of "No harm, no foul." However, some persons recall the expression "No blood, no foul" from rough-and-tumble playgrounds of the 1950s (the record in print is meager); possibly, then, "No blood, no foul" is the older form, and "No harm, no foul" is something like a euphemistic adaptation.

## The bigger the **hat** (The wider the brim), the smaller the property (holding, ranch, herd).

1922 William MacLeod Raine, *The Fighting Edge* (New York: Grosset & Dunlap) 135 (chapter title): "The Bigger the Hat the Smaller the Herd." Later in the chapter: ". . . [H]e knew instinctively that real riders would resent any attempt on his part to swagger as they did. A remark dropped by Blister came to mind. 'The b-bigger the hat the smaller the herd, son. Do all yore b-bragging with yore actions.'" 1962 Dymphna Cusack, *Picnic Races* (London: Heinemann) 189: "'I can understand why you chappies wear wide brims with a sun like this.' Harry grunted: 'There's a rule for it: "The smaller the property the wider the brim."'" 1966 Randolph Stow, *The Merry Go Round in the Sea* (New York: William Morrow) 206: "'I dunno,' Hugh said, 'you bloody squatters and your delusions of grandeur. . . . Just so you can wear a big hat.' 'It works the other way,' the boy said. 'They say: The bigger the hat, the smaller the property.'" Many occurrences of the proverb are Australian. Cf. "Big HAT, no cattle."

## Big (All) **hat**, no cattle.

1944 "The Editor's Page," *Agricultural Leaders' Digest* 25, no. 3 (Mar.) 15 (filler item): "An Indian's definition of a tenderfoot on a dude ranch—'Big hat, no cattle'" (credited to "*Adv. Age*"). 1954 "Bank Accounts," *Coronet* 36, no. 6, 10: "The banker asked a neighboring Indian if he regarded the rancher as a good credit risk. The Indian pondered the question a moment, then grunted: 'Big hat, no cattle'" (credited to *Indianapolis Times*). Cf. "The bigger the HAT, the smaller the property."

## You are (become) what you **hate**.

1905 Benjamin De Casseres, "The Great Wonder," *Mind* 15: 60: "Hate is comic, for you shall in time become that which you hate; and the thing you scorn—behold! that thou art." 1958 Victor M. Victoroff, "The Assumptions We Live By," *Etc.* 16: 26: "Seeking a way to prevent oneself from performing an act which would be disapproved and punished, security is found by seeking those evils in others, then vindictively punishing them for one's own contemplated crime. There is a saying 'We become what we hate.' Often the quotation should be, 'We *are* what we hated'" (italics as shown). 1979 Virgil Parsons and Nancy Sanford, *Interpersonal Interaction in Nursing* (Menlo Park CA: Addison-Wesley) 36: ". . . [T]here is a saying, 'You are what you hate.' This means simply that we often feel negatively about someone or something because an unacceptable or undesirable piece of ourselves is reflected." The proverb possibly originated as an anti-proverb patterned after "You are what you eat." It epitomizes the psychology of "projection."

## You either **have** (got) it or you don't (Some have it and some don't).

1921 Joseph Ralph, *Character and Vocational Analysis* (Los Angeles: Pacific Institute of Vocational Analysis) 233: "Financial ability and trading capacity is [*sic*] not a matter of intellect. It is a developed sense. You either have it or you don't." 1921 Mae Marsh, *Screen Acting* (New York: Frederick A. Stokes) 87: "I have never heard anyone give a very good definition of 'screen personality.' The most that can be said is that some seem to have it and some don't." 1923 Raymond Blathwayt, *The Tapestry of Life* (New York: E. P. Dutton) 373: "But the money-making faculty is a distinct faculty. . . . It is not, or only very rarely, an acquired talent. You either have it or you don't, like a talent for music, or for painting, or for sport." The phrasing can be used in other ways (in reference to a disease or to

divine election, for instance), but the proverb (or the *it* in the proverb) refers to some innate talent or hard-to-define ability or attribute. *DAP* 271(2).

## A hard **head** makes a soft (sore) behind (back, butt, ass, tail).

1905 Monroe N. Work, "Some Geechee Folk Lore," *Southern Workman* 34: 633: "A hard head makes a soft back. This is equivalent to, If a child will not be admonished, he will be beaten." *MP* H123; Daniel et al. (1987) 503; Prahlad (1996) 230–32.

## Keep your **head** down and your feet moving.

1990 *Washington Times* 6 Feb.: "Motto 'Keep your head down and your feet moving'" (attributed to "Coach Jack Taylor, circa 1962"). 1992 *Washington Post* 15 Feb.: "[Dan] Jansen earned that respect by his diligent effort to right his own misfortune. For four years he's kept his head down, his feet moving and his mind focused." Probably originating as advice to a running back in (American) football, the proverb counsels humble or inconspicuous perseverance.

## Use your **head** for something besides a hat rack.

1910 *Syracuse Post-Standard* 19 Dec. "Use your head for something else than a hatrack." 1918 *Lockport [NY] Leader* 2, no. 10 (Jan.) 2 (filler item): "If you would get ahead and keep ahead, use your head. Anyway, use it for more than a hat rack." *DAP* 288(43).

## What drops off the **head** falls on the shoulders.

Speirs (1902) 35 lists the saying as a Guyanan proverb: "Wha' fall from head go a-shouldah." Franck (1921) 106 lists it as a Jamaican proverb: "What drop off a head go down 'pon shoulder." So does Beckwith (1925) 113: "What fall off a head mus' drop 'pon shoulder. . . . i.e. what you do not give to the man you give to his children." Prahlad (2001) 253.

## What you haven't got in your **head**, you have in your feet (What you lack in your head you make up in your heels).

1933 J. Mason Brewer, "Old-Time Negro Proverbs," *Publications of the Texas Folklore Society* 11: 103: "*Whut yuh don' hab in yo' haid yuh got ter hab in yo' feet.* 'Dat me'ns lak dis,' said Uncle George McKay. 'Lak ef yuh goes to de sto' fer some grub an' yuh fergits ter git it all, den yo' feet hab ter take yuh back anudder time fer whut yuh didn' git de fus' trip'" (italics as shown). *DAP* 288(47); Whiting (1952) 421. Versions of the international proverb are less common in English than in other European languages.

## It takes a **heap** of living (loving) in a house to make a (it) home.

See "It takes a LOT of living to make a house a home."

## The **heart** has a mind of its own.

1960 The saying probably entered oral tradition as a proverb from a song by Howard Greenfield and Jack Keller (popularized by Connie Francis). However, the conceit was anticipated in 1948 in Betsey Barton's novel *The Long Walk* (New York: Duell, Sloan & Pearce) 48: "His attraction to Candy seemed to him at the moment to be heavier and stronger than the hospital walls. No one can help me, I guess, he thought as he hurried his stride. My heart has a mind of its own." Cf. Blaise Pascal's aphorism "The heart has its reasons which reason knows nothing of" ("Le coeur a ses raisons, que la raison ne connaît point").

## You can't measure **heart**.

1967 *Lawrence [KS] Daily Journal-World* 17 Aug.: "'We may be the Puny Cats instead of the Chesly

Lions,' [the football coach Al] Woolard said in jest. 'Fortunately, you can't measure heart and enthusiasm by pounds and inches.'" 1976 *Daily Item [Sumter SC]* 26 May: "'The potential is there,' he [the football coach Bobby Ross] continued, 'but you can't measure heart.'"

## If you can't stand (don't like) the **heat**, get out of the kitchen.

1931 *Independence [MO] Examiner* 1 Jan. (quoting Jackson County judge E. I. "Buck" Purcell): "But if a man can't stand the heat, he ought to stay out of the kitchen." 1942 *Charleston [WV] Gazette* 12 Jul.: "Favorite rejoinder of Senator Harry S. Truman, when a member of his war contracts investigating committee objects to his strenuous pace. 'If you don't like the heat, get out of the kitchen.'" *RHDP* 157–58; *YBQ* Harry Vaughan; Rees (1984) 70; *ODP* 152; Pickering et al. (1992) 265; Bertram and Spears (1993) 117; Flavell and Flavell (1993) 148; Rees (1995) 239; Mieder and Bryan (1997) 60, 147; Pickering (2001) 332. The saying was made famous by President Truman, but he acknowledged having heard it from "an old friend and colleague on the Jackson County Court"—presumably Judge Purcell.

## Everybody wants to go to **heaven**, but nobody wants to die.

1950 The proverb originated with—or gained popularity from—the title of Tommy Dorsey's song "Everybody Wants to Go to Heaven (but No One Wants to Die)." Dundes and Pagter (1991) 68.

## **Heaven** (God) protects (will protect) the working girl.

1909 The saying probably entered oral tradition as a proverb from a song by Edgar Smith and A. Baldwin Stone, "Heaven Will Protect the Working Girl," sung by Marie Dressler in the show *Tillie's Nightmare* (1910). *DAAP* 375; *YBQ* Edgar Smith.

## In **heaven** an angel is nobody in particular (nobody special).

1904 The saying passed into oral tradition as a proverb from George Bernard Shaw's *Man and Superman* (the appended "Maxims for Revolutionists"). 1936 Carl Sandburg, *The People, Yes* (New York: Harcourt, Brace) 165 (in a poetic montage of proverbs and other sayings): "In heaven an angel is nobody in particular." *DAAP* 21.

## Never take more on your **heels** than you can kick off with your toes.

1925 "Folklore from St. Helena, South Carolina," *Journal of American Folklore* 38: 228 (in a list of proverbs collected at a coastal school): "Take no more on your heels than you can kick off with your toes." A possible variant is listed as a Jamaican proverb by Anderson and Cundall (1927) 67: "Heel nebber go before toe" (gloss: "Important matters must be dealt with first"). *DAP* 296(2). Usually the proverb appears to mean "Don't claim more than rightfully belongs to you" or "Don't profess more than you can deliver."

## It's **hell** being (to be) poor.

1904 *Washington Post* 29 Jan.: "'Checkers' is the first play to run up against the censor. . . . [H]e spied a half sheet with this line, spoken by Checkers in the second act, and which is welcomed nightly by applause and cheers which come from the heart: 'Gee, ain't it hell to be poor?'" The play *Checkers*, by Henry Martyn Blossom, written in 1904 and never published, was based on the popular novel by Blossom, *Checkers: A Hard-Luck Story* (1896), in which the saying does not appear. 1907 *Freight Shippers' Forum* 7: 123 (a filler item): "John D. Rockefeller's soliloquy: 'Ain't it hell to be poor.'" *DAP* 474(16); *DAAP* 378.

## Always drink upstream from the **herd** (Don't drink downstream from the herd).

1983 *San Diego Union-Tribune* 11 Dec.: "A terrific trio called Riders in the Sky gave some sage advice to Yankee boss George Steinbrenner: 'Remember, always drink upstream from the heard.'" Eventually the cowboy singing group Riders in the Sky issued a CD titled *Always Drink Upstream from the Herd* (1995).

## **Heroes** are made, not born.

1905 Ármin Vámbéry, *The Story of My Struggles* (London: T. Fisher Unwin) 167: "But I still hold to my opinion, that heroes are not born but made, and that the most timid home-lover can by a gradual process of compulsory self-defense become a very lion of strength and valour." *DAP* 299. Vámbéry was a Hungarian-born Jew who published mostly in German, but his autobiography was (evidently) written in English. Cf. the much older "Poets are born, not made."

## **Heroes** often (sometimes) fail (Even heroes fail).

1922 Ierne L. Plunket, *Europe in the Middle Ages* (Oxford: Clarendon) 264: "This kingly achievement was denied him [The Cid], for even heroes fail." 1970 Gordon Lightfoot, "If You Could Read My Mind" (song): ". . . The hero would be me. / But heroes often fail." 1998 James M. Prichard, review of *Theodore O'Hara: Poet Soldier of the Old South* by Nathaniel Hughes Jr. and Thomas Ware (1998), *Register of the Kentucky Historical Society* 96: 389: "Heroes sometimes fail. However, Hughes and Ware capture the nobility of this demon-haunted knight-errant. . . ."

## Everybody has something to **hide**.

1900 Marie Corelli, *The Master-Christian* (London: Methuen) 559: "'Oh, you are happy—happy!' he exclaimed. '. . . Then indeed you

should not be here—for we all have something
to hide, and we are afraid even of the light. . . .'"
1902 Henry van Dyke, "Spy Rock," *Scribner's
Magazine* 32: 476: "Do you remember
Hawthorne's story of 'The Minister's Black Veil'?
It is the best comment on human life that ever
was written. Everyone has something to hide."
*DAAP* 248.

## Hindsight is (always) twenty-twenty.

1949 *Van Nuys [CA] News* 17 Feb. (a witticism,
printed as a filler, attributed to Richard Armour):
"Most people's hindsight is 20–20." *DAAP* 386;
*YBQ* Billy Wilder (2). Cf. the older "Hindsight
is better than foresight" and "Foresight is better
than hindsight" (in the first proverb, "better than"
means "clearer than"; in the second, it means
"preferable to"). Also, cf. the older, playfully
versified "If our foresight were as good as our
hindsight, we'd be better off by a damn sight."

## Last **hired**, first fired.

1918 Charles A. King, "Vocational Guidance:
Part III," *Educational Administration &
Supervision* 4: 482: ". . . [T]he subject will
probably give evidence of subnormality or
feeblemindedness. . . . At any rate, it is probable
that no amount of training will make an
acceptable workman of him. He will in many
cases become a member of the unemployed,
so unskilled as to be 'last hired, first fired.' . . ."
Person (1958) 181; Dundes (1975) 970; Prahlad
(1996) 232; Winick (2003); Prahlad (2006)
1022–27. Cf. "LAST in, first out."

## History (The past) does not repeat itself, but it (often) rhymes.

1970 *New York Times* 25 Jan.: "W. D. M. is
seeking to locate the source of the following
line, attributed to Mark Twain: 'History never
repeats itself, but it rhymes.'" 1970 John
Robert Colombo, "A Said Poem," in *Neo Poems*
(Vancouver: Sono Nis) 46 (the poem consists of
attributed aphorisms): "'History never repeats

itself but it rhymes,' said Mark Twain." 1971
James Eayrs, *Diplomacy and Its Discontents*
(Toronto: U of Toronto P) 121: "The trouble with
history is that while historians repeat each other,
history never repeats itself. Not, at any rate,
exactly. (When Mark Twain declared 'History
does not repeat itself, but it rhymes,' he went
about as far as he could go.)" 1973 David Pratt,
"The Functions of Teaching History," *The History
Teacher* 7: 419: "The relationship between the
continuities and the discontinuities of history
have rarely been better expressed than in Mark
Twain's epigram, 'The past does not repeat itself,
but it rhymes.'" The proverb probably originated
as an anti-proverb, based on "History repeats
itself"—perhaps with the spurious attribution to
Mark Twain already attached.

## History is bunk.

1916 *Chicago Tribune* 25 May (quoting Henry
Ford): "'Say, what do I care about Napoleon?'
he rambled on. 'What do we care what they did
500 or 1,000 years ago? . . . History is more or
less bunk. It's tradition. We don't want tradition.
We want to live in the present.'" 1919 Andrew
F. West, "Our Use of English," *American Review
of Reviews* 60: 393: "Those who think history is
'bunk' should read it and discover that one of
the surest means of weakening a race or nation
is to deprive it of the free use of its language."
*RHDP* 133; *DAAP* 386; *YBQ* Henry Ford (2);
Rees (1984) 21; Pickering et al. (1992) 274. The
saying entered oral tradition as a proverb from a
misquotation of the statement by Ford.

## History is fiction with the truth left out.

Kin (1955) 120 lists the saying as an American
proverb. 1971 B. F. Jones, review of *The Trial
Record of Denmark Vesey* by John Oliver Killens
(1970) and *Denmark Vesey: The Slave Conspiracy
of 1822*, edited by Robert Starobin (1970), *North
Carolina Historical Review* 48: 203: "Starobin's
statement . . . is a curious one coming from a
historian ostensibly engaged in investigating
*a slave plot* and not the attitudes of the ghetto

population. One is reminded of the old saw: 'History is fiction with the truth left out'" (italics as shown). *DAP* 301(2).

## History is written (penned) by the victors (winners, survivors).

1903 Clement A. Evans, "Introduction," *History of the Doles-Cook Brigade, Army of Northern Virginia, C.S.A.*, by Henry W. Thomas (Atlanta: Franklin) ix: "It is an old saying, that the victor writes the history of a struggle. . . . Lands overrun by conquerors have been blighted, their resistance defamed and their heroes maligned in story. . . ." 1904 W. J. Murray, *History of the Twentieth Tennessee Regiment* (Nashville: privately printed) 10: "The victors write the history of the vanquished and control public sentiment whether it be true or false. . . ." 1916 William Elliot Griffis, *Bonnie Scotland and What We Owe Her* (Boston: Houghton Mifflin) 61: "The accepted history of almost all wars is that written by the victors. The beaten foe is always in the wrong." 1919 Alfred von Tirpitz, *My Memoirs* (New York: Dodd, Mead) 1:254: "If ever this idea were to establish itself in German minds, it could be taken as proof of the saying that history is written by the victors. . . ." (The famous admiral and politician published his *Erinnerungen* in German the same year; the English edition does not carry any notation that identifies it as a translation. In German, the proverb appears as "Der Sieger schreibt die Geschichte.") 1931 James H. S. Bossard, "The Concept of Progress," *Social Forces* 10: 14: "Since history is written by the survivors, it is easy to understand the universal belief in progress." *YBQ* Modern Proverbs (43).

## Hit it and quit it.

1991 *Washington Post* 8 May: "One of the set's hottest pieces is 'Get It Together' (1967) on Disc 2, . . . with [James] Brown the taskmaster putting his horn section through an airtight 'hit it and quit it' drill." 1996 Darrell Dawsey, *Living to Tell about It: Young Black Men in America*

*Speak Their Piece* (New York: Doubleday) 140: "I've heard him ridicule mercilessly any of our friends who've dared suggest they might be in love. . . . Paul's is the 'jizz and whiz, hit it and quit it' school of romance." In one of its several applications, the proverb advises (from a crudely male perspective) that sexual relationships be kept carnal and brief. Cf. "FUCK them and forget them" and the older "Love them and leave them."

## You can't get a hit if you don't swing.

See "You can't hit the BALL if you don't swing."

## Every hoe (in the shop) has a stick in the bush.

Beckwith (1925) 46 gives the saying as a Jamaican proverb: "Every hoe da shop, him 'tick da bush" (gloss: "Every hoe in the shop has a stick [for a handle] in the bush; i.e. every man has his mate"). Anderson and Cundall (1927) 67; Prahlad (2001) 255.

## It's easier to dig a hole than to build a pole.

1993 Melissa Hendricks, "Is It a Boy or a Girl?" *Johns Hopkins Magazine* (Nov.) 15: "Doctors who work with children with ambiguous genitalia sometimes put it this way: 'You can make a hole but you can't build a pole.'" 1995 Anne Fausto-Sterling, "How to Build a Man," in *Constructing Masculinity*, edited by Maurice Berger et al. (New York: Routledge) 131: "When surgeons turn 'Sammy' into 'Samantha,' they also build her a vagina. . . . As one surgeon recently commented, 'It's easier to poke a hole than build a pole.'"

## When you are in a hole, stop digging.

1911 *Washington Post* 25 Oct.: "Nor would a wise man, seeing that he was in a hole, go to work and blindly dig it deeper, as [William Jennings] Bryan did when he shifted ground and assailed the integrity of the President and the Judges." 1977 *Wall Street Journal* 16 Sep.: "A senior official concerned about the [Bert] Lance affair suggests the administration [of President Jimmy Carter] needs to learn 'the rule of holes': When you're in a hole, you don't keep digging." 1981 *Washington Post* 16 Nov.: "At Rochester and in junior hockey (at Saskatoon), we had some tough times. But when you're in a hole, don't dig it deeper." 1984 *New York Times* 17 Feb.: "The [Reagan] administration will do well to remember an old maxim: If you find yourself in a hole, for heaven's sake, stop digging." 1984 *New York Times* 11 Sep.: "There is a Law of Holes that says, when you are in one, stop digging. That is a law Congress finds it almost impossible to observe." *ODP* 155; Doyle (2001a) 462–63. In British publications, the "Law of Holes" is often referred to as "Healey's Law," after the statesman Denis Healey, a popularizer of the expression in the later 1980s.

## Always go **home** while you're still having fun.

See "Always leave the PARTY while you're still having fun."

## Go big (large) or go **home**.

See "GO big or go home."

## Go **home** with the one (man) who brought you.

See "Go home with the ONE who brought you."

## Go strong or go **home**.

See "GO strong or don't go at all."

## **Home** is where the mortgage is.

1904 Charles Wayland Towne (pseudonym "Gideon Wurdz"), *A Foolish Dictionary* (Boston: John W. Luce) [fol. 311] (unpaginated; filler item): "Home is where the mortgage is." *DAP* 304(15); Litovkina and Mieder (2006) 169. The proverb originated as an anti-proverb based on the old expression "Home is where the heart is."

## Keep the **home** fires burning.

See "Keep the home FIRES burning."

## You can't go **home** again.

1940 The saying probably entered oral tradition as a proverb from the title of Thomas Wolfe's novel, published posthumously (Wolfe died in 1938). *RHDP* 382.

## You can't hit a **home run** every time.

1959 *Windsor [Ontario] Daily Star* 13 Aug. (quoting the minister of labor for Saskatchewan, C. C. Williams): "When our party first came to power, we directly entered the industrial field. . . . Some of those ventures were not too successful, but you can't hit a homerun every time." 1971 *Wall Street Journal* 1 Oct. (quoting Ford Motor Company president Philip Caldwell): "You can't hit a home run every time at bat. Sometimes you have to strike out." 1981 Robert DuPont, "Coping with Controversial Research," in *Communicating University Research*, edited by Patricia L. Alberger and Virginia Carter (Washington DC: CASE) 91: "If the reporter's story displeases the researcher, then I think I would put a little salve on the wounds, sort of like my friend who took me aside and said you win a few and you lose a few. . . . If you have to hit a home run every time you step up to the plate, you are not going to play baseball." Cf. "Nobody BATS a thousand."

## *Honesty* is (such) a lonely word.

1979 The saying probably entered oral tradition as a proverb from a line in Billy Joel's song "Honesty": "Honesty is such a lonely word."

## When you hear **hoofbeats**, think horses, not zebras (When you hear hoofbeats, don't look for zebras).

1969 John A. Koepke, *Guide to Clinical Laboratory Diagnosis* (New York: Appleton-Century-Crofts) 79: "These three causes [of edema] should always be prime considerations, and after they have been ruled out, other less common causes may be considered. As one 'philosopher' put it: 'When you hear hoofbeats, think of horses, not zebras.'" Dundes et al. (1999). The proverb is a figurative statement of the so-called principle of parsimony, a corollary of "Occam's razor."

## Keep your **hook** baited.

Whiting (1952) 426 lists the saying as a North Carolina proverb. 1989 *Sacramento Bee* 5 Nov.: "The important thing, of course, is to keep your hook baited with a little conviction. Basketball teams are notoriously impatient." Cf. the older proverbs "The hook without bait catches no fish" and "Keep your gun loaded."

## **Hope** floats.

1995 *Daily Variety* 28 Jul.: "Twentieth Century Fox acquired scribe Steven Rogers' spec script 'Hope floats' for Fox-based Lynda Obst to produce." The motion picture appeared in 1998. In the dialog, it is implied that the saying is proverbial, but no earlier record of it—in that form and usage—can be found. It probably entered oral tradition from its use in the movie.

## **Hope** is dangerous (a dangerous thing).

1941 George Derwent Thomason, *Aeschylus and Athens* (London: Lawrence & Wishart) 164 (summarizing the tenets of "Orphism"): "Hope is dangerous, love is dangerous, it is dangerous to strive overmuch, dangerous to emulate the gods. . . ." 1988 Allan Mayer, *Gaston's War* (Novato CA: Presidio) 158 (a fictionalized diary of a Belgian resistance fighter): "It's a year since I was arrested. . . . Hope is a dangerous thing. It can sustain you, but it also can drive you mad." 1989 *Washington Post* 9 Jun.: "The prospects of accord are remote. Hope is a dangerous will-o'-the-wisp." 1994 *The Shawshank Redemption* (motion picture): The character Red (portrayed by Morgan Freeman), says, "Hope is a dangerous thing. Hope can drive a man insane."

## **Hope** is for sissies.

2001 *Times [London]* 23 Mar.: ". . . [T]he Manics remain able to get pointlessly, amusingly irate about things no one else cares about, otherwise, nihilism is everywhere . . . , and love and hope is [sic] for sissies." 2009 *Globe and Mail [Canada]* 19 Jan.: "House [the television show] is all about hope, even though the publicity shots for the new season feature the entire cast in softball-team jerseys with the words, 'Hope is for sissies' emblazoned on front."

## **Hope** is for suckers.

1994 *Los Angeles Times* 8 Jun.: "Fear will be the operative emotion in this [California gubernatorial] race. Hope is for suckers." 2000 *Santa Rosa [CA] Press Democrat* 18 Sep.: "'Hope is for suckers, baby.' That's been the Raiders' six-year plan. . . ."

## **Hope** (A hope) is not a plan (strategy).

1948 *Military Functions, National Military Establishment Appropriation Bill for 1949: Hearings before the Subcommittee of the Committee on Appropriations, House of Representatives* (Washington DC: Government Printing Office) III: "Mr. [Francis] CASE. Do you expect to have some ammunition left over? Colonel [T. F.] WESSELS. That is a hope; not a plan, sir." 1956 *New York Times* 13 May: "But a hope is not a plan, and the Southerners need both a plan and a candidate. So far they have neither." 1996 Kim Campbell, *Time and Chance* (Toronto: Doubleday) 393: "We flew to Winnipeg that afternoon [22 Oct. 1993] . . . where Premier Gary Filmon made a wonderful speech of introduction. Among his best lines: 'Hope is not a strategy.'"

## Always ride the (your) **horse** in the direction it's going (it wants to go).

1975 *Amarillo [TX] Globe-Times* 10 Mar.: "Ride a horse in the direction he is going." 1979 Althea J. Horner, *Object Relations and the Developing Ego in Therapy* (New York: Jason Aronson) ix:

"It has been a pleasure to work with my editor, Joan Langs, and with Jason Aronson, who wisely recommended, 'Ride the horse in the direction he wants to go.'" 1992 Frank J. Haluch et al., "Negotiating," in *Purchasing Handbook*, 5th ed., edited by Harold E Fearon et al. (New York: McGraw-Hill) 242: "As President Reagan said on many occasions, it is easier to ride a horse in the direction that the horse wants to go."

## If you can't ride two **horses** at once, you shouldn't be in the circus.

1935 Gilbert McAllister, *James Maxton: The Portrait of a Rebel* (London: John Murray) 232: "He had been told [in 1930] that he could not ride two horses. 'My reply to that is,' he said, . . . 'that if my friend cannot ride two horses—what's he doing in the bloody circus?'" *ODP* 268; Rees (1984) 227. The proverb may derive from "No one can ride two horses except in a circus," itself an anti-proverb based on "You can't ride two horses at once."

## There are more **horses**' asses than horses (in the world).

1957 Ed Lacy, *Room to Swing* (New York: Harper & Brothers) 5: "As somebody once said, there are more horses' asses than horses in the world, and at the moment I felt like the number-one rear." The proverb is sometimes referred to as the "equine paradox" and abbreviated "eqn prdx"; 2001 Dean Stahl and Karen Kerchelich, *Abbreviations Dictionary*, 10th ed. (Boca Raton FL: CRC) 376.

## There was never a **horse** that couldn't be ridden.

1921 N. Howard "Jack" Thorp, *Songs of the Cowboys* (Boston: Houghton Mifflin) 106–8 (in an African American "dialect" poem by the white easterner cowboy-poet Thorp); the refrain: "Oh, dere ain't no horse what can't be rode, / Dat's what de white folks say! / En dere ain't a man what can't be throwed, / OH, MAH!—I finds

it jest dat way!" (capitalization as shown). 1925 Charles Simpson, *El Rodeo* (London: John Lane) 85: "The only amateurs who succeeded had been bronco-busters in their youth, but as Tex Austin said—and he shook hands with all of them—'Well, boys! we always say out West: "There was never a horse that could not be rode, or a man who could not be throwed," and I guess we're right.'" The two-clause rhyming version of the proverb is common. *DAP* 312.

## When you fall off a **horse** (bicycle), you have to get (right) back on.

1962 Fred Down, "Will Paret's Ghost Ruin Griffith's Career?" *Negro Digest* 11, no. 11 (Sep.) 20 (quoting Emile Griffith's boxing manager, Gil Clancy): "There are two schools of thought. Some say, 'when you fall off a horse, get right back on another,' and others say, 'go slow.' I don't know which is right for Emile." 1983 *Fort Scott [KA] Tribune* 20 Oct.: "I think there's a philosophical bonbon that even says if you fall off a bicycle, it's better to get right back on again. Or is that a horse?"

## If greedy waits, **hot** will cool.

See "If GREEDY waits, hot will cool."

## What's **hot** is hot (and what's not is not).

1982 Michael Fitzgerald, "Antitrust, Discounting, and RPM in the Sporting Goods Industry," *Antitrust Law and Economics Review* 14: 49: ". . . [T]here are certain brands that are very hot—though the quality of skis from many manufacturers is very similar—what's hot is hot." The two-clause rhyming version of the proverb is common. Cf. "When you're HOT, you're hot."

## When you're **hot**, you're hot (and when you're not, you're not).

1969 The saying may have entered oral tradition as a proverb from a song by Jerry Reed, recorded by Porter Wagner in 1969 (and by Reed himself in 1971). 1971 Louie Robinson, "The Expanding World of Sidney Poitier," *Ebony* 27, no. 1 (Nov.) 104: "When you're hot, you're hot. 'But nobody can sustain that kind of popularity,' Poitier said recently. . . ." The two-clause rhyming version of the proverb is common.

## Never ask (You don't want to know) what's in a **hotdog**.

See "Never ask what's in a SAUSAGE."

## Someone who kicks his **hound** will beat his wife.

See "A MAN who kicks his dog will beat his wife."

## My **house**, my party (Your house, your party).

1979 Joyce Carol Oates, *Unholy Loves* (New York: Vanguard) 82: "Oliver . . . rather enjoys these oases of time after the excitement of a party, during which he can walk from room to room, partly dressed, in his bedroom slippers. . . . *His* house, *his* party" (italics as shown). 1984 John Coriolan, *A Sand Fortress*, rev. ed. (San Francisco: Gay Sunshine) 214: "Nobody could shut Nina up: it was her house, her party, and she insisted on telling us a lot more than anybody wanted to hear. . . ." 1990 Heather Graham (Pozzessere), *Wedding Bell Blues* (New York: Harlequin) 108: "'You think I've been—' 'Drinking too much champagne, yes. But hey, it's your house, your party.'" 1991 *Daily Pennsylvanian* (University of Pennsylvania) 3 Dec.: "And partygoers are encouraged to act within the context of the fraternity's attitudes rather than vice-versa. 'Remember, this is my house, my party. I'm inviting you.'" Cf. "My HOUSE, my rules" and "My MONEY, my rules."

## My **house** (room), my rules (Your house, your rules).

1983 *Pittsburgh Courier* 27 Aug.: "Risky Business [the 1983 motion picture] is about an affluent all-American boy whose parents go away on vacation. At home he lives by his father's motto 'It's my house, my rules.'" 1985 Tracy Kidder, *House* (Boston: Houghton Mifflin) 7: "She remembers Jules closing out disputes, when she was still a child, by saying to her, 'My house, my rules.' Now when he visits her house and takes out a cigar, she says, 'My house, my rules. No cigar.'" Cf. "My PARTY, my rules," "My MONEY, my rules," "My GAME, my rules," and "My HOUSE, my party."

## **Hunger** makes a monkey blow fire.

See "MONKEYS in hard times eat red peppers."

## Don't **hurry**, start early (Start early, don't hurry).

1915 New Jersey Department of Public Instruction, *The Teaching of Hygiene and Safety* (Union Hill NJ: Dispatch) 104 (in a list of safety tips): "Start early. Don't hurry." 1928 Patrick F. Shea, *Accident Prevention through Education in the Elementary Schools* (Boston: D. C. Heath) 61 (in a list of "safety slogans"): "Don't hurry, start early." *DAP* 319(1).

## **Hurry** (up) and wait.

1930 Harry A. Franck, *A Scandinavian Summer* (New York: Century) 212: "Of course, it was hurry and wait, as at all army functions the wide world over, since Hannibal halted to feed his elephants. Though we had been summoned for nine, not a wheel turned until ten." 1942 E. J. Kahn Jr., *The Army Life* (New York: Simon & Schuster) 125: "In fact, there is a little Army game, played perhaps more often at a big camp like Bragg than in smaller posts, known as 'Hurry and Wait' . . . First you rush pell-mell to get somewhere quickly in order to do something there, and then you wait endlessly in line to do it." 1942 *Hartford [CT] Courant* 22 Mar.: "'Hurry up and wait,' the soldier says truthfully."

## If it **hurts**, it's good for you (it's doing you good).

1950 *Reading [PA] Eagle* 10 Apr. (column by Lilly March): "I am one of that misguided lot which believes that if it hurts it must be good for you— iodine in open wounds, for example." 1982 Karel Rose, *Teaching Language Arts to Children* (New York: Harcourt Brace Javanovich) 384: "For these people, the old 'iodine treatment,' if it hurts it's good for you, may have been replaced by 'If it doesn't feel good right now, forget it.'" 1984 Helen Waite, "Culture and the Production of Aggression II," in *Apocalypse No: An Australian Guide to the Arms Race*, edited by Rachel Sharp (Sydney: Pluto) 240: "In fact, an old coaching adage states, 'If it hurts, it's doing you good.'"

## Sometimes you're the (fire) **hydrant**, and sometimes you're the dog."

See "Sometimes you're the DOG, and sometimes you're the fireplug."

## There is no *I* (*me*) in *team*.

1960 *Los Angeles Times* 14 Aug.: "Star pitcher Vernon Law's rules for success are as meaningful off the field as on. . . . Into Law's book, along with the usual baseball information, go shrewd observations that apply to life as well as baseball. If you read them carefully, you'll find yourself thinking twice: . . . There is no 'I' in team." 1995 Jill Smolowe, "Tumbling's New Titans," *Time* 146, no. 9 (28 Aug.) 73: "Says [gymnastics coach Peggy] Liddick: 'Our motto for '96 is "There's no *me* in *team*."'" *YBQ* Modern Proverbs (46).

## Don't skate on thin **ice**.

1935 Ray Wesley Sherman, *If You're Going to Drive Fast* (New York: Thomas Y. Crowell) 36: "If you don't approach accidents you won't have any that are your own fault. . . . Leave yourself a reserve, some leeway, and don't skate on thin ice. It's *poor* driving" (italics as shown). As literal advice, the sentence is older—as is the idiomatic verb phrase "skate on thin ice." *MP* I9; Whiting (1952) 429.

## Laugh and show your **ignorance**.

1912 C. C. Quale, "The Judge Who Did Not Know His Own Daughter," in *Thrilling Stories of White Slavery* (Chicago: Hamming) 10: "After all, we are all judges and as a rule we are blind to our own faults. Laugh and show your ignorance! The echo means weeping if you are sinning against Nature." *DAP* 325(21).

## One ought to try everything once except **incest** and folk dancing.

1943 Arnold Bax, *Farewell, My Youth* (London: Longmans, Green) 17: "The folk-song phase was inevitably followed by an enthusiasm for folk-dancing, and as to this infliction I, for one, would have been happy to cry: 'The nine men's morris [dance] is choked up with mud.' A sympathetic Scot summed it all up very neatly in this remark, 'You should make a point of trying every experience once, excepting incest and folk-dancing.'" 1972 *Wall Street Journal* 17 Aug.: "When [George S.] Kaufman was a very young boy, his father told him to 'try everything in life but incest and folk-dancing.' He did." *YBQ* Bax. The proverb originated as an anti-proverb based on "You should try everything (anything) once."

## **Information** wants to be free.

1984 *Washington Post* 18 Nov.: "'Information wants to be free,' said Stewart Brand. . . . 'But it also wants to be valuable,' a paradox he said is giving the fledgling software industry such fits." 1993 Mike Holderness, "Hackers Come in from the Cold," *New Scientist* 140, no. 1900 (20 Nov.) 23: "If there is a hacker's credo, it's that 'information wants to be free.'" *YBQ* Brand (4).

## Any **ink** (All ink, Even bad ink) is good ink.

1990 Rob Allyn, *Front Runner* (New York: Crown) 240: "But Callahan sent photocopies to every small-town weekly in the state. 'Right now, any ink is good ink,' he explained." 1991 Ralph Wiley, *Why Black People Tend to Shout* (New York: Penguin) 16: "They say any ink is good ink, but black men, above all other ethnic groups in America with the exception of the Native Americans, know this is not so." The proverb is analogous to (and synonymous with) "Any PUBLICITY is good publicity."

## Never argue (quarrel) with someone who buys **ink** by the barrel (gallon).

See "Never argue with a MAN who buys ink by the barrel."

**Insanity** is doing the same thing (the same thing over and over, what you've always done) and expecting a different result (outcome).

1983 Rita Mae Brown, *Sudden Death* (Toronto: Bantam) 68: "Unfortunately, Susan didn't remember what Jane Fulton once said. 'Insanity is doing the same thing over and over again, but expecting different results.'" *YBQ* Rita Mae Brown (2). The saying is sometimes attributed to Albert Einstein.

If at first you don't succeed, try reading the **instructions** (directions).

1962 Harry Stine, "Rocket Trails," *American Modeler* 58, no.6 (Sep.) 55: "Desire more information about model rocketry or the National Association of Rocketry? . . . Just mail me a postcard. . . . And remember, if at first you don't succeed, try reading the instructions!" 1968 Evan Esay, *20,000 Quips and Quotes* (Garden City NY: Doubleday) 432: "If at first you don't succeed, try reading the directions" (unattributed). The proverb originated as an anti-proverb based on the old saying "If at first you don't succeed, try and try again." Cf. "When all else fails, read the DIRECTIONS."

When all else fails, read the **instructions**.

See "When all else fails, read the DIRECTIONS."

A little **insurance** never hurt (anyone).

1965 David Rogers, *Boys and Ghouls Together* (Chicago: Dramatic) 43: "DIRGA. If you're so sure he'll like me, why did you lock that Barbara in the tower? COUNT. A little insurance never hurt anybody." 1986 Mark Vaniman, "Flight Insurance—Service Style," *Fish and Wildlife News* (Sep.–Oct.) 11: "As with anything else, it pays to be prepared. A little insurance never hurt anyone."

No one ever went broke (went bankrupt, got poor, etc.) underestimating the **intelligence** of the American people.

1926 The saying entered oral tradition as adapted from H. L. Mencken, writing in the *Chicago Tribune* 19 Sep.: "No one in this world, so far as I know—and I have searched the records for years, and employed agents to help me—has ever lost money by underestimating the intelligence of the great masses of the plain people." *RHDP* 246; *YBQ* Mencken (35).

## If you love your **job**, you don't have to work (a day in your life).

1991 *Chicago Tribune* 11 Sep.: "[Bruno] Maciuszek can't imagine doing anything but what he's been doing. 'If you love your job, you don't have to work a day in your life.'" 1993 *Press-Telegram [Long Beach CA]* 11 Oct.: "And if you love your job, then it's not work at all." 1998 "Heritage Tourism and Cultural Presentation," *Historic Preservations Forum* 13, no. 4 (Summer) 59: "'If you love your job, then you will never work another day in your life.' This may not be exactly the way Confucius said it, but it is close."

## The **job** isn't over (finished) until the paperwork is done (You aren't finished till you've done the paperwork).

1969 Lawrence L. Steinmetz, *Managing the Marginal and Unsatisfactory Performer* (Reading MA: Addison-Wesley) 194: "The word in the Office is: 'A job is not over until the paperwork is done.'" 1971 Thomas G. Sanborn (letter to the editor), *Datamation* 17, no. 21 (15 Nov.) 18: "I recently saw a cartoon. . . . Beneath a picture of an outhouse was a caption, 'You haven't finished till you've done the paper work.'" 1974 L. Joseph Kaiser, "How to Write Reports," *Industrial Education* 63, no. 8 (Nov.) 57: "'Document your work' and 'The job's never over until the paper work is done' are common remarks in industry." Dundes and Pagter (1975) 160–62.

## Just do your **job**.

1934 Dennis Wheatley, *Black August* (New York: E. J. Dutton) 283: "She nodded quickly. 'I'll be all right—don't worry about me, sweet—just do your job.'" 1938 James Hanley, *Hollow Sea* (London: John Lane) 366: "Just do your job and keep your mouth shut." 1957 *Christian Science Monitor* 23 May: "My working buddy said, 'Why ask questions? Just do your job.'"

## If you can't take a **joke**, you shouldn't have joined (enlisted).

1954 Kenneth Poolman, *The Kelly* (London: William Kimber) 92 (recalling experiences in the British Royal Navy during World War II): "But you mustn't be downhearted. 'Shouldn't have joined if I can't take a joke,' you said. You lurched and vomited your way through the miserable round of watchkeeping. . . ." The proverb also occurs in other branches of the military, both British and American—as well as in other sectors of the labor force.

## The **joy** is in the journey.

1915 Winston Churchill (the American novelist), *A Far Country* (New York: Macmillan) 483: "'The joy is in the journey,' he answered. 'The secret is in the search.'" 1918 T. B. Rudmose-Brown, *French Literary Studies* (New York: John Lane) 112 (paraphrasing Francis Viele-Griffin): "The joy is in the journey and in the breaking of the gates. And the last gate we break is death." Cf. "HAPPINESS is a journey, not a destination" and "GETTING there is half the fun."

## Don't **judge** yourself by others.

1909 Robert F Horton, *My Belief* (New York: Fleming H. Revell) 222: ". . . [Y]our spiritual experience must be entirely your own; you must not expect it to resemble that of any one else. . . . But the second point will disincline you even more to judge yourself by others, or even to compare yourself with them." 1953 Catherine Marshall and Peter Marshall, *God Loves You* (New York: McGraw-Hill) [9] (the designation of a parable, as listed in the table of contents): "Their faces fell[.] *Don't Judge Yourself by Others*" (italics as shown; the subtitle or appended clause does not appear with the parable itself). Perhaps the proverb originated as an anti-proverb based on "Don't judge others by yourself."

## It's a **jungle** out there.

1951 Louis Paul, *A Father in the Family* (New York: Crown) 211: "'Children can be very cruel to one another.' 'So can people. I told you on New Year's Eve it was a jungle out there.'" 1963 *Southeast Missourian [Cape Girardeau]* 25 Feb.: "'I end up washing dishes,' the youth was quoted, 'and being called dirty names. Like I say, it's a jungle out there.'"

## **Just** (Only just, Barely) is (just) good enough.

1968 Frederic Raphael, *Orchestra & Beginners* (New York: Viking) 43: "'How are you?' 'Alive.' She remembered Lawson Redfellow. 'Just.' 'Just is good enough for me,' he said." 1985 *Orlando [FL] Sentinel* 11 Nov.: "Armstrong caught the ball on the 1 [yard line] and barely got across the goal line. But 'barely' is good enough." Cf. "CLOSE enough is close enough," "GOOD enough is good enough," "CLOSE doesn't count," and "ALMOST is not good enough."

## Karma is a bitch.

1995 *Hollywood Reporter* 7 Aug.: "Hello? Hello? HELLO? Nobody answers . . . Did somebody say Tommy on line 2? Karma is a bitch" (ellipsis dots and capitalizaton as shown). 2000 David Moody and Maureen Callahan, "Don't Drink the Brown Water," in *Da Capo Best Music Writing 2000*, edited by Peter Guralnick (New York: Da Capo) 88: "Many audience members were hot and pissed off. Some shoes were thrown. Everlast [pseudonym of the rapper/rock musician Erik Schrody] paused and addressed this. 'Karma's a bitch,' he said. 'You better recognize that and act accordingly.'" Cf. "PAYBACK is a bitch" and "LIFE is a bitch."

## It's cheaper to **keep** her.

1972 The saying probably entered oral tradition as a proverb from the title and refrain of a popular song by Mack Rice, performed by Johnnie Taylor.

## **Keep** it real.

1975 Joanne Hendrick, *The Whole Child* (Saint Louis: C. V. Mosby) 220: "*Keep it real.* Cognitive learning should be based on actual experience . . ." (italics as shown). 1985 William Katz, *Open House* (New York: McGraw-Hill) 260: "But he looked at Laura, his face flashing surprise. Anyone hearing that message would *have* to look at her. Keep it real. Even now, keep it real!" (italics as shown).

## **Keep** it simple (Keep it short and simple, Keep it simple, stupid!).

1919 "The Show Exhibit—How to Make It Pay," *Printers' Ink* 108, no. 3 (17 Jul.) 40: "But if you really want to build an effective exhibit: Keep it simple! Keep it simple! KEEP IT SIMPLE!" (capitalization as shown). 1947 Paul W. White, *News on the Air* (New York: Harcourt, Brace) 17: "'Much of the news these days,' he [Earl Johnson] told his writers, 'is of such vital importance that it deserves to be presented in terms that can be understood easily by the widest possible audience. . . . *Watch that lead sentence. Keep it short and simple*" (italics as shown). 1958 *Robesonian [Lumberton NC]* 23 Jul.: "Signs with the single word, KISS, are being tacked up on walls in offices and other places of business. . . . What could the word KISS mean? The mystery continued until one day, said Mr. [James] Webb, . . . he asked the boss point blank, 'What do the four letters K-I-S-S mean?' 'Keep It Simple, Stupid'" (credited to the *Rocky Mount Telegram*). YBQ Sayings (32); Lighter (1994– ) 2: 364. The acronym KISS is sometimes taken to represent "Keep it short and simple" or "short and sweet."

## **Keep on** trucking.

1936 The saying probably entered oral tradition as a proverb from a song by Fulton "Blind Boy" Fuller: "Keep on truckin', baby, truckin' my blues away / . . . / Keep on truckin', mama, truckin' both night and day. . . ." YBQ B. Fuller; Rees (1995) 277.

## You can't (Don't try to) kid a **kidder**.

1924 *Lincoln [NE] State Journal* 15 Feb.: "You can't kid a kidder so why try?" 1939 William March, "The Shoe Drummer," in *Some Like Them Short* (Boston: Little, Brown) 171: "'You're a sweet little girl, and I'm pretty lucky, I guess.' 'Go on with that stuff, don't try to kid a kidder.'" Cf. "Don't bullshit a BULLSHITTER" and "You can't con a CON."

## The worst **kind** of ride is better than the best kind of walk.

See "The worst RIDE is better than the best walk."

## A **kiss** is just a kiss.

1931 The song "As Time Goes By," lyrics by Herman Hupfeld (in the musical *Everybody's Welcome*), contained the lines "A kiss is still a kiss, / A sigh is just a sigh"; the saying entered oral tradition (and many performances of the song itself) with the lines conflated: "A kiss is just a kiss." 1933 *Chicago Tribune* 7 May: "Sally Blane, the movie actress who recently got herself reported engaged to an earl by kissing him goodbye at a Hollywood airport, let it be known today that a kiss is just a kiss as far as she is concerned." More recently, the song has been featured in the BBC television series *As Time Goes By* (1992–2005). *YBQ* Hupfeld (1).

## Don't get your **knickers** in a twist.

See "Don't get your PANTIES in a twist."

## Don't (try to) catch a falling **knife**.

1915 James Wilson, *Lowland Scotch* (London: Oxford UP) 194 (among "proverbs and sayings"): "Nair kep a fawin tnief. [translated:] Never catch a falling knife." 1919 Harry Johnston, *The Gay-Dombeys* (New York: Macmillan) 287: "I'm only infectious now as a political and social delinquent, and if you've much regard for your own welfare you oughtn't to mix yourself up with my affairs. . . . What's that saying? 'Never catch a falling knife, or save a falling friend! . . .'" (ellipsis dots as shown).

## Never (You don't) bring (take) a **knife** to a gunfight.

1988 *Charlotte Observer* 25 Feb.: [Eugene] Easter pulled a pistol and [Robert] Seibert a knife. . . . 'It was an old lock-blade and I didn't even get it open,' Seibert's statement said. 'Shouldn't never take a knife to a gunfight.'" The phrasal

counterpart of the proverb is perhaps older; it is uttered by Sean Connery's character (an Irish cop) in the 1987 film *The Untouchables*—or the phrase may allude to an existing proverb.

## The same **knife** cuts the sheep and the goat.

Anderson and Cundall (1927) 75 give the saying as a Jamaican proverb: "De same knife dat cut goat troat can cut sheep troat." Prahlad (2001) 256.

## Don't **knock** it till you've tried it.

1960 *Washington Post* 13 Sep. (title of a five-line poem): "Don't Knock It Until You Try It / Moise Tshombe of Katanga, / Kasarubu and Lamumba, / Names of music, now you're free: / Try a little harmony." 1962 John Shea, "Pretrial Amendments," *Journal of the State Bar of California* 37: 470: "I feel that the proposed rules should be adopted and I would add an appropriate cliche—'Don't knock it until you've tried it.'"

## It's not whether you get **knocked down** that matters but whether you get back up.

See "It's not how many TIMES you get knocked down that matters but how many times you get back up."

## Everything you **know** is (probably) wrong.

1974 Title of a record album (by Firesign Theater): *Everything You Know Is Wrong.* 1976 *Times-News* [Hendersonville NC] 18 Jun.: "'Practically everything we know is wrong,' says Joe Kane. 'The stuff in history books are [sic] fairy tales.'" The concept is older—in the vein of the venerable "paradox of the liar."

If you don't **know** what it is, (then) don't mess with (fool with, touch, eat) it.

1950 Marshall W. Stearns, "Rebop, Bebop, and Bop," *Harper's* 200 (Apr.) 89: "When an eager undergraduate once demanded, 'What is jazz, Mr. Waller?' the great pianist is said to have growled: 'Man, if you don't know what it is, don't mess with it!'" (the unverifiable attribution to Fats Waller is common—an attribution that may have been influenced by Waller's famous quip, subsequently proverbial, about jazz: "If you got to ask, you ain't got it"). 1974 Carolyn Niethammer, *American Indian Food and Lore* (New York: Macmillan) xxix: "The acute pain subsided in two days. . . . [T]he moral of the story is obvious—don't eat it unless you know what it is." 1980 Wendell Berry, "The Native Grasses and What They Mean," *The New Farm* 2, no. 1 (Jan.) 56: "'I don't know what they are,' the farm wife said to Bill Martin, 'but I don't want anybody fooling with them.' That is an ecological principle, and a religious one. If you don't know what it is, don't fool with it." Cf. "If you have to ASK, you'll never know."

It's not what you **know**, it's who (whom) you know (that counts).

1914 H. W. Jacobsen, letter to the editor, *The Electrical Worker* 13: 233: "Many devious forces apparently also control the conditions of advancement and preference, and a phrase that is often heard is to the effect that it's not what you know that counts so much, as who you know!" 1918 *New York Tribune* 22 Sep.: "The shipyard workers along the Delaware River have adopted a war slogan all of their own. It is: 'It's not what you know, it's who you know.'" *DAP* 352(17); *RHDP* 184; *YBQ* Modern Proverbs (49); *ODP* 344.

You can't (You never) **know** what you don't know.

1953 Clark Kerr, "The University in a Progressive Society," *Pacific Spectator* 7: 273: "New insights cannot be demanded, cannot be blueprinted in advance—for we cannot know what we do not know." 1968 Curtis E. LeMay, *America in Danger* (New York: Funk & Wagnalls) xiv: "How good is our intelligence? . . . What have we *not* been able to learn? As one Chief of Staff put it, 'We never know what we don't know'" (italics as shown). 1979 *Hearings on Military Posture and H. R. 1872 . . . Committee on Armed Services, House of Representatives* (Washington DC: Government Printing Office) 336; Roland Herbst testifies: ". . . I do believe we got very good cooperation. I cannot know that because you never know what you don't know, but I think we did."

You can't **know** where you're going unless you know where you've been.

1937 "Power Plant Held Bar to Air Growth," *American Aviation* 1, no. 3 (1 Jul.) 5: "Predicting is like rowing a boat. The only way you know where you're going is to see where you've been." 1956 Transcript of discussion following Jason Berger's presentation "Dialogue Concerning Art and Creativity," in *Conference on Creativity as a Process* (Boston: Institute of Contemporary Art) 18: "[James S.] PLANT: Then you mean a cold and analytic phase is an indispensable part of creative work. BERGER: Oh, definitely. You have to know where you've been to know where you're going, I think." Cf. "In order to GET where you want to go, you have to start from where you are now" and the nineteenth-century aphorism "Don't forget where you came from."

You don't **know** it's too late till it's too late.

See "It's NEVER too late until it's too late."

You don't **know** you've got it till you get it.

See "You haven't GOT it till you get it."

You have to **know** when to hold them and know when to fold them.

1977 The saying probably passed into oral tradition as a proverb from Don Schlitz's song "The Gambler" (popularized by Kenny Rogers).

You never **know** what you have till it's gone (you've lost it).

1952 William Goyen, *Ghost and Flesh* (New York: Random House) 82: "'Well,' I said, 'I guess that's the way life is, you don't know what you have till you don't have it any longer, till you've lost it, till it's too late.'" 1954 A. C. Friend, "The Proverbs of Serlo of Wilton," *Medieval Studies* 16: 212 (given as a loose translation or equivalent of Seneca's "nihil magis placent quam quod amissum est"): "You don't know what you have until you have lost it."

**Knowledge** is like manure (fertilizer): it's only good when spread (around).

1962 Charles H. Cotter, *The Master and His Ship* (London: Maritime) xiv: "Knowledge is like money—no good at all if it is stowed away. If it is to be put to some good purpose it must be spread." 1980 Robert E. Johnson, "Pearl Bailey, Student at 62, Brings Wisdom and Wit with Her to Campus," *Jet* 58, no. 18 (17 Jul.) 56: "And to paraphrase one of her lines from [*Hello*] *Dolly*, 'Knowledge is like manure. It has to be spread around so something can grow.' And those who give her an audience usually wind up knee deep in knowledge." The proverb is perhaps a new application of the image in the very old proverb "Riches are like muck—of no value unless spread around."

Real **knowledge** is what you learn after you know it all.

See "It is what you LEARN after you know it all that counts."

Respect **knowledge**, but doubt is what gives you an education.

See "Respect FAITH, but doubt is what gives you an education."

To gather **knowledge**, roam; to use it, stay (bide) at home.

1924 The saying probably passed into oral tradition from an epigram by Arthur Guiterman, in *A Poet's Proverbs* (New York: E. P. Dutton) 75: "To gather Knowledge, roam; / To use it, bide at home."

**Labels** are for cans (not people).

1984 *Anchorage [AK] Daily News* 5 Nov.: "When he first ran for office in Texas, [George H. W.] Bush dodged questions about whether he was a moderate or a conservative by asserting: 'Labels are for cans, not for people.'" 1994 *Washington Post* 11 Oct. (quoting Michael Stipe of the musical group R.E.M.): "In terms of the whole queer-straight thing, my feeling is that labels are for canned food." 1998 Daryl Dance, *Honey, Hush* (New York: W. W. Norton) 88 (in a list of sayings titled "Sister to Sister"): "Girl, don't pay no tention to what dey call you. Labels are for canned goods, and you sho don't sit aroun' on nobody's grocery shelf."

Don't tell me about the **labor** pains; just show me the baby.

See "Don't tell me about the PAIN; just show me the baby."

It ain't over till the fat **lady** sings.

See "The OPERA isn't over till the fat lady sings."

When the fat **lady** sings, the opera is over.

See "The OPERA isn't over till the fat lady sings."

**Lady Luck** is a jealous (cruel, fickle, hard) mistress.

See "LUCK is a jealous mistress."

They don't (God doesn't) make **land** anymore (Buy land; they don't make it anymore).

1968 *Reading [PA] Eagle* 16 Oct. (in a classified ad for real estate): "You know they don't make land anymore." 1970 *New York Times* 12 Sep. (heading of a classified ad): "Buy Land: They Ain't Making It Anymore!" 1970 John L. Springer, *Consumer Swindlers* (Chicago: Henry Regnery) 87: "Widely used by land promoters is Will Rogers's adage: 'Buy land, they're not making it anymore.'" 1976 Erik Berganst, *Colonizing the Sea* (New York: G. P. Putnam's Sons) 17: "It is not quite true that 'they don't make land anymore.' We *can* make more land by expanding into the sea . . ." (italics as shown). 1978 Raleigh Barlowe, *Land Resource Economics* (Englewood Cliffs NJ: Prentice-Hall) 333: "These promoters frequently use effective selling tactics . . . and the obvious clincher that 'God doesn't make land anymore' to sell their lots."

A shady **lane** breeds mud.

1922 A. E. Coppard, "A Broadsheet Ballad," in *Adam & Eve & Pinch Me* (New York: Alfred A. Knopf) 287: "'Well, a' [i.e., she] called for it [a beating], sure,' commented Sam. 'Her did,' agreed Bob, 'but she was the quietest known girl for miles round those parts, very shy and quiet.' 'A shady lane breeds mud,' said Sam." Taylor (1931) 12 glosses the proverb: "secrecy creates wrong-doing or scandal." *DAP* 359(1).

You can't rise with the **lark** if you've been on one the night before.

1908 Grace Donworth, *The Letters of Jennie Allen to Her Friend Miss Musgrove* (Boston: Small, Maynard) 12–13: "A man next door has jest fell down the seller [*sic*] stairs and they have sent for me. . . . Mr. Spinney says you can't rise with the lark if you've been on one the night before." *DAP* 360(2).

**Last** in, first out.

1914 *Popular Mechanics* (Jan.) 173 (advertisement for Velvet tobacco, depicting a tin of tobacco on top of clothing packed in an open suitcase): "Last in, first out. . . . Put it on the top so it will be handy." 1914 Joseph Kennedy, "Essentials in the Professional Preparation of Teachers," *American Schoolmaster* 7: 67: "College graduates had gone into these schools without any professional preparation and had begun to pour down upon high school children the most recent results of their own studies. It was like putting potatoes in a sack,—last in, first out." *MP* L48; Room (2000) 390–91. In recent decades the proverb has been used as a technical term in reference to inventory accounting and control—and still more recently in reference to computer storage in memory. It is now sometimes abbreviated *LIFO*. Cf. "Last HIRED, first fired."

## What happens (goes on) in **Las Vegas** (etc.) stays in Las Vegas (etc.).

2002 *Las Vegas Review-Journal* 25 Nov.: "The Las Vegas Visitors and Convention Authority, meanwhile, continued its saucy come-to-Vegas-baby advertising campaign with six new spots filmed over a three-day period last week. Depicting the theme 'what happens in Las Vegas stays in Las Vegas,' the national commercials, produced by Hungry Man Productions, feature Vegas visitors indulging fantasies in locations ranging from a limousine to a tattoo parlor." 2002 Kellye M. Garrett et al., "Everything the Top Football Stars Can't Live Without," *Vibe* Nov. 62 (quoting the football player Adam Archuleta): "Favorite city: Las Vegas. . . . You party and have a good time with your friends. What happens in Vegas stays in Vegas." Whether the advertising campaign originated the saying or merely employed an existing proverb, "What happens in Las Vegas stays in Las Vegas" has become, by far, the most common of the popular sayings that follow the formula; it is widely assumed to be the prototypical version, and currently it can be uttered (figuratively) in reference to any site of conduct that calls for nondisclosure. However, it was anticipated—at least as early as the 1970s—by parallel sayings about secrecy or discretion

of various sorts: "What's said (What happens) at home stays at home," an expression sometimes used to lament the secrecy of child abuse or spousal abuse; the clinical or psychotherapeutic adage "What happens in the group (at the meeting, at the session) stays . . ."; the professional baseball maxim "What happens in the clubhouse stays . . .". Even in the dissipated-vacation usage, other versions are apparently older: 1996 *San Antonio Express-News* 13 Nov.: "But there was one condition. Drill sergeants told them repeatedly: 'Whatever happens in Mexico stays in Mexico.'" 1998 *Orlando Sentinel* 30 Mar.: "'What happens in Daytona, stays in Daytona,' he tells the others."

## Better **late** than pregnant.

1995 *Albuquerque [NM] Journal* 19 Feb.: "'College was an interlude to make sure writing was what I wanted to do. It did confirm it. . . . I figured it out. So better late than pregnant,' she half-joked." 2001 Divad Yvel (presumably a pseudonym for David Levy), *You've Got Funny Mail* (Bloomington IN [?]: 1st Books Library) 74 (in a chapter titled "Kids"): "And the favorite: Better late than . . . . . . pregnant" (ellipsis dots as shown). The proverb originated as an anti proverb based on "Better late than never."

## It's never too **late** until it's too late.

See "It's NEVER too late until it's too late."

## It isn't against the **law** if they don't catch you.

See "The only CRIME is getting caught."

## The old make **laws**, the young die for them.

See "Old MEN make wars, and young men fight them."

## Never play **leapfrog** with a unicorn.

1977 *Ironwood [MI] Daily Globe* 23 Feb.: "At times I came perilously close to breaking one of my basic rules: never play leapfrog with a unicorn." 1979 Laurence Peter, *Peter's People* (New York: William Morrow) 191: "FELDSTEIN'S LAW: Never play leapfrog with a unicorn" (capitalization as shown). 1979 John Peers, *1,001 Logical Laws* (Garden City NY: Doubleday) "Feldstein's Law: Never, ever, play leapfrog with a unicorn."

## It is what you **learn** after you know it all that counts (Real knowledge is what you learn after you know it all).

1921 *Spartenburg [SC] Herald* 21 Jul. (in a list titled "Abe Martin Says"): "It's what we learn after we think we know it all that counts." 1950 *Chicago Tribune* 20 Feb. (filler item, titled "Advanced Education," credited to "The Fatheaded Janitor"): "It's what you learn after you know it all that counts." 1964 *Register-Guard [Eugene OR]* 27 Jun.: "A fine basketball coach, John Wooden . . . , is credited with the line which says real knowledge is what you learn after you 'know it all.'" The attribution to Wooden is common; the saying has also been credited to President Harry S. Truman.

## Always **leave** them laughing.

1903 The saying probably entered oral tradition as a proverb from a song by George M. Cohan, "Always Leave Them Laughing When You Say Good-bye."

## If you get **lemons** (If anyone hands you a lemon), make lemonade.

See "If LIFE hands you lemons, make lemonade."

## **Less** is the new more.

2001 *Los Angeles Times* 16 Dec.: "But not all businesspeople welcome an age in which less is the new more." 2006 *Observer [London]* 30 Apr.: "More pages and sections need to equal more sales. Extra! Extra! Read all about it—or Less is the new More." The proverb asserts

the trendiness of "minimalism"—in economic behavior, environmental stewardship, sartorial fashion, and so on. Cf. the older paradoxical proverb "Less is more." The pattern "_____ is the new _____" is productive: "Gray is the new black," "Small is the new large," "Fifty is the new thirty," etc.

## If it's yellow, **let** it mellow; if it's brown, flush it down.

1977 Deborah Johnson, "Californians Find Two Years of Sun Too Much," *Seven Days* 1, no. 4 (28 Mar.) 16: ". . . [S]uch signs as 'If it's yellow, let it mellow' are appearing above toilets in even the swankiest homes." 1979 Lester A. Herr, "Introductory Remarks," *Proceedings of the Conference on Water Conservation: Needs and Implementing Strategies* (New York: American Society of Civil Engineers) 20: "Unfortunately, engineers and public officials, as well as the general public, wait until we have drought conditions . . . and react with slogans such as 'If it's yellow let it mellow and if it's brown flush it down' and then pray for the rains to come!" The reference is to economizing on the use of water in a flush toilet.

## **Let** it all hang out.

1962 Jim Brosnan, *Pennant Race* (New York: Harper), 88: "'Hope he has a couple of easy innings,' said Turner. 'Sit down and cool off, young man.' 'Let it all hang out now, Tits,' said Whisenant. 'Don't hold back out there.'" *DAAP* 20; Lighter (1994– ) 2: 22–23.

## Never (Don't) **let** them see you sweat.

1970 E. M. Broner, "The Bagger," *Epoch* 20: 12: "I rush back to my bags, one inside the other. . . . [D]on't sweat, don't let them see you sweat—it shows white on your face, shiny on your face." In 1984 the slogan "Never let them see you sweat" was featured in an advertising campaign for Dry Idea (Gillette) underarm deodorant.

## A **liberal** is a conservative who has been arrested.

1983 Peter Kreeft, *The Unaborted Socrates: A Dramatic Debate on the Issues Surrounding Abortion* (Downers Grove IL: InterVarsity) 93 (an imaginary conversation): "TARIAN: What's the mystery, Socrates? A liberal is just the opposite of a conservative. HERROD: (Entering, with drinks.) And a conservative is a liberal who just got mugged. TARIAN: Oh, Rex. Thanks. For the drinks and for the definition. But couldn't you also say a liberal is a conservative who just got arrested?" 1987 Tom Wolfe, *Bonfire of the Vanities* (New York: Farrar, Straus & Giroux) 504: "He was learning for himself the truth of the saying 'A liberal is a conservative who has been arrested.'" YBQ Tom Wolfe (9). Cf. "A CONSERVATIVE is a liberal who has been mugged."

## A **liberal** is a conservative who has not been mugged.

See "A CONSERVATIVE is a liberal who has been mugged."

## **Lick** (it) before you stick (it).

2003 Denise LaSalle, "Lick It before You Stick It" (song, perhaps being performed in "live" venues as early as the 1980s): "You're making her feel good but you can make her feel better, / If you treat your lady like a stamp on a letter: / You've got to lick it before you stick it." 2004 *New York Times* 8 Aug.: "Mr. [Bill] Gates, unlike [the disk jockey called] Grandwizard, probably wouldn't use the phrase 'You gotta lick it before you stick it.'" 2007 Noire [pseudonym], *Thong on Fire: An Urban Erotic Tale* (New York: Simon & Schuster) 257: "You gotta lick before you stick! That's a rule for vaginas!"

## If you are not **lying**, you are not trying.

2004 *Atlanta Journal* 20 Apr.: "As former Eagles [football] coach Buddy Ryan, who drafted a player two days after declaring him a medical reject, once put it: 'If you ain't lyin', you ain't tryin'.'" 2007 *Philadelphia Inquirer* 7 Jan.: ". . . [The football coach Nick] Saban probably was just prepping for his foray back into college recruiting, where the motto is: 'If you ain't lyin', you ain't tryin'.'" Cf. "If you are not CHEATING, you are not trying."

## Little **lie**, big lie.

1999 John R. Maxim, *Mosaic* (New York: Avon) 275: It was not quite a lie. Not a big lie, at least. . . . Grayson settled back again. He closed his eyes. Little lie, big lie. . . ." The proverb means that the telling of a minor lie suggests that the teller (a criminal suspect or witness, for example) is prevaricating about or concealing matters of greater importance. Cf. the legal maxim "Falsus in uno, falsus in omnibus" (a lie regarding one point can invalidate testimony on all related points).

## Repeating a **lie** doesn't make it true.

1969 W. J. E. Crissy and Robert Kaplan, *Salesmanship* (New York: John Wiley & Sons) 286: "Repeating a lie does not make it true, but an uncritical person may lose his perspective in the face of repetition. Hitler's constant claims about the 'Master Race' lulled many persons into this belief, but did not result in creating a different type of person." 1971 James William Johnson, *Prose in Practice* (New York: Harcourt Brace Javanovich) 440: "Repeating a falsehood again and again will not make it true; nor will outshouting another opinion demonstrate the validity of one's own."

## **Lie back** and enjoy it.

See "RELAX and enjoy it."

## Anything good in **life** is either illegal, immoral, or fattening.

See "Anything GOOD is either illegal, immoral, or fattening."

**Don't take life too seriously; you'll never get out of it alive.**

1911 The saying was probably authored by Elbert Hubbard, *A Thousand & One Epigrams* (East Aurora IL: Roycrofters) 74: "Do not take life too seriously—you will never get out of it alive." 1915 *Atlanta Constitution* 7 Jun.: "C. R. Vance, the original Musket Ridge Philosopher of The Dalton [GA] Citizen, has written these rules and bylaws for the health and happiness club: 'Don't take life too seriously, for you will never get out of it alive, anyway.'"

**Eighty percent (Ninety percent, etc.; Most) of life (success) is (just) showing up.**

1977 *New York Times* 21 Aug. (quoting Woody Allen's friend Marshall Brickman): "I have learned one thing. As Woody says, 'Showing up is 80 percent of life.'" 1978 *Pittsburgh Post-Gazette* 20 Oct.: ". . . [S]he thinks of a newspaper interview she once read in which the ballerina Gelsey Kirkland said that, when things get difficult, she reminds herself that '99 percent of life is showing up.'" 1979 Louise Colligan and Doug Colligan, *The A+ Guide to Good Grades* (New York: Scholastic) 29: "Woody Allen once gave an anxious friend a T-shirt inscribed: 'Most of life is showing up.' Not a bad piece of advice. . . ." 1982 Thomas J. Peters and Robert H. Waterman Jr., *In Search of Excellence* (New York: Harper & Row) 119 (epigraph): "Eighty percent of success is showing up.—Woody Allen." *YBQ* Woody Allen (41).

**If life hands you lemons, make lemonade.**

1910 William G. Haupt, *The Art of Business College Soliciting* (Chicago: for the author) 89: "Don't be a pessimist, but be optimistic. If anyone 'hands you a lemon' take it home and make lemonade of it." 1911 "Health Hints," *Illinois Medical Journal* 19: 675: "If anyone hands you a lemon, make lemonade of it. It is both

healthful and pleasant to take." (The proverb there seems to have been understood—and misapplied—*literally!*) 1917 *Plumbers, Gas and Steam Fitters' Journal* 21, no. 4 (Apr.) 29: "If life hands you a lemon adjust your rose-colored glasses and start to selling pink lemonade." 1919 Homer Randall, *Army Boys in the French Trenches* (Cleveland: World Syndicate) 132: "'I wish I had your cheery disposition,' growled Tom. 'When any one hands you a lemon—' 'I make lemonade out of it,' came back Billy, and there was a general laugh." *YBQ* Modern Proverbs (51); *ODP* 184. The proverb's imagery had been anticipated: 1908 *The Real Optimist [Reno NV]* 25 Apr.: "An optimist is a man who can make lemonade out of all the lemons handed to him" (credited to *Biddleford Journal*).

**If life hands (gives, throws) you scraps, make a quilt.**

1992 Florence Cope Bush, *If Life Gives You Scraps, Make a Quilt: Short Stories of the Smoky Mountains* (Concord TN: Misty Cove). 2007 Larry L. Murdock, *Why Did the Chicken Cross the Road* (Raleigh NC: Lulu) 155: "Stone fence-building materials were right there at the farmers' feet, in the way, and had to be removed from the fields anyway, so they simply made the best of it. As the old saying goes, 'if life gives you scraps, make quilts.'" MacDowell and Mieder (2010). The proverb parallels "If LIFE hands you lemons, make lemonade."

**It's a good (great, gay) life if you don't weaken.**

1914 *Chicago Daily Tribune* 5 Jul.: "Miss Elizabeth Murray, the comic singer, told an interviewer that to her rather than to Otto Hauerbach belonged the effective lines of [the 1913 operatic farce by Hauerbach and Leo Dietrichstein] 'High Jinks,' in which she performed here last season. She laid stress upon the statement that she interpolated what she said was the best 'laughing line' in the libretto—'It's a great life if you don't weaken!'" *MP* L125; *DAP* 373(13); *DAAP* 459–60; *YBQ* Buchan; Partridge (1977) 78.

## Life begins at forty.

1932 The saying probably entered oral tradition as a proverb from the title of the best-selling book by Walter B. Pitkin and the 1935 motion picture made from the book, starring Will Rogers. *DAP* 373; *RHDP* 209; *YBQ* Pitkin; *ODP* 184; Pickering et al. (1992) 208–9; Rees (1995) 293; Room (2000) 400; Pickering (2001) 212.

## Life comes at you fast.

2004 The saying probably entered oral tradition as a proverb from a slogan in an advertising campaign for the Nationwide insurance company.

## Life deals us each a hand.

1997 Jim McCue, *Edmund Burke and Our Present Discontents* (London: Claridge) 119: "Yet the peers [members of the House of Lords] are a healthy reminder that life deals each of us a hand, and that we must make the best of it, not waste our precious time complaining that we ought to have other cards." 2007 Robert L. Davis, *Cop Out* (New York: iUniverse) 58: "I simply deduced that life deals everyone a hand and you simply play that hand as best you can." 2007 Poster (Kaufman Hall, UCLA) for an "HIV-Positive" exhibit (May): "Life deals us each a hand." Cf. "You play the HAND you are dealt."

## Life is a bitch.

1940 Langston Hughes, *The Big Sea* (New York: Alfred A. Knopf) 183: "'And here we'll be,' he affirmed. 'Life's a bitch, but I'll beat it—and stay here too.'" 1946 Kenneth Patchen, *Sleepers Awake* (New York: Padell) 191: "Sometimes life is a bitch, huh? How about it? Don't you think so?" The phrase *chienne de vie* ("bitch of life") was attributed (without authentication) to Mme. de Sévigné by Anatole France, *La vie en fleur* (Paris: Calmann-Lévy, 1926) 319.

## Life is a bitch, and then you die.

1982 Sara Rimer, "Brainchild," *Washington Post Magazine* (10 Oct.) 17: "... Marc and Valerie and eight of Valerie's other friends discussed ... the meaning of life, a question that was addressed cynically by the composer, 15-year-old Tony Daniels, who said, 'Life's a bitch, then you die.'" 1983 Pat Cadigan, "Nearly Departed," *Isaac Asimov's Science Fiction Magazine* 7, no. 6 (Jun.) 107: "... I lay down on the couch again, and I blew smoke at the ceiling. 'Life's a bitch. Then you die.'" 1984 *Mother Jones Magazine* 9, no. 11 (Feb.–Mar.) 61 (ad for sweatshirts: inscription): "LIFE'S A BITCH AND THEN YOU DIE" (capitalization as shown). *YBQ* Modern Proverbs (53); Rees (1995) 294. Probably the proverb originated as an elaboration of (or anti-proverb based on) "LIFE is a bitch."

## Life is a bitch, and then you marry one.

1987 *Advertising Age* 16 Feb. (regarding an entrepreneur who sells printed buttons): "This is the most recent list of his best sellers: ... 3. Life's a bitch and then you marry one." Casselman (2002) 88. The proverb originated as an anti-proverb based on "LIFE is a bitch, and then you die."

## Life is (just) a bowl of cherries.

1931 *New York Times* 15 Sep.: "Lew Brown and Ray Henderson have written a jovial score [for *Scandals: A Revue*]—'Life Is Just a Bowl of Cherries' and 'Ladies and Gentlemen, That's Love' for the inexhaustible voice of Ethel Merman...." 1932 E. G. Cousins, *Filmland in Ferment* (London: Denis Archer) 71: "It's just one of those things, and life is a bowl of cherries, and you don't have to be crazy but it helps a lot ... and murmuring these time-honored comments Hollywood and Elstree go about their business...." (the first set of ellipsis dots as shown). *MP* L126; *DAP* 374(32), 94(1); *RHDP* 209–10; *DAAP* 461–62; *YBQ* Lew Brown; Barbour (1963); Mieder (1988); Pickering et al.

(1992) 355; Rees (1995) 293; Pickering (2001) 212. Lew Brown's song is widely cited as the origin, but Brown may himself have been employing the proverb. Cf. "LIFE is not a bowl of cherries."

## Life is (just) a cabaret.

1966 The saying entered oral tradition as a proverb from the featured song in the musical *Cabaret*, lyrics by Fred Ebb (music by John Kander). *YBQ* Ebb (1). The proverb updates the venerable Elizabethan commonplace of the world as a stage (and men and women merely players).

## Life is a dance you learn as you go.

1992 The saying perhaps entered oral tradition as a proverb from the song "Life's a Dance," lyrics by Allen Shambin and Steve Seskin (popularized by John Michael Montgomery): "Life's a dance you learn as you go / Sometimes you lead, sometimes you follow / Don't worry about what you don't know / Life's a dance you learn as you go."

## Life is a funny (strange) old dog.

1976 Dan Jenkins and Edwin Shrake, *Limo* (New York: Atheneum) 8: "D. Wayne Cooper made sense as usual. It was time to move it on down the road, as he would say. . . . I said to Cooper, 'I know you're right, D. Wayne, but it still hurts.' 'Yeah, I know,' he said. 'Life's a funny old dog, ain't she?'" 1988 *Free Lance-Star [Fredericksburg VA]* 7 Oct.: "In the words of an eminent philosopher, life is a strange old dog. Things circle around; things continue to fascinate." Cf. "LIFE is a bitch."

## Life is a garden.

1914 Otto Harbach, "Life Is a Garden"—song in the stage musical *Suzi*. 1924 *Gazette [Montreal]* 19 Apr.: "Arimathea lustrates life's enigma and consummates its marvels. Life is a garden. The everlasting sunrise touches its hidden roots."

## Life is a garden; dig it.

1972 U.S. copyright registered for "Marijuana plants: sticker" with the inscription "Life is a garden, dig it." 1977 *New York Times* 18 Dec.: "My tree was selected last May by George Newman (of Bloomin' Newman's—Life Is a Garden, Dig It) . . ."; the saying was the motto of the landscape designer Newman. It originated as an anti-proverb based on "LIFE is a garden," with the punning addition of the hip 1960s expression "dig it."

## Life is a journey, not a destination.

1941 Staff of First Community Church (Columbus OH), "Senior and Young People's Departments," *International Journal of Religious Education* 18, no. 1 (Jan.) 29: "By its very nature life seems not a destination but a journey, not an ending but a beginning." 1957 *Mason City [IA] Globe-Gazette* 11 Oct.: "In our attempt to find security . . . we sometimes live as if intent on arriving and not living. Life is a journey, not a destination." Cf. "SUCCESS is a journey, not a destination" and "HAPPINESS is a journey, not a destination."

## Life is a party.

1944 Channing Pollock, "Must We Be Glum?" *Coronet* 17, no. 1 (24 Nov.) 26: "My son, life is a party. The more you enjoy it, the more the other guests will and the more successful the whole thing will be." 1946 Horace Annesley Vachell, *Now Came Still Evening On* (London: Cassell) 47: "I have a last word for you. Life is a party. As one of the guests, do your damnedest to be as pleasant as possible to the other guests."

## Life is a picture; paint it well.

1956 *Spencer [IA] Reporter* 23 May: "Fourteen Peterson high school seniors were graduated. . . . [The class] motto was 'Life is a picture, paint it well.'" 1958 William W. Harper, "Summary of a Presentation [at the forty-ninth annual convention, 15–19 Feb.]," *Bulletin of the National*

*Association of Secondary-School Principals* 42: 245: "Remember, the school program should be organized in such a manner that it is effective in helping students to meet their needs, explore their abilities, and extend the range of their interests. Life is a picture, let us attempt to teach our boys and girls to paint it well." *DAP* 374(27).

## Life is (like) a shit sandwich (without bread) (and every day we take another bite).

1966 Daniel Spoerri, *An Anecdoted Topography of Chance*, translated by Emmett Williams (New York: Something Else) 9: "Just this morning MONSIEUR GEORGES expanded the philosophical observation of one of his customers, CAMILLE, that 'Life is a shit sandwich' with; 'Yes, and we take a bite every day'" (capitalization as shown). 1976 James Kirkwood, *P.S. Your Cat Is Dead: A Comedy* (New York: Samuel French) 24: "My God—What's happening to me? . . . So—well, life is a shit sandwich and every day we have to take another bite!" Attributed (without documentation) to the pro football player Joe Schmidt (1976) in 1982 Jonathon Green, *Morrow's International Dictionary of Contemporary Quotations* (New York: William Morrow) 45: "Life is a shit sandwich and everyday [*sic*] you take a bite."

## Life is a shit sandwich: the more bread you have, the less shit you eat.

1978 Dick Donnelly, "Comic Book Capitalism," *Socialist Standard* 74 (1978) 189: "One of them [witticisms submitted to the magazine *New Musical Express*] struck me as being rather less silly than most; it stated, 'Life is a shit sandwich. The more bread you have, the less shit you have to eat.'" The word *bread* has the punning sense of "money." The proverb probably originated as an anti-proverb based on "LIFE is a shit sandwich."

## Life is hard by the yard, but by the inch it's a cinch.

1947 *Tucson Daily Citizen* 20 Jun. (set as verses): "Life is hard / By the yard; / But by the inch / Life's a cinch.—Jean J. Gordon, in Better Homes and Gardens." *RHDP* 209.

## Life is like (is just) a box of chocolates (chocolate).

1994 The saying entered oral tradition as adapted from the motion picture *Forrest Gump*: "Life is a box of chocolates, Forrest. You never know what you're going to get."

## Life is not a bowl of cherries.

1931 *New York Times* 13 Nov.: "But the score was 7–6 in favor of Georgia, leading N.Y.U. rooters to the conclusion that there is no justice, life is not a bowl of cherries and Russia may have the right idea after all." 1932 Ad for subscription, *Life Magazine* 99 (Apr.) 62: "Contrary to the popular phrase, life is NOT a bowl of cherries— and LIFE treats it with respect but always with a smile" (that is, *Life* the magazine treats the phenomenon life with respect and a smile; capitalization as shown). *DAAP* 461–62. Presumably the proverb originated as a counter-proverb rebutting "LIFE is a bowl of cherries"—or vice versa.

## Life is not a spectator sport.

1958 *Albuquerque [NM] Tribune* 19 Aug.: "Life is not a spectator sport. We are all on the team." 1964 *Chicago Tribune* 9 Aug. (title of an article): "Life Is Not a Spectator Sport."

## Life is not life without a wife (There's no life without a wife).

1952 Bishambhar Das Chowhan, "Ceremonial Life among the Gaddi People of Bharmour Chamba State, Himachal Pradesh," *Man in India* 32: 23: "All Gaddi consider marriage a normal state for people and believe in the saying 'No life without a wife.'" 1962 R. E. S. Tanner, "The Relationship between the Sexes in a Coastal Islamic Society: Pangani District, Tanganyika," *African Studies* 21: 73 (in a list of "slogans which are embroidered on their pillows, counterpanes and curtains. . . . It is interesting to note that they are usually written in English"): "No life without a wife." *DAP* 374(57).

## Life is (just) one (damn) thing after another.

1909 *Wilkes-Barre [PA] Times* 5 Mar.: "Life: (A new definition) One damn thing after another." 1909 *Anaconda [MT] Standard* 20 Jul.: "As the pessimistic philosopher puts it: 'Life is just one damn thing after another.'" 1909 Ad for carbon-paper duplicated books, *The Practical Printer* 11, no. 7 (Jul.) 107: "Life is one darn thing after another" (playing on the wording of the proverb). *MP* L128; *DAP* 374; *YBQ* Modern Proverbs (52); Stevenson (1948) 1401. Sometimes the proverb is allusively abbreviated "ODTAA," which was the title of a novel by John Masefield (1926); whether it is to be pronounced as an acronym or an initialism is unclear.

## Life is so daily.

1943 *Christian Science Monitor* (29 Jun.): "The piece [a choral/dance rendition of Sandburg's *The People, Yes*], run off smoothly in three sections . . . , presented . . . (2) Life is So Daily—the rhythm of daily living, its buying and selling, its work and play and dreams." 1951 James Keller, *One Moment Please* (Garden City NY: Doubleday) 270: "Then suddenly one morning she seemed strangely dispirited. 'Mattie,' asked one of the girls, 'what's wrong?' 'Nothing at all, Miss Annie,' Mattie replied. 'It's just that life is so daily, isn't it?'"

## Life (The main thing in life, Everything) is (about) timing (Timing is everything).

1919 C. W. Saleeby, *The Whole Armour of Man* (Philadelphia: J. B. Lippincott): 370: "Just

contrast the exercise and delight of games like cricket and tennis, in which 'timing' is everything." 1929 *Los Angeles Times* 28 Dec.: (quoting Buster Keaton): "In vaudeville we . . . make laughter and we hold on to it. Timing is everything." 1963 Jean Dalrymple, *September Child* (New York: Dodd, Mead) 231: "Everything is timing. Even an almost unfunny line will bring a laugh if it's properly timed. . . ." 1967 J. J. Clark, *Carrier Admiral* (New York: David McKay) 36: "Among his [Adm. William Moffett's] many good traits he possessed a remarkable sense of timing; he used to tell me, 'Life is timing. Everything you do must be timed.'" 1973 *New York Times* 7 Jan. (quoting Richard Tucker): ". . . I said there's a boy next door at the City Opera. Get him. Bing and his assistants had called [Placido] Domingo provincial. Everything in life is timing." *RHDP* 336 (said to be of ancient Greek origin); *YBQ* Modern Proverbs (93).

## Life is too short (to wait) for someday.

1969 *On Her Majesty's Secret Service* (motion picture). "[FATHER:] 'Bond—he's in love with you?' [DAUGHTER:] 'That may come too, someday.' [FATHER:] 'Life's too short for someday, Tereza.'" 1992 John Newman, *How to Stay Cool, Calm & Collected When the Pressure's On* (New York: American Management Association) 165: "After every funeral, I say to myself, 'Life is too short for putting fun times off until "someday."' Life is for living, loving, laughing right now."

## Life is too short to drink (too short for) bad wine.

1985 *San Diego Union-Tribune* 20 Aug.: "Janet and Michael Asher arrived at the Bonita League party wearing grape purple T-shirts. . . . His insisted: 'Life Is Too Short—To Drink Bad Wine.'" 1986 *Advertiser [Adelaide, Australia]* 17 Dec.: "His [Robert Dundon's] philosophy is that life is too short to drink bad wine." A comical variant of recent provenence: "Life is short; drink the good wine first."

**Life** (Time, etc.) is too short (too precious) to waste it sleeping (Don't waste your life sleeping).

1944 Warren Miller, "The Animals' Fair," *Harper's Bazaar* 78, no. 2 (Feb.) 145: "Richard started to say . . . that when you got old you realized there was not much of your life left to you and you didn't want to waste it sleeping." 1959 *Milwaukee Journal* 28 Nov.: ". . . Christmas Eve is a pretty splendid occasion and it seems a pity to waste it sleeping." 1966 Jan Peerce, "A Week-end in Suburbia," *Music Journal* 24, no. 4 (Apr.) 25: "I have always been an early riser, and Sundays are no exception. We have so little time to do everything we want, so why waste it sleeping?" 1977 Frank Brady, *Onassis: An Extravagant Life* (Englewood Cliffs NJ: Prentice-Hall) 42: "His [Aristotle Onassis's] avoidance of sleep was a studied and tutored habit. 'Why waste your life sleeping?' he once asked. 'I don't have time for it!'" 1985 Diane Hoh, *Betrayed* (New York: Scholastic) 95: "'Look, Pres,' she'd said angrily when he'd just casually mentioned going home to get some sleep, 'life is too short to waste it sleeping.'"

**Life** is tough (Life is hard, Life sucks); wear (get) a helmet.

1992 Denis Leary, *No Cure for Cancer* (New York: Anchor) 28: "'My life didn't turn out the way I thought it would.' Hey. . . . Life sucks. Get a helmet." 1995 In the ABC television series *Boy Meets World*, season 3, episode 2 (29 Sep.), the character Eric speaks: "Little bro, life's tough; get a helmet." 1998 James D. Meadows, *Measurement of Geometric Tolerances in Manufacturing* (New York: Marcel Decker) 53: "What we have to accept is that our individual situations are no more difficult than the situations of others. Life is tough. Wear a helmet!"

**Life** is what happens while you are making other plans.

1957 "Quotable Quotes," *Reader's Digest* 70, no. 1 (Jan.) 32: "Allen Saunders: Life is what happens to us while we are making other plans." 1957 Harold W. Felton, *Bowleg Bill, Seagoing Cowpuncher* (Englewood Cliffs NJ: Prentice-Hall) x–xi: "It [the 'saga' of Bowleg Bill] also seems like life, because life is what happens to people while they are hoping for other things, and making other plans. Bowleg always planned to quit the sea and go back to punchin' cows." *YBQ* Allen Saunders. More recently, the saying has often been attributed to John Lennon.

**Life** sucks.

1979 Albert Ellis and Robert Harper, *Guide to Rational Living*, 3rd ed. (North Hollywood CA: Wilshire) 247: "You can take the negative thought, 'Life sucks and will always be miserable,' and can change it to the positive thought, 'Life sometimes sucks but can also be very enjoyable. . . .'" The *OED* traces the verb *suck* (in that sense) back no farther than 1971.

**Life** sucks, and then you die.

1984 *Schenectady [NY] Gazette* 21 Jul.: "It will be interesting to see if [Bruce] Springsteen can take his listeners that next step beyond the fatalism of life sucks-and-then-you-die. . . ." 1984 *Adweek* Nov.: "Strange as it seems, even little old ladies in Greenville go for 'The Morning Sickness Show' on Dallas' KTXQ-FM. The theme song of this morning-drive-time monument to poor taste suggests the general flavor of the show: 'Life Sucks and Then You Die.'" Perhaps the proverb originated as a blend of "LIFE sucks" and "LIFE is a bitch, and then you die."

**Life** sucks, but it's better than the alternative.

2002 Michael Flynn, *Falling Stars* (New York: Tom Doherty) 370: "Or maybe the water will slowly poison out. Or there'll be a solar storm and I'll get sleeted by radiation without ever knowing it happened. Life sucks; but it beats the alternative." Cf. "Old AGE is better than the alternative."

The **life** you save may (could) be your own.

1947 *Los Angeles Times* 10 Aug. (public service advertisement): "BE CAREFUL. . . . The Life You Save May Be Your Own! / Check Your Car / Check Your Driving / Check Accidents" (capitalization as shown). *DAP* 375(77).

Live **life** like you mean it.

See "LIVE like you mean it."

Live **life** to the fullest.

1934 Clifford Kirkpatrick, "Student Projects and the Sociology of Religion," *Social Forces* 12: 59 (summarizing the philosophical views of college students): "Life is short and after death we are dust, so why not live life to the fullest." 1940 *Washington Post* 15 Sep. (advertisement): "Live LIFE to the Fullest . . . Wear Vitality Shoes" (capitalization and ellipsis dots as shown). The proverb could be thought of as a paraphrase of "Carpe diem."

Nobody ever said **life** is easy (Who ever said life is easy?).

1965 *Chicago Tribune* 18 May: "SO WHO EVER SAID LIFE WAS EASY? OK, OK—but at least Evie can make it easier for you to enjoy . . . by looking pretty and fresh—and FLIRTY, why not!" (capitalization as shown). 1978 *New York Times* 19 Jul. (beginning of a poem titled "Whatthehell, c'est la guerre" by Elliott Nonas): "Nobody said life was easy. / Nobody said life was fair." Cf. the older proverb—from which this one perhaps evolved—"Life is not meant to be easy."

Nobody ever said **life** is fair (Who ever said life is fair?).

1929 *Washington Post* 5 Mar.: "Many say it is horribly unfair. . . . But who said life was fair?" 1937 Mary Hastings Bradley, *Pattern of Three* (New York: D. Appleton) 3: "Oh, it wasn't fair! But whoever [*sic*] said life is fair?" Cf. the

older proverb—from which this one perhaps evolved—"Life is unfair."

Take (Grab) **life** by the balls.

See "Take the BULL by the balls.

Take (You must take) what **life** gives you.

1908 Neith Boyce, *The Bond* (New York: Duffield, 1908) 134: "Take what life gives you, Teresa; take it with both hands, don't be afraid." 1912 Mary Helen Fee, *The Locusts' Years* (Chicago: A. C. McClurg) 67: "We must just take what life gives us, and if by and by comes sorrow, why, we've had a little taste of joy."

To lengthen your **life**, lessen your meals.

1947 *Nashua [IA] Reporter* 26 Mar. (cartoon caption): "To lengthen life, lessen the meals." *DAP* 375. The proverb has been spuriously credited to Benjamin Franklin.

You get out of **life** (the world, something, anything) what you put into it.

1901 Joseph F. Flint, *The Boy Puzzle* (New York: Pacific) 136: "We get out of life what we put into it, and reap what we sow." 1921 E. L. Blair, "Upon Whom Does the Burden Fall When Death or Disability Removes a Producer from Our Midst?" *Proceedings of the National Safety Council: Tenth Annual Safety Congress* (Boston) 744: "As this splendid man from the south said this morning, you get out of the world what you put into it." 1943 Robert N. Cunningham and Frank W. Cushwa, *Reading, Writing & Thinking* (New York: Charles Scribner's Sons) 42: "You and Dr. Johnson are both uttering versions of the old truth: You get out of anything what you put into it." *DAP* 250(9), 375(90). Cf. the older "The more you put into something, the more you get out."

You only go around (round) once in **life**.

c. 1966 The proverb—which is the current form of the older proverb "We only live once"—was popularized by a slogan in television advertisements for Schlitz beer: "You only go around once in life, so grab all the gusto you can!"

## There's no **lifeguard** in the gene pool.

1985 *The Economist* 294, no. 7381 (16 Feb.) 100 (lead-in of a classified ad for the 1984 book *Reality in Transition*, by Michael Spiegel): "Does our gene pool need a lifeguard?" 2004 "Countdown with Keith Obermann for August 25" (transcript), MSNBC television (reporting an inscription on a T-shirt allegedly marketed by Abercrombie and Fitch): "West Virginia: No Lifeguard In The Gene Pool." 2005 Karin Gillespie, *A Dollar Short* (New York: Simon & Schuster) 99 (epigraph to a chapter): "The problem with the gene pool is there's no lifeguard" (credited to "Sign tacked to a bulletin board in the Senior Center"). The proverb comments on what might be perceived as a declining "quality" in the human species, or some subset of it.

## The **light** at the end of the tunnel may be a train.

1974 Edward J. Schack, "ICC Energy Policy and Procedures," *ICC [Interstate Commerce Commission] Practitioners' Journal* 41: 666: "But yet the only predictable factor is that things will get worse before they get better. If you see the light at the end of the tunnel, don't forget that it may just be a train coming in the other direction." 1977 Robert Lowell, "Since 1939," in *Day by Day* (New York: Farrar, Straus & Giroux) 31: "We feel the machine slipping from our hands, / as if someone else were steering; / if we see a light at the end of the tunnel, / it's the light of an oncoming train." *YBQ* Dickson. The proverb satirizes the cliché "the light at the end of the tunnel," which was prevalently used by optimistic supporters of the Vietnam War. See "There's always LIGHT at the end of the tunnel."

## A **light** (candle) that burns (shines) twice as bright burns (shines) half as long.

1982 The saying entered oral tradition as a proverb from the movie *Blade Runner* (screenplay by Hampton Fancher and David Peoples).

## There's always (a) **light** at the end of the tunnel.

1971 Joseph Rees, *Titus Brandsma* (London: Sidgwick & Jackson) 175 (in reference to the Dutch priest Brandsma when he was interned at Dachau in 1942): "More than once he encouraged his fellow prisoners by saying: 'We are here in a dark tunnel. We have to pass through it. Somewhere at the end shines the eternal light.'" 1974 *Valparaiso [IN] Vidette-Messenger* 5 Jun.: "Somewhere there is always a light at the end of the tunnel of darkness." 1974 *New York Times* 25 Aug.: "To a wartime President, there is always light at the end of the tunnel, even in the midst of an enemy offensive." *RHDP* 323.

## It is not what you **like** (want) that makes you fat (it is what you eat).

1917 Kenneth C. Cardwell, "Eliminating the Dull Season," *The Furniture Worker* 34: 486: "'Of course, I'd love to sell loads of furniture in March,' retorted a fretful, hard-headed furniture man. . . . 'But, as they used to say down in the country when I was a kid, it ain't what you want that makes you fat.'" 1937 Mrs. Morgan Smith and A. W. Eddins, "Wise Saws from Texas," *Publications of the Texas Folklore Society* 13: 244: "It's not what you want that makes you fat, but what you get." *DAP* 200.

## Until the **lions** have their own historians, the stories will glorify the hunters.

1971 Willard R. Johnson, "The Responsibility of Africanists," *Africa Today* 18, no. 1 (Jan.) 23: "How many Africanists have moved to help the victim recover . . . and then write his own story of how he overcame his enemies[?] Until the lions have their own historians, stated W. E. B. DuBois, the tales will continue to glorify the hunters." *ODP* 186. The attribution to W. E. B. DuBois cannot be authenticated. The proverb is sometimes referred to as an African proverb. Cf. "HISTORY is written by the victors."

## Loose **lips** sink ships (A slip of the lip might sink a ship).

1942 "Slogans," *Time* 39, no. 2 (12 Jan.) 58: "Around Los Angeles harbor signs read: 'A slip of the lip may sink a ship.'" 1942 *Frederick [MD] News* 12 May: "In the high school lobby before the opening of the meeting, they were surrounded on all sides by placards bearing such admonitions as 'Loose Lips Might Sink Ships.'" *DAP* 546(2); *RHDP* 215–16; *YBQ* Advertising Slogans (139); Room (2000) 411. The proverb originated as a wartime "security" slogan. Cf. "Careless (Loose) TALK costs lives."

## You can put **lipstick** on a pig but it's still a pig (A pig wearing lipstick is still a pig).

1985 *Washington Post* 16 Nov.: "The board of commissioners, reluctant to commit to such a project, asked if they couldn't use the money to renovate Candlestick Park. 'That,' replied KNBR personality Ron Lyons, 'would be like putting lipstick on a pig.'" 1986 *Dallas Morning News* 8 Jan.: "'It's like putting lipstick on a pig. It can't hide its ugliness,' said [Jim] Hightower, a self-styled 'progressive' Democrat. . . ." 1992 *Virginian-Pilot* 16 Oct. (regarding a character on the television series *Designing Women*): "She speaks her mind and tosses around such Bubba-isms as this one: 'You can put lipstick on a pig and call it Matilda. But it's still a pig.'" The *lipstick-on-a-pig* version is the predominant modern form of older expressions that assert the futility of dressing or decorating pigs or other animals. Mieder (2009b): 83–85.

## **Little** by little does the trick.

1906 Franklin T. Baker, George Carpenter, and Katharine Owen, *Second Year Language Reader* (New York: Macmillan) 2 (the moral at the end of the Aesopic fable "The Crow and the Pitcher"): "Little by little does the trick." *DAP* 379.

## **Live** fast (hard), die young.

See "Live fast, die young, leave a good-looking CORPSE."

## **Live** (Live life) like you mean it.

1972 Robert Cohen, *Acting Professionally* (Palo Alto CA: National) 31: "So live as if you mean it, and become an artist in the same way." 1992 David James Duncan, *The Brothers K* (New York: Doubleday) 512: . . . [T]here it'll be—the cold, empty world we came from [that is, the moon]. . . . And still trying to maybe tell us, *Enjoy it down there. Live like you mean it. 'Cause once upon a time, this was a world too*" (italics as shown).

## **Live** like you're dying.

2004 The proverb was popularized in a song (so titled) by Tim McGraw. 2004 *New York Times* 25 Oct.: "It's like the song says: You gotta live like you're dying." 2007 Charles Carroll, *Leadership Lessons from a Chef* (Hoboken NJ: John Wiley & Sons) 139: "There is a saying, 'Live Like You're Dying.' I wonder how many of us take life for granted?"

## **Live** now, pay later.

1946 *Mason City [IA] Globe-Bazette* 20 Apr. (advertisement): "MR. AND MRS. BRIDE TO BE AND GROOM TO BE. LIVE NOW—PAY LATER" (capitalization as shown). 1958 *Modesto [CA] Bee* 17 Feb. (headline): "Psychiatrist Hits Live Now, Pay Later Philosophy." Rees (1984) 56.

## We **live** too short and die too young.

1991 Title of a book by Walter Bortz (New York: Bantam); Bortz may have coined the saying—or

he may have been using an existing proverb.
1993 *The State [Columbia SC]* 28 Oct.: "Too many people of all ages live too short and die too young."

## You have to (be able to, learn to) **live** with yourself.

1902 William Travers Jerome, "Address," *Report of Special and Regular Meetings of the Colorado Bar Association* 5: 72: "Suppose you go down in the fight? You have kept your self-respect, and you have got to live with yourself most of the time." 1903 [Anne] Constance Smedley [Armfield], *An April Princess* (New York: Dodd, Mead) 53: "You've got to live with yourself when all's said and done."

## It takes a lot of **living** to make a house a home.

See "It takes a LOT of living to make a house a home."

## A rolling **loan** gathers no loss.

1984 Scott E. Pardee, "Prospects for LDC Debt and the Dollar," *Economic Review* (Federal Reserve Bank of Kansas City) 69, no. 1 (Jan.) 6: ". . . [N]ew loans are being made to pay interest on old loans. The current comment on this topic is 'a rolling loan gathers no loss.'" 1984 *Morning Call [Allentown PA]* 15 Mar.: "He [Robert H. Stovall] said failure of these nations to pay debts to American money center banks would be handled by the banks, some of which are lending these nations more money to make the interest payments on the debts. He joked: 'A rolling loan gathers no loss.'" The proverb originated as an anti-proverb based on "A rolling stone gathers no moss."

## **Location**, location, location.

See "The most important CONSIDERATIONS for buying a home are location, location, and location."

## In the **long run** (long range), we are all dead.

1923 John Maynard Keynes, *A Tract on Monetary Reform* (London: Macmillan) 80: "But this *long run* is a misleading guide to current affairs. *In the long run* we are all dead" (italics as shown). 1970 Samuel Lenher, "A View from the Private Sector: Industry and Environment," in *Ecology and Politics in America's Environmental Crisis* (Princeton NJ: Center for International Studies, Princeton University) 76: "It [the automobile] presents a problem that can only be solved nationally, and long range the problem undoubtedly will be solved. . . . But as the old saying has it, in the long range we are all dead." *YBQ* Keynes (4). Keynes is often cited as the author of the saying. It is to be understood not as a commonplace observation on human mortality but rather as a comment on the possible futility of long-range planning.

## A **long shot** is better than no shot (at all).

See "A long SHOT is better than no shot."

## Don't (Never) **look** back; something (someone, they) might be gaining on you.

1953 *New York Times* 5 Jun. (advertisement for forthcoming issue of *Collier's Magazine*): "Satch [baseball player Satchel Paige] gives his own six rules for longevity ending with the warning: 'Don't look back. Something might be gaining on you.'" 1953 Richard Donovan, "The Fabulous Satchel Paige [part 3]: 'Time Ain't Gonna Mess with Me,'" *Collier's* 131, no. 24 (13 Jun.) 55 (quoting Paige's six precepts for "How to Stay Young"): "6. Don't look back. Something might be gaining on you." *YBQ* Paige (6).

## If something **looks** too easy, it probably is.

See "If something SEEMS too easy, it probably is."

If you keep **looking** back, you can't see where you are going (It is hard to see where you are going if you keep looking back).

1990 *Los Angeles Times* 24 May: "It's hard to see where you're going when you're looking back. David Bowie's 'Sound + Vision' tour offers a peculiar promise. . . ." 2004 Charles Carroll, *Life Is an Inside Job* (Lincoln NE: iUniverse) 182: "Remember, life moves forward. If you keep looking back, you won't be able to see where you are going."

It is better to **look** good than to be good.

1986 *Atlanta Constitution* 13 Mar. (review of the movie *Highlander*): "Clearly Mulcahy believes it's better to look good than to be good. 'Highlander' has more optic nerve than brains. . . ." 1986 *Atlanta Journal and Constitution* 24 Aug. (at the top of a list): "Best uniforms [among southern college football teams.] Sometimes it's better to look good than be good."

It's better to **look** good than to feel good.

1978 *Cancer-Causing Chemicals—Part 1: Safety of Cosmetics and Hair Dyes. Hearings before the Subcommittee on Oversight and Investigations . . . House of Representatives* (Washington DC: Government Printing Office) 136; James Merritt, president of the cosmetics trade association, is being questioned by Congressman Henry Waxman (26 Jan.): "[Waxman:] 'Are you telling us that it is as important, that is, that it is more important to look good than to feel good?' [Merritt:] 'I think looking good and feeling good perhaps could be equally important. On the other hand, there are certain individuals to which one might be better than the other.'" 1984 *Washington Post* 25 Dec.: "We look to Joe [Theismann] for these beauty tips because Joe looks *mah-velous*. And you know I always say, better to look good than to feel good" (italics as shown). The allusion is probably to phrasing employed by Billy Crystal's character Fernando,

introduced on *Saturday Night Live* (NBC-TV) earlier in 1984. Cf. "BEAUTY is pain."

**Look** before you leave.

1958 *Traffic Safety* 53, no. 3 (Sep.) 29 (depiction of a poster urging drivers' caution in lane-changing): "Squeeze plays are preventable / Look before you leave." 1960 *Look before You Leave: A Primer for Communities Facing Change* (Chicago: Mayor's Commission on Human Relations). Litovkina and Mieder (2006) 205. Originating as an anti-proverb based on "Look before you leap," the proverb has had a wide range of applications, urging caution about withdrawing one's money from an investment, about ascertaining that no body lies on the bottom of a private swimming pool, about ensuring that no children or pets are left locked in a car, and so on.

Praise the **Lord** and pass the ammunition.

1942 *Tucson Daily Citizen*, 3 Feb. (attributed to "an unnamed Navy chaplain at Pearl Harbor"): "Cromwell said, 'Put your trust in God, but mind to keep your powder dry,' and an unnamed Navy chaplain at Pearl Harbor on December 7 said in the midst of the hell, 'Praise the Lord and pass the ammunition, I got one of the sons-of-b—— (Belial)!'" Later in 1942 the popular song with the saying as its title (and recurring line) was published, recorded, and widely sung and alluded to. The saying came to be attributed to Chaplain William McGuire, but he discounted the attribution, and Chaplain Howell Forgy claimed it: 1942 *New York Times* Nov. 1. *RHDP* 275; *YBQ* Forgy.

You never **lose** (You don't get defeated, You aren't beaten, You can't fail) unless (until) you quit (trying).

1909 "Addison Div., No. 108," *The Railroad Telegrapher* 26: 1979: "Boys, you seem slow in sending in any items, write them on a card . . . and send to your chairman, so we can have a good report. We cannot fail unless we quit." 1951 "Tangles Take Time," *The Rotarian* 78, no. 6 (Jun.) 60 (credited to *Carleton Place Canadian*): "Fixing a tangled line is more exciting even than fishing. You know you can do it if you stay with it. You can't lose unless you quit."

## A good **loser** is (still) a loser (Show me a good loser, and I'll show you a loser).

1948 Howard Roberts, *The Big Nine* (New York: G. P. Putnam's Sons) 83: "These Illini teams went down to defeat but they went down fighting, true always to Zup's [coach Bob Zuppke's] contention that 'a good loser is no good.'" 1965 *Valley Independent [Monessen PA]* 6 Apr.: "'The losers will join hands and march on the British embassy,' he [Bob Hope] said. This wasn't quite as lasting a remark as the one expressed elsewhere by Boston Celtic Coach Red Auerbach—'show me a good loser, and I'll show you a loser'—but it did the job." 1966 Sam P. Wiggins, *Higher Education in the South* (Berkeley CA: McCutchan) 115: "In other quarters the words of Grantland Rice about 'how you played the game' fall on deaf ears. The operational slogan is that a good loser is a *loser*" (italics as shown). Perhaps originating as an anti-proverb based on an aphorism like "A good loser is a winner" or "A good loser is better than a bad winner," the saying has also been attributed to Knute Rockne, Vince Lombardi, Bear Bryant, Woody Hayes, Leo Durocher, Adm. Hyman Rickover, Paul Newman, and others. *YBQ* Auerbach.

## It takes a **lot** (heap) of living (loving) to make a house a home.

1916 The saying entered oral tradition as a proverb adapted from a line in Edgar A. Guest's poem "Home": "It takes a heap o' livin' in a house t' make it home." 1923 *Los Angeles Times* 27 Jun.: "'It takes a lot of loving to make a house a home.' Occupied only since March 17, the beautiful new clubhouse of the Tuesday Afternoon Club of Glendale underwent yesterday

the magic of love and became a home." *DAP* 382(2), 392(2); *RHDP* 169; *YBQ* Guest.

## All you need is **love**.

1967 The saying passed into oral tradition as a proverb from the title and refrain of the Beatles' song (lyrics by John Lennon).

## If you **love** something, let it go (set it free); if it comes back to you, it is yours.

1972 Jess Lair, *I Ain't Much, Baby—But I'm All I've Got* (Garden City NY: Doubleday) 203 (among unattributed thoughts or sayings submitted by college students): "If you want something very, very badly, let it go free. If it comes back to you, it's yours forever. If it doesn't, it was never yours to begin with." 1975 Leonard Gasparini, *If You Love* (Ottawa: Borealis) 7 (epigraph to the collection of poems; set as verse): "If you love something, / Set it free. / If it comes back, / It is yours. / If it doesn't, / It never was" (the author is said to be "Unknown"). 1978 Donald M. Joy, "Adolescents in Socio-Psychological Perspective," in *Youth Education in the Church*, edited by Roy B. Zuck and Warren Benson (Chicago: Moody) 96: "There is risk involved in allowing certain freedoms to children. . . . One of the newer adages makes the point poetically: 'If you love something, set it free. If it comes back, it's yours. If it doesn't, it never was.'" 1979 David Klimek, *Beneath Mate Selection and Marriage* (New York: Van Nostrand Reinhold) 229: "Recently I attended an art festival where I found an inscription burned into a small piece of weathered barn siding. It read, 'If you love something, let it go. If it returns, it's yours; if it doesn't, it wasn't.' Whoever wrote it must have known something about the process of human intimacy. . . ."

## *Love* is (just, only, nothing but) a four-letter word.

1937 Harold Petersen, "Rewrite," *Los Angeles Time Sunday Magazine* (9 May) 10: ". . . I'm liable to excuse him where a lot of his readers will too. But when the guy says that 'Love is just a four-letter word. . . .' Well, you get the idea" (second set of ellipsis dots as shown). 1948 Leonard Ralph Casper, "My Soul Doth Magnify Itself" (undergraduate thesis in creative writing, University of Wisconsin) 29 (in a poem titled "Swimmers Out of Water"): "Whatever her private life, one should be stirred / To trust her, but his suggestive eyes / Insist that love is a four-letter word." 1948 April Taylor, *Love Is a Four-Letter Word* (New York: Beechhurst). In the form "Love is just a four-letter word," the proverb was made highly popular by Bob Dylan's 1967 song with that title and refrain (famously recorded by Joan Baez).

## Love is where you find it.

1938 The saying possibly entered oral tradition as a proverb from the title and lyrics of a song by Johnny Mercer and Al Dubin—or else the song employed a sentence that was already proverbial. A different song, by Earl K. Brant in 1948, bore the same title. The proverb may derive from the older proverb "Gold is where you find it." Cf. "HAPPINESS is where you find it."

## Love it or leave it.

1901 D. A. Knuppenburg, "Qualifications Essential to Be the Successful Farmer," *Seventh Annual Report of the Pennsylvania Department of Agriculture*, part 1, 660: "To be successful, I say, he must first, love his occupation. . . . So, on this point, I would say, love it, or leave it." 1905–6 Elizabeth B. Andrews, "Farming as an Art," *Farmer's Institutes* (Commonwealth of Pennsylvania Department of Agriculture Bulletin no. 161) 10: "An old farmer put into five short words such advice as this: 'Love it or leave it.' Perhaps you say this is a text for a forcible sermon for people in all professions and callings." More recently, the proverb usually occurs as a jingoistic slogan. 1921 *Chicago Daily Tribune* 2 Aug.: "William Valle, congressman from the First Colorado district, a member of the house immigration committee, said his message to aliens in this country was: 'Love it or leave it.'" Rees (1984) 211.

## Love means never having to say you're sorry.

1970 The saying entered oral tradition as a proverb from Erich Segal's best-selling novel *Love Story* (New York: Harper & Row), which first appeared (somewhat condensed) in *Ladies' Home Journal* 87, no. 2 (Feb.) 124: "She cut off my apology, then said very quietly, 'Love means not ever having to say you're sorry.'" In the popular motion picture, "never" replaces "not ever." The novel was written after Segal's screenplay but published before the release of the movie in Dec. 1970. *YBQ* Segal (2).

## The love you take is equal to the love you make.

1969 The saying probably passed into oral tradition as a proverb from the Beatles' song "The End": "And in the end the love you take is equal to the love you make." *YBQ* Lennon-McCartney (24).

## Make love, not war.

1965 *Observer [London]*, 14 Mar.: "Recent visitors to Berkeley have been charmed by the sight of long-legged, barefoot Californian beauties parading with posters saying 'Mr. President, let's make love, not war.'" *DAAP* 486; *YBQ* Legman (2); Rees (1984) 216; Pickering et al. (1992) 368; Rees (1995) 310. The saying has been credited to Gershon Legman, speaking in 1963. The zeugma itself had been anticipated: 1921 K. L. Montgomery, "Quarrelling of Queens," *Cornhill Magazine* 124: 299: "'Then it's not for war, for the spear is silent!' said he. For the smith who had wrought the spear had uttered ranns [Irish for 'verses'] as he hammered and cooled. . . . 'Yerra, they are for making love, not war,' said Rosaleen." 1955 Hugh Mills, *The Little Glass Clock*, in *Plays of the Year*, vol. 11, edited by

J. C. Trewin (New York: Frederick Ungar) 406: "If every husband were adored as much as mine and every wife as much as I, they would make love instead of war."

## It takes a lot of **loving** to make a house a home.

See "It takes a LOT of living to make a house a home."

## Bad **luck** comes (runs) in threes.

1907 Eleanor Gates, *Cupid, the Cow Punch* (New York: McClure) 92: "I feel better. Was worried 'cause I've had bad luck lately, and bad luck most allus runs in threes." *DAP* 392(3). The proverb acknowledges a common superstition.

## The harder you work (practice), the more **luck** you have.

See "The harder you WORK, the luckier you get."

## Luck (Good luck, Bad luck) does not just happen.

1965 Robert Kroetsch, *But We Are Exiles* (New York: St. Martin's) 95: "'Bad luck doesn't just happen,' Pottle said. 'We've got a right to ask a few questions.'" 1982 Douglas G. Dean, "The Impact of a Juvenile Awareness Program on Select Personality Traits of Male Clients," *Journal of Offender Counseling, Services, & Rehabilitation* 6, no. 3 (Spring) 80: "Likewise, with regard to chance expectations, the experimental group was able to shed their magical thinking and realize that luck does not just happen."

## Luck (Lady Luck) is a jealous (cruel, fickle, hard) mistress.

1916 Bennet Copplestone, "The Luck of the Navy: How the 'Sydney' Met the 'Emden,'" *Cornhill Magazine* 114: 717: "Luck is no bungler, but Luck is a most jealous mistress." 1928 Emil Engstrom, "Mushing the Arctic Trails," *The Frontier* 9: 137:

"'Lucky Swedes' is a common expression in Alaska, and includes all Scandinavians. But Luck is a hard task-mistress, as the old prospectors know only too well." 1938 Howard Woolston, *Metropolis: A Study of Urban Communities* (New York: D. Appleton-Century) 256: "This psychology explains the excitement, superstition, sharp dealing and touchiness that prevail in gaming resorts. Lady Luck is a fickle mistress."

## Luck is the residue of design.

1946 *Valley Morning Star [Hurlingen TX]* 16 Feb.: "The other day [the baseball manager and executive Branch] Rickey discoursed at length on 'luck—the residue of design.'" 1946 *Sporting News* 21 Feb. (quoting Branch Rickey): "I say once again, that time is of the essence and luck is the residue of design." *RHDP* 218; *YBQ* Rickey.

## Luck is when (what happens when) preparation meets opportunity.

1912 "Fact and Comment," *The Youth's Companion* 86, no. 17 (25 Apr.) 222 (in a series of sagacious sayings): "He is lucky who realizes that 'luck' is the point where preparation meets opportunity." 1926 "Savings Bank Division Meeting," *Bankers' Magazine* 113, no. 5 (Nov.) 670: "Some are inclined to call it luck, but we can only agree if we define luck as that thing which happens when preparation meets opportunity." Since the late 1990s, the saying has been widely attributed (on no discernible basis) to the Roman philosopher Seneca.

## You can't trust **luck**.

1928 Konrad Bercovici, *Alexander: A Romantic Biography* (New York: Cosmopolitan) 248: "And now even Iskander's best friends and admirers remembered what Philotas had said: that Iskander's luck was greater than his bravery and courage combined. . . . For you cannot trust luck!" 1939 John Steinbeck, *The Grapes of Wrath* (New York: Viking) 420: "Maybe you're lucky. Look out for luck. You can't trus' luck." 1966

*Palouse [WA] Republic* 24 Jun. (public service ad): "You can't trust luck. You can trust seat belts."

## It's better to be **lucky** than good.

1939 *New York Times* 27 Nov.: "The singular [baseball player] Lefty Gomez has always subscribed to the theory that it is better to be lucky than good." 1940 Richard D. Chapman and Ledyard Sands, eds., *Golf as I Play It* (New York: Carlyle House) 123 (quoting Charlie Yates): "On the first extra hole in my match against John Fischer in the British Amateur Championship [in 1938], I laid him a dead stymie, winning the match. As I told Johnny, 'It's better to be lucky than good.'" Cf. "If you can't be GOOD, be lucky," and the older "It's better to be lucky than wise" and "It's better to be (born) lucky than rich."

## There is no free **lunch**.

See "There is no such THING as a free lunch."

### Don't get **mad**, get ahead.

See "Don't GET mad, get ahead."

### Don't get **mad**; get even.

See "Don't GET mad, get even."

### Don't (try to) **make** something out of nothing.

See "Don't (try to) make something out of NOTHING."

### If you (can) **make** it here, you can make it anywhere.

1959 *New York Times* 8 Feb. (quoting the actress Julie Newmar): "That's why I came to New York. Because if you make it here, you make it anywhere." *RHDP* 155–56; *YBQ* Ebb (6). The reference, in the world of professional entertainment, is usually to New York City. The proverb plays on the older "If you can't make it here, you can't make it anywhere," referring to some specific place: 1931 Robert Cantwell, *Laugh and Lie Down* (New York: Farrar & Rinehart) 36: "I can't make any sense in all this moving around. If we can't make it here, on our own territory, we'll certainly never be able to make it anywhere else."

### Make it do, wear it out, use it up, or do without.

See "EAT it up, wear it out, make it do, or do without."

### If **Mama** ain't happy, ain't nobody happy (When Mama is happy, everybody's happy).

1982 Ferrol Sams, *Run with the Horsemen* (Atlanta: Peachtree) 27: "There is an unspoken Southern axiom that if a lady complains about something, a gentleman immediately assumes the responsibility of rectification. It is based on the principle that if Mama ain't happy, ain't nobody happy. . . ." 1987 Carole Marsh, *Grits R Us* (n.p.: Gallopade) 27: "'IF MAMA AIN'T HAPPY—NOBODY'S HAPPY': Sign on kitchen wall in Hominy Valley, North Carolina" (capitalization as shown). 1994 *Argus Press [Owasso MI]* 5 Dec. (ad for Singer sewing machines): "GET HER A SINGER—'CAUSE IF MAMA'S HAPPY, EVERYBODY'S HAPPY" (capitalization as shown). The proverb most often occurs with one or both "dialect" *ain't*'s.

### Whatever (What) **Mama** wants, Mama gets.

1975 *Los Angeles Times* 28 Apr. (advertising supplement): "One little girl not too long ago said, 'ALL I WANT FOR CHRISTMAS IS MY TWO FRONT TEETH.' But not my ma. All she wanted was a GRAND OLD FLAG. So what mama wants mama gets. So please wave at mama's flag" (capitalization as shown). 1985 Jonathan Coleman, *At Mother's Request* (New York: Atheneum) 421 (prosecuting attorney Ernie Jones is quoted): "I suppose the defense is telling us that Marc Schreuder was so tied to his mother's apron strings that he . . . was virtually a puppet. What Mama wants, Mama gets."

### All **men** put their pants on the same way (one leg at a time).

See "Everyone puts his PANTS on one leg at a time."

## The best **man** for the job may be a woman.

1974 Helen W. Diamond, "The Best Man for a Job May Be a Woman," *Educational Horizons* 52 (the article describes a course on management training for women at the University of California, Irvine, in 1972). 1978 Fran McKee, "A Historical Sketch of the Naval Air Station[,] Pensacola . . . ," in *Military Presence on the Gulf Coast*, edited by William S. Coker (Pensacola FL: Gulf Coast History and Humanities Conference) 123: "What I guess I'm getting at is that sometimes the best man for the job is a woman!"

## Beware (of) a smiling **man**.

Whiting (1952) 440 lists "Beware of a smiling man" as a North Carolina proverb. 1956 Samuel W. Taylor, *I Have Six Wives* (New York: Greenberg) 210: "'I thought of the old proverb,' Becky said, telling of the incident. '*Beware the smiling man*'" (italics as shown). MP M25. Cf. "Beware a smiling FACE."

## The bigger a **man's** head gets, the easier it is to fill his shoes.

1945 *Business Education World* 26: 130 (filler item): "The bigger a man's head gets, the easier it is to fill his shoes" (unattributed, credited to *Magazine Digest*). 1948 "Wise and Otherwise," *Coronet* 25, no. 2 (Dec.) 66 (in a small gathering of witty sayings): "The bigger a man's head gets, the easier it is to fill his shoes"—there attributed to Joseph A. Mullins. *DAP* 288(35).

## Don't judge a **man** until you have walked a mile in his boots.

See "Don't judge someone till you have walked a MILE in his shoes."

## Don't take a lazy **man's** load.

1918 C. M. Barbeau, "Canadian-English Folklore," *Journal of American Folklore* 31, 35, reports the proverb from Ontario; Whiting (1952) 440

from North Carolina. The term "lazy man's load," attested as early as the eighteenth century, refers to an excessively heavy load by means of which a lazy man would attempt to avoid making two trips. The proverb figuratively advises against burdening oneself with futile or excessive cares.

## Every **man's** dung is (smells) sweet to him (to his own nose).

1905 Havelock Ellis, *Studies in the Psychology of Sex*, vol. 4 (Philadelphia: F. A. Davis) 56: " . . . [W]hile the exhalations of other people's bodies are ordinarily disagreeable to us, such is not the case with our own; this is expressed in the crude and vigorous dictum of the Elizabethan poet, Marston, 'Every man's dung smells sweet i' his own nose.'" MP M30. The attribution to John Marston appears to be spurious; however, Ellis must have thought he was quoting someone! The orator in Erasmus's *Praise of Folly* (1511) declares that "dogs' dung smells sweet as cinnamon to them, I suppose" ("Opinor etiam, cum excrementa canum odorantur, illis cinnamomum videri"), but there it is the hunters—not the dogs—that experience the sweetness of the smell, in their ardor for the chase. Cf. "Nobody minds the SMELL of his own farts."

## Every **man** must pull his own weight.

See "Everyone must pull his own WEIGHT."

## Every **man** to his own poison (To every man his own poison).

1922 H. L. Mencken, *Prejudices: Third Series* (New York: Alfred A. Knopf) 278: "Every man, as the Psalmist says [?], to his own poison, or poisons, as the case may be. One of mine, following hard after theology, is political economy." 1928 Jim Tully, *Shanty Irish* (New York: Albert & Charles Boni) 112: " . . . [H]e got so drunk—When I scolded him he said—'Oh it's ivery man his own poison and the divil take us all.'" Perhaps the proverb originated as an anti-proverb based on "Every man to his own taste" or "To each his own." *DAP* 399.

## Go home with the **man** who brought you.

See "Go home with the ONE who brought you."

## A good **man** is hard to find.

1918 Eddie Green, song title (the song was first performed by Alberta Hunter and first recorded, in 1918, by Marion Harris). *RHDP* 118; *YBQ* Eddie Green; Rees (1995) 189; Doyle (2007b). The proverb is the twentieth-century incarnation (or equivalent) of the older proverb "Good men are scarce."

## If you must strike (hit) a **man** from behind, slap him on the back.

1955 Jacob M. Braude, *Speaker's Encyclopedia of Stories, Quotations, and Anecdotes* (New York: Prentice-Hall) 136: "If you must strike a man from behind, slap him on the back" (unattributed). *DAP* 400(112). A slap on the back is a friendly or complimentary gesture; a strike from behind is a treacherous act.

## If you want something done, ask a busy **man**.

See "If you want something done, ask a busy PERSON."

## Inside every fat **man** there's a thin man trying to get out.

See "Inside every fat PERSON there's a thin person trying to get out."

## Inside every old **man**, there is a young man.

See "Inside every old PERSON, there is a young one."

## **Men** are from Mars, women are from Venus.

1992 The saying entered oral tradition as a proverb from the book so titled, by John Gray. *YBQ* John Gray.

## **Men** are like buses; if you miss one, another will come along.

See "Never run after a WOMAN or a streetcar; if you miss one, another will come along soon."

## **Men** are only good for one thing.

1954 Jerome Chodorov, *Anniversary Waltz* (New York: Random House) 103: "A man is only good for one thing, Miss Revere. It's been true since the dawn of time. Send him out with his spear, let him kill a bear. . . . What *else* are we good for?" (italics as shown; in this instance, it is not clear that the saying has its current sexual meaning, unless we apply a Freudian analysis). 1981 Aurora Levins Morales, ". . . And Even Fidel Can't Change That" (ellipsis dots as shown), in *This Bridge Called My Back: Writings by Radical Women of Color*, edited by Cherríe Moraga and Gloria Anzaldúa (Watertown MA: Persephone) 53: ". . . [G]randmother, aunts and greataunts all decked out in sex, talking about how I'm pretty, talking about how men are only good for one thing. . . ." 1986 Danny Peary, *Guide for the Film Fanatic* (New York: Simon & Schuster) 149 (review of *Femmes Fatales*): "The trick [director Bertrand] Blier plays on his men in this film is that they become sexual objects to be used and humiliated and the women become the aggressors who think that men are only good for one thing."

## **Men** are only good for one thing—and sometimes they aren't even good for that.

1994 *The Age [Melbourne, Australia]* 29 Aug.: "'You know girls, men are only good for one thing,' said Sandy 'Pepa' Denton. (Much whooping from the crowd.) 'And sometimes they're not even good for that.'" 1994 João

Ubaldo Ribeiro, *The Lizard's Smile*, translated from Brazilian Portuguese by Clifford Landers (New York: Atheneum) 174: "I never liked black men anyway. They're only good for one thing, and you're not even good for that" ("*negro só serve para uma coisa e nem para isso você serve*"). The proverb originated as an anti-proverb based on "MEN are only good for one thing."

## Men (All men) are pigs.

1910 Anna Costantini, *Ragna* (New York: Sturgis & Walton) 374: "'All men are pigs,' opined the cook. 'Some things are above the comprehension of females,' retuned Nando, loftily, his masculine vanity ruffled. . . ." 1915 Rachel Crothers, *A Man's World* (Boston: Richard G. Badger) 94: "Men are pigs, of course. They take all they can get and don't give any more than they have to. It's a man's world. . . ."

## A man's got to do what a man's (he's) got to do.

1939 John Steinbeck, *Grapes of Wrath* (New York: Viking) 306: "Casy said quickly, 'I know this—a man got to do what he got to do. I can't tell you.'" 368: "Pa took the dirty bill and gave Uncle John two silver dollars. 'There ya are,' he said. 'A fella got to do what he got to do. Nobody don' know enough to tell 'im.'" *RHDP* 222–23; Pickering et al. (1992) 380; Rees (1995) 313.

## A man's got to do what a man's got to do; a woman has to do what he can't.

1998 Roz Warren, *Women's Lip* (Naperville IL: Hysteria) 77: "A man's got to do what a man's got to do. A woman must do what he can't" (attributed to the comediene Rhonda Hansome). The proverb originated as an anti-proverb based on "A MAN's got to do what a man's got to do."

## A man is entitled to his own opinions, not his own facts.

See "Everyone is entitled to his own OPINIONS, not his own facts."

## A man is no better than his horse.

1905 *Commonwealth of Australia Parliamentary Debates* 26: 2140: "A mounted man is no better than his horse, and the rider of an animal with a sore back is of no use." 1940 J. Frank Dobie et al., "Introduction," *Publications of the Texas Folklore Society* 16: ix: "'A man is no better than his horse,' as a saying [in Texas] went, and another: 'A man on foot is no man at all.'"

## A man is not a camel.

1911 R. E. Vernède, *An Ignorant in India* (Edinburgh: William Blackwood) 223–24: "I . . . considered myself amply provident to take with me a pint flask of whisky and soda ready mixed and some sandwiches. Fool, in that I did not remember that man is not a camel, whereas Bengal, for the most part, is undoubtedly a desert." 1931 Walter Owen, *The Cross of Carl* (Boston: Little, Brown) 72: "But a man is not a camel, no . . . not a camel . . . and it is time to make an end" (ellipsis dots as shown). 1986 *Wall Street Journal* 25 Jun. (the dialog being recounted occurred in Barrow Creek, Australia): "Mr. Roberts drains a glass of beer and orders another. 'A man's not a camel,' he explains." Most often currently, the proverb jocularly justifies a need for the frequent slaking of human thirst, especially with alcoholic decoctions.

## A man may be down but never (not) out.

See "DOWN is not out."

## The man most down on a thing is he who is least up on it.

1909 [Elbert Hubbard], *The Philistine: A Periodical of Protest* 29: 176: "The people simply do not know, and not knowing they do not care. That which we are not up on we are down on." 1911 Helen Barrett Montgomery, "The Woman's Jubilee Campaign," *Missionary Review of the World* 34: 410: "'What one is least up on, she is apt to be most down on,' as one of the speakers wittily put it." *DAP* 403(214). Cf. "PREJUDICE is being down on what you are not up on."

## A **man** on foot is no man at all.

1927 J. Frank Dobie, "The Pacing White Mustang," *American Mercury* 12: 435: "A man on foot is no man at all. The proverb belonged to the West when the West was a land of two radical facts: horses and horsemen." 1940 J. Frank Dobie et al., "Introduction," *Publications of the Texas Folklore Society* 16: ix: "'A man is no better than his horse,' as a saying [in Texas] went, and another: 'A man on foot is no man at all.'" 1947 Robert Moorman Denhardt, *The Horse of the Americas* (Norman: U of Oklahoma P) xv: "While it lasted, men who belonged to the Age [of Horse Culture] said truly, 'A man on foot is no man at all.' . . ."

## **Men** seldom make passes at girls who wear glasses.

See "BOYS seldom make passes at girls who wear glasses."

## **Man** stumbles over pebbles but never over mountains.

1925 Earl Derr Biggers, *Behind That Curtain*, in *Charlie Chan Omnibus* (New York: Grosset & Dunlap) 84 (second numbering): "But it is wise in our work, Miss Morrow, that even the smallest improbabilities be studied. Men stumble over pebbles, never over mountains." *DAP* 401(148).

## A **man** who kicks his dog (hound) will beat his wife.

Whiting (1952) 428 gives the saying as a North Carolina proverb. Wilson (1969) 15, lists it as a Kentucky proverb. Champion (1938) 230 records a Livonian proverb, "The man who strikes his horse strikes his wife too."

## The **man** who marries for money earns it.

See "Those who marry for MONEY earn it."

## The **man** who reads is the man who leads (He who reads leads).

1915 *Efficiency Magazine* 5, no. 8 (Aug.) 14 (filler item in the book review section): "The man who reads is the man who leads." 1916 *Photo-Era* 36: 309 (filler item; the words are attributed to Glen Buck): "Under his feet the reading man puts the printed record of what men have thought and done, and thereby gets his head up in the fog-free atmosphere of the everlasting morning. . . . The man who reads is the man who leads." *DAP* 500(5). Occasionally the proverb is adapted as a slogan asserting that "the community (nation) that reads leads."

## A **man** without a woman is like a fish without a bicycle.

1983 Philip Howard, *A Word in Your Ear* (New York: Oxford UP) 30: "I do not know what to make of the Sikh student I saw on the campus of Delhi University wearing a T-shirt with the strange device: 'A man without a woman is like a fish without a bicycle.'" 1990 *Boston Globe* 28 Nov. "The [Gloria] Steinem quotation works even better for the male of the species than it does for the female—i, e,. 'A man without a woman is like a fish without a bicycle.'" The proverb may have originated as an anti-proverb based on "A MAN without a woman is like a fish without a tail"—or (as in the 1990 instance) an anti-proverb based on the much more recent "A WOMAN without a man is like a fish without a bicycle." Cf. "A MAN without a woman is like a ship without a sail."

## A **man** without a woman is like a fish without a tail.

1909 The proverb may represent a collapsing of two lines in an old song, alluded to by W. F. Oliver, "What Have You to Offer," *Wilson's Photographic Magazine* 46: 178: "The author of that beautiful ballad, 'A Man without a Woman,' was unquestionably a philosopher. Let me paraphrase a bit and sing: An Association without an object / Is like a ship without a sail, / A boat without a rudder, / Or a fish without a tail." 1958 George M. Lott, *The Story of Human Emotions* (New York: Philosophical Library) 106: "An old toast recites, 'A man without a woman is like a fish without a tail, a shirt without a collar button, or a ship without a sail.'" Cf. "A MAN without a woman is like a ship without a sail" and "A MAN without a woman is like a fish without a bicycle." The conceit of the proverb had been anticipated in a humorous article from 1859, by one "Launcelot Gossenberry, esq., Poet Laureate," entitled "What Is a Bachelor?" in *Hutchings' Illustrated California Magazine* 3: 379; the article consists of a long series of metaphors for a bachelor, one of which is "a fish without a tail."

## A **man** without a woman is like a ship without a sail.

1909 The saying occurs as the first two lines of an old song, alluded to by W. F. Oliver, "What Have You to Offer," *Wilson's Photographic Magazine* 46: 178: "The author of that beautiful ballad, 'A Man without a Woman,' was unquestionably a philosopher. Let me paraphrase a bit and sing: An Association without an object / Is like a ship without a sail, / A boat without a rudder, / Or a fish without a tail." A full text of the song appears in Ray B. Browne, *Alabama Folk Lyric* (Bowling Green OH: Bowling Green UP, 1979) 198. *DAP* 397. Cf. "A MAN without a woman is like a fish without a tail." The conceit of the proverb had been anticipated in a humorous article from 1859, by one "Launcelot Gossenberry, esq., Poet Laureate," entitled "What Is a Bachelor?" in *Hutchings' Illustrated California Magazine* 3: 379; the article consists of a long series of metaphors for a bachelor, one of which is "a ship without a sail."

## A **man** without faith (religion, God) is like a fish without a bicycle.

1958 *Swarthmore [PA] Phoenix* (7 Apr.) 2: "A

man without faith is like a fish without a bicycle" (Charles S. Harris claims the credit for having coined the expression). 1975 *New York Times* 20 Aug.: "'A man without God is like a fish without a bicycle,' reads one enigmatic injunction" (among "graffiti scrawled on a wall in the weathered riverfront shack" in the Alaskan tundra). 1977 Arthur Bloch, *Murphy's Law and Other Reasons Why Things Go Wrong!* (Los Angeles: Price/Stern/Sloan) 86: "VIQUE'S LAW: A man without religion is like a fish without a bicycle" (capitalization as shown). *YBQ* Charles S. Harris. The image occurs independent of the proverb, as a simile: 1976 Kurt Vonnegut, *Slapstick* (New York: Delacorte) 69: "We need a mother's and father's love about as much as a fish needs a bicycle, as the saying goes." 1977 *Bangor [ME] Daily News* 18 Nov.: "He [Ron Bose] ended up buying a filleting knife, . . . which he said he needed 'like a fish needs a bicycle.'" Cf. "A WOMAN without a man is like a fish without a bicycle" and "A MAN without a woman is like a fish without a bicycle."

## Never argue (quarrel) with a **man** (someone) who buys ink by the barrel (gallon).

1931 John F. Steward, *The Reaper* (New York: Greenberg) 239: "The manufacture of self-raking reapers was then at its height, and the makers of those machines were . . . led to believe that the Marsh harvester might become a competitor. So, with printer's ink, by the barrel, the new comer was cried down." 1964 Irving Leibowitz, *My Indiana* (Englewood Cliffs NJ: Prentice-Hall) 76: "Pulliam's power lies in the relentless, scorching heat of his newspapers. . . . Former Congressman Charles Bornson . . . used to say, 'I never quarrel with a man who buys ink by the barrel.'" 1965 William L. Rivers, *The Opinionmakers* (Boston: Beacon) 177: "One Indiana Congressman said resignedly of [newspaper owner Eugene] Pulliam, 'I never argue with a man who buys ink by the barrel.'" 1970 Jack L. Davidson, *Effective School Board*

*Meetings* (West Nyack NY: Parker) 105: "No one benefits when the school system and the press are at odds. An experienced superintendent said wisely once that 'you cannot afford to carry on a feud with anyone who buys ink by the barrel.'" 1985 Tommy Lasorda and David Fisher, *The Artful Dodger* (New York: Arbor House) 207: "Fortunately, I had learned early in my career that . . . it is impossible to win an argument with anyone who buys ink by the gallon."

## No **man** is above the law, and no man is below it.

1903 Theodore Roosevelt, third annual message to Congress, 7 Dec.—as quoted in *The Forum* 35 (1904) 334: "No man is above the law, and no man is below it; nor do we ask any man's permission when we require him to obey it." *DAP* 363(17), 403(188); *YBQ* T. Roosevelt (13). Roosevelt uttered the saying as a sort of anti-proverb, elaborating on the much older proverb "No man is above the law."

## Old **men** make wars, and young men fight them (pay the price).

1912 *Tyrone [PA] Herald* 19 Sep.: "In the current issue of Farm and Fireside appears the following: 'In the civil war on the Union side there were 844,588 boys enlisted 17 years of age or under. There were 2,270,588 enlistments, and only 188,000 were over 21 years old. Men make the wars and then push the boys up in front of the enemy's guns.'" 1917 St. John G. Ervine, *Changing Winds* (New York: Macmillan) 569: "It was fore-ordained that old men would make wars and that young men would pay the price of them. . . ." Whiting (1952) 453 gives what seems like a variant (it is too rare to be deemed a separate proverb): "The old make laws, the young die for them."

## One **man's** floor is another man's ceiling.

1929 *Sun [Baltimore]* 28 Apr.: "One night when the convivial Mr. Jones was demonstrating

Spanish dances to a group of his playmates[,] the Fimbles went upstairs to remonstrate with him. 'I'll have to ask you to be a little more quiet,' said Mr. Fimble. 'Our plaster is coming down.' . . . 'I declare, some people are never contented. There's no accounting for tastes. One man's floor is another man's ceiling.'" 1967 Patricia McGerr, *Murder Is Absurd* (Garden City NY: Doubleday) 102–3: "'Do you know what, to me, is the most exciting line in the whole play? . . . It's what Gertie says, "One man's floor is another man's ceiling."' . . . 'And one man's meat is another man's poison,' Savannah quipped. 'It takes genius to find new words for an old adage.'"

## One **man's** fortune is another man's folly (misfortune, etc.).

1962 *Washington Post* 14 Apr.: "One man's fortune is another man's tough luck. When Grant was put back on the roster, the Indians sent Bill Bailey, a right-hander, back to the minors." 1964 Elinor Langer, "Industrial R&D," *Science* 144: 273: ". . . [T]he ACIL arguments . . . deserve some attention, if only as a reminder that one man's fortune is another man's headache." 1970 John Ferguson, *The Religions of the Roman Empire* (Ithaca NY: Cornell UP) 80: "There's the rub; it so often happens that one man's good fortune is another man's misfortune." 1985 Roger G. Kennedy, *Architecture, Men, Women and Money in America* (New York: Random House) 445: "[Jacob] Shuh . . . was bankrupted when a flash flood piled up behind the abutments of James Lanier's new railroad (one man's fortune is another man's grief)." 1989 *Los Angeles Times* (San Diego County edition) 6 Dec.: "One man's fortune is another man's downfall. Hopefully he understands the situation and can stay with friends." 2001 *Daily Telegraph [Sydney, Australia]* 21 Jul.: "One man's fortune is another man's sorrow. When stewards black-flagged the championship leader Mark Skaife last weekend, the main beneficiary was his teammate, Jason

Bright." *DAP* 230(31). Cf. "One MAN's trash is another man's treasure" and the older "One man's meat is another man's poison."

## One **man's** freedom fighter is another man's terrorist.

See "One MAN's terrorist is another man's freedom fighter."

## One **man's** terrorist is another man's freedom fighter (One man's freedom fighter is another man's terrorist).

1970 Christian E. Hauer Jr., *Crisis and Conscience in the Middle East* (Chicago: Quadrangle) 41: "One man's terrorist is another man's heroic freedom fighter. But terrorist activity was a fact of daily life in Palestine." 1971 G. G. Norton, *The Red Devils: The Story of the British Airborne Forces* (London: Leo Cooper) 138: "Of course, one man's terrorist is another man's freedom fighter; and it was in the latter guise that the IZL and the Stern Gang were presented to world opinion by the highly-organized Zionist propaganda machine." *YBQ* Sayings (44).

## One **man's** trash is another man's treasure.

1924 *Washington Post* 17 May: "Mrs. Gouverneur Hoes will be chairman for the opportunity table at the House of Mercy garden party Wednesday, and promises to have the usual tempting bargains under the caption, 'One man's trash is another man's treasure.'" *RHDP* 258.

## Stand by your **man.**

1919 *Union Record* 1 Feb.: "The eyes of the working class of Americans today are turned upon you [women]. . . . Stand by your man in this, his hour of trial. Fight by his side in the age-long fight for freedom"; quoted in Philip S. Foner, *History of the Labor Movement in the United States* (New York: International, 1947–94) 7:66.

1926 Charles G. Booth, *Sinister House* (New York: Grosset & Dunlap) 201: "Now, don't you get het up, dearie! You've got to stand by your man! Besides, I'm not saying he done it!" *DAAP* 494; *YBQ* Wynette (3–4). The use of the proverb in the 1968 song (so titled) by Tammy Wynette and Billy Sherrill vivified its currency.

## Trust all **men**, but cut the cards.

See "Trust everyone, but cut the CARDS."

## You can take a **man** out of the country, but you can't take the country out of a man.

See "You can take a BOY out of the country, but you can't take the country out of a boy."

## You can take the **man** out of Texas, but you can't take Texas out of the man.

1944 *Brownsville [TX] Herald* 17 Jan.: "Said [Chester] Nimitz: 'This gathering . . . shows that you can take a man out of Texas but you can't take Texas out of the man.'" A report of an address by Adm. Nimitz two days later (19 Jan.) gives slightly different wording: the gathering "shows that you can take a man out of Texas, but you can't take Texas out of a man"; 1944 Stuart M. Long, "That Texas Club in the United States Marines," *Southwestern Review* 29, no. 4 (Summer) 560. Cf. "You can take a BOY out of the country, but you can't take the country out of a boy."

## You can't blame a **man** for trying.

See "You can't blame a FELLOW for trying.

## You win like a **man**, you lose like a man (Win like a man and lose like a man).

1992 *USA Today* 26 Oct.: "And [I think] of Mark Lemke, trying to put in some perspective the Braves' torment of seven World Series one-run losses in two years: 'It's not easy. But life isn't easy. You win like a man and you lose like a man.'" 1997 *Daily News [New York]* 20 May (quoting the basketball player Karl Malone): "They kicked our butts today. They outplayed us in every facet of the game. I always say you've got to win like a man and lose like a man."

## Manners matter (much).

1909 E. J. Hardy, *How to Be Happy though Civil* (New York: Charles Scribner's Sons) 11 (title of chapter 1): "Manners Matter Much." 1929 Gwladys Evan Morris, *Tales from Bernard Shaw* (London: George G. Harrap) 77: ". . . I mean, he had no manners, and manners matter a lot."

## The **map** is not the territory.

1933 The saying probably entered oral tradition as a proverb (condensed and slightly misquoted) from a philosophical treatise by Alfred Korzybski, *Science and Sanity* (Lancaster PA: International Non-Aristotelian Library) 58: "A map *is not* the territory it represents, but, if correct, it has a *similar structure* to the territory, which accounts for its usefulness" (italics as shown). *YBQ* Korzybski. The proverb emphasizes the distinction between symbols (including words) and their referents.

## Marriage is a journey, not a destination.

1943 *St. Petersburg [FL] Times*, 8 Aug.: "Our authority urges that the couple concerned act like grownups instead of children, to bear in mind that marriage is a journey, not a destination." Cf. "success is a journey, not a destination," "happiness is a journey, not a destination," and "life is a journey, not a destination."

## All the good ones are (already) **married**.

See "All the good ones are taken."

## Just because you're **married** (Being married) doesn't mean you're blind.

1961 Shelagh Delaney, *The Lion in Love* (London: Methuen) 72: "KIT: . . . You're a very pleasant looking young man. PEG: Hey! Just you think

on you're a married woman. KIT: Just because I'm married doesn't mean to say I'm blind." 1992 *Times-News [Hendersonville NC]* 9 Feb.: "I had always thought Ray was gorgeous, with the prettiest blue eyes I'd ever seen—just because you're married doesn't mean you're blind." 2001 Bruce Kreisman, *Off the Bench* (Bend OR: Salvo) 121: "What's the old saying, just because a guy's married doesn't mean he's blind. Hell, we aren't even married."

## The **master's** tools cannot (be used to) destroy (dismantle) the master's house.

1981 The saying probably passed into oral tradition (commonly misquoted) as a proverb from Audre Lorde's influential feminist essay "The Master's Tools Will Never Dismantle the Master's House," in *This Bridge Called My Back: Writings by Radical Women of Color*, edited by Cherríe Moraga and Gloria Anzaldúa (Watertown MA: Persephone), 98–101.

## Use the **master's** tools to destroy the master's house.

1996 James G. Ladwig, *Academic Distinctions* (New York: Routledge) 164: "To the extent feminist methodologies have demonstrated that the master's tools can be used to bring down the master's house, it seems that a wider, heterodox stance toward methodology could only aid RSSK ['radical sociology of school knowledge']." 1997 Harriet Rubin, *The Princessa: Machiavelli for Women* (New York: Doubleday) 28: "'Use the master's tools to destroy the master's house,' Aesop's small, clever animals are always advised in their war against big predators." The Aesopic reference is obscure. The proverb should probably be regarded as a counter-proverb rebutting "The master's tools cannot destroy the master's house"—or vice versa.

## What **matters** is what works.

1958 George Walker, "The Development and Organisation of Associated Electrical Industries

Limited," in *Business Enterprise*, edited by Ronald Stanley Edwards (London: Macmillan) 316: "Preconceived ideas and abstract theories have no place in running companies; what matters is, *what works*" (italics as shown). 1963 Walter Weir, *Truth in Advertising* (New York: McGraw-Hill) 67: "But it [the voice of conscience] is quickly stifled because 'science'—and the philosophy of pragmatism . . . —clearly indicate that all that matters is what 'works,' what achieves the desired end, what overcomes competition." *ODP* 207; Ratcliffe (2006) 483.

**Maturity** is a high price to pay for growing up.

See "AGE is a high price to pay for maturity."

### Sell in **May** and (then) go away.

Champion (1938) 39 gives the saying as a proverb from the "British Isles," concerned with (or commonly heard at) the "Stock Exchange." 1943 J. W. B. Worsley, "Stock Exchange Speculation," *Quarterly Review* 281: 77: "And, to complete the picture, these crashes do frequently fall on 'a summer's day' ('sell in May, and go away!') when the people who made their profits in the Spring bloom and have lost them again . . . would like to see the light of love and not the fact of ruin." *ODP* 282.

### There is no *me* in *team*.

See "There is no *I* in *team*."

### Just because you're paranoid doesn't **mean** they aren't after you (doesn't mean they aren't out to get you, doesn't mean you aren't being persecuted, doesn't mean they aren't watching you).

1970 The saying's occurrence in the motion picture *Catch-22* ("Just because you're paranoid doesn't mean they aren't after you") may have helped fix it as a proverb in something like that form. 1974 Warren Hinckle, *If You Have*

*a Lemon, Make Lemonade* (New York: G. P. Putnam's Sons) 245 (epigraph to a section of a chapter): "Just because you're paranoid doesn't mean you aren't being followed"; the saying is there ascribed (perhaps spuriously—though not implausibly) to Thomas Pynchon. The concept of the proverb was anticipated in various other phrasings: 1933 Dorothy Sayers, *Murder Must Advertise* (New York: Harcourt, Brace) 265: "Because a person has a monomania she need not be wrong about her facts. She might have imagined or invented a good deal, but she couldn't possibly imagine or invent anything so fantastic. . . ." 1960 C. P. Snow, *The Affair* (New York: Charles Scribner's Sons) 107: "Laura's letters were a curious mixture of business-like information and paranoia. Margaret said: 'Has it ever struck you that when people get persecution mania, they usually have a good deal to feel persecuted about?'" *YBQ* Sayings (31). Cf. "Even PARANOIDS have enemies."

### The blacker the **meat**, the sweeter the bone (piece).

1935 David L. Cohn, *God Shakes Creation* (New York: Harper & Brothers) 297: "Ashore, Henry bought presents in the five-and-ten-cent stores and the fleeting favors of bright-skinned girls. 'Some niggers say de blacker de meat de sweeter de bone, but I doesn't bleeve dat.'" 1941 William James Blake, *The Copperheads* (New York: Dial) 444: "'That high yaller by the post office,' a Wisconsin looie called out. 'Don't like her,' said an experienced campaigner. 'In Sherman's army we say 'The blacker the meat the sweeter the piece.'" *MP* M123. Person (1958) 179 gives the (seemingly rare) variant "The darker the meat, the richer the gravy." The proverb praises blackness, usually in regard to sexual desirability. Cf. "The blacker the BERRY, the sweeter the juice."

### Don't let your **meat** loaf (meatloaf).

1969 Earl M. Rauch, *Dirty Pictures from the Prom* (Garden City NY: Doubleday) 246: "I'll be seeing you around, Tom. Take it easy on the ass, but don't let your meat loaf either." 1970 Michael Mewshaw, *Man in Motion* (New York: Random House) 64: "'How's it hanging, Walker? . . . out of work?' 'No, I'm leaving for California.' . . . 'Good luck.' 'Same to you. Don't let your meat loaf.'" The punning reference is to male sexual activity (*meat* "penis"). Lighter (1994– ) 2: 531 illustrates the expression from a 1963 manuscript.

## If you don't eat your **meat**, you can't have any pudding.

See "You can't have any PUDDING if you don't eat your meat."

## It's not the **meat**, it's the motion.

1951 The saying may have entered oral tradition as a proverb from the title and recurring line of a rhythm and blues song written by Henry Glover (and recorded by the Swallows): "It Ain't the Meat (It's the Motion)." Or the song may have been built around an existing proverb. Proverbial uses of the expression do not appear in print until the 1980s, after Maria (D'Amato) Muldaur's popular rendition of Glover's song in 1974 had nudged it—and the saying—toward the (white) mainstream. Interestingly, in the version recorded by the Swallows the slang word *meat* refers sexually to a woman—a "skinny" woman: "It ain't the meat, it's the motion / Makes your daddy want to rock." However, Muldaur's version regarded *meat* as a slang reference to the penis ("Makes your mama want to rock"), and that has remained the prevailing—though not invariant—referent of the proverb. 1983 Hob Broun, *Odditorium* (New York: Harper & Row) 49: "Okay, so she's not exactly stacked, but you know what they say: It's not the meat, it's the motion." 1983 Cynthia Heimel, *Sex Tips for Girls* (New York: Simon & Schuster) 187: "Stop any girl on the street and ask her if she cares if a man is well hung, and she will look at you aghast. 'Of course not,' she'll say, 'it's not what you've got, it's how you use it. It's not the meat, it's the motion.'" Cf. "It's not the SIZE of the boat but the motion of the ocean" and "SIZE doesn't matter."

## Move your **meat**, lose your seat.

See "Move your FEET, lose your seat."

## Same **meat**, different gravy.

1967 *The Observer [London]* 12 Nov.: William Hill's casual observation when told about the formation of the Turf Board—'Same meat, different gravy'—is proving all too prophetic." 1970 Joan G. Robinson, *Charley* (New York: Coward-McGann) 52: "Well, it makes no odds. Same meat, different gravy." In the proverb *meat* has the sense of "essence"; *gravy* represents superficial trappings or accompaniments.

## The **medium** is the message.

1964 The saying entered oral tradition as a proverb from its memorable appearance in Marshall McLuhan's *Understanding Media* (the title of chapter 1)—whether or not the locution had been uttered earlier (by McLuhan or someone else). The saying was presumed familiar enough by 1967 that McLuhan gave the allusive title *The Medium Is the Massage* to another book.

## Just because you've ordered (Just because you've eaten) doesn't mean you can't look at the **menu**.

See "Just because you're on a DIET doesn't mean you can't look at the menu."

## In the **middle** of difficulty lies (there is) opportunity.

1975 Ilene Wright and Noel McInnis, "The End of Naïveté," in *What Makes Education Environmental?* edited by McInnis and Don Albrecht (Louisville KY: Data Courier) 452: "Realism lies in the ability to identify the presence of opportunity in the midst of difficulty, and then to transform difficulty into advantage." 1978 Jack Culbertson, "Challenge and Opportunity," in *The Changing Politics of Education*, edited by Edith K. Mosher and Jennings Waggoner Jr. (Berkeley CA: McCutchan) 342: "I am told that the Chinese have a word for 'crisis' that combines the symbols of danger and opportunity. Thus, whether one looks at the educational institutions today from a macro- or a microview, there is even in the midst of difficulty, much opportunity." 1979 John Archibald Wheeler, "The Outsider," *Newsweek* 93, no. 11 (12 Mar.) 67: "There are three additional rules of [Albert] Einstein's work that stand out for use in our science, our problems, our times. First, out of clutter find simplicity. Second, from discord make harmony. Third, in the middle of difficulty lies opportunity." 1994 *Miami Herald* 20 Jul.: "A wise woman once told me that in the middle of every difficulty lies opportunity." The saying—especially as presented among three "rules"—is commonly credited to Einstein, although it has not been found in his published writings, and his friend Wheeler did not exactly attribute the saying to him.

## The **middle** of the road is where people get run over.

1953 *Observer [London]* 9 Dec. (quoting Aneurin Bevan): "We know what happens to people who stay in the middle of the road. They get run over." 1954 *Pittsburgh Post-Gazette* 11 Jan. (Dorothy Thompson, commenting on President Eisenhower's "moderate" politics): "The middle of the road is not to be recommended in heavy traffic. Those who pursue it are likely to be knocked down from the left lane and run over from the right." 1966 William R. Manning, "Negotiations: The Process in Collective Bargaining," *American School Board Journal* 153, no. 2 (Aug.) 15: "I say this despite the fact that the superintendent stands in the middle of the road, and those who do, as we know, often get run over." *YBQ* Bevan (2). Cf. "There is NOTHING in the middle of the road but yellow stripes and dead skunks."

## Don't judge (criticize) someone (a man) till you have walked a **mile** in his shoes (moccasins, boots).

1930 *Lincoln [NE] Star* 10 Oct.: "Never criticize the other boy or girl unless you have walked a mile in his moccasins" (the saying is described as an "Indian maxim"). 1957 Else Wendel, *Hausfrau at War* (London: Odhams) 76: "What it means to be without parents and without a country, only those will understand who have experienced these things. As the Chinese say: 'to know what another man feels it is necessary to walk a mile in his shoes.'" 1957 Ralph Pfau (pseudonym "Father John Doe"), *Golden Book of Sanity* (Center City MN: Hazelden) 21: "This should make us realize that had we been born and raised in the same circumstances as the other fellow we might not be nearly so likable! Even old Confucius say 'Never judge a man until we have walked a mile in his shoes.'" *RHDP* 62; *YBQ* Modern Proverbs (19). The Chinese—much less Confucian—connection is questionable (especially in the moccasins version!).

## The longest **mile** is the last mile home.

1949 The saying may have entered oral tradition as a proverb from the song "The Last Mile Home," by Walter Kent and Walton Farrar (popularized by Doris Day)—or else the song was employing a proverb. *DAP* 304(22).

## Why buy **milk** when a cow is so cheap (when you've got a cow at home)?

1957 Otis Carney, *When the Bough Breaks* (Boston: Houghton Mifflin) 180: "Well, I could go get one of the cuties at the Orph, but that's a little juvenile, isn't it? Or, I could go first-class at Mary Taylor's . . . but why buy milk when a cow's cheap?" (ellipsis dots as shown). 1963 Gerald Kersh, "Ghost Money," *Playboy* 10, no. 4 (Apr.) 135 (an anomalous use?): "'Married?' 'Not as far as I know. He's smart. Why buy milk if you're friendly with the cow?'"; there, buying milk seems to refer to being married, while being "friendly with the cow" implies less formal relationships. 1979 Stella Allan, *A Mortal Affair* (New York: Charles Scribner's Sons) 34: "'Why don't you get yourself a car and learn to drive?' Duncan went on munching. 'Oh, I don't think I'm temperamentally suited to driving—not like Fran. . . . Besides—' She halted herself in time. When you've already got a cow, why buy milk?" The proverb probably originated as an anti-proverb responding to the anti-marriage saying "Why buy the cow when you can get milk for free?" 1987 Mark Glazer, *Dictionary of Mexican American Proverbs* (Westport CT: Greenwood) 171 gives as a Mexican American proverb "Para que compras lelche teniendo tan buena vaca"—perhaps adapted from the English equivalent. Cf. the more genteel-sounding "Why go out for HAMBURGER when you can get steak at home?"

## A **million** here and a million there—pretty soon it adds up to real money.

See "A BILLION here and a billion there—pretty soon it adds up to real money."

## A (The) **mind** is a terrible thing to waste.

1972 The saying entered oral tradition as a proverb from a slogan of the United Negro College Fund. *RHDP* 227; *YBQ* Advertising Slogans (121).

## The **mind** is the most important erogenous zone.

See "The most important erogenous ZONE is the brain."

## Everybody will be famous for fifteen **minutes**.

1968 The saying entered oral traditon (slightly misquoted) as a proverb from a remark by Andy Warhol, quoted in *Andy Warhol*, exhibition catalog for the Moderna Museet in Stockholm (Stockholm: for the museum) [fol. 7v] (unpaginated): "In the future everybody will be world famous for fifteen minutes." *RHDP* 86; *YBQ* Warhol (2); Rees (1995) 156; Room (2000) 226.

## If you are fifteen (ten, etc.) **minutes** early, you are on time (already five minutes late).

1963 *Los Angeles Times* 10 Jan.: "'If you show up to a workout or a meeting 15 minutes early, you're on time. If you're 10 minutes early, you're a straggler and if you're five minutes early you're the last one there,' he [the football player Jerry Kramer] explained." 1975 Anne Ortlund, *Up with Worship* (Glendale CA: Regal) 64: "Churchgoer, when do you walk in the door? Henrietta Mears used to say, 'If you're not five minutes early, you're late!'" 1981 James Clavell, *Noble House* (New York: Delacorte) 4: "Five minutes early is on time, tai-pan. Isn't that what Father hammered into me?"

## A **minute** on the lips is a lifetime on the hips.

See "A MOMENT on the lips, a lifetime on the hips."

## **Miracles** take (a lot of) hard work.

1946 Archie Binns, "People of the Oregon Coast Range," in *Pacific Coast Ranges*, edited by Roderick Peattie (New York: Vanguard) 257: "A miracle takes hard work, and $200 is small change." 1959 Robert St. John, *Ben-Gurion: The Biography of an Extraordinary Man* (Garden City NY: Doubleday) 54: "[Chaim] Weizmann . . . was credited with two classic remarks; one of which he denied originating, although he did at least popularize it: 'Miracles do happen, but you have to work hard for them.'" 2001 Lisa Lewis, *Special Diets for Special Kids Two* (Arlington TX: Future Horizons) 18 (in a list headed "Rules to Live By"): "Miracles take a lot of hard work!"

They don't make **mirrors** like they used to.

1949 Jerome Beatty, "High, Low, Ace and Jane," *American Magazine* 147, no. 1 (Jan.) 59: "They don't make mirrors like they used to. I can remember when I used to look in a mirror and I looked almost like a schoolgirl." 1956 Frederic Wakeman, *Deluxe Tour* (New York: Rinehart) 186: "He reminds me . . . of the old fellow staring at himself in the mirror on his sixtieth birthday. This old character studied himself rather pensively and then muttered, 'They don't make mirrors like they used to.'" Dundes and Pagter (1991) 238–39. The proverb may be regarded as a joking anti-proverb based on the more general lament, "They don't make things like they used to."

A **miss** is as good as a male.

See "A MS. is as good as a male."

You are only as good as your last (latest) **mistake**.

1979 David Ascoli, *The Queen's Peace* (London: Hamish Hamilton) 301–2: "A present-day deputy assistant commissioner has summed up the sterile philosophy of the command structure of the [London] Metropolitan Police in a bleak phrase which still colours attitudes within the force today: 'You are only as good as your last mistake.' As a prescription for managerial inertia, that could hardly be bettered." 1991 Brian H. Maskell, *Performance Measurement for World Class Manufacturing: A Model for American Companies* (Cambridge MA: Productivity) 38–39: "This practice leads to fear and nervousness, rather than to innovation and improvement. People make comments like, 'You're only as good as your last mistake in this company,' or 'Successes are soon forgotten, but failures are remembered forever.'"

A **moment** (minute) on the lips, a lifetime (forever) on the hips.

1940 *Daily Times-News [Burlington NC]* 16 Nov. (end of a recipe): "It melts in the mouth! But, oh, a moment on the lips, forever on the hips!" 1940 William Engel, "Lamb Chops & Pineapple," *Cosmopolitan* 108, no. 5 (May) 113: "If you are one of those people who can resist anything *but* temptation, where food is concerned, then bear in mind the time-honored adage: 'A minute on the lips and forever on the hips'" (italics as shown). *DAP* 412(2).

Follow the **money**.

1974 *Nomination of Earl J. Silbert to be United States Attorney: Hearings before the Committee on the Judiciary . . . Senate* (Washington DC: Government Printing Office) 399; Henry Peterson testifies: "I would say, 'Follow the money, Earl, because that's where it's going to be.' Unfortunately, we did not get it following the money because the records were either nonexistent or were destroyed." 1975 Clive Borrell and Brian Cashinella, *Crime in Britain Today* (London: Routledge & Kegan Paul) 98–99: ". . . Mr [James] Crane usually offers this piece of sound advice to all new officers joining his fraud department: 'Always follow the money. Inevitably it will lead to an oak-panelled door and behind it will be Mr Big.' It is a tip that has paid off in scores of cases." 1976 In the motion picture *All the President's Men*, the shadowy informant called Deep Throat advises emphatically, "Follow the money." In the film, based on Carl Bernstein and Bob Woodward's memoir *All the President's Men* (New York, Simon & Schuster, 1974), Deep Throat is a composite of several anonymous sources. The saying does not appear in the book, in which one of Bernstein's sources (not the one whom the journalists nickname Deep Throat) says, "The money is the key to this thing" (34), and Woodward (as he paraphrases himself) tells Senator Sam Ervin that "the key was the secret campaign cash, and it should all be traced. . . ." *YBQ* Film Lines (8).

## Money has no memory.

1991 *Colorado Springs Gazette* 11 Oct.: "'Your inventory is money, and money has no memory,' said Dan Douglass, part-owner of the Narrow Gauge Gaming Depot and Saloon. . . ." 1993 *The Age [Melbourne, Australia]* 24 Jul.: "The crucial thing to remember is that money has no morality. Money has no memory. In 10 years' time, when the economy is booming again, business entrepreneurs will return."

## Money has no morality.

1905 "Tainted Money," *The Watchman* 87, no. 3 (3 Aug.) 66: "In itself money has no moral quality. Coins and bills do not contract any taint of moral evil by passing through the hands of evil men." 1906 *Boston Daily Globe* 17 Oct. (a speech by Congressman George Fred Williams): "'Money Has No Morality' [section head]. . . . But the forces of money have no morality. The forces of money have but the motive of gain at any cost, only gain." 1937 David Milton Proctor, *False Faces on Quality Street* (Kansas City MO: Brown Book) 22: "It will . . . pay you handsome dividends which some people might call tainted. This is bunkum. Money has no morality. I never saw a dollar in my life that had either conscience or angel's wings." In its ambiguous wording, the proverb can mean either that money itself is amoral or that it—or the greed it represents—is immoral.

## Money never sleeps.

1907 Jeff Davis (governor or Arkansas), speech before a joint session of the legislature, in *Journal of the House of Representatives, State of Arkansas* (Hot Springs: Sentinel-Record) 55: "Money does not sleep; and you who have memories may recall what was said by the enemies of the people when the Fishback amendment was adopted. . . . They then said, 'there will be another day—money does not sleep.'" 1918 Paul Myron (Linebarger), *Bugle Rhymes from France* (Chicago: Mid-Nation) 102 (in a poem "Li-Ber-Ty Bo-onds," advocating the purchase of bonds): "Money doesn't sleep. (Alas! . . . that's why I weep) / Hide your money in a bag, buried deep beneath the mould, / Still you'll find it gets away; money's hard to hold" (ellipsis dots as shown). 1930 *New York Times* 15 May (an ad for Henry Mandel Associates, an investment firm): "Money never sleeps. It doesn't get sick or old. It can work in any industry and in any part of the world. It need never be without a job." The proverb has two (related) meanings: the value of money that is merely hoarded can slip away, and the value of money that is prudently invested will grow relentlessly.

## Money talks, bullshit walks.

1969 Jerry L. Simmons, *Deviants* ([Berkeley CA]: Glendessary) 115: "These factors are manipulated by skillful lawyers and the more sophisticated culprits, and they are summarized in the cynical convict adage: 'Money talks and bullshit walks.'" Lighter (1994– ) 1: 304–5. The proverb probably originated as an anti-proverb based on "Money talks."

## My money, my rules (Your money, your rules).

1975 Patricia Traxler, *Blood Calendar* (New York: William Morrow) 21 (in a poem titled "Allow Me"—perhaps creatively alluding to the proverb): "Allow me to help you on with your / coat, your hat, my baby, my name, / my money, my rules, my roles." 1996 Linda Foust, *The Single Parent's Almanac* (Rocklin CA: Prima) 139: "Let's answer that question [i.e., 'Who's in charge?'] immediately. You are. Your house, your money, your rules." 2003 John Mickey, *Poisoned Medicine* (Honolulu: PageFree) 12: "So all this unnecessary security gets in the way of doing science. Okay, we can work around that. Their money, their rules." 2007 Jerome B. Friedman, U.S. district judge, *Cars Unlimited II, Inc., v. National Motor Co.* (LEXIS 59745): "Greenberg's testimony reveals that he took a 'my money, my rules' approach to the business relationship. . . ." 2009 Kelly Armstrong, "A Haunted House of

Her Own," in *Twilight Zone: 19 Original Stories*, edited by Carol Serling (New York: Tom Doherty) 55: "There'd been no chance of that while Tanya was alive. Her money. Her rules. Always." Cf. "My HOUSE, my rules."

## Never (Don't) marry for **money**; it's cheaper to borrow it (you can borrow it cheaper).

1927 *Parliamentary Debates: Commons* 205: 1201; F. A. Macquisten speaks (29 Apr.): "I always remember what the late Lord Tennyson said, putting the words into the mouth of an old farmer: 'Don't 'e marry for money, you can borrow for cheaper.'" 1931 *Parliamentary Debates: Commons* 248: 1682: Macquisten speaks again (20 Feb.): "One recalls a remark of the late Poet Laureate, Lord Tennyson, about a farmer who said to his sons, 'Don't 'ee marry for money, boys; you can borrow for cheaper.'" Almost certainly the MP was misremembering Tennyson's 1869 "dialect" poem "The Northern Farmer (New Style)," in which the farmer advises (using a different proverb—or coining an expression that became a proverb), "Doänt thou marry for munny, but goä wheere munny is!" Cf. "Those who marry for MONEY earn it."

## No one ever lost **money** making (taking) a profit.

See "No one ever went bankrupt taking a PROFIT."

## Put your **money** where your mouth is.

1913 *New York Tribune* 24 Aug.: "'Put your money where your mouth is,' retorted Senator [Morris] Sheppard. 'I am surprised that that remark should be made by any Senator, even from Texas,' replied Senator [Reed] Smoot." *DAP* 418(72); *RHDP* 280; *YBQ* Modern Proverbs (63); Room (2000) 555. The proverbial phrase "put (one's) money where his mouth is" is older.

## Rich or poor, it's good to have **money**.

1949 *Increasing the Salaries of Federal Judges: Hearings before Subcommittee No. 1 of the Committee on the Judiciary, House of Representatives* (Washington DC: Government Printing Office) 41; statement of Judge Sherman Minton: "I never had any money, I do not have any now, and I never expect to have any. But as the comedian Joe Lewis once said, whether you are rich or poor it is nice to have money." 1952 *Migrant Labor: Hearings before the Subcommittee on Labor and Labor-Management Relations . . . Senate* (Washington DC: Government Printing Office) 307–8; an untitled speech by Secretary of Labor Maurice J. Tobin (14 Feb.): "And like the farmer, he wants to earn as much as he can. Both the farmer's and the laborer's viewpoints are expressed in the current quip: 'Whether you are rich or poor, it's good to have money.'" 1955 George Gobel, "Confessions of a Southpaw," *American Magazine* 160, no. 1 (Jul.) 102: "What I always say, what's the difference whether you're right-handed or left-handed as long as you're rich? That's what I always say. Rich or poor, it pays to have money." The saying is sometimes attributed to Milton Berle.

## Those who marry for **money** earn it.

1903 *Dubuque [IA] Telegraph-Herald* 26 Apr. (among "Pointed Paragraphs"): "The man who marries for money certainly earns it." 1904 Emily Post, *The Flight of the Moth* (New York: Dodd, Mead) 131: "It is certainly true: A man who marries for money earns it! Every penny!" 1908 *Hunter-Trader-Trapper* 17, no. 3 (Dec.) 9 (a small collection of sayings in an ad for the Herman Reel fishing supplies company): "Those who marry for money always earn more than they get." *DAP* 415(11). Cf. "Never marry for MONEY; it's cheaper to borrow it."

## You can only spend **money** once.

See "You can only spend a DOLLAR once."

You can't get **money** from a dead man.

1964 *Chicago Tribune* 15 Aug. (the accused murderer Richard Maddox claims that his collaborator Larry Shelton—whom he quotes himself addressing here—had killed someone who owed them money): "Shelton, that was a crazy thing to do. You can't get money from a dead man." 1985 *Atlanta Journal* 27 Oct. "'Loan sharks don't kill people. There's no percentage in it,' said homicide Sgt. Dean Gundlach. 'You can't get money from a dead man.'"

**Monkeys** in hard times eat red peppers (Hunger makes a monkey blow fire).

Anderson and Cundall (1910) 34 give the saying as a Jamaican proverb: "Hungry mek monkey blow fire" (glossed: "Necessity teaches him new habits. Cf. 'Necessity is the mother of invention.'"). Beckwith (1925) 60, glossing the same Jamaican proverb, perhaps misunderstands its meaning: "'Hunger makes monkey blow the fire,' (so as to hasten the meal)." 1929 Bata Kindai Amgoza Ibn Lobagola, "An African Savage's Own Story," *Scribner's Magazine* 87: 430: "Finally my money all went, and I could not get work in any of the theaters. I . . . asked the owner of a boarding-house for something to eat. He laughed and said, 'Hard times in New York will make a monkey eat red pepper.'" *MP* T156; *DAP* 419(6); Prahlad (1996) 239.

One **monkey** don't stop no show.

1961 *Los Angeles Sentinel* 28 Sep. ". . . Nathaniel 'Nat the Cat' Butts arrived in Los Angeles and settled down to the hard-fashioned task of making a success. . . . His dogged perseverance began to pay off in some degree recently when he recorded 'One Monkey Don't Stop No Show.'" 1965 Presumably a different song with the same title was performed by Joe Tex and others, and Joe Tex claimed authorship. Daniel et al. (1987) 503; Prahlad (1996) 238–39.

Only **monkeys** work for peanuts (If you pay peanuts, you get monkeys).

1953 *New York Times* 16 Feb. (classified ad for salesmen): "ONLY MONKEYS WORK FOR PEANUTS. But YOU will be working and making BIG MONEY with us" (capitalization as shown). 1966 Leslie Coulthard, "Directors' Pay," *Director* (Aug.) 228: "Shareholders want the best available businessmen to lead the companies and recognise that you get what you pay for. If you pay in peanuts, you must expect to get monkies [*sic*]." 1966 *Free Press [Winnepeg]* 3 Sep.: "If you pay peanuts, you must expect to get monkeys." *ODP* 245–46; Pickering (2001) 277.

Don't throw a **monkey wrench** (spanner) into the works (machinery).

1920 Philander Johnson, "The Colyumists' [*sic*] Confessional. V.," *Everybody's Magazine* 42, no. 5 (May) 36: "I think that two widely circulated phrases were first used by me; both of them in conversation, not in print. I never saw either until after I had used them; one, the rather unfeeling invitation to end a hard-luck story: '*Cheer up! The worst is yet to come!*' and the other, the admonition, '*Don't throw a monkey-wrench into the machinery*'" (italics as shown). *MP* M238; *DAP* 682; *RHDP* 70; *DAAP* 715. The proverbial phrase "throw a monkey wrench into the machinery" may be somewhat older than the sentence form, the proverb. Cf. the even older proverbial phrase "throw sand into the gears (wheels)."

The older the **moon**, the brighter it shines (The old moon shines brightest).

1991 The proverb appears as a line in Bob Marley's song "Easy to Catch": "The older the moon, the brighter it shines / I'm a want to tell you this from a very long time." 1998 Easton Lee and Owen Minott, *From behind the Counter: Poems from a Rural Jamaican Experience* (Kingston, Jamaica: Ian Randle) 195: "'You never hear say the older the violin the sweeter it play and the older the moon the brighter it shine' he said smiling." Prahlad (2001) 260. Cf. "The older the FIDDLE, the sweeter the tune."

## Moonlight does not dry mittens.

1924 George Allan England, *Vikings of the Ice* (Garden City NY: Doubleday, Page) 256 (in a list of proverbs that exemplify the "shrewd native wisdom [that] has developed among the Newfoundlanders"): "Moonlight dries no mittens." 1936 Carl Sandburg, *The People, Yes* (New York: Harcourt, Brace) 57 (in a poetic montage of proverbs and other sayings): "Fine words butter no parsnips. Moonlight dries no mittens." *MP* M47; *DAAP* 518.

## That's how the mop flops.

See "That's the WAY the mop flops."

## Always leave them wanting (wishing for) more.

1910 George Barr McCutcheon, *The Butterfly Man* (New York: Dodd, Mead) 21: ". . . [H]e knew when to stop singing and playing. He left them wanting more, not calling him a bore—which is a truth as well as a rhyme." 1918 Clay Smith, "Artists Who Helped to Popularize Classics: The Chicago Operatic Company," *Lyceum Magazine* 28 (Oct.) 24: "'Any longer is too long,' says Mr. [John H.] Miller [director of the operatic company]. 'We stop before they weary, leave them wanting more and the appreciation is higher.'" 1922 Herbert J. Mangham, "His Public," *The Smart Set: A Magazine of Cleverness* 68, no. 4 (Aug.) 58: "Simons had never heard that infallible axiom of the theatre: '*Always leave them wanting more*'" (italics as shown).

## More can be (mean) worse.

1960 A. D. C. Peterson, "The Higher Education of Teachers," *Hibbert Journal* 59: 150–51: "The answer to 'More will be worse' may be that many of them would indeed be worse Honours specialists, but very worth-while students in

general courses. . . ." 1960 Kingsley Amis, "Lone Voices: Views of the 'Fifties," *Encounter* 15, no. 1 (Jul.) 9: "University graduates, however, are like poems or bottles of hock, and unlike cars or tins of salmon, in that you cannot decide to have more good ones. All you can decide is to have more. And MORE WILL MEAN WORSE" (typefaces as shown). 1965 Nellie Alden Franz, *English Women Enter the Professions* (Cincinnati: for the author) 25: "Purists fear that *more* [college students enrolled] may mean *worse* in their struggle for learning" (italics as shown). Rees (1984) 15–16.

## A mother can take care of ten (etc.) children, but (sometimes) ten children can't take care of one mother.

1956 Ardyth Kennelly, *Marry Me, Carry Me* (Boston: Houghton Mifflin) 404: "It seemed rather novel to think that the Winnies of this earth could be and were everywhere, in fine apartment houses such as these, with one visitor, or hovels with fifty. And in a way it was like that old saying, a mother can take care of fourteen children, but fourteen children can't take care of one mother." 1962 Theodore Rosen, "The Significance of the Family to the Resident's Adjustment to the Home for the Aged," *Social Casework* 43: 242: "To intensify her children's guilt she would often comment, 'One mother can take care of four children, but four children can't take care of one mother.'" *RHDP* 233.

## A mother's wish is a daughter's duty.

1972 The saying may have passed into oral tradition as a proverb from a song (so titled) in the musical comedy *Lady Audley's Secret*, lyrics by John B. Kuntz. *DAAP* 522.

## It isn't nice to fool Mother Nature.

1970 The saying probably entered oral tradition as a proverb from television advertisements for "butter-tasting" Chiffon margarine. It has found wide use in ecological discussions.

If you do not climb the **mountain**, you cannot see the view.

See "To see the VIEW, you have to climb the mountain."

The **mountains** are calm even in a tempest.

1912 Arthur W. Ryder, *Kalidasa: Translations of Shakuntala* (New York: E. P. Dutton) 69: "A good man never lets grief get the upper hand. The mountains are calm even in a tempest." Whiting (1952) 447 gives the saying as a North Carolina proverb. The proverb seems to have originated in India.

The second **mouse** gets the cheese.

1997 *Sydney [Australia] Morning Herald* 13 Sep.: "Thought for the weekend, culled by Greg Cocks, of Brooklyn, from the Internet: The early bird may get the worm, but the second mouse gets the cheese." The proverb might be thought of as an anti-proverb responding to "The early bird gets the worm"; often (as in the quotation) it appears in conjunction with the older proverb.

Big **mouth**, small brain (mind).

1958 Raymond Chandler, *Playback* (Boston: Houghton Mifflin) 116: "He looked me over coolly. 'Big mouth, small brain,' he said. 'Save it for Thursday when they set the trash cans out. You don't know nothing, friend.'" 1973 *Schenectady [NY] Gazette* 17 May (in a letter to the editor): "It is only Martha's egotistical self-adoration, and bid for attention that blinds her to accept the very appropriate saying, 'A big mouth is Nature's compensation for a small mind.'" 1991 *Pittsburgh Press* 1 Feb.: "From Barry Bonds—big mouth, small brain—you expect the kind of mindless, senseless, totally-lacking-in-logic harangue he dumped on the Pirates Wednesday." *MP* M293.

Big **mouth**, small pecker (dick, prick).

1993 Joseph Flynn, *The Concrete Inquisition* (New York: Penguin) 319: "'Big mouth, little pecker,' Glenna said. *Another idiom*, Armando thought. This one insulting" (italics as shown). 2010 James Albert, *Tom, Dick and Harley: 666 Jokes and Comic Situations* (Indianapolis IN: Dog Ear) 110: "'I like my women with big boobs and nice and tight down below.' 'Just like ALL you Harley Riders. Big Mouth and small pecker'" (capitalization as shown). Cf. "Big MOUTH, small brain" and "Big CAR, small dick."

A closed **mouth** does not get fed.

1989 *Sun-Sentinel [Fort Lauderdale FL]* 8 Jan.: "Florida State defensive back and probable top-five selection Deion Sanders on why he talks so much: 'Because I feel a closed mouth never gets fed.'" 1992 Sonya Brooks, "Grandma Talks," in *In the Tradition: An Anthology of Young Black Writers*, edited by Kevin Powell and Ras Baraka (New York: Harlem River) 120: "Chile, I don't know what's botherin you, / but whatever it is, / always remember this, / 'a closed mouth won't get fed.'" The proverb means that one must "speak up" in order to be noticed or rewarded.

A closed (shut) **mouth** gathers (catches) no feet.

1956 *Reader's Digest* 68, no. 1 (Jan.) 178 (in a short list of witty sayings): "A closed mouth gathers no feet" (credited to Bob Cooke, from the *New York Herald Tribune*). 1959 *Christian Science Monitor* 28 Feb.: "Possibly on the theory that a closed mouth gathers no foot, Coach Red Auerbach has been understandably reluctant to discuss the formula. . . ." Baldwin (1965) 140 lists the saying as a Pennsylvania proverb. Litovkina and Mieder (2006) 75. The proverb probably originated as an anti-proverb blending two proverbs, "A closed mouth catches no flies" and "A rolling stone gathers no moss," with the idiom "put one's foot in one's mouth."

Don't let your **mouth** write (Don't write) a check that your ass (behind) can't cash.

1966 Charles Portis, *Norwood* (New York: Simon & Schuster) 184: "Watch it now. You're taking liberties. Don't make things worse than they are. Don't let your mouth write a check that your ass can't cash, son." 1980 Edith A. Folb, *Runnin' Down Some Lines: The Language and Culture of Black Teenagers* (Cambridge MA: Harvard UP) 235: "Don't let your mouth overload your ass; don't let your mouth write a check your ass can't cash" (with the gloss "Don't talk too much, in such a belligerent manner, or there's going to be a fight"). Lighter (1994– ) 1: 30; Prahlad (1996) 239–40.

If you keep your **mouth** shut, you won't put your foot in it.

1915 Austin O'Malley, *Keystones of Thought* (New York: Devin-Adair) 192 (in a list of unattributed sayings): "If you keep your mouth shut you will never put your foot in it." Cf. "A closed MOUTH gathers no feet" and the older "Open mouth, insert foot."

If it **moves**, nail it (if it doesn't, paint it).

1986 Jackie Collins, *Hollywood Husbands* (New York: Simon & Schuster) 37–38: "*It was not exactly love at first sight for Mannon: more,* If it moves—nail it. *And delectable Whitney was the most nailable girl he'd seen all week*" (italics as shown). 1999 Stephen Parr, *North to the Future* (Birmingham UK: Windhorse) 100 (beginning of the poem "Flatlanders"): "They're all do-it-yourselfers. / If it moves, nail it. / If it cracks, slap Polyfilla / in it before teatime. . . ." The proverb can refer either to male sexual predation (a slang sense of the verb *nail*) or to excessive neatness, an eagerness to "fix" everything. A slightly different sense is noted by Casselman (2002) 135 (as a "Canadian saying"): "If it moves, nail it. If it doesn't, paint it. A command from the boss when his workers think more than they sweat." It has probably been influenced by the military adage "If it MOVES, salute it."

If it **moves**, salute it (if it doesn't pick it up) (if it doesn't, paint it) (if you can't pick it up, paint it).

1944 *Chicago Defender* 16 Dec.: "'If it moves salute it. If it doesn't move pick it up. If you can't pick it up paint it.'—That's the slogan for discipline that originated at Camp Lee [VA]; a slogan that has since been adopted by Army camps all over the country." *YBQ* Sayings (22).

If it **moves**, shoot it.

1934 Josephine Herbst, *The Executioner Waits* (New York: Harcourt, Brace) 43 (a young socialist "agitator" is speaking): "And what I remember best about that Colorado mess [the 'Ludlow Massacre']. . . . What was the command? *Shoot everything that moves.* There you are. The perfect slogan of the system. If it moves, shoot it" (italics as shown). 1970 *New York Times* 7 Mar.: "For the marines here [in a Vietnam 'free-fire zone'], the rule of thumb after dark is simple: 'If it moves, shoot it.'"

If it **moves**, shoot it; if it doesn't, cut it down.

1964 Bill Wannan, *Fair Go, Spinner* (Melbourne, Australia: Lansdowne) 87: "The 'national motto of Australia'[:] If it moves shoot it; if it doesn't, chop it down." 1966 Sidney J. Baker, *The Australian Language* (Sydney: Currawong) 78: "He [the 'axeman'] has . . . hacked his way into and out of the bush, and, probably, as much as anyone, given point to the old Australian saying, 'If it grows, cut it down; if it moves, shoot it!'" Pickering et al. (1992) 416. The proverb, which satirizes ravagings of the environment, evidently originated in Australia—perhaps as an anti-proverb elaborating on "If it MOVES, shoot it."

You **move**, you lose (When you move, you lose).

1925 Guy W. Ellis, "Making Sales Points of Objections," *National Real Estate Journal* 26, no. 12 (15 Jun.) 42: "A wise old philosopher one time [Benjamin Franklin in 1736] said that three moves are equal to a fire. Every time you move, you lose; every time you buy, you gain." 1953 Langston Hughes, "Picture for Her Dresser," in *Simple Takes a Wife* (New York: Simon & Schuster) 43 (a photographer is speaking to a "sitter"): "Now look pleasant, please! You have observed the sign yonder which is the rule of the company: IF YOU MOVE, YOU LOSE. IF YOU SHAKE—NO RETAKE! So kindly hold your position" (capitalization as shown). 1964 "People Are Talking About," *Jet* 27, no. 13 (31 Dec.) 42 (regarding a woman whose Canadian husband, while she was out of the country, had sold the house that she had paid for): "That Jamaican wife . . . learned the bitter truth about the old adage, 'When you move, you lose.'" 1983 *Washington Post* 29 Aug.: "In the view of the street dealers, there simply is no time for standing in unemployment or welfare lines. Out here on the streets, if you move, you lose." As the quotations reveal, the proverb can have a wide range of applications. Cf. "Move your FEET, lose your seat."

### A ms. (miss) is as good as a male.

1942 *Chicago Daily Tribune* 25 May: "Now that women are to be inducted into the army we may revise the old saying to read, 'A miss is as good as a male.'" 1948 Aldous Huxley, *Ape and Essence* (New York: Harper) 13: "I picked up the nearest of the scripts. 'A Miss is as good as a Male, Screenplay by Albertine Krebs.'" 1974 *Interim Study by the Select Committee on Inter-School Activities, the Montana High School Association and Montana Inter-School Activities* (Helena: Montana Legislative Council) 27, citing the title of a speech by New York state commissioner of education Ewald Nyquist (3 Jul. 1973): "Equity in Athletics; or, A Ms. Is as Good as a Male." Litovkina and Mieder (2006) 72. The proverb originated as an anti-proverb based on "A miss is as good as a mile."

### If you have to ask how **much** it costs, you can't afford it.

See "If you have to ask the PRICE, you can't afford it."

### If you sift through enough **mud**, you may find gold.

See "If you sift through enough DIRT, you may find gold."

### **Mud** thrown is lost ground (He who slings dirt loses ground; The easiest way to lose ground is to throw mud).

1923 *New Castle [PA] News* 27 Nov.: "It is encouraging to know that politicians who throw mud eventually lose ground." 1924 *Atlanta Constitution* 5 May: "A Missouri exchange wonders 'if political parties won't find, before the campaign is over, that mud thrown is ground lost.'" 1949 *Billings [MT] Herald* 8 Dec.: Somebody said that if you throw dirt you lose ground." *DAP* 26(10), 421(4); Dundes and Pagter (1991) 94. The proverb is sometimes regarded as a "Confucianism" (especially with the formulaic "He who . . ." beginning); it has also been attributed to Texas governor W. Lee "Pappy" O'Daniel and to Adlai Stevenson.

### **Mules** don't kick according to rules.

1968 *Federal Constitutional Convention: Hearings before the Subcommittee on Separation of Powers . . . Senate* (Washington DC: Government Printing Office) 72; Senator Sam Ervin speaks: ". . . I have found that when we go to court, we have certain principles of law that must be allowed to prevail; but individual Congressmen are like Josh Billings says, 'They do not kick according to any rule whatsoever, except their own political notions.'" 1972 *Professional Basketball: Hearing before the Subcommittee on Antitrust and Monopoly . . . Senate* (Washington DC: Government Printing Office) 247; Sam Ervin gives a more cogent version of the proverb:

"... [M]aybe the owners of these teams are like Josh Billings' philosophy instead of the philosophy of law, Josh Billings had a mule and said the mule didn't kick according to no rule whatsoever. ..." Ervin employed the proverb on still other occasions; the attribution to Josh Billings appears to be erroneous. *DAP* 421(3).

## **Murder** is easier the second time (The second murder is easier).

1933 Agatha Christie, "13 for Dinner," *American Magazine* 115, no. 5 (May) 140: "One life is removed, perhaps after a terrific struggle with the conscience. Then—danger threatens—the second murder is easier." 1980 Robert Barnard, *Death of a Literary Widow* (New York: Charles Scribner's Sons) 190: "'If he suspects ... It's easier the second time, they say.' 'What about you? ... Then I'd watch out for yourself too'" (first set of ellipsis dots as shown; the novel was published in England in 1979 with the title *Posthumous Papers*). *DAAP* 526.

## A **murderer** returns to the scene of the crime.

See "A CRIMINAL returns to the scene of the crime."

## The better the **music**, the better the dance.

1991 *Record [Kitchener-Waterloo, Ontario]* 6 Mar.: "Other people will tell you that ballet music is mostly bad music to begin with. But I'm convinced that the better the music, the better the dance." 2003 Twyla Tharp, *The Creative Habit* (New York: Simon & Schuster) 106: "That's why finding a great piece of music is key to making a great dance. The better the music, the better the dance."

## **Mustard** with mutton is a sign of a glutton.

1927 Patrick Hamilton, *Craven House* (Boston: Houghton Mifflin) 74: "Master Wildman was reproved for taking mustard with mutton, which Mrs. Nixon, with a proverb ready for any child on any occasion, affirmed to be the sign of a glutton." *MP* M348.

## The **nail** that sticks out gets pounded (hammered down).

1969 Richard Halloran, *Japan: Images and Realities* (New York: Alfred A. Knopf) 215 (quoting): "Conformity is important to us, and we Japanese soon hammer down the nail that sticks up." 1972 John Hohenberg, *New Era in the Pacific* (New York: Simon & Schuster) 145: "It will be a long time before the Japanese give up faith in the group creed: 'The nail that sticks up must be hammered down.'" 1973 F. T. Hauer and James Ford, *Contemporary Management* (Columbus OH: Charles E. Merrill) 61: "The decision makers can react negatively to 'the squeaky wheel gets the oil' principle. In fact, the Chinese have a saying, 'The nail that sticks out gets the whack.'" *DAP* 423(2): "A nail that sticks out is struck"; *ODP* 221. Widely quoted in English—in reference to Asian societies as well as to organizations in general—the proverb has been attributed to several Asian languages.

## **Names** are for tombstones.

1973 *Live and Let Die* (motion picture). Retorts a Harlem gang boss, after James Bond has introduced himself: "Names is for tombstones, baby!" 1980 Rock Brynner, *The Ballad of Habit and Accident* (New York: Wyndham) 123: "'By the way, what's your name?' 'I haven't figured that out yet.' 'Well, names are for tombstones anyhow.'"

## **Nearly** doesn't count.

See "CLOSE doesn't count."

## **Nearly** is not good enough.

See "ALMOST is not good enough."

## Don't stick your **neck** out.

1937 *Los Angeles Times* 2 May: "Pomona meets the Oxy freshmen and Bob Strehle turns around and forfeits the relay to the Tigers. . . . Only Bob says he told Oxy before the meet that he wouldn't run the relay even if his team was behind . . . which it wasn't. . . . Moral for sports writers: Never stick your neck out, there are too many geezers eager to wedge an ax in it." *DAP* 425; *RHDP* 68; *YBQ* Modern Proverbs (87). The proverbial phrase "stick one's neck out" may be older.

## Love thy **neighbor**, but don't get caught.

1967 *Washington Post* 18 Oct.: "Members' felt-pen scrawls ornament the men's room: . . . 'Love thy neighbor—but don't get caught.'" Litovkina and Mieder (2006) 209. The proverb is an anti-proverb based on the biblical mandate to "love thy neighbor" (e.g., Galatians 5:14).

## It's **never** too late until it's too late.

1988 *Advocate [Baton Rouge]* 8 Nov.: "It's never too late until it's too late . . . It's too late at 8 pm. We're going to vote first thing in the morning." 1995 *San Diego Union* 31 Dec.: "Of the team's slim playoff hopes, [Chargers coach Bobby] Ross said, 'It's never too late until it's too late. Right now, it still isn't too late.'" *DAP* 361. "You never know (realize) it's too late till it's too late" could be regarded as a separate proverb: 1918 *Plumbers, Gas and Steam Fitters' Journal* 23, no. 7 (Jul.) 15 (filler item): "One of the great drawbacks in this world is that a man never knows it is too late until it is too late." 1957 *Daily News [Virgin Islands]* 21 Mar.: "Many a man loses his chance in this life because he never knows it is too late until it is too late." Cf. "It's not OVER till it's over."

Never say *never*; never say *always* (Never say *never* or *always*).

1967 John H. McGovern, "Discussion," in *Ureteral Reflux in Children*, edited by James F. Glenn (Washington DC: National Academy of Sciences–National Research Council) 206: "One should never say 'never' or 'always.' I don't believe one should make a hard and fast rule; each case is different." 1986 Bonnie Runyan McCullough, *Totally Organized* (New York: St. Martin's) 249: "If your rules are absolute, you may forfeit your opportunity to influence or help your children. . . . Never say *never*; never say *always*" (italics as shown). The proverb represents an extension of the older "Never say never."

## Nice (Being nice) doesn't win games (awards, elections, etc.).

1981 Earle Rice Jr., *Fear on Ice* (Belmont CA: Simon & Schuster) 36: "Coach Hall wasn't happy. He stormed up and down the locker room. 'What are you guys doing out there? . . .' he shouted. 'Being nice doesn't win games.'" 1992 *Times-News [Hendersonville NC]* 11 Sep.: "It would be nice to think that politicians have evolved, psychologically speaking, in 200 years. But nice doesn't win elections."

## Don't take any wooden nickels.

1912 *Cedar Rapids Evening Gazette* 16 Nov.: "So long. Don't take any wooden nickels, will you?" *MP* N68; *DAP* 430(2), 670–71; *RHDP* 69; *DAAP* 540–41; Pickering et al. (1992) 432; Prahlad (1996) 240. The proverb advises against gullibility or credulity.

## Whatever gets (helps) you through the night (day).

1974 John Lennon's song "Whatever Gets You through the Night" probably helped establish the elliptical sentence as a proverb, which licenses certain indulgences to help one endure a difficult or painful time.

## Only Nixon could go to China.

1981 *Confirmation Hearing on Edward C. Schmults, Nominee, to Be Deputy Attorney General . . . before the Committee on the Judiciary . . . Senate* (Washington DC: Government Printing Office) 36; Senator Joseph Biden speaks (5 Feb.): "Quite frankly, just as only Nixon might have been able to go to China, maybe only President Reagan can really take some of the very tough approaches that need to be taken with regard to cutting down some of the bureaucratic thickets. . . ." 1981 *Washington Post* Nov. 29: "If only Nixon could go to China, perhaps only a liberal can go to Middle America." 1984 *Genocide Convention: Hearing before the Committee on Foreign Relations . . . Senate* (Washington DC: Government Printing Office) 70; Senator Joseph Biden speaks: "The difference here is we have a president, to use the old cliché, like Nixon could go to China and only Nixon, probably only Reagan could pass the genocide treaty." *YBQ* Modern Proverbs (66).

## Just say no.

1983 The slogan entered oral tradition from the Reagan administration's publicity campaign (headed by Nancy Reagan) against the use of drugs, especially by young people. As an allusion to the slogan, the sentence is often uttered derisively, satirizing the ineffectiveness of such a facile admonition. Proverbially, the sentence can now be used (most often jocularly) to discourage succumbing to any temptation or indulging in any particular behavior. *YBQ* Advertising Slogans (2). Of course, nonproverbial uses of the clause are older.

## No means "no."

1980 Court of Appeals of Wisconsin, *State v. Lederer* 99 Wis 2d 430 (decided 28 Oct.) 436: "'No' means no, and precludes any finding that the prosecutrix consented to any of the sexual acts performed during the night." The proverb refers to the definitiveness of a woman's rebuff of sexual overtures. Of course, the clause is older in other uses (for example, as something a parent might say to a recalcitrant child).

## Keep your **nose** clean.

1903 J. L. Smith, "Moral Characteristics of Pupils," *American Annals of the Deaf* 48: 420: "'If you are going to teach the young idea [*sic*] how to shoot, you must keep your nose clean.' That homely sentence comes back to me now. . . ." 1904 Frank E. Kellogg, *The Boy Fisherman* (Akron: Saalfield) 288 (addressing the Mississippi River): "Goodby, old man! Keep your nose clean, and don't go on a rampage next spring and knock things galley west." *MP* N104; *RHDP* 194. Before the clause came to be used proverbially, it was common as literal advice in "hygiene" manuals.

## You can pick your **nose**, and you can pick your friends, but you can't pick your friend's nose.

See "You can pick your FRIENDS, and you can pick your nose, but you can't pick your friend's nose."

## You can pick your **nose**, but you can't pick your family (relatives).

1997 Jeff Gomez, *Geniuses of Crack* (New York: Simon & Schuster) 157: "'What's the old phrase about picking your nose and not your friends?' Mark laughs. 'I think it's "You can pick your nose, but you can't pick your relatives." Your friends you can pick.'" 1998 *The Age [Melbourne, Australia]* 2 Oct.: "As a wise dad once said: You can pick your friends and you can pick your nose but you can't pick your family." 2002 E. Lynn Harris, *Any Way the Wind Blows* (New York: Anchor) 219: "I don't talk about mine either. You can pick your nose, but not your family." The proverb probably originated as an anti-proverb based on "You can choose your friends, but you can't choose your family." Cf. "You can pick your FRIENDS, and you can pick your nose, but you can't pick your friend's nose."

## Your (The) **nose** knows.

1905 Herman Kuehn (pseudonym "Evelyn Gladys"), *Thoughts of a Fool* (Chicago: E. P. Rosenthal) 146: "Suppose your nose, which is an important factor on your face, should say there is no liver, because it nosed and found it not. Does that prove that the nose knows?" 1916 *McClure's* 48 (Apr.) 50 (advertisement for Tuxedo brand smoking tobacco): "Can anyone fool you on a rose—with your eyes blindfolded? Of course not! 'Your nose knows.'" 1916–19 Various texts featuring the slogan appeared in ads placed by the American Tobacco Company in North American magazines. 1920 Herbert C. Hamilton, "Purified Cresol (Cresylic Acid)," *American Journal of Pharmacy* 92: 251: "The time necessary to vaporize the impurities varies with amount present, and can be determined by smelling. 'The nose knows' when the pyridine is gone."

## **Nostalgia** is not what it used to be.

1959 Peter De Vries, *Tents of Wickedness* (Boston: Little, Brown) 6: "No. Nostalgia, as his Uncle Joshua had said, ain't what it used to be. Which made it pretty complete. Nothing was what it used to be—not even nostalgia." *YBQ* De Vries (2); Ratcliffe (2006) 325. Cf. "The PAST is not what it used to be."

## Don't (try to) make something out of **nothing**.

1907 Shan F. Bullock, *Robert Thorne* (London: T. Werner Laurie) 189: "'Nell,' I said, 'for goodness sake be sensible. Don't make something out of nothing. You know what I meant.'" *DAP* 551. The proverb may be thought of as an anti-proverb based on the very old metaphysical aphorism "Nothing can be made from nothing." It usually counsels against exaggerating the importance of a thoughtless comment or other social slight.

He who stands for **nothing** will fall for anything (everything).

See "If you don't STAND for something, you will fall for anything."

Most of us know how to say **nothing**, but few of us know when.

1902 *The Smart Set* 7, no. 2 (Jun.) 114 (in a short collection of witticisms): "Most of us know how to say nothing; few of us know when." *DAP* 352.

**Nothing** ain't worth nothing, but it's free.

1969 The saying probably entered oral tradition as a proverb from the song "Me and Bobby McGee," written by Kris Kristofferson and Fred Foster (popularized by Janis Joplin, Willie Nelson, and others). *YBQ* Kristofferson. It might be regarded as a modern incarnation of the ancient adage "Nothing comes from nothing"—or as an anti-proverb responding to a version of that adage.

**Nothing** comes easy (in this world, that is worth having, etc.).

1900 *New Castle [PA] News* 19 Dec.: "Nothing comes easy in this world. Even that $90,000 which Terry McGovern 'cleaned up' during the past year came only through hard knocks." 1914 *American Club Woman* 7, no. 9 (Sep.) 50 (in some untitled, unattributed verses): "Nothing comes easy, the strife is hard / But the thing worth doing—ah that repays." 1914 Maurice Switzer, *Letters of a Self-Made Failure* (Boston: Small, Maynard) 53: "On general principles nothing comes easy that's worth having." 1915 Peggy ("Peggy from Paris"), "No. 200, Paris," *International Bookbinder* 16: 292: "I know it must be hard in a long strike, but you know nothing comes easy that is worth anything." Cf. "Nobody ever said LIFE is easy" and the older "Life is not meant to be easy."

**Nothing** grows forever.

1978 *Chicago Tribune* 10 Apr.: "Nothing grows forever. Most well-known stocks at one time or another rise speculatively to heights considerably above where they deserve to sell on the basis of logically projected prospects." 1986 *Sacramento [CA] Bee* 6 Nov.: "On top of that, many ignore the basic rule of economics that says nothing grows forever. A tree can't reach the sky." The proverb typically refers to finance or economics.

**Nothing** happens until it happens (before its time).

1901 "Editorial Notes," *The Inland Printer* 27: 835–36: ". . . [I]t must be borne in mind that the old adage, 'Nothing happens until it happens,' is exceedingly applicable to the insidious planting of tubercular disease. . . ." *DAP* 279(1); Prahlad (2001) 260–61.

**Nothing** in life is simple (Nothing is simple in life).

1901 Horace Annesley Vachell, *Sport and Life on the Pacific Slope* (New York: Dodd, Mead) 170: "Had he been taught that nothing in life is simple, that in the strenuous competition of to-day no hour may be wasted with impunity, no dollar squandered, no trifle ignored . . . , he might—who knows?—have graduated with honours." 1919 Leslie Burton Blades, *Claire* (New York: George H. Doran) 35: "'Neither sounds very simple.' 'Nothing in life is simple,' he replied." 1947 Hewlett Johnson, *Soviet Success* (London: Hutchinson) 35: "Dr. Koulakofskaya had rejected religion . . . but possessed a profound belief that good would triumph over evil, that nothing is simple in life, that duty to family and country are of paramount importance. . . ."

**Nothing** is as dead as yesterday's newspaper.

1921 Glenn Frank, "The Tide of Affairs," *Century* 103: 315: "Few of us carry over from day to day and from week to week a sense of the accumulating information that our newspaper has given us in any field of interest. Nothing is as dead as yesterday's newspaper." The proverbial comparison "dead as yesterday's newspaper" may be somewhat older than the proverb.

## Nothing is as easy (simple) as it looks (seems, appears).

1905 Norma Lorimer and Douglas Sladen, *More Queer Things about Japan* (London: Anthony Treherne) 65: "In Japan nothing is as simple as it looks, for everything has a double meaning, too subtle for the ordinary tourist to discover." 1934 John Houston Craige, *Cannibal Cousins* (New York: Minton, Balch) 279: "President Borno planned to get himself reëlected. . . . As he could appoint and remove the members of the Council, this might seem simple, but nothing is as simple as it looks in Haiti." 1936 Hiralal Haldar, "Realistic Idealism," in *Contemporary Indian Philosophy*, edited by S. Radhakrishnan and J. H. Muirhead (New York: Macmillan) 230: "Nothing is as simple as it seems. A lump of sugar is no doubt sweet, but who will undertake to prove that it is sweet to me in precisely the same way it is to you?" 1954 *Use of Funds Raised in Behalf of the Disabled American Veterans: Hearings before the Committee on Veterans' Affairs, House of Representatives* (Washington DC: Government Printing Office) 3514; Millard W. Rice testifies: "It is true that there were diminishing returns. . . . But there were reasons. Nothing is as simple as it appears to be." 1963 "A Fantastic Journey," *Life* 54, no. 21 (24 May): 31: "But before Faith-7 [a manned NASA space mission] had plunked into the Pacific 34 hours later, everyone knew that nothing is as easy as it looks in the realm of space. . . ." Occasionally referred to as "Allen's Law," versions of the proverb are also commonly given as an article of "Murphy's Law"; in Morris and Morris (1962–71) 3: 184, it appears as the first "article" of that law: "*Murphy's Law. . . .* 1. Nothing is as easy as it looks. 2. Everything will take longer than you think it will. 3. If anything can go wrong, sometime it will."

## Nothing ruins a duck but (like) its bill (A wise duck takes care of its bill).

1955 Sigman Byrd, *Sig Byrd's Houston* (New York: Viking) 175: "I asked what it was like in the old days here, when she was a child. Pinkie gazed down at the toes of her rubber boots. 'Nothing ruins a duck but his bill,' she said. 'There's some things I don't like to bill about.'" 1959 Marilyn Schlesinger, "Proverbs from High School," *Western Folklore* 18: 322 (from a California student's Arkansan mother): "Nothing ruins a duck but his bill." *DAP* 171(4); Prahlad (1996) 225–26. The proverb warns against excessive or injudicious talking.

## Second best is better than nothing (at all).

See "SECOND BEST is better than nothing."

## There is nothing in the middle of the road but yellow stripes and dead skunks (armadillos, possums, etc.).

1967 Richard Mathison, "Curse You, Red Peril!" *West Magazine (Los Angeles Times)* 3 Dec.: "But, he [William Penn Patrick] adds, he is tired of wishy-washy me-tooism. 'The middle of the road is where there's a yellow line and dead cats,' he says." 1970 *Florence [AL] Times–Tri Cities Daily* 27 Sep.: "Criticizing Americans for their moderation in facing the 'creeping gradualism,' he [Jack Mohr] said there is no virtue in being moderately wrong and added, 'the middle of the road is where you find the yellow stripe and dead skunks.'" 1983 *Kentucky New Era [Hopkinsville]* 11 Apr.: "He [Grady Stumbo] said his grandfather always told him to take a stand . . . because 'you only find two things in the middle of the road—yellow lines and dead possums.'" 1984 *New York Times* 22 Jul.: "Jim Hightower, state agriculture commissioner [of Texas], on why he's not a middle-of-the-road politician: 'Ain't nothing in the middle of the road but yellow stripes and dead armadillos.'" *YBQ* Hightower (2). Cf. "The MIDDLE of the road is where people get run over."

## There is **nothing** worse than an educated fool.

1904 Edgar G. Doudna, "The Boy and the Farm," *Handbook of Agriculture* (Wisconsin Farmers' Institutes) 18: 279: "Knowledge without power to apply it is wasted, is dead. There is no such monstrosity as an educated fool." 1942 Edgar Maass, *Don Pedro and the Devil* (Indianapolis: Bobbs-Merrill) 90: "We consider it dangerous for our knowledge to lodge in heads not fit to contain it, for who can tell how they may misuse their power? There's nothing worse than an educated fool." Daniel et al. (1987) 503.

## When you have **nothing**, you have nothing to lose.

1965 *Liberator* 5, no. 6 (Jun.) 29 (letter to the editor, by Marilyn Dyling): "This country is in the worse [sic] state it has ever been. . . . One thing in our favor, when you have nothing, you have nothing to lose." 1965 Vernon Howard, *Psycho-Pictography* (West Nyack NY: Parker) 163: "You now see that you cannot lose anything because, psychologically speaking, you never really owned anything. When you have nothing, you have nothing to lose." 1965 Bob Dylan's song "Like a Rolling Stone" contains the line "When you got nothing, you got nothing to lose." 1982 Betsy Bowden, *Performed Literature* (Bloomington: Indiana UP) 77: "[Dylan's line] may be spoken to express sympathy at another's loss or else bravado before a coming challenge." The idea encapsulated in the proverbial forms is much older—for instance, the medieval commonplace that a poor man may sing in the presence of thieves.

## You can't beat something with **nothing** (somebody with nobody).

1909 *Nebraska State Journal* [Lincoln] 25 Oct.: "'You can't beat somebody with nobody' is an axiom of very practical politics." 1919 *New York Times* 30 Jul. (quoting Gifford Pinchot): "We [Republicans] must beat [President Woodrow] Wilson and the Democrats. But you cannot beat something with nothing." 1923 Solomon Bulkley Griffin, *People and Politics Observed by a Massachusetts Editor* (Boston: Little, Brown) 388: "The situation was put in an extreme way by Nicholas Murray Butler of New York when he said to Mr. [Mark] Hanna, 'You cannot beat something with nothing.'" 1934 D. W. Brogan, "The President and Politics," *Fortnightly Review* 142: 20: "It is a maxim of American politics that you cannot beat something with nothing." *DAP* 40; *RHDP* 380.

## Any **notice** is good notice.

See "Any PUBLICITY is good publicity."

## **Number two** tries harder (When you're number two, you try harder; Second best has to try harder).

1962 The saying probably entered oral tradition as a proverb from an advertising campaign for Avis: "We're Number Two. We try harder" (Avis was second to Hertz in the car-rental business). 1970 *Victoria [TX] Advocate* 13 Jan. (section heading of a column about a Little League team): "Second-Best Tries Harder." 1972 Sheilah Graham, *A State of Heat* (New York: Grosset & Dunlap) 240: "I have often wondered why some of the homeliest women get the handsomest, nicest husbands. Perhaps, like the Avis car, the second best has to try harder." *YBQ* Advertising Slogans (17); Dundes and Pagter (1987) 43.

## There's a **nut** on every family tree (Every family tree has a nut on it).

1915 "Jimmy McGlade Says" (a collection of witticisms), *The Gateway* 23, no. 6 (Jan.) 21: "Many a family tree has produced a nut." 1936 Carl Sandburg, *The People, Yes* (New York: Harcourt, Brace) 111 (in a poetic montage of proverbs and other sayings): "There's always a nut on every family tree." *DAAP* 553.

## The **obstacle** is the path.

1985 China Galland, "The Joy of Risk-Taking," *Ms.* 14, no. 3 (Sep.) 106: "Learning to read the river [while white-water rafting] has disclosed the meaning of the Chinese proverb, 'The obstacle is the path.'" 1987 Rachel V., *Family Secrets: Life Stories of Adult Children of Alcoholics* (San Francisco: Harper & Row) xxii: "There is an old saying that never fails me: 'The obstacle is the path.'" The proverb is common among participants in addiction "recovery" programs.

## It is (is always, must be) five (six) **o'clock** somewhere (in the world).

1964 *Wisconsin State Journal* [Madison] 5 Mar. (cartoon: two women at a restaurant table): "I promised my doctor that once I've had my lunch I wouldn't eat again until six o'clock, but I'm sure it's six o'clock somewhere." 1967 Lewis W. Gillenson, *Billy Graham and Seven Who Were Saved* (New York: Trident) 129: "For a while he kept to the time schedule—no drinking before five—but then he began to rationalize. He told himself it was always five o'clock somewhere in the world. . . ."

## **Offense** sells tickets, defense wins games.

1976 *Daily Record* [Ellensburg WA] 8 Jul.: "'Offense sells tickets, defense wins games,' he [football coach Jack Patera] told Seahawk owners in a recent clinic." 1978 *Washington Post* 8 Jan.:

"Aware of what the fans prefer, he [football coach Marv Levy] says, 'It's an oversimplification, but the offense sells tickets, the defense wins games, and the kicking game wins championships.'" The proverb can apply to football, basketball, soccer, hockey, and other sports.

## It isn't how **old** you are but how old you look (feel).

1922 Carl Sandburg, "The Windy City," in *Slabs of the Sunburnt West* (New York: Harcourt, Brace) 6–7: "Hush baby, / It ain't how old you are, / It's how old you look. / It ain't what you got, / It's what you can get away with." 1949 Lester D. Crow and Alice Crow, *Eighteen to Eighty* (Boston: Christopher) 111: "How old should a person be before he retires . . . ? The question could be answered facetiously by the statement that it is not how old you *are* but how old you *feel* that counts" (italics as shown). *DAAP* 558.

## The **old** make laws, the young die for them.

See "Old MEN make wars, and young men fight them."

## We get **old** too soon and smart too late.

1942 H. L. Mencken, *New Dictionary of Quotations* (New York: Alfred A. Knopf) 25 (designated as anonymous): "Ve get too soon old, and too late smart." 1963 *The Shape of Education* 2: 53: ". . . [I]n today's world there is too much to learn and too little time in which to do it. Or, as the Pennsylvania Dutch put it, 'We get old too soon and smart too late.'" *DAP* 438(19). As in Mencken's version, the proverb is sometimes pronounced or written in a jocular German American dialect—such as, "Vee get too soon olt unt too late schmart." Cf. the German "Alt genug und doch nicht klug."

## You're only **old** once.

1927 *Life Magazine* 90 (22 Sep.) 28 (filler item, credited to *Farm and Fireside*): "'Old men,' reads a scolding editorial, 'are too frisky these days. . . .' Why not? After all, a man's only old once." 1940 Mildred Meiers and Jack Knapp, *Thesaurus of Humor* (New York: Crown) 31: "'I wish to goodness we could go home, mother, but dad wants to stay for three more dances.' 'Yes, dear, your father is a trial, isn't he? But, after all, one can be old only once.'" The proverb probably originated as an anti-proverb based on "You are only young once (Youth comes but once)."

## Old age is better than the alternative.

See "Old AGE is better than the alternative."

## Old age is hell.

See "Old AGE is hell."

## Old age is not for sissies.

See "Old AGE is not for sissies."

## Dance (Always dance) with the one who brought you.

1950 Peggy Lamson, *The Charmed Circle* (Philadelphia: Lippincott) 172: "He put his arm around her. 'Come on then, dance with the guy that brung you.' She held back." 1979 "Jimmy versus Teddy," *Newsweek* 39, no. 2 (14 May) 37: "'You dance with the one who brung you,' shrugged an unenthused Jimmycrat in Iowa— and [Jimmy] Carter's early-bird campaigning was aimed at keeping it that way." The proverb often occurs in a "rustic" dialect form (" . . . with the one what brung you"). Cf. "Go home with the ONE who brought you."

## Go home with (Leave with) the one who brought you.

1941 Isabel Currier, *The Young and the Immortal* (New York: Alfred A. Knopf) 225: "Halleck sneered, rising so quickly that Gretchen hardly realized his intention. 'Fun running into you, O'Callaghan. Goodnight, Gretchen.' 'Rude not to leave with the guy what brung you,' Kevin muttered." 1978 Charlton Heston and Hollis

Alpert, *The Actor's Life: Journals 1956–1976* (New York: E. P. Dutton) 381 (journal entry for 18 Jun. 1969): "Stuart is not the ideal director for us, but we have no other course at this point. You have to go home with the guy that brung you." The proverb often occurs in a "rustic" dialect form (" . . . with the one what brung you"), like its analog "Dance with the ONE who brought you."

## It takes one to know one.

1946 Gore Vidal, *Williwaw* (New York: E. P. Dutton) 45: "'I've got a bad egg,' said Bervick. 'I guess this was a pre-war egg.' 'It takes one to know one,' said the Chief, referring back to the eggs." 1947 Arthur William Row, review of *Shakespeare as Poet and Lover* by Louis Anspacher (1944), *Poet Lore* 53: 280: "Anyone who appreciates Shakespeare as this author unquestionably does is another Shakespeare—it takes one to know one!" *MP* O30; *RHDP* 170–71; *YBQ* Modern Proverbs (9); *ODP* 312; Prahlad (1994); Doyle (2001a). Cf. the considerably older "It takes a fool to know a fool" and "It takes a thief to catch a thief."

## One is the loneliest number.

1967 The saying probably entered oral tradition as a proverb from Harry Nilsson's popular song "One": "One is the loneliest number that you'll ever do."

## One (by) one, cocos [i.e., coconuts] fill a basket.

1979 Bob Marley, "Wake Up and Live," on the album *Survival*: "You see, one-one cocoa full a basket; / When they use you, live big today, tomorrow you bury in a casket." 1991 G. Llewellyn Watson, *Jamaican Sayings* (Tallahassee: Florida A & M UP) 161 explains: "Wan-Wan coco full basket. . . . This is a simple way of encouraging thrift. . . . Persistent frugality, in a word, will pay off." Prahlad (2001) 244.

## The **one** who smelt it dealt it.

1971 James Fritzhand, *Son of the Great American Novel* (New York: George Braziller) 176: "While his peers were busy saying, 'See ya later, alligator,' listening to Elvis Presley and holding their noses with two fingers to the tune of 'he who smelt it dealt it,' Arden Hoffstetter was busy laying away plans for his future." The reference is to making note or mention of the odor of flatus. Sometimes the proverb is rhymingly elaborated: "The one who denied it, supplied it," etc.

## **Only just** is good enough.

See "JUST is good enough."

## The **opera** isn't over till the fat lady sings (When the fat lady sings, the opera is over).

1976 *Dallas Morning News* 10 Mar.: Ralph Carpenter, sports information director of Texas Tech University, is quoted using the expression during a basketball game. *RHDP* 261–62; *YBQ* Ralph Carpenter; *ODP* 240–41; Rees (1984) 58; Rees (1995) 369; Room (2000) 745; Pickering (2001) 271. Cf. "CHURCH is not out till the fat lady sings" and "The GAME is not over till the fat lady sings."

## Everyone is entitled to his own **opinions**, not his own facts.

1950 *Deming [NM] Headlight* 6 Jan. (epigraph): "'Every man has a right to his own opinion, but no man has a right to be wrong in his facts.'—Bernard M. Baruch." 1976 *Milwaukee Journal* 31 Jul. (letter to the editor by Congressman Les Aspin): "In a democracy everyone may have his own opinions, but that doesn't mean he may have his own facts. [D. F.] Shaw should know that I voted against the pay raises he says I supported." 1978 Francis P. Hoeber, "To the Editor," *Orbis* 21: 976: "As former Secretary of Defense James Schlesinger tartly observed, 'One is entitled to his own opinions but not his own

facts.'" The saying is also commonly attributed to Senator Daniel Patrick Moynihan.

## **Opinions** are like assholes (armpits)—everybody's got one (and they all stink).

1972 Dave Wolf, *Foul! The Connie Hawkins Story* (New York: Holt, Rinehart & Winston) 337 (regarding Hawkins's fellow basketball player Elvin Hayes): "Hawkins was less than mortified by Elvin's put-down. 'Opinions are like assholes,' he told reporters. 'Everybody's got one.'" 1996 Coke Newell, *Cow Chips Aren't for Dippin'* (Salt Lake City UT: Gibbs-Smith) 37: "A common bit of wisdom in the West is that opinions are like armpits: we all have them and most of them stink." The proverb can occur, elliptically or allusively, with the first clause alone: "Opinions are like assholes." The proverb probably originated as an anti-proverb based on "Everyone has his own opinion." Cf. "EXCUSES are like assholes; everybody has them."

## Never miss an **opportunity** to relieve yourself (Never pass up a chance to pee).

1936 Logan Pearsall Smith, *Reperusals and Recollections* (London: Constable) 163: ". . . [T]he sayings of the greatest man of action of his time, the Duke of Wellington, have become . . . famous. . . . 'Always make water when you can.' . . ." 1951 Edward Windsor, *A King's Story* (New York: G. P. Putnam's Sons) 134: "Perhaps one of the only positive pieces of advice that I was ever given was that supplied by an old courtier who observed: 'Only two rules really count. Never miss an opportunity to relieve yourself; never miss a chance to sit down and rest your feet.'" Rees (1984) 4. The attribution to the Duke of Wellington cannot be authenticated.

## Just because you've **ordered** doesn't mean you can't look at the menu.

See "Just because you're on a DIET doesn't mean you can't look at the menu."

It's (The game is) not **over** till it's over.

1921 Roy Sahm, "It Is Believed Rotarians Won," *The Delta of Sigma Nu Fraternity* 38: 667: "It is said the score was 23 to 21 in favor of Rotary, they having tied the score in the seventh. They passed Kiwanis in the eighth and held Kiwanis in the ninth. All of which goes to prove that a ball game's never over until it's over" (credited to the *Indianapolis News*). *RHDP* 183; *DAAP* 566; Rees (1995) 261. Often, the saying is apocryphally attributed to Yogi Berra. Cf. the older expression "When it's over, it's over," which has a different meaning.

What you don't **owe** won't hurt you.

1968 Evan Esar, *20,000 Quips and Quotes* (Garden City NY: Doubleday) 418: "Another thing about the income tax—what you don't owe won't hurt you" (unattributed). Litovkina and Mieder (2006) 328. The proverb originated as an anti-proverb based on "What you don't know won't hurt you."

You can't tell what's in a **package** by the box (wrapping).

1961 George Garrett, *Which Ones Are the Enemy?* (Boston: Little, Brown) 61: ". . . [S]he looked pretty and clean and sweet and innocent enough to take home to meet Mama. Which only goes to prove one more time that you can't tell what's in a package by the wrapping paper." 1976 Lilly Bruck, ed., *Consumer Rights for Disabled Citizens* (New York: City of New York, Department of Consumer Affairs) 51: "You can't tell a Book by its Cover . . . and you can't tell what's in a package by the box" (ellipsis dots and capitalization as shown). *DAP* 447.

Don't tell me about the **pain** (labor pains); just show me the baby.

1979 Tom Melvin, *Practical Psychology in Construction Management* (New York: Van Nostrand Reinhold) 41: "Regardless of obstacles and difficulties, the owner expects the general [contractor] to complete the project in accordance with the contract documents—so well expressed by 'Don't tell me about the labor pains, just show me the baby.'" 1999 Mike Stewart, *Close More Sales!* (New York: American Management Association) 12: ". . . [H]e told a supplier who was having a problem delivering an order as promised, . . . 'Don't tell me about the pain, just show me the baby!'" 2005 John C. Maxwell, *The 360° Leader* (Nashville: Thomas Nelson) 131: "I haven't met a leader yet who didn't want to get quickly to the bottom line. . . . Their motto is, 'Never mind about the delivery, just show me the baby.'"

**Pain** is beauty.

1993 *Mrs. Doubtfire* (in the motion picture the title character, portrayed by Robin Williams, is being transformed into an elderly woman at a theatrical makeup shop): "'This going to hurt?' 'Don't whine, just relax.' 'Are you sure?' 'Just remember, pain is beauty. OK, here we go. Take a deep breath.'" 2001 Jayne Young, *Savvy in the City: New York* (New York: Macmillan) 148: "And no, Tootsi Plohound does not stand for 'uncomfortable shoes made in Europe' although beauty is pain and pain is beauty." Cf. "BEAUTY is pain."

**Pain** is just weakness leaving the body.

1991 *Washington Post* 6 Jun. (regarding Quantico VA): "The town's major industries are barbershops specializing in crew cuts and variety stores selling T-shirts with slogans such as 'Pain is Weakness Leaving the Body.'" The proverb is an unofficial slogan in the U.S. Marine Corps; it is also common among "extreme" athletes.

**Pain** (Fatigue) is nature's way of telling you to slow down (you need a rest).

1920 M. V. O'Shea and J. H. Kellogg, *Making the Most of Life* (New York: Macmillan) 159: "Fatigue is nature's way of telling us that the body requires rest. What the alcohol does is to make one unconscious of fatigue. . . ." 1943 "'Willie Everlearn': Perhaps You've Met Him?" *Business Education World* 24: 124 (in a piece of text to be transcribed as a shorthand exercise): "But Nature sends pain. Every time we have a headache or any other ache, high or low, it is Nature's way of saying, Willie Everlearn?" 1967 *Register-Guard [Eugene OR]* 20 Mar.: "Fatigue is Nature's way of saying that the patient needs some rest, and he ought to have it." 1988 Jim Fox and Rick McGuire, *Save Your Knees* (New York: Dell) 133: "Yes, you will feel better, but you must realize that the disease is still there. Pain, like death, is nature's way of saying 'Slow down.'" Cf. "DEATH is nature's way of telling you to slow down."

## Pain is (Tough times are) temporary; failure (quitting) is forever.

2003 Lance Armstrong (with Sally Jenkins), *Every Second Counts* (New York: Random House) 3–4: "But the fact is I wouldn't have won a single Tour de France without the lesson of illness. What it teaches is this: pain is temporary. Quitting lasts forever." 2003 Lysa Mateu, *Psychic Dairies* (New York: Harper-Collins) 217: "Beautiful things . . . are available to all who are willing to work hard by doing what they love and never quitting. Tough times are temporary. Quitting is forever." 2005 *Telegraph [UK]* 10 May (quoting the Paralympic athlete Darren Kenny, on his "sporting motto"): "I'm stealing from Lance Armstrong, although he probably stole it from someone else, too. 'Pain is temporary, failure is forever.'"

## Pain is temporary; victory (glory, pride) is forever.

1988 *Spokesman Review [Spokane WA]* 3 Dec.: "The shirt, made up at the start of the season by seniors Jeff Nelson and Jason Scott, read, 'Pain is temporary. Pride is forever.'" 1989 *Herald-Journal [Spartanburg SC]* 3 Dec. (quoting the football player Jerry Rice): "Pain is temporary; victory is forever. I was 23–1, and that record will always be with me." 1996 Alyce M. McKenzie, *Preaching Proverbs: Wisdom for the Pulpit* (Louisville KY: Westminster John Knox) 84: "But the chuckle fades as one continues flipping through the shirts on the rack, reading saying after saying. . . . 'Pain is temporary. Glory is forever.'" 2000 *The Replacements* (motion picture); Keanu Reeves's character speaks: "Pain heals; chicks dig scars; glory lasts forever." 2004 Lorna Davies, "Having a Baby Is Like Running a Marathon," in *Midwifery: Best Practices 2*, edited by Sara Wickham (Edinburgh, Scotland: Elsevier) 203: ". . . I think the maxim which sums up

both experiences for me, when I look at my children, and of course my marathon medal, was extolled [*sic*] on the T-shirt of a runner at about the 22 mile point: 'The pain will subside, but the pride lasts forever!'" Especially in the *glory* form, the proverb resembles certain triumphant exclamations attributed to early Christian martyrs.

## Pain is the price of glory.

2005 *Adweek* 19 Sep.: "I guess we ask for this, those of us who choose this profession [i.e., advertising] that lies at the intersection of art and commerce. It is an unholy alliance, and pain is the price of glory." 2006 *Oakland Tribune* 4 Feb. (title of an article): "Pain Is the Price of Glory for Many Old-time Football Players."

## A thin **pan** will get hot quicker than a thick one (and cold, too).

c. 1938 Transcribed (as part of the WPA Federal Writers' Project) from a seventy-nine-year-old ex-slave in South Carolina: "Cold climate lak they has up dere [in the North] is too hard on him. He has thin blood and you know dat a thin pan gwine to git hot quicker than a thick one and cold the same way"; 1971–79 George P. Rawick, ed., *The American Slave: A Composite Autobiography* (1941; rpt. Westport CT: Greenwood) 3 (pt. 3): 43. *DAP* 448(1); Prahlad (1996) 241.

## Don't get your **panties** (knickers, undies, drawers, etc.) in a twist (bunch, wad, knot, etc.).

1965 Wilbur Smith, *Train from Katanga* (New York: Viking) 145: "'Well, bugger off, then,' snarled Bruce. 'Okay, okay, don't get your knickers in a knot, bucko.' He sauntered off down the corridor." 1970 John Summers, *Dylan* (London: New English Library) 96: "'I don't know what your standards were when you helped on the college magazine they tell me about but we like to get the *Evening Globe* Final Edition out a damn sight faster than we did today—.' . . . 'All right, all right—don't get your knickers in a twist.'" 1973 Johnny Reggae, "Don't Get Your Knickers in a Twist" (song title). 1987 Edgardo Vega Yunqué, *Mendoza's Dreams* (Houston: Arte Publico) 86: "'Quiet, Pancho,' Mandlestein said. 'Everything's under control.' 'My name is not Pancho,' Comacho said. 'Okay, then Cisco,' Mandlestein said. 'Just don't get your panties in a wad, all right?'" *DAAP* 442; Lighter (1994– ) 2: 370. Often the sentence is merely a rebuke to someone displaying agitation or anger, but sometimes it is used proverbially—as general counsel against incurring or succumbing to needless irritation.

## Don't get caught with your **pants** (trousers, britches) down.

1944 James Rawls, poster: "This war will be over some day / Don't get caught with your pants down / Buy G. I. Bonds" (the poster depicts a bewildered-looking G.I. with his trousers down around his ankles). 1944 *Glascow [Scotland] Herald* 15 Sep.: "Denver curio shops sell mildly bawdy postcards—'Remember Pearl Harbour [*sic*]; don't get caught with your pants down.'" The proverb cautions against unpreparedness.

## Everyone puts his (All men put their) **pants** on one leg at a time (the same way).

1932 *Berkeley [CA] Daily Gazette* 28 Sep.: ". . . Lonnie Warneke summed up the Yankees [baseball team] when he said: 'Hell, they're just like all the rest of us. They put on their pants one leg at a time.'" 1933 Thames Williamson, *The Woods Colt: A Novel of the Ozark Hills* (New York: Harcourt, Brace) 14: "'That hound o' his'n ain't no 'count,' puts in Clint. . . . 'Wal, maybe so, but Ed *he's* all right.' 'Puts on his pants same as I do,' says Clint . . . " (italics as shown). 1934 *Pittsburgh Press* 3 Mar.: "When reminded that Ohio State hasn't won the Big Ten football title since 1920 and that Michigan has been the principal obstacle, he [OSU coach Francis Schmidt]

remarked dryly: 'They put on their pants one leg at a time the same as everybody else.'"

## **Paper** bleeds little (Paper does not bleed).

1940 Ernest Hemingway, *For Whom the Bell Tolls* (New York: Charles Scribner's Sons) 166: "'On paper the bridge is blown at the moment the attack starts. . . . It is very simple.' 'That they should let us do something on paper,' El Sordo said. . . . '"Paper bleeds little,"' Robert Jordan quoted the proverb" (the reader is probably expected to assume that a Spanish proverb has been quoted, although—thanks, perhaps, to the novel's popularity—it has become common in English). 1974 *Palm Beach [FL] Post* 27 Jan.: "The Spanish had a saying during their civil war that paper doesn't bleed—a reference to maps and orders from headquarters as opposed to soldiers in the lines." 1982 *Philadelphia Inquirer* 17 Sep.: "'It's not Medicare. It's paper care,' he [physician José Garcia Oller] said. 'Paper doesn't bleed, doesn't have high blood pressure, doesn't have a mother-in-law, doesn't have a job.'" *DAP* 449(3); *RHDP* 267.

## You aren't finished till you've done the **paperwork**.

See "The JOB isn't over until the paperwork is done."

## Even **paranoids** (can) have enemies.

1967 "Eutychus III" (pseudonym), "Dear Slogan-Lover," *Christianity Today* 11, no. 21 (21 Jul.) 20: "When it comes to expressing their views on life, they ['young radicals'] say by button: 'I Want To Be What I Was When I Wanted To Be What I Am Now,' . . . and 'Even Paranoids Have Real Enemies.'" 1967 Mark Harris, "The Flowering of the Hippies," *Atlantic* 220, no. 7 (Sep.) 68: "Their paranoia was the paranoia of youthful heretics. *Even Paranoids Have Real Enemies.* True" (italics as shown). 1969 Herman Lebovics, *Social Conservatism and the Middle Classes in Germany,*

*1914–1933* (Princeton NJ: Princeton UP) ix: ". . . Moreover, as the poet Gregory Corso reminds us, 'even paranoids have enemies.'" More often, the saying has been attributed to the poet Delmore Schwartz and, more recently, to the political pundit Henry Kissinger. Cf. "Just because you're paranoid doesn't MEAN they aren't after you."

## Just because you're a **paranoid** doesn't mean they aren't out to get you.

See "Just because you're paranoid doesn't MEAN they aren't after you."

## **Parasites** don't kill their host.

1971 William E. Brown, *Islands of Hope* (Washington DC: National Recreation and Park Association) 113: ". . . [S]ome parasites restrain themselves so as not to kill their hosts. . . . Potential analogies with human behavior are almost infinite. . . . Generally, predators consume their capital but parasites live off the interest." 1971 Colin Wilson, *The Black Room* (London: Weidenfeld & Nicolson) 109 (regarding CIA agents): "So by the very nature of their business, they've got to exercise restraint. You could say that they're professional parasites, and they have to take care not to kill their host." 2009 *Kansas City [MO] Star* 27 Jan.: "Perhaps the government could learn something from biology. Successful parasites don't kill their hosts."

## If you're not **part** of the solution (answer), you're part of the problem.

1937 John R. Alltucker, "Guidance in a Medium-Sized High School," *California Journal of Secondary Education* 12: 158: "Does the individual citizen so live, act, and react that he becomes a part of the problem or a part of its solution?" 1941 Harry Emerson Fosdick, *Living under Tension* (New York: Harper & Brothers) 120: "We need Christ's radical remedy . . . by which, one by one, men and women are transferred from being part of the problem to being part of the solution." 1947 Ashley Montagu, "The

Improvement of Human Relations through Education," *School and Society* 65: 469: "We know the problem, we know the solution. Let us ask ourselves the question: Are we part of the problem or are we part of the solution?" 1950 George Ernest Thomas, *Faith Can Master Fear* (New York: Revell) 44: "In one of his prayers before the United States Senate [11 Mar. 1947], the Rev. Peter Marshall, chaplain, said: '. . . May we resolve, God helping us, to be part of the answer, and not part of the problem.'" *RHDP* 159; *YBQ* Cleaver (2); *ODP* 292–93; Pickering (2001) 275. In recent decades, the proverb has been associated with Eldridge Cleaver, who said in a 1968 speech, "You're either part of the solution or you're part of the problem."

## If you're not **part** of the steamroller, you're part of the road.

1987 Stewart Brand, *The Media Lab: Inventing the Future at MIT* (New York: Viking) 9: "Once a new technology rolls over you, if you're not part of the steamroller, you're part of the road." 1994 James Jorgensen, *It's Never Too Late to Get Rich* (Dearborn MI: Financial) 136 (quoting a letter received): "It pays to know the ins and outs of IRAs because if you're not part of the steamroller you're part of the asphalt." *YBQ* Brand (2). The proverb perhaps originated as an anti-proverb modeled on the dichotomy "If you're not PART of the solution, you're part of the problem."

## There are no small **parts** (roles), only small actors.

1924 The saying may have entered English-speaking tradition as a proverb from Russian; Konstantin Stanislavski, *My Life and Art*, translated by J. J. Robbins (Boston: Little, Brown) 298: "We also spoke of artistic ethics and entered our decisions into the minutes, at times even using aphorisms. 'There are no small parts, there are only small actors.'" 1929 "Drama, Dead as—the Sunrise" (editorial), *Theatre Magazine* 49 (Jun.) 40: "George Horace Lorimer, of the

*Saturday Evening Post*, coined the editorial gem that there are no dull subjects; only dull writers! Similarly, Mr. [Edward G.] Robinson says there are no small parts; only small actors." Cf. "There are no dull SUBJECTS, just dull writers."

## Always leave the **party** (leave, go home, quit) while you're still having fun (a good time).

1953 *Spokane [WA] Daily Chronicle* 8 Apr.: "Don't stay out too late. Go home while you're still having fun and you both wish the evening—and the date—were longer." 1977 *News and Courier [Charleston SC]* 24 Jan.: "Quit while you're still having fun. Accidents happen when a skier is tired." 1990 *Eugene [OR] Register-Guard* 11 Mar.: "Emily Post said you should always leave a party while you're still having fun, not after you've stopped having fun." *DAP* 450(1).

## Every **party** has (needs) a pooper.

1967 *Hartford Courant* 15 Feb.: "Every party needs a pooper, and in this case it may be the state Alcoholic Beverage Control Board (ABC)." Sometimes the proverb is expanded and used an an insult: 1978 Sonia Pilcer, *Teen Angel* (New York: Coward, McGann & Geoghegan) 106: "'Come on don't be a party pooper.' 'Every party needs a pooper that's why we invited you, party pooper. . . .'"

## My **party**, my rules (Your party, your rules).

2003 *Fresno Bee* 16 May: "I call the shots. It's my party. It's my rules." 2005 Jamie Denton, *Hard to Handle* (Toronto: Harlequin) 19: "She usually preferred the role of the aggressor. Her party, her rules. As long as she called the shots." 2009 James W. Fuerst, *Huge* (New York: Random House) 242: "Dudes, everybody knows this is *my* party and *my* house and like rules, and the first rule is just totally *no fighting* . . . " (italics as shown). Cf. "My HOUSE, my rules," "My MONEY, my rules," and "My HOUSE, my party."

## No **pass**, no play.

1984 The saying probably entered oral tradition as a proverb from the wording of a controversial bill—and the popular designation of the bill itself—passed by the Texas legislature (and influentially advocated by the mogul-politician Ross Perot in the preceding months). The law mandated a minimum level of academic achievement for student participation in sports and other extracurricular activities. 1990 Gladys Peterson Meyers (oral history contributor), *Hill Country Teacher*, edited by Diane Manning (Boston: Twayne) 75: "She was a very strong teacher. . . . With her it was, 'no pass, no play.' That was the first I ever heard of it." 1990 Paul Zane Pilzer, *Unlimited Wealth* (New York: Crown) 120: "Perhaps the concept of 'no pass—no play,' would have been much more effective if it had been 'no pass—no *pay*,' and applied to teachers and administrators" (italics as shown). 1991 "Knight Commission Places Presidents at Center of Athletic Reform," *AGB Reports* 33, no. 2 (Mar.–Apr.) 3: "'No Pass, No Play' will be the byword of college sports in admissions, academic progress, and graduation rates."

## The **past** does not equal the future.

1991 Anthony Robbins, *Awaken the Giant Within* (New York: Summit) 85: "The reason success eludes most people is that they have insufficient references of [sic] succeeding in the past. But an optimist operates with beliefs such as 'the past doesn't equal the future.'" 1991 *New York Magazine* 24, no. 16 (22 Apr.) 133 (classified ad titled "New Age Male Seeking Soul Mate"): "You must see the glass of life half full not half empty, be able to laugh at yourself and have the knowledge that the past does not equal the future." Eret (2001).

## The **past** does not repeat itself, but it rhymes.

See "HISTORY does not repeat itself, but it rhymes."

The **past** is not what it used to be.

1950 Mordecai M. Kaplan, "Random Thoughts," *The Reconstructionist* 16, no. 2 (Mar.) 30: "Men say the future isn't what it used to be. Neither is the past. Both are in need of reconstruction, if we are to have a livable present." 1963 C. Vann Woodward, *New York Times Book Review* 28 Jul. (title of an essay): "Our Past Isn't What It Used to Be." Cf. "THINGS are not what they used to be—and they never were," "The FUTURE is not what it used to be," and "NOSTALGIA is not what it used to be."

**Patience** moves mountains.

1930 Frederick Houk Law, ed., *Stories of To-day and Yesterday* (New York: D. Appleton-Century) 308 (in a list of subjects for a student wishing to compose a story similar to Harriet Prescott Spofford's "Circumstance"): "2. 'Patience moves mountains.' A person has such patience that he brings about an apparent miracle." 1947 Robert Penn Warren, "The Circus in the Attic," *Cosmopolitan* 123, no. 3 (Sep.) 84: "Knowledge is power and patience can move mountains. Mrs. Parton was nothing if not patient." *MP* P53. Cf. the biblical *faith* that can move mountains (Matthew 17:20).

It **pays** to look well (good).

1902 *Lima [OH] Times Democrat* 6 Jun. (advertisement): "Young men are apt to be very particular about their clothes; even a little fussy, cranky. It's all right; a good appearance means a whole lot to a young fellow sometimes; may even be his chief asset; it pays to look well." 1972 Harcourt Roy, *Physical Fitness for Boys* (London: Pelham) 27: "And remember, you are noticed and weighed up in most situations. It pays to look good." *DAAP* 481.

It **pays** to pay attention.

See "It pays to pay ATTENTION."

You have to **pay** to play.

See "If you're going to PLAY, you have to pay."

You **pay** now (You can pay) or pay later (with interest).

1974 *Livestock Feeding Problems: Hearings before the Subcommittee on Agricultural Production, Marketing, and Stabilization of Prices . . . Senate* (Washington DC: Government Printing Office) 89; statement by Erhart Pfingsten: "And so by lowering those prices, we put this Nation right into the position where it's no better off for our meat production or our supplies, than the oil industry is. . . . So it's either pay now, or pay later." 1976 *You Can Pay Now or You Can Pay Later: LR 127: Maintenance of State Buildings* (Lincoln: Nebraska Legislative Council). 1982 Fritz Ridenour, *What Teenagers Wish Their Parents Knew about Kids* (Waco TX: Word) 170: "Of course it's a lot of trouble. But as the mechanic in the oil filter ad on TV puts it, 'You can pay now or you can pay later.'"

**Payback** is a bitch.

1970 Jack E. White Jr., *Black Politics in a Dying City* (Nashville TN: Race Relations Information Center) 8: "In December 1969, Mayor [Hugh] Addonizio was indicted by a federal grand jury for income tax evasion and extortion. One black Newarker remarked, 'payback is a bitch.'" 1972 Nathan C. Heard, *To Reach a Dream* (New York: Dial) 97: ". . . [S]uppose she said 'get out' tomorrow morning? Some of the things he'd said to girls in the past came flooding into his mind and he remembered what some wit had told him once: 'Payback is a bitch.'" Cf. "KARMA is a bitch" and "LIFE is a bitch."

Give **peace** a chance.

1923 *Christian Science Monitor* 14 Nov.: Editorial titled (in a box) "Give Peace a Chance": "He [Prime Minister David Lloyd George] believed, and many others believe with him, that Great Britain and America might give peace its needed chance." The 1969 song (so titled) recorded by John Lennon / Plastic Ono Band familiarized later generations with the proverb. *RHDP* 112; *YBQ* Lennon and McCartney (25).

## Everything is not (all) **peaches** and cream.

1928 *Hartford [CT] Courant* 1 Aug.: "Every day the cables from Amsterdam bring convincing evidence that everything is not peaches and cream for the Yankee athletes in that Olympic games. . . ." 1931 "The Ritzy All-Europe Taxi Tour," *Literary Digest* 111, no. 10 (5 Dec.) 32: "His past customers tell their friends about his good services, and they call on him whenever they get to Paris. All is not peaches and cream for the driver, however. . . ." *DAP* 185(11); *RHDP* 87; *DAAP* 578.

## If you pay **peanuts**, you get monkeys.

See "Only MONKEYS work for peanuts."

## Don't put **peas** in the baby's ears.

See "Don't put BEANS in the baby's ears."

## Don't dip your **pen** in the company ink (inkwell).

1979 Thomas Walker, *Recall* (New York: Seaview) 267: "Generally it was a good idea to avoid personal relations with business colleagues or people who lived in the same apartment building. Don't dip your pen in the company ink, so to speak." 1980 R. N. Whitehurst and G. V. Booth, *The Sexes: Changing Relationships in a Pluralistic Society* (Toronto: Gage) 98: "The modern proverb, 'Don't dip your pen in the company's ink,' seems to accord with this temptation." 1982 Michael Blodgett, *Hero and the Terror* (New York: Crown) 174: "One thing he learned back in Chicago, you don't shit where you eat. Don't dip your pen in the company inkwell."

## A **penny** spent is a penny earned (A penny saved is a penny lost).

1901 *Oakland Tribune* 23 Aug. (advertisement): "Saturday is the last day of the final reduction sale in our ready-to-wear garment department. Tomorrow you may reverse the old adage and say A PENNY SPENT IS A PENNY EARNED" (capitalization as shown). 1901 *Report of the Industrial Commission on the Condition of Foreign Legislation upon Matters Affecting General Labor*, vol. 15 (Washington DC: Government Printing Office) 224: ". . . [T]here is little inducement to the laborer to become a capitalist. [set as verse:] A penny spent is a penny had, / A penny saved is a penny lost." 1930 *Reading [PA] Eagle* 19 Sep.: "A penny saved is a penny lost to [the economist] William Trufant Foster of Boston. He told the Retail Jewelers' Association that America is wasting her substance in 'riotous saving.'" The proverb originated as an anti-proverb responding to "A penny saved is a penny earned (got)."

## Be nice to **people** on your way up because you'll meet them on your way down (The people you meet on the way up are the same ones you will meet on the way down).

1932 *Pittsburgh Press* 8 Jul.: "Walter Winchell . . . did give some good advice to bigheaded movie actors. 'Be nice to those you meet on the way up. They're the same folks you'll meet on the way down.'" 1939 *Pittsburgh Courier* 1 Jul.: "If you're smart you'll remember that old but true saying: 'Remember the folks you meet on your way up because as sure as preaching the gospel, you'll meet them on your way down.'" *RHDP* 19.

## Happy **people** don't get (fall) sick.

1906 [Elbert Hubbard?], "Heart to Heart Talks with Philistines by the Pastor of His Flock," *The Philistine* 23: 125: "Happiness and health are synonymous. Happy people do not get sick, unless run over by an automobile or something like that." 1988 Pelé, "with Herbert Resnicow" (ghostwriting in English), *World Cup Murder* (New York: Wynwood) 192: "For therapeutic reasons, Dahliah had allowed him a second helping of the carob soufflé; happy people don't get sick, was one of her precepts." 2007 Barbara Ehrenreich, "The Cancer Blame Game," *The Progressive* 71, no. 9 (Sep.) 12 (quoting from an e-zine article titled "Breast Cancer Prevention Tips"): "You must have heard the slogan 'happy people don't fall sick.'"

## If three (four, etc.) **people** tell you you're drunk, lie down (sit down, believe it).

Champion (1938) 259 lists the saying as a Russian proverb. 1973 Harry Kenelman, *Tuesday the Rabbi Saw Red* (New York: Arthur Fields) 215: "You know the old Talmudic proverb: when three people tell you you're drunk, go home and lie down." 1974 Tom Dietz, *Dancing in the Dark* (New York: Quadrangle) 110: "He was not opinionated and he gave good advice, such as, 'If four or five guys tell you that you're drunk, even though you know you haven't had a thing to drink, the least you can do is to lie down.'" 1975 Leopold Bellak, *Overload: The New Human Condition* (New York: Human Sciences) 58: "'If three people tell you you are drunk, you'd better believe it,' expresses the idea of the social consensus versus one's own inner reality testing."

## **People** who live in glass houses should (always) wear clothes (dress in the dark).

1904 Charles Wayland Towne (pseudonym "Gideon Wurdz"), *A Foolish Dictionary* (Boston: John W. Luce) [12r] (unpaginated; filler item): "People who live in glass houses should dress in the dark." 1906 J. F. Percy, "Some of the Problems of the Internist Which Concern the Surgeon," *Illinois Medical Journal* 10: 107: "No one appreciates better than I the force of

the ancient saying that individuals living in glass houses 'should dress in the dark.' We all have our difficulties." 1997 *Buffalo News* 8 Apr.: "Allure magazine . . . passed out Chinese takeout containers holding fortune cookies with such messages as 'Great minds believe in aromatherapy' and 'People who live in glass houses should wear clothes.'" The proverb originated as an anti-proverb based on "People who live in glass houses shouldn't throw stones."

## **People** who stay in the middle of the road get run over.

See "The MIDDLE of the road is where people get run over."

## The smaller the **pepper**, the hotter (sharper) the bite (sting, taste).

1958 Premendra Mitra, "Where the River Meets the Sea," in *Green and Gold: Stories and Poems from Bengal*, edited by Humayun Kabir (London: Chapman & Hall) 222: "She did not like chillies, she said, and added wisely, 'Size doesn't matter, does it? The smaller the pepper, the sharper it is.' Dakshayani laughed at her and said, 'One has only to look at you to know that what you said is true.'" 1991 *Los Angeles Times* 10 Oct.: ". . . [A] friend from Bangkok told me . . . that the Thai way of saying 'Good things come in small packages' is 'The smaller the pepper, the hotter the taste.'" 2007 *Africa News* 3 May: "He [soccer coach Christian Chukwu] noted that smaller teams trouble the [Nigerian] Eagles more than their established counterparts. . . . 'I hope you know that smaller pepper is more potent than the bigger ones.'" 2009 *New York Times* 23 Dec.: "Koreans used to value what was perceived as grittiness on the part of shorter people. 'A smaller pepper is hotter,' the saying went." Distinct from the application of the proverb to horticulture and cookery, it means figuratively that small persons (or groups) tend to be energetic, assertive, or hot-tempered.

## Perception is everything (is reality).

1911 H. Wildon Carr, "The Theory of Psycho-Physical Parallelism," *Proceedings of the Aristotelian Society* n.s. 11: 136: "The idealist contention is that perception is everything; there is nothing lying hidden behind it." 1946 Mark Schorer, *William Blake: The Politics of Vision* (New York: Henry Holt) 379: "That Blake's visions of eternity appeared to him on Primrose Hill and in South Moulton Street is of great importance. It is the evidence for his belief . . . that perception is everything." 1947 Earl C. Kelley, *Education for What Is Real* (New York: Harper & Brothers) 44: "Probably we have not departed from reality, if perception is reality, but have ceased to use our clues. . . ." Perhaps the saying did not become fully proverbial until the 1960s (or so), when it moved beyond the epistemological use to refer (often cynically) to politics, show business, commercial advertising, and the like. It is partly synonymous with the more colloquial-sounding (and apparently older) "It's all in the way you look at it." Cf. "In POLITICS perception is reality" and "There are no FACTS—just interpretations."

## Perception is reality in politics.

See "In POLITICS perception is reality."

## If you want something done, ask a busy person.

1905 Jennie Jameson, *Annals and Antics of the Homestead Club* (Springfield MA: Phelps) 40: "It is an old saying, 'If you want something done ask a busy woman,' and Katy lives in the same town with our energetic president. . . ." 1914 Margaret E. Sangster, *Eastover Parish* (New York: Fleming E. Revell) 105: "'I am the busiest person in Eastover,' said Kathleen, flushing, 'but mother has always said that when you want a thing done, you must ask a busy person to do it.'" 1916 "The Brotherhood World," *St. Andrew's Cross* 31, no. 3 (Dec.) 49: "In reading the communication, one is reminded of the saying, 'Ask a busy man if you want something done.'" 1957 C. Northcote

Parkinson, *Parkinson's Law and Other Studies in Administration* (Cambridge MA: Houghton Mifflin) 2: "Work expands so as to fill the time available for its completion. General recognition of this fact is shown in the proverbial phrase 'It is the busiest man who has time to spare.'" *DAP* 339(11) ("If you want a job well done, give it to a busy man"), 675(13) ("If you want work well done, select a busy man"); *YBQ* Modern Proverbs (11); *ODP* 340; Doyle (2001a) 459–60. Cf. the older proverb "Idle folks have the least leisure."

## Inside every fat person (man, woman) there's a thin person trying (struggling, crying, anxious) to get out.

1939 George Orwell, *Coming Up for Air* (London: V. Gollancz) 29: "Has it ever struck you that there's a thin man inside every fat man, just as they say there's a statue inside every block of stone?" 1944 Cyril Connolly, *The Unquiet Grave* (London: Horizon) 44 (in a series of French and English *bons mots* regarding obesity, among other topics): "Imprisoned in every fat man is a thin one wildly signalling to be let out." *YBQ* Cyril Connolly (3), Orwell (10). Cf. "Inside every old PERSON, there is a young one."

## Inside every old person (man, woman), there is a young one (trying to get out, saying "What the hell happened?" etc.).

1973 *New York Times* 5 May: "Inside every old person, so the saying goes, there is a young person trying to get out. This tug is especially visible in summertime. . . ." 1974 *The Age* [Melbourne, Australia] 1 Feb.: "Thus does [the television character] Ada remind us that inside every old lady there's a heedless girl, skipping on time-ambered sands." 1976 *Los Angeles Times* 8 Aug.: ". . . [Y]ou saw that Sylvia had very young eyes, and it almost seemed a reminder that inside every old person there is a young one wondering what happened." 1986 Kenneth Hurren, review of the play *I'm Not Rappaport* by Herb Gardner, *Mail on Sunday* [London] 6

Jul.: "Inside every old man is a young man's spirit resentful of the crumbling flesh." 1988 *Spokesman-Review [Spokane WA]* 1 May: "'Inside every old person is a young person,' said Mike Green. . . ." Cf. "Inside every fat PERSON there's a thin person trying to get out."

## One **person's** floor is another person's ceiling.

See "One MAN's floor is another man's ceiling."

## To love another **person** is to see the face of God.

1985 The saying probably entered oral tradition as a proverb from the finale of the stage musical *Les Miserables*, lyrics by Herbert Kretzmer: "And remember the truth that once was spoken: / To love another person is to see the face of God." The song, however, implies that the saying has a "source." *YBQ* Kretzmer.

## The **personal** is political.

1970 Carol Hanisch, "The Personal Is Political"; title of an often-reprinted and often-cited essay in *Notes from the Second Year: Women's Liberation,* edited by Shulamith Firestone (New York: Radical Feminist) 76–78. c. 1974 Stephanie Jenkins et al., "From Survival: For Our Times, for Our Movement," *Women* 3, no. 4 (n.d.) 58: "We are told that the personal is political until we bring up the realities of our life differences." *YBQ* Hanisch. Cf. "The POLITICAL is personal."

## **Pick** yourself up (You've got to pick yourself up) and dust yourself off.

1915 Walter Weyl, "The Average Voter," *Century Magazine* 90: 904: "The loser is supposed to pick himself up, dust himself off, shake hands with the victor, and for a suitable period refrain from all criticism." 1922 Elsie Singmaster, *Bennett Malin* (Boston: Houghton Mifflin) 190: "This morning's sunshine must shake off the power of last night's sundown. Pick yourself up

and dust yourself off after you have been flung." 1932 *New York Times* 13 Mar.: "The beginners [at gardening] rush blissfully to their falls, pick themselves up, dust themselves off and try again." 1934 Elsie Robinson, *I Wanted Out!* (New York: Farrar & Rinehart) 104: "Hurt? Too bad. But you've got to take it, kid. So pick yourself up, dust yourself off, and walk along with Life." 1936 A line in a popular song from the motion picture *Swing Time,* lyrics by Dorothy Fields, music by Jerome Kern: "Pick yourself up, dust yourself off, start all over again." The proverb often concludes with a third clause or verb phrase, the wording of which is highly variable ("and keep on going," "and start all over," etc.). Mieder (2009b) 140–41.

## One **picture** is worth a thousand words.

1911 Arthur Brisbane, "Newspaper Copy That People Must Read," *Printers' Ink* 75, no. 3 (20 Apr.) 17: "Use a picture. It's worth a thousand words." 1915 *New Orleans Item* 26 Jul. (among quoted comments by Arthur Brisbane): "A picture is worth a thousand words." 1917 Herbert F. DeBower, *Advertising Principles* (New York: Alexander Hamilton Institute) 253: "According to an old Japanese proverb, 'a picture is worth a thousand words.'" *DAP* 463(4); *RHDP* 260; *YBQ* Folsom; *ODP* 249; Rees (1984) 159; Hoffman and Honeck (1987); Mieder (1989b); Mieder (1990); Rogers (1990); Mieder (1992); Mieder (1993b) 41–57, 135–51; Mieder (1994) 297–316; Prahlad (1996) 241–42; Room (2000) 500; Pickering (2001) 269; Winick (2003); Mieder (2004) 79–88; Prahlad (2004); Rees (2006) 538. The common attribution to Frederick Barnard is not to be credited.

## There'll be **pie** in the sky when you die.

1911 The saying probably entered oral tradition as a proverb from a song by the laborite singer Joe Hill (sometimes titled "The Preacher and the Slave")—unless Hill was himself using a proverb: "Work and pray, live on hay, / You'll get pie in the sky when you die." *MP* P134; *RHDP* 374; *YBQ* Joe Hill (1); Pickering et al. (1992)

473. The song parodies the old Protestant hymn "The Sweet By and By"; Hill's song—like the proverb itself—satirizes the concept of patiently enduring earthly misery and injustice in hopes of a heavenly reward.

## If you lie down with **pigs**, you get up smelling bad (covered with shit, etc.).

1966 In the famously "bad" motion picture *The Oscar*, the character Hymie Kelly (played by Tony Bennett) remarks, "If you lie down with pigs, you get up smelling like garbage." 1981 Eric Van Lustbader, *Sirens* (New York: M. Evans) 326: "But she felt no pity for Dr. Geist or his family. When you lie down with swine, you're sure to get fouled." 1983 Nicholas Proffitt, *Gardens of Stone* (New York: Carroll & Graf) 68: "Well, if you lie down with pigs, you're going to get covered with shit." 1996 James Glickman, *Sounding the Waters* (New York: Crown) 219: "The old saying 'If you lie down with pigs, you get up dirty' pops into my head." The proverb parallels to the older "If you lie down with dogs, you get up with fleas."

## Never try to teach a **pig** to sing; it wastes your time, and it annoys the pig.

1973 Robert A Heinlein, *Time Enough for Love* (New York: G. P. Putnam's Sons) 51: ". . . [A] fool cannot be protected from his folly. If you attempt to do so, you will not only arouse his animosity but also you will be attempting to deprive him of whatever benefit he is capable of deriving from experience. Never attempt to teach a pig to sing; it wastes your time and annoys the pig." 1980 Paul Dickson, *The Official Explanations* (New York: Delacorte) 27 (under the heading "Business Maxims"): "Never Try to Teach a Pig to Sing; It Wastes Your Time and It Annoys the Pig." *YBQ* Heinlein (13); Dundes and Pagter (1991) 70–71.

## Never wrestle (wallow with) a **pig**; you will both get dirty, and the pig likes it.

1946 Richard P. Calhoon, *Moving Ahead on Your Job* (Toronto: Collins) 171: "And when you begin refuting one another's reasons, fussing back and forth, you generally do what a nationally known industrial relations authority warns you against: you wallow in the mud with a pig. He says, 'Never wallow in the mud with a pig, because the pig likes it.'" 1948 *Daily Mail [Charleston WV]* 31 May: "Some politicians were discussing hecklers. One of them said he never made reply. 'Many years ago,' he explained, 'my father told me never to roll in the mud with a pig. Because you both get covered with mud—and the pig likes it.'" 1950 "The Administration: Come & Get It," *Time* 56, no. 17 (23 Oct.) 212: "'I learned long ago never to wrestle with a pig,' [Cyrus] Ching likes to say. 'You get dirty and besides the pig likes it.'"

## **Pigs** get fat; hogs get slaughtered (killed, butchered).

1967 *Dispatch [Lexington NC]* 14 Nov. (column by Paul Harvey): "Such excesses of union power . . . will invite drastic labor-curtailing legislation. Pigs get fat; hogs get slaughtered." 1978 *Southeast Missourian [Cape Girardeau]* 1 Nov. ("Ann Landers" column): "After considering all the facts, my advice is settle for less—temporarily. Remember—pigs get fat. Hogs get slaughtered." 1980 "Bad Luck Forces Updating at Lloyd's of London," *Business Week*, no. 2625 (25 Feb.) 97: "'Pigs get fat, hogs get killed, and they got a little bit hoggish,' notes B. P. Russell. . . ." 2001 Kent D. Redfield, *Money Counts: How Dollars Dominate Illinois Politics* (Springfield IL: Institute for Public Affairs, U of Illinois at Springfield) 11: "Professional politicians have had to develop their own sense of how much the public will bear. But, as an old Chicago adage warns, 'Pigs get fat. Hogs get butchered.'"

## **Pigs** smell their own smells first.

1966 Nicholas Monsarrat, *Life Is a Four-Letter Word* (London: Cassell) 1: 66: ". . . [S]he had a store of rough phrases which, imported from her Liverpool slum home, ripped through our supposedly sheltered nursery like wasps at a church picnic. 'Pigs smell their own smells first!'

she would say, when our surreptitious sniffing traced a sudden odour to its true source, herself." *MP* P154. Cf. "The ONE who smelt it dealt it."

## A **pig** wearing lipstick is still a pig.

See "You can put LIPSTICK on a pig but it's still a pig."

## Some days (Sometimes) you're the **pigeon**, and some (other) days you're the statue.

1993 Roger C. Anderson, *Some Days You're the Pigeon—Some Days You're the Statue: Comic Confessions of a College President* (Saratoga Springs NY: Humor Project). 1995 *Toronto Star* 6 Jun.: "'The moral of the story,' says Connie Chung, 'is that some days you're the pigeon and some days you're the statue.' Since getting dumped from CBS Evening News two weeks ago, the diminutive Chung has been feeling awfully statue-esque." Cf. "Sometimes you're the DOG, and sometimes you're the fireplug."

## **Pile** it high, sell it cheap.

1955 Max Mandell Zimmerman, *The Super Market* (New York: McGraw-Hill) 18 (quoting T. A. Von Der Ahe, son of the founder of Von's supermarket chain in California): "I prefer to think of a Super Market as a new method of food merchandizing, based on the theory of 'Pile it High and Sell it Cheap,' plus the elimination of service and introduction of self-service techniques." Pickering et al. (1992) 272; Room (2000) 527.

## **Pioneers** get (take) arrows in their backs (Pioneers get the arrows, settlers get the land).

1972 "The Video Cassette Runs Even Slower," *Business Week*, no. 2210 (8 Jan.) 21: "'It will take a multimillion dollar investment to get the home entertainment market off the ground,' he [John R. North] explains. 'And the pioneers are often

the guys who wind up with the arrows in their backs.'" 1972 Angeline Pantages, "CSC and New York's Off-Track Betting: Pioneers Get Arrows," *Datamation* 18, no. 9 (Sep.) 101–9; the article ends, "And CSC [Computer Sciences Corp.] is left wincing over the adage: 'Pioneers get little but arrows in the derriere.'" 1996 Kim Laughlin and John Monberg, "Horizons of Interactivity: Making the News at Time Warner," in *Connected: Engagements with Media*, edited by George E. Marcus (Chicago: U of Chicago P) 262: "A friend of mine has a great expression: pioneers get the arrows and settlers get the land. I wouldn't mind getting a couple of arrows in the back. . . ."

## There must be **pioneers**, and some of them get killed.

1928 *Free-Lance-Star [Fredericksburg VA]* 15 Feb. (quoting Charles A. Lindbergh): "At the outset when new methods of transportation are coming into use there must be pioneers to show the way and some of them are killed." 1928 Carl Sandburg, *Good Morning, America* (New York: Harcourt, Brace) 18 (in a poetic montage of proverbs and other sayings): "There must be pioneers and some of them get killed." *DAAP* 590. The proverb may have originated as an anti-proverb elaborating on the saying "There must be pioneers."

## It's better to be **pissed** off than pissed on.

1974 John Wood, *How Do You Feel? A Guide to Your Emotions* (Englewood Cliffs NJ: Prentice-Hall) 37: "I have a friend who says, 'It's better to be pissed off than pissed on.' That's kind of the way I feel about anger. . . ." The proverb is often uttered in response to someone's exclamation that he is "pissed off" (angry or acutely annoyed).

## Never get into a **pissing** contest (match) with a skunk.

1943 *Study and Investigation of the Federal Communications Commission: Hearing before the Select Committee to Investigate the Federal*

Communications Commission, House of
Representatives (Washington DC: Government
Printing Office) 691; Stefano Luotto testifies,
quoting Gene Dyer: ". . . [Y]ou boys have
to understand that I have to deal with a
combination of Hartley-David [two individuals
being investigated]; it is like having a pissing
contest with a skunk." 1953 Ira Wolfert, *Married
Men* (New York: Simon & Schuster) 278: "'I
hate a blackmailer, but pay her off,' he shouted
at John E. 'You can't win a pissing match with
a skunk.'" 1962 Morris L. Ernst, *Untitled: The
Diary of My 72nd Year* (New York: Robert B. Luce)
50: "I'll not even correct the press, on an old
theory—don't ever get into a pissing match with
a skunk." MP P220.

## Good **pitching** beats good hitting.

1969 *New York Times* 6 Oct.: "It was going to
be a very simple weekend, a pair of tight ball
games that would answer a classic question—
can good pitching beat good hitting?" 1971
*Herald [Spartanburg SC]* 15 Oct.: "Yes sir, good
pitching beats good hitting any time." 1973 John
Wilson, "Rollie Fingers: The Man Who Shut the
Door," *Baseball Digest* 32, no. 1 (Jan.) 43: "The
Reds scored two or less runs in five of the seven
games. What's the old saying? Good pitching
beats good hitting everytime [*sic*]."

## The best (easiest, safest) **place** to hide is in plain sight.

1920 Alice Grown, *The Wind between the Worlds*
(New York: Macmillan) 151: "Remember the rule,
Andrea: if you want to hide a thing, put it in
plain sight." 1921 Charles J. Dutton, *Underwood
Mystery* (New York: A. L. Burt) 190: "You know
that they say the safest place to hide anything is
in plain sight. You remember that story of Poe's?"
The concept—but not the saying—occurs in
Edgar Allan Poe's story "The Purloined Letter."

## The only **place** where success comes before work is in a dictionary.

1955 Elizabeth Gregg MacGibbon, *Fitting Yourself
for Business*, 3rd ed. (New York: McGraw-Hill)
226: ". . . [Y]ou must from the first day absorb
the instructions given you and put them into
practice as quickly as possible. Bear in mind that
the dictionary is the only place where Success
comes before Work." 1955 *Chicago Daily Tribune*
28 Nov.: "Monday morning foolosophy: The
dictionary is the only place where success comes
before work!" Ratcliffe (2006) 435.

## Second **place** is first loser.

1994 *Houston Chronicle* 26 Feb.: [The baseball
player Joe] Collins showed up wearing a T-shirt
with 'Second place is the first loser' on it." 1994
*St. Petersburg [FL] Times* 6 Jun.: "The key words
[on T-shirts] this summer are, 'No Fear.' Or
maybe they're 'Second Place is First Loser,' or
something like 'He Who Dies With the Most
Toys, Still Dies.'" Cf. "There is no second PLACE"
and the older "If you are not first, you might as
well be last."

## There is no second **place** (in battle, in war) (There is no such thing as winning second place—there's just winning and losing).

1929 John W. Thomason Jr., "The Hope of the
World," *McCall's Magazine* 57, no. 3 (Dec.) 81:
". . . [Y]ou can respect the man you fight, because
he believes in something of his own. One of
you must be beaten; and there is no second
prize in battle. But after it is over, you can meet
on common ground." 1936 Ernest Boyd, "The
Library: Report on Rugged Proletarianism,"
*American Mercury* 37: 371: "But in war, offensive
tactics are the only tactics from which decisions
may be expected. There is no second place in
battle. The second-best navy never wins." 1941
*Washington Post* 26 Oct.: "Admiral [Adolphus]
Andrews said the Juneau . . . would be manned

by fighting Americans who believe there is no second place in anything." Cf. "Second PLACE is first loser" and the older "If you are not first, you might as well be last." In the form "In war there is no prize for second place (second best, runner-up)," the saying is often attributed to Gen. Omar Bradley.

## Plans are nothing, planning is everything.

1950 Dwight D. Eisenhower, letter to Hamilton Fish Armstrong, 31 Dec.: "I always remember the observation of a very successful soldier who said, 'Peace-time plans are of no particular value, but peace-time planning is indispensable'"; in *Papers of Dwight David Eisenhower*, edited by Alfred D. Chandler Jr. et al. (Baltimore: Johns Hopkins UP, 1970–89) 11: 1157. 1962 Richard M. Nixon, *Six Crises* (Garden City NY: Doubleday) 235 (quoting Eisenhower, Nixon calls the saying a "maxim—one of President Eisenhower's favorites"): "In preparing for battle I have always found that plans are useless, but planning is indispensable." Much later, in an interview, Nixon recalled the "maxim" somewhat differently: "I remember at a National Security Council meeting once, President Eisenhower said, 'Planning is absolutely vital. Plans are useless'"; 1970 Jules Witcover, *The Resurrection of Richard Nixon* (New York: G. P. Putnam's Sons) 301. 1964 J. Fred Weston, *Defense-Space Market Research* (Cambridge MA: M.I.T. Press) 23: "It has been said, 'Plans are nothing. Planning is everything.' The statement emphasizes that the planning process has value in stimulating a systematic analysis of a company's history and prospects. . . ." *YBQ* Eisenhower (13).

## Step up (You have to step up) to the plate.

1965 Jerome Weidman, *The Death of Dickie Draper* (New York: Random House) 54–55: "No matter how many automobile plants they own,

they're just potential clients, that's all. You can't let yourself be intimidated by their money and their reputations. You have to step up to the plate and take your cut at the old apple as though they were no different from any other pitchers." 1989 Tim Hansel, *Eating Problems for Breakfast* (Dallas: Word) 141: "Kathy Seligman, a journalist, once said, 'You can't hit a home run unless you step up to the plate. . . . You can't reach your goals unless you actually do something.'" 1998 Helen Lippman, "Step Up to the Plate," *Business and Health* 16, no. 6 (Jun.) 6 (the editorial so titled challenges businesses to pay more heed to quality control and to the wishes of consumers). *RHDP* 303. The proverb (obviously its metaphor comes from baseball) signifies that it is necessary—or at least admirable—for one to accept the challenge at hand. "Step up to the plate" also exists as a proverbial phrase.

## Don't play if you can't win.

See "If you can't WIN, don't play."

## If you're going to play, you have to pay (You have to pay to play).

1955 Song: "If You Play, You Must Pay," written and performed by "Enyatta Holta" (Laverne Holt). 1964 "Must Pay to Play" (headline), *[Hopkinsville] Kentucky New Era* 12 Aug.: "If a fellow doesn't pay his dues to the club, he doesn't play golf there any more. Period and paragraph. That's the rule. Nikita Krushchev doesn't understand this simple rule." 1969 Eldridge Cleaver, *Eldridge Cleaver: Post-prison Writings and Speeches* (New York: Random House) 120 (a speech delivered at Stanford University, 1 Oct. 1968): "I knew what the penalty for that was, and I would say, if you play you have to pay. I did a little playing and I did a little paying. . . ." In one application, currently prevalent, the proverb can refer to sexual intercourse and the possible price to be paid by a woman: pregnancy.

**Play** big (You have to play big) to win big.

1978 *Ocala [FL] Star Banner* 19 Jul.: "But she took one last chance Tuesday. It was worth $97,750. 'I've always believed you have to play big to win big and it sure paid off for me,' the middle-aged woman said." 1997 *Daily News [Bowling Green KY]* 5 Mar.: "She returned to her West Warwick, R.I., home and stuffed 16 hundred dollar bills under her mattress. . . . The next day, she went back to the $25 machines to spin those hundreds into thousands. You have to play big to win big." 1998 Daryl Dance, *Honey, Hush* (New York: W. W. Norton) 88 (in a list of sayings titled "Sister to Sister"): "you got to play big to win big."

**Play** it as (where) it lays (lies).

1917 Nancy Mann Waddell Wilson (pseudonym "Mrs. Wilson Woodrow"), *The Hornet's Nest* (Boston: Little, Brown) 96: "All right, we'll play it as it lays. You go out and round up that missing package for me, and I'll draw the lightning off you." In recent decades the metaphorical extension—and proverbial use—of the golfing maxim owes much to its appearance in 1970 as the title of Joan Didion's novel, *Play It as It Lays*. The plural version of the proverb, in some instances, seems more like a card-game metaphor: 1923 Ledyard M. Bailey, "Locoes," *McClure's Magazine* 55, no. 4 (Jun.) 68: "After he had done what he could to make his patient comfortable he stood staring down at the man. . . . 'Well, maybe he's got folks somewhere. Anyway, we play 'em as they lie, I guess.'" 1941 *Washington Post* 3 Mar.: "The important thing, however, is that exchanges will not be possible . . . because the demand for seats is the largest in the history of the Theater Guild–A.T.S. plays. You will have to play them as they lie and like it." Cf. "You play the HAND you are dealt."

**Play** to win or don't play (at all).

1938 *Hartford [CT] Courant* 23 Jan. (quoting the baseball player Rogers Hornsby): "If you're not going to play to win, don't play anything. Don't play cards or even bean bags." 1981 *Washington Post* 30 Sep. (quoting the football player Greg Washington): "We were used to being told, 'Go out, play hard and if hard doesn't do it, okay.' It was the first time someone said, 'If you aren't going to play to win, don't play at all.'" Cf. "If you can't WIN, don't play."

Don't hate the **player**; hate the game.

1992 *Chicago Sun-Times* 12 Mar.: "'Hate the game, don't hate the player,' [the football player Sean] Gilbert said. 'That's what's afforded to us in our business and what we do.'" 1998 Kristal Brent Zook, "21st Century Foxx," *Vibe* 6, no. 2 (Mar.) 72: "He [Jamie Foxx] knows us. Even better, he has much love for us despite our flaws. As Foxx says, 'Don't hate the player, hate the game.'"

You can't tell the **players** without a scorecard.

1910 Bruce Farson, "Excess Baggage," *Hampton Magazine* 25: 98 (a hawker in the stadium shouts): "Here's where you get your soda, gents! . . . Score card? You can't tell the players without a score card." 1947 A. J. Liebling, *The Wayward Pressman* (Garden City NY: Doubleday) 279: "But here are a few books, pamphlets, and articles that will help the habitual newspaper reader to understand what the habitual newspaper writer is habitually writing. You can't tell the players without a scorecard." 1953 Warren Eyster, *Far from the Customary Skies* (New York: Random House) 264: "You see, I was only twelve, and I didn't really care about seeing her naked. Hell, I wouldn't of knowed what to look for. You can't tell the players without a scorecard."

**Playing** hard is not (good) enough.

See "TRYING is not enough."

What has been **plowed** once is easier the second time.

1956 Holger Cahill, *The Shadow of My Hand* (New York: Harcourt, Brace) 35: "'They go for the married stuff. What's been plowed once is easier the second time.' 'My wife is a virgin,' the Bemidji Kid said with gloomy finality." *MP* P254.

The **plural** of *anecdote* is *data* (*evidence*).

1980 Roger G. Noll, "The Game of Health Care Regulation," in *Issues in Health Care*, edited by Richard S. Gordon (New York: McGraw-Hill) 136: "Most of the evidence is anecdotal. Nevertheless, in the words of a leading political scientist, Raymond Wolfinger, the plural of anecdote is data. . . ." 1994 Robert Wade, "World Bank Economics versus East Asian Economics," *Miracle or Design?* by Albert Fishblow et al. (Washington DC: Overseas Development Council) 69: ". . . [T]he evidence provided by the so-called revisionists . . . is less than compelling. It leaves them open to the quip that a revisionist is someone who thinks the plural of 'anecdote' is 'evidence.'" Cf. "The PLURAL of *anecdote* is not *data*."

The **plural** of *anecdote* is not *data* (*evidence*).

1982 Kenneth Kernaghan, "Merit and Motivation: Public Personnel Management in Canada," *Canadian Public Administration* 25: 703: "In that the plural of the word anecdote is not data, it is difficult to provide hard information on selection problems." 1997 Mark Thompson, "Letting the Air Out of Tort Reform," *ABA Journal* 83 (May) 69: "'Despite the lack of evidence . . . there is no shortage of conjecture and anecdotes about the triumphs of tort reform,' says [Cynthia] Lebow, but 'the plural of anecdote is not evidence.'" Presumably the proverb originated as a counter-proverb responding to the waggish "The PLURAL of *anecdote* is *data*"—or vice versa.

Be **polite** but not too polite.

1911 Ford Madox Ford (Hueffer), *Memories and Impressions* (New York: Harper & Brothers) 189–90 (quoting an unnamed newspaper editor's instruction): "The German journalists' deputation is coming to London tomorrow. . . . Be polite, but not too polite, you understand." 1936 Carl Sandburg, *The People, Yes* (New York: Harcourt, Brace) 107 (in a poetic montage of proverbs and other sayings): "Polite words open iron gates. / Be polite but not too polite." *DAAP* 600.

The **political** is personal.

1975 Jonathan Katz, *Coming Out!* (New York: Arno), [76] (in an unpaginated afterword): "The personal is political, the political is personal. Although much now divides lesbians and gay males, and gays of different ages, lifestyles, and values, the play seeks, ecumenically, to emphasize that which unites all gay people against our common oppressor." 1980 Lynne Sharon Schwartz, *Rough Strife* (New York: Harper & Row) 179: "'The political is personal! I mean, the personal is political.' She had read that in a magazine the other day. It had seemed profound but now it sounded stupid. . . ." Presumably, "The political is personal" originated as an anti-proverb based on "The PERSONAL is political"—though the reverse is possible; as in the quotations, both forms often appear together as a chiasmus.

In **politics** a man must learn to rise above principle.

1927 "So They Say" (a collection of notable quotations), *Golden Book Magazine* 5: 608 (quoting F. N. Tincher, member of the House of Representatives from Kansas): "I heard of a reputable Congressman on the Democratic side of the aisle, and I am glad he is there, although we have some like him, who said—and some of you will know who it is—'Gentleman, the time finally comes in our service here when we must rise above principle.'" 1928 Duff Gilford,

"Gentlemen of the Ensemble," *American Mercury* 14: 441: "There comes a time in the life of every statesman when he must rise above principle" (Gilford attributes the declaration to Representative Percy Edwards Quin of Mississippi). The form "In politics a man must learn to rise above principle," which has become more or less standard as the wording of the proverb, was quoted by H. L. Mencken, who referred to it as one of "the familiar maxims of American statecraft"; 1941 *Newspaper Days* (New York: Alfred A. Knopf) 143. *DAP* 472(1), 484(2).

## In **politics** perception is reality.

1975 Richard Scammon, "Political Elections in the 1970's," in *The State of American Society*, edited by Dennis J. Murray (Long Beach: California State UP) 144: "I would emphasize, however, that the turn toward the other candidates . . . was not an acceptance of either so much as it was a reaction to the *perceived* extremism of Goldwater and McGovern. I use the word perception because in politics perception is reality and there really is no reality but perception" (italics as shown). 1987 William M. Lunch, *The Nationalization of American Politics* (Berkeley: U of California P) 52: "The image-makers will often cheerfully accept that they are engaged in an exercise in make-believe, but now more than ever, perception is reality in politics." Cf. "PERCEPTION is everything."

## **Politics** is a contact sport.

1960 *Gazette [Montreal]* 14 Jun.: "But with millions on the streets how can the public prevent at a minimum an inter-faction fight among the Japanese who consider politics a contact sport even when it is carried on in the House of Parliament itself?" 1986 Richard Brookhiser, *The Outside Story* (Garden City NY: Doubleday) 120: "Hypocrisy on procedure is rarely fatal; people know politics is a contact sport." 1987 *Daily News [Bowling Green KY]* 8 Jul.: "Well, politics is a contact sport, and I suppose we mustn't complain too much."

## **Politics** (All politics) is local.

1905 *Washington Post* 25 Jun.: "The foregoing extract, if it came from him [John C. Calhoun], only shows that politics—all politics—is a local question." 1911 *Washington Post* 31 Oct. (in a small collection of witticisms and observations): "As the campaign progresses the suspicion deepens that politics is a local issue." 1939 Herbert Read, *Poetry and Anarchism* (New York: Macmillan) 92: "In short, real politics are local politics. If we can make politics local, we can make them real." *YBQ* Thomas O'Neill. In recent times the proverb (in the form "All politics is local") is commonly associated with Congressman Thomas P. "Tip" O'Neill Jr.

## There is (There must be, There just has to be, I know there is) a **pony** (in) there somewhere.

1958 H. K. Beecher, "Relation of Drugs to Reaction Components in Subjective Responses," in *Psychopharmacology*, edited by Harry H. Pennes (New York: Hoeber-Harper) 353 (relating a story, which "many of you have heard," by way of illustrating the hypothesis "that whether one is optimistic or pessimistic is a matter of inborn temperament"): "The optimistic child was similarly locked in a room, containing only a large pile of manure. At the end, the child emerged covered with manure and smiles. 'I could not find it, but there must be a pony somewhere!'" 1960 James Kirkwood, *There Must Be a Pony! A Novel* (Boston: Little, Brown). 1966 Marvin J. Gersh, *How to Raise Children at Home in Your Spare Time* (New York: Stein & Day) 104: ". . . When he came out they asked him what he was so happy about. 'Of course I'm happy,' he said. 'With all that manure in there, there must be a pony somewhere.'" The allusive proverb satirically cautions against credulity or excessive optimism. Cf. "If you sift through enough DIRT, you may find gold."

## If it exists, there is **porn** of it.

2010 *The Gazette [Montreal]* 20 Jun.: "Soon we will be buried in Smurf comics, Smurf lunch boxes, Smurf cups at fast-food joints, overpriced Smurf merch of all kinds, Smurf parodies (some of them helping prove Rule 34). . . . What's that? You don't know Rule 34? Keep up! Rule 34: If it exists, there is Internet porn of it. No exceptions." The proverb began appearing on Internet postings in 2008, often with its (seemingly arbitrary) designation as "Rule 34."

## Everyone **poops**.

See "Everybody SHITS."

## Accentuate the **positive** (eliminate the negative).

1944 Earlier instances of advice to "accentuate the positive" in preference to the negative occur, but as a proverb the saying probably entered oral tradition from Johnny Mercer's song "Ac-cent-tchu-ate the Positive," popularized that year by Bing Crosby in the motion picture *Here Come the WAVEs*: "You've got to accentuate the positive, / Eliminate the negative, / Latch on to the affirmative. . . ." *RHDP* 2–3; *YBQ* Mercer (4).

## An empty **pot** does not boil over.

Anderson and Cundall (1910) 38 give the saying as a Jamaican proverb: "You neber see empty pot bwoil over"—gloss: "Poor people have nothing to give away." Beckwith (1925) 126, on the other hand, glosses the Jamaican proverb (somewhat obscurely), "[A] person who is quiet enough if you do not anger him, will speak his mind in a quarrel." Parsons (1943) 465 lists the saying as a Granadan proverb, Whiting (1952) 461 as a proverb from North Carolina.

## Shit (Piss) or get off the **pot**.

c. 1935 Djuna Barnes, *Nightwood*: "Beating her head against her heart. Sprung over, her mind closing her life up like the heel of a fan,

saying; I do not know which way to go. . . . Tell the story of the world to the world; shit or get off the pot." The saying does not appear in the first edition of the novel, 1936, but rather in one of the surviving typescript leaves printed in Cheryl J. Plumb's scholarly edition (Normal IL: Dalkey Archive, 1995) 269. The typescript fragments seem to represent versions of the text that Barnes originally (in 1935) submitted to the publishers and editors, one of whom was T. S. Eliot, who recommended the excision of several indelicate passages. 1939 Alvah Cecil Bessie, *Men in Battle: A Story of Americans in Spain* (New York: Charles Scribner's Sons) 198: ". . . [I]t would be a smart move now for the Government to repatriate us; they could say, 'See, we sent home our volunteers,' to Franco, 'now shit or get off the pot.'" 1949 Merle Miller, *The Sure Thing* (New York: William Sloane) 267: "And once, not too long ago, he would have said, Look, chum, either pee or get off the pot. I'm going to fight this thing, and if you don't want to go along, I'll take it to the White House." 1952 John Steinbeck, *East of Eden* (New York: Viking) 309: "Maybe I was wrong, but by telling him I also forced him to live or get off the pot" (it is unclear whether that instance represents an anti-proverb or a mere accommodation of the censors). *MP* P298; *RHDP* 295; *YBQ* Modern Proverbs (84).

## You can't put ten (six, etc.) **pounds** of shit in a five-pound bag.

1980 P. F. Kluge, *Eddie and the Cruisers* (New York: Viking) 65: "He wants to tag along, that's fine. But put him up on the stage? Sounds to me like you're trying to carry six pounds of shit in a five-pound bag." 2001 Kent Beck and Martin Fowler, *Planning Extreme Programming* (Boston: Addison-Wesley) 33 (epigraph to a chapter that begins "How big is the bag? The shopping [?!] metaphor is all well and good, but what is the budget?"): "You can't put ten pounds of shit in a five-pound bag"; attributed to "Anyone who has tried" (perhaps here *shit* is understood in the figurative sense of "stuff"). The imagery of the proverb may bear some relationship to the joke word *blivet* (widely known among military personnel since the World War II era) for a person, thing, or situation that is useless, offensive, or unattractive; the traditional, jocular definition is "ten pounds of shit in a five-pound bag" or "two pounds of shit in a one-pound bag." Lighter (1994– ) 1: 187–88.

## A little **powder** and a little paint makes a woman look like what she ain't.

1908 *A Thousand Laughs from Vaudeville* (Baltimore: I. & M. Ottenheimer) 45 (in a list of sayings attributed to the actor "Harry Gilfoil as 'Baron Sands'"): "A little bit of powder and a little bit of paint makes a woman what she ain't." *DAP* 478.

## The faster you go, the less **power** you need.

1903 George Chetwynd Griffith, *The Lake of Gold* (London: F. V. White) 133: "At sea the faster you go the more resistance you get. In the air it's the other way about. The higher your speed, the less power you have to use for support, and the more you have to give for driving." 1936 Carl Sandburg, *The People, Yes* (New York: Harcourt, Brace) 230 (in reference to the Wright brothers): "They proved 'the faster you go the less power you need.'" 1959 Carl Sandburg, "Carl Sandburg[,] Drawing from His Own Rich Experience, . . . Eloquently Describes the First Passenger Jet Flight across the Country," *Better Homes and Gardens* 37, no. 4 (Apr.) 56 (the article is Sandburg's second person account, addressing himself): "You remember back to many years ago when you talked in Dayton, Ohio, with Orville Wright, and how he told you, 'The faster you go, the less power you need.'" *DAAP* 249.

## Never underestimate the **power** of a woman (of women).

1941 *Tide: Of Advertising and Marketing* 15, no. 7 (1 Apr.) [inside front cover] (heading of a full-page ad for *Ladies' Home Journal*): "Never Underestimate the Power of a Woman." *DAP* 478(5); *YBQ* Advertising Slogans (69); Rees (1995) 340.

## **Power** has its price.

1966 Mary Renault, *The Mask of Apollo* (New York: Random House) 7: "It was like a lover's touch, which says, Be what I desire. All power has its price. . . . As they [hands] molded me like wax and sculptured me into one, I knew the many-headed lover had caught him too. . . ." 1977 Ronald G. Corwin and Roy A. Edelfelt, *Perspectives on Organizations: The School as a Social Organization* (Washington DC: American Association of Colleges for Teacher Education) 76: "Power has a price: teachers will be held accountable for the failures and the successes of schools as they enter more fully into decision making." Earlier, two books were published with the apparently allusive title *The Price of Power*, one by Hanson W. Baldwin (New York: Harper & Brothers, 1948), the other by Herbert Agar (Chicago: U of Chicago P, 1957); both discuss the obligations—sometimes onerous—imposed on the United States by the nation's emergence as the preeminent world power following World War II. In older uses of the locution "Power has a price," extending back to the late nineteenth century, or the phrase "the price of power," the reference is to the effort, sacrifice, or resources necessary for the desirable attainment of power (for example, a strenuous regimen of exercise to acquire bodily strength)—not the pain or burden consequent to achieving power, the point of the proverb. Cf. "FAME has a price."

## Any (All) **P.R.** is good P.R.

See "Any PUBLICITY is good publicity."

## The harder you **practice**, the luckier you get.

See "The harder you WORK, the luckier you get."

The longest **prayer** has an "Amen."

c. 1975 G. A. Seaman, *Not So Cat Walk: The Philosophy of a People and an Era Expressed in Proverbs* ([St. Croix, Virgin Islands]: Crown) 59: "DE LONGES' PRAYER GOT AMEN. How true and how wonderful. The inference being that all things, both good and evil, come to an end" (capitalization as shown). 1987 John R. Rickford, *Dimensions of a Creole Continuum* (Stanford CA: Stanford UP) viii: "I wish to remember and thank my father and mother . . . for their unstinting support and their shared pleasure in seeing the project bear out the Guyanese proverb: 'De longes' road gat a en'; de longes' prayer gat Amen.'" 1998 Patrick Ibekwe, *Wit & Wisdom of Africa: Proverbs from Africa & the Caribbean* (Trenton NJ: Africa World) 50: "De langes' prayer got a amen" (listed as a "Guyanan" proverb). 2006 *Bahama Journal* 13 Apr.: "'Every prayer has an Amen. Maybe the situation in Haiti also,' Mr. [Bolivar] Gustave told The Bahama Journal." The proverb, principally from Anglo-Caribbean countries and nearby places, is often (as in the instance from 1987) coupled with the older—and more widely distributed—proverb "The longest road has an end."

When all else fails, try **prayer**.

See "When all else FAILS, pray."

Never make **predictions** (It is difficult to prophesy, It is dangerous to prophesy), especially about the future.

1956 "Proceedings of the Meeting," *Journal of the Royal Statistical Society* (series A, General) 119: 147 (Bradford Hill speaks): "Alas, it is always dangerous to prophesy, particularly, as the Danish proverb says, about the future." 2004 *Toledo [OH] Blade* 15 Sep.: "An old adage holds, 'Never make predictions, especially about the future.'" *YBQ* Bohr (2). The proverb is frequently referred to as Danish (or Chinese or Romanian) or attributed to a particular Dane (often the physicist Neils Bohr) or to Yogi Berra, Casey Stengel, Samuel Goldwyn, or Mark Twain.

You can't be (There is no such thing as) a little **pregnant**.

1942 "Coverage of the [Fair Labor Standards] Act," *Wage and Hour Manual* (Washington DC: Bureau of National Affairs) 62: "You are either one or the other [a retailer or a wholesaler]; you can't be both. As the doctor remarked to the lady patient, you can't be just a little bit pregnant— you either are or you aren't." 1948 *Public Health Economics* 5: 634 (abstracting an article from *New York Star*, 3 Nov., which quotes William B. Rawls): "Call it what you will, but you can't be a little bit socialistic any more than you can be a little bit pregnant." 1949 Lindsay Rogers, "Notes on the Language of Politics," *Political Science Quarterly* 64: 485: "Apparently the Chamber of Commerce would have agreed with Gabriel Heatter, who is reported to have said . . . 'You can't be a little bit socialist or communist any more than you can be a little bit pregnant.'"

**Prejudice** is being down on what you are not up on.

1922 Alfred Dwight Sheffield, *Joining in Public Discussion* (New York: George H. Doran) 39–40: "Prejudice, too, is a defensive reaction of ignorance—'you're apt to be "down" on what you're not "up" on'—and you have to rouse yourself from its instinctive level to the level of attention to facts." 1935 John Garland Pollard, *A Connotary: Definitions Not Found in Dictionaries*, 3rd ed. (New York: Thomas Y. Crowell) 90 (definition): "Prejudice—(a) A vagrant opinion without visible means of support.—Bierce. (b) Being down on anything you are not up on." 1938 "Women at Work in Diocese and Parish," *Spirit of Missions* 103: 524: "Will Rogers used to say that 'prejudice is being down on the thing you are least up on.' Could it be that the average antipathy toward 'missions' and 'missionaries' was due to prejudice?" *DAP* 481. Cf. "The MAN most down on a thing is he who is least up on it."

## Be **prepared**.

1908 Robert S. S. Baden-Powell, *Scouting for Boys* (London: Horace Cox) 20 (and passim): "That [badge] of the first class scout consists of a brass arrow head with the motto 'BE PREPARED'" (capitalization as shown). YBQ Baden-Powell. The official Boy Scout motto paraphrases the older Latin motto "Semper paratus." It is sometimes said to have been based on the initials of Baden-Powell's name.

## All **press** is good press.

See "Any PUBLICITY is good publicity."

## Even bad **press** is good press.

See "Any PUBLICITY is good publicity."

## **Pressure** makes diamonds.

1973 B. J. Mason, "The Lawyer Is Truly a Lady," *Ebony* 28, no. 6 (Apr.) 151: ". . . Mrs. Lafontant welcomes it [pressure], for she remembers that pressure makes diamonds and other gems. After all, her name is Jewel." 1983 Bob McDill, song, "Pressure Makes Diamonds" (music by John Schweers): "'Cause if pressure makes diamonds, our love's a diamond now" (popularized by Don Williams). 1986 Ken Smikle, "Inside Hollywood," *Black Enterprise* 17, no. 5 (Dec.) 52: "As he [casting director Reuben Cannon] is fond of saying, 'pressure makes diamonds,' and his persistence has turned up some rare gems." 1988 Kevin S. Donahue, "'No Slack'—A Blueprint for Combat Excellence," *Field Artillery* (Oct.) 51: ". . . [A] Ranger class motto says it well: 'Pressure makes Diamonds'" (capitalization as shown).

## If you have to ask the **price** (the cost, how much it costs), you can't afford it.

1926 *Wall Street Journal* 14 Sep.: "A banker . . . went to the late J. P. Morgan. 'John,' he said (that's the kind of banker he was), 'do you think I could afford a yacht?' And the answer was: 'If there is any doubt in your mind, you can't.'"

1931 Harry Evans, "Movies," *Life Magazine* 97 (1 May) 22: "Maybe you've heard this old one: A man went to a very rich friend and said, 'I am thinking of buying a yacht. How much does it cost to keep one?' The friend replied, 'If you have to ask how much it will cost you can't afford it.'" YBQ J. P. Morgan (3).

## There is no second **prize**.

See "There is no second PLACE."

## There are no **problems**, only opportunities (challenges).

1948 "Necktie Sale," *School Activities* 19: 271: "Advertising, displaying, and selling offer no problems—only opportunities." 1961 Coy V. Farrell, "The Role of the Family on the Cooperative Frontier," in *American Cooperation, 1961* (Washington DC: American Institute of Cooperation) 89: "To acknowledge the title of this topic ['A Problem We Converted into an Opportunity'] would be to repudiate an earlier statement, 'there are no problems, only opportunities.'" 1962 Murray L. Bob, "Those Damn Teenagers," *Library Journal* 87: 3613: "In the promoter, press-agent parlance of the times there are no problems, only opportunities, no difficulties, only challenges." 1968 Helen J. Mandigo, "1967–68 Report of AHEA Activities: From the President," *Journal of Home Economics* 60: 530: "I hope that what I have learned is true for each of you. 'There are no problems—just challenges.'" Cf. "A CRISIS is an opportunity."

## He **profits** most who serves best.

1909 James Wood Pogue, "Science of Practice Building," *Dental Digest* 15 (Sep.) 648: "You tell me you [dentists] are not peddlers, nor agents; but, not withstanding, you and I are selling service, and he profits most who serves best. . . ." DAP 486. In 1910 the proverb became the unofficial motto of Rotary International (adopted officially in 1950, now in the form "They profit most who serve best").

No one ever went bankrupt (went broke, lost money) taking (making) a **profit**.

1902 Frederick Upham Adams, *John Brock*, serialized in *Munsey's Magazine* 28: 84: "A mere trifle of a few thousands, don't you know, but a fellow never goes broke taking profits." 1914 Maurice Switzer, *Letters of a Self-Made Failure* (Boston: Small, Maynard) 76: "No man ever went broke taking profits, and every day you're out of work is a loss of that day's proceeds." 1922 "Averaging Down," *The Outlook* 130: 233: "When prices are advancing, no problem is presented, and one of the oldest sayings on Wall Street is that no one ever lost money taking a profit." *DAP* 485(4); *DAAP* 610. The proverb is often attributed to J. P. Morgan.

**Progress** comes in small steps (one step at a time, step by step).

1935 *Norwalk [CT] Hour* 20 Nov. (letter to the editor): "Certainly even Mr. London will have to admit we cannot expect our whole social system to be changed over night, for he must realize that all growth comes gradually, and progress comes step by step." 1957 *Florence [AL] Times* 12 Oct.: ". . . Mr. Threadgill realizes that education is big business and that progress comes a step at a time." 1975 George M. Van Dyne, "Long-Term Development Strategies in Relation to Environmental Management in the Sahel," in Agency for International Development, *Arid Lands of Sub-Saharan Africa* (Washington DC: National Academy of Sciences) 90: "There are not [*sic*] quick and easy solutions, for progress comes in small steps and only after much struggle, effort and time."

**Prosperity** is always just around the corner.

1936 *New York Times* 19 Jul.: "Jurisprudence, as he wittily puts it, like prosperity, is always just around the corner" (the reference is to Thurmond W. Arnold's *Symbols of Government*, published in 1935—though Arnold's book

did not include the "prosperity" analogy). 1937 J. P. Watson, *Economic Backgrounds of the Relief Problem* (Pittsburgh: Bureau of Business Research, University of Pittsburgh) 9: "Consequently, even to very competent workmen, need, like prosperity, is always 'just around the corner'; and the wolf lives at the door of the less competent workman." 1945 P. S. Brenner, *Uncommon Common Sense* (New York: Field-Doubleday) 78 (the book is a classified collection of anonymous aphorisms): "Prosperity is always just around the corner . . . but somehow when you reach that corner it is just around another corner" (ellipsis dots as shown). *YBQ* Political Slogans (19). In its origins, the saying mocked the Hooverite slogan applied to the Great Depression, "Prosperity is just around the corner," from 1931.

Any (All, Even bad) **publicity** (P.R., press, notice) is good publicity (P.R., press, notice).

1925 "The Comity of the Northwest," *Outlook* 141: 588: "On the theory of P. T. Barnum that any publicity is good publicity, the Seattle criticism is good" (quoted from an editorial in the *Seattle Times*). 1925 *Fresno [CA] Bee* 1 Aug.: "The prevailing psychology of Hollywood is that any publicity is good publicity." 1927 *New York Times* 8 Jun.: "People wonder whether the theatres were sincere when they agreed that 'any publicity is good publicity.'" *YBQ* Modern Proverbs (71); *ODP* 259; Rees (1984) 60; Rees (1995) 9; Pickering (2001) 21. The saying is widely attributed to P. T. Barnum. It perhaps originated as a counter-proverb rebutting "Not all PUBLICITY is good publicity"—or vice versa. Cf. "There is no such THING as bad publicity" and "Any INK is good ink."

Not all **publicity** (press) is good publicity.

1915 C. A. Upton, "President's Address," *Journal of the American Osteopathic Association* 14: 634: "We are in just a little danger of going publicity mad, in connection with this newspaper advertising. All publicity is not good publicity." 1921 John M. Cooper, "The Next Steps in Social Hygiene," *Proceedings of the National Conference on Social Welfare* 48: 118: "The third step is the awakening of a sane and abiding public interest that will be neither hysterical nor morbid. In the sex field, not all publicity is good publicity." 1926 "Editorial," *Library World* 29: 114: "Daily experience proves that librarians should be very careful in giving interviews to journalists. . . . All publicity is *not* good as some librarians seem to think" (italics as shown). 1945 *Atlanta Constitution* 26 Mar.: "It taught [boxing manager James J.] Johnson that not all publicity is good publicity." 2004 Chris Baty, *No Plot? No Problem* (San Francisco: Chronicle) 66: "As two-time NaNoWriMo winner Irfon Ahmad can tell you, not all press is good press." The proverb perhaps originated as a counter-proverb rebutting "Any PUBLICITY is good publicity"—or vice versa.

## Publish or perish.

1927 Clarence Marsh Case, "Scholarship in Sociology," *Sociology and Social Research* 12: 325: "If it be true that . . . the quality of American sociological writing is in inverse relation to its quantity, the reason is to be sought, among other things, in the fact, first, that the system of promotion used in our universities amounts to the warning, 'Publish or perish!'" 1938 Isaiah Bowman, "Education through Discovery," *Liberal Education* 24: 465: "We have too often let records of experience take the place of experience. 'Read or barbarise,' says a humanist, and a scientist seconds the motion by adding, 'publish or perish.'" *DAAP* 614; *YBQ* Logan Wilson; Arora (1988); Winick (2003).

## You can't have any pudding if you don't eat your meat.

1983 Michael R. Perkins, *Modal Expressions in English* (Norwood NJ: Ablex) 34 (illustrating the use of the auxiliary verb *can* in the sense of

"deontic possibility" or permission): "If you don't eat your meat, you can't have any pudding." 1995 Matthew Naythons and Anthony Catsimatides, *The Internet Health, Fitness & Medicine Yellow Pages* (Berkeley CA: Osborne McGraw-Hill) 220 (in an ad for the online *Electronic Gourmet Guide*): "How can you have any pudding if you don't eat your meat?"

## You can't tell how deep a puddle is till you step into it.

1977 Arthur Bloch, *Murphy's Law and Other Reasons Why Things Go Wrong!* (Los Angeles: Price/Stern/Sloan) 79: "Miller's Law: You can't tell how deep a puddle is until you step in it." 1978 Edward E. Shaw, "The Research Libraries Information Network," in *Changing Environment for Research Library Development: Minutes of the Ninety-second Meeting* (Washington DC: Association of Research Libraries) 49: "I have been involved in this effort some 18 months. When I got into it, I should have remembered another small law that has crossed my desk more than once. That is, 'You can't tell how deep a puddle is until you step into it.'"

## The one who throws the second punch (always) gets caught (blamed, punished).

1987 *Philadelphia Daily News* 10 Jun.: "The problem with that is, it's usually the guy who throws the second punch that winds up getting caught." 2000 *New York Times* 6 Jan. (quoting the football player Peter Warrick): "He hit me in the face; I retaliated and hit him back in the face. But you know how that goes. They always catch the person that throws the second punch."

## A good pupil never forgets a good teacher.

See "Nobody forgets a good TEACHER."

**Push** can get you there, but it takes character to stay there.

1935 "Wilson v. Rudolph Wurlitzer Co.," *North Eastern [Law] Reporter* 194: 443 (quoting a page-filler in a booklet issued by Wurlitzer to its employees): "A man with push can get there, but it takes a man with character to stay there" (attributed to one "Shepherd"). A probable earlier allusion: 1920 *Touchstones of Success by 160 Present-Day Men of Achievement* (Philadelphia: Vir) 91: "It takes men with character to stay there after they get there" (a page-filler, attributed to "Shepard"—the same, though spelled differently?). In 1912, *Meyer Brothers Druggist* (33: 383) printed, as a page-filler, what is perhaps a witty anti-proverb based on the proverb, replacing *character* with "a character": "A Man of force can get there, but it takes a character to stay there." Cf. "ABILITY can take you to the top, but character is what will keep you there" and "BULLSHIT can get you to the top, but it won't keep you there."

If you buy **quality**, you only cry once.

See "Buy the BEST and you only cry once."

If you have two **quarterbacks**, you don't have one (any).

1993 *Dallas Morning News* 22 Aug.: "[Coach] Wayne Fontes' wavering over starting Rodney Peete or Andre Ware reminds of an old philosophy from longtime Rice [football] coach Jess Neely: 'If you have two quarterbacks, you don't have any.'" 1995 *St. Petersburg [FL] Times* 23 Oct.: "There is a saying about coaches when it comes to choosing a quarterback. If they have two quarterbacks, they really have none." 1998 *Orlando [FL] Sentinel* 27 Sep.: "Johnson and Palmer are making shambles of the old saw that goes: If you have two quarterbacks you don't have one." Beyond its use as a football adage, the proverb can refer to the necessity in general of making hard choices.

The only stupid (dumb, foolish) **question** is the one you don't ask.

1957 Raymond Will Burnett, *Teaching Science in the Secondary School* (New York: Rinehart) 304: "I continually kept them aware of the fact that the only stupid question was the question that wasn't asked. . . ." 1959 Melvene D. Hardee, *The Faculty in College Counseling* (New York: McGraw-Hill) 354 (slogan at the end of Kent State University's brochure "Your Guide to Personnel Services,"

which the book reproduces): "The only foolish question is the one you don't ask." Cf. "There are no foolish QUESTIONS."

There are no foolish (stupid, silly) **questions** (There is no such thing as a stupid question).

1915 "Railway Courtesy Is Good Advertising," *Railway World* 59: 145: "From the standpoint of a courteous employe there should be no such thing as a foolish question." 1922 "The Romance of an Engineering Genius," *Current Opinion* 73: 339: "I said something, in fact, concerning a hope that he [Charles P. Steinmetz] would not consider my questions foolish. 'There are no foolish questions,' he said, with an engaging grin. 'No man really becomes a fool until he stops asking questions.'" 1938 George Lawton, "A Preliminary Study of Questions Which Adolescents Find Unanswerable," *Journal of Experimental Education* 7: 99: "Next, they were informed that there were no silly questions; anything which had genuinely baffled them was precisely the thing that was wanted." Cf. "The only stupid QUESTION is the one you don't ask."

You have to ask the right **questions** to get the right answers (To ask the right question is halfway to the right answer; To get the right answer, ask the right question; Finding the right answer starts with asking the right question).

1937 *Sarasota [FL] Herald* 12 Dec.: "There is an old adage that to ask the right question is to provide at least half the right answer." 1944 A. K. Coomaraswamy, "Sir Gawain and the Green Knight: Indra and Namuci," *Speculum* 19: 121: "Moreover in India we are dealing with an unbroken tradition; and proverbially, one has only to ask the right question . . . to receive the right answer." 1952 Clarence Ayres, *The Industrial Economy* (Boston: Houghton Mifflin) 35: "Thus it is often said that in order to get the right answer one must ask the right question."

**Quit** while you're ahead.

1919 Charles E. Van Loan, *Score by Innings* (New York: George H. Doran) 245: "'That's right!' growls Sam Horgan, who was down on the floor with the dice. 'Quit while you're ahead, you cheap skates!'" 1923 J. P. McEvoy, "The Potters" (first installment of a play), *Los Angeles Times Illustrated Magazine* (26 Aug.) 18: "You were just lucky that time . . . you better quit while you're ahead" (ellipsis dots as shown). *YBQ* Modern Proverbs (73).

Everyone hates a **quitter**.

See "The WORLD hates a quitter."

A **quitter** never wins, and a winner never quits.

See "A WINNER never quits, and a quitter never wins."

**Quitters** (Only quitters) quit.

1929 Earl Reeves, "The Fog Fighter," *Youth's Companion* 103: 378: "Those who want soft jobs apply elsewhere; quitters quit; the proven men are baked, hardened, toughened." 1961 Jesse L. Lasky, *Naked in a Cactus Garden* (Indianapolis IN: Bobbs-Merrill) 77: "Wasn't it you who always said, 'Only quitters quit?'"

## Little **rabbits** have big ears.

1935 *Chester [PA] Times* 20 Dec. (in an "Uncle
Wiggily's Corner" narrative): "'What is it you're
going to tell Daddy?' asked Jingle. 'Never you
mind,' said Mrs. Longears, laughing. 'Little
rabbits have big ears,' she said to her husband,
and this made Baby Bunty and all the others all
the more anxious to know the secret." Pickering
et al. (1992) 359, where the proverb is identified
as Australian. It is an analog of the older "Little
pitchers have big ears."

## When the **race** gets tough, step on the gas.

See "When the GOING gets tough, step on the
gas."

## No one is born a **racist**.

See "No one is born a BIGOT."

## Everything is (It's all) a **racket**.

1928 Daniel Robert Maue, "Fame While It's
Hot," *New Outlook* 149: "I get all his stuff into the
papers. He gets all the money. That's the racket—
everything's a racket nowadays." 1930 *New York
Times* 17 Oct. (quoting Albert Ottinger): "The
city of New York is controlled by racketeers and
stick-up men. Everything is a racket." *DAAP* 249.

## You can't win the **raffle** if you don't buy a ticket.

1983 Rosalind Miles, *Danger! Men at Work*
(London: Macdonald) 131 (filler item): "You
can't win the raffle if you don't buy a ticket"
(attributed to "Joe Mercer, football manager").
1992 Anthony Simmons, *A Little Space for Issie
Brown* (Oxford: Oxford UP) 71: "But he was . . . a
great believer in the notion that if you presented
yourself in certain situations, something might
turn up. In other words, if you didn't buy a ticket,
you couldn't win a raffle." Cf. "You can't WIN if
you don't play," "You have to be in it to WIN it,"
and the older "You can't win if you don't bet."

## One **rain** won't make a crop.

1905 Monroe N. Work, "Some Geechee Folklore," *Southern Workman* 34: 633: "One rain won't
make a crop. This rather farfetched interpretation
is given [by 'the oyster Negroes of Thunderbolt,
Georgia':] If you do a person a favor he may
surprise you by doing you an injury. . . . This
answers to the English saying 'One swallow does
not make a summer.'" Whiting (1952) 465 gives
the saying as a North Carolina proverb in the
form "One raindrop can't make a crop." Person
(1958) 178 gives it as a Washington State proverb
in the form "One rain won't make a crop."

## The **rain** doesn't know broadcloth from jeans.

See "RAINDROPS can't tell broadcloth from jeans."

## **Rain** is the best policeman.

1950 MacKinlay Kantor, *Signal Thirty-two*
(New York: Random House) 235: ". . . [He]
could . . . taste the wet whip of the great Harlem
policeman. . . . Yes, yes (they always said)—
rain—the best policeman in Harlem" (the
third set of ellipsis dots as shown). 1970 Peter
Laurie, *Scotland Yard* (New York: Holt, Rinehart
& Winston) 96: "Rain, the best policeman of all,
begins to fall. . . ." Pickering et al. (1992) 506. The
point is that lawbreakers are likely to stay indoors
in bad weather. Cf. the older "Light is the best
policeman" (sometimes attributed to Emerson).

To see a **rainbow**, we have to (be willing to) stand a little rain.

1986 The saying probably passed into oral tradition as a proverb from lines in the song "Stand a Little Rain," written by Donny Lowery and Don Schlitz (popularized by the Nitty Gritty Dirt Band).

**Raindrops** can't tell broadcloth from jeans.

Champion (1938) 631 lists the saying as a "Negro" proverb. Whiting (1952) 465 gives it as a North Carolina proverb: "The rain doesn't know broadcloth from jeans."

In the long **range**, we are all dead.

See "In the LONG RUN, we are all dead."

If **rape** is inevitable, you might as well relax and enjoy it.

See "RELAX and enjoy it."

Old **rats** like cheese too.

1977 Will D. Campbell, *Brother to a Dragonfly* (New York: Seabury) 69: ". . . Grandpa married Miss Daisy Sandifer. . . . He assigned me the task of going home one weekend and finding out what the daughters were saying about him. When I reported that it was less than favorable he said, 'Well, Jack, old rats like cheese too.'" 1984 Roy Wilder Jr., *You All Spoken Here* (New York: Viking Penguin) 23 (in a list of "Southern" sayings): "Old rats like cheese, too." The proverb refers to an old person's (usually a man's) sexual desire.

Too many **rats** never dig a good hole.

Anderson and Cundall (1910) 40 give the saying as a Jamaican proverb: "Too much rat can't dig good hole" (gloss: "Cf. Too many cooks spoil the broth"). Beckwith (1925) 110 ("Too much rat dig bad hole"); Prahlad (2001) 263.

**Reach** out and touch someone.

1970 Eliot Tiegel, "Reach Out and Touch Someone," *Billboard* (15 Aug.) 26; the title of the review of a live performance by Diana Ross presumably alludes to Ross's song "Reach Out and Touch Somebody's Hand." 1972 *Los Angeles Sentinel* 21 Sep.: "THE PILGRIM CONGREGATIONAL CHURCH . . . schedules its Annual Musical. . . . 'Reach Out and Touch Someone,' is the theme" (capitalization as shown). 1973 *Los Angeles Times* 18 Feb. (quoting Chris George): "I've met some of my best friends at phony Hollywood cocktail parties. I met John Derek. I fell in love with Joe Namath. He's like wild. This is what we all should do—reach out and touch someone." Beginning in 1978 the proverb was featured in an advertising campaign for AT&T's long-distance phone service. *YBQ* Advertising Slogans (18).

You don't **realize** it's too late till it's too late.

See "It's NEVER too late until it's too late."

Everything (that happens) happens for a **reason**.

1916 Fred Jackson, "Young Blood," *Munsey's Magazine* 59: 640: "'Do you really think that everything that happens to us happens for a reason—to teach us something?' asked Bucky. 'I do, for a fact.'" 1931 Kathleen Norris, *Hands Full of Living* (Garden City NY: Doubleday, Doran) 62: "And believing in a scheme, which is to say believing in God—or Primal Force, or Elementary Intelligence, or whatever you choose to call the idea that everything that happens to us happens for a reason, and because Someone or Something arranges that it shall happen— believing in God, one can't believe in Luck." 1944 James Thomas Flexner, *Steamboats Come True* (New York: Viking) 6: "Of course, in history as in science everything happens for a reason."

## Better **Red** than dead.

1958 *Oakland Tribune* 12 Dec.: "The popular phrase 'better red than dead' has lost what appeal it ever had." 1961 Bertrand Russell, *Has Man a Future?* (London: George Allen & Unwin) 96: "We have formerly considered the rhetorical war propaganda embodied in the slogan, 'Liberty or Death,' but there is an opposite slogan invented by West German friends of peace: 'Better Red than dead.' One may guess that in some sections of Russian public opinion there is an opposite slogan: 'Better capitalists than corpses.'" *YBQ* Political Slogans (7); Barrick (1979); Rees (1984) 214; Pickering et al. (1992) 512–13; Rees (1995) 52; Room (2000) 67. Bertrand Russell has often been credited with coining the expression, but in the 1961 quotation he disclaims having originated it. Cf. "Better DEAD than Red."

## **Regulations** were made for the obedience of fools.

See "RULES were made for the obedience of fools and the guidance of wise men."

## If you ain't the lead **reindeer**, the view never changes.

See "If you aren't the lead DOG, the scenery never changes."

## **Relax** (You might as well relax, You might as well lie back) and enjoy it.

1926 Claude C. Crawford, *Methods of Study* (Moscow ID: for the author) 98: "When you are reading a library book for recreation it is ordinarily best to take it home and read it during your leisure hours. Take a play attitude toward it rather than a work attitude. Relax and enjoy it." 1938 "At the Pictures," *Punch* 194: 262 (reviewing *The Big Broadcast of 1938*): "Two super ocean greyhounds are supposed to be racing from New York to Cherbourg, but under pressure of W. C. Fields' nonsense, diverse broadcasters and love scenes, we forget that we are on the deck of the *Gigantic*. . . . Since it is all mad, let us relax and enjoy it." 1939 Clifford Odets, "The Stage & Screen," *Commonweal* 29: 216: "There's an awful lot of cuteness in a little number called 'Spring Madness.' . . . Exhausted Burgess Meredith sums it all up with: 'When defeat is inevitable, relax and enjoy it.'" 1947 *Chicago Tribune* 22 Jun. (Charles Goren on playing bridge): "It is my belief that when it becomes clear that the lead switch is inevitable, one should adopt the oriental philosophy, relax and enjoy it." The proverb can have numerous applications; an especially pernicious one is advice to a woman being raped. 1945 "Notes for a Political Dictionary," *Politics* 2: 112: "Modern usage [of the term *rape*] is exemplified by the motto of the Lublin Government [of Poland]. 'When rape becomes inevitable, just relax and enjoy it.'" 1946 Frederic Wakeman, *The Hucksters* (New York: Rinehart) 24: "All you professional advertising men are scared to death of raping the public; I say the public likes it, if you got the know-how to make 'em relax and enjoy it." 1948 Scott Graham Williamson, *Convoy through the Dream* (New York: Macmillan) 250: "This joke was one I heard when the 'Confucius say' jokes were popular. I think it was 1939—when the war began. . . . 'Confucius say, "When rape is inevitable, relax and enjoy it."'" 1950 James Lansdale Hodson, *Thunder in the Heavens* (London: Wingate) 52 (journal entry for 26 Oct. 1947): "A story is being told about a British general. . . . Then at last the General said: 'Gentlemen, this is a rape. But I will say no more. As the Spanish saying has it, "If it is to be rape, then lean back, relax and enjoy it."'" 1954 John Marlowe, *History of Modern Egypt* (New York: Praeger) 349: "The Egyptian Government of the day had, in fact, seen the wisdom of the allegedly Chinese proverb: 'If rape is inevitable, lie down and enjoy it.' But this attitude, although enlightened, does make it difficult for the assaulted one to complain about it afterwards." 1957 Jan De Hartog, *The Spiral Road* (New York: Harper & Brothers) 238: "So—think of old Confucius: 'If rape is inevitable, lie back and enjoy it,' and you'll be surprised how true it is, once you've got rid of your Dutch inhibitions. Another drink?" *MP* R75; *DAP* 503. Of course, the attribution to Confucius is fanciful.

## **Rename** it and claim it.

1951 Herbert O. Brayer, "Introduction," *Stock Raising in the Northwest* by G. Weis (Evanston IL: Branding Iron) ii (quoting an unnamed Scotsman): "You Americans are indeed a strange people. You take the best the world has to offer, adapt it, improve it, rename it and then claim it as your own." 2002 Marcyliena Morgan, *Language, Discourse and Power in African American Culture* (Cambridge UK: Cambridge UP) 4: "Americans hypocritically want to get rid of it [African American speech], speak it, keep it, regulate it, stereotype it, write it, call it a language, call it a dialect, rename it, claim it, and blame it for the problems of black youth!" 2007 Kurt Link, *Understanding New, Resurgent, and Resistant Diseases* (Westport CT: Praeger) 163 (the limerick—printed as prose—is said to satirize Stanley B. Prusiner's coining of the term *prion* for a certain pathogenic protein): "There was a young Turk named Stan who embarked on a devious plan. 'If I simply rename it, I'm sure I can claim it,' said Stan as he pondered his scam." The currency of the proverb may have owed something to a term for popular commercial "give-away" contests called "Name It and Claim It" (for instance, by identifying a snippet of music, one wins the entire album).

## That which one **resists** persists.

1976 Tony Velie and Leonard Fusselman, *Mind Games* (Chicago: Henry Regnery) 22: "What you resist persists automatically, but seeing is freeing." 1980 Sam Keen, *What to Do When You're Bored and Blue* (New York: Wyden) 14: The fundamental rule of the psyche is: *whatever you resist will persist*" (italics as shown).

## Give (Show) **respect**, get (gain, take) respect.

1925 David R. Craig and W. W. Charters, *Personal Leadership in Industry* (New York: McGraw-Hill) 33 "To get respect one must give respect. . . . Moreover, the leader who wants respect from others must have some self-respect. . . . Respect breeds respect" ("Respect breeds respect" is an older proverb). 1981 Robert L. Woodson, ed., *Youth Crime and Urban Policy: A View from the Inner City* (Washington DC: American Enterprise Institute) 98 (Darryl "Tee" Rodgers speaks, May 1980): "See, he doesn't lose anything. He keeps that manly respect. . . . In order to get respect, you have to give respect." 1984 *Sarasota [FL] Herald-Tribune* 29 Nov.: "[The crime boss Meyer] Lansky taught his children a simple rule: 'To gain respect, you have to give respect.'"

## You (Only you) are **responsible** for you.

1912 "A Pertinent Post-election Question," *Medical Brief* 40: 790: "But what about you, the proud, haughty, vote-casting, independent American sovereign, what are *you* to amount to? That is the important question for *you*, for *you* are responsible for *you*" (italics as shown). 1965 *Chicago Tribune* 26 Dec.: "First, the future is contingent on each one of us accepting responsibility for himself. I am responsible for me, and you are responsible for you."

## If you **rest**, you rust.

1906 Karl Breul, *New German and English Dictionary* (New York: Funk & Wagnalls) 468: In the dictionary's entry for the word *rasten*, for the proverb "Wer rastet, der rostet," the translation "if you rest you rust" appears. 1912 Sanford Bennett, *Old Age: Its Cause and Prevention* (New York: Physical Culture) 65: "There is an old German proverb, 'If you rest you rust.' It is true, and if you would be healthy and prolong your life, don't get into a rusty condition, either mentally or physically." 1922 *Chicago Daily Tribune* 28 Jul. (announcing the winner of a

$5 award "for the best motto submitted by a reader"): "If you rest, you rust; get busy." *DAP* 507(1).

## Don't **retreat**, reload.

2009 *Contra Costa [CA] Times* 19 Jan.: "However, he [Rev. Paul Baines] recited a motto often said at St. Samuel Church: 'We never retreat, we reload. We reload with faith, love, unity, peace, and more joy.'" 2010 *Dallas Morning News* (blog) 2 Mar.: "'Just like the founding generation, we are showing the world that when faced with adversity, Texans do not retreat, we reload,' [Senator John] Cornyn said." 2010 *Anchorage [AK] Daily News* 24 Mar.: "Honestly, where in any decent civilized society is there room for Sarah's [Sarah Palin's] latest tweet, 'Don't retreat, RELOAD!'?" (capitalization as shown). 2010 *The Australian [Sydney]* 29 Mar.: "Democrats accused Tea Party advocates of . . . threatening violence against congress members. But Mrs. [Sarah] Palin, an avid hunter, urged: 'Don't retreat, reload.'"

## The best **revenge** is success.

See "SUCCESS is the best revenge."

## The best **revenge** is survival (to survive).

See "SURVIVAL is the best revenge."

## There's no **reward** for bad behavior.

1998 *Syracuse [NY] Post-Standard* 23 Dec.: "We've got to let kids know that there is no reward for bad behavior." 2004 Stephen R. Shalom and Mark Selden, "Making Sense of the Korea Crisis," *Z-Magazine* 17, no. 4 (Apr.) 44: "The security guarantee of North Korea that it had long refused to consider was on the table. Its position of 'no reward for bad behavior' was in tatters. . . ." As a phrase, the paradox "reward for bad behavior" has been current since the late nineteenth century—usually suggesting that such a reward *does* commonly occur.

## The **rich** are different.

1926 The proverb probably originated as a misquotation from F. Scott Fitzgerald's story "The Rich Boy": "Let me tell you about the very rich. They are different from you and me." *YBQ* F. Fitzgerald (36).

## The **rich** get richer and the poor get children (kids).

1920 The saying may have entered oral tradition as a proverb, slightly misquoted, from Gus Kahn's song "Ain't We Got Fun": "The rich get rich and the poor get children." *DAP* 508(2); *RHDP* 285–86; *DAAP* 637; *YBQ* G. Kahn (1). The proverb may be regarded as an anti-proverb based on "The rich get richer and the poor get poorer."

## A bad **ride** is better than walking.

See "The worst RIDE is better than the best walk."

## No one **rides** (for) free.

See "There is no such THING as a free ride."

## The worst (kind of) **ride** is better than the best (kind of) walk.

Fogel (1929) 57 gives "A bad ride is better than walking" as the equivalent of the Pennsylvania German "Schlecht gfâre is besser as gūt gelofe" (Old-World German versions are "Besser schlecht fahren als stolz laufen" and "Bäter armsölig färn as grôt herrsch gahn"). 1934 Francis Edward Abernethy, *Texas Folklore Society, 1909–1943*, Publications of the Texas Folklore Society 51 (1992) 199 (quoting from the minutes of the 1934 meeting of the society): "Second prize [in a contest of favorite proverbs] was won by Dan Storm, Austin, with the saying 'The worst kind of ride is better than the best kind of walk.'" 1993 Hans Halberstadt, *U.S. Marine Corps* (Osceola WI: Motorbooks International) 51: "These big vehicles . . . are noisy, smelly, and cramped—but as Marines like to say, the worst ride is better than the best walk." Baldwin (1965) 142 (reporting the English proverb from Pennsylvania). Both Texas and Pennsylvania have hosted waves of immigrants from Germany, so the English proverb could have entered the language (more than once) as a calque from German.

## Everyone has a **right** to his own opinions, not his own facts.

See "Everyone is entitled to his own OPINIONS, not his own facts."

## A **ring** on the finger is worth two on the phone.

1911 The jocular saying may have entered oral tradition as a proverb from Jack Mahoney's song "A Ring on the Finger Is Worth Two on the 'Phone." *DAAP* 640; Barbour (1965) 153. The proverb is modeled on "A bird in the hand is worth two in the bush."

## No **risk**, no fun.

1953 David Noel Francis, *No Risk—No Fun: Talks and Sermons* (London: Epworth). 1982 Bobbe L. Sommer, *Never Ask a Cactus for a Helping Hand* (Dubuque IA: Kendall/Hunt) 29: "Another reason for this withdrawal often stems from fear of risk-taking. . . . No risk, no fun."

## No **risk**, no reward.

1907 General Staff, War Office [Great Britain], *Official History of the Operations in Somaliland, 1901–04* (London: His Majesty's Stationery Office) 2: 406: "The details of such rewards must be left to the judgment of the intelligence officer, but the following rough rules give a guide:—1. No risk, no reward." 1929 Stephen McKenna, *The Shadow of Guy Denver* (New York: Dodd, Mead) 206: "No risk, no reward. If I fail . . . I shan't whimper" (ellipsis dots as shown). 1990 *Modesto [CA] Bee* 25 Feb.: "You've heard the old adage 'No risk, no reward.' It's true."

## **Risk** is the price you pay for opportunity.

1981 *Ottawa [Ontario] Citizen* 29 Aug. (ad for a "total marketing" firm—soliciting new agents): "Risk is the price you pay for opportunity. Investment required: $7,500.00." 1983 *Chicago Tribune* 31 Jul.: "In reality, risk is the price pay for opportunity." 1992 *San Antonio Express* 6 Jul.: "I agree with the phrase 'Risk is the price you pay for opportunity.'"

## A noisy **river** never drowned anybody.

Anderson and Cundall (1910) 40 give the saying as a Jamaican proverb: "Braggin' riber never drown s'mody" (glossing *s'mody* as "somebody" or "anybody," and comparing the proverb "Still waters run deep"). Parsons (1943) 458 gives it as a Granadan proverb: "Bragging riber neber drowns smaddy." Whiting (1952) 467 lists it as a North Carolina proverb.

## If you don't know where you are going, any **road** will take you there.

1942 M. N. Chatterjee, "Measurement in Education," *Social Science* 17: 164: "Does this bring us any nearer to the goal which still remains undefined? Means are easily developed, but without proper consideration of aims, are not all means equally good? If one does not know where he is going, any road will take him there." 1945 M. N. Chatterjee, "India and World Peace," *The Humanist* 5: 82: "The Hindus remember the ancient saying, 'If you do not know where you are going any road will take you there.'" 1958 Daniel Bell, "Ten Theories in Search of Reality," *World Politics* 10: 358: "Now that we have investigated many roads, are there some which can lead us to reality better than others? (Says a passage in the Talmud: 'If you don't know where you are going, any road will take you there.')" 1997 George Harrison, "Any Road" (song), with the refrain line "And if you don't know where you're going any road will take you there" (first recorded on the 2002 album *Brainwashed*).

The **road** to Easy Street goes (runs) through the dump (sewer).

1970 *Chicago Tribune* 25 Jun. (quoting Flip Wilson): "We're building a set called Easy Street. The [character] Reverend LeRoy says, 'The road to Easy Street runs thru the sewer,' and the church is a storefront on Easy Street." 1982 Sam Toperoff, "Mind Games," *Inside Sports* 4 (Jun.) 51 (quoting the football coach John Madden): ". . . I'd say to myself when I knew the game was won . . . 'Piss on the fire and call in the dogs. The hunt's over.' When things were going tough, I'd always tell myself, 'The road to Easy Street goes through the dump.'"

A **robin's** song is not pretty to the worm.

Champion (1938) 635 lists the saying as a "Negro" proverb: "The worm don't see nothing pretty in the robin's song." Whiting (1952) 467 gives it as a North Carolina proverb.

When you're on a **roll**, you're on a roll.

1984 *Los Angeles Times* 7 Sep.: "'When you're on a roll, you're on a roll,' [the movie producer Terry] Moore bubbled in a phone interview." 1986 Marvin T. Levin, *How to Profit on a Real Estate Roller Coaster* (New York: Prentice Hall) 21: ". . . [Y]ou don't want to think about anything that creates anxiety. When you're on a roll, you're on a roll!" Cf. "When you're HOT, you're hot."

Fix (Mend, Patch) the **roof** before it rains.

1910 Hanford Lenox Gordon, *Laconics* (Salem MA: Salem) 67 (in a thematically categorized list of sayings): "Fore-thought. Patch the roof before it rains." 1935 *Banking Act of 1935: Hearings before a Subcommittee of the Committee on Banking and Currency . . . Senate* (Washington DC: Government Printing Office) 964; J. J. Thomas testifies: "I am inclined to feel as Mr. Hamlin does, that we should patch the roof before it rains. . . . No one can tell when that will be."

My **room**, my rules.

See "My HOUSE, my rules."

There is always **room** (You can always find room) on a bandwagon.

1944 *Atlanta Constitution* 31 Jan.: "There's plenty of room on the bandwagon, of course. But I can't help but feel they're just along for the ride." 1980 *Lewiston [ME] Sun Journal* 17 May: "If you aren't on the bandwagon, hurry up and get aboard. There is always room for one more, and it may as well be you." 1989 *Boston Globe* 20 Sep.: "I suppose there's always room on the bandwagon for one more."

A **rooster** one day, a feather duster the next.

1907 *Life Magazine* 50 (24 Oct.) 781: Ad for a color print of a cartoon, the artwork said to be "after Mark Fenderson," that shows a despondent-looking rooster leaning against the outside of a barn; the caption reads, "What's the use, anyway? Nothing but an egg yesterday and a feather duster to-morrow." 1920 *Public Health* (Michigan Department of Health) n.s. 8: 26 (filler item—presumably describing the Mark Fenderson cartoon and paraphrasing its caption): "The old rooster leaned disconsolately against the hen-house. 'After all, what's the use? An egg today—a feather duster tomorrow.'" 1972 A[rthur] A. Calwell, *Be Just and Fear Not* (Victoria, Australia: Lloyd O'Neil) 266: "I also know that few politicians are remembered very long once they leave the scene of their labours. Years ago I told the House of Representatives a basic truth that I had read in a United States publication. The writer said that a politician is 'a rooster one day and a feather duster the next.'" The proverb is commonly identified as Australian, even though the Australian statesman A. A. Calwell specifically credited it to an American source. Arthur Delbridge in *Aussie Talk* (McMahon's Point, Australia: Macquarie, 1984) glosses it: "an expression describing the uncertainty of continued popularity or success." Cf. "CHICKEN today, feathers tomorrow."

## A **rose** is a rose is a rose.

1913 The saying passed into oral tradition as a proverb—misquoted and misinterpreted—from Gertrude Stein's poem "Sacred Emily" (published in 1922): "Rose is a rose is a rose is a rose"; the intended reference was to the painter Sir Francis Rose. 1948 John Wild and J. L. Coblitz, "On the Distinction between the Analytic and the Synthetic," *Philosophy and Phenomenological Research* 8: 654: "Now a sentence such as 'red is red' or Gertrude Stein's 'A rose is a rose is a rose' is, we contend, no proposition at all. . . ." *YBQ* Stein (1); Rees (1984) 90–91. The proverb can refer to the impenetrability (perhaps the tautology) of a statement or explanation.

## Stop and smell the **roses**.

See "Stop and smell the FLOWERS."

## Don't (You can't) change the **rules** in the middle of the game (while the game is in progress).

1921 Charles Seymour, *The Rise to World Power* (New Haven CT: Yale UP) 2: 44: "The United States could not change the rules in the middle of the game for the advantage of one side." 1927 Louis Martin Sears, *History of American Foreign Relations* (New York: Thomas Y. Crowell) 505: "Allied command of the ocean routes deprived Germany of this opportunity, but similarly to have handicapped the allies by declaring an embargo on munitions, would have meant to change the rules while the game was on for the benefit of one contestant." 1935 Walter Millis, *Road to War* (Boston: Houghton Mifflin) 328: "The novel principle of international law, however, failed to impress the State Department officials who had been so often browbeaten by the Allies' insistence that one could not 'change the rules in the middle of the game.'" 1935 Frank

Monaghan, *John Jay* (New York: Bobbs-Merrill) 421: "Jay reasoned that the will of the people had been expressed in the April elections. Was it fair to change the rules in the midst of the game?" *RHDP* 58. The proverb may have been patterned after "Don't change horses in the middle of a stream."

## **Rules** (Regulations) were made (written) for the obedience of fools and the guidance of wise men (for fools to obey and wise men to consider, for fools to obey and wise men to ignore).

1915 Frank Parker Stockbridge, "The Editorial Point of View," *The Editor* 41: 10 (quoting advice from a newspaper editor): "Don't you know that rules are made to be broken? I really thought you had more sense than that. Rules are for fools! . . . Make your own rules—then break them every time they ought to be broken." 1938 Bernard M. Allen, "The Book of the Quarter," *Journal of the Royal African Society* 37: 475: "On a certain occasion one of his officers objected to a proposal he [H. H. Kitchener (1850–1916)] had made on the ground that it was contrary to regulations. 'Don't quote regulations to me,' said Kitchener, 'they are made for the guidance of fools.'" 1958 George Walker, "Appendix V: The Development and Organisation of Associated Electrical Industries Limited" (dated 14 May 1957), in *Business Enterprise: Its Growth and Organisation*, by Ronald S. Edwards and Harry Townsend (London: Macmillan) 316: "Fleet-Paymaster Foe's maxim: 'Rules are made for the guidance of fools: the wise man knows when to break 'em' ought to be the motto of all senior executives" (the reference to "Fleet-Paymaster Foe" is obscure). 1972 *Wall Street Journal* 29 Jun. (in an ad for an advertising agency): "'Rules are for the obedience of fools and the guidance of wise men.' At Ogilvy & Mather we believe in knowing what the rules *are*—even though we may sometimes decide to break them" (italics as shown). 1974 Andrew Boyle, *Poor, Dear Brendan* (London: Hutchinson) 70: "In his view rules were made for fools to keep and wise men to break, always provided that the reasons for breaching or ignoring rules proved sound or sophisticated enough." Rees (2006) 30. Cf. the older "Rules are made to be broken."

## There are no **rules** in a knife fight.

1969 The saying entered oral tradition as a proverb, garbled, from dialog in the motion picture *Butch Cassidy and the Sundance Kid*: "[Butch:] 'No, no, not yet. Not until me and Harvey get the rules straightened out.' [Harvey Logan:] 'Rules? In a knife fight? No rules!'" (at which instant Butch kicks Harvey in the groin). 1990 Stephen Coonts, *Under Siege* (New York: Simon & Schuster) 199: "'You're not playing by the rules,' he objected, finally. 'There ain't no rules in a knife fight,' Hooper growled. 1994 Linda Vaccariello, "Cancer in Changing Times," *Cincinnati Magazine* 27, no. 8 (Jun.) 82: "Different physicians do, indeed, treat and follow-up the same cancer in different ways. . . . As Butch Cassidy quipped, There ain't no rules in a knife fight." 1994 Earl M. Maltz, "No Rules in a Knife Fight: Chief Justice Rehnquist and the Doctrine of Stare Decisis," *Rutgers Law Journal* 25: 669.

## When (If) you change the **rules**, you change the game.

1945 Lee Emerson Boyer, *Introduction to Mathematics for Teachers* (New York: Henry Holt) 399 (picture caption): "Officials in charge of competitive athletic contests must make their decisions on the basis of rules. Change the rules and you will change the game!" 1959 William S. Vincent, *Roles of the Citizen* (Evanston IL: Row, Peterson) 311: "The rules that govern a jury's deliberations are clear and specific. . . . [T]hey are exceedingly important. For if you change the rules, you change the game." Cf. "Don't change the RULES in the middle of the game."

## If you don't **run**, you can't win.

1964 Marshall Loeb and William Safire, *Plunging into Politics* (New York: David McKay) 32: "But every hopeful politico can take a lesson from him [William Proxmire, quoted as follows]. 'If you don't run, you can't win. . . . Hundreds of people could have run for the state assembly back in Madison in 1950. But they didn't. I did.'" The proverb here refers to "running" for electoral office; as applied (literally) to racing, it is older. Cf. "You can't WIN if you don't play" and "You have to be in it to WIN it."

## In the long **run** (long range), we are all dead.

See "In the LONG RUN, we are all dead."

## You can **run** but you can't hide.

1946 *New York Times* 20 Jun.: "'He can run but he can't hide.' That bit of homespun philosophy was offered in his training camp by [the boxer] Joe Louis less than a fortnight ago. Philosophers can't always prove their theories, but the Dark Destroyer can—and did. Billy Conn ran, but he couldn't hide." *RHDP* 379; *YBQ* Joe Louis (2); Pickering et al. (1992) 271; Rees (1995) 524.

## The **rush** (Sometimes the rush) is worth the risk.

See "The THRILL is worth the risk."

in proportion as we know how they are made"—often credited to Otto von Bismark, but the attribution is uncertain. *YBQ* Bismark (11).

## You can't (Don't try to) saw **sawdust**.

1931 *Tyrone [PA] Daily Herald* 18 Feb.: "Willard Keefe writes . . . , 'How are you going to satirize people who insist on doing it themselves? After all, you can't saw sawdust.'" 1936 *Gazette [Montreal]* 4 Jun.: "He [Denton Massey] entitled his remarks 'you cannot saw sawdust,' and said the moral was that one must never cease trying, but always continue to saw new wood."

## Sacred cows make great hamburger.

See "Sacred cows make great hamburger."

## Only **saps** work for a living.

See "Only suckers work."

## Never ask (You don't want to know) what's in a **sausage** (hotdog).

1929 Oscar Asche, *Oscar Asche: His Life* (London: Hurst & Blackett) 220: "Thank you no, Charles—you never know what sausages are made of" (declining to order sausages for dinner). 1978 Mischa Richter, cartoon, *New Yorker* 54, no. 10 (24 Apr.) 52 (corporate board members around a table, in the middle of which lies a hotdog): "Granted the public has a *right* to know what's in a hot dog, but does the public really *want* to know what's in a hot dog?" (italics as shown). 2002 Rich Page, *Hope Is Not a Strategy: The 6 Keys to Winning the Complex Sale* (New York: McGraw-Hill) 55: "There is an old saying that you really don't want to be around to see sausage being made. But in this case, you need to know exactly how the requirements were made and where each element came from." The proverb mostly occurs metaphorically, in reference to situations that are best left unexamined because, upon close inspection, they may reveal unattractive aspects. The proverb may have evolved from the older conceit "Laws are like sausages; it's best not to see them being made" or "Laws, like sausages, cease to inspire respect

## What can't be **said** is often whistled.

1904 George Bernard Shaw, *Man and Superman* (New York: Brentano's) 69: "Now you seem to think that which is too delicate to be said can be whistled. Unfortunately your whistling, though melodious, is unintelligible." 1931 Frank Plumpton Ramsey, "General Propositions and Causality" (written in 1929, a year prior to Ramsey's death), in *Foundations of Mathematics and Other Logical Essays*, edited by R. B. Braithwaite (London: Kegan Paul, Trench, Trübner) 238 (an allusion or anti-proverbial adaptation): "But what we can't say we can't say, and we can't whistle it either." 1947 Fanny Butcher, "The Literary Spotlight," *Chicago Tribune Magazine of Books* (3 Aug.) 4: "From World Books' little treasury of humor, 'Counterpoints,' I gather that 'What can't be said can be whistled.'" *DAP* 525(18).

## What everybody **says** nobody knows.

1917 E[liza] Aria, "About Conversation," *Fortnightly Review* 107: 703–4: "We have ever with us the inexhaustible topic of Ministerial mistakes—or at least we had; now we are rather uniting in a chorus of applause, a claque for the common good, and, as Oscar Wilde observed succinctly, 'What everybody says, nobody knows.'" 1922 [Eliza] Aria, *My Sentimental Self* (London: Chapman & Hall) 88–89: "This is a small matter but indicative of the lies which spring up round the great dead, and of the truth of the dictum, 'what everybody says nobody knows.'" *DAAP* 248. The attribution to Wilde cannot be authenticated. The proverb may represent a variant of "What everyone knows no one knows"—about the unreliability of gossip, rumors, or popular opinions.

## The **scenery** only changes for the lead dog.

See "If you aren't the lead DOG, the scenery never changes."

## Never let **school** interfere with education.

See "Never let EDUCATION interfere with your intelligence."

## There's no **school** like (the) old school.

1922 Augustus Thomas, *The Copperhead* (New York: Samuel French) 61: The character Philip, whose mother has just exited after behaving in an embarrassing manner, says, "No school like the old school," to which Madeline responds consolingly, "I think your mother's wonderful." 1998 *San Antonio [TX] Express-News* 22 May: "There is no school like old school when it comes to funk [music]." 2003 *The Advocate [Baton Rouge LA]* 17 Jan.: "There's no school like old school. That said, not all the zydeco acts . . . really are old school. . . ." 2004 *The Incredibles* (motion picture)—as reported in *USA Today* 3 Nov.: "During that small moment, one geezer observes of the on-screen goings-on, 'That's the way to do it. That is old school.' Says another, 'No school like old school.'" As a nonproverbial tribute to some particular institution of learning, the locution is older.

## You can't **score** if you don't shoot.

1965 Glenn Warner, "Soccer Shots," in *Soccer Anthology*, edited by Alva C. Moore and Melvin R Schmid ([Gainesville FL]: for the editors) 57: "Don't over-do the passing when shooting territory is reached (bang away—you can't score if you don't shoot)"; the article is said to be reprinted from the *Newsletter* of the National Soccer Coaches Association of America (1951). 1971 Bill Jeffrey, "Soccer," in *Sportsman's Encyclopedia*, edited by Bill Burton (New York: Grosset & Dunlap) 488: "In dribbling to the [soccer] goal he must get his shot off before being tied up. The important thing is to get a shot off if possible; you cannot score without shooting." 1995 Mario Cuomo, *Reason to Believe* (New York: Simon & Schuster) 106: "But we can't score without shooting. Since the mid-1970s, the United States has wandered away from the path to better education, higher skills, and higher wages." 1999 Claire Turenne Sjolander, "How Canadians (Dis)connect," in *Canada: The State of the Federation 1998/99*, edited by Harvey Lazar and Tom McIntosh (Montreal: McGill-Queen's UP) 134: "As [Sergio] Marchi argued colloquially, 'You know, anyone who played hockey as a child . . . will remember what every good coach drills into young players: "You can't score if you don't shoot." The same is true of international trade negotiations: You can't score a good deal if you don't take your best shot at negotiating it.'" Cf. "You miss 100 percent of the SHOTS you don't take," "You can't hit the BALL if you don't swing," and "You can't score unless you have the BALL."

## The **scoreboard** doesn't lie.

1973 *Sun-Herald [Sydney, Australia]* 2 Apr. (report about a rugby game): "There is an old saying that the scoreboard doesn't lie." 1976 *Gazette [Montreal]* 3 Jan. (report about a hockey game): "Spare me those bleats that the Canadiens should have won by seven or eight goals. . . . The scoreboard doesn't lie."

## Calm **seas** do not make good sailors.

1944 Powell Spring, *What Is Truth?* (Winter Park FL: Orange) 77: "The billows of emotionalism rise in multi-colored spray as they beat upon the rock of destiny, said Hoelderlin. How true! Calm seas do not train good sailors." *DAP* 528(1); Barbour (1965) 159. The proverb is sometimes referred to as an African proverb, but it seems like an elaboration or counterpart of the older American proverb "Rough (Stormy) seas make good sailors."

## Sloppy **seconds** are for losers.

See "SLOPPY SECONDS are for losers."

## You can't steal **second base** while your foot is on first base (if you keep one foot on first).

1942 "Shorthand Practice Material" (passages of text to be transcribed), *Business Education World* 22: 932: "Progress always involves risks. You can't steal second base and keep your foot on first" (credited to *Rays of Sunshine*). DAP 529.

## **Second best** has to try harder.

See "NUMBER TWO tries harder."

## **Second best** is better than nothing (at all).

1923 Percy Dearmer, *The Church at Prayer and the World Outside* (London: James Clarke) 98: "Father Tyrrell justified such practices on the ground that they helped ignorant people, and that a second-best is better than nothing at all; but such justification of the second-best is very dangerous to the principle of truth." 1937 Arthur Calder-Marshall, *Pie in the Sky* (New York: Scribner) 471: "'I want Annie to have what she wants,' Ma said. 'Or rather what she can get. Second best is better than nothing at all.'"

## **Secrets** are no fun (Secrets, secrets are no fun).

The proverb perhaps represents a truncation of a cautionary couplet, "Secrets, secrets are no fun; / Secrets, secrets hurt someone." 2002 Hilary Chermiss and Sara Jane Sluke, *Complete Idiot's Guide to Peer Pressure for Teens* (Indianapolis IN: Alpha) 65: "You feel completely in the dark, left out in the cold to freeze alone in an

information-less tundra. Secrets are no fun now, are they?" 2004 *The Hotline* 8 Apr. (a parody, used as a section heading): "Saddam secrets are no fun, Saddam secrets hurt someone."

## **Secrets** are no fun (Secrets, secrets are no fun) unless you share (they're shared) with everyone.

1995 Roslyn Bresnick-Perry, "Riding with the Moon," in *Chosen Tales: Stories Told by Jewish Storytellers*, edited by Peninnah Schram (Northvale NJ: Jason Aronson) 60: "But I quietly closed the door and went back to bed, smiling to myself because I now had a secret. Having a secret is no fun if you can't share it with someone." 2002 *Ocala [FL] Star-Banner* 29 Sep.: "Well, 'secrets, secrets are no fun, unless you share with everyone,' right?" 2005 *The Hotline* 10 Nov. (headline): "Iraq: Secrets, Secrets Are No Fun, Unless They're Shared with Everyone." 2006 Bart King and Jennifer Kalis, *Big Book of Girl Stuff* (Layton UT: Gibbs Smith) 58: The couplet, appearing as an epigraph to a chapter titled "Secrets," is attributed to one Lynn Adair. The proverb probably originated as an anti-proverb based on "SECRETS are no fun" or the rhyme "Secrets, secrets are no fun; / Secrets, secrets hurt someone."

## A **secret** shared is no secret.

1922 Carolyn Wells, *The Vanishing of Betty Varian* (New York: George H. Doran) 132: "'I'll use the same combination Fred used,' she said, 'nobody on earth knows it but myself.' 'Keep it to yourself, Mrs Varian,' North counseled her, 'a secret shared is no secret.'" MP S87; DAP 529(3). Cf. the older "A secret's a secret until it is told" and "Three can keep a secret if two of them are dead."

## You are only as sick as your **secrets**.

1984 Julia Cameron, "The Petty Passion," *Cosmopolitan* 90, no. 5 (May) 184: "There is a truism in pop psychology that we are only as sick as our secrets." 1985 *Evening News*

*[Newburgh-Beacon NY]* 9 Jun.: "'You are only as sick as your secrets,' is one of the many slogans in the [Alcoholics Anonymous meeting] room."

## If you can **see** it, you can be (achieve) it.

1973 James Morris, *The Preachers* (New York: St. Martin's) 184 ("a little poem" attributed to Frederick J. Eikenkoetter II, popularly known as "Reverend Ike"): "If you can see it, you can be it!! / If you can see it, you can have it!! / If you can see it, you can do it!!" 1988 Connie Sitterly and Beth Duke, *A Woman's Place: Management* (Englewood Cliffs NJ: Prentice Hall) 134: "Concentrate on what is really important so that you can visualize your goals. If you can see it, you can achieve it." Cf. "If you can DREAM it, you can do it."

## If you **saw** it, you missed it.

1981 Richard Whelan, *Double Take: A Comparative Look at Photographs* (New York: Clarkson N. Potter) 22: ". . . [P]hotographers who shoot rapidly changing scenes with single lens reflex cameras must develop the ability to anticipate the gestures that they will capture on their film. As new photographers say, 'If you saw it, you missed it.'" Winick (2003) 579.

## It is hard to **see** where you are going if you keep looking back.

See "If you keep LOOKING back, you can't see where you are going."

## *See me* (*Come see me*) is one thing; *come live with me* is a different (another) thing.

Anderson and Cundall (1910) 9 give the saying as a Jamaican proverb: "'Come see me' is one ting, but 'come lib wid me' is anuder" (gloss: "One learns by experience of living with a person what mere acquaintance will not teach" or "the former is an empty civility, the latter a valuable offer"). Beckwith (1925) 26 ("'Come see me' a

not'ing; 'come lib wid me' a de t'ing," and "'Come see me' an' 'come lib with me' a two different t'ing," and "'Come see me' no 'tan' like 'come lib wid me,'" and "'Come see me' a one; 'come lib wid me' a de odder"); Prahlad (2001) 264.

## What you **see** is what you get.

1936 *Chicago Tribune* 2 May (in an ad for home movie cameras): "What you see is what you get." *RHDP* 358; *YBQ* Television Catchphrases (19); *ODP* 280; Folsom (1993). The proverb is sometimes represented by the initialism *WYSIWYG*.

## The **seed** of crime bears bitter fruit.

See "The WEED of crime bears bitter fruit."

## **Seeing** is freeing.

1942 "Seeing Is Freeing" (article title), *Washington Post* 2 May: "Before Pearl Harbor, Ray and Robert Graham, twins, tried to join the Navy to 'see the world.' . . . On their seventeenth birthday, the twins returned. 'This time we want to help free, not just see, the world,' they chorused." 1976 Tony Velie and Leonard Fusselman, *Mind Games* (Chicago: Henry Regnery) 22: "What you resist persists automatically, but seeing is freeing."

## If something **seems** (sounds, looks) too easy (to be true), it probably is.

1972 Terry M. Walker, *Introduction to Computer Science* (Boston: Allyn & Bacon) 397: "Now, this all seems too easy to be true, and it is to an extent." 1985 *Orlando Sentinel* 5 Sep.: "'If it sounds too easy or too good to be true, it's not going to work,' said Edward R. Atkins. . . ." 1987 David Dreman, "The Hustler's Best Friend: You," *Forbes* 139, no. 2 (26 Jan.) 105: "Here are a few antigreed rules. . . . The point is, if it looks too easy, it probably is. Avoid it." Cf. "If something SOUNDS too good to be true, it is."

If something **seems** too good to be true, it probably is.

See "If something SOUNDS too good to be true, it is."

Bad **sex** is better than no sex (Any sex is better than no sex, The only bad sex is no sex).

1969 Thomas Nagel, "Sexual Perversion," *Journal of Philosophy* 66: 17: "Finally, even if perverted sex is to that extent not so good as it might be, bad sex is generally better than none at all." 1971 Richard R. Roach, "Theological Trends: Sex in Christian Morality II," *The Way: Contemporary Christian Spirituality* 11: 236–37: "The problem common to these three areas is summed up in the popular aphorism: 'Bad sex is better than no sex.' . . ." Cf. "No SEX is better than bad sex" and "There is no such THING as bad sex."

Everybody lies about **sex.**

1973 Robert Heinlein, *Time Enough for Love: The Lives of Lazarus Long* (New York: G. P. Putnam's Sons) 267 (in a collection of sayings titled "Excerpts from the Notebooks of Lazarus Long"): "Everybody lies about sex." 1977 J. D. Gilman and John Cleve, *KG200: A Novel* (New York: Simon & Schuster) 92: "Some of her friends had told her stories that sounded very different from the sort of thing she had experienced, but people always told lies about sex." 1986 Dagmar O'Connor, *How to Make Love to the Same Person for the Rest of Your Life* (Garden City NY: Doubleday) 117: "We all know that everyone lies about sex—it began in the locker room and never stops." The proverb usually refers to boasts about one's own sexual experience or prowess, not to misinformation such as might be conveyed to children by parents or peers.

No **sex** is better than bad sex.

1984 "Better No Sex Than Bad Sex," *Sunday Times [London]* 15 Jan. The title was given to the first installment of "pre-published" excerpts from Germaine Greer's *Sex and Destiny* (New York: Harper & Row, 1984). The saying has generally been ascribed to Greer, though it is unclear that she herself was responsible for the title in the *Sunday Times*; the phrasing does not appear in the book itself. The proverb possibly originated as an anti-proverb—woman's response to the (presumably) male "Bad SEX is better than no sex" or "There is no such THING as bad sex."

**Sex** sells.

1926 "The Literature of Opportunism" (editorial), *Journal of Social Hygiene* 12: 550: "To the opportunist publisher and news dealer the main point is embodied in the slogan 'Sex sells.'" 1938 Frank Irving Fletcher, *Lucid Interval* (New York: Harper & Brothers) 167–68: "Nobody can contemplate the grotesque spectacle of modern advertising without being serious. . . . The fact remains, sex sells goods."

You can't have too much **sex.**

See "There is no such THING as too much sex."

You cannot trust **shadows** (after dark).

Anderson and Cundall (1910) 10 record two versions of the proverb as featured in Jamaican semi-wellerisms: "Crab say him don't trus' no shadow after dark" (gloss: "Land-crabs are generally caught at night"), and "Crab say no trus' shadow: when you tink it a shadow it a man." Beckwith (1925) 30 adds another variant, also from Jamaica: "Crab say him no trust no shadder a'ter dark—may be a hand."

Better to burp (belch) and bear the **shame** than swallow the burp (belch) and bear the pain.

1953 Charles Allan Birch, *Common Symptoms, Described and Explained for Nurses* (Edinburgh: E. & S. Livingstone) 183: "Relief of flatulence by bringing up wind, however, may be preferable to the great discomfort of unrelieved flatulence. 'It is better to belch and bear the shame than squelch the belch and bear the pain.'" Person (1958) 177 lists the saying as a Washington State proverb. *DAP* 75.

## Shape up or ship out.

1953 *New York Times* 14 May (in the form of a punning anti-proverb): "In Supreme Headquarters, Allied Powers, Europe—better known as SHAPE—there had been a witticism, 'SHAPE up or ship out.' This meant that officers must conform to the philosophy and doctrine of the North Atlantic Treaty Organization headquarters or transfer elsewhere." 1956 Arthur M. Z. Norman, "Army Speech and the Future of American English," *American Speech* 31: 108: "The soldier's language is cemented by more or less ephemeral idioms: . . . *Shape up or ship out!* (start soldiering or be sent to a combat zone) . . ." (italics as shown). 1956 Howard M. Brier, "Yogi's PR Client," *Boys' Life* 46, no. 10 (Oct.) 39: "Shape up or ship out. Those are my terms." Partridge (1977) 188; Room (2000) 617; Winick (2003).

## One clean sheet will not soil another (Two clean sheets don't smut).

1935 David L. Cohn, *God Shakes Creation* (New York: Harper & Brothers) 258–59: "'Elder,' I said, 'how can you mess about with the sisters all week long, and be a Christian man in the pulpit on Sunday?' 'Well, I tell you how dat is,' he replied without hesitation. 'If a Christian man goes to bed wid a Christian lady dat's just like rubbing two clean sheets together: dey can't soil each other.'" *DAP* 534(2); Prahlad (1996) 246.

## Don't shit where you eat.

1953 Saul Bellow, *Adventures of Augie March* (New York: Viking) 20–21: "What he had to say was usually on the Spartan or proconsular model, quick and hard. 'You can't go to war without smelling powder.' 'If granny had wheels she'd be a cart.' 'Sleep with dogs and wake up with fleas.'

'Don't shit where you eat.' One simple moral in all, amounting to 'You have no one to blame but yourself.' . . ." 1963 Edward Lewis Wallent, *The Tenants of Moonbloom* (New York: Harcourt, Brace & World) 158: "I never, never brung a woman here, even while Sheryl was away. . . . Here I get my spirit nourishment and I know that much—you don't shit where you eat."

## Don't sweat the small shit.

See "Don't sweat the small STUFF."

## Don't sweat the small shit—and it's all small shit.

See "Don't sweat the small STUFF—and it's all small stuff."

## Everybody shits (poops).

1968 Brock Brower, *Other Loyalties* (New York: Atheneum) 306: "'Shit,' Marie insisted, 'is a good word. Everybody shits'" (italics as shown). 1970 Martin Shepard and Marjorie Lee, *Games Analysts Play* (New York: G. P. Putnam's Sons) 121: "Everybody shits and takes a leak, you know." In 1993 the title of a popular Japanese children's book by Tarō Gomi was rendered in English as *Everyone Poops* in Amanda Mayer Stinchecum's translation (New York: Kane/Miller).

## If you sift through enough shit, you may find gold.

See "If you sift through enough DIRT, you may find gold."

## If you stir (up) shit, it will stink (you raise a stink).

1982 Ed Linn, *Steinbrenner's Yankees* (New York: Holt, Rinehart & Winston) 156: "Almost the last thing Gabe [Paul] told him, as Billy [Martin] was ready to leave, was that he was only going to hurt himself if he persisted in taking on the front office in the press. He had told Billy that before, too—'If you stir shit, it stinks.'" 2003 *Guardian*

*[UK]* 8 Mar.: "A non-political man, he [Bonifacio Morcuende] is dubious about the merits of delving into that period [the Spanish Civil War]. 'If you stir up shit, the stink rises,' he says." Doyle (1996) 79.

## Ninety percent of everything is **shit**.

See "Ninety percent of everything is CRUD."

## Same **shit**, different day (Different day, same shit; New day, same old shit).

1988 Robert L. Schattner, *Acronymal Dictionary . . . Medical Edition* (Maple Shade NJ: Omnimed) 188: "SSDD [glossed:] same shit, different day." 1988 Howard Lewis Russell, *Rush to Nowhere* (New York: Donald I. Fine) 151: "On Silas's head perches a baseball cap that says, DIFFERENT DAY SAME SHIT" (capitalization as shown). 1996 *Moonlight and Valentino* (motion picture): The character Rebecca (played by Elizabeth Perkins) says, "Same old shit, brand new day."

## **Shit** flows (runs, rolls) downhill.

1971 Thomas J. Cottle, *Time's Children* (Boston: Little, Brown) 280: "Everything comes down, right? It all goes downhill, right? Shit runs downhill. It's all bullshit, right?" 1972 Carl Franz, *People's Guide to Mexico* (Santa Fe NM: John Muir Publications) 123: "Be wary of houses located in a low spot if rain is imminent. That saying that shit flows downhill is quite true." 1975 Joseph Wambaugh, *The Choirboys* (New York: Delacorte) 111: "I know shit rolls downhill. But why am I *always* livin [sic] in the valley?" (italics as shown). The proverb suggests that onerous tasks or blame for mistakes will get passed from superiors to underlings. The 1972 quotation ironically *literalizes* a proverb that is nearly always applied metaphorically; that is one way in which an anti-proverb can work.

## **Shit** (Stuff) happens.

1944 Lee Thayer, *Five Bullets* (New York: Dodd, Mead) 232: "Was it just chance? Is there such a thing as pure chance? As 'Vic and Sade' are wont to say, 'Stuff happens.' Yes. Stuff does happen" ("Vic and Sade" was a comic radio show popular in the 1930s and 1940s). 1969 Jean Hersey and Robert Hersey, *These Rich Years* (New York: Charles Scribner's Sons) 236: "I always like to remember the simple comment of an intelligent friend of ours in the face of a family crisis that came out of the blue. 'Oh, well, stuff happens,' she said with a sigh as she began to plan the next step ahead." 1978 Wesley Brown, *Tragic Magic* (New York: Random House) 98: "Once you know the reason why shit happens, you shouldn't have to ask the question anymore." 1983 Connie Eble, "UNC-CH Campus Slang— Spring 1983" ([Chapel Hill NC: for the author] Ditto-reproduced): "Shit happens" (saying collected from a student). *YBQ* Modern Proverbs (83); Mieder (2005a); Rees (2005) 6. The proverb commonly expresses a sort of stoic resignation at the vagaries and sorrows of life. Even though the citations for "Stuff happens" antedate ones for "Shit happens," it is not unreasonable to suspect, in some instances at least, that *stuff* represents a euphemistic replacement of *shit*—*stuff* having been more acceptable in print (and in polite oral discourse as well). The "Shit happens" form achieved notoriety in the 1980s when its appearance on bumper stickers occasioned arrests and criminal prosecutions—giving rise to allusive (anti-proverbial) variants that substituted for *shit* the name of some disliked public figure or group.

## **Shit** happens, and then you die.

1991 Jasper Neel, "Where Have You Come from, Reb Derissa, and Where Are You Going?" in *(Inter)Views*, edited by Gary A. Olson and Irene Gale (Carbondale: Southern Illinois UP) 145: "The teenager who murders his girlfriend in the film *River's Edge* explains, 'You're born, shit happens, and you die'" (the character in the

1986 film actually says, "You do shit, and it's done, and then you die"). 1991 Don C. Hall and Annette Hall, *I Served* (Bellevue WA: A. D. Hall) 122: "I had smiled cynically at Barajas, who was still busy with the chicken leg, but seriously gazing at the pale dead body. 'Shit happens and then you die, hey, Sarge?' I had commented." 1991 Stephen King, *Needful Things* (New York: Viking) 248: "Arthritis, yes, terrible, such a shame, shit happens, life's a bitch and then you die. . . ." The proverb probably originated as a blended anti-proverb (as in the Stephen King novel) based on "SHIT happens" and "LIFE is a bitch, and then you die."

## Shit rubs off.

1997 William Diehl, *Reign in Hell* (New York: Random House) 48: "People are going to jail, Roy. You'd be advised to distance yourself from them. Shit rubs off." 2000 William W. Johnstone, *Code Name: Survival* (New York: Kensington) 299: "'You really are one sorry piece of crap, Sugar.' 'I guess I've been hanging around you too long, Nick. Shit rubs off, I suppose.'"

## You can't kill shit (Shit never dies).

1997 Robert Marion, *Rotations: The Twelve Months of Intern Life* (New York: HarperCollins) 226: "'Did Sanchez make it through the surgery?' I asked. 'Sure did,' Gordon told me. 'You know the old saying, "You can't kill shit."'" Winick (2003); Winick (2004).

## You can't put ten pounds of shit in a five-pound bag.

See "You can't put ten POUNDS of shit in a five-pound bag."

## Don't (You can't, Don't try to) shit a shitter.

See "Don't bullshit a BULLSHITTER."

## Shoes are made for walking.

See "BOOTS are made for walking."

## Shop till you drop.

1984 *Los Angeles Times* 21 Oct. (classified ad for a Volkswagen dealership): "Shop till you drop / You can't beat our deals." 1985 *Los Angeles Times* (San Diego County supplement) 10 Aug.: "As skywriting pilots circled a blue sky with the exhortation 'SHOP TILL YOU DROP,' thousands of San Diegans and visitors seemed intent on doing just that. . . ." (capitalization as shown). 1986 *San Diego Union-Tribune* 8 May: "You know the saying, 'Shop till you drop.'"

## A long shot is better than no shot (at all).

1947 John Alden Knight, *Ruffed Grouse* (New York: Alfred A. Knopf) 252: "Friends to whom I have talked about this stunt of running out at right angles when a bird flushes criticize the maneuver because it takes too much time. Well, it does take time, but I'd rather have a long shot than no shot at all" (there the term *long shot* is to be understood literally—and perhaps not yet proverbially) 1974 *New York Times* 7 Sep. (headline of a column about bridge strategy): "Long-Shot Bid for Contract Better Than No Shot At All." 1975 *Sarasota [FL] Herald Tribune* 6 Dec. (quoting a policeman): "We have nothing to tie him into the case, but a long shot is better than no shot at all."

## The shot you don't hear is the one that gets you.

See "The BULLET you don't hear is the one that gets you."

## You miss 100 percent of the shots you don't take.

1991 Burton W. Kanter, "AARP—Asset Accumulation, Retention and Protection," *Taxes* 69: 717: "Wayne Gretzky, relating the comment of one of his early coaches who, frustrated by his lack of scoring in an important game, told him, 'You miss 100% of the shots you never take.'" 1998 Ron Louis and David Copeland, *How to Succeed with Women* (Paramus NJ: Reward) 34: "The Effective Seducer does not allow rejections to mean that he is unworthy or bad in any way. Though we dislike the overly new age/positive thinking movement, we saw a poster recently that poignantly sums up our point. It said, 'You miss 100% of the shots you don't take.'" The saying is often attributed to the hockey player Gretzky (sometimes to his father or to a coach). Cf. "You can't SCORE if you don't shoot."

## Drive for **show**, putt for dough.

1942 *Milwaukee [WI] Journal* 22 Jul.: "The 18 year old . . . made the mistake of concentrating practice on wooden clubs and long irons. . . . She knows now what the nation's pro headliners mean when they say: 'You drive for show, and putt for dough.'" 1943 *Los Angeles Times* 6 Jul.: "Some golfing wag once said, 'You drive for show and putt for dough.'" The proverb is encountered both in golfing and in more general applications—where it refers to the importance of nonglamorous aspects of a process or enterprise. It is sometimes attributed to the golfer Bobby Locke.

## **Show** beats tell.

1988 Elna Dimock, *Teacher Certification Tests*, 2nd ed. (New York: Arco) 105 (tersely explaining the designated correct answer to the question "'Counting their toes and counting candles on a birthday cake are some of the ways that children can learn math.' How can you use this information in the classroom?"): "*Show beats tell*" (italics as shown). 1999 Laurence G. Boldt, *Zen and the Art of Making a Living*, rev. ed. (New York: Penguin) 401: "Additionally, studies have shown that most people process information visually—show beats tell every time." 2008 *Contra Costa [CA] Times* 16 Jul.: "As for the festival, [Leslie] Carrara said getting

children interested in performing arts young is important. 'I think it's awesome, "show" beats "tell,"' she said. 'You can't beat a live theatrical experience.'"

## **Showing** up is eighty percent of life.

See "Eighty percent of LIFE is showing up."

## Nobody likes a **show-off**.

See "Nobody likes a SMART-ASS."

## Keep your sunny **side** up.

The saying probably entered oral tradition as a proverb from the 1929 song (so titled) by Lew Brown. *DAP* 574(1); *YBQ* Lew Brown (1).

## Neither **side** (ever) wins a war.

See "No one wins a WAR."

## There are three **sides** to every question (argument) (Every argument has three sides): my side, your side (his side, her side), and the right side (the truth, God's side).

1903 Edward Wadsworth Peterson, response to Edward Quintard, "A Study of Typhoid Cases Treated in the Hospital Wards during the Past Two Months," *The Post-Graduate* (New York Post-Graduate Medical School and Hospital) 18: 143–44: "A distinguished teacher once said, 'There are three sides to every question, your side, my side and the right side.'" *DAP* 26(15); Rees (2006) 326. The proverb probably originated as an anti-proverb based on the much older "Every argument (question) has two sides." As an allusive variant, "There are three sides to every question" also occurs standing alone.

## There are two **sides** to every pancake.

1915 A. L. Studer, "Trade Union Influence on War," *Machinists Monthly Journal* (International Association of Machinists) 27: 207: "There are always two sides to every pancake, no matter how thin. Let us advert to the saying that 'A little charity covers a multitude of sins' to remove the charity and discover the sin and by whom perpetrated." 1935 *Evening Courier* [Champaign-Urbana IL] 21 Dec.: "Asked recently for his version of the great fortune hunt, [Oscar M.] Hartell sagely remarked: 'There are two sides to every pancake.'" The proverb may have originated as an anti-proverb based on "There are two sides to every argument (story, coin)."

## Don't apologize; it's a **sign** of weakness (An apology is a sign of weakness).

1949 *She Wore A Yellow Ribbon* (motion picture, screenplay by Frank S. Nugent): The character Captain Brittles (played by John Wayne) says, "Don't apologize; it's a sign of weakness." 1958 John O'Hara, *From the Terrace* (New York: Random House) 880: "'Also, knowing him as well as I do, I know what he thinks of apologies.' 'Yes. He'd only see it as a sign of weakness. Don't apologize.'"

## **Signs** don't vote.

1981 *Spokane [WA] Daily Chronicle* 1 Oct.: "Well, I've never used yard signs before. . . . Anyway, yard signs don't vote." 1983 *Milwaukee Journal* 20 Feb.: "'If you're nailing a sign to a tree, you're blowing a vote,' the captain says. 'Signs don't vote. People vote.'" Originally, the proverb referred to the trend, which effloresced in the late 1970s, of campaign signs for political candidates posted in the front yards of homes.

## **Silence** has a price.

1943 Cale Young Rice, "Yolanda of Cyprus," in *Best Poetic Work* (Lebanon TN: Cumberland UP) 77: "Your silence has a price. Name it briefly. / I will not see her betrayed." 1967 "For Apartments Only—A Really Quiet Air Conditioner," *House & Home* 32, no. 1 (Jul.) 87: "It's the quietest on the market, claims the manufacturer—an old-line regional firm now going national. But

silence has a price—$80 to $100 higher than other makers' units of equal size." The proverb can have a range of applications: blackmail, the frustration of keeping a secret, and the luxury of quiet living, for example.

## **Silent** is deadly (Silent but deadly, Silent is violent).

1969 Howard Junker, "As They Used to Say in the 1950's," *Esquire* 72, no. 2 (Aug.) 71 (in a list of expressions popular in the 1950s): "Who cut the cheese? The true clue: he who smelt it dealt it. Silent but deadly." 1999 Jim Dawson, *Who Cut the Cheese? A Cultural History of the Fart* (Berkeley CA: Ten Speed) 23: "In America it's a 'whiffer,' a 'one-cheek sneak,' 'a slider,' 'a trouser cough,' 'a cushion creeper,' or if accompanied by a stench out of proportion to its stealth, an 'S.B.D.' (silent but deadly) or 'S.A.V.' (silent and violent)." The collocations have had older and other applications; currently, however, they can probably no longer be used without an expected awareness of the proverb's flatulent implications.

## **Sins** can be forgiven, but stupid is forever.

See "STUPID is forever."

## **Sinners** can repent, but stupid is forever.

See "STUPID is forever."

## **Sisters** before misters.

2006 Title of an episode (season 1, no. 8) of the Nickelodeon television series *Just for Kicks* (11 Jun.): "Sisters before Misters." 2008 Nancy Robards Thompson, *Accidental Princess* (New York: Harlequin) 110: "When Sophie was a teenager, she and her friends had a 'sisters before misters' pact, meaning they'd never date each other's exes and they'd never let a guy come between [sic] their friendship." Cf. "CHICKS before dicks" and "BROS before hos."

Where you **sit** is (determines) where you stand.

See "Where you STAND depends on where you sit."

## Situation normal—all fucked (fouled, etc.) up (SNAFU).

1941 *San Francisco Chronicle* 15 Jun.: "'Snafu' means 'situation normal, all fuddled up.'"
1941 *Kansas City Star* 27 Jul.: "The word was 'snafu' and his family was curious about its precise meaning. . . . 'But surely the word didn't just pop out of somebody's head,' his mother protested. . . . 'Well, you hear two versions of that. Most of the fellows say that's the way it happened. Then, after snafu got pretty well spread around, somebody decided it was a bunch of letters that stood for words.' 'What words, son?' 'The way I heard it, it goes "Situation normal. All fixed up."'" 1941 "National Defense," *Time* 38, no. 7 (18 Aug.) 36: "Another [U.S. Army] outfit used another word as response to almost any question: Snasu ('Situation normal: all screwed up')" (a rare—euphemistic?—variant). 1941 Private "W," "Army Air Slang," *American Notes & Queries* 1, no. 6 (Sep.) 94: "There is very little, in all, that could be called really new: and most of it is unprintable. But if *AN&Q* would like these three—just for the record—here they are: *latrinogram* . . . / *snafu*—situation normal / *susfu*—situation unchanged" (that is, "situation unchanged, still fucked up"). 1942 "The Administration," *Time* 39, no. 24 (15 Jun.) 11: "The Army has a laconic term for chronic befuddlement: *snafu*" (glossed in a footnote, "Situation normal: all fouled up"). 1943 Philip Jordan, *Jordan's Tunis Diary* (London: Collins) 38 (diary entry for 12 Nov. 1942): "SNEFU as an American officer said at dinner when told of to-day's orders. . . . Snefu means Situation Normal: Everything F——d Up" (capitalization as shown). Sheidlower (2009) 255–58.

It is (always) **six o'clock** somewhere.

See "It is five O'CLOCK somewhere."

## It's not the **size** of the boat (ship) but the motion of the ocean (that matters).

1968 Charlie Cobb, "Ain't That a Groove?" (a prose poem) in *Black Fire*, edited by LeRoi Jones and Larry Neal (New York: William Morrow) 519: "Reply to whitey taken from words of black Atlanta DJ: 'It ain't the size of the ship / that makes the waves / it's / the . . . / motion of the ocean.'" 1976 *Miami News* 30 Aug.: "'It's not the size of the boat that counts, you know,' [Al] Jones told the manager. 'It's the motion of the ocean.' Jones used to be a big boat." 1980 *Dispatch [Lexington NC]* 11 Dec. (letter to "Ann Landers" advice column): "Ann, please tell 'Rhode Island' [a man who feared he was 'underendowed'] that it's not the size of the ship that counts, it's the motion of the ocean." Prahlad (1996) 246–47. In the 1968 example the application of the proverb is nonsexual, referring to political struggle, and in the 1976 example to boxing; currently, however, it most often refers to male sexual proficiency in satisfying a woman. Cf. "It's not the MEAT, it's the motion" and "SIZE doesn't matter."

## It's not the **size** of the dog in the fight that matters; it's the size of the fight in the dog.

1911 Arthur G. Lewis, "Stub Ends of Thoughts," *Book of the Royal Blue* (magazine of the Baltimore & Ohio Railroad) 14, no. 7 (Apr.) 21 (in a collection of sayings): "It is not the size of the dog in the fight that counts, but the fight in the dog that matters." *DAP* 100(78). The proverb has become a common slogan among competitive athletes.

## Size does matter.

1964 Phyllis Kronhausen and Eberhard Kronhausen, *The Sexually Responsive Woman* (New York: Grove) 75 (quoting a therapy client): "Someone said the *size* doesn't matter, but it certainly seems to matter to *me*. The times I came nearest to orgasm were all with men who were rather well endowed" (italics as shown). 1977 Lonnie Myers, "Size *Does* Matter" (italics as shown), *Penthouse Forum* 6, no. 4 (Jan.) 38. The proverb, with the emphatic auxiliary verb *does*, probably originated as a counter-proverb rebutting the proverb "SIZE doesn't matter."

### **Size** doesn't matter (it's what you do with it, it's how you use it).

1903 J. L. Sammons, "Sexual Sense" (letter to the editor), *Medical World* 21: 21: ". . . [A]s for the sexual act, the size of the penis has not much to do with it; the pleasure derived from the act does not depend on the size. I know a family in this section of a father and three sons, and there is not a penis in the lot that will pass for more than three inches during erection; and they and their wives seem to be happy, and each has a large family." 1952 Frank S. Caprio, *The Adequate Male* (New York: Medical Research) 52: "He [a patient] was told that a woman's gratification is not entirely dependent upon the size of the penis, but rather on the technique of lovemaking." 1963 Maxine Davis, *Sexual Responsibility in Marriage* (New York: Dial) 129: "The size of the penis has nothing whatever to do with a husband's ability to satisfy his wife." 1964 Phyllis Kronhausen and Eberhard Kronhausen, *The Sexually Responsive Woman* (New York: Grove) 75 (quoting a therapy client): "Someone said the *size* doesn't matter, but it certainly seems to matter to *me*. The times I came nearest to orgasm were all with men who were rather well endowed" (italics as shown). 1979 Lorna J. Sarrel and Philip M. Sarrel, *Sexual Unfolding* (Boston: Little, Brown) 197–98: "Until they are examined, some men can say to themselves, 'They may say penis size doesn't matter, but they haven't seen how small mine is!'" 1980 Jerry Rubin and Mimi Leonard, *War between the Sheets* (New York: Richard Marek) 110: "Many other women sincerely do not care about penis size. They have done market research and concluded,

in the words of a woman from Santa Barbara, 'Size doesn't matter.'" 1983 Cynthia Heimel, *Sex Tips for Girls* (New York: Simon & Schuster) 187: "Stop any girl on the street and ask her if she cares if a man is well hung, and she will look at you aghast. 'Of course not,' she'll say." 1998 Terry Kelley, *Don't Put Socks on the Hippopotamus* (Brookfield VT: Gower) 145: "Rules of business life no. 50 / Size doesn't matter—it's how you use it that counts." 1999 Tess Gerritsen, *Gravity* (New York: Simon & Schuster) 306: "He gazed at the rocket, a snub-nosed blip on the horizon. 'From this far away, she's [!] not much to look at, is she? So small.' . . . 'Well, you know what they say, Mr. Rashad. It's not the size that matters. It's what you do with it.'" *YBQ* Modern Proverbs (86). Of course, the locution "Size doesn't matter" has had older and other uses, but as a current proverb, it most often refers to—or at least glances jokingly at—the concept that penis size is irrelevant per se to female sexual gratification. Nowadays, commonly, the use of the expression in other connections will evoke snickers on account of its perceived sexual allusiveness—intended or not. Cf. "It's not the SIZE of the boat but the motion of the ocean" and "It's not the MEAT, it's the motion."

### The **sky** is the limit.

1909 "Glidden Tour to Evolve Winners," *Cycle and Automobile Trade Journal* 13, no. 12 (1 Jun.) 56: "Nothing seems to be considered too much of an effort—the sky is the limit—and next July . . . the tourists will all be more than surprised at the enthusiasm met with through the Western towns. . . ." *MP* S257.

### Nothing comes to a **sleeper** but a dream.

1968 Larry Williams, song title: "Wake Up (Nothing Comes to a Sleeper but a Dream)." 1969 "Words of the Week," *Jet* 36, no. 12 (26 Jun.) 34: "Sonny Wilcox, Cleveland bail bondsman, discussing his office on wheels in his $9,100 Lincoln Continental Mark III: 'I'm out there working, man—sometimes 16–18 hours a day. Nothing comes to a sleeper but a dream.'" Prahlad (1996) 247–48.

### A **slip** of the lip might sink a ship.

See "Loose LIPS sink ships."

### **Sloppy seconds** are for losers.

2001 Richard B. Rosse, *The Love Trauma Syndrome* (New York: Perseus) 135: "'Why did she get married so quickly,' he said, 'and to such a loser?' 'What does that make me, an even greater loser, getting sloppy seconds?'" 2004 Jonathan Kellerman, *Therapy* (New York: Random House) 378: "After Ray said he wasn't dating her anymore, I told him I'd give her a try. He got irritated with me, told me sloppy seconds was for losers." 2007 David Corbett, *Blood of Paradise* (New York: Random House) 149: "A toast. May the best man win. Loser gets sloppy seconds." The slang term *sloppy seconds* denotes "sexual intercourse with a woman (usually) who has recently had intercourse with another man."

### A **smack** on (in) the mouth often (sometimes) offends.

1985 *Globe and Mail [Toronto]* 3 Aug.: "Apparently this particular style of notice amuses even the natives, as it was parodied in this sign in a Yorkshire pub: 'Customers are requested not to ask for credit as a smack in the mouth often offends.'" 1986 D. J. Enright, *The Alluring Problem: An Essay on Irony* (Oxford UK: Oxford UP) 160: "A lower class of customers is to be found, one supposes, in the City of London pub which declares, with pleasing litotes, 'Don't ask for credit as a smack in the mouth sometimes offends.'"

### **Small** is beautiful.

1971 John V. Taylor, "Small Is Beautiful," *International Review of Missions* 60: 328–38 (the article so titled urges that Christian mission efforts focus on local concerns). 1973 E. F. Schumacher, *Small Is Beautiful: Economics as If People Mattered [sic]* (London: Blond & Briggs). *YBQ* Schumacher; *ODP* 291; Wescott (1981); Pickering et al. (1992) 565; Flavell and Flavell (1993) 217–18; Rees (1995) 430; Room (2000) 630; Pickering (2001) 323. Schumacher's book is largely responsible for popularizing the expression, which may have originated as an anti-proverb responding to "BIG is beautiful."

### **Small** is the new big (large).

2003 *New York Times* 2 Feb.: "Still, it is refreshing this fall to see that Chuck Close, a pioneer of the supersize photograph . . . , has been making daguerreotypes. Maybe small is the new big." Most often, the proverb acknowledges or promotes "downsizing" as regards food consumption, automobile purchasing, and other lifestyle and environmental issues. Cf. "LESS is the new more."

### If you're so **smart**, why aren't you rich?

1909 "Gathered Notes," *The Friend* 82: 271: "The mate said to me one day, 'I want to ask you a question. We've been talking it over. You're a smart man, why ain't you rich?'" 1927 *Life Magazine* 89 (12 May) 39 (in a miscellany of amusing tidbits): "Sign behind the clerk's desk in the hotel Albert, Selma AL: 'If You're So Damn Smart Why Ain't You Rich?'" (credited to the *Cleveland Plain Dealer*).

### Nobody likes a **smart-ass** (show-off).

1930 Alice Sowers, "In Our Neighborhood," *Parent-Teacher Magazine* 30, no. 3 (Nov.) 16: "However, no one likes a 'show-off,' and Sidney is apt to become one if she continues her present behavior." 1964 William Goldman, *Boys and Girls Together* (New York: Atheneum) 179: "'Nobody likes a smart-ass,' Walt told her. 'Bear that in mind.'"

Nobody minds the **smell** of his own farts (Everyone likes to smell his own farts; Everyone thinks his own farts smell sweet; Only your own farts smell sweet).

1937 W. H. Auden, *Letters from Iceland* (New York: Random House) 151 (in a list of Icelandic proverbs): "Every man likes the smell of his own farts." 1968 Frederic Prokosch, *Missolonghi Manuscript* (New York: Farrar, Straus & Giroux) 297: "Human vanity reaches its highest, most idiotic pinnacle in the field of flatulence. Our own farts we accept with composure and sometimes even relish." 1976 Patricia E. Raley, *Making Love* (New York: Dial) 78: "Smell is an important and often unsung sense. Think about your body scents. W. H. Auden once said that everyone loves the smell of his own farts." 1981 James Morrow, *Wine of Violence* (New York: Holt, Rinehart & Winston) 156: "Wouldn't you agree that the average person likes the smell of his own farts far more than is commonly supposed?" 1993 Eric Gabriel Lehman, *Quaspeck* (San Francisco: Mercury House) 145: "He never got to know me as a normal person who eats and sleeps and likes the smell of his own farts." Possibly Auden was an agent in the importation of the saying (if not the concept) into English-speaking tradition (although occasionally it has been identified as a Polish or an Inuit proverb); he included it in the collection that he compiled (along with Louis Kronenberger), the *Faber Book of Aphorisms* (London: Faber & Faber, 1962) 37, there identified as an "Icelandic Proverb," under the heading "Self-Love." Cf. the older "Every man's dung is (smells) sweet to him."

You **smelt** it, you dealt it.

See "The ONE who smelt it dealt it."

A **smile** is just a frown turned upside down.

See "Turn a FROWN upside down."

A **smile** pays the bills.

See "A BABY's smile pays the bill."

Don't **smoke**, exercise, eat right, and die anyway.

See "EAT right, stay fit, die anyway."

If she **smokes**, she pokes.

1996 *Washington Times* 25 Nov.: "Maj. [Michael] Cloutier commented to Lt. [Julie] Clemm, 'You know what they say about a girl who smokes: If she smokes, she pokes.'" 2007 Jeremy Wisnewski, *Family Guy and Philosophy* (Malden MA: Balckwell) 186: "Lois sternly disapproves of Vanessa, despite her earlier motherly advice on girls to Chris ('Find a girl who smokes. Remember: *if she smokes, she pokes*')" (italics as shown). Here *pokes* has the slang sense of "performs sexual intercourse promiscuously."

**Smoke** them if you've got them (If you've got them, smoke them).

1972 Joe W. Haldeman, "Hero," *Analog* 89, no. 4 (Jun.) 12: "'Awright, soldier boys and girls, ten minutes. Smoke 'em if you got 'em.' He reached into his pocket and turned on the control that heated our coveralls." 1976 Herb Caen, *One Man's San Francisco* (Garden City NY: Doubleday) 50: "World War II made smoking patriotic. . . . 'Smoke 'em if you've got 'em,' barked every top sarge at every rest period. The K and C rations came with cigarettes included." As adapted from the World War II saying—widely remembered though not recorded in print, evidently, till much later—the proverb can mean simply "Relax" or "Rest" or it can mean "Don't defer an opportunity (especially for pleasure)."

He who has been bitten by a **snake** fears even a rope.

1901 Charles Arthur Mercier, *Psychology: Normal and Morbid* (London: Swan Sonnenschein) 193: "Several proverbs testify to the cohesion of a relation which has been determined by a highly impressive experience. 'The scalded dog fears cold water.' 'He who has been bitten by a snake fears a rope.'" *ODP* 28. The proverb is usually identified as Arabic, Hebrew, Persian, or Chinese.

## You **snooze** (If you snooze), you lose.

1950 *Waterloo [IA] Daily Courier* 6 Jun. (advertisement): "If You Snooze You Lose / So BUY NOW From Us" (capitalization as shown). The proverb discourages procrastination or laziness. Winick (1998) 74–77.

## Don't eat yellow **snow**.

1971 Robert Reisner, *Graffiti* (New York: Cowles) 136: "Don't eat yellow snow"; credited to "men's toilet, bar in Alaska." 1971 *Appleton [WI] Post Crescent* 7 Feb.: "One of the hottest selling patches is one with an Eskimo and the warning, 'Don't Eat Yellow Snow.'" Yellow snow would mark the site of someone's (or something's) having urinated.

## Just because there's **snow** on the roof doesn't mean the fire is out inside (there's no fire in the furnace/chimney/ kitchen).

1943 Chester E. Seltzer, "A Peddler's Notebook," *Southwest Review* 28: 423: "'Don't look right fur an old white-haired man tuh be runnin' round the country like this.' Waters laughed weakly. 'There may be snow on the roof but they's still fire in the furnace, ma'am.'" *DAP* 550(3).

## A live **soldier** is better than a dead hero.

1904 *New Zealand Parliamentary Debates* 129 (29 Jul.–31 Aug.) 96; Thomas Mason Wilford speaks: "I do not believe in all the tinsel show that appertains to some of the Volunteer regiments, and lean rather toward the creed of Tom Dooley in regard to the Boer war, that it was 'better to be a live soldier than a dead hero.'" *DAP* 551. Cf.

the older "It's better to be a live coward than a dead hero."

## Old **soldiers** never die (they just fade away).

1916 Bruce Bairnsfather, *Bullets & Billets* (London: Grant Richards) 52–53: "Occasionally, in the silent, still, foggy mornings, a voice from somewhere in the alluvial depths of a miserable trench, would suddenly burst into a scrap of song, such as—Old soldiers never die, / They simply fade away.—a voice full of 'fed-upness,' steeped in determination." In the same book (202) appears a drawing of a singing "Tommy" in a trench, holding a raised umbrella; over the umbrella appears a line of music with the words "old soldiers never die, they simply fades [*sic*] a-way." Snippets of the song (said to be to the tune of "Kind Words Can Never Die") appear in other reminiscences of World War I, with slight variations ("they fade away"; "they always fade away"). In 1920 the song was copyrighted by one J. Foley, but there is no good evidence that he was the actual author. The proverb is now popularly associated with its use by Gen. Douglas McArthur in his farewell address to Congress in 1951. The proverb has given rise to a cycle of parodic jokes, which are anti-proverbs ("Old doctors never die, they just lose their patients"; "Old golfers never die, they just lose their balls"). *MP* S337; *DAP* 551(10); *RHDP* 253–54; *YBQ* Foley; *ODP* 237; Rees (1984) 71; Pickering et al. (1992) 447; Rees (1995) 362; Hernadi and Steen (1999); Pickering (2001) 265; Litovkina and Mieder (2006) 244–48.

## Old **soldiers** never die; young ones do.

1951 *Daily Review [Hayward CA]* 26 Apr.: "There were two discordant notes today in Chicago's otherwise harmonious tribute to Gen. Douglas MacArthur: Small, single-page handbills were distributed among passers-by in the loop. 'Old soldiers never die, but young ones do,' the sheets said. . . ." 1951 Tris Coffin, "The MacArthur Rebellion," *New Republic* 124 (14

May) 13: "Old soldiers never die. But young soldiers die by hundreds of thousands in world war." Litovkina and Mieder (2006) 248. The proverb evolved as an antiwar anti-proverb responding to "Old SOLDIERS never die." Cf. "WARS are not started by warriors."

### Soldiers do not start wars.

See "WARS are not started by warriors."

### Every solution creates new problems.

1920 Edward Caldwell Moore, *West and East* (New York: Charles Scribner's Sons) 169: "Every solution leads to new problems. We are never at the end of these difficulties." 1920 Abraham Myerson, *The Nervous Housewife* (Boston: Little, Brown) 137: "Moreover the contraceptive measures, according to the law that every 'solution' breeds new problems, have their place in causing nervousness."

### If you're not part of the solution, you're part of the problem.

See "If you're not PART of the solution, you're part of the problem."

### There are no final solutions.

See "There are no final ANSWERS."

### You win some, you lose some.

See "You win a FEW, you lose a few."

### There is someone for everyone.

1920 D. O. Knapp, song (copyrighted): "If There Is Someone for Everyone Then There Must Be One for You." 1932 Leonard Ehrlich, *God's Angry Man* (New York: Simon & Schuster) 282: "'Ain't there no girl you like?' 'Me? With my face?' 'Hell! There's someone for everyone, Tidd.'"

### Don't (try to) make something out of nothing.

See "Don't make something out of NOTHING."

### It is (always) five (six) o'clock somewhere.

See "It is five O'CLOCK somewhere."

### You have to come from somewhere before you can go back.

See "You have to COME from somewhere before you can go back."

### If something sounds too easy, it probably is.

See "If something SEEMS too easy, it probably is."

### If something sounds (seems) too good to be true, it (probably) is.

1908 Winston Spencer Churchill, *My African Journey* (London: Hodder & Stoughton) 90: "The air is soft and cool. Except that the picture actually looks more English in its character, one would imagine it was the Riviera. It must be too good to be true. [New paragraph] It *is* too good to be true" (italics as shown). 1935 Major Greenwood, "University Education: Its Recent History and Function," *Journal of the Royal Statistical Society* 98: 28: "To segregate the best teachers among the best students is a proposal that appeals very strongly. . . . It sounds too good to be true! Perhaps it *is* too good to be true" (italics as shown). 1949 Langston Hughes, "Madam and Her Might-Have-Been," in *One-Way Ticket* (New York: Alfred A. Knopf) 24: "When you grow up the hard way / Sometimes you don't know / What's too good to be true, / Just might be so." ODP 294; Doyle (2001a) 460. Cf. "If something SEEMS too easy, it probably is."

### Don't throw a spanner into the works.

See "Don't throw a MONKEY WRENCH into the works."

**Speak** (Talk, Walk) softly and carry a big stick.

1900 Theodore Roosevelt, letter to Henry Sprague (26 Jan.): "I have always been fond of the West African proverb: 'Speak softly and carry a big stick; you will go far.' If I had not carried the big stick the organization would not have gotten behind me. . . ."; *Letters*, edited by Elting E. Morison (Cambridge MA: Harvard UP, 1951–54) 2: 1141. On several occasions Roosevelt uttered the saying, without the last clause and without the West African connection. In oral tradition, the proverb often varies the first verb. *DAP* 556(20), 582(13); *RHDP* 302; *DAAP* 725; *YBQ* T. Roosevelt (7); Rees (1984) 65–66; Rees (1995) 437; Pickering (2001) 329; Mieder (2005b) 9. An interesting prior analog: 1882 C. H. Spurgeon, "Colportage a Want of the Age," in *Booksellers and Bookbuyers*, by Spurgeon et al. (London: Passmore & Alabaster) 12: "Amid abundant laughter, our friend [an evangelist] declared that he had not fought wild beasts at Ephesis, but . . . he had found it well to trust in God *and carry a big stick*" (italics as shown).

If you don't **speculate**, you can't accumulate.

1903 *Commonwealth of Australia Parliamentary Debates*, 3 Edward VII: 13 (10 Jun.) 694: "Mr. [James Whiteside] McCAY.— . . . My experience has been that it is the parsimonious man who prospers rather than the extravagant man. Sir JOHN FORREST.—If we do not speculate we cannot accumulate" (capitalization as shown). 1919 "A Losing Hazard," *Punch* 157: 202: "'If you don't speculate you don't accumulate,' replied Frederic, borrowing the vocabulary of the Crown and Anchor expert. 'Foller my system an' you comes in wheelbarrows an' goes away in motor-cars." *ODP* 297–98.

**Speed** is born with the foal.

1903 "No. 171. Observer," in *Old Glory Horse Auction at Madison Square Garden* (New York:

Fasic-Tipton), unpaginated: "This is certainly a great pedigree and a good colt is the result. Observer is one of the trotters that has *speed born with the foal*" (italics as shown). 1915 Arthur C. Thomas and William Shields, *Care and Training of Trotters and Pacers* (Chicago: Chicago Horseman Newspaper) 66: "If it is true, as I believe, that owing to our advance in breeding, 'speed is born with the foal' more frequently every year, it may be that the mile on mile system . . . will now produce more useful colts than the brush system." *DAAP* 715.

**Speed** kills.

1939 *Atlanta Constitution* 30 Apr. (headline): "Carelessness Causes Wrecks but Speed Kills, Constitution Poll Shows." 1948 *Christian Science Monitor* 5 Mar.: "'Speed kills,' said the Registrar. 'We have been trying to make the public realize it for years. . . .'" The proverb could be regarded as a specialized updating of the old proverb "Haste makes waste." "Speed kills" usually refers to issues of highway safety, though more recently is has punningly referred to the drug informally known as *speed*.

You have to **spend** to get.

1904 Eden Phillpotts, *The American Prisoner*, 2nd ed. (London: Methuen) 81: "'I know you have had to spend a great deal lately.' 'Yes, yes; we must spend to get, and Dartmoor wants a good deal of cash down in advance on a bargain.'" 1954 Grace Carstens, *Born a Yankee* (New York: Macmillan) 23: "'You ought to hire a woman to do that kind of work, Ben.' 'Then where would the profits be?' 'Sometimes you have to spend to get.' Mama dropped in a tablet of cold logic, but Father refused to swallow."

Even a blind **squirrel** can sometimes find a nut (an acorn).

1928 *N.A.R.D. Journal* (National Association of Retail Druggists) 47: 1034 (filler item): "Make a play for more business—Keep *after it*—even

a blind squirrel gets a *nut* once in a while"
(italics as shown). 1964 *Washington Post* 20
Mar.: "Bill Bennings, The Washington Post's
old handicapper, proved yesterday that a blind
squirrel sometimes finds an acorn." The proverb
seems to be the prevalent modern version of
"Even a blind hog can occasionally find an
acorn." *RHDP* 81.

## If you don't **stand** for something (If you stand for nothing, If you stand for everything), you will fall for anything.

1945 Clayton W. Fountain, "Industrial Mental
Health," *Mental Hygiene* 29: 103: "So many of
these boys have only a very hazy idea of the real
issues of the war. . . . This is a dangerous state.
If they don't stand for something, they will fall
for anything." 1950 James Keller, *One Moment
Please!* (Garden City NY: Doubleday) 6: "For
this reason, those who have no convictions are
dangerous to society. In short, *'those who stand
for nothing are apt to fall for anything'*" (italics
as shown). 1962 *Pittsburgh Post-Gazette* 23 Jun.
(quoting Neal C. Wilson): "[W]e have come to
an appalling time in the history of the world
when most people stand for nothing and fall for
everything."

## Where you **stand** depends on where you sit (Where you sit determines where you stand).

1966 Anthony Downs, *Bureaucratic Structure
and Decisionmaking* (Santa Monica CA: Rand)
110. ". . . [T]he particular position he takes will
usually be strongly influenced by its incentive
effects upon him. As a bureaucratic proverb
puts it, 'Where you stand depends upon where
you sit.'" 1966 Kermit Gordon, "Reflections on
Spending," *Public Policy* 15: 14: "One has to live
with the truth which is known in Washington
as Miles' Law, which holds that where you
stand depends on where you sit." 1974
Jessica Pernitz Einhorn, *Expropriation Politics*
(Lexington MA: D. C. Heath) 3: "The central

dictum of the approach is a succinct statement
of the relationship between organizational and
personal goals in matters of U.S. government
debate; that is, 'where you sit is where you
stand' in bureaucratic debates. The meaning
of this phrase is that when issues arise for
discussion, . . . bureaucrats will take positions
in accordance with the organizational norms by
which their outlooks are shaped." The proverb is
often referred to as "Miles's Law" in reference to
the distinguished government bureaucrat Rufus
E. Miles.

## If you shoot (aim) for the **stars**, maybe at least you will hit the moon (get over the trees, etc.).

1955 *Postal Pay and Classification: Hearings before
the Committee on Post Office and Civil Service,
House of Representatives* (Washington DC:
Government Printing Office) 105; Congressman
Elford Cederberg speaks (3 Feb.): "There is an old
saying that if you shoot for the stars, sometimes
you will get over the trees." 1984 *Boston Globe* 1
Jul. (quoting Billy Sullivan): "I was taught that if
you did your best, that was okay. Of course, I was
*also* taught that if you shoot for the stars and land
on the moon, that's okay" (italics as shown). 1985
Mary McCarty, "Bob Kalfin," *Cincinnati Magazine*
18, no. 9 (Jun.) 52 (quoting Kalfin): ". . . I got
farther than I thought possible. If you aim for the
stars and only get to the moon, that's all right."
1987 *Spokesman-Review [Spokane WA]* 20 Feb.:
". . . Chuck still thinks they're going to win state.
'Even if you shoot for the stars and miss,' he
likes to say, 'you might land on the moon.'" 2008
*Dayton [OH] Daily News* 16 Aug · "As a teacher of
mine used to say: 'If you shoot for the stars, you
will no doubt get over the fence!'" The proverb
perhaps originated as an anti-proverb enlarging
on "Shoot (Aim) for the stars."

## Don't **start** something you can't finish.

1915 P. L. Mathews, "Don'ts. For Those Who
Want to Get Ahead," *Colorado School of Mines*

*Magazine* 5: 284 (a collection of admonitions): "Don't start something you can't finish." 1916 Louise Burleigh and Edward H. Bierstadt, *Punishment: A Play* (New York: Henry Holt) 101: "Don't start something you can't finish, Warden. . . . You can see you aren't fitted for this job. You take things too hard." *DAP* 551(4). Cf. "Don't start a FIGHT you can't finish."

## Everybody has to **start** somewhere.

1926 Homer Croy, *They Had to See Paris* (New York: Grosset & Dunlap) 262: "'A common ordinary salesman!' She curled her tongue over the words. . . . 'That ain't anything against him,' he said. 'He won't always be. Everybody's got to start somewhere.'" 1930 Martin Flavin, *Broken Dishes* (New York: Samuel French) 22: "JENNY. I won't have Elaine going around with the delivery boy for Bascom's store. Now that's all there is to it. BILL. I don't figure to do that all my life. Everybody's got to start somewhere."

## A good **start** often means a bad finish.

1905 H. Rider Haggard, *Ayesha* (New York: Grosset & Dunlap) 61: "As Leo said, things were 'going like clockwork,' but I reminded him that a good start often meant a bad finish. Nor was I wrong, for now came our hardships." 1910 *Washington Post* 25 Mar. (in a list of sayings titled "Pointed Paragraphs," credited to "the Chicago News"): "A good start is all the requirements of a bad finish." *MP* S415.

## **Start** early, don't hurry.

See "Don't HURRY, start early."

## **Statistics** (Stats) are for losers.

1960 *Miami News* 26 Oct.: "Boston College has outgained its opposition this season by 1,267 yards to 1,260, sustaining the aphorism of old Bob Neyland [a legendary football coach]: 'Statistics are for losers.'" 1966 *New York Times* 26 Sep.: "But [the football coach Al] Sherman has often said that statistics are for losers. It's

the score that counts." 1974 *Telegraph-Herald* [*Dubuque IA*] 31 Jan. (quoting the high-school basketball coach Bill Fleming): "'All I know is we're leading the league. We only have one loss. I think stats are for losers[;] we don't care who scores,' he concluded."

## The **steam** that blows the whistle won't turn the wheel (do the work).

1910 *Evening Post* [*Wellington, New Zealand*] 8 Jan. (in a small collection of witticisms titled "Alleged Humour"): "Unto those who talk and talk / This proverb should appeal: / The steam that blows the whistle / Will never turn the wheel" (credited to *Chicago News*). 1967 George W. Boswell, "Folk Wisdom in Northeastern Kentucky," *Tennessee Folklore Society Bulletin* 33: 16 (in a list of proverbs): "The steam that blows the whistle never does the work." *DAP* 562.

## The hardest **steel** comes from the hottest fire.

See "The hottest FIRE makes the hardest steel."

## Baby **steps** first.

1985 *Lakeland [FL] Ledger* 9 Jan.: "If the statewide prosecutor is kept from local cases, much of the opposition to the concept may be avoided, [Florida Supreme Court justice Alan] Sundberg said. 'There is some thought of us trying to take some baby steps first.'" 1991 In the motion picture *What about Bob?* the psychotherapeutic mantra of Dr. Marvin (played by Richard Dreyfuss) is "Baby steps." 1993 Sue Miller, *For Love* (New York: HarperCollins) 145: "Lottie reached over and touched him. 'I want to do everything.' 'Baby steps first,' he said. He rose above her."

## Whether the **stone** bumps the jug or the jug bumps the stone, it is bad for the jug.

1936 Carl Sandburg, *The People, Yes* (New York: Harcourt, Brace) 57 (in a poetic montage of proverbs and other sayings): "Whether the stone bumps the jug or the jug bumps the stone it is bad for the jug. / One hand washes the other and both wash the face." *DAP* 341(3); *DAAP* 731.

## Don't spoil a good **story** with facts.

See "Never let the FACTS stand in the way of a good story."

## Every **story** ends (Stories always end).

1923 James Joyce, early manuscript draft of a section of *Finnegans Wake*: "Well, you know or don't you know but every story has an end look look, the dusk is growing"; *Anna Livia Plurabelle: The Making of a Chapter*, edited by Fred H. Higginson (Minneapolis: U of Minnesota P, 1960) 34 (the passage emerged in the 1939 edition of *Finnegans Wake* as "Well, you know or don't you kennet or haven't I told you, every telling has a taling and that's the he and the she of it. Look, look, the dusk is growing" [New York: Viking] 213; *kennet* presumably represents a dialect derivative of *ken* "know"). 1935 *Pittsburgh Press* 23 Jan.: "Love stories always end. But marriage doesn't end." 1970 Gordon Lightfoot, "If You Could Read My Mind" (song): "If you could read my mind, love, / What a tale my thoughts could tell. / . . . / But stories always end." 1973 Elie Wiesel, *The Oath*, translated by Marion Wiesel (New York: Random House) 281: "Every story has an end, just as every end has a story" (in the original French: "Toute histoire a une fin comme toute fin a une histoire"). The proverb most often acknowledges the transitory character of especially happy times. Cf. the older "No dream lasts forever."

## There will always be another **streetcar**.

See "There will always be another BUS."

## Three **strikes** and you're out.

1901 Peter P. McLoughlin, "A Stenographer as a Witness," *Proceedings of the New York State Stenographers' Association . . . Twenty-sixth Annual*

*Meeting . . . Buffalo, N.Y.*: 94: "Q. Well, is that your explanation of why you omitted to read that from your notes? A. Yes sir, because anything I do not strike out [i.e., "delete"] that way, anything I strike out during the examination I strike out that way. And I thought I heard the stenographer in the court room say, 'Three strikes, you're out,' but he didn't—he just went out for a ball.'" *RHDP* 3332–33; *YBQ* Modern Proverbs (92); Room (2000) 690. The proverb generalized the baseball rule to refer to other kinds of shortcomings that exceed a limit and result in failure.

## You cannot push a **string** (of spaghetti).

1935 *Banking Act of 1935: Hearings before the Committee on Banking and Currency, House of Representatives* (Washington DC: Government Printing Office) 377: "GOVERNOR [Marriner S.] ECCLES. . . . Under present circumstances there is very little, if anything, that can be done. MR. [Congressman T. Allen] GOLDSBOROUGH. You mean you cannot push a string. GOVERNOR ECCLES. That is a good way to put it, one cannot push a string." 1943 *Los Angeles Times* 4 Apr.: "His [Gen. George S. Patton's] tank is always well up in front. . . . This he calls his spaghetti theory of leading men into battle. Many commanders take charge of their forces by following, so they can see the formations spread out before them. 'This is like trying to push a string of spaghetti; it won't work,' says Patton. 'It's much better if you pull.'" 1962 *Telegraph-Herald [Dubuque IA]* 18 Dec. (column by Paul Harvey): "The point, it seems to me, in handouts at home or abroad, is that you can't push a string."

## Different **strokes** for different folks.

1945 *Philadelphia Tribune* 19 May: "Yes, I realize that 'times have changed' and that, as a jitterbug friend told me the other day, 'one has different strokes for different folks.'" In the late 1960s the proverb moved from preponderantly African American parlance into the "mainstream," largely on account of the popularity of the song "Everyday People," by Sly and the Family

Stone (1968). *DAP* 569; *RHDP* 49–50; *YBQ* Modern Proverbs (25); *ODP* 77; Mieder (1989a) 317–32; Mieder (1991); Mieder (1992); Mieder (1993b) 3–17, 41–57; Mieder (1994) 297–316; Rees (1995) 118–19; McKenzie (1996); Prahlad (1996) 253; Room (2000) 183; Prahlad (2004); Mieder (2006); Prahlad (2006) 1022–27. *ODP* glosses the word *strokes* in the proverb ("of US origin") as "comforting gestures of approval or congratulations"; however (in North America, at least), the proverb retains sexual implications— *strokes* as "techniques of stimulation" (and, by extension, "tastes" or "approaches"). Cf. "Different WAYS for different days."

## Strong and wrong beats weak and right (Better strong and wrong than weak and right).

1912 Edward Abbott Parry, *What the Judge Saw* (London: Smith, Elder) 136: "Sir Charles Russell once said to a new County Court judge, 'Better to be strong and wrong than weak and right.' It is a counsel of perfection to all judges of first instance." In recent times the saying is often attributed to Bill Clinton, referring specifically to the election of President George W. Bush in 2002.

## A good student never forgets a good teacher.

See "Nobody forgets a good TEACHER."

## There are no bad students, just bad teachers.

1958 Chester S. Williams, "Teacher Education in America as Challenged by the Soviet Education Effort," *Teachers College Journal* 30: 114: "It is wonderful to be a Soviet teacher. . . . It is marvelous to know that there are no poor students, only poor teachers, and it is always a stimulation and a challenge to work in this exalted profession" (the writer is being ironic). 1984 *The Karate Kid* (motion picture): The old martial arts master says to the protagonist, "No such thing as bad student; only bad teacher.

Teacher say, student do." Cf. "There are no bad CHILDREN, only bad parents" and "There are no bad DOGS, only bad owners."

## Study long, (and) study wrong (Think long, think wrong).

1923 *San Antonio Express* 21 Jan. (in an ad for real estate): "Study Long You Study Wrong." 1984 "Khalilah Ali, Boxer's Ex, Weds Teacher in Las Vegas," *Jet* 66, no. 10 (14 May) 53: "After all, 'Muslims don't believe in long engagements. You think long. You think wrong,' she said confidently." *DAP* 569(3), 591(9); Prahlad (1996) 235. The proverb can refer to the impropriety or imprudence of delay in a board game; a card game; an athletic contest; or a financial, political, or amorous quandary.

## Don't sweat the small stuff (shit).

1960 *Massillon [OH] Evening Independent* 12 May (advertisement for a clothing store): "WOMEN'S SWEATERS / Don't sweat the small stuff because the price of cotton is dropping." 1964 Allen Saunders and Ken Ernst, "Mary Worth" (comic strip), *Washington Post* 5 Nov.: "'Oh Jim! . . . I despise myself! . . . for what I said . . . and did!' 'It's okay, honey! . . . Like they say . . . "Don't sweat the small stuff"!'" (ellipsis dots as shown). 1975 McCarthy Coyle, *The Root*, in *Playwrights for Tomorrow*, vol. 12, edited by Arthur H. Ballet (Minneapolis: U of Minnesota P) 50: "Don't sweat the small shit, Kevin. I can handle him." *YBQ* Sayings (11). It is possible that *stuff* represents a euphemistic replacement of *shit*; however, the *stuff* versions are not only older in print but also seemingly more common in current oral discourse.

## Don't sweat the small stuff (shit)—and it's all small stuff (shit).

1979 *New York Times* 23 Oct.: "But perhaps the most easily remembered advice came from Dr. [Kenneth] Greenspan as he opened the seminar. He quoted a friend's prescription for dealing with stress. 'Don't sweat the small stuff,' he said. 'And try to remember it's all small stuff.'" 1993 Jim Northrup, *Walking the Rez Road* (Stillwater MN: Voyageur) 22: "Don't sweat the small shit, Lug thought, it's all small shit unless they're shooting at you." *YBQ* Sayings (11). The proverb originated as an anti-proverb elaborating on "Don't sweat the small STUFF."

## It's just **stuff**.

See "THINGS are just things."

## **Stuff** happens.

See "SHIT happens."

## **Stupid** is forever (Sins can be forgiven, but stupid is forever; Sinners can repent, but stupid is forever).

1969 *Washington Post* 19 Dec.(review of the stage musical *Coco*): ". . . [Alan Jay] Lerner has fashioned a score of tight epigrams: 'A sinner can reform, but stupid is forever.'" 1986 Don Hellriegel et al., *Organizational Behavior*, 4th ed. (St. Paul MN: West) 138 (regarding a company executive "in the late 1970s and early 1980s"): "Many of his subordinates have heard him use his favorite phrase, 'Stupid is forever,' behind an employee's back." *YBQ* Modern Proverbs (88). Cf. "You can't fix STUPID."

## You can't fix **stupid**.

1995 *St. Louis Post-Dispatch* 28 Dec. "What do the bumper stickers given out by KMOX Radio's Jim White say? . . . You Can't Fix Stupid." 2003 Michael S. Piazza, *Queeries: Questions Lesbians and Gays Have for God* (Dallas: Sources of Hope) 119: "Bill and I have a refrigerator magnet that says, 'You can't fix stupid.' I know it's not nice to call anyone stupid, but sometimes they just are." Doyle (1996) 79. Cf. the older "He who is born a fool can never be cured."

## If you keep anything (a dress) long enough, it will come back in **style**.

1938 *Palm Beach [FL] Post-Times* 11 Dec.: "'Fashions move in cycles.' We've heard this statement so often that most of us accept it and are inclined to believe that if we keep anything long enough, it will come back into style." 1950 Joseph Fort Newton, *Everyday Religion* (New York: Abingdon-Cokesbury) 146–47: "Fads of thought, fashions in clothes, come, go, and return. . . . Keep a dress long enough and it will come back in style."

## There are no dull **subjects**, just dull writers (teachers, students).

1922 *Lewiston [ME] Evening Journal* 9 Dec.: "George Horace Lorimer, editor of the Saturday Evening Post, . . . declared that modern fiction had reached the lowest level of merit in its entire existence. 'There are no dull subjects in this world to write about, but the world is full of mighty dull writers,' he said." 1929 Arthur E. Bostwick, *The American Public Library*, 4th ed. (New York: D. Appleton) 150: "That 'there are no dull subjects but only dull writers,' has been lately evidenced by the success of some authors in making nonfiction popular and entertaining with no sacrifice of dignity or value." 376: ". . . [A]s some one aptly puts it, 'there are no dull subjects; there are dull writers.'" 1943 Roscoe Spencer, "Mental and Social Health in Health Education," *School and Society* 57: 240: "Perhaps this accounts partly for the notorious dullness of courses in personal hygiene, for we have been reminded that there are no dull subjects—only dull teachers and dull pupils." 1953 Howard A. Murphy, "Music in General Education," *Teachers College Record* 54: 389: "The old quip that there are no dull subjects, only dull teachers, is well known." Cf. "There are no small PARTS, only small actors."

There is no **substitute** (In war there is no substitute) for victory.

1932 Percy Elliott Lindley, *Human Nature and the Church* (New York: Macmillan) 184: "Oftentimes the sympathizers try to console the less fortunate players by lauding the merits of the game and extolling the virtues of a 'good loser.' This is all semi-apologetic talk. Such philosophy is no substitute for victory." 1941 "Face the Facts" (editorial), *New Republic* 104: 650: "A combatant who fights bravely but without adequate preparation may go down in history as one of the heroic vanquished; but that is no substitute for victory." 1942 Tom Carlyle Smith, "Anglo-French Policy and the Question of American Mediation, 1916," *The Historian* 4: 234: "No substitute for victory, neither a collective guarantee such as [Edward M.] House associated with his plan nor the pledged word of Germany would suffice." 1944 Dwight D. Eisenhower, letter to Mamie Eisenhower (2 Aug.): "Right now the morale on our front is exceedingly high—as I suppose you could guess. In war there is no substitute for victory. I'll be glad when we get the final one, and I can come home to you"; in *Letters to Mamie*, edited by John Eisenhower (Garden City NY: Doubleday, 1978) 203. *RHDP* 163–64; *YBQ* Eisenhower (3). Cf. "WINNING isn't everything; it's the only thing."

Eighty percent (Ninety percent, etc.) of **success** is just showing up.

See "Eighty percent of LIFE is showing up."

**Success** comes in *cans*, failure in *can'ts*.

1910 W. C. Jenkins, "Battleground to Playground," *National Magazine* 32: 280: "However, in all its difficulties, the road has been under the control and management of ambitious men, who looked far into the future and realized that '*success comes in cans, failure in can'ts.*' This motto hangs in a conspicuous place in the office of the general passenger agent of the railroad" (italics as shown). *DAP* 571(18).

**Success** (Victory) has many (a hundred) fathers, but failure (defeat) is an orphan.

1961 John F. Kennedy, "The President's News Conference of April 21, 1961," in *Public Papers of the Presidents of the United States: John F. Kennedy . . . 1961* (Washington DC: Government Printing Office, 1962) 312: "There's an old saying that victory has 100 fathers and defeat is an orphan. And I wouldn't be surprised if information is poured into you [the press corps] in regard to all of the recent activities." 1962 Edmund Wright, "Foreign Policy since Dulles," *Political Quarterly* 33: 123: "His [President Kennedy's] apology [for the Bay of Pigs fiasco] was that he had failed, not that he had erred. 'Success,' he said grimly, 'has a hundred fathers; failure is an orphan.'" *RHDP* 348–49; *YBQ* John Kennedy (18), Ciano; *ODP* 306; Rees (1984) 78. President Kennedy used variants of both the "victory/defeat" and the "success/failure" forms of the proverb on several occasions.

**Success** is always preceded by preparation.

1981 Bill Glass, *Expect to Win* (Waco TX: Word) 82: ". . . [S]pectacular success is always preceded by unspectacular preparation. The everyday drudgery of getting in shape is an important part of the formula of success." *DAP* 570(8).

**Success** (Accomplishment) is a journey, not a destination.

1933 *Chicago Daily Tribune* 19 Jul.: "Standing straight and strong at the banquet board in Hotel Stevens tower[,] the commandant of the Ninth naval district says in a sailor's ringing tones: *Success is action. Success is a journey, not a destination. Italy cannot stand still. She will move on*" (italics as shown). 1957 Dwight D. Eisenhower, *New York Times* 17 Dec. (addressing NATO, 16 Dec.): "We shall be successful. But the task will not be easy or short. Accomplishment will prove to be a journey, not a destination." Cf. "LIFE is a journey, not a destination."

## Success is fleeting; failure is (lasts) forever.

1985 Beth Brennan, *Who's Who and Why of Successful Florida Women* (Winter Park FL: Currier-Davis) 1: 466 (quoting Emma Lee Twitchell): "I am reminded of the adage, 'success is fleeting, failure is forever." 1997 *Times [London]* 25 Jan.: "Invariably, Natalie came last. . . . [T]he memory of losing the tiny mini-golf trophy . . . has not lost its sting. The boys scarcely remember it; success is fleeting, failure dogs a rival forever." Cf. "PAIN is temporary; victory is forever."

## Success is never final (and failure is never fatal).

1920 George Starr White, *Think* (Los Angeles: for the compiler) 73 (the book is a collection of sagacious sayings): "Success is never final." 1954 "What Is Failure?" *Coronet* 36, no. 3 (Jul.) 70 (a small collection of sayings): "Success is never final and failure never fatal. It's courage that counts" (credited to George F. Tilton). *DAP* 571(27); *RHDP* 306. Cf. the somewhat older proverb "Failure is never final (is not forever)."

## Success is the best revenge.

1974 "America's Rising Black Middle Class," *Time* 103, no. 24 (17 Jun.) 19: "'Success is the best revenge [for racial oppression],' says Richard Clarke, owner of a large black employment agency." 1975 Dennis Forsythe, "The Dialectics of Black Separation," in *Black Alienation*, edited by Forsythe (Washington DC: College and University) 26. "Moreover, white society likes to point to the existence of the Black middle class as proof that Blacks have now entered the open society and . . . that 'success is the best revenge against whites.'" 1988 Alexander Theroux, *An Adultery* (New York: Macmillan) 104: "'I once read that the best revenge is success,' said Farol." The proverb is a prevalent modern form of the older "Living well is the best revenge." Cf. "SURVIVAL is the best revenge."

## Never (Don't) give a sucker an even break.

1923 *Boston Daily Globe* 9 Sep. (in reference to the stage musical *Poppy*, in which W. C. Fields reportedly ad-libbed the line—which passed into oral tradition as a proverb): "In the last act the old swindler is bidding farewell to his daughter. He calls her back for a parting word of advice and says, 'Never give a sucker an even break.'" *MP* S533; *DAP* 572; *RHDP* 240; *DAAP* 744; *YBQ* W.C. Fields (19); *ODP* 307; Rogow et al. (1957); Rees (1984) 20; Olinick (1987); Rees (1995) 339; Room (2000) 474; Pickering (2001) 253.

## Only suckers (saps) work (for a living).

1930 Courtenay Terrett, *Only Saps Work: A Ballyhoo for Racketeering* (New York: Vanguard). 1931 Louis Joseph Vance, *The Trembling Flame* (Philadelphia: J. B. Lippincott) 98: "'Work!' Flink snorted—'only saps work for a livin', they's too much jack lyin' around loose in this country. . . .'" 1937 John P. McCaffrey, "The Anatomy of Theft," *Commonweal* 26 (Apr.–Oct.) 95: "The mental slant of the professional thief is: 'only suckers work'; 'only fools work'; 'never give a sucker an even break.'" The proverb perhaps originated as an adaptation of the older proverb "Only fools work."

## You can't sprinkle sugar on shit (bullshit) and make (call) it candy (dessert, a treat, etc.).

1999 George Elliott Clarke, *Beatrice Chancy* (Victoria BC: Polestar) 99 (verses): "You talkin like you been fuckin Lustra, / Like, if you pile enough sugar on shit, / It'll start to look and smell like chocolate cake." 1999 Martin Malone, "Elliot's Really Dead," *Books Ireland* 225 (Oct.) 291: "George shook his head, and said Elliot never changed, sugar on shit doesn't sweeten the taste any." Cf. "You can't polish (gild) a TURD."

### The **sun** doesn't shine on (up) the same dog's ass every day.

1976 Gary Cartwright, "Orange Peril," *Texas Monthly* 4, no. 11 (Nov.) 124: "What DKR [former University of Texas football coach Darrell K. Royal] really talks about is how ol' ugly is better than ol' nothing and why the sun don't shine on the same ol' dog's ass every day and how when that big scorekeeper finally comes to write against your name all he really wants to know is who won." 1981 Lou Crabtree, "Holy Spirit," *Laurel Review* 15, no. 2 (Summer) 63: "Old man, feeling sorry for himself, said, 'The sun don't 'spose to shine on the same dog's ass all the time.'" 1982 Roger Angell, *Late Innings: A Baseball Companion* (New York: Simon & Schuster) 62: "[Jim "Catfish"] Hunter, a lighthearted hero of many previous Octobers, smiled and shrugged in response to the postgame questions. 'The sun don't shine on the same dog's ass every time,' he said." 1993 *Moscow [ID]–Pullman [WA] Daily News* 7 Sep.: "Because of the crowds and these rules of order on any given day some anglers will be more successful than others. But like a wizened surgeon friend of mine likes to say, 'The sun can't shine on the same dog's ass every day.'" Casselman (2002) 11.

### The **sun** will come out tomorrow.

1938 "The First Robin" (anonymous poem), *American Childhood* 23, no. 2 (Feb.) 55: "It is raining. / The wind blows. / There is snow on the fence. / But the sun will come out tomorrow." In those verses, it is uncertain whether the expression is being used proverbially. A song in the stage musical *Annie* (1976), lyrics by Martin Charnin, is at least partly responsible for the current popularity of the proverb.

### On any given **Sunday** (day), any team can beat any other team.

1952 *Hartford Courant* 13 Nov.: "'The teams are so closely matched,' said [National Football League commissioner Bert] Bell, 'that on any given Sunday, any one team can beat any other team.'" 1979 Robert J. Samuelson, "The New Trade Bill—At Last, a Carter Victory," *National Journal* 11: 1118: "'There hasn't been any consistency in the administration [of these rules],' said Don deKieffer, who mostly represents domestic industries. 'On any given Sunday, almost any team could win'" (square brackets as shown). 1995 Phil G. Goulding, *Classical Music* (New York: Random House) 545: "Officials of the National Football League like to say that on any given Sunday any team in the league can beat any other team. The same is true for the top orchestras."

### **Sunshine** is the best disinfectant.

1913 Louis D. Brandeis, "What Publicity Can Do," *Harper's Weekly* 58, no. 2974 (20 Dec.) 10: "Publicity is justly commended as a remedy for social and industrial diseases. Sunlight is said to be the best of disinfectants. . . . And publicity has already played an important part in the struggle against the Money Trust." As advice given by experts in medicine and domestic hygiene, the saying has been applied literally. As a proverb, it is understood metaphorically: A lack of secrecy (what Brandeis calls "publicity") is the best way to prevent dishonest dealings in politics or in other areas.

### Don't tug (pull) on **Superman's** cape.

1972 The saying perhaps entered oral tradition as a proverb from Jim Croce's song "You Don't Mess Around with Jim": ". . . [N]ow they say / You don't tug on Superman's cape / You don't spit in the wind. . . ."

### Don't get high on your own **supply**.

1983 The rhymed saying occurred in (possibly originated as a proverb from) the motion picture *Scarface*. It offers advice or a warning to drug dealers who are also drug users.

**Survival** (Surviving) is the best revenge.

1980 "The Editing Room," *American Film* 6, no. 1 (Jan.–Feb.) 4: "Survival is the best revenge. At the age of ninety-one, the extraordinary French director Abel Grance has survived his critics and decades of neglect." 1984 *Kentucky New Era [Hopkinsville]* 26 Apr.: "'As Mort Sahl (the comedian) recently told me, survival is the best revenge,' [Blake] Edwards said." The proverb is a somewhat grim updating (perhaps an anti-proverb) of the much older "Living well is the best revenge." Cf. "SUCCESS is the best revenge."

Francine Wyeth said [of her daughter]. 'Look at her'. . . . 'She can't win if she's not at the table, Francine.' Harry Wyeth threw his napkin and stood up. 'You wouldn't understand that'" (there the usage is actually an anti-proverb, altering the traditional sense of *table* from a site for gambling to the family dinner table). 1976 *Wall Street Journal* 11 Jun.: "But while all those things are happening to you, you will be at the table, and you cannot win if you're not at the table. And eventually, if you have even a modicum of talent, you will make your point, even if the bet is small at first." Cf. "You can't WIN if you don't play."

## All the good ones are (already) **taken** (married).

1935 Bess Streeter Aldrich, *Spring Came on Forever* (New York: D. Appleton-Century) 160–61: "'What girl would look at a gnarled old bachelor, nearing forty?' 'Oh, there's a plenty,' Amelia told him. . . . But Fritz would not stop. . . . 'The good ones are all married already,' he said laconically. . . ." 1975 Jerry A. Greenwald, *Creative Intimacy* (New York: Simon & Schuster) 95: "T people ['toxic' people] often complain that they never seem to find nourishing people interested in an Intimacy of Two. That all the 'good ones' are taken." 1977 Arthur Bloch, *Murphy's Law* (Los Angeles: Price, Stern, Sloan) 61: "Harris's lament: All the good ones are taken" (Harris was a character in the television sitcom *Barney Miller*; he had trouble finding an apartment to rent). 1985 *Washington Post* 12 Apr.: "[Melvyn] Kinder and [Connell] Cowan are married men: 'What someone else has always looks better. "All the good ones are married" is a myth.'" Most often the proverb expresses the perceived difficulty of a person's—usually a woman's—finding a suitable companion or spouse.

## Everything (always) **takes** longer than it should (than it does, than it takes, than you expect).

1900 Florence Converse, *The Burden of Christopher* (Boston: Houghton, Mifflin) 139: "To be sure, we're still profit sharing, we have n't gone into real coöperation yet; but then,

## Get up from (Leave, Push away from) the **table** while you are still hungry (before you are full).

1953 *Daytona Beach [FL] Morning Journal* 24 Apr.: "Work hard, but don't forget to play a little—and push yourself away from the table while you're still hungry." 1959 Cornelius Vanderbreggen, *A Leatherneck Looks at Life* (Philadelphia: Westbrook) 157: "Always rise from the table when you are still hungry. Never take a nap in the middle of the day." 1961 *New York Times* 5 Feb. (quoting Charles S. Ball, age 103): "It's a good thing to push away from the table before you're full." 1961 *Telegraph [Nashuka NH]* 4 Oct.: "The best diet we've heard of is the simplest: Get up from the table while you're still hungry."

## If you are not at the **table**, you may be on the menu.

1993 "Lebanon—At the Table or on the Menu?" *Middle East Insight* 10, no. 6 (Sep.–Oct.) 5 (commentary on a pending Syria-Israel accord). 2002 *Salt Lake [City UT] Tribune* 30 Jul. (quoting the education activist Pat Rusk): "I am often reminded of the adage, 'If you are not at the table, then you could be on the menu.' If I am not getting out and having my voice heard by those who make decisions, I am not doing my job."

## You can't win if you're not at the **table**.

1970 Joan Didion, *Play It as It Lays* (New York: Farrar, Straus & Giroux) 88: "'She's too thin,'

things always take longer than you think they will. . . ." 1919 Viola Meynell, *Modern Lovers* (Boston: Four Seas) 283: "But I suppose I can't be sure of that, can I? I mean, as a matter of fact things always take longer than one thinks." 1954 Folco Quilici, *The Blue Continent* (New York: Rinehart) 17: "Everything takes longer than you expect, especially the things you want the most." 1973 Gershon Rosenblum, "Community Psychology and Mental Health Administration," in *Current and Future Trends in Community Psychology*, edited by Stuart E. Golann and Jeffrey Baker (New York: Human Sciences) 97: "An administrative colleague of mine in another state, recognizing the agonizingly slow process of change, coined a 'law' which states: 'It always takes longer than it takes.'" 1979 Art Fettig, *How to Hold an Audience in the Hollow of Your Hand* (New York: Frederick Fell) 89: "There is an old maxim that really shows up as truth in the speaking profession. It says, 'Everything takes longer than it does.'" Especially in absurdly worded forms like "Everything takes longer than it takes," the proverb is often given as one of "Murphy's Laws."

It **takes** one to know one.

See "It takes ONE to know one."

Take while the **taking** is good.

1921 *Extension of Ball Rent Act: Hearing before the Committee on the District of Columbia . . . Senate* (Washington DC: Government Printing Office) 27; Senator Frank Gooding speaks: "Is that not a growing tendency in other lines, to take all they can get, take while the taking is good?" 1927 H. E. Raabe, *Cannibal Nights* (New York: Payson & Clarke) 34: "I have often wondered why we were called privateers. . . . I suppose the name was applied to let us off gently. Take while the taking is good was the law, and may the devil take the fainthearted." *DAP* 580. Cf. "Get while the GETTING is good" and "Go while the GOING is good."

**Talent** can get you to the top, but it takes character to stay there.

See "ABILITY can take you to the top, but character is what will keep you there."

All **talk**, no action.

1946 Nelms Black, *How to Organize and Manage a Small Business* (Norman: U of Oklahoma P) 20 (a line in a personal-assessment scale, headed "Initiative"): "real go-getter," "self-starter," "all talk no action," "sack artist." 1947 Fred Hamlin, *Land of Liberty* (New York: Thomas Y. Crowell) 176: "[Civil War general George] McClellan was 'a humbug'—all talk, no action." 1948 Caroline Pratt, *I Learn from Children* (New York: Simon & Schuster) 160 (the proverb is used in the manner of an anti-proverb): "When they were ready, they would play out the scene to the rest of the group, who would then evaluate it in terms of . . . whether or not the scene was 'boring' (meaning all talk, no action)." *MP* T21. Cf. the older "All talk, no do" and "All talk, no cider (grog)."

All **talk**, no game.

1995 *Wilmington [NC] Morning Star* 18 Feb.: "Business as usual in baseball—all talk, no game." 1999 *St. Louis Post-Dispatch* 2 Mar. (caption to a photo of the basketball player Charles Barkley): "Barkley: All talk, no game. . . ." 2003 David Kushner, *Masters of Doom* (New York: Random House) 259: "On game sites with names such as Evil Avatar . . . players had a feeding frenzy around Ion Storm. 'All talk, no game,' a typical post read." In the proverb *game* has the slang sense of "skill or savvy." Cf. "All TALK, no action" and "All TALK, no walk."

All (Big) **talk**, no walk.

1965 *Los Angeles Times* 3 Feb. (playfully allusive title of an article that begins, "British scientists have developed a walkie-barkie which could be the ultimate answer to the lazy dog owner's biggest problem—how to exercise the dog without exercising the master"): "Rover Roves with Radio. Dog Dilemma Solved: All Talk and No Walk." 1993 *Ocala [FL] Star-Banner* 28 Jan.: "'We remember what happened last year,' says [the football player] Thurman Thomas, referring to the Bills' big-talk, no-walk 37–24 loss to Washington." The proverb perhaps derives from (or alludes to) "If you want to talk the TALK, you've got to walk the walk," probably in combination with "All TALK, no action."

## Careless (Loose) **talk** costs lives.

1940 *Times [London]* 7 Feb.: "'Careless talk costs lives' is the motto that has inspired a series of posters about to be distributed all over the country by the Ministry of Information in what is described as a 'nation-wide anti-gossip campaign.'" 1942 *St. Petersburg [FL] Times* 5 May (Walter Winchell's column "On Broadway"): "Sudden thought: 'Loose talk costs lives' . . . How about loose writing?" (ellipsis dots as shown). *DAP* 581(5); Rees (1984) 124; Room (2000) 121. The proverb originated as a wartime "security" slogan in Britain and North America. Cf. "Loose LIPS sink ships."

## Good **talk** saves the food.

2006 "The Week Ahead," *Forbes.com* (21 Jan.): "Good talk saves the food, they say. Which is just as well, because shareholder activist and Gotham hedge fund manager William Ackman has been chewing the fat on a proposed restructuring of McDonald's. . . ." The proverb usually refers to substandard food that is nonetheless enjoyed with conversation. In 2006 Jon R. Stone, *Routledge Book of World Proverbs* (London: Routledge) 284, it is listed (without documentation) as a Portuguese proverb.

## If you want to talk the **talk**, you've got to walk the walk.

1967 David Deitch and Daniel Casriel, "The Role of the Ex-Addict in Treatment of Addiction," *Federal Probation* 31, no. 4 (Dec.) 47: "In summary, whoever the man and whatever his labels, to be useful in the new treatment setting he must walk the walk as well as talk the talk." 1971 Margaret Lamb, "Possession," *Aphra* 2, no. 2 (Spring) 26: "Remember how I always looked up to you? How I liked to talk like you, that strung-out way? You told me: 'You wanna talk the talk, you gotta walk the walk.'"

## You can't **talk** black and sleep white.

See "You can't THINK black and sleep white."

## Some **tasks** require a strong back and a weak mind.

See "Strong BACK, weak mind."

## Each one **teach** one.

1913 "The Lucy Perry Noble Bible Training School, Madura," *Annual Report, American Board of [Congregational] Commissioners for Foreign Missions* 103: 151: "They taught 85 pupils, of whom 29 were Christian women unable to read but willing to learn. Their motto has been, 'Each one teach one.'" 1922 Cora Wilson Stewart, *Moonlight Schools for the Emancipation of Adult Illiterates* (New York: E. P. Dutton) 48: "The citizens of the county were enlisted. The slogan 'Each one teach one' was adopted. . . . Doctors were soon teaching their convalescent patients, ministers were teaching members of their flocks, children were teaching their parents. . . ."

## Nobody forgets (You never forget, Students never forget, A boy never forgets, etc.) a good **teacher**.

1911 Thomas William Bicknell, *History of the Rhode Island Normal School* ([Providence]: for the author) 79: "A good pupil never forgets a good teacher. Each lives in the other." 1997 *The Independent [London]* 15 Oct.: "The advertisement featured 17 celebrities naming their favourite teachers under the slogan, 'no one forgets a good teacher.'" Ratcliffe (2006) 446.

There is no *I* (*me*) in **team**.

See "There is no *I* in *team*."

**Tell** it like it is.

1939 "Lewis v. State [of Mississippi]," *Southern [Law] Reporter* (ser. 1) 184: 55 (quoting from the transcript of trial testimony, in which an African American man hesitantly recounted a conversation with his daughter after she had allegedly been raped): "I said 'come and tell me what kind of playing you done . . ,' Tell it like it is?" 1965 Ralph Ellison, "Tell It Like It Is, Baby," *Nation* 201 ("One Hundredth Anniversary" issue, for 12 and 20 Sep.; separately paginated): 129. *DAAP* 759.

Won't **tell**, won't swell, grateful as hell.

1953 J. M. Elgart, ed., *More Over Sexteen* (New York: Grayson) 121 (printed as verse): "We like Women over forty / They don't tell / They don't yell / They don't swell / And they're grateful as Hell!" 1960 Theodor Reik, *Sex in Man and Woman* (New York: Noonday) 219: "In a bar in lower Manhattan is a board on which the following advice is inscribed: Always take a woman past forty / They don't tell / They don't swell / And they are grateful as hell." 1972 *Washington Post* 13 Jul. (letter to "Ann Landers" advice column): "I take a dim view of the theory that younger men like older women because they don't swell, they don't tell, and they are grateful as hell. Let's face it, older women are just nicer to be with."

Keep your **temper**: nobody else wants it.

1904 William J. Shearer, *The Wisdom of the World, in Proverbs of All Nations* (NY: Richardson, Smith) 192: "Keep your temper; no one else wants it"—listed as a proverb under the heading "Temper" (with no other information). *DAP* 586(6).

What gets **tested** (is what) gets taught.

1941 *1941 Survey of Maryland Public Schools and Teachers Colleges* (Baltimore: Maryland State School Survey Commission) 86: "A standardized testing program tends to formalize the teaching. Teachers tend to teach what is tested. . . ." 1967 Arthur Percival and Bernard Bryan, *Talking About: A Course in Spoken English for Secondary Schools* (London: Methuen) 148: "The usual alternative to sampling skills at random is the examination testing of a very narrow range of skills—and 'what gets tested gets taught.' There is direct teaching, coaching, or cramming: call it by any name. . . ." 1993 Sally Hampton, "The Education of At-Risk Students," in *Theory and Practice in the Teaching of Writing*, edited by Lee Odell (Carbondale: Southern Illinois UP) 206: "There is a great deal of truth in the old adage that what gets tested gets taught." The proverb usually criticizes a preoccupation with testing as a gauge of student progress.

Don't mess with **Texas**.

1985 *Adweek* 24 Jun.: "GSD&M was selected last week to handle a $2 million anti-litter campaign for the Texas Department of Highways and Public Transportation. During presentations, the agency suggested multimedia campaigns with the themeline 'Don't mess with Texas.'" The environmentally sensitive slogan came to be reinterpreted and used as a somewhat belligerent declaration of state pride. As a proverb it can refer to the desirability of avoiding contentious or complicated issues.

All the **things** I like are either immoral, illegal, or fattening.

See "Anything GOOD is either illegal, immoral, or fattening."

The best **things** in life are not things.

1977 *Inclusion of Alaska Lands in National Park, Forest, Wildlife Refuge, and Wild and Scenic Rivers Systems . . . Hearings before the Subcommittee*

on *General Oversight and Alaska Lands . . .
House of Representatives*, part 11 (Washington
DC: Government Printing Office) 286; Ginny
Moore testifies: "Americans are just beginning
to discover that the best things in life are not
things. It is time to stop looking for more
resources to use up. . . ." The proverb likely
originated as an anti-proverb based on "The best
things in life are free."

### *Come see me* is one **thing**; *come live with me* is a different thing.

See "*SEE me* is one thing; *come live with me* is a
different thing."

### Do your own **thing**.

1929 Wilbur Daniel Steele, "Survivor," *Pictorial
Review* 30 (May) 92: "Splendid, Mary! Do your
own thing in your own way, and don't bother
about the fatheads. They come to scoff now.
They'll remain to pray." *DAAP* 766; *YBQ* Perls
("I do my thing, and you do your thing").

### If you want a **thing** done, ask a busy person.

See "If you want something done, ask a busy
PERSON."

### It's just **things**.

See "THINGS are just things."

### Little **things** mean a lot (to a woman).

1901 Anna Fuller, *Katherine Day* (New York:
G. P. Putnam's Sons) 287: "Little things mean a
lot to her,—I suppose they stand for other things,
and that's why she cares so much." 1921 Eugene
L. Pearce, *The Seventh Wave* (New York: Moffat,
Yard) 293: "I've found out in the last two years or
so that little things mean a lot to a woman, and I
expect to remember those little things . . . "

### Not all **things** that can be counted count (Some things that count cannot be counted).

See "Not everything that can be COUNTED counts."

### The only **thing** in the middle of the road is yellow stripes and dead skunks (armadillos, possums).

See "There is NOTHING in the middle of the road
but yellow stripes and dead skunks."

### Some **things** are best (better) left undone.

1900 Florence Burlingame, "The Rural School
Problem," *School Journal* 61: 597: "Some things
are best left undone. Because a thing has been
done here or elsewhere is not reason for doing
it now." 1973 Amos Oz, *Elsewhere, Perhaps* (New
York: Harcourt Brace Jovanovich) 171–72: "I
didn't look inside the gun to see what would have
happened if I'd pressed [the trigger] a fifth time.
Better not to know. Some things are better left
undone." The proverb may be based on the older
"Some things are best left unsaid."

### Some **things** (in life) you can't change.

1935 *Popular Science* 126, no. 1 (Jan.) 101 (in an
ad for the International Correspondence School):
"There are some things you *cannot* change—
and some things you *can* change. One thing you
*can* change . . . is the size of your pay envelope"
(italics as shown).

### There is no such **thing** as a definitive study (text, edition, etc.).

1936 Oliver Carlson and Ernest Bates, *Hearst,
Lord of San Simeon* (New York: Viking) ix:
"There is, of course, no such thing as a
'definitive biography,' for the simple reason that
biographers, like their subjects, are products
of their times." 1936 W. A. Amiet, *The Practice
of Literary History* (Sydney, Australia: Angus &

Robertson) 109: "... [T]here can be no such thing as a definitive history of literature." 1937 Addison Leroy Phillips, "Shakespeare Not Closet Drama," *School and Society* 46: 690: "... [T]he scholars themselves have to concede that there is no such thing as a definitive edition."

## There is no such **thing** as a free lunch (There is no free lunch).

1917 *Eau Claire [WI] Sunday Leader* 27 May: "Liquor men gathered ... to advocate passage of an ordinance forbidding free lunch in saloons. Michael Montague, one of the delegation, held an opposite view to the others. 'There is no such thing as free lunch,' he said. 'First of all you have to buy something from the saloonkeeper before you can partake of the lunch'" (there the saying is literal—probably not yet proverbial). 1938 *El Paso [TX] Herald-Post* 27 Jun.: Applied figuratively, the proverb appears as the "punch line" of a fable: A king asks his counselors to summarize economics in a brief and simple way. They respond with 87 volumes, more than 600 pages each, drawing the king's wrath and incurring executions. Further demands and more executions encourage ever-briefer summations until, finally, the last economist, "a man of profound wisdom," speaks: "Sire, in eight words I will reveal to you all the wisdom that I have distilled through all these years from all the writings of all the economists who once practiced their science in your kingdom. Here is my text: 'There ain't no such thing as free lunch.'" *RHDP* 327; *YBQ* Lutz and W. Morrow; Kanfer (1983); Bassin (1984); Rees (1984) 249; Kauffman (1990); Pickering et al (1992) 212; Galef (1993); Rees (1995) 351; Room (2000) 485; Pickering (2001) 344. An interrogative quip resembling the locution appeared as far back as 1898 in the *Nebraska State Journal [Lincoln]* 23 Oct.: "Why is it that a free lunch is never free?" (credited to the *Chicago Daily News*). Cf. "There is no such THING as a free ride."

## There is no such **thing** as a free ride (Nobody rides for free).

1949 L. B. Perkins and W. D. Cocking, *Schools* (NY: Reinhold) 10 (concerning expenditures for education): "Let's watch our step. There's no such thing as a free ride." *RHDP* 327. Cf. "There is no such THING as a free lunch" and "GAS, grass, or ass: Nobody rides for free."

## There is no such **thing** as a little pregnant.

See "You can't be a little PREGNANT."

## There is no such **thing** as bad publicity (press, P.R., ink).

1941 Clifton Fadiman, "The Reviewing Business," *Harper's Magazine* 183: 479: "One of the paradoxes of book selling ... is that a book may be helped by one or more of the so-called competitive media. ... There is no such thing as bad publicity for books." Cf. "Any PUBLICITY is good publicity."

## There is no such **thing** as bad sex (a bad fuck, a bad piece).

1971 Don Carpenter, *Getting Off* (New York: E. P. Dutton) 184: "Captain Poontang got his nickname from the fact that he was very interested in girls. 'There is no such thing as a bad fuck,' he was fond of saying." 1981 Paula Trachtman, *Disturb Not the Dream* (New York: Crown) 61–62: "'It's O.K., sweetheart. There's no such thing as bad sex. Just relax and enjoy it,' he breathed into her ear. ... Inadvertently, and unnoticed, Richard was a frightened witness to his parents' couplings. ... Never would he forget—or forgive. *No such thing as bad sex*— O.K.!" (italics as shown). 1982 Brenda Maddox, *Married and Gay* (New York: Harcourt Brace Jovanovich) 81: "'There is no such thing as Bad Sex,' she [Bette Midler] tells her audience sagely, 'just people who don't fit together.'" 2005 Arthur Elmo Jackson, *Confessions of a Bumbling Sex*

*Addict* (College Station TX: Virtualbookworm .com) 83–84: "Wary though I was, I remembered the immortal words of Frank Sinatra: 'There's no such thing as a good war or a bad piece.'" In the form "There is no such thing as a good war or a bad piece" (*piece* in the slang sense of "woman considered sexually" or "sex act"), the proverb is probably to be understood as a (punning) orthographic anti-proverb based on the much older "There is no such thing as a good war or a bad peace." Cf. "Bad SEX is better than no sex."

## There is no such **thing** as bad weather, only the wrong clothes.

1979 David Wiggins, "Ayer on Monism, Pluralism and Essence," in *Perception and Identity*, edited by G. F. Macdonald (Ithaca NY: Cornell UP) 153 (illustrating the fallacies of "anti-essentialism"): "If it were right to say that there is no such thing as bad weather, only the wrong clothes, then I suppose it might follow that, in some weird sense, tempests were the creatures of our interests." *ODP* 12.

## There is no such **thing** as (You can't have) too much sex.

1961 Paul Goodman, "Pornography, Art & Censorship," *Commentary* 31: 210: "It is said that the pornography artificially stimulates, and no doubt this is true (though there is no evidence that there can be such a thing as 'too much' sex). . . ." 1963 Lesley Styles, *The Outer Gate* (Adelaide: Rigby) 39: "I bet your family crest bears the words, 'Ain't no such thing as too much sex.' In Latin. And in neon lights." 1969 LeMon Clark, "Your Personal Questions Answered," *Sexology* 36, no. 2 (Sep.) 42: "At any rate, there is no such thing as 'too much sex,' and no amount of sexual activity will debilitate a person." The proverb is perhaps patterned after the older proverb "There's no such thing as too much money." Cf. "There is no such THING as bad sex" and the older "You can't have too much of a good thing."

## There is no such **thing** as winning second place (prize); there's just winning and losing.

See "There is no second PLACE."

## They don't make **things** like they used to.

1959 George Garrett, "3 Fabliaux," *Transatlantic Review* 1: 110: "Jack is in the kitchen . . . and he's got the washing machine disemboweled and parts of the motor spread all over the floor.—I tell you, Jack says, they just don't make things like they used to. Look at that mess!" Frequently the complaint will specify a category of poorly made "things" or substitute the pronoun *them*.

## **Things** always take longer than you expect.

See "Everything TAKES longer than it should."

## **Things** are just things (It's just stuff; It's just things).

1929 Sidney Hook, "What Is Dialectic?" *Journal of Philosophy* 25: 85: "There is no sense in arguing or disputing about things, Adler's position implies, since things are just things, and that's all there is to it" (there the locution occurs in a metaphysical discussion—not proverbially). 1953 Saul Bellow, *Adventures of Augie March* (New York: Viking) 525: "'He was the one that gave you the coat? . . . And the car? . . . And all the things in the house?' '. . . Why, it's just stuff. It's only you that matters.' Gradually she calmed me." 1955 Virginia Brown, "Is Getting Ahead Worth It?" *Farm Journal* 79 (Feb.) 98: "We saved everything for the bank account. Now we are sitting pretty—on our front porch. Things are just things. We don't seem to want them . . ." 1972 Neil Simon, *Prisoner of Second Avenue* (New York: Random House; the play was first performed in 1971) 28 (the main characters' dwelling has been robbed): "It's just things, Mel. Just some old suits and coats. We can replace them. We'll buy new ones." As a proverb, the locution refers to the essential unimportance of material belongings, such as might be lost through misfortune.

## Things are not what they used to be— and they never were.

[1912] Luther Munday, *A Chronicle of Friendships* (London: T. Werner Laurie) 177: "Ah well! if things are not what they used to be, at least it is consoling that they never were." 1917 *Munsey's Magazine* 60: 453 (verses titled "The Poet Speaks," attributed to Lyon Mearson): "The truth is plain, it seems to me— / Things are not what they used to be; / And perhaps I do not err / In saying that they never were." 1927 *Lewiston [ME] Evening Journal* 30 Jun. (a news report about a lecture): "His subject was, 'Things are not as they used to be and never were.'" The proverb originated as an anti-proverb based on the old lament "Things are not what they used to be." Cf. "The PAST is not what it used to be."

## Things turn up for a man who digs.

1920 Edward Earle Purinton, *Triumph of the Man Who Acts* (New York: Robert M. McBride) 289: "Prepare by action. Things turn up for the man who digs." 1922 *Chicago Tribune* 2 Mar. (a prize-winning "best motto" contributed by a student-reader): "Things turn up for the man who digs." The proverb may have originated as a variant of the older proverb "Things don't turn up; they must be turned up."

## Think big **things**.

"See "THINK. big "

## Whether you think you can do a **thing** or not, you are probably right.

See "Whether you THINK you can or not, you are probably right."

## You can never do merely (just, only) one **thing**.

1963 Garrett Hardin, "The Cybernetics of Competition," *Perspectives in Biology and Medicine* 7, no. 4 (Autumn) 80: "The moral of the myth [a narrative of the magically granted three wishes] can be put in various ways. One: wishing won't make it so. Two: every change has its price. Three (and this one I like the best): we can never do merely one thing. Wishing to kill insects, we may put an end to the singing of birds. Wishing to 'get there faster,' we insult our lungs with smog." *YBQ* Hardin (1). In *Living within Limits* (New York: Oxford UP, 1993) 199–201, Hardin traces the tradition and background of the principle that the proverb encapsulates, which came to be called "Hardin's Law"—but Hardin himself prefers to think of it as the "First Law of Ecology."

## You don't know a good **thing** till it's gone (you've lost it, you lose it).

See "You never KNOW what you have till it's gone."

## **Think** big (big thoughts, big things).

1907 [C. D. Kellogg], "Another Year Begun," *Railway Conductor* 24: 32: ". . . [I]f we think little thoughts we are apt to be little, if we think big thoughts, of big things, we are apt to grow larger. . . ." 1907 "One Reason Some of Us Don't Succeed," *Agricultural Advertising* 16: 356 (beginning of the essay): "Think big things. Do not let yourself become so wrapped up in the trifling details that your vision is obscured as regards the larger—broader possibilities." 1911 Guy Potter Benton, "Education and the State" (inaugural address as president of the University of Vermont), *U.V.M. Notes* 8, no. 1 (Nov.) 23: "We must think big if we are to accomplish big things." 1914 "Thinking Big in Medicine," *Medical Council* 19: 126: "And it is becoming increasingly evident that the whole profession must think big if medicine is to hold its place in the march of world progress."

**Think** globally, act locally (Think global, act local).

1942 W. H. Cameron, "Personal Challenge," *Safety Education* 21: 387: "Our vision of a better world is limited to our vision of better communities. We must think globally, but first act locally" (the words are said to be quoted from Edgar Dale, in the Feb. 1942 issue of the newsletter of the Bureau of Educational Research, Ohio State University). 1947 *Vidette-Messenger [Valparaiso IN]* 27 Mar. (quoting from a letter from Jane Sense): ". . . [T]he objective and slogan of the right worthy grand matron and the general grand chapter [of the Indiana Order of the Eastern Star]: 'World Friendship' and 'think globally, act locally.'" *YBQ* Dubos; *ODP* 316–17; Rees (2006) 665.

**Think** long, think wrong.

See "STUDY long, study wrong."

Whether you **think** you can or not, you are probably right.

1949 Percy Roy Hayward, *This Business of Living* (New York: Association) 23: "She was getting at what someone meant in saying, whether you think you can or can't, *you are right!*" (italics as shown). 1965 "Thoughts" (a collection of sayings), *Think* 31, no. 3 (May–Jun.) 32: "Whether you believe you can do a thing or not, you are right." 1968 Richard R. Gariépy, *Your Child Is Dying to Learn* (Barre MA: Barre) 46 (filler item): "Whether you think you can, or whether you think you can't . . . you are right!" (ellipsis dots as shown). 1972 Elmer L. Towns, *America's Fastest Growing Churches* (Nashville TN: John T. Benson) 116: "He [Rev. Bob Moore] points to the motto of Henry Ford as a good criterion [*sic*] for his mental attitude toward growth, 'Whether or not you think you can, you're right.'" 1973 Robert H. Schuller, *You Can Become the Person You Want to Be* (New York: Hawthorn) 40: "Henry Ford said, 'Think you can, think you can't: either way you'll be right.' Be careful of what you imagine yourself

becoming." There exist no apparent grounds for the frequent attribution to Ford.

You can't **think** (talk) black and (if you) sleep white.

1969 Fletcher Knebel, *Trespass* (Garden City NY: Doubleday) 103: "Sure, maybe some black men would like a go at you. We gotta line for that kind. We say, 'They talk black and sleep white.' . . . Me, I'm black all the way. . . . I won't soil my hands on a honky body. I think black and I sleep black." 1971 Sophia F. McDowell, "Black-White Intermarriage in the United States," in *Intermarriage in a Comparative Perspective*, edited by Ruth S. Cavan and Jordan T. Cavan, special issue of *International Journal of Sociology of the Family* 1 (May) 52: "Today, among those who are ideologically Black, there is [*sic*] scorn and charges of race disloyalty against colleagues who 'talk Black and sleep White.'" 1973 Carolyn Jetter Greene, *70 Soul Secrets of Sapphire* (San Francisco: Sapphire) [fol. 40r] (unpaginated; no. 34): "[Sapphire] has no respect for Black men who talk black and sleep white" ("Sapphire," as the book's introduction explains, is a generic "jive name used to refer to a Black woman"). 1989 Nathan Hare and Julia Hare, *Crisis in Black Sexual Politics* (San Francisco: Black Think Tank) 92: "Many Black females [in the late 1960s] raised the question to their Black male: 'how can you think Black and sleep White?'" The African American proverb suggests that amorously consorting with a white person will compromise one's psychological or ideological "blackness."

It's the **thought** that counts.

1907 Charles Fillmore, "Bible Lessons," *Unity: A Monthly Magazine Devoted to Practical Christianity* 27: 17–18: "Do not have anything to do with destructive thoughts in mind or in form. This carried to the ultimate will make you an abstainer from all food that has been wantonly killed. It is the *thought* that counts" (italics as shown). 1914 Harris Franklin Rall, *New Testament History* (New York: Abingdon) 310: "The early writers are very careful to quote the exact words of the Old Testament. Not so with the writings of the New Testament. Here it is the thought that counts, not the words." 1922 B. L., "It's Not So Much the Gift—It's the Thought That Counts," *Life Magazine* 80 (28 Dec.) 29 (title of article). *MP* T87; *YBQ* Modern Proverbs (91); Galef (1993). The proverb is often used as a sort of apology for a seemingly unsatisfactory gift or a carelessly phrased utterance.

## A kind **thought** is never lost.

1914 Ardelia M. Barton, *Short Sermons for Myself* (San Francisco: Philopolis) 23: "In giving material things we may wound a sensitive heart sometimes but a kind thought is never lost. . . ." *DAP* 593(1). Cf. "It's the THOUGHT that counts."

## Think big **thoughts**.

See "THINK big."

## The **thrill** (rush) is worth the risk.

1936 *Portsmouth [OH] Times* 16 Feb. (quoting Helen Wills Moody on fox hunting): "Every once in a while, you hear of someone taking a bad fall—breaking their necks or crippling themselves. But the thrill is worth the risk." 1981 Grace Lichtenstein, *Machisma: Women and Daring* (Garden City NY: Doubleday) 119: "A true daredevil, however, experiences the eleation in the midst of the act itself, and determines that the 'rush' or 'thrill' is worth the risk again." 1999 *Sun [Baltimore]* 10 Sep. (headline "Is the Rush Worth the Risk?"): "The accidents have cast a harsh light on roller coasters and made many folks wonder if the rush is worth the risk." 2002 *Korea Times* 8 Feb.: "With their noses mere inches from the ice, there is little to protect the ['skeleton'] racers if they make a mistake. However, many of the competitors say the adrenaline rush is worth the risk." 2009 Judy Dutton, *How We Do It: How the Science of Sex Can Make You a Better Lover* (New York: Random House) 228: ". . . [F]ans of edgeplay argue that

with training and by taking some necessary precautions, these activities can remain fairly safe—and that the rush is worth the risk."

## If you don't buy a **ticket**, you can't win the raffle.

See "You can't win the RAFFLE if you don't buy a ticket."

## You buy the **ticket**, you see the show (take the ride).

1977 *Boston Globe* 15 May: "They could alter the terms of the merger. . . . But there would probably be some sentiment against that among established NBA clubs, who subscribe to a buy-the-ticket-take-the-ride philosophy." 1988 Angela Neumann Clubb, *Love in the Blended Family* (Toronto: NC Press) 20–21: "I realize now that my friend still operated under some very unyielding values . . . with the message, 'You've made your bed, now lie in it,' or 'When you buy a ticket, you see the show.'" 1988 Hunter S. Thompson, *Generation of Swine* (New York: Simon & Schuster) 10: "Buy the ticket, take the ride. I have said that before, and I have found, to my horror, that it's true." The proverb asserts that one must accept the consequences of decisions.

## It's only when the **tide** goes out that you see who's swimming naked.

1988 Hoare Govett, "The Next Agony for American Banks," *The Economist* 306, no. 7539 (27 Feb.) 66: "As Mr. [George] Salem says: 'You don't know if someone is swimming naked until the tide goes out.' The tide is still in." 1989 *Rock Hill [SC] Herald* 4 Feb.: "As the comptroller of the currency, Robert Clarke, says of bank failures, 'When the economic tide goes out, you find out who is swimming naked.'" 1993 "Avoiding the Wreckage," *U.S. News & World Report* 114, no. 24 (21 Jun.) 50: ". . . Warren Buffett reached for a typically whimsical image: 'It's only when the tide goes out that you learn who's been swimming naked.'" 1998 Mortimer B. Zuckerman, "Happy New Year to All," *U. S. News & World Report* 124, no. 1 (13 Jan.) 68: "Federal Reserve Chairman Alan Greenspan on the financial difficulties of Korea: 'It is only when the tide goes out that you see who has been swimming naked.'" The attribution to Buffett is most common.

## A rising **tide** lifts all boats (ships).

1915 *Charlotte [NC] Observer* 26 Sep.: "'The rising tide lifts all ships.' A direct plan for improvement by every Christian Endeavor society is to identify itself with all union movements. A sense of solidarity in fellowship and service increases the 'esprit de corps.'" 1916 H. D. Chase et al., "Woman's Home Missionary Society," *Minutes of the One Hundred and Seventeenth Session of the New York Conference of the Methodist Episcopal Church . . . March 22, 1916*, 101: "Wherever there is an active, interested, wide-awake Woman's Missionary Organization there will be found . . . a permeating spirit of the Christ-love that is most helpful. 'The rising tide lifts all boats.'" *RHDP* 286; *YBQ* J. F. Kennedy (26); *ODP* 269.

## A **tie** is like kissing your sister.

1953 *Washington Post* 9 Nov.: "Navy coach Eddie Erdelatz came up with a classic definition for a tie [*sic*] football game . . . —'It's like kissing your sister.'" *YBQ* Erdelatz. The image itself had been anticipated: 1931 *Lime Springs [IA] Sun Herald* 15 Oct.: "Listening to a radio service is like kissing your sister, it fails to give the proper stimulation."

## Always leave (quit) while you're still having a good **time**.

See "Always leave the PARTY while you're still having fun."

## The best **time** to fish is when they are biting.

See "You've got to FISH while they are biting."

## Hard **times** make a monkey blow fire.

See "MONKEYS in hard times eat red peppers."

## If you can't do the **time**, don't do the crime.

See "Don't do the CRIME if you can't do the time."

## It's not how many **times** you get knocked down that matters but how many times you get back up.

1954 R. J. Minney, *Viscount Southwood* (London: Oldhams) 177: "His speeches [those of J. S. Elias, Lord Southwood (1873–1979)] were always playful, but embedded in them were maxims which are still remembered: . . .'Success depends on your ability to get up again after a fall. It doesn't matter how many times you are knocked down; if you are able to get up, you're all right.'" 1966 *Baltimore Afro-American* 20 Sep. (quoting Emmett Ashford, one of the first African American baseball umpires in the American League): "I've been knocked down a few times along the way. I think they wanted to see how I'd react. But after all, it's not how many times you get knocked down; it's how you get up." Cf. "To win, you only have to get up one more TIME than you fall down" and "FAILURE is not falling down but staying down."

## Once seen is better than a hundred **times** heard.

1947 Holger Cahill, *Look South to the Polar Star* (New York: Harcourt, Brace) 78: "Don't ask me about it now. Wait until tomorrow morning. Once seen is better than a hundred times heard." 1985 Roy McConkey, *Working with Parents* (London: Croom Helm) 253 (epigraph at the head of the chapter "Learning through Video"):

"'*To be seen once, is better than hearing a hundred times.*' (Chinese Proverb)" (italics as shown). *MP* S88. Cf. "One PICTURE is worth a thousand words," "SHOW beats tell," and the much older "Seeing is believing."

## Take **time** to smell the flowers (roses).

See "Stop and smell the FLOWERS."

## There comes a **time** in the life of a statesman when he must rise above principle.

See "In POLITICS a man must learn to rise above principle."

## Time flies when you're having fun.

1939 George S. Kaufman and Moss Hart, *The Man Who Came to Dinner* (New York: Random House) 179: "Just the family circle gathering at Christmas. (*A look at his watch*) My, how time flies when you're having fun" (italics as shown). Rees (1995) 122. The proverb elaborates on the very old "Time flies."

## Time spent wishing is time wasted.

1922 Gus Kahn, "Carolina in the Morning" (song): "Wishing is good time wasted." 1995 *The Independent [London]* 4 May: "This is not 30 years ago, and time spent wishing it was is wasted time." 2004 *Sunday Independent [Dublin]* 18 Jan.: "Time spent wishing is time truly wasted. And money too."

## The **time** to shoot (catch) bears is when they are out (around).

1914 *Chicago Tribune* 27 Jun. (in a classified ad for bungalows "in charming Oak Lawn"): "The time to shoot bears is when bears are around" (presumably meaning that such desirable domiciles are seldom available). *DAP* 40. Cf. "Go hunting where the DUCKS are" and "Fish where the FISH are."

## Time wounds all heels.

1938 Frank Case, *Tales of a Wayward Inn* (New York: Frederick A. Stokes) 232: ". . . [T]ime eventually catches up with them and they live to regret their evil ways. What I always say is, Time wounds all heels." 1940 In the motion picture *Go West*, Groucho Marx (perhaps ad-libbing) utters the proverb. *MP* T144. It originated as an anti-proverb based on "Time heals all wounds."

## Time you enjoy wasting is not (always) wasted time.

1912 Marthe Troly-Curtin, *Phrynette Married* (London: Grant Richards) 256: "'Your father, for instance, don't you think he would have done three times as much work if it had not been for your—what shall I say—"bringing up"?' 'He liked it—time you enjoy wasting is not wasted time.'" 1912 *Ashburton [New Zealand] Guardian* 18 Dec. (among "Thoughts for the Day"): "Time you enjoy wasting is not wasted time." 1920 *Washington Post* 27 Oct. (among "Words of Wise Men"): "Time you enjoy wasting isn't always wasted time." The proverb represents a prevalent twentieth-century formulation of older commonplaces asserting that time spent on certain seemingly idle pursuits is not "wasted."

## Tough **times** are temporary; failure (quitting) is forever.

See "PAIN is temporary; failure is forever."

## Tough (Hard, Difficult) **times** call for tough (hard, difficult) decisions (choices).

1955 P. J. Young, *Boot and Saddle* (Cape Town: Maskew Miller) 28: Finally, he voluntarily proposed to go himself to his disobedient subjects and fetch the cattle. No one could see what lay ahead; difficult times call for difficult decisions. . . ." 1979 *Import of Fuel Shortages during Harvest: Hearings before the Committee on Agriculture . . . Senate* (Washington DC:

Government Printing Office) 101; Jim Wooten testifies: "These are tough times and call for tough decisions. Congress must be willing to make those decisions and level with the American people." 1985 *Chicago Tribune* 28 Oct.: "Tough times call for tough decisions. . . . For the first time since 1914, the U.S. is now a debtor nation. . . ." Cf. the older "Desperate times call for desperate measures."

## Tough **times** don't last; tough people do.

1983 Robert H. Schuler, *Tough Times Never Last, but Tough People Do* (Nashville: Thomas Nelson). In chapter 1, the evangelist Schuler recounts his impromptu invention of the expression during a 1982 lecture.

## Tough **times** make monkeys eat red peppers.

See "MONKEYS in hard times eat red peppers."

## To win, you only have to get up one more **time** than you fall down.

1941 *Evening Citizen [Ottawa, Ontario]* 24 Sep. (quoting the boxer Lou Nova): "We'll probably both go down, maybe more than once. But I'll get up one more time than Joe [Louis], and that's the one that counts." 1953 *Chicago Tribune* 9 Dec. (among miscellaneous tidbits, this one titled "Such Is Life"—presumably versified): "There's only one rule for success . . . That's all . . . Get up one more time . . . Than you fall" (attributed to "The Barber's Wife"; ellipsis dots as shown— apparently to represent line endings). 1993 Gladiola Montana, *Never Ask a Man the Size of His Spread: A Cowgirl's Guide to Life* (Layton UT: Gibbs Smith) 106 (an uncontextualized saying): "To win, all you gotta do is get up one more time than you fall down." Cf. "It's not how many TIMES you get knocked down that matters but how many times you get back up" and "FAILURE is not falling down but staying down."

## When it's **time** to go, it's time to go.

1936 Negley Farson, *The Way of a Transgressor* (New York: Harcourt, Brace) 59: "'Don't argue,' he was saying, 'when I say it's time to go, it's time to go.'" 1975 *Los Angeles Times* 1 Jun.: "He likes to play too much. When it's time to go, it's time to go. 'My friend, Ruben, be ready to go in seven, seven or less.'" Cf. "When you've got to GO, you've got to go." The proverb "When it's time to go, it's time to go" usually refers to dying or, literally, to departure from a meeting or a social gathering, whereas "When you've got to go, you've got to go" very often refers, at least glancingly, to urinating or defecating.

## **Timing** is everything (It's all about timing; Everything is timing).

See "LIFE is timing."

## You have to kiss a lot of **toads** before you find a prince.

See "You have to kiss a lot of FROGS to find a prince."

## Don't chew your **tobacco** twice.

1937 Paul Green, *Johnny Johnson* (New York: Samuel French) 159: "Gentlemen, we've passed this covenant once and let's let it stay passed. As Johnny says, don't chew your tobacco twice." Whiting (1952) 487 lists the saying as a North Carolina proverb. *DAP* 601(1). Figuratively, the proverb means "Don't repeat yourself" or "Don't ponder overly long." The proverbial phrase "chew (one's) tobacco twice" may be older than the actual proverb.

## **Today** (This, Tomorrow) is the first day of the rest of your life.

1968 *Helena [MT] Independent Record* 29 Jan.: "The colorful fluorescent posters lining the walls of the crowded Student Union theatre bore such messages as: . . . 'Today is the first day of the rest of your life.'" 1968 *Vocational*

*Education Amendments of 1968: Hearings before the General Subcommittee on Education . . . House of Representatives* (Washington DC: Government Printing Office) 1070; written statement by Donald F. Fowler: "Where does the future begin? Maurie Reetz has a definition of the future—'Today marks the first day of the rest of our lives.'" 1968 *Chicago Tribune* 7 Jul.: "Eve [Arden] has a favorite saying that she finds helpful. 'It's a marvelous phrase,' she said, quoting it. 'Today is the first day of the rest of my life.'" 1969 *The Blade [Toledo OH]* 10 Feb.: ". . . Lou Thomson, Jr., was impressed by this sign on a wall at old Heidelberg College in Tiffin [OH]: 'Tomorrow is the first day of the rest of your life.'" 1969 C. C. Courtney and Peter Link, *Salvation* (title of a song in the stage musical): "Tomorrow Is the First Day of the Rest of Your Life." *YBQ* Abbie Hoffman (1); Rees (1984) 62; Hoffman and Honeck (1987); Keyes (1992) 39; Pickering et al. (1992) 611; Rees (1995) 470; Room (2000) 697–98.

**Today** is the tomorrow that you worried about (dreaded, dreamed about) yesterday.

1910 William C. Hunter, *Brass Tacks* (Chicago: Reilly & Lee) 72 (the book is a collection of "optimistic" sayings): "Today is the tomorrow you worried about yesterday, and that dreadful thing didn't happen, did it?" *DAP* 601(10).

The **toes** you step on today may be attached (connected) to the ass you have to kiss tomorrow.

1999 Bruce Klatt, *Ultimate Training Workshop Handbook* (New York: McGraw-Hill) 448: "Timing is important. Thus a quip like, 'Be careful who's [sic] toes you step on today, they may be connected to the ass you have to kiss tomorrow' is funny if it's timed right." Casselman (2002) 55.

**Tomorrow** is the first day of the rest of your life.

See "TODAY is the first day of the rest of your life."

If the only **tool** you have is a hammer, everything will look like a nail.

See "When all you have is a HAMMER, everything looks like a nail."

You can't put **toothpaste** back in the tube.

1936 Jay Dratler, *Manhattan Side Street* (New York: Longmans, Green) 318: "It would be as hopeless as . . . well . . . trying to put toothpaste back into the tube" (ellipsis dots as shown). 1939 "Charivaria," *Punch* 196: 29: "Stand outside the Bank of England at night and watch the home-going crowds oozing like toothpaste into the tube railway" (quoted from the *Daily Express. Punch's* response:) "So it *is* possible to get toothpaste back into the tube?" (italics as shown). *YBQ* Haldeman. Cf. the older "You can't put the bullet back in the gun."

It is lonely at the **top**.

1930 A. F. C., "Backstage in Washington," *Outlook and Independent* 156, no. 11 (12 Nov.) 411: "Though it is not generally known, or even suspected, Vice-President [Charles] Curtis has discovered that it is always lonely at the top." 1931 [Ray Thomas Tucker], *The Mirrors of 1932* (New York: Brewer, Warren & Putnam) 161: "A man can be lonely—or indulge his loneliness—at the top, as Mr. [Herbert] Hoover demonstrates." *YBQ* Modern Proverbs (56).

If it is wet and not yours, don't **touch** it.

1996 Laura K. Hamilton, "Sparkle Plenty," in *Early Embraces*, edited by Lindsey Elder (Los Angeles: Alyson) 96: "Amid a general conversation about AIDS, I repeated for the group the safe-sex advice I had heard: 'If it's wet and it's not yours, don't touch it.'" 1998 *Salt Lake*

*City [UT] Tribune* (1 Mar.): "If it's wet and not yours, don't touch it with your bare hands, Dye instructs [prison guard] cadets, all of whom wear rubber gloves."

## He who dies with the most **toys** still dies.

1993 *New York Times* 16 Aug.: "The young people, who had come to Denver for World Youth Day, wore T-shirts that read, 'Life is Short—Pray Hard'; 'Whoever Dies With The Most Toys—Still Dies.' . . ." The proverb originated as an anti-proverb based on "Whoever dies with the most TOYS wins."

## Whoever dies with the most **toys** wins.

1983 *New York Times* 9 May: "Dozens of people congregated around BG's car, its hood propped open by his trophy, with lettering across the radiator top that read: 'Those who die with the most toys win.'" 1983 George R. R. Martin, *The Armageddon Rag* (New York: Simon & Schuster) 185: "You can't do diddly-shit in this world, Blair, and neither can I. So why tear ourselves up about it? Get drunk, get laid, get rich. He who dies with the most toys wins."

## **Tragedy** (Every tragedy) is an opportunity.

1978 Daniel C. Maguire, *The Moral Choice* (Garden City NY: Doubleday) 363: "The tragic experience introduces a new horizon. . . . In this sense, tragedy is an opportunity and may be an opening to creativity." 1992 *CBS Evening News* (transcript), 15 Sep.: "As with every tragedy, there's an opportunity." Cf. "A CRISIS is an opportunity."

## There's no stopping the **train** (once it leaves the station) (There is no boarding the train once it leaves the station).

1915 *The Freeman [Indianapolis IN]* 23 Oct.: "The case [to enjoin the showing of the film *Birth of a Nation*] has been in court more than a month, but the same thing has been said, 'You can't catch the train after it leaves the station.'" 1944 Halford E. Luccock, *In the Minister's Workshop* (New York: Abingdon-Cokesbury) 191: "The only kind of humor which, in sermons, is more than, at its best, an interruption and, at its worst, an impertinence is that which is struck off incidentally while the preacher is moving directly on his way, just as sparks are struck off by the wheels of a railroad engine while it is going to a destination. There is no stopping the train for the purpose of showing off the sparks." 1956 E. C. V. Foucar, *I Lived in Burma* (London: Dennis Dobson) 68: "There is nothing as terrifying as an earthquake. . . . There is no stopping the train. In a moment it will overwhelm everything and everyone."

## When you get hit by a **train**, it isn't the caboose that kills you.

1992 Peter Holmes and Peggy Holmes, *Out of the Ashes* (Minneapolis: Deaconess) 178: "'When you get run over by a train, it's not the caboose that kills you.'—A. A. [Alcoholics Anonymous] axiom. / For an addicted smoker, lighting a cigarette is not just lighting a cigarette." 1993 Kenneth K. Gorman, "Addicted and Disabled: One Man's Journey from Helplessness to Hope," in *Substance Abuse and Physical Disability*, edited by Allen W. Heinemann (New York: Haworth) 15: "There's a saying that when you get hit by a train, it's not the caboose that kills you. So, I do not take the first drink."

## You cannot tell which way the **train** went (is going) by looking at the tracks.

1977 Stuart A. Sandow, *Durations* (New York: New York Times) 293 (citation in the bibliography): "Sandow, Stuart A., 'You Can't Tell Which Way the Train Went Just by Looking at the Tracks' privately published by the author, 1973." 1980 Suzette Haden Elgin, *The Gentle Art of Verbal Self Defense* (Englewood Cliffs NJ: Prentice-Hall) 275: "If I knew where I learned it, I would credit its author, but I first heard it years and years ago. It is a totally empty Popular Wisdom line that means nothing at all and goes like this: 'You can't tell which way the train went by looking at the tracks.'"

## All **trash** goes before (out with) the broom.

1920 "A Happy Little Girl," *Herald and Presbyter* 91, no. 18 (5 May) 16: "There's the old man that sweeps the crossings. . . . He always tells me that all trash goes before the broom and pretends he is going to sweep me out of the way." 1949 Henry Hornsby, *Lonesome Valley* (New York: William Sloan) 63: "'You better take care,' she warned him. 'All trash goes before the broom.' That was an old saying, when people got in the way of a broom." *DAP* 608.

## If you fool (play) with **trash**, it will get (blow) in your eyes.

1953 Ruby Berkley Goodwin, *It's Good to Be Black* (Garden City NY: Doubleday) 145: "Without so much as another look at Bristol she pulled us along saying loudly enough for him to hear, 'Let's go. Mama always told me if you fool with trash it would fly in your eyes.'" *DAP* 608(3); Prahlad (1996) 254; Prahlad (2001) 269. Whiting (1952) 489 gives the analogous "If you associate with trash, you'll flounder with trash." The word *trash* in the proverb commonly signifies "person(s) of low moral standing or low social class"—with the implication that associating with such a person will "lower" one.

## Every family **tree** has a nut on it.

See "There's a NUT on every family tree."

## The **tree** of crime bears bitter fruit.

See "The WEED of crime bears bitter fruit."

## The **trend** is your friend (Trend is friend).

1983 *American Banker* 18 Jul.: "At the Geldermann Group, the sage advice was not to fight the markets. 'The trend is your friend,' analysts there advised their customers." 2002 *Desert News [Salt Lake City UT]* 7–8 Aug.: "This type of movement is called a trend, and in FOREX [the parlance of the Foreign Currency Exchange], A Trend Is A Friend."

## Either make light of your **troubles** or keep them in the dark.

1941 *Wall Street Journal* 11 Mar. (in a small collection of witty sayings): "If you can't make light of your troubles, keep them in the dark." *DAP* 613.

## If you can't dodge **trouble**, step on the gas.

See "When the GOING gets tough, step on the gas."

## It's easier to stay out of **trouble** than to get out of trouble.

1920 "Financial Conditions of Gas Companies Dependent upon Meter Efficiency," *American Gas Engineering Journal* 113: 505: "R. E. Davis . . . said in part: Speaking of meters and the care of them, it is well to bear in mind that it is much easier to stay out of trouble than to get out of trouble. The mill will never never grind with the water that has passed and a meter will never register the gas that has by-passed." *DAP* 612.

## Pack up your **troubles**.

1915 The saying probably entered oral tradition as a proverb from the song by George Asaf, "Pack up your troubles in an old kit-bag, / And smile, smile, smile." *DAP* 612(18); Prahlad (2001) 270.

**Trouble** loves company.

1909 *New York Tribune* 10 Dec. (headline to
a brief article about difficulties encountered
by Tammany Hall "boss" Charles T. Murphy):
"Trouble Loves Company" (the article ends,
"Misfortunes never come singly"). 1947 Mary
Overholt Peters, "Talks with Beginning Social
Workers," *Journal of Social Casework* 28: 225: ". . .
[M]ost of those who come to you are in trouble.
It may be only a financial difficulty, but trouble
loves company and rarely travels alone." *DAP*
612(29). Cf. the older "Misery loves company"
and "Troubles never come singly (always come in
bunches)."

**Trouble** never sets like rain.

Anderson and Cundall (1910) 45 give the saying
as a Jamaican proverb: "Trouble neber set like
rain," with the gloss "In Jamaica rain is usually
seen long before it comes. Trouble hardly ever
gives warning"—perhaps construing *set* to mean
something like "have its onset." Beckwith (1925)
III gives an alternative interpretation, taking *set*
to mean "cease" (as in the "setting" of the sun?):
"'Trouble never ends like rain'; applied to one
who gets himself into trouble by trying to get out
of it." Prahlad (2001) 269–70.

Don't get caught with your **trousers**
down.

See "Don't get caught with your PANTS down."

Keep on **trucking**.

See "KEEP ON trucking."

**Trust** but verify.

1966 Michel Tatu, "Soviet Reforms: The Debate
Goes On," *Problems in Communism* 15, no. 1 (Jan.–
Feb.) 31: "Supplemented by the Khrushchevian
motto, 'Trust but verify' (*dovierat no provierat*),
this attitude leaves agricultural producers [in
the USSR] very little freedom of action." *YBQ*
Modern Proverbs (94). Ironically, the proverb is
often attributed to Ronald Reagan, even though
Reagan himself stated that he had learned it (as a
Russian proverb) from Mikhail Gorbachev.

**Trust** is (must be) earned.

1947 Ross N. Young, *Personnel Manual for
Executives* (New York: McGraw-Hill) 60: "People
will generally talk to those they trust deeply.
That trust must be earned." 1961 *Hartford [CT]
Courant* 28 Nov.: ("Ann Landers" advice column):
"Trust must be earned—and it must be earned
one day at a time."

Never let the **truth** get in the way of
opinions.

See "Never let FACTS get in the way of opinions."

Speak **truth** to power.

1955 *Speak Truth to Power* ([Philadelphia:
American Friends Service Committee]). As a
verb phrase, "speak truth to power" is older, but
the fame of the anonymous Quaker antiwar
pamphlet, with its imperative title, popularized
the expression as a proverb.

Tell the **truth**; it's easier to remember
what you said.

1955 Dean Acheson, letter to President Harry
S. Truman (23 Nov.); in *Among Friends: Personal
Letters of Dean Acheson*, edited by David S.
McLellan and David C. Acheson (New York:
Dodd, Mead, 1980) 108: "However, Bill
Leonard . . . asked me what I thought of Adlai's
announcement of his candidacy. I thought of—
who was it?—Mark Twain's? admonition that it
was better to tell the truth because it was easier
to remember what you said." 1960 *Modesto [CA]
Bee* 27 Nov. (in a collection of witty sayings): "It's
a lot easier to remember what you said when you
tell the truth." 1971 James K. Van Fleet, *How to
Put Yourself Across with People* (West Nyack NY:
Parker) 78: "If you're going to be yourself, you'll
always use the words that really represent you.

Just tell the truth; it's easier to remember what you said when you do."

## The **truth** is out there.

1993 The saying probably entered general oral tradition as a proverb from the television show *The X-Files*, though it may have circulated earlier within groups interested in paranormal occurrences and UFOs. Of course, the sentence can be found in earlier contexts—though not with the sense in which it became proverbial in the 1990s, meaning "Enigmas remain to be solved" or "The usual explanations or reassurances (especially 'official' ones) are not to be credited." *YBQ* Television Catchphrases (89).

## **Truth** is the first casualty of war (The first casualty of war is truth).

1915 Mrs. Philip Snowden, "Women and War," *Journal of Proceedings and Addresses of the National Education Association* 53: 55: "Someone has finely said that 'truth is the first casualty in war'; and never was a greater untruth spoken than that war is waged for the protection of women and homes." 1916 E. D. Morel, *Truth and the War* (London: National Labour Press) vii: "'Truth,' it has been said, 'is the first casualty of war.'" *DAP* 86; *YBQ* Modern Proverbs (98); *ODP* 328. Currently the proverb is often attributed to Aeschylus, but the attribution seems to be no older than the 1980s.

## Don't **try** to be someone you are not.

1956 Paul Witty, *How to Improve Your Reading* (Chicago: Science Research Associates) 240: "If you need glasses when you read, wear them. Don't try to be someone you are not." 1964 *Kentucky New Era [Hopkinsville]* 22 Jan. (column by Billy Graham): "Be yourself; be natural. Don't try to be someone you are not. God only made one person exactly like you, so you be that person." Cf. the older counsel of sincerity and authenticity "Be yourself."

## You **try** it, you buy it.

1983 *Chicago Tribune* ("North Shore" section) 4 Mar.: "In Morton Grove, if you try it, you buy it. That's what the village board decided this week. . . ."; the reference is to the opening of jars on supermarket shelves. The proverb can have various mercantile applications, among them the display of toys in a store and the presentation of powdered cocaine for sale.

## **Trying** (Trying hard, Working hard, Playing hard) is not (good) enough.

1934 *Daily Times [Rochester PA]* 29 Mar.: "'I can certainly *try* to make Sandra happy.' Arthur shook his head. 'Trying isn't enough, Fred. It's got to be something a whole lot more than that'" (italics as shown). 1936 *Rochester [NY] Journal* 29 Dec. (a poem by Elsie Robinson, titled "Listen, World!"): "Working hard / Isn't enough / In this new world." 1974 *Schenectady [NY] Gazette* 31 May: ". . . [Prospective juror Joseph] Bush responded, 'I can try my best [to remain open-minded].' [District attorney William] Intemann said, 'Trying is not good enough,' and Bush said, 'Then I'd have to say I'm not sure.'" 1983 *Pittsburgh [PA] Press* 14 Jan.: "But [the basketball coach] Roy Chipman knows against the competition in the Big East [athletic conference] . . . , playing hard isn't enough." 1986 *Anchorage [AK] Daily News* 26 Mar. (quoting the baseball manager Jim Leyland): "We've got to start winning for the fans. Playing hard isn't good enough."

## You can't blame someone for **trying**.

See "You can't blame a FELLOW for trying."

## Don't kick a (fresh) **turd** on a hot day.

1980 Merle Miller, *Lyndon: An Oral Biography* (New York: G. P. Putnam's Sons) 541 (quoting Richard Bolling): "Once someone asked him [President Harry S. Truman] what his philosophy of life was. I'll never forget his answer: 'Never kick a fresh turd on a hot day.'" 1997 *BCD*

*[Bankruptcy Court Decisions] News and Comments* 3 Jan.: "Among his [Judge Russell Eisenberg's] other great one liners: . . . 'One of the truths we live with in Wisconsin is that if the day is hot, you never kick a turd.'"

## You can't polish (gild) a **turd**.

1976 Geoffrey Stokes, *Star-Making Machinery* (Indianapolis IN: Bobbs-Merrill) 137: "As one exasperated producer finally screamed to a performer who was complaining about the quality of the mix: 'Listen, you can't polish a turd.'" 1989 *Adweek* 20 Feb.: "Pat Burnham's rules for producing great commercials . . . [:] (1) The production budget can't buy you an idea. (2) The director can't give you an idea. (3) You can't polish a turd." Cf. "You can't sprinkle SUGAR on shit and make it candy."

## There will be some **turkeys** in any group of eagles.

See "In any GROUP of eagles, there will be at least one turkey."

## **Turn** on, tune in (Tune in, turn on), drop out.

1966 Timothy Leary, "The Politics, Ethics, and Meaning of Marijuana," in *The Marihuana Papers*, edited by Alfred R. Lindesmith (Indianapolis IN: Bobbs-Merrill) 88: "And on college campuses and in the art centers of the country hundreds of thousands of the creative young take LSD and millions smoke marijuana to explore their own consciousness. The new cult of visionaries. They turn on, tune in, and often drop out of the academic, professional and other games-playing roles they have been assigned." 1966 *East Village Other* 15 Apr.–1 May: "'The End of the World is coming,' someone kept insisting and Tim Leary said, 'No, don't worry, it's only a party.' Later on stage, after a standing, cheering ovation when he was introduced, he spoke about the younger generation and ended by advising them to, 'TURN ON, TUNE IN, AND DROP OUT'" (capitalization as shown). *YBQ* Leary; Rees (2006) 689–90.

## You can't take the **twist** out of a grapevine by cultivating it.

See "You can tame a GRAPEVINE, but you won't take the twist out of it."

## It takes **two** to tango.

1952 The saying entered oral tradition as a proverb from the song "It Takes Two to Tango," by Al Hoffman and Dick Manning. *RHDP* 171; *DAAP* 805; *YBQ* Al Hoffman; *ODP* 333; Mieder (1983); Mieder (1985) 151–54; Mieder (1988); Mieder (1991); Pickering et al. (1992) 597; Mieder (1993b) 3–17; Chlosta and Grzybek (1995); Rees (1995) 263; Room (2000) 356; Pickering (2001) 358. The proverb may have originated as an anti-proverb based on "It takes two to quarrel."

**Ugly** (Winning ugly) is better than nothing (is better than not winning, is still winning).

1976 Gary Cartwright, "Orange Peril," *Texas Monthly* 4, no. 11 (Nov.) 124: What DKR [former University of Texas football coach Darrell K. Royal] really talks about is how ol' ugly is better than ol' nothing and why the sun don't shine on the same ol' dog's ass every day and how when that big scorekeeper finally comes to write against your name all he really wants to know is who won." 1987 *New York Times* 4 Sep.: "He had learned, however, that winning ugly is better than not winning at all. It is a lesson [Ivan] Lendl learned several years ago." 1987 *Atlanta Constitution* 30 Nov.: "But hey, winning ugly is better than losing ugly. Just ask the Falcons. . . ." 1989 *Wilmington [NC] Morning Star* 22 Sep.

(quoting Mark Rypien): "The bottom line is winning football games. If it's winning ugly, fine, it's still winning." 1989 *Union Democrat [Sonora CA]* 22 Nov.: "If winning ugly is better than losing pretty, then Summerville High's basketball team didn't want to confront any mirrors last night." Cf. "SECOND BEST is better than nothing."

If you leave your **umbrella** at home, it is sure to rain.

1906 Gelett Burgess, *Are You a Bromide?* (New York: B. W. Huebsch) 24: "And this piece of ancient cynicism has run through a thousand changes: '*Of course if you leave your umbrella at home it's sure to rain*'" (italics as shown). *DAP* 623. The proverb can have nonmeteorological applications.

Don't get your **undies** in a twist.

See "Don't get your PANTIES in a twist."

What one is least **up on**, he is apt to be most down on.

See "The MAN most down on a thing is he who is least up on it."

**Use** it up, wear it out, make it do, or do without.

See "EAT it up, wear it out, make it do, or do without."

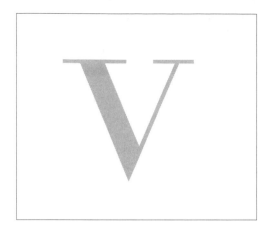

No **victim**, no crime (Where there is no victim, there can be no crime).

1971 *Southeast Missourian [Cape Girardeau]* 23 Oct.: ". . . [T]here is a new wrinkle in the theory of criminal behavior. It says that if there are no victims there is no crime." 1977 *Reform of the Federal Criminal Laws: Hearing before the Subcommittee on Criminal Law and Procedure . . . Senate* (Washington DC: Government Printing Office) 9075 (John Shattuck testifies, 20 Jun.): "The first principle is one that Professor [Alan] Dershowitz alluded to, and that is that where there is no victim, there should be no crime." 1979 *Pittsburgh Press* 1 Mar.: "Citing the legal proposition, 'no victim, no crime,' attorneys for the young men yesterday asked District Magistrate William Ivill to dismiss the charges." Cf. "No BODY, no crime."

**Victory** has a hundred fathers, but defeat is an orphan.

See "SUCCESS has many fathers, but failure is an orphan."

To see the **view** (If you want to see the view), you have to climb the mountain (If you do not climb the mountain, you cannot see the view).

1945 Robert Ormond Case and Victoria Case, *Last Mountains: The Story of the Cascades* (Garden City NY: Doubleday, Doran) 109: "These eyes that must remain forever empty of the view were scorned by the Mazamas, who asserted that anybody who couldn't climb a mountain—or wouldn't climb a mountain—didn't deserve to see the view." 1990 Croft M. Pentz, *Complete Book of Zingers* (Wheaton IL: Tyndale House) 60: "If you don't climb the mountain you can't see the view."

It takes a (whole) **village** to raise a child.

1981 Toni Morrison, "A Conversation with Toni Morrison" (interview by Judith Wilson), *Essence* 12, no. 3 (Jul.) 86: ". . . I don't think one parent can raise a child. I don't think two parents can raise a child. You really need the whole village." 1984 Louise Meriwether, "Teenage Pregnancy," *Essence* 14 (Apr.) 151: "As author Toni Morrison has said, it takes a village to raise a child, not one parent, not two parents, but the whole village." *RHDP* 170; *YBQ* Modern Proverbs (97); Mieder (2011). The saying is often referred to as an "African" or a "West African" proverb; however, no prototype from Africa has been discovered—though several sayings from that continent do urge cooperation in child rearing and other enterprises ("One hand cannot nurse a child," "One finger cannot crush a louse," etc.).

The older the **violin**, the sweeter the tune.

See "The older the FIDDLE, the sweeter the tune."

## You have to pull your own (little red) **wagon**.

1907 *Prescott [AZ] Weekly Courier* 15 Mar.: "'Hitch your wagon to a star' was Emerson's advice. But wouldn't it be better to pull your own wagon yourself and travel in the direction of the star?" 1949 Charles A. Graham and Robert Perkins, "Denver, Reluctant Capital," in *Rocky Mountain Cities*, edited by Ray B. West Jr. (New York: W. W. Norton) 317: "The issue is not where Denver is going; but whether she is going to continue to coast in, or start being a big girl and pull her own little red wagon." 1961 Thomas A. Clark, "Africa Awakening," *Quarterly Review of Higher Education among Negroes* 29: 116: "They cannot rely upon the Europeans to face responsibilities for them. . . . These problems are the young African nations['] 'Little Red Wagon,' they can pull it or push it." 1962 Zenna Henderson, "Shadow on the Moon," *Magazine of Fantasy and Science Fiction* 22, no. 3 (Mar.) 117: "You told me—this is my own little red wagon and I'll find some way of dragging it, even if a wheel comes off along the way."

## If greedy **waits**, hot will cool.

See "If GREEDY waits, hot will cool."

## *Wait* broke the wagon down (broke the mule's back, broke the camel's back).

1936 *Philadelphia Tribune* 16 Jan.: "Don't wait but do it now as weight broke the wagon down."

1986 *Atlanta Constitution* 2 Nov.: "And besides, as the old-timers were quick to tell you, 'wait' is what broke the wagon down." 1994 Jan Karon, *At Home in Mitford* (Colorado Springs CO: Lion) 32: "'I don't know that this is what we need to do just now. I think we should wait on that.' 'Wait? Wait was what broke the camel's back!'" 1998 Daryl Dance, *Honey, Hush* (New York: W. W. Norton) 88 (in a list of sayings titled "Sister to Sister"): "Wait for you! I don't wait. Weight broke the mule's back / Weight broke the wagon down" (virgule as shown). *DAP* 648; Prahlad (1996) 186. The proverb is mostly used as a punning remonstration to being asked to *wait*. The "camel's back" variant has perhaps been influenced by the proverbial "last straw that broke the camel's back."

## If you can **walk**, you can dance.

1940 Drayton E. Marsh, "'If You Can Walk—You Can Dance': A Social Dance Plan for Pupils," *Clearing House* 15: 243: "They had learned to know each other and had found out that those boys and girls with whom they only spoke casually were really nice people. Simple. 'If you can walk, you can dance.'" 1947 "In One Easy Lesson," *Negro Digest* 5, no. 9 (Jul.) 40: "But for dancing, it's 'Walk-'em' rhythm that brings in the customers and sells records, no matter what the tune. 'If you can walk you can dance' is still a fine slogan as far as Buddy [Johnson] is concerned." *ODP* 338. The proverb is sometimes referred to as African.

## A **walk** is (just) as good as a hit.

1946 Tommy Henrich, "How to Hit," *Boys' Life* 36, no. 7 (Jul.) 20: "Remember the old baseball saying, 'a walk is as good as a hit.'" 1983 Sam Koperwas, *Easy Money* (New York: William Morrow) 46–47: "*Life is funny*, Del repeated to himself. *That is so true, so absolutely right. And God helps those who help themselves. A walk is as good as a hit.* Everything he could think of was wisdom, the experience of generations. . . . *No taxation without representation. What goes up must come down*" (italics as shown). Metaphorically, the proverb from baseball can suggest that different means enable one to reach a goal, and sometimes unspectacular means are just as satisfactory.

### Don't tear down a **wall** unless you are sure why it was put up.

See "Don't take down a FENCE unless you are sure why it was put up."

### If you don't **want** it known, don't do it.

1943 Virginia Armstrong ["Vanya"] Oakes, *White Man's Folly* (Boston: Houghton, Mifflin) 26 (chapter title): "If You Don't Want It Known, Don't Do It." *DAP* 355.

### If you **want** to get along, you have to go along.

See "You've got to GO ALONG to get along."

### It is not what you **want** that makes you fat—it is what you eat (get).

See "It is not what you LIKE that makes you fat."

### In **war** there is no prize for second place (second best, runner-up).

See "There is no second PLACE."

### In **war** there is no substitute for victory.

See "There is no SUBSTITUTE for victory."

### No one (ever) wins a **war**.

1928 *Christian Science Monitor* 9 May: "To serve in peace as we served in war is our present purpose [that of the American Peace Society]. No one ever wins a war." 1931 *Atlanta Constitution* 20 Dec.: "Incidentally we will give the world a great lesson— . . . that wars are uneconomic and that no one ever wins a war." 1940 "In Brief," *American Mercury* 49: 127: "Neither side ever wins a war, insists Warren L. Howell. . . . 'We want the democracy to win' is on the foolish side." 1940 *Kentucky New Era [Hopkinsville]* 4 Jan.: "No one wins a war these days. That is a truism few dispute."

### Someday they will give a **war** and nobody will come.

1936 Carl Sandburg, *The People, Yes* (New York: Harcourt, Brace) 43: "The girl held still and studied [the parading soldiers]. . . . 'Sometime they'll give a war, and nobody will come.'" 1939 *Los Angeles Times* 12 Dec. (quoting from a recent lecture by Alexander Woollcott): "Some day they are going to give a war and nobody will come." 1962 *Spokane [WA] Daily Chronicle* 12 Mar.: "A little girl, after hearing Carl Sandburg describe a Civil War battle, looked up and asked him innocently, 'Suppose they gave a war and no one came?'" 1968 *Ramparts* 6, no. 8 (Mar.) 65 (in an advertisement for inscribed "protest buttons"): "What if they gave a war and nobody came?" *DAAP* 818. Cf. "WAR will cease when men refuse to fight."

### **Wars** are fought one battle at a time.

See "You must fight one BATTLE at a time."

### **Wars** are not started by warriors (Soldiers do not start wars).

1907 James Barr, "Inaugural Address on 'Preventive Medicine, the Medicine of the Future,'" *Journal of the Royal Institute of Public Health* 15: 516: "It is not the mastiff that starts a fight, but a yelping cur. Wars are not started by military men but by politicians and low bred financiers, and some newspaper editors who will never do any fighting themselves. . . ." 1930 William Lyon Phelps, *Essays on Things* (New York: Macmillan) 93: "Although wars are not started by warriors, but only by politicians and tradesmen, . . . there is no doubt that high officers have a ripping time during a great war. . . ." 1971 Walter Cronkite, *Eye on the World* (New York: Cowles) 56: "Soldiers do not start wars; failed politicians and generals do."

## War will cease when men refuse to fight.

1933 Albert Einstein, *The Fight against War*, edited by Alfred Lief (New York: John Day) 37 (excerpted from Einstein's interview with George Sylvester Viereck, Jan. 1931): "I am not only a pacifist but a militant pacifist. I am willing to fight for peace. Nothing will end war unless the peoples themselves refuse to war [*sic*]." 1933 James T. Shotwell et al., *Preliminary Draft of a Survey of the Study of International Relations in the United States* (New York: [Social Science Research Council], mimeographed) 69: "The central philosophy of this organization [War Resisters League] might be summed up as wars will cease when men refuse to fight." Ratcliffe (2006) 330. Cf. "Someday they will give a WAR and nobody will come."

## Warriors do not start wars.

See "WARS are not started by warriors."

## Don't make waves.

1934 "J. Mortimer Hall" (pseudonym), *Anecdota Americana II* (Boston: Humphrey Adams) 187: "Well, for Christ's sake, Pat, be careful not to make any waves when you come in." That plea from the Irishman Pat's deceased friend Mike to Pat, himself newly expired, culminates a joke featuring hell as a pool of raw sewage in which the damned must stand on their tiptoes, with their mouths and noses barely above the surface. In some versions, Satan circles the excremental lake in a motorboat, occasioning an anguished cacophonous chorus of "Don't make waves!" Gershon Legman, in *Rationale of the Dirty Joke*, vol. 2 (New York: Breaking Point, 1975) 944, identified that as "the most popular joke told at the present time in America." 1939 *Palm Beach [FL] Daily News* 2 Feb. (an uncontextualized snippet quoted by—or from?—Arthur "Bugs" Baer): "Here's a little thing we learned that the boys over there might use. When you're in trouble up to your neck don't make waves." 1941

*Washington Post* 6 Jan. (another column by Baer): "I still follow my old formula for not aggravating the inevitable. When you are in trouble to your neck don't make waves." *YBQ* Modern Proverbs (58). It is impossible to determine whether the proverb originally alluded to the joke or the joke was built with the proverb as its punch line.

## The best way to get over someone is to get under (on top of) someone else.

2000 Kim Louise, *Destiny's Song* (Washington DC: BET) 114: "'Jacq, I'm not sure if I'm completely over Rico.' 'Girl, don't you know? The best way to get over someone is to get under someone?'" 2001 Mark Welsh, *Sweetie: From the Gutter to the Runway* (New York: Time Warner) 107 (an allusive adaptation—spoken by a canine fashion model as advice to other female dogs—among "a furry floozy's lessons learned"): "The best way to get over a dog is to get under another one." 2003 *Belfast [UK] News Letter* 22 Jan.: "Everybody wants to cut to the chase these days—or rather the boudoir. The best way to get over a man, is to get under another one." 2006 Elizabeth L. Paul, "Beer Goggles, Catching Feelings, and the Walk of Shame: The Myths and Realities of the Hookup Experience," in *Relating Difficulty*, edited by D. Charles Kirkpatrick et al. (Mahwah NJ: Lawrence Erlbaum) 150: "Another male explained, 'If I have a bad hookup, I'll hook up with someone else. . . . The best way to get over a girl is to get on top of another one.'"

## The best way to kill time is to work it to death.

1914 "Light Verse," *Munsey's Magazine* 52: 464 (a little poem titled "Killing Time," attributed to Faye N. Merriman): "If you want to kill time, / I'll advise you in a rime / How to do it; / It will go in a breath, / If you work it to death! / Now go to it!" 1919 "Quips and Quirks Department," *Western Electric News* 8, no. 4 (Jun.) 32: "If you want to kill time, why don't you work it to death?" *DAP* 597(37).

## The best **way** to make money is to save it (is not to lose it).

1922 "Economy and Thrift," *American Cookery* 27: 350: "This was the burden of advice given recently to the Young Men's Bible Class of the Park Avenue Baptist Church by John D. Rockefeller, Jr. 'The best way to make money is to save it,' he declared." 1923 "The Disadvantages of High-Yield Investments," *Outlook* 134: 196: "As we have many times endeavored to point out, the best way to make money is not to lose it." 1980 Paul Dickson, *The Official Explanations* (New York: Delacorte) 28: "The Easiest Way to Make Money Is to Stop Losing It." Cf. the old "A penny saved is a penny earned."

## The best **way** to rob a bank is to own one.

1986 *Oversight on Civil RICO Suits: Hearings before the Committee on the Judiciary . . . Senate* (Washington DC: Government Printing Office) 213; statement by Daniel W. Persinger (20 May 1985): "Over the past few years, the FDIC has encountered tangible evidence of the harm that can result when certain individuals are willing to translate [*sic*] the following maxims of 'common wisdom' for their own illegal ends: 'The best way to rob a bank is to own it' and 'Borrow a thousand dollars and the bank owns you; borrow a million and you own the bank.'" 1987 *Fraud and Abuse by Insiders, Borrowers, and Appraisers in the California Thrift Industry: Hearing before a Subcommittee of the Committee on Government Operations, House of Representatives* (Washington DC: Government Printing Office) 10; statement by William J. Crawford: "Well, you can steal far more money, and take it out the back door. The best way to rob a bank is to own one. If you have 100 percent control, you can make yourself the chairman of the audit committee. . . ."

## Different **ways** for (on) different days.

1971 Charles E. Wilson, "The Case for Black Studies," in *Curricular Concerns in a Revolutionary Era*, edited by Robert R. Leeper (Washington DC: Association for Supervision and Curriculum Development) 130: "The young people of America . . . speak out against homogenization in their own words. 'There are indeed different strokes for different folks.' 'Different ways on different days.'" 1981 Ron Zemke, Linda Strandke, and Philip Jones, *Designing and Delivering Cost-Effective Training* (Minneapolis MN: Lakewood) 246: ". . . [T]he guideline for finding usable reinforcing stimuli is often characterized by the maxim 'different strokes for different folks and different ways on different days.' Letting the behaver choose his own reinforcer—a process called contracting—is sometimes the only practical solution." As in the quoted instances, the proverb is often paired with the parallel "Different STROKES for different folks."

## The easiest **way** to lose ground is to throw mud (dirt).

See "MUD thrown is lost ground."

## Go all the **way** or don't go at all.

See "GO all the way or don't go at all."

## If you don't know the **way**, walk (go) slowly.

1995 Sean Desmond, *A Touch of the Irish: Wit and Wisdom* (Stamford CT: Longmeadow) 72 (in a list headed "Proverbs"): "If you don't know the way, walk slowly." 1998 Una McManus, *Wild Irish Roses* (Uhrichsville OH: Heartsong Presents) 72: "'Och, it's like the old saying, "If you don't know the way, walk slowly."' 'You and your moldy old maxims!'" 2004 Martin R. Carbone and Matthew Carbone, *Teach the Short Words First* (Carlsbad CA: for the authors) 133 (in a list of "short-word proverbs, aphorisms, quotations and sentences"): "It's good to go slow if you are lost or don't know the way."

## Lead, follow, or get out of the **way**.

1912 Ameen Rihani, "The Crisis of Islam," *The Forum* 47: 568: "'Either lead the way, or get out of the way!' will soon be the cry of Islam to the Turks." 1939 Jack M. Potter, *Cattle Trails of the Old West* (Clayton NM: Leader) 39: "He was the 'follow me or get out of the way kind,' and he has proved that I figured him right as a leader." 1967 *Abilene [TX] Reporter-News* 11 Feb. "[Mayor D. D.] McClatchy said that Olney [TX] has developed a slogan for the people which indicated the spirit of the town. This slogan is 'Either Lead, Follow or Get out of the way.'" Cf. "Push, pull, or get out of the WAY."

## Push, pull, or get out of the **way**.

1909 *Motorcycle Illustrated* 4, no. 13 (1 Jul.) 17 (filler item): "PUSH! If you can't push, PULL—if you can' [*sic*] pull, please get out of the way" (capitalization as shown); attributed to "R. A. Pickens, in Sparks." 1932 A. E. Winters, letter to the editor, *Living Age* 342: 280: "We need everyone these days. Push, pull, or get out of the way!" Cf. "Lead, follow, or get out of the WAY."

## That's the **way** (how) the ball bounces.

1952 Bill Mauldin, *Bill Mauldin in Korea* (New York: W. W. Norton) 150: "We'd say what a shame it is that a new generation of kids have to have their education and their life messed up like we did. But we'd have another drink and say that's the way the ball bounces. . . ." 1952 George Mandel, *Flee the Angry Strangers* (Indianapolis IN: Bobbs-Merrill) 249: "You think you can have everything the way you like it? You have to lean over sometimes. Because that's the way the ball bounces, see?" *MP* W85; *YBQ* Modern Proverbs (4); Lighter (1994– ) 1: 75. Proverbs that follow the "That's the way the <noun> <verbs>" pattern usually express or encourage resignation in the face of difficult circumstances. Cf. the older "That's how the world wags."

## That's the **way** (how) the cookie crumbles.

1955 *Evening Standard [Uniontown PA]* 3 Mar. "With so many different activities going on in the last couple of weeks most everyone is melted out! (Translated: broke) Well that's the way the cookie crumbles." 1956 Marion Hargrove, *The Girl He Left Behind* (New York: Viking) 50: "If they are not clean, there's people up front who are going to chew me, and then I'm going to chew you, because that's the way the cooky crumbles." *MP* W86; *RHDP* 315; *DAAP* 176; *YBQ* Modern Proverbs (16); Rees (1984) 185; Lighter (1994– ) 1: 473; Rees (1995) 458; Room (2000) 684. Proverbs that follow the "That's the way the <noun> <verbs>" pattern usually express resignation at the reality of circumstances. Cf. the older "That's how the world wags."

## That's the **way** (how) the mop flops.

1956 *Dispatch [Lexington NC]* 4 May: "'That's the way the mop flops' is added to expressions of Eastern young people. It's supposed to take the place of such antiquated phrases as the 'way the wind blows' etc." 1957 *News and Courier [Charleston SC]* 27 Oct.: "High schoolers now emulate the advertising crowd with such expressions as: 'that's the way the mop flops,' . . . 'that's the way the cookie crumbles.' . . ." *RHDP* 315. Proverbs that follow the "That's the way the <noun> <verbs>" pattern usually express resignation at the reality of circumstances. Cf. the older "That's how the world wags."

## There's more than one **way** to peel an orange (banana, egg, etc.)

1954 *New York Times* 8 Aug.: "It is the misfortune of any conductor that he has to run against the competition of Toscanini . . . ; but there is more than one way to peel an orange, and [Ferenc] Fricsay's way loses none of the juice." 1976 "Coping with Fear through Behavior Modification," *Intellect* 105: 127 (quoting Chester B. Scrignar): "There's more than one way to peel a banana, and behavior modification utilizes a variety of methods. . . ." 1977 *Pittsburgh Press* 12 Oct.: "If natural enthusiasm faintly embarrasses you, relax . . . there's more than one way to peel an apple" (ellipsis dots as shown). Cf. the older "There are more ways than one to skin a cat."

## When you're down (at the bottom), the only **way** is up.

1933 "Artists in the Bread Line," *Literary Digest* 115, no. 1 (Jan.) 16 (quoting Henry McBride): "What is to be done for them? Nothing much physically. . . . [B]ut for their souls I have a specific. It is nothing less than the reminder that for those already at the bottom there is nowhere to go but up." 1938 "There's Nowhere to Go but Up" (song title), in Maxwell Anderson and Kurt Weill's stage musical *Knickerbocker Holiday*: "And you're down at the bottom looking up at the top, / When you're at zero, when you're a has-been, / Then there's nowhere to go but up." *DAP* 63(1); *DAAP* 825.

## **Wear** it out, use it up, make it do, or do without.

See "EAT it up, wear it out, make it do, or do without."

## The **weed** (tree, seed) of crime bears bitter fruit.

1930s In the radio show *The Shadow*, "The weed of crime bears bitter fruit" was a recurring tagline. 1943 "The Shadow" (review of the radio show), *Billboard* 55, no. 42 (16 Oct.) 12: "However, as the author so aptly puts it, 'the mead [*sic*] of crime bears bitter fruit.' It did, albeit we all knew *The Shadow* would be there with the final sock and the laugh." 1950 Edward John Carnell, *Television: Servant or Master?* (Grand Rapids MI: Wm. B. Eerdmans) 67: "All mature men know that 'the weed of crime bears bitter fruit,' but the problem is how to show it to those immature minds who may turn to crime. . . . On the wings of video

the bitter fruits of crime can be borne into the living room for public exhibition." 1978 Arthur W. Campbell, *Law of Sentencing* (Rochester NY: Lawyers Co-operative) 27: "Both the individual lawbreaker and the community at large . . . will be forestalled from criminal behavior by the knowledge that the tree of crime bears bitter fruit." 1990 Associated Press, *World War II: A 50th Anniversary History* (New York: Henry Holt) 21: "There was an appeal to Americans in the omniscient crimefighter [i.e., the Shadow] who knew what evil lurks in the hearts of men and that the seed of crime bears bitter fruit." *DAP* 126(15).

## A **week** is a long time in politics.

1961 Richard Cox, "Nyerere Sees a Middle Way for Africa," *New York Times Magazine* (3 Dec.) 121: "He [Prime Minister Julius Nyerere] will undoubtedly find it difficult to negotiate federation when it comes to the details, but as the weeks pass—and a week is a long time in African politics—it seems more and more likely that he will succeed." 1962 George Wolfskill, *Revolt of the Conservatives* (Boston: Houghton, Mifflin) 34: "From the noncommittal reply that [Stephen] Early relayed to him from the President, [Jouett] Shouse was reminded once more that in politics a week is a long time." Rees (1984) 149–50; Pickering et al. (1992) 644; Room (2000) 740. The expression is commonly attributed to Prime Minister Harold Wilson; however, no record of his using it can be found from earlier than 1968, and Wilson himself is on record saying he cannot remember when he first uttered it.

## Everyone must (Every man must) pull his own **weight** (You must pull your own weight).

1902 *New York Times* 31 Aug. (report of a speech by Theodore Roosevelt in Windsor VT): "The man who cannot pull his own weight, that man is not any good in our public life. Now we have got to do it in widely different ways; each man has got to at least pull his own weight, and if he is worth his salt he will pull a little more." 1905 Theodore Roosevelt, speech in Upper Divide Creek CO (30 Apr.). "You must pull your own weight first before you can do more than be a passenger in the boat"; *Presidential Addresses and State Papers*, vol. 3 (New York: Review of Reviews, 1910) 347. 1927 *St. Petersburg [FL] Times* 26 Feb.: "Afer all, we cannot hire anybody else to be a neighbor on our behalf. Every man must pull his own weight in the race of life." *DAP* 399(93); Prahlad (2001) 272.

**Weight** broke the wagon down (broke the mule's back, broke the camel's back).

See "*WAIT* broke the wagon down."

## Don't (try to) reinvent the **wheel**.

1970 *New York Times* 20 Sep.: "[Jack] Davies says he's using the French method of making champagne with a few modern technological twists, 'because I don't see any reason to reinvent the wheel.'" 1972 Stanton Leggett, "For Boardmen and Superintendants Only: How to Keep Tabs on Your District's Curriculum," *American School Board Journal* 159, no. 8 (Feb.) 43: "Don't reinvent the wheel. Turn to many areas where you can get constructive help." The verb phrase "reinvent the wheel" is older.

## The squeaking (squeaky) **wheel** gets the grease.

1903 Cal Stewart, *Uncle Josh Weathersby's "Punkin Centre" Stories* (Chicago: Regan) 6 (a poem): "I don't believe in kickin', / It aint apt to bring one peace; / But the wheel what squeaks the loudest / is the one what gets the grease." 1911 O. D. Skelton, "The Canadian Reciprocity Agreement," *Economic Journal* (Royal Economic Society) 21: 284: "But the western farmer, . . . resentful of the methods by which protection is secured—'the wheel that squeaks the loudest gets the grease,' as the president of the Canadian Manufacturers'

Association recently admitted— . . . is not willing to wait." 1919 "Around the Circuit," *Western Electric News* 7, no. 12 (Feb.) 31: "So saying, 'Old Scrooge' was about to turn on his heel when Charlie, in his winning way, piped up, 'It's the squeaking wheel that gets the grease.'" *MP* W128; *DAP* 650(8); *RHDP* 361; *YBQ* Billings (2); *ODP* 299. Versions of the little poem, often titled "The Kicker," were frequently printed (sometimes in an expanded form) in newspapers and magazines up through the 1930s—usually unattributed, occasionally labeled "anonymous," and in at least one instance credited to Kipling. The eleventh edition of *Bartlett's Familiar Quotations* (1937) 518—on no discernible basis—gave Josh Billings as the author, and that attribution has been customary ever since. The poem may itself represent the origin of the proverb, or it may simply have enlarged on an existing proverb.

## No one likes a **whiner**.

See "The WORLD hates a whiner."

## Happy **wife**, happy life.

1980 *Vancouver [British Columbia] Sun* 2 Feb. (classified ad): "HAPPY WIFE HAPPY LIFE / In this 2 storey home on 1/4 acre" (capitalization as shown). 1998 *Jeff Allen Live: Happy Wife, Happy Life* (a motion picture consisting of the comedian's performances). Cf. "If MAMA ain't happy, ain't nobody happy."

## The **wife** is (always) the last to know (hear, find out).

1901 Percy White, *The Grip of the Bookmaker* (New York: R. F. Fenno) 221: "The opening sentence flung her pride into purgatory. 'A wife is the last to know her husband is deceiving her,' said the letter." 1911 *San Francisco Chronicle* 15 Oct.: "A man's wife is always the LAST one to find out!" (capitalization as shown). 1929 Elmer L. Rice, *Street Scene* (New York: Samuel French) 30: "An' what I always say is . . . the husband or the wife is always the last to know." 1934 *New York Times* 26 Aug.: "One of the best bits [in Cecil B. De Mille's staging of *Cleopatra*] is when one of the Roman wives declares that 'a wife is always the last to hear,' and another woman puts in, 'And the husband, too.'" *MP* H377; *RHDP* 138–39; *ODP* 161. The proverb may derive from the complementary (and considerably older) "The husband (cuckold) is always the last to know," but the "wife" form seems to occur more prevalently in recent decades.

## If you can't **win**, don't play (the game).

1958 *Register-Guard [Eugene OR]* 18 Aug.: "War is no athletic encounter. The rules of sportsmanship do not apply. It is not enough to play the game. The object is to win. . . . If you can't win, don't play. Wait until circumstances favor you." 1985 *[Lakeland FL] Ledger* 19 Apr.: "The lesson here appears to be that if you can't win, don't play, which teaches our children very little about life." 1988 Cartoon caption, *New Yorker* 64, no. 9 (18 Apr.) 43 (two fierce-looking tycoons sitting in their "club"; one speaks): "I say if you can't win don't play the game." Cf. "PLAY to win or don't play."

## Sometimes you **win**, sometimes you lose (You win some, you lose some).

See "You win a FEW, you lose a few."

## To **win**, you only have to get up once more than you fall down.

See "To win, you only have to get up one more TIME than you fall down."

## You can't **win** if you don't play.

1940 Albert Maltz, "Sunday Morning on Twentieth Street," *Southern Review* 5: 473: "'You win at bingo.' 'I don't win,' the old woman said. 'And my husband wallops me.' 'But you can't win if you don't play,' Mary persisted." *DAAP* 844.

Cf. "You have to be in it to WIN it," "You can't win the RAFFLE if you don't buy a ticket," "You can't hit the BALL if you don't swing," "You can't SCORE if you don't shoot," and the older "You can't win if you don't bet."

## You can't **win** them all.

1918 William Heyliger, *Don Strong, Patrol Leader* (New York: Grosset & Dunlap) 217: "The end of the game returned him a loser. 'Can't win them all,' Ted Carter said philosophically." *MP* A70 (intermingled with "You win some, you lose some"); *RHDP* 386; *YBQ* Modern Proverbs (100); *ODP* 347; Room (2000) 767; Pickering (2001) 374. Cf. "You win a FEW, you lose a few."

## You can't **win** them all if you don't (unless you) win the first one.

1947 *Ottawa Citizen* 1 Mar.: "It is an old saying that 'you can't win them all, unless you win the first one.'" 1955 *Spokane [WA] Daily Chronicle* 3 Dec.: "You can't win 'em all if you don't win the first one—and Gonzaga and Whitworth did just that last night as the collegiate basketball season got underway. . . ."

## You have to be (get) in it to **win** it (You can't win it unless you are in it).

1953 L. A. Downey and A. D. North, "Pork and Bacon-Pig Competition," *Journal of Agriculture* (Victoria, Australia) 51: 510: "Pig breeders who recognize the advertising value of this competition should realise that if their pigs are not in it they cannot win it." 1953 T. A. G. Hungerford, *Riverslake* (Sydney, Australia: Angus & Robertson) 42: "Murdoch lifted his shoulders in a curiously un-Australian gesture he had copied from the Balts. '*Comme ci, comme ça*,' he said. 'Like everything else—you've got to be in it to win it'" (italics as shown). Cf. "You can't win the RAFFLE if you don't buy a ticket" and "You can't win if you're not at the TABLE."

You **win** some, you lose some.

See "You win a FEW, you lose a few."

Sometimes (Some days) you're the **windshield**, and sometimes you're the bug (bird).

1981 *Choices* (motion picture, written by Jon Stevens): Pops the bartender (played by Pat Buttram) addresses the main character, a despondent and rebellious teenager: "Just a word of advice: Life is funny. Sometimes you're the bug, and sometimes you're the windshield." 1986 William Mastrosimone, *The Woolgatherer* (Garden City NY: Nelson Doubleday) 56: "You really want to help the guy, but why should you? Hey, sometimes you're the bird, and sometimes you're the windshield. Today, you get to be the bird." 1988 Terry L. Paulson, *They Shoot Managers, Don't They* (Santa Monica CA: Lee Canter) 23: "As one manager so aptly expressed, 'Some days you're the bug, and some days you're the windshield.' Everyone has those days."

**Winners** learn from mistakes (losers repeat them).

1956 *Milwaukee Sentinel* 22 Apr (title of a column on bridge playing): "Winners Learn from Mistakes." 1980 Mary Jo Trapp Bulbrook, *Development of Therapeutic Skills* (Boston: Little, Brown) 62: "Winners learn from mistakes; losers repeat them. She [a psychotherapist] was also still my friend in spite of my mistakes. . . . She taught me that you never really fail unless you quit trying." 1989 Mitzi Chandler, *Gentle Reminders for Co-dependents* (Deerfield FL: Health Communications) 19: "Winners learn from their mistakes and go on."

A **winner** never quits, and a quitter never wins (A quitter never wins, and a winner never quits).

1922 Wilfred H. Osgood, "In Memoriam: Charles Barney Cory," *The Auk: A Quarterly Journal of Ornithology* 39: 166: ". . . [H]e played it like other games, to win, and none knew better than he that winners never quit." 1924 *Chicago Tribune* 29 Feb.: "He [U.S. Attorney General Harry M. Daugherty] said he had received more than 2,000 telegrams during the last two days complimenting him on the stand he had taken. . . . One telegram which pleased him greatly read: 'A winner never quits and a quitter never wins.'" 1924 "Senate Stagnates," *The Independent* 112: 167: "To be sure a slight trace of manhood made its appearance among them [the U.S. senators] after [Attorney General Harry M.] Daugherty announced that 'a fighter sometimes loses but a quitter never wins.'" *DAP* 658(1); *RHDP* 370; *YBQ* Modern Proverbs (74). As the quotations illustrate, either clause can stand alone as a proverb. Cf. "QUITTERS quit."

You can't have **winners** without losers.

1956 Jim Bonder, *Fundamentals of the "T" Formation* (Dubuque IA: Wm. C. Brown) 2: "Emerging victorious is dependent on the other team losing. There just cannot be a winner without a loser." 1965 *Herald Tribune [Sarasota FL]* 17 Jan.: "He was born to lose, always defeated in his campaigns, a situation with which he was perfectly happy, for how can one have winners without losers?" 1981 *Victoria [TX] Advocate* 22 Jan.: "Today anyone whose home mortgage is 10 years old is having over half of his notes being paid by inflation at the expense of my life's savings and retirement funds. There can be no winners without losers."

It's not **winning** that counts, it's playing the game.

See "It isn't whether you win or lose; it's how you play the GAME."

**Winning** isn't everything.

1912 *Atlanta Constitution* 11 Feb. (Theodore Roosevelt, in an interview): ". . . I am inclined to give just as much credit to those who go and do their best and don't win. Winning isn't everything." 1914 Francis Ouimet, "The Game I Love," *St. Nicholas* 41: 486: "They [boys learning golf] should be taught that winning is not everything in the game: that a prize won through trickery . . . gives no lasting pleasure." *YBQ* Modern Proverbs (101); Rees (1984) 220.

## Winning isn't everything; it's the only thing.

1950 *Los Angeles Times* 18 Oct.: "Here's one of Red [UCLA coach Henry] Sanders, as told by himself this summer. . . . Speaking about football victories, Sanders told his group: 'Men, I'll be honest. Winning isn't everything. (Long pause.) Men, it's the only thing!' (Laughter.)." 1953 *Trouble along the Way* (motion picture, screenplay by Jack Rose and Melville Shavelson): A child welfare agent says to the young daughter of a football coach (portrayed by John Wayne, to whose character the saying is sometimes erroneously attributed), "Is winning so important?" and the girl (played by Sherry Jackson) replies, "Listen, like Steve says, 'Winning isn't everything; it's the only thing.'" 1956 Ben Padrow, "Let's Stop Calling Them [speech 'tournaments'] Educational," *Speech Teacher* 5: 206: "If this is not to be the case, then we should put education by the wayside and adopt the slogan, 'Winning isn't everything, it is the *only* thing'" (italics as shown). 1958 John R. Tunis, *The American Way in Sport* (New York: Duell, Sloan & Pearce) 95: "Jim Tatum, successful football coach of the University of North Carolina, made this point cogently, 'I don't think winning is the most important thing. I think it's the only thing.'" *YBQ* Sanders; Rees (1984) 220; Rees (1995) 511. The proverb originated as an anti-proverb based on "WINNING isn't everything." Red Sanders's friend, the sportswriter Fred Russell, remarked (in an interview), "I remember hearing him saying it back in the mid-1930s"; 1999 David Maraniss, *When Pride Still Mattered* (New York: Simon & Schuster) 239. It has often been attributed to Vince Lombardi.

**Winning** ugly is better than nothing (is better than not winning, is still winning).

See "UGLY is better than nothing."

Always take a **woman** past forty: She won't tell, won't swell, is grateful as hell.

See "Won't TELL, won't swell, grateful as hell."

A good **woman** is hard to find.

1942 *Baltimore Afro-American* 19 Dec.: "I am 46; 5 feet 4, light brown, weigh 120, and have a steady job. My object is matrimony if I can meet the right one. I'm not hard to suit but as is said, a good man or a good woman is hard to find." 1964 Alice S. Rossi, "A Good Woman Is Hard to Find: Does Anyone Get Hurt When Mother Goes Back to Work?" *Trans-action* 2, no. 1 (Nov.–Dec.) 20. Doyle (2007b) 13. The proverb originated as an anti-proverb based on "A good MAN is hard to find."

If you want something done, ask a busy **woman**.

See "If you want something done, ask a busy PERSON."

Inside every fat **woman** there's a thin woman trying to get out.

See "Inside every fat PERSON there's a thin person trying to get out."

Inside every old **woman**, there is a young woman.

See "Inside every old PERSON, there is a young one."

Never run after a **woman** or a streetcar (Girls are like busses); if you miss one, another will come along soon.

1910 Robert Rudd Whiting, *Four Hundred Good Stories* (New York: Baker & Taylor) 172: "Most Southerners are gallant. An exception is the Georgian who gave his son this advice: 'My boy, never run after a woman or a street car—there will be another one along in a minute or two.'" 1924 "Why Buy Securities?" *Outlook* 127: 158: "We heard a man say one time that he believed it never paid to run after a girl or a trolley car, because another one would come along in just a minute. This advice might well apply to investments also." 1928 E. Arnot Robertson, *Cullum* (New York: Henry Holt) 227: "His attitude is, never run after a woman or a bus, because there's sure to be another coming round the corner in a minute. Women are all alike to him." *DAP* 519(3) ("Never run after a worrier or a bus"), 667(52); Pickering et al. (1992) 429; Rees (1995) 338.

## Well-behaved **women** rarely (seldom) make history.

1976 The proverb may have originated with Laurel Thatcher Ulrich, "Vertuous Women Found," *American Quarterly* 28: 20: "Well-behaved women seldom make history; against Antinomians and witches, these pious matrons have had little chance at all."

## **Women** and elephants never forget.

1904 H. H. Munro ("Saki"), "Reginald on Besetting Sins," in *Reginald* (London: Methuen) 77: "Miriam Klopstock came to lunch next day. Women and Elephants never forget an injury." *DAP* 668; *YBQ* Modern Proverbs (26); Stevenson (1948) 675. The proverb probably originated as an anti-proverb, an ironic extension of the old saying (or belief), "Elephants never forget."

## A **woman's** place is any place she wants to be.

1918 Horace Traubel, "Whitmania," *The Conservator* 29: 41–42: "They say woman's place is in the home. I say woman's place is any place she can make good in." 1921 *The Freeman* 16 Mar.: "The writer of the advertisement seems to be something of a feminist. . . . We agree with him that woman's place is any place she wants

and can get. . . ." 1929 *Alberta Labor News*, 23 Feb.: "In speaking to the argument that 'a woman's place is in the home' Miss [Agnes] Macphail said: 'I take it a woman's place is any place she wants to be'", quoted by Doris Pennington, *Agnes Macphail, Reformer: Canada's First Female M.P.* (Toronto: Simon & Pierre, 1989) 80. The proverb originated as an anti-proverb rebutting "A woman's place is in the home" or "A woman's place is beside her husband."

## A **woman** should be (kept) barefoot and pregnant (barefoot, pregnant, and in the kitchen).

1947 Marjorie M. Kimmerle, "A Method of Collecting and Classifying Folk Sayings," *Western Folklore* 6: 365 (given as an example of proverbs about "people and parts of the human body"): "Keep 'em barefooted and pregnant." 1948 "Alabama: Going Around in Circles," *Time* 51, no. 20 (17 May) 27 (quoting "Alabama's caveman Governor James E. Folsom"): "And hadn't he said: 'Billy, us men ought to keep our wives barefooted and pregnant'?" 1959 George J. W. Goodman, *The Wheeler Dealers* (Garden City NY: Doubleday) 175: "'Well, King Lear, he was sort of a nice old guy, but he let his daughters just run all over the place. . . .' 'That's a fairly original interpretation. Is that what you think, too, keep 'em barefoot and pregnant?'" 1959 Milton Crane, *New York Times* 27 Sep. (review of *The Wheeler Dealers*, misquoting): "The love affair between Henry and Molly, with its remarkable excursion into high culture ('So I'd say the moral [of "King Lear"] was, keep the women in the kitchen, barefoot and pregnant, or they'll be all over the place') remains this side of absurdity" (parentheses and square brackets as shown). *DAAP* 40.

## A **woman** without a man is like a fish without a bicycle (A woman needs a man like a fish needs a bicycle).

1976 *Corpus Christi [TX] Times* 5 May (quoting Barbara Hower): ". . . [A] feminist said recently an independent woman needs a man like a fish needs a bicycle. That's horse feathers, at least for me. I like what I'm doing but I'd like someone to scratch and giggle with" (credited to *Chicago Daily News*). 1976 *Seattle Times* 5 Jun.: "Sign in a (feminist?) dress shop in Seattle, Wash.: 'A woman without a man is like a fish without a bicycle.'" 1976 *People* 6, no. 4 (26 Jul.) 20 (photo caption): "Gloria Steinem (left) planned to wear a shirt that said, 'A woman without a man is like a fish without a bicycle,' but, like Candy Bergen, arrived unlettered at a [Democratic Party] women's fund raiser." 1976 Mary Murphy, "Superstar Women and Their Marriages," *New York Magazine* 9, no. 32 (9 Aug.) 26: "[Gloria] Steinem sums it up: 'Today a woman without a man is like a fish without a bicycle." 1979 Deborah Goleman Wolf, *The Lesbian Community* (Berkeley: U of California P) [vi] (epigraph): "'*A woman without a man is like a fish without a bicycle.*' (Graffito in the women's lavatory, Student Union, University of California Berkeley, 1975, attributed to Flo Kennedy)" (italics as shown). *YBQ* Dunn; *ODP* 350; Mieder (1982); Mieder (1993b) 70–71, 94; Room (2000) 401. The proverb perhaps originated as an anti-proverb patterned after "A woman without a man is like a handle without a pan" (or other old similes suggesting uselessness or absurdity). Steinem, in *Time* 156, no. 15 (9 Oct. 2000) 20, disclaimed credit for originating the feminist expression: "Irina Dunn, a distinguished Australian educator, journalist and politician, coined the phrase back in 1970. . . ." The image of a fish without (or not needing) a bicycle has had a life of its own. Cf. "A MAN without faith is like a fish without a bicycle," "A MAN without a woman is like a fish without a bicycle," and "A WOMAN without a man is like a fish without a net."

## A **woman** without a man is like a fish without a net (A woman needs a man like a fish needs a net).

1993 Cynthia Heimel, *Get Your Tongue Out of My Mouth, I'm Kissing You Goodbye* (New York: Atlantic Monthly) 15: "It's the boys who are desperate now, but . . . they figure if they don't say anything maybe we won't notice. . . . A woman without a man is like a fish without a net." That is the end of an essay titled "Boyfriends: Why?" which begins, "I just want to reiterate something here. *A woman without a man is like a fish without a bicycle. Old news, you're thinking? An expression that's just too seventies for words?*" (italics as shown). The proverb, then, probably derives from "A WOMAN without a man is like a fish without a bicycle"—now with a man being not just an absurd irrelevancy to a woman but an actual impediment to her success or happiness, even a danger to her.

## A **woman's** word is never done.

1905 Thomas Lansing Masson, *A Corner in Women, and Other Follies* (New York: Moffat, Yard) 51 (filler item): "A woman's word is never done." Litovkina and Mieder (2006) 80. The proverb originated as an anti-proverb based on "A woman's work is never done."

## The harder (more) you **work** (practice), the luckier you get (the more luck you have).

1940 Esther Eberstadt Brooke, *Career Clinic* (New York: Farrar & Rinehart) 246: "Luck, if you will, is something you work for, and the harder you work the more luck you have." 1949 *Spartanburg [SC] Herald* 6 Jun.: "'Isn't it wonderful how lucky your boy is?' said the man. 'Yes,' replied Mr. [J. J.] Lerner [about his son, Alan J. Lerner], 'isn't it wonderful. The harder he works the luckier he gets.'" 1961 Jack Youngblood and Robin Moore, *The Devil to Pay* (New York: McCann) 218: "'One shot,' he muttered. 'You were lucky.' 'That's right. And the more I practice, the luckier I get.'" A different proverb, probably older, asserts, "The more you know, the more luck you have." *DAP* 676(5).

**If it works, don't fix it.**

See "If it ain't broke, don't FIX it."

**It works (It will work) if you work it.**

1922 Warren W. Denison et al., "Forward
Movement of the Christian Church," *Herald of
Gospel Liberty* 114: 85: "It was a beautiful sight
to see the pastor charging thirty-four of his
members to go out on a mission. . . . Go and do
likewise. It works if you work it." 1949 Geraldine
Saltzberg, *Our Teachers Mold Our Nation's
Future* (New York: Macmillan) viii: "Whatever is
suggested here has been tried out sufficiently to
recommend it. It works if you work it."

**Work expands to fill the available
(allotted) time.**

1955 "Parkinson's Law," *The Economist* 177: 633
(the reference is to C. Northcote Parkinson):
"It is a commonplace observation that work
expands so as to fill the time available for its
completion. . . . Before the discovery of a new
scientific law—herewith presented to the public
for the first time, and to be called Parkinson's
Law—there has, however, been insufficient
recognition of the implications of this fact
in the field of public administration." 1957
C. Northcote Parkinson, *Parkinson's Law and
Other Studies in Administration* (Cambridge
MA: Houghton Mifflin) 2 (chapter 1 is the 1955
essay, but with the first sentences changed):
"Work expands so as to fill the time available
for its completion. General recognition of
this fact is shown in the proverbial phrase 'It
is the busiest man who has time to spare.'"
1971 Margaret J. Early and Harold L. Herber,
"Parkinson and Priorities," *Journal of Reading*
14: 155: ". . . [I]t is enlightening to speculate
on the implicit presence of his [Parkinson's]
first law, that work expands to fill the available
time, in the organizational structure of our
educational system. It seems that decisions
related to the content of the curriculum are

based more on the number of days available
in the school year than the reverse." *YBQ*
Parkinson (1); *ODP* 352; Pickering (2001)
380. There exist countless anti-proverbs based
on "Parkinson's Law," an early one being the
title of chapter 10 in *The Feminine Mystique*
by Betty Friedan (New York: W. W. Norton,
1963): "Housewifery Expands to Fill the Time
Available." Others are "Debts expand to fill the
available credit," "Book reviews expand to fill
the space allowed," and "Medical treatment
expands to fill the insurance coverage."

**Work is worry's worst enemy (the best
antidote to worry).**

See "ACTION is worry's worst enemy."

**Work smart, not hard (smarter, not
harder).**

1951 "Hood Plants Now Work Smarter," *Ice
Cream Field* 57, no. 3 (Mar.) 38 (quoting Harold
G. Dunlap): "In other words, the idea is to
adhere to a Hood [H. P. Hood & Sons] slogan
which is publicized on posters throughout the
building: —'Be alert; work smarter, not harder!'"
1965 *Chicago Tribune* 14 Mar. ("Help Wanted"
ad for insurance salesmen—number 5 in a list
of the announced position's advantages): "Work
smart, not hard."

**Working hard is not (good) enough.**

See "TRYING is not enough."

**All the world (Everybody) loves a clown.**

1929 *Christian Science Monitor* 7 Feb. (review of
an art show): "Miss [M. Elizabeth] Price exhibited
flower decorations, with . . . their glint of gold
and silver as accent to flower forms or to animals
and humans on the decorative panel 'Everybody
Loves a Clown.'" 1929 Claude Bragdon, "Clowns
and Clowning," *Outlook and Independent* 151:
491: "'All the world loves a lover' because we are

all—potentially at least—lovers, and all the world loves a clown because in one department of our manifold nature we are all clowns." *YBQ* Cole Porter (21) 601.

## It is a dog-eat-dog **world**.

1935 Edward Anderson, *Hungry Men* (Garden City NY: Doubleday, Doran) 71: "'Do you approve of a system that operates so one man can have enough to buy a billion meals and another can't raise the price of one?' 'Like I've told you before, this is a dog-eat-dog world, and if I don't get mine I'm not going to whine.'" 1946 *New York Times* 24 Mar. (an article about the Nuremburg Trials): "'This is a dog-eat-dog world,' he [Hermann Goehring] explained, and if the Communists had won instead of the Nazis he would have expected worse treatment from them." The proverb probably alludes to the proverb "Dog does not eat dog."

## It is (is always, must be) five (six) o'clock somewhere in the **world**.

See "It is five O'CLOCK somewhere."

## The **world** (Everyone) hates a quitter.

1903 *Terril [IA] Tribune* 21 Aug.: "It has been said that the world hates a quitter." 1921 *Atlanta Constitution* 14 Sep.: "From the men your eye will wander to the walls, which are covered with mottoes. Here are a few from the [Georgia] Tech dressing room: 'For Tech my all.' 'Everybody hates a quitter, but the whole world loves a fighter.'" The proverb may derive from—or respond to—the somewhat older "God hates a quitter."

## The **world** hates (Nobody likes) a whiner.

1905 *Bruce [New Zealand] Herald* 23 Jun.: "The advice recently given to his race by Booker T. Washington fits all of us. . . . Those are brave words and true. The world hates a whiner."

1920 "Fire Insurance Salesman," *The Standard* [Boston, "a Weekly Insurance Newspaper"] 87: 727: "Don't unjustly criticise or cast aspersions on your competitor. Nobody likes a whiner."

## The **world** is a place.

1976 "The World Is a Place" (song recorded by the group Rhythm, on RCA): "The world is a place / For the whole human race." 1995 Barack Obama, *Dreams from My Father* (New York: Random House) 228–29 (a friend speaks and Obama responds): "'I'm telling you, man, the world is a *place*.' 'Say, the world is a place, huh.' 'That's just what I'm saying. . . . Crazy shit going on. You got to ask yourself, is this kinda stuff happening elsewhere? . . . You ever ask yourself that?' 'The world's a place,' I repeated" (italics as shown). Mieder (2009b) 56–57. The proverb means "The world is full of strange, distressing events."

## A **worm** does not find the robin's song beautiful.

See "A ROBIN'S song is not pretty to the worm."

## Don't **worry**, be happy.

1908 *Puck* 64 (29 Jul.) 14 (an advertisement for Evans Ale): "Keep Cool! / Don't Worry! / Be Happy!" 1919 C. J. L. Almquist, *Sara Videbeck*, translated (from Swedish) by A. B. Benson (New York: American-Scandinavian Foundation) 52: "Forgive me, it's none of my business. Don't worry, be happy, and go wherever you like!" The proverb acquired renewed popularity from the 1988 hit song by Bobby McFerrin, "Don't Worry, Be Happy." *YBQ* Baba; Pickering et al. (1992) 259.

## **Worry** is interest paid on trouble before it is due.

1909 William Meade Pegram, *Past-Times* (Baltimore: John H. Saumenig) 120 (in a small collection of sayings—mostly not proverbial—

titled "Proverbs"): "Worry—interest paid on trouble before it falls due." *DAP* 679(5).

## Worry is like a rocking chair: it gives you something to do but doesn't get you anywhere.

1916 Harry Leslie Stroupe, *The Vegetarian* (Jamaica NY: for the author) 35: "Worry is lost energy. It is like a rocking chair, it keeps going but never gets anywhere. Stop the habit, form new plans of thought, work, expression, activity, and living one day at a time." 1920 Thomas Parker Boyd, *Prospectus of Life* (San Francisco: for the author) 68: "*Don't worry*! Like a rocking chair worry gives a vast amount of agitation and no progress. Get the calmness of trust and move forward" (italics as shown). *DAP* 679(6).

## Anything **worth** doing is worth overdoing.

1962 *New York Times* 29 Apr. (in an ad for Jantzen sportswear): "[D]o you have to dress for this kind of life? Of course you do; as Frank Gifford once said, if a thing is worth doing, it's worth overdoing." 1965 *New York Times* 21 Nov.: "It may be significant that he [Peter Falk] includes, when describing what he finds appealing in O'Brien, that character's feeling that 'anything worth doing is worth overdoing.'" The proverb originated as an anti-proverb based on "Anything worth doing is worth doing well."

## Don't throw a monkey **wrench** into the works.

See "Don't throw a MONKEY WRENCH into the works."

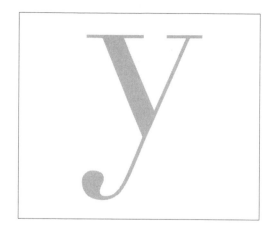

## The first five (six, etc.) **years** are the hardest.

1918 *100%: The Efficiency Magazine* (Feb.) 53: "When Sir Douglas Haig was asked how long he thought the war would last he replied: 'I think the first five years will be the hardest,' and a famous French general is credited with the opinion on the same subject that the first seven years would be the hardest and then every fourteenth year." 1919 "From and About Those Serving under the Grand Old Flag," *Santa Fe Magazine* 13, no. 6 (May): 34: "It's a gay life if you don't weaken. They say the first six years [in the army] are the hardest." 1924 Jane Littell, "Meditations of a Wage-Earning Wife," *Atlantic Monthly* 134: 730: "When we announced our marriage to a friend she laughed and said, 'Well, the first five years are the hardest.'" Pickering et al. (1992) 199; Pickering (2001) 136. The proverb is usually intended jocularly—specifying a seemingly long interval as the "hardest." Cf. "The first hundred YEARS are the hardest."

## The first hundred **years** are the hardest.

1918 *Bridgeport [CT] Telegram* 29 Jul. (heading of a sequence of cartoon panels depicting the difficulties of a golfer over the years): "The first hundred years are the hardest." *MP* Y3; *DAP* 685(10); *RHDP* 97; *YBQ* Modern Proverbs (31). The proverb probably originated as an anti-proverb, exaggerating (from absurdity to impossibility) the already-jocular proverb "The first five YEARS are the hardest."

## It's not the **years**, it's the mileage (miles).

1957 "Sport: The Suicide Circuit," *Time* 70, no. 21 (18 Nov.) 83 (quoting the rodeo rider Jim Shoulders): "'Lots of boys who've been traipsin' around this suicide circuit have to tie their legs before they ride. It's not the years,' he says sorrowfully, 'it's the mileage.'" The expression literally (and originally) would refer to the value of a used automobile, but as a proverb it usually applies to persons whose physical state differs from what their age or experience might predict.

## **Youth** is wasted on the young.

1931 *New York Times* 28 Dec. (headline): "[Harry Emerson] FOSDICK SAYS RELIGION KEEPS PEOPLE YOUNG: Declares Youth is Wasted by Children Who Are Unaware of the Treasure They Possess" (capitalization as shown). 1933 Michael Arlen, *Man's Mortality* (Garden City NY: Doubleday, Doran) 69: "How the young enjoy those trifles! How enormous those trifles seem. To be hungry, to snatch, and to eat. The appetite of youth! What a pity it's wasted on young men." 1934 Frank H. Lee, *Tokyo Calendar* (Tokyo: Hokusiedo) 59: "The cheap and tawdry café, the frequently malodorous dance-hall, and the unrealities, even deceptions, of the cinema, are all calling the youth away from the old paths. I often think of Bernard Shaw's remark, that youth is a wonderful thing, but that it is wasted on the young." *YBQ* Modern Proverbs (104). On no evident basis, the saying is commonly attributed to Shaw.

There is no **zealot** like a convert (The latest convert is the greatest zealot).

1906 Ednah Proctor Clarke, "A Special Messenger," *Harper's Bazaar* 40 (Oct.) 10: "There is no zealot like a convert, and all my Father's brain and energy were spent now in search, not for Truth, but for Error. . . ." 1910 "The Paulist Fathers' Jubilee," *Outlook* 94 (5 Feb.) 280: "On the principle that there is no zealot like a convert, these men were certainly the ones to undertake the work. . . ." 1934 Christopher Morley, "Old Loopy," *Saturday Review of Literature* 11, no. 21 (8 Dec.) 340: "I can still remember my strong prejudice against her [the city of Chicago] before we met. Perhaps the convert is always the greatest zealot. . . ."

The most important (The most potent, The most) erogenous **zone** is the brain (mind).

1969 *New York Times* 7 Dec.: "Sometimes [David] Frost simply manages to bring out somebody in a small way, as when he coaxed out of a shy Raquel Welch . . . the notion that 'the mind is the most erogenous zone.'" 1974 *Newsweek* 83, no. 11 (18 Mar.) 43: "There cannot be winners in the battle of erectile tissues. Surely the most erogenous zone in both men and women lies not between the legs but behind the eyes." 1977 *Lawrence [KS] Daily Journal* 24 Oct. ("Ann Landers" advice column): "The most erogenous zone in both male and female is located between the eyebrows and the hairline." 1980 Mike Grace and Joyce Grace, *A Joyful Meeting: Sexuality in Marriage* (St. Paul MN: National Marriage Encounter) 26: "If there is competition from other things—distractions, other feelings— foreplay may have no erotic effect. This is why we emphasize that the most important erogenous zone is the brain."

The compilers of this book began by searching proverb dictionaries and other published collections for sayings that were not shown to be any older than the twentieth century. Those lists were then greatly expanded to include material from the present compilers' own extensive (and ever-growing) files of previously unnoticed and undocumented proverbs, ones that appeared to be somewhat recent in their coinage. Next, the compilers studiously investigated each of the putatively "modern" proverbs, discovering that the ones in the following list are, in fact, older than 1900. The proverbs are sequenced alphabetically, by key words.

**Advice** is cheap.
**Anger** improves nothing but the arch of a cat's back.
**Anticipation** is better than realization.
**Anticipation** is nine-tenths of (half) the fun (pleasure).
Never **apologize**, never explain.
An **apple** a day keeps the doctor away.
An **army** marches on its stomach.
There's no harm in **asking**.
**Attack** is the best form of defense.

You have to take the **bad** with the good.
If you can't **beat** (lick) them, join them.
**Beauty** is in the eye of the beholder.
**Beauty** is only skin deep, but ugly is clear to the bone.
An empty **belly** is no epicure.
Save the **best** until last.
Don't rock the **boat**.
When a new **book** appears, read an old one.

You can't judge (tell) a **book** by its cover.
Don't send a **boy** to do a man's job (work, duty).
Two **boys** are half a boy, and three boys are no boy at all.
Don't burn your **bridges** behind you.
You can't put the **bullet** back in the gun.
**Business** before pleasure.
Don't mix **business** with pleasure.
**Busybodies** never want a bad day.
**Buy** low, sell high.
Don't monkey with a **buzz saw**.

Don't let a **camel** get its nose under the tent.
The **camera** cannot (does not) lie.
*Can't* never did anything.
There is always a **catch**.
A **change** is as good as a rest.
**Change** is the only constant in life.
**Character** is what we are; reputation is what others think we are.
**Children**: One is one, two is fun, three is a household.
You can't build a **chimney** from the top down.
**Chivalry** is dead.
**Chivalry** is not dead.
Extraordinary **claims** require extraordinary evidence (proof).
Even a stopped (broken) **clock** is right twice a day (sometimes).
All **coons** look alike (in the dark).
It doesn't **cost** anything to ask.
It doesn't **cost** anything to look.
It's what's inside that **counts**.
**Courage** breeds courage.
**Courtesy** is contagious.
Faraway **cows** have long horns.

Why buy the **cow** when milk is cheap?
It's better to be a live **coward** than a dead hero.
**Curiosity** killed the cat.

The best **defense** is a good offense (Offense is
the best defense).
The **devil** lays (places) pillows for drunken men
to fall on.
We all **die** alone.
The **dogs** bark but the caravan moves on.
Every **dog** is allowed one bite.
Like **dog**, like master.
When a **door** closes, a window opens (When God
shuts a door, he opens a window).
When in **doubt**, don't.
No **dream** lasts forever.
**Duty** is duty.

You are what you **eat**.
You can't spoil a rotten **egg**.
An **elephant** never forgets.
Every **elm** has its man.
The **enemy** of my enemy is my friend.
The absence of **evidence** is not evidence.
See no **evil**, hear no evil, speak no evil.
**Explanations** don't explain.

One's **face** is his fortune.
**Failure** teaches success.
**Father** knows best.
You can't get **feathers** from a horse (toad).
A **fence** should be horse-high.
Don't go down (give up) without a **fight**.
The same **fire** that melts butter hardens an egg.
Give a man a **fish**, and he will eat for a day; teach
a man to fish and he will eat for a lifetime.
Don't shoot a **fly** (mosquito) with a cannon (an
elephant gun, etc.).
**Flies** have their virtues.
Keep your **feet** on the ground.
**Foresight** is better than hindsight.
If our **foresight** were as good as our hindsight,
we'd be better off by a damn sight.
**Form** follows function.
My **friend's** friend is my enemy.
The **future** is already here.

He is the best **general** who makes the fewest
mistakes.
**Genius** is one percent inspiration and ninety-
nine percent perspiration.
Let **George** do it.
What **goes** up must come down.
**God's** help is nearer than the door.
**God** knows, but He won't tell.
The **gods** send nuts (almonds) to those who have
no teeth.
Thank **God** for small favors (blessings).
The **good** is the enemy of the best.
One **guess** is as good as another.

Cold **hands**, warm heart.
There's no **harm** in looking.
It is better to be a **has-been** than a never-was.
Don't use a **hatchet** to break eggs.
If you can't **have** what you like, you must like
what you have.
Them as **has**, gets.
What you've never **had** you never miss.
You can't **have** everything.
Hard **head**, soft heart (mind).
A wise **head** is better than a pretty face.
**Hindsight** is better than foresight.
**Home** is where one hangs his hat.
**Hope** lost, all lost.
It never **hurts** to ask.

Where the **jackals** are, the lion cannot be far away.
The longest **journey** begins with a single step.
**Justice** delayed is justice denied.

There are three **kinds** of lies: Lies, damned lies,
and statistics.
One **kisses**, the other turns a cheek.
To **know** all is to forgive all.
All **knowledge** is useful.

**Land** (The land) won't burn.
He who **laughs** last laughs longest (loudest).
**Laughter** is the best medicine.
Where there's been no **learning**, there's been no
teaching.
You never know the **length** of a snake until it is
dead.

Life is a gamble.
A little can go a long way.
Come live with me and you'll know me.
Looks break no bones.
The more (farther) you look, the less you see.
If you don't look out for yourself, nobody else will.
Love them and leave them.
Plain and loved, loved forever.
You can't live on love.
Don't press (push, crowd) your luck.
You never know your luck.

All men are liars.
Behind every great man there's a great woman.
It takes a smart man to know he's stupid.
A man is known by the enemies he makes.
The rich man has his ice in the summer, and the
    poor man gets his in the winter.
What man can do man has done.
You can judge a man by his shoes.
You can't keep a good man down.
A young man married is a young man marred.
Like master, like dog.
Don't shoot (kill) the messenger.
The second million (dollars) is always easier
    (than the first).
You can do anything you put your mind to.
Don't make the same mistake twice.
If you don't make mistakes, you don't make
    anything.
Money cannot buy happiness.
Money cannot buy love.
Money has no smell.
Money isn't everything.
Money makes the world go around.
Money works miracles.
Monkey see, monkey do.
Softly, softly, catchee monkey.
You can't legislate morality (morals).
Open mouth, insert foot.
Too much is enough.

No names, no pack drill.
Nature cures the disease.
No needle is sharp on both ends.
Never say never.

Good news travels fast.
Night (Sunset) makes no difference to a blind
    man.
Anything is better than nothing.
Nothing is forever.
Nothing is impossible.
Say nothing and saw wood.
There is nothing so good for the inside of a man
    as the outside of a horse.
There is nothing to fear but fear itself.

The ocean has no memory.
Opposites attract.
An ounce of fact is worth a pound of theory.

No pain, no gain.
Distant pastures (fields) are greener.
Patience moves mountains.
It pays to advertise.
Don't let the perfect (the best) be the enemy of
    the good.
Nobody is perfect.
The only good pig is one with its throat cut.
Pleasure shared is doubled.
Poison is a woman's weapon.
Anything is possible.
Power is an aphrodisiac.
Presentation is everything.
A stiff prick has no conscience.
A bad professional is better than a good amateur.
Promises cost little.

Ask a stupid question, you'll get a stupid answer.
Shoot first and ask questions later (afterwards).

A cornered rat will fight.
Records are set to be broken.
There's always room at the top.
Don't make rules that can't be enforced.
Rules are made to be broken.
Rules are rules.

Safety first.
If you can't say something nice, don't say anything.
A secret's a secret until it is told.

Once **seen**, never forgotten.

Fool me once, **shame** on you; fool me twice, shame on me.

From **shirtsleeves** to shirtsleeves in three generations.

**Silence** is the best policy.

Old **sins** have long shadows.

Old **sins** will find one out.

Pick on someone your own **size**.

Everybody is **smarter** (wiser) than anybody (None of us is as smart as all of us).

A **Smith & Wesson** beats four aces (A pair of six-shooters beats a pair of aces).

*Sorry* (Saying you're sorry, Apologizing) doesn't help (doesn't change anything).

The darkest **spot** is just under the candle (light, lamp).

Only when it's dark can you see the **stars**.

Shoot (Aim) for the **stars**.

You can prove anything with **statistics**.

One **step** (Take things one step) at a time.

**Stop**, look, listen.

**Success** breeds success.

You can't argue with **success**.

**Suspicion** breeds suspicion.

What you lose on the **swings** you gain on the roundabouts.

Don't judge a **tale** before its end.

A moving **target** is hard to hit.

**Thanks** would starve a cat.

The best **things** (in life) are free.

First **things** first.

Good **things** come in small packages.

If it isn't one **thing**, it's another.

It's never too late to do the right **thing**.

Little **things** please little minds.

The more **things** change, the more they stay the same.

The only **thing** we have to fear is fear itself.

Some **things** are best left unsaid.

Some **things** never change.

There are some **things** money can't buy.

**Things** have a way of working (themselves) out.

It's later than you **think**.

First **thoughts** are best.

No **tickee**, no washee (shirtee).

He who has a **tiger** (wildcat, bear, etc.) by the tail dares not let go.

Desperate **times** call for desperate measures.

One is a long **time** dead.

**Time** wasted is time lost.

There's always **tomorrow**.

**Travel** broadens the mind.

Don't go looking for **trouble**.

A **trouble** shared is a trouble halved.

**Trust** and be trusted.

The **truth** harms no man.

**Truth** is more important than facts.

You should **try** anything (everything) once.

**Two** can live as cheaply as one.

**Use** it or lose it.

**Violence** begets violence.

Empty **wagons** make the most noise.

Every **war** has casualties.

It's all in the **way** you look at it.

There is no right **way** to do a wrong thing.

The (only) **way** up is down.

You can't have it both **ways**.

A **win** is a win.

You can't **win** if you don't bet.

Be careful what you **wish** (pray) for; you might get it.

The **woman** pays.

**Women**: You can't live with them and you can't live without them.

There is no such **word** as *can't*.

Hard **work** never hurt (killed) anyone.

**Work** is work (and play is play).

**Work** with what you have.

All the **world** loves a lover.

Don't try to save the **world**.

Give to the **world** your best, and it will come back to you.

The **world** is what people (you) make it.

You are only **young** once.

You can tell a **zebra** by its stripes.

A **zebra** cannot change its stripes.

# WORKS CITED

Albig, William. 1931. "Proverbs and Social Control." *Sociology and Social Research* 15: 527–35.

Allinson, Robert E., and A. L. Minkes. 1990. "Principles, Proverbs and Shibboleths of Administration." *International Journal of Technology Management* 5: 179–87.

Anderson, Izett, and Frank Cundall. 1910. *Jamaica Negro Proverbs and Sayings*. Kingston: Institute of Jamaica.

———. 1927. *Jamaica Negro Proverbs and Sayings*. Second edition. London: Institute of Jamaica.

Arora, Shirley L. 1988. "'No Tickee, No Shirtee': Proverbial Speech and Leadership in Academe." In *Inside Organisations: Understanding the Human Dimension*. Edited by Michael Owen Jones, Michael Dane Moore, and Richard Christopher Snyder. Newbury Park CA: Sage. 179–89.

Baldwin, L. Karen. 1965. "A Sampling of Housewives' Proverbs and Proverbial Phrases from Levittown, Pennsylvania." *Keystone Folklore Quarterly* 10: 127–48.

Barbour, Frances M. 1963. "Some Uncommon Sources of Proverbs." *Midwest Folklore* 13: 97–100.

——— 1965. *Proverbs and Proverbial Phrases of Illinois*. Carbondale: Southern Illinois UP.

Barrick, Mac E. 1979. "Better Red than Dead." *American Notes and Queries* 17: 143–44.

———. 1986. "Where's the Beef?" *Midwestern Journal of Language and Folklore* 12: 43–46.

Bassin, Alexander. 1984. "Proverbs, Slogans and Folk Sayings in the Therapeutic Community: A Neglected Therapeutic Tool." *Journal of Psychoactive Drugs* 16: 51–56.

Beckwith, Martha Warren. 1925. *Jamaica Proverbs*. Poughkeepsie NY: Vassar College.

Bertram, Anne, and Richard Spears. 1993. *NTC's Dictionary of Proverbs and Clichés*. Lincolnwood IL: National Textbook.

Bohn, Henry G. 1857. *A Polyglot of Foreign Proverbs*. London: for the author. Rpt. Detroit MI: Gale Research, 1968.

Bradley, F. W. 1937. "South Carolina Proverbs." *Southern Folklore Quarterly* 1: 57–101.

Bryan, George B. 2001. "An Unfinished List of Anglo-American Proverb Songs." *Proverbium* n.s. 18: 15–56.

Casselman, Bill. 1999. *Canadian Sayings: 1,200 Folk Sayings Used by Canadians*. Toronto: McArthur.

———. 2002. *Canadian Sayings 2: 1,000 Folk Sayings Used by Canadians*. Toronto: McArthur.

Cassidy, Frederic G., and Joan Houston Hall. 1985–. *Dictionary of American Regional English*. 4 volumes (to date). Cambridge MA: Harvard UP.

Champion, Selwyn Gurney. 1938. *Racial Proverbs*. New York: Macmillan.

Champion, Selwyn Gurney, and Ethel Mavrogordato. 1922. *Wayside Sayings*. London: Duckworth.

Chlosta, Christoph, and Peter Grzybek. 1995. "Empirical and Folkloristic Paremiology: Two to Quarrel or to Tango?" *Proverbium* n.s. 12: 67–85.

Christy, Robert. 1888. *Proverbs, Maxims and Phrases of All Ages*. 2 volumes. New York: G. P. Putnam's Sons.

DAAP. Bryan, George B., and Wolfgang Mieder. 2005. *A Dictionary of Anglo-American Proverbs & Proverbial Phrases Found in Literary Sources of the Nineteenth and Twentieth Centuries*. New York: Peter Lang.

Daniel, Jack L., Geneva Smitherman-Donaldson, and Milford A. Jeremiah. 1987. "Makin' a Way Outa No Way: The Proverb Tradition in Black Experience." *Journal of Black Studies* 17: 482–508.

DAP. Mieder, Wolfgang, Stewart A. Kingsbury, and Kelsie B. Harder. 1992. *A Dictionary of American Proverbs*. New York: Oxford UP.

Doyle, Charles Clay. 1972. "Smoke and Fire: Spenser's Counter proverb." *Proverbium* o.s. 18: 683–85.

———. 1983. "The Power of Not Thinking: A Jocular Toothache Cure." *Kentucky Folklore Record* 29: 24–29.

———. 1996. "On 'New' Proverbs and the Conservativeness of Proverb Dictionaries." *Proverbium* n.s. 13: 69–84. Reprinted in Mieder (2003) 85–98.

———. 2001a. "Is the Third Time a Charm? A Review of *The Concise Oxford Dictionary of Proverbs*." *Proverbium* n.s. 18: 453–68.

———. 2001b. "Seeing through Colored Glasses." *Western Folklore* 60: 67–91.

———. 2007a. "Collections of Proverbs and Proverb Dictionaries: Some Historical Observations on What's in Them and What's Not (with a Note on Current 'Gendered' Proverbs)." In *Phraseology and Culture in English.* Edited by Paul Skandera. Berlin: Mouton de Gruyter. 181–203.

———. 2007b. "A Good Man Is Hard to Find: The Proverb." *Flannery O'Connor Review* 5: 5–22.

———. 2009. "'Use It or Lose It': The Proverb, Its Pronoun, and Their Antecedents." *Proverbium* n.s. 26: 105–18.

Dundes, Alan. 1975. "On the Structure of the Proverb." *Proverbium* o.s. 25: 961–73.

Dundes, Alan, and Carl R. Pagter. 1975. *Urban Folklore from the Paperwork Empire.* Austin TX: American Folklore Society.

———. 1987. *When You're Up to Your Ass in Alligators: More Urban Folklore from the Paperwork Empire.* Detroit: Wayne State UP.

———. 1991. *Never Try to Teach a Pig to Sing: Still More Urban Folklore from the Paperwork Empire.* Detroit: Wayne State UP.

———. 1996. *Sometimes the Dragon Wins: Yet More Urban Folklore from the Paperwork Empire.* Syracuse NY: Syracuse UP.

Dundes, Lauren, Michael Streiff, and Alan Dundes. 1999. "'When You Hear Hoofbeats, Think Horses, Not Zebras': A Folk Medical Diagnostic Proverb." *Proverbium* n.s. 16: 95–103. Reprinted in Mieder (2003) 99–107.

Eret, Dylan. 2001. "'The Past Does Not Equal the Future': Anthony Robbins' Self-Help Maxims as Therapeutic Rhetoric." *Proverbium* n.s. 18: 77–103.

Flavell, Linda, and Roger Flavell. 1993. *Dictionary of Proverbs and Their Origins.* London: Kyle Cathie.

Fogel, Edwin Miller. 1929. *Proverbs of the Pennsylvania Germans.* Lancaster PA: Lancaster. Rpt. (with introduction and bibliography by Wolfgang Mieder) Bern Switzerland: Peter Lang, 1995.

Folsom, Steven. 1993. "A Discography of American Country Music Hits Employing Proverbs: Covering the Years 1986–1992." In *Proceedings for the 1993 Annual Conference of the Southwest-Texas Popular Culture Association.* Edited by Sue Poor. Stillwater OK: Southwest-Texas Popular Culture Association. 31–42.

Franck, Harry A. 1921. "Jamaica Proverbs." *Dialect Notes* 5, part 4: 98–108.

Galef, David. 1993. "How to Gain Proverbial Wisdom; or, It Takes One to Know One." *Verbatim: The Language Quarterly* 19, no. 4 (Spring): 5–7.

Hernadi, Paul, and Francis Steen. 1999. "The Tropical Landscape of Proverbia: A Crossdisciplinary Travelogue." *Style* 33: 1–20. Reprinted in Mieder (2003) 185–204.

Hoffman, Robert R., and Richard P. Honeck. 1987. "Proverbs, Pragmatics, and the Ecology of Abstract Categories." In *Cognition and Symbolic Structures: The Psychology of Metaphoric Transformation.* Edited by Robert E. Haskell. Norwood NJ: Ablex. 121–40.

Jente, Richard. 1932. "The American Proverb." *American Speech* 7: 342–48.

Kanfer, Stefan. 1983. "Proverbs or Aphorisms?" *Time* 122, no. 2 (11 Jul.) 74.

Kauffman, Draper. 1990. "System Proverbs." *Etc: A Review of General Semantics* 47: 20–29.

Keyes, Ralph. 1992. *"Nice Guys Finish Seventh": False Phrases, Spurious Sayings, and Familiar Misquotations.* New York: HarperCollins.

Kin, David. 1955. *Dictionary of American Proverbs.* New York: Philosophical Library.

Lau, Kimberly J., Peter Tokofsky, and Stephen D. Winick, editors. 2004. *What Goes Around Comes Around: The Circulation of Proverbs in Contemporary Life.* Logan: Utah State UP. (Wolfgang Mieder festschrift.)

Lighter, Jonathan E. 1994–. *(Random House) Historical Dictionary of American Slang.* 2 volumes (to date). New York: Random House.

Litovkina, Anna T., and Wolfgang Mieder. 2006. *Old Proverbs Never Die, They Just Diversify: A Collection of Anti-proverbs.* Burlington: University of Vermont; Veszprém, Hungary: Pannonian University of Veszprém.

MacDowell, Marsha, and Wolfgang Mieder. 2010. "'When Life Hands You Scraps, Make a Quilt': Quiltmakers and the Tradition of Proverbial Inscriptions." *Proverbium* n.s. 27: 113–72.

Manser, Martin H. 2002. *Facts on File Dictionary of Proverbs.* New York: Facts on File.

McKenzie, Alyce M. 1996. "'Different Strokes for Different Folks': America's Quintessential Postmodern Proverb." *Theology Today* 53: 201–12.

Mieder, Wolfgang. 1982. "'Eine Frau ohne Mann ist wie ein Fisch ohne Velo.'" *Sprachspiegel* 38: 141–42.

———. 1983. "'Zum Tango gehören zwei.'" *Der Sprachdienst* 27: 100–102, 181. Reprinted in Mieder (1985) 151–54.

———. 1985. *Sprichwort, Redensart, Zitat: Tradierte Formelsprache in der Moderne.* Bern Switzerland: Peter Lang.

———. 1988. "Proverbs in American Popular Songs." *Proverbium* n.s 5: 85–101.

———. 1989a. *American Proverbs: A Study of Texts and Contexts.* Bern Switzerland: Peter Lang.

———. 1989b. "'Ein Bild sagt mehr als tausend Worte': Ursprung und Überlieferung eines amerikanischen Lehnsprichworts." *Proverbium* n.s. 6: 25–37.

————. 1990. "'A Picture Is Worth a Thousand Words': From Advertising Slogan to American Proverb." *Southern Folklore* 47: 207–25. Reprinted in Mieder (1993b) 79–88.

————. 1991. "General Thoughts on the Nature of the Proverb." *Revista de ethnografie si folclor* 36: 151–64. Reprinted in Mieder (1993b) 3–17.

————. 1992. "Paremiological Minimum and Cultural Literacy." In *Creativity and Tradition in Folklore.* Edited by Simon J. Bronner. Logan: Utah State UP. 185–203. Reprinted in Mieder (1994) 297–316.

————. 1993a. "'The Grass Is Always Greener on the Other Side of the Fence.'" *Proverbium* n.s. 10: 151–84. Reprinted in Mieder (1994) 515–42.

————. 1993b. *Proverbs Are Never Out of Season: Popular Wisdom in the Modern Age.* New York: Oxford UP.

————, editor. 1994. *Wise Words: Essays on the Proverb.* New York: Garland.

————, editor. 2003. *Cognition, Comprehension, and Communication: A Decade of North American Proverb Studies (1990–2000).* Baltmannsweiler Germany: Schneider.

————. 2004. *Proverbs: A Handbook.* Westport CT: Greenwood.

————. 2005a. "'A Proverb Is Worth a Thousand Words': Folk Wisdom in the Modern Mass Media." *Proverbium* n.s. 22: 167–233.

————. 2005b. *Proverbs Are the Best Policy: Folk Wisdom and American Politics.* Logan: Utah State UP.

————. 2006. "'Different Strokes for Different Folks.'" In Prahlad (2006) 1: 324–27.

————. 2009a. "New Proverbs Run Deep: Prolegomena to a Dictionary of Modern Anglo-American Proverbs." *Proverbium* n.s. 26: 237–74.

————. 2009b. *"Yes We Can": Barack Obama's Proverbial Rhetoric.* New York: Peter Lang.

————. 2010a. "The Golden Rule as a Political Imperative for the World: President Barack Obama's Proverbial Messages Abroad." *Millî Folklor* 22, no. 85: 26–35.

————. 2010b. *Making a Way Out of No Way: Martin Luther King's Sermonic Proverbial Rhetoric.* New York: Peter Lang.

————. 2011. "'It Takes a Village to Change the World': Proverbial Politics and the Ethics of Place." *Journal of American Folklore* 124: 4–28.

Mieder, Wolfgang, and George B. Bryan. 1997. *The Proverbial Harry S. Truman.* New York: Peter Lang.

Morris, William, and Mary Morris. 1962–71. *Dictionary of Word and Phrase Origins.* 3 volumes. New York: Harper & Row.

*MP.* Whiting, Bartlett Jere. 1989. *Modern Proverbs and Proverbial Sayings.* Cambridge MA: Harvard UP.

Nierenberg, Jess. 1983. "Proverbs in Graffiti: Taunting Traditional Wisdom." *Maledicta* 7: 41–58. Reprinted in Mieder (1994) 543–61.

Nussbaum, Stan. 2005. *American Cultural Baggage: How to Recognize and Deal with It.* Maryknoll NY: Orbis.

*ODP.* Speake, Jennifer. 2008. *The Oxford Dictionary of Proverbs.* Fifth Edition. Oxford: Oxford UP. (The first three editions—1982, 1992, and 1998—were titled *The Concise Oxford Dictionary of Proverbs.*)

Olinick, Stanley L. 1987. "On Proverbs: Creativity, Communication, and Community." *Contemporary Psychoanalysis* 23: 463–68.

Page, Mary H., and Nancy D. Washington. 1987. "Family Proverbs and Value Transmission of Single Black Mothers." *Journal of Social Psychology* 127: 49–58.

Parker, Carol. 1975. "'White Is the Color.'" *Western Folklore* 34: 153–54.

Parsons, Elsie Clews. 1943. *Folk-lore of the Antilles, French and English.* Part 3. New York: American Folk-lore Society.

Partridge, Eric. 1977. *Dictionary of Catch Phrases.* New York: Stein & Day.

Pasamanick, Judith R. 1985. "Watched Pots Do Boil: Proverb Interpretation through Contextual Illustration." *Proverbium* n.s. 2: 145–83.

Person, Henry A. 1958. "Proverbs and Proverbial Lore from the State of Washington." *Western Folklore* 17: 176–85.

Petrova, Roumyana. 1996. "Language and Culture: One Step Further in the Search for Common Ground." In *Europe from East to West: Proceedings of the First International European Studies Conference.* Edited by Martin Dangerfield, Glyn Hambrook, and Ludmilla Kostova. Varna, Bulgaria: PIC. 237–48.

Pickering, David. 2001. *Cassell's Dictionary of Proverbs.* Second edition. London: Cassell.

Pickering, David, Alan Isaacs, and Elizabeth Martin. 1992. *Brewer's Dictionary of 20th-Century Phrase and Fable.* Boston: Houghton Mifflin.

Prahlad, Sw. Anand. 1994. "'No Guts, No Glory': Proverbs, Values and Image among Anglo-American University Students." *Southern Folklore* 51: 285–98. Reprinted in Mieder (2003) 443–58.

————. 1996. *African-American Proverbs in Context.* Jackson: UP of Mississippi.

————. 2001. *Reggae Wisdom: Proverbs in Jamaican Music.* Jackson: UP of Mississippi.

————. 2004. "The Proverb and Fetishism in American Advertisements." In Lau, Tokofsky, and Winick (2004) 127–51.

————, editor. 2006. *Encyclopedia of African American Folklore.* 3 volumes. Westport CT: Greenwood.

Ratcliffe, Susan. 2006. *Oxford Dictionary of Phrase, Saying, and Quotation*. Third edition. Oxford: Oxford UP.

Rees, Nigel. 1984. *Sayings of the Century: The Stories behind the Twentieth Century's Quotable Sayings*. London: Allen & Unwin.

———. 1995. *Phrases & Sayings*. London: Bloomsbury.

———. 2005. "'Shit Happens.'" *"Quote . . . Unquote" Newsletter* 14, no. 2: 6.

———. 2006. *A Word in Your Shell-like: 6,000 Curious and Everyday Phrases Explained*. London: HarperCollins.

*RHDP*. Titelman, Gregory. 2000. *Random House Dictionary of America's Popular Proverbs and Sayings*. Second edition. New York: Random House.

Rogers, Tim B. 1990. "Proverbs as Psychological Theories . . . Or Is It the Other Way Around?" *Canadian Psychology/Psychologie canadienne* 31: 195–207, 215–17. Reprinted in Mieder (2003) 459–82.

Rogow, Arnold, Gloria Carey, and Calista Farrell. 1957. "The Significance of Aphorisms in American Culture." *Sociology and Social Research* 41: 417–20.

Room, Adrian. 2000. *Brewer's Dictionary of Modern Phrase & Fable*. London: Cassell.

Russell, Melissa Anne. 1999. "Kill 'Em All and Let God Sort 'Em Out: The Proverb as an Expression of Verbal Aggression." *Proverbium* n.s. 16: 287–302.

Scott, W. T. 1996. "Proverbs, Postmodernity, and Unacknowledged Legislation." In *Law and Literature Perspectives*. Edited by Bruce L. Rockwood and Roberta Kevelson. New York: Peter Lang. 341–52.

Sheidlower, Jesse. 2009. *The F-Word*. Oxford: Oxford UP.

Speight, E. E. 1911. "A Few Norwegian Proverbs." *Folklore* 68: 213–18.

Speirs, James. 1902. *The Proverbs of British Guiana*. Demerara Guyana: Argosy.

Stevenson, Burton. 1948. *Home Book of Proverbs, Maxims and Familiar Phrases*. New York: Macmillan.

Taft, Michael. 1994. "Proverbs in the Blues: How Frequent Is Frequent?" *Proverbium* n.s. 11: 227–58.

Taylor, Archer. 1931. *The Proverb*. Cambridge MA: Harvard UP. Rpt. (with introduction and bibliography by Wolfgang Mieder) Bern Switzerland: Peter Lang, 1985.

———. 1958. "'The Customer Is Always Right.'" *Western Folklore* 17: 54–55.

Wescott, Roger W. 1981. "From Proverb to Aphorism: The Evolution of a Verbal Art Form." *Forum Linguisticum* 5: 213–25.

White, Geoffrey M. 1987. "Proverbs and Cultural Models: An American Psychology of Problem Solving." In *Cultural Models in Language and Thought*. Edited by Dorothy Holland and Naomi Quinn. Cambridge UK: Cambridge UP. 151–72.

Whiting, B. J. 1952. "Proverbs and Proverbial Sayings." In *The Frank C. Brown Collection of North Carolina Folklore . . . Collected by Dr. Frank C. Brown during the Years 1912 to 1943, in Collaboration with the North Carolina Folklore Society*. 7 volumes. Edited by Newman Ivey White. Durham NC: Duke UP, 1952–64. 1: 329–501.

Williams, Derek Antonio. 1997. "The Proverbial Zora Neale Hurston: A Study of Texts and Contexts." Ph.D. dissertation, Emory University.

Wilson, Gordon. 1969. "Some Mammoth Cave Sayings." *Kentucky Folklore Record* 15: 12–21.

Winick, Stephen D. 1998. "The Proverb Process: Intertextuality and Proverbial Innovation in Popular Culture." Ph.D. dissertation, University of Pennsylvania.

———. 2001. "'Garbage In, Garbage Out,' and Other Dangers: Using Computer Databases to Study Proverbs." *Proverbium* n.s 18: 354–64.

———. 2003. "Intertextuality and Innovation in a Definition of the Proverb Genre." In Mieder (2003) 571–601.

———. 2004. "'You Can't Kill Shit': Occupational Proverb and Metaphorical System among Young Medical Professionals." In Lau, Tokofsky, and Winick (2004) 86–106.

*YBQ*. Shapiro, Fred. 2006. *Yale Book of Quotations*. New Haven CT: Yale UP.